D1735000

Gerald Moers (ed.)

Narrative and Narrativity in Ancient Egypt. Case Studies on Narrative Difference in Various Media

Lingua Aegyptia
Studia Monographica

Herausgegeben von

Frank Kammerzell, Gerald Moers und Kai Widmaier

Band 29

Institut für Archäologie
Humboldt Universität
Berlin

Widmaier Verlag
Hamburg

Institut für Ägyptologie
Universität Wien
Wien

Narrative and Narrativity in Ancient Egypt

Case Studies on Narrative Difference in Various Media

edited by

Gerald Moers

Widmaier Verlag · Hamburg
2023

Titelaufnahme:
Gerald Moers (ed.),
Narrative and Narrativity in Ancient Egypt:
Case Studies on Narrative Difference in Various Media,
Hamburg: Widmaier Verlag, 2023
(Lingua Aegyptia – Studia Monographica; Bd. 29)
ISSN 0946-8641
ISBN (paperback) 978-3-943955-29-3
ISBN (PDF) 978-3-943955-92-7
DOI: https://doi.org/10.37011/studmon.29

Druck und Verarbeitung: Hubert & Co., Göttingen
Printed in Germany

www.widmaier-verlag.de

CONTENTS

EDITORIAL

This book collects the results of the research-project entitled "Altägyptische Erzählungen in Texten und Bildern: Ägyptologische Perspektiven auf zentrale Axiome einer historischen Text- und Bildnarratologie", which was funded by the *Jubiläumsfond der Österreichischen Nationalbank* under the project-number 18121 from December 2019 to May 2022.

The research was conducted in difficult times under difficult circumstances by different scholars who have enriched the project with their personalities, their enthusiasm, and their vision that Egyptology might indeed contribute to a better understanding of the different historical and cultural circumstances of *narrative* in Ancient Egypt as well as to the relatively recent subfield of narratology called *historical narratology*. The contributions shed light on Egyptian narrative phenomena in different media and sound the possibilities not only of a narratological perception of Egyptian objects but also, if necessary, of the Egyptological adjustment of narratological methodology.

I would like to thank Camilla di Biase-Dyson and Claus Jurman for their inspiring collegiality and their intellectual commitment that went way beyond the ordinary and continued also after their contracts had ended, until the present day. Kristina Hutter and Dina Serova decided to enhance the volume with a contribution that originated independently from the project (see appendix). It could have easily been published elsewhere but was considered a perfect thematic fit from all parties involved. I am grateful for their dedication to publish with us.

Thanks go also to many colleagues in Vienna and elsewhere and to a decent number of peer-reviewers for their will to involve in various and sometimes rather detailed discussions on specific topics of relevance for the contributions.

I am most grateful for the generous funding by the *Jubiläumsfond der Österreichischen Nationalbank* and for the kind assistance by all its representatives, especially Mag. Robert Patterer.

Gerald Moers, Vienna, Fall 2023

Egyptological narratology as *historical narratology*

A brief history and some (im-)possibilities

Gerald Moers[1]

Abstract

The contribution presents a history of the Egyptological discussions of 'narrative' in different media. It does so by classifying relevant contributions according to their explicit use of narratological theory and methods as *pre-narratological* (section 1 and 2) or following *classical* (section 2), or *postclassical* (sections 3 and 4) approaches in narratology. It is argued for a design of Egyptological narratology as *historical narratology* (section 4) in order to offer appropriate possibilities to understand the *narrative difference* (section 5) of Egyptian objects which nevertheless remains defined in a clear-cut framework of narratological concepts and methods.

1 Egyptological narratology?

As "narrative communities" ("Erzählgemeinschaften"),[2] all cultures narrate. Still, different cultures do so in a different manner, even if 'narrative' is often considered a "panglobal fact of culture"[3], to be "everywhere"[4], or simply to be "there", "like life itself [...], international, transhistorical, transcultural"[5], as a "human universal",[6] or as a "form of life". But as this notion of "narrative as a form of life" already implies the shift from *classical* to *postclassical narratology* (see below section 3) and does not contrive narrative as based on a "normative model or a universal ontology" but as "culturally situated",[7] modelling cultural difference is epistemologically mandatory. This is especially the case when it comes to the (re-)construction of the narrative behaviour of an alien culture like Ancient Egypt that wants to be informed by *narratology* – "a humanities discipline dedicated to the study of the logic, principles, and practices of narrative representation"[8]. This volume thus

---

1 I like to thank Camilla Di Biase-Dyson, Martin Fitzenreiter, Kristina Hutter, Claus Jurman, and Dina Serova for their comments on previous versions of this introduction. I am also grateful for the comments of two anonymous peer reviewers.

2 Müller-Funk 2008: 14.

3 White 1980: 5.

4 Bal 1999: 19.

5 Barthes 1975 [1966]: 237.

6 See the discussions in Mellmann 2017 or Meister 2018.

7 Brockmeier 2012: esp. 448–449, 459; Brockmeier 2015: passim.

8 See Meister 2014, who gives a thorough discussion of the scope of the term.

Gerald Moers (ed.), *Narrative and Narrativity in Ancient Egypt*, 1–25
DOI: https://doi.org/10.37011/studmon.29.01

tries to analyse some paradigmatic specialties of the narrative culture of Pharaonic Egypt by developing a critical perspective on some very basic concepts from the methodological toolkit of contemporary narratologies (see sections 4 and 5).[9]

Especially since the much-quoted *narrative turn*,[10] cultural studies have likewise cultivated a rather unspecific and/or polyphonic discourse on 'narrative' that is no longer inspired just by the core discipline of narratology, but also feeds from other disciplines as, for example and most prominently, cognitive sciences[11]. In this interdiscourse, the term 'narrative' covers a variety of uses, both as a noun and as an adjective. Apart from the colloquial understanding of the act of storytelling (German: 'Erzählen'; French 'raconter une histoire'), the term figures specifically as reference to both sides of the difference between a 'story' ('fabula'; German: 'Geschichte', French: 'histoire': "the temporal-causal sequence which is, however it may be told, the 'story' or story-stuff [...,] an abstraction from the 'raw materials'"[12]) and its medial manifestation for example as 'text' ('sujet', 'plot'; German: '(Text-)Erzählung', '(Bild-)Erzählung', French: 'récit': "the 'narrative structure' [of] the artistically ordered presentation"[13]) (see fig. 1). Furthermore, 'narrative' refers to the processual act of 'narration' (German: 'erzählende Darstellung', French: 'narration') and not least to the nowadays ubiquitous understanding of the term as a legitimising '(master-) narrative' (German: 'Narrativ'; French: grand récit').[14]

In Egyptology, research on 'narrative' has initially been embedded rather implicitly in the discipline's project of the mid-1970s to the early 2000s to analyse parts of the Egyptian textual universe as 'literature' by an import of concepts and theories from the field of literary studies.[15] However, over the last 20 years or so, 'narrative' itself has increasingly been put at issue in Egyptological textual scholarship. Recent thematic volumes edited by Hu-

---

9 For the plural see for example Nünning 2003; Sommer 2012; Meister 2014; see also below section 3.

10 See Kreiswirth 1992; Fahrenwald 2011: 82–96; Roussin 2017.

11 For example Fludernick 1996; Brockmeier 2012; Herman 2013; Brockmeier 2015; Breithaupt 2022.

12 Wellek & Warren 2019: 194.

13 Wellek & Warren 2019: 194.

14 See for example the overview in Schmidt-Haberkamp 2017. For a lucid introduction to the history of the – often blurry – terminological distinctions see Schmid 2010. For recent Egyptological processings of some aspects of the issue see Braun 2019: 19–20, 29–30, Di Biase-Dyson 2019: 39–42, and Roeder 2018, esp. 107, who prefers to cover the German terms 'Erzählung' und 'Narration' under the heading of "narrative Präsentation". In the cognitive approach of Fritz Breithaupt, the basic concept of *narration* (German: 'Narration') covers phenomena as diverse as "Erzählung (Text) und Narration (mentale Repräsentation von Handlung)" as well as "*grand narrative* (italics Fritz Breithaupt) oder sogenanntes »Narrativ«", see Breithaupt 2022: 61–79, 185–209, esp. 61, 185. For the difference between the German terms 'Erzählung' und 'Narrativ' see the recent proposal in A. Assmann 2023: esp. 94–95.

15 See pars pro toto Loprieno (ed.) 1996, Moers 2001, Parkinson 2002, Simon 2013, Enmarch & Lepper (eds.) 2013. For a thorough analysis of the main shortcomings of this approach (the modernistic Egyptological fiction of an Egyptian 'literature' defined by anachronistic criteria, the use of a concept of 'literary genre' as opposed to 'types of texts', the conception of Egyptian 'literature' as being based on a 'language of art') see now Roeder 2018: 109–129.

Tomaševskij 1925	Fabel		Sujet	
Todorov 1966	histoire		discours	
Genette 1972	histoire		récit	
Rimmon-Kenan 1983	story		text	
Bal 1977	histoire		récit	texte
Bal 1985	fabula		story	text
García Landa 1998	acción		relato	discurso
Stierle 1973	Geschehen	Geschichte	Text der Geschichte	
Schmid 1982	Geschehen	Geschichte	Erzählung	Präsentation der Erzählung

Fig. 1 | The opposition between 'fabula'/'story' and 'sujet'/'plot' (Schmid 2010: 34)

bert Roeder, Fredrik Hagen & al., and Dina Serova & al. are symptomatic for this trend.[16] From an institutional viewpoint, the initial Egyptological presence in the *Bonner Zentrum für Transkulturelle Narratologie*[17] as well as the early-career-network *Norm und Narration in antiken Gesellschaften* of the *Deutsche Forschungsgemeinschaft* (2007–2013) under the Egyptological principal investigator Anke Illona Blöbaum,[18] may also be interpreted as signals of this development. While some of the papers that resulted from these contexts offer highly interesting case studies of various phenomenological aspects of Egyptian narrativity that could also be put into narratological perspectives,[19] many of them from especially the earlier volumes of this list are rather classical Egyptological studies that are located somewhere at the borders between Egyptological varieties of cultural and literary studies. They thus maintain a rather conventional and *pre-narratological* understanding of 'narrative' and often presuppose their objects' 'narrativity'[20] instead of analysing it from a narratological point of view.

16 Roeder (ed.) 2009; Roeder (ed.) 2018; Hagen & al. (eds.) 2011; Serova & al. (eds.) 2019. Also some of the contributions in Fitzenreiter (ed.) 2009 deal with the issue of 'narrative' in the widest sense.

17 https://www.bztn.uni-bonn.de/de, last access Oct. 25, 2022. See El Hawari & Tawfik 2009; Yacoub 2009.

18 https://gepris.dfg.de/gepris/projekt/47162201, last access Nov. 25, 2022.

19 See for example Verhoeven 2009 on the topic of repetition. For repetition in Demotic narratives see now Tait 2011.

20 See for example Yacoub 2009: 61: "Die Narrativität dieses Textes steht außer Frage". The same observation now in Roeder 2018: passim. This use of the term is colloquial, as opposed to its narratological definitions, as for example in Abbott 2014. As the contribution of Kristina Hutter and Dina Serova in this volume shows, Egyptology often also presupposes the non-narrativity of certain objects like the *Pyramid Texts*.

2 Egyptological narratology as *classical narratology*

Apart from the rather circumstantial interest in 'narrative' outlined above, recent Egyptological scholarship has also appropriated specifically narratological methods and concepts for the analysis of texts that are by default perceived as 'narrative literature'. Some – basically philological – studies as for example by John Tait touch upon narratological terminology as "conscious choice" while discussing for example phenomena such as repetition or stories within stories in Demotic narratives in order to explore "the expectations of an ancient audience" and not to provide "criteria for a modern reader to classify types of composition".[21]

This take on narratology differs from approaches in which a strict narratological analysis in terms of what is called *classical narratology*[22] is conducted. In these studies, narratology is a prerequisite for the proper solution of a lingering Egyptological question or part of the studies' methodological frameworks and of their conceptual goals. In 1977, Jan Assmann brought forward an analysis of the plot-structure of the *Tale of the Two Brothers* on the basis of Vladimir Propp's classic *Morphology of the Folktale*[23] which resulted in the following hardcore-structuralist formula of parts II and III of the text:

$$i\ a_1\ b_1\ c_1 \begin{Bmatrix} I\ d_1\ e_1\ f_1\ g_3\ A_1 \\ II\ d_1\ e_1\ A_{13} \end{Bmatrix} \alpha_1\ B_4\ C\ L_9 \downarrow X\ E\ \dot{U}\ P\ T'_1\ St$$

Fig. 2 | Assmann 1977: 6, fn.17

Since this analysis was based on Assmann's introduction of the narratological possibility to distinguish between narrative as 'text'/'narration', as 'sujet'/'plot', and as 'fabula'/'story' (see above section 1) to Egyptology, these narratological distinctions were the necessary condition to eventually address and account for the prevailing Egyptological perception that there was a lack of thematic coherence between the different parts of the analysed text.[24]

After Assmann's early contribution, it took almost 25 years until the emergence of studies in which the application of *classical narratology* has been an implicit or explicit conceptual decision or even a prime objective in itself. In 1999, Claudia Suhr used narratological tools straightforwardly in order to analyse the way in which texts display their

---

21 See Tait 2011: 279 and especially Tait 2015: 392 w. fn. 3, both with reference to the 3rd edition of Mieke Bal's *Narratology* (here Bal 2017). While concepts as for example the 'external narrator' are mentioned (Tait 2015: 400), it does not become entirely clear in other passages whether for example the use of the term 'fable' (Tait 2015: 395) relates to the narratological concept of 'fabula' or the genre of 'animal-fables' (Tait 2015: 396). Quotations in Tait 2015: 392 w. fn. 2 and 491.

22 For the difference between *classical* and *postclassical narratology* see Nünning 2003; Alber & Fludernik 2010; Sommer 2012; Pier 2018.

23 Propp 1968.

24 Assmann 1977a: 1 and Assmann 1977b: 3. Interestingly enough, Jan Assmann (1977a: 4) cancels the distinction between 'fabula'/'story' and 'sujet'/'plot' since, as he holds, the former "truly represents" the latter. The structure-formula above thus describes both.

conceptual control of the communication between their producers and their audiences.[25] Other authors used narratological concepts to enrich what would otherwise have been rather conventional Egyptological analyses. For example, Steve Vinson's 2008 article of the highly complex patterns of *focalization* in the *First Tale of Setne Khaemwas* engages with embedding the research into a clearly marked narratological framework.[26] The same holds true for Gerald Moers' 2013 comparison of the striking similarities between the complexity of narrative levels in the *Tale of Shipwrecked Sailor* with the modern children's book *The Gruffalo*. He was able to show that the way in which its 'fabula' is structurally emplotted is at least equally important for the meaning of the tale as its content.[27] Steve Vinson's narratological analysis of the same text's diegetic and discursive levels as *mise en abyme* from 2015 is another example of this kind of approach, though more explicitly aimed not only at offering a "convenient vocabulary" but also to "open to the interpreter a wide corpus of comparative texts [...] from many literary traditions".[28]

Of greater relevance for the evolution of a conceptual understanding of what an Egyptological narratology may be are the monographic studies of Anja Wieder, Claudia Suhr, and again Steve Vinson.[29] They all approach their objects within a descriptive framework that belongs to the field of *classical narratology*: Gérard Genette's *Discours du récit* in the cases of Anja Wieder and Claudia Suhr, and again Genette's *Discours du récit*, Roland Barthes' *Introduction to the Structural Analysis of Narrative*, and Mieke Bal's *Narratology* in the case of Steve Vinson.[30] In her *Altägyptische Erzählungen* from 2017, Anja Wieder recombines the Egyptological 'genre-theory' of the time with the basic concepts of Genette's structuralist narratology (order, duration, frequency, mood, voice) in order to "synthesise an independent method" in which the integration of a "narratological perspective is obligatory".[31] While her study aims to "offer a detailed and *genre-defining* (italics G.M.) description" of Egyptian narrative texts which "interdisciplinarily" tests their "narrative value",[32] it eventually remains bound to Egyptological preconceptions of literary genre and thus mainly reinforces the disciplinary understanding of the analysed

25 Suhr 1999, esp. 91.

26 Vinson 2008: passim and esp. 306 with fn. 11, likewise with reference to the 3rd ed. of Mieke Bal's *Narratology* (here Bal 2017) and to Seymour Chatman's *Coming to Terms* (Chatman: 1990); for even finer narratological distinctions that add to Vinson's observations see Suhr 2016: 55. Vinson's (2008: 404 n. 2) claim that the concepts of 'fabula' and 'sujet' "have only recently found their way into Egyptological literary scholarship" with reference to Dieleman 2005: 230 is wrong, see above (Assmann 1977a: 1).

27 Moers 2013a with references to Genette 2010 and the 1st ed. of Mieke Bal's *Narratology* (here Bal: 2017). See also the Egyptological interpretation of the text as "enduring catastrophe through narrating" in Parkinson 2002: 188.

28 Vinson 2015 with references to the 3rd edition of Mieke Bal's *Narratology* (here Bal 2017). The quotations are from Vinson 2015: esp. 482.

29 Wieder 2007; Suhr 2016; Vinson 2018.

30 Here: Genette 2010, Barthes 1975, and Bal 2017; see Wieder 2007: esp. 89; 95–97; Suhr 2016: esp. 10–11; Vinson 2018: esp. 11–13 with a glossary on narratological vocabulary on pp. 226–231.

31 Wieder 2007: 98.

32 Wieder 2007: 97–98.

texts.[33] As in Claudia Suhr's 1999 article "Zum fiktiven Erzähler in der ägyptischen Literatur", Suhr's book *Die ägyptische „Ich-Erzählung"* from 2016 likewise sends Egyptian texts through the black box of Gérard Genette's structuralist *classical narratology*.[34] In comparison to Anja Wieder's study, Claudia Suhr's contributions appear more rigidly narratological and also posit "new insights into the interpretation of texts" as "works of art", while Anja Wieder had argued rather defensively about the potential interpretative gains of her narratological imports.[35] Taxonomically and historically, both studies can be situated within the relatively advanced stage of the Egyptological project to establish the literariness of Egyptian texts by the import of concepts from literary studies (see above section 1). One means to this end among many is the adaption of classical narratology. Like Anja Wieder, Steve Vinson, in his analysis on the *First Tale of Khaemwas* from 2018, subscribes to the conviction that narratology "cannot actually interpret".[36] In his use of the toolbox of classical narratology – which might be considered an enlarged version of the approach he took in his previous article on the same text (see above) – he thus confines himself to offering, in the rather philological context of a "fresh look" at a well-known Egyptian text, a "vocabulary and conceptual framework within which to systematically describe and discuss aspects of our story's construction, framed in terms whose meanings have been defined in advance, so as to eliminate ambiguity".[37]

3 Egyptological narratology as *postclassical narratology*

This typologising and instrumental use of classical narratology in terms of rather disciplinary agendas or for the sake of categorising objects *as* narrative or *by* narratological categories should be distinguished from attempts to adapt concepts from the so-called *postclassical narratology*.[38] *Postclassical narratology* tries to transform its *classical* counterpart by being inter- and transdisciplinary, historicising, and oriented towards the cultural contexts of its objects.[39] Due to a phase-shift which is typical for the always deferred Egyptological appropriation of non-disciplinary concepts and methods, the existence of these different kinds of practising narratology has been rarely discussed in Egyptology. While the field of narratology has constantly and productively reinvented itself, Egyptology was still occupied with picking up standard concepts from the field of *classical narratology*. Thus, it still does not explicitly reflect on the fact that the difference

33 See the summary in Wieder 2007: 214–230.

34 Suhr 1999; Suhr 2016.

35 Suhr 2016: 165–166; Wieder 2007: 97. Still, also Wieder 2007: 51, 80 classifies her objects as "works of art" by reference to Umberto Eco's concept of *Opera Operta* (here Eco 2006).

36 Vinson 2018: 12

37 Vinson 2018: 3 and 12.

38 For the differences between *classical* and *postclassical narratology* see once more Nünning 2003; Alber & Fludernik 2010; Sommer 2012; Pier 2018.

39 See the summarising table in Nünning 2003: 243–244. As the mutual permeation of the both varieties is complex from a synchronous point of view, my use of the terms *classical* and *postclassical* is rather descriptive. It refers to different historical stages of the field of 'narratology' as if it were were *one* and not to two separate and independently operating subfields of the discipline.

between types of narratologies can make a difference. But in fact, this difference allows the scholar to mediate appropriately between the narratological concepts which are used and the culturally contextualised objects which are brought into contact with these concepts (see below section 4).[40] Tonio Sebastian Richter's studies on non-literary Coptic acts of child-donation can be regarded as an exception, as he subscribes to the field of *cultural narratology* (*Kulturgeschichtliche Narratologie*).[41] Gerald Moers' article on the "Emplotment of Master-Narratives in the *Tale of Sinuhe*" from 2011 also belongs to this category, as he thematises the differences between *classical* and *postclassical* approaches in narratology and equally opts for the *postclassical* variety of *cultural narratology*.[42]

A particular field within the domain of interdisciplinary *postclassical narratology* is related to the study of 'narrative' in other than textual media, as for example in music, dance and theatre, oral storytelling, film and television, comics, computer-games, or in multiple media.[43] Rather prominently in a list like this would also feature the analysis of visual narrative in architecture,[44] sculpture,[45] and, above all, in images.[46] It goes without saying that the phenomenon of visual narrativity has also been addressed in Egyptology. But until very recently, Egyptological art-history did mostly without any reference to narratological concepts (of whatever kind) or made rather eclectic use thereof. Initially, only those images were awarded narrativity that present, in the eye of the modern beholder, a particular or, even better, historical event,[47] especially in form of a 'cinematographic'[48]

40 Also in recent studies as Braun 2015, Roeder 2018, Braun 2019, or Di Biase-Dyson 2019, the difference does not yet figure explicitly. In her study on visual narrativity, Nadja Braun 2020: 10–11 describes narratology in terms of its *postclassical* variety as if they were one, but remains bound to a rather *classical* framework (Braun 2020: 11, 391). The direct import of some non-historicised concepts of *classical* narratology may explain some shortcomings of her study (see below). Also Frederik Rogner's study on visual narrativity remains – however more loosely – bound to *classical* narratology, see Rogner 2022: 23–27 and below.

41 Richter 2005; Richter 2011: esp. 170–173.

42 Moers 2011: esp. 165–167. For *cultural narratology* see Bal 1999, Erll & Roggendorf 2002, and Sommer 2018.

43 See for example Nünning & Nünning (eds.) 2002, Ryan 2014 and the sections "Erzählen jenseits der Literatur" in Huber & Schmid (eds.) 2018, 441–565 as well as "Medien des Erzählens" in Martínez (ed.) 2017: 24–114.

44 See for example Chiesa 2016. I thank Kristina Hutter for this reference.

45 See for example Wolf 2011.

46 For an overview of the ongoing discussion see Varga 1990; Wolf 2002: esp. 53–75; Wolf 2003; Wolf 2011; Giesa 2011; Speidel 2013; Klein 2017; Kemp 2018. Further references can be found in Moers, Ägyptische Monochrone Einzelbilder als Erzählungen, in this volume.

47 Gaballa 1976: 5, 28; as such perpetuated for example in Lashien 2011: 101; see also Bochi 2003: 55.

48 See now Rogner 2022: 30, 115–118 for a more detailed discussion of the (potential) 'narrativity' of 'kinetic' and 'cinematographic' images (with references to some relevant older studies); while Fitzenreiter 2017: 179, n. 6, denies the connection of 'cinematographic' and 'narrative', Ludwig Morenz speaks of "narrative compaction" ("narrative Verdichtung"; 2014: 193); see also the short notes in Braun 2020: 144–145 and in Förster 2022: 43, both with additional references.

series of images[49]. On the other hand, the great majority of Egyptian images from tombs and temples has been analysed as *non-narrative* without asking for their potential narrativity by an appropriate appropriation of narratological concepts, since they were interpreted as just symbolically intended representations of stereotypical, static, and thus uneventful practices.[50]

This oversimplified perception in Egyptological art-history has been analysed by Whitney Davis as "lacking minimally necessary narratological distinctions" in his 1992 monograph on late prehistoric Egyptian images.[51] To establish the narrative character of many, if not most of these images as "a prior and overarching consideration",[52] Davis sets out to develop – in what he has named an "appendix" on "pictorial narrative" – a rough sketch of what he thinks a minimal narratological frame of analysis may be and could, in combination with some very general thoughts on the media-specificities of images, contribute "to determine that an investigation of the images *as narrative* (italics G.M.) is appropriate".[53] In the early 1990s, his field of potential narratological imports was naturally limited to concepts from classical narratology, as for example the basic structuralist (see above section 1) distinction between 'story' ('histoire'; 'fabula'), 'text' ('récit'; 'text'), and 'narration' (narrative presentation) of Gérard Genette – a distinction Davis holds to be "fundamental to narrative theory. No study of verbal or pictorial denotation can attend to their 'narrative' dimensions without making these distinctions in some way".[54] In any case, the images "work as pictorial narratives" for Whitney Davis.[55]

Despite Whitney Davis' methodological warnings against the Egyptological practice to conceive of large parts of the Egyptian pictorial material as non-narrative, the preconception has been perpetuated repeatedly by Nadja Braun,[56] especially in her important Habilitationsschrift *Bilder erzählen* from 2020.[57] As Braun's studies are the first full-blown Egyptological examples of a thematic import of media-specific approaches from narratology, they have to be regarded taxonomically as *postclassical* approaches despite their rather *classical* conceptual layout (see below).[58] As such, they present and discuss many important issues of the theory of two- and three-dimensional visual narrative and

49 Thus for example El Hawari & Tawfik 2009: 42, 48–51 concerning the narrative appeal of the "seriality" of different versions of the vignette of chapter 1 of the *Book of the Dead*. Typically, series of images in Egyptian battle-scenes are considered 'narrative', see for example Heinz 2002.

50 See for example Groenewegen-Frankfort 1951: 33–34; Kantor 1957: 44; Gaballa 1976: 5–6; Bochi 2003: 55–56; Lashien 2011 maintains the criterion of eventfulness to define 'narrative', but enlarges the amount of potentially narrative images for the Old Kingdom. See now however Förster 2022: 43, who understands also "the sequential representation" of "typical behavior" as 'narrative'.

51 Davis 1992: 243; see also Davis 1993: 53.

52 Davis 1992: 22.

53 Davis 1992: 234–255, quotation on p. 254.

54 Davies 1992: 242. He uses the terms 'fabula' (for Genette's 'histoire'), 'story' (for Genette's 'récit'), and 'text' (for Genette's 'narration').

55 Davis 1992: 22.

56 Braun 2015: esp. 351–352; Braun 2019: 23; see also Braun 2009.

57 Braun 2020: passim, esp. 17, 84, 108.

58 See Sommer 2012: 153 with fig. 5: postclassical – contextual – corpus-based – media-specific.

their Egyptological adoption for the first time. But despite this methodological progress in many aspects of the narrativity of sources as diverse as picture-series or monochronic (i.e. single still) pictures, they rather consolidate standard Egyptological positions.[59] This applies especially to the allegedly non-narrative scenes of everyday life in tombs and ritual-scenes from temples. As Nadja Braun decides to adopt most of the definitions that are relevant for her study in the universalistic and quite technical understanding of structuralist *classical narratology*,[60] she fails to historicise important concepts such as for example 'narrativity' and 'narrative' itself.[61] Instead, she defines 'narrative' "prototypically" by so-called 'narratemes' or 'narremes' in combination with an equally transhistorical understanding of 'event', 'eventfulness', and esp. 'tellability'.[62] Since she shapes 'tellability' as the decisive criterion of 'narrativity' and defines it as the occurrence of "norm-violating and thus exceptional events"[63] without considering what would potentially define a tellable event in Egypt in difference to other cultural settings,[64] Nadja Braun cannot but conclude as a direct response to Whitney Davis that his theory lacks the criterion of a "special event from which to deduce tellability".[65] Accordingly, standard-scenes of everyday life from tombs as well as ritual images from temples cannot count as 'narrative' in her conceptual framework.[66] As a matter of fact, it is this *specific* amalgam of prototype theory and structuralist *classical narratology* as such that defines, in a prescriptive and "revisionary" manner,[67] the possibility to verify visual narrativity for *only some* types of Egyptian images.[68] This is because Nadja Braun excludes cases of equally prototypical *natural narrative* from her conceptual setup[69] and proposes "more complex verbal and epic-literary narrative as the best examples of the category 'narrative'".[70] From this perspective, every

59 So now also Rogner 2021 for a summarizing critique.

60 Braun 2020: esp. 10, 391.

61 See also Rogner 2021: 576. For definitions of 'narrativity' see Abbott 2014.

62 Braun 2020: 9–18, esp. 17. For some general problems implicit in this setup see Rogner 2019: 74, Rogner 2021: 574–578, and Rogner 2022: 19–20. For definitions of 'eventfulness' see Hühn 2013, for a definitions of 'tellability' as „a notion referring to features that make a story worth telling" see Baroni 2014.

63 Braun 2020: passim, esp. 17, 84 (quotation), 108.

64 As she should have done, since she quotes several authors who refer to the cultural character of the narratem 'tellability', see Braun 2020: 13.

65 Braun 2020: 84. For an alternative perspective on what would potentially define 'tellability' in Ancient Egypt see now Gerald Moers, Ägyptische monochrone Einzelbilder als Erzählungen, in this volume.

66 Braun 2020: 84 and passim. What remains 'narrative' despite this classification is presented in Braun 2020: 134–176. Nadja Braun does not discuss the extension of the corpus of potentially narrative images from the Old Kingdom in Lashien 2011, which was based on the very same criterion of 'eventfulness' as Braun's own studies.

67 See Speidel 2018: 77, who defines "revisionary" as "prescribing how to think about the objects in the world rather than describing how we actually think about them".

68 See also Rogner 2021: 574–575.

69 Braun 2020: 12 with reference to Monika Fludernik's classic *Towards a "Natural" Narratology* (Fludernik 1996).

70 Braun 2020: 12, 15–16 (quotation), 391; despite this claim, Braun's setup remains blurry, as she explains that "the prototype of narrative is equally represented by *natural* (italics G.M.), more

form of Egyptian everyday communication cannot be, by definition and in whatever media, narrative.[71] Since Nadja Braun furthermore does not distinguish especially between 'fabula' ('histoire'; 'story')[72] and 'text' ('sujet'; 'plot'), her concept of visual narrativity in Egypt remains implicitly bound to the existence of a prior verbal or textual narrative that might only secondarily legitimate the scholarly claim for visual narrativity.[73] In the same way, also Braun's concept of 'illustration' favours text over image, as images are rather "illustrations relating to" verbal or textual narratives than narratives in their own rights.[74] Especially the possibility that Egyptian monochronic (i.e. single still) pictures might be regarded as self-contained autonomous narratives is thus conceptually excluded in Nadja Braun's studies from the beginning.

Very recently, Frederik Rogner has also proposed an approach to the 'narrativity' of Egyptian images with special regard to New Kingdom data.[75] As he claims, his approach is the inductive result of an analysis of Egyptian sources and not bound to the instrumentalization of "abstract" considerations.[76] Indeed, narratological theory does not play an integral role in his methodological framework as such. Still, his studies are well-informed by *classical* structuralist textual narratology as well as by *postclassical* works on the narrativity of images.[77] It includes several discussions of the relevance to distinguish between 'fabula', 'story', and 'text' (see above and section 1)[78] and is enriched by literary reader-response criticism[79]. In order to analyse especially those kinds of representations of everyday life as narrative that were excluded in Nadja Braun's studies by her conceptual frame, and in opposition to Nadja Braun, whose attempt was primarily[80] to define which types of Egyptian images might have been *narratives* by criteria like their degree of 'narrativity', Frederik Rogner designs *narrativity* itself as his prime concept and defines it

---

complex verbal, and epic-literary narrative" (Braun 2020: 16).

71 In contrast to this, Frank Förster 2022: 43 has proposed, with reference to Braun 2015, Braun 2020, Rogner 2019, and Rogner 2022 an understanding of 'narrativity' not "in an anecdotal or even historical sense", but as the "sequential representation of an activity or behaviour *typical* (italics G.M.) of a human or animal".

72 In Braun 2020, 'fable' is exclusively used as a notion of the genre of 'animal-fables' and not as the narratological concept of 'fabula'.

73 Braun 2020: 97, 335, 372: "related story", 388 and esp. 128: "Interessant sind in Hinblick auf bildliches Erzählen nur von bekannten Geschichten inspirierte Darstellungen"; see also Braun 2015: 354: "original story".

74 See Braun 2020: 65, 176, 248, 258, 290; see esp. p. 26 w. fn. 76: "an image that belongs to a narrative" and the distinction between "visual narration *or* illustration" (italics G.M.) on p. 285.

75 Rogner 2019; Rogner 2021; Rogner 2022.

76 Rogner 2021: 578; Rogner 2022: 33.

77 Rogner 2022: 23–32; main references from the realm of *classical* narratology are Gérard Genette's *Discours du récit* (here Genette 2010) and Mieke Bal's *Narratology* (here Bal 2017). Well-known postclassical contributions are for example Ryan 2004, Steiner 2004, Speidel 2013 and Cohn 2016.

78 Rogner 2022: 18, 24, 34–35 (n. 240).

79 Rogner's (2022: 25–27, 33–37) central notion of "reference" draws mainly on Eco 1979, Ricœur 1983, and Bal 2017: 108–126.

80 Of course, also Nadja Braun (2020: 29–30) discusses the potential of images to induce a "narrativization" even if the "original story" remains unknown.

as the *narrative effect*, that is the potential of images to evoke a narrative impression in the eye of the ancient beholder. Whether images *are* 'narratives' that actually tell a story or not is only of secondary interest.[81] Although Frederik Rogner's Egyptological focus does not aim to contribute to the discussion of narratological theory in the first place,[82] his studies can be regarded taxonomically as *postclassical*.[83]

4 Egyptological narratology as *historical narratology*

As can be inferred from this overview, Egyptological attempts which offer to historicise central narratological concepts are quite generally rare, although an adequate adaption is mandatory for their appropriate use at the interface of narratological practice and Egyptian objects. On the other hand, the lack of reflection on the conditions of adequacy that have to be fulfilled in order to enable the analysis of ancient Egyptian objects by modern non-Egyptian concepts is not solely an Egyptological problem. It is rather rooted in the trans-historically generalised key assumptions that resulted from the context-free, text-centred, and synchronous practice of *structuralist classical narratology*, which had designed its concepts originally for and based on the analysis of linear and modern literary texts, especially the 19th and 20th century novel.[84] In this original setup, there was no need to model narratological concepts in a way that would allow for their customized use also in the analysis of objects from different historical and medial contexts. But if, as Wolfgang Müller-Funk has argued, cultures are "Erzählgemeinschaften, die sich gerade in Hinblick auf ihr narratives Reservoir unterscheiden",[85] the mere instrumentalization of narratological concepts is, while always possible, not enough. Even though a narratological analysis of narrative levels may result in an adequate description of the narrative complexity of Egyptian texts,[86] or could even offer another potential solution for a lingering Egyptological problem, as in the case of line 183 of the *Tale of the Shipwrecked Sailor*, in which an usually emended personal pronoun indicates the existence of another narrative level and an Egyptian example of what Gérard Genette has termed "pseudodiegetic narrative",[87] such an approach involves a narratological appropriation of Egyptian objects rather than the promotion of ideas of what is specifically Egyptian within the Egyptian objects of allegedly narrative character (see section 2). Thus, while theoretical concepts

81 Rogner 2019: esp. 75; Rogner 2021: esp. 578; Rogner 2022: esp. 33–34.

82 Nevertheless, see Rogner 2020: 228–229 for potential methodological consequences of his study for the realm of textual narratology.

83 See Sommer 2012: 153 with fig. 5: postclassical – contextual – corpus-based – media-specific.

84 See for example Hausken 2004: 393–397; Speidel 2018: 77; Brockmeier 2012: 454; Veits 2020: 125–126.

85 Müller-Funk 2008: 14; see also Nünning 2013.

86 For example Moers 2013a; Vinson 2015; Suhr 2016: 73–89 w. fig. 3.

87 Blackman 1932: 48; for an emendation see for example Vinson 2015: 477; besides a "more complex corruption", John Baines (1990: 68–69) has proposed a reconstruction of the tale as being part of a larger cycle; for the claim for "pseudodiegetic narrative" (see Génette 2010: 154–158) see Moers 2013b: 34 w. fn. 35.

and methodical tools might "travel" (in Mieke Bal's words)[88] also from *narratology*[89] to Egyptology (and hopefully back), their one-directional Egyptological application might rather transform Egyptian objects into artefacts that are epistemologically situated in the no man's land between Egyptology and narratology.[90] What is needed instead is a proper Egyptological appropriation of narratological concepts to "confront"[91] Egyptian objects in order "to understand them on their *own terms*" (italics Mieke Bal).[92]

An Egyptological example which takes account of this need to historicise narratological concepts in terms of Egyptian specificities is a study on the phenomenon of 'metalepsis' in Egyptian texts by Gerald Moers.[93] Although the existence of the phenomenon in Ancient Egypt has not been denied as such,[94] the study argues for the reconceptualization of the structuralist-narratological original from the perspective of the history of media: while the original concept of 'metalepsis' is based on the modern ontological distinction between fiction(ality) and reality especially in modern literary texts, this distinction has to be regarded as largely inappropriate for Egyptian texts. Due to their virtually oral and aural nature, their actual performance transforms almost every extradiegetic voice into the voice of an intradiegetic character by metaleptic immersion.[95] Taxonomically, this study has likewise to be regarded as *postclassical*.[96]

A different approach has been proposed by Hubert Roeder in his recent attempts to decolonise the Egyptological discourse on 'narrative' from the problematic impact of such far-travelled concepts as 'literature' and maybe even 'narratology'.[97] While his framework is restricted to textual narrative and does not include narrative in other media like images,[98] Hubert Roeder also argues for necessary modifications to be made to existing modern(istic) narratological concepts[99] in order to promote the "interdisciplinary founda-

88 For the concept of 'traveling concepts' see Bal 2002, esp. 3–55.

89 For the scope of the term see again Meister 2014.

90 Widmaier 2017 has shown impressively how Egyptology has transformed *Egyptian* objects into "*Egyptological* art" (italics G.M.) by applying the very concepts of 'art' or 'style'. As Roeder 2018: 109–129, esp. 116, 120–122 has shown (with reference to the potentially problematic 'traveling' of concepts, see above), the same holds true for the Egyptological construction of the allegedly Egyptian 'literature'.

91 See Bal 2002: 24 for the opposition of 'application' and 'confrontation'.

92 Bal 2002: 8.

93 Moers 2013b.

94 As misunderstood by Manisali 2015: 57–58.

95 For similar observations concerning the "oral dimensions of narrative texts" in Demotic which is in part even terminologically inscribed into them by referring to their 'stories' as "speech" or "voice" see Agut-Labordère 2022: 138. I am indebted to Claus Jurman for hinting to this study.

96 Sommer 2012: 153 with fig. 5: postclassical – formal – diachronic.

97 Roeder 2009; Roeder 2018; in Roeder 2018: 160–161, he puts into question the "relevance of the narratological concept of narrative for the linguistic culture of Ancient Egypt" ("Relevanz des naratologischen Erzählkonzepts für die altägyptische Sprachkultur") and even the "relevance of narratology".

98 Roeder 2009: 15.

99 Roeder 2009: esp. 46–47.

tion of an Egyptological narratology"[100] as an "*archaeological narratology*"[101]. According to Hubert Roeder, these modifications must take account for the difference within Egypt's narrative practices, as opposed to the "sometimes too universalistic assumptions of historical narratology".[102]

However, while Hubert Roeder has shaped his *archaeological narratology* as a project which may contribute to *historical narratology* by amplifying the difference between the two,[103] the approach taken in the present volume would rather suggest that these types of narratology exist on a continuum. Firstly, what Hubert Roeder has marked as the "universalistic assumptions" of *historical narratology* would likely be attributed to a branch of narratology that can be distinguished as *diachronic narratology*.[104] Thus, in the introduction to their *Handbuch historische Narratologie*, Eva von Contzen and Stefan Tilg have argued for a strict discrimination between these two narratological varieties: "Der Ansatz der historischen Narratologie betont in der Regel eher die Differenz oder die Alterität, jener der diachronen eher die Kontinuität der Untersuchungsgegenstände".[105] While the basic assumption of *diachronic narratology* is that "moderne narratologische Parameter gleichsam a- oder transhistorische Gültigkeit besitzen und sich bereits in der Antike vielfach belegen lassen",[106] there is the "Alterität herausarbeitende[n] Anliegen der ›historischen Narratologie‹" and its "Relativierung des universalen Anspruchs der ›allgemeinen Narratologie‹".[107]

Secondly, as Hubert Roeder himself has insightfully shown, questioning or negating the applicability of narratological concepts sets the comparative frame of narratology as well and presupposes its full understanding. Thus, also his call for a "recollection of basic definitions of narrative" is framed by narratology, as his quote of "the core definition of narrative" as "Geschichte" ('story'; 'histoire') by the German narratologist Mathias Martínez clearly shows.[108] And how, if not narratologically by implication, would Hubert Roeder have been able to redefine the meaning of the Egyptian term *sḏd* as "*narrative* presentation" (italics G.M.) in an attempt to replace the old translation "to tell" by the not less infelicitous etymological rendering "to let speak"?[109] Furthermore, it is rather doubtful that the application of "linguistic methods" as an alternative to literary narratology in the narratological analysis of Egyptian sources is, as Hubert Roeder holds, "more innocuous"

100 Roeder 2018: 109, fn. 10.
101 Roeder 2018: 183–191.
102 Roeder 2009: esp. 46–47; Roeder 2018a: 183–191.
103 Roeder 2018: 189.
104 See De Jong 2014a.
105 See Von Contzen & Tilg 2019: VIII.
106 An example would be De Jong 2014b.
107 See Von Contzen & Tilg 2019: VII–VIII. See also Von Contzen 2014 and Bleumer 2015. For an alternative perspective on *historical narratology* as just another "heuristics of interpretation" see Hübner 2015: 17.
108 Roeder 2018: 159, quoting Martínez 2011: 11.
109 Roeder 2018: 159–166, esp. 165.

than any other contemporary academic discourse – as if modern linguistics would by nature be a more appropriate tool to confront the otherness of Egyptian objects.[110]

The approach taken in this volume thus starts from the conviction that any Egyptian object is first and foremost *alien* in comparison to objects which are actively *communicated* in any potential observer's contemporary culture.[111] On the other hand, Egyptian objects necessarily possess what Armin Schulz, in an analysis of mediaeval narrative practices, has termed "alien coherence" ("Fremde Kohärenz").[112] It is therefore the analysts' frame of observation alone that construes an alien object no longer as alien but as *understandably and coherently different*. Understanding difference, however, presupposes a framework of comparison. For an analysis of the specificities of the Egyptian narrative behaviour which likes to perceive itself as *Egyptological narratology*, the comparative framework for any potential understanding must inevitably be a narratological one. Only the narratological perspective allows for the observation that an Egyptian object might indeed be fundamentally different from the objects shaped by *classical narratology*. Therefore, as *historical narratology*, Egyptological narratology cannot do without a profound knowledge of concepts from the various narratologies (for the plural see above section 3). The decision whether or not to use them, why to use them or why not, and for what reason, can only come after a proper understanding of these concepts in their original contexts and after an evaluation of their potential (in)applicability. There is no contemporary observation of an Egyptian object which would be natural in itself or more natural than another. But contemporary scholarship might define what an adequate observation may be and how it negotiates its own alienness towards the narrative culture of Ancient Egypt.

Eventually, the contrast between Hubert Roeder's *archaeological narratology* and the *historicising* approach taken in this volume is likely a matter of perspective rather than of fundamental difference, as both argue for the adjustment of narratology itself in order to master the genuine alterity of the Egyptian narrative behaviour in an appropriate manner. In any case, as the contributors of the present volume would argue, their results are compatible with Hubert Roeder's proposals. This holds especially for Camilla Di

---

110 Roeder 2018: 183. This does of course not imply that modern linguistics would not be able to substantially contribute to the extension of narratological knowledge. But also a contemporary "grammar of narration" (for example Zeman 2020) should be put into a historical and cultural perspective. I am grateful to Dina Serova for this reference and according discussions.

111 My use of the term 'alien' is thus not intended to refer to the scholarly idea of a specific Egyptian form of natural otherness, not least since such an idea might rather be the effect of an undisclosed scholarly process of 'alienation' based on a methodological misappropriation of objects. As for example Moreno-Garcia 2014 has shown, the reason for what is called the "Egyptian exception" is the "Egyptological exception" of the discipline's sometimes "trivial" and regularly "isolated" alienness to current methodological frameworks in cultural studies and related fields of historical research (quotes from pp. 51, 53–55; my gratitude for this reference goes to a peer-review). Since the discussion is too complex and full of philosophical implication, I will not even try to go into more detail here. For a first impression see Jaeggi 2014. My gratitude for a short but very enlightening discussion on the larger topic goes to Kristina Hutter who also pointed out the last reference to me.

112 Schulz 2010.

Biase-Dyson's analysis of the semantics of the Egyptian term *sḏd* (see Di Biase-Dyson in this volume), which expands upon, rather than contradicts, Hubert Roeder's findings.

5 *Narrative difference*: the contributions

As determined by the layout of the project, this volume does not intend to offer a conceptual blueprint or a consistent theory of a full-blown Egyptological narratology. This is neither necessary nor expedient. Instead, it presents paradigmatic examples of how narratological concepts can be either used or appropriated in an Egyptological practice that is able to enrich both fields at the same time. While, from the perspective taken above, the narratological framework of any potential analysis of Egyptian narrative in whatever medium is given by default, its (also partial) applicability is a matter of Egyptological evaluation and, if necessary, appropriation.

The common conviction that is shared by all contributors to this volume is that 'narrative' is a transmedial phenomenon that has to be considered as existing independently from the narrow text-centred definitions of structuralist classical narratology which in some cases live on even in postclassical approaches. These have implicitly hindered not only an adequate perception of *narrative difference* from a historical and cultural perspective, but have done so already synchronously with respect to narrative in forms other than written verbal media.[113] With Jens Brockmeier, we do not think "that there are universal components of […] 'narrative' that exist prior to and independent from a culturally situated event" or that there is "an abstract entity called 'story'". Instead, we look at "concrete contexts of action and interaction in which a *linguistic or otherwise performed action sequence* (italics G.M.) is perceived as a story".[114] Specifically, the approach taken here implicates a modified understanding especially of narrative key-factors as 'narrative coherence' or 'event' and 'eventfulness'[115], as well as of 'tellability' and of 'tell-', 'news-' or 'noteworthiness'[116]. All these factors are rather dependent on historical and medial contexts as well as on cultural dispositions than on trans-everythingly valid conceptualizations that are sovereignly controlled by narratology.[117] Thus, the overarching main hypothesis of this volume is that an Egyptian emplotment of 'events' which possess culture-specific 'tellabilities' will more often than not result in untoward forms of coherence that might

---

113 Even postclassical narratology may suffer from what Liv Hausken 2004: 392–393 has termed 'medium blindness', which she discriminates into two forms: 'Total' and 'nonchalant medium blindness. Total medium blindness relates to the fact that "that the medium itself matters is simply neglected, but at the same time a particular medium is silently presumed. In short, theories that are seemingly independent of the medium are usually implicitly tied to a particular medium […]. Nonchalant blindness is most readily apparent in those approaches that uncritically borrow ideas from medium-specific or medium-sensitive studies of media other than the medium under consideration".

114 Quotations from Brockmeier 2012: 458.

115 Hühn 2013.

116 Baroni 2014.

117 For this claim see already Moers 2019: 324.

differ fundamentally from familiar sequential or linear forms of modern western textual narratives. Only such kind of an expanded narratological understanding of what is not only 'narrative' but might also be 'a narrative' goes well in line with what may have been considered 'narrative' objects in Ancient Egypt. The narratological implications of this shift in perspective is clear: "When definitions are modified to include non-paradigmatic entities, the ways we analyse paradigmatic ones change too."[118]

As Camilla Di Biase-Dyson shows in her contribution "What does *sḏd* tell?", the semantics of the Egyptian term *sḏd* and its nominal derivates, which have often wrongly been exclusively associated with modern western conceptions of linear verbal and especially textual narrativity ('to tell'; 'story'), does in fact relate quite generally to the verbalization or verbal re-presentation of mentally pre-existent complex-objects that have either a specifically contextual or a general cultural relevance.[119] Thus *sḏd* is generally used in contexts that would not qualify as having specific 'narrativity' by modern standard definitions, as for example in the *Instruction of Ptahhotep*. Here, *sḏd* designates the – by modern criteria – non-narrative form of a paradigmatic 2nd person instructional discourse.[120] It might be worth noting for reasons of comparison that 'narration', in English Renaissance rhetoric, was similarly conceived of as "a plain and manifest pointing of the matter".[121] On the other hand, and from the very beginning of the use-life of the term in the early Middle Kingdom, it is also used to designate objects that would in fact very well meet the criteria of narratological standard-definitions of having 'narrativity' as well as being 'a narrative'. One very early example is the metanarrative[122] introduction of hypodiegetic and hypohypodiegetic narratives in the *Tale of the Shipwrecked Sailor* as an act of 'telling' (*sḏd*) 'events' (*ḫpr.w*/*ḫpr.t*) which obviously have 'tellability',[123] for example by relating traumatic experiences. In fact, the line "how happy is he who can *tell* what he has experienced *after* the *suffering* has passed"[124] reads like an Egyptian preview of the definition a "type II event" as the "narration as the representation of changes with certain qualities".[125] This specific use of the term is then stabilized over time to designate what Camilla Di Biase-Dyson calls a "complete 'metanarrative form'". An example is the introduction of what is "listened to" as (probably hypodiegetic) 'stories' in many Demotic tales.[126] From the perspective of historical narratology, the data can be interpreted in two different ways: *sḏd* might simply designate non-narratives and, as a matter of chance, also objects that *look like* narratives by comparison to modern definitions. Preferable,

118 Speidel 2018: 79.

119 This interpretation is largely compatible with the observations in Roeder 2018: 161–165 (see above section 4).

120 pPrisse 17,10–12, ed. Žába 1956: 62.

121 See Thomas Wilson, *Art of Rhetorique*, I. f. 4 from 1553. The hint to this source can be found via Breithaupt 2022: 62.

122 On metanarration see Neumann & Nünning 2014.

123 pPetersburg 1115, 21–23, 125, 142–143, ed. Blackman 1932: 42,7, 45,4, 46,1; see also Moers 2019: 323.

124 pPetersburg 1115, 124, ed. Blackman 1932: 45,3.

125 See Hühn 2013.

126 Tait 2015: 392–396 (*Djed-her*, *The Swallow and the Sea*, *Myth of the Sun's Eye*).

however, is a perspective on the semantic scope of *sḏd* in which the root can designate objects that do not only *look like* narratives but *are* narratives from an Egyptian as well as from a modern perspective, because the semantic core of the term is categorically related to the realm of 'narrativity'. Seen from this perspective, the use of *sḏd* would define any Egyptian object of verbal re-presentation as conceptually being 'narrative' or being 'a narrative'. This historically enriched – and likely Egyptian – understanding of 'narrativity' would thus not only include narrative objects that would conceptually meet the modern and rather narrow text-centred definitions of classical narratology, but also objects which have 'narrative coherence' despite the fact that they would not qualify as 'narrative' by the very same modern definitions.

This point is explicated in detail also in the contribution of Kristina Hutter and Dina Serova on "Narrated Spaces in the Pyramid Texts" (see Appendix). As the Pyramid Texts are still largely considered as non-narrative in Egyptology, the contribution of narrativity to the textual coherence of at least some of the spells of the genre is well-contested. The discussion was triggered by Jan Assmann's conception of Egyptian myths as "genotexts" that transcend genre and media and are considered 'narrative' only in form of written mythological literary narratives. According to Assmann, these so-called "phenotexts" are attested only from the New Kingdom onwards, while earlier processings of mythical material was considered as lacking narrative coherence and thus being only "iconic" or "constellative".[127] Kristina Hutter and Dina Serova, for their part, enhance an understanding of their object that subscribes to previous analyses that, as we would hold, support an interpretation of the Pyramid Texts' narrativity as *different* from modern standard conceptions of linear or sequential narrative coherence.[128] This form of narrativity is not only embedded in the Pyramid Texts' non-linear linguistic structure that nevertheless displays eventful and obviously coherently emplotted actions,[129] but also in the *performative*[130]

127 See Assmann 1977c: esp. 14–15, 37–40; for the "iconicity" of mythical constellations see esp. Assmann 1982: 39–42. Assmann's distinction of "genotext" and "phenotext" can be translated into the narratological distinction between 'fabula'/'story' and 'sujet'/'plot', see section 1 above.

128 The main point of discussion concerns the appropriateness of Jan Assmann's use of standard definitions of 'narrative' and 'narrative coherence'. John Baines (1991: 94) refers to the specificities of Egyptian narratives which might not meet our expectations of linear sequentiality and points out that "realization of myths [...] might range from a minimal transitive element to a tale"; see also Baines 1999: 32: "myths have a *narrative core* [italics G.M.), but the extent of this core [...] may exhibit little of what one might call narrative 'quality' or even and especially 'coherence'"; Katja Goebs 2002: 29–38, esp. 33 argues that "narrativity [...] was not required", while she otherwise assumes that myths have a "narrative structure" already before they might be "fixed" by "their writing down" (p. 35); Harco Willems 1996: 13 rightfully pinpoints the problem in that a definition of narrativity as an exclusive "characteristic of a *written* (italics Harco Willems) story" is too "narrow" and holds that already "mythological patterns" (G.M.: Assmann's "constellations") "can have a narrative structure". But while Harco Willems sees a solution in the possibility of oral narrative myths, the present volume argues for a *problematization of verbal linearity* as the main criterion of 'narrativity'.

129 See Zeidler 1993: esp. 86–89 and 95–104.

130 See again Brockmeier 2012: 458, quoted above.

and spatial[131], or, as Martin Pehal has put it, "configurational" translation of the narrative potential of the mythical "genotexts" (=> 'fabula'; 'histoire') in ritual contexts.[132] Thus, at least some spells of the Pyramid Texts sketch complete narrative structures despite the fact that they lack, although being verbal themselves, the verbal sequentiality of written narrative texts.

This idea of *narrative difference* is deepened from a transmedial and cognitive perspective in Claus Jurman's all-encompassing re-definition of Old Kingdom life-writing from non-royal tombs as "portfolio-biographies": the interrelated assemblages of texts, images, statuary, and architecture into well-integrated, non-linear, three-dimensional, and "multimodal iconotexts".[133] As multimedial and multimodal complex-objects, tombs have narrative coherence despite not being translatable only one and a purely linear narrative text, as their inherent temporal and causal structures relate by default to what can be regarded as the underlying *cultural* rather than *individual* 'histoire', 'fabula', or 'Narrativ' of the perfect life of a member of the Egyptian Old Kingdom elite. Tombs are, as Claus Jurman puts it, the "syndiegetic" medial sources of any actual reçit of any personalised version of this cultural "Narrativ", as they offer focal points for recipients to *perform* the narrativization of the tomb owner's perfect life – a narrativization that would never result in only one single linear story.

Gerald Moers discusses the *narrative difference* of Egyptian monochronic (i.e. single still) pictures. He argues in favour of overcoming the revisionary Egyptological practice of importing prescriptive definitions of 'narrativity' and 'narrative' which still leads to the exclusion of this type of images from the realm of artefacts that can be considered potential autonomous narratives[134] – a perspective which is meanwhile contested in transmedial narratology itself.[135] He thus shows that non-sequential monochronic pictures do not only have 'narrative' potential, as it may trigger and induce the construction of a narrative based on the recipients' culturally defined knowledge and cognitive frame of perception. Instead, they can also be full-fledged autonomous 'narratives', depending on their contextually defined 'tellabilities' and 'narrative interests' as well as on the specific temporality which is presented also by non-sequential visual media.

---

131 The performative construction of narrated spaces is a multi-medial and multimodal effort, as it does not only involve verbal representation, but also physical dimensionality and sound, see for example Huwiler 2005: 296–300.

132 See the summary of the ongoing discussion in Di Biase-Dyson 2019: 43–45 with further references; for the concept of "configurational" instead of "narrative coherence" see Pehal 2015: 35–40.

133 In terms of his Egyptological and narratological framework, Claus Jurman's concept goes way beyond a similar idea (in the broadest possible sense) that was proposed in a short article on the narrative qualities of Amarna tomb-paintings in Meyers 1985: esp. 49–50: "Instead of the sequential development of a narrative, the theme is generated by the meaningful juxtaposition of images. And pictorial narrative, instead as being presented as a sequence of images, is derived from the interplay of relationships in which the underlying narrative process aspires to the space-logic rather than a time-logic alone and a structure of juxtaposition rather than linear sequences".

134 Braun 2020: passim. As Rogner 2022: esp. 33–34 shapes 'narrativity' as the "effect [...] to cause a narrative impression in the act of perception", he does not discuss this question as such.

135 See Speidel 2013 and Speidel 2018.

Bibliography

Abbott, H. Porter 2014. Narrativity, in: Peter Hühn et al. (eds.), *The Living Handbook of Narratology*, Hamburg, URL = https://www-archiv.fdm.uni-hamburg.de/lhn/node/27.html [last view date 08 Nov 2022].

Agut-Labordère, Damien. 2022. Inserting or Ruminating: How Demotic Became Canonic, in: Damien Agut-Labordère & Miguel John Versluys (eds.), *Canonisation as Innovation: Achoring Cultural Formation in the First Millennium BCE*, Euhormos: Greco-Roman Studies in Anchoring Innovation 3, Leiden & Boston, 130–151.

Alber, Jan & Monika Fludernik. 2010. Introduction, in: Jan Alber & Monika Fludernik (eds.), *Post-classical Narratology: Approaches and Analyses*, Theory and Interpretation of Narrative, Columbus, 1–31.

Assmann, Aleida. 2023. Was ist ein Narrativ? Zur anhaltenden Konjunktur eines unscharfen Begriffs, in: *Merkur* 889, 88–96.

Assmann, Jan. 1977a. Textanalyse auf verschiedenen Ebenen: Zum Problem der Einheit des Papyrus d'Orbiney, in: Wolfgang Voigt (ed.), *Zeitschrift der Deutschen Morgenländischen Gesellschaft Supplement III/1, XIX. Deutscher Orientalistentag vom 28. September bis 4. Oktober 1975 in Freiburg im Breisgau, Vorträge*, Wiesbaden, 1–15.

Assmann, Jan. 1977b. Das ägyptische Zweibrüdermärchen: Eine Textanalyse auf drei Ebenen am Leitfaden der Einheitsfrage, in: *Zeitschrift für ägyptische Sprache und Altertumskunde* 104, 1–25.

Assmann, Jan. 1977c. Die Verborgenheit des Mythos in Ägypten, in: *Göttinger Miszellen: Beiträge zur ägyptologischen Diskussion* 25, 7–43.

Assmann, Jan. 1982. Die Zeugung des Sohnes: Bild, Spiel Erzählung und das Problem des ägyptischen Mythos, in: Jan Assmann, Walter Burkert & Fritz Stolz (eds.), *Funktionen und Leistungen des Mythos: Drei altorientalische Beispiele*, Orbis Biblicus et Orientalis 48, Freiburg/Schweiz & Göttingen, 13–61.

Baines, John. 1990. Interpreting the Story of the Shipwrecked Sailor, in: *Journal of Egyptian Archaeology* 76, 55–72.

Baines, John. 1991. Egyptian Myth and Discourse: Myth, Gods, and the Early Iconographic Record, in: *Journal of Near Eastern Studies* 50/2, 81–105.

Baines, John. 1999. Prehistories of Literature: Performance, Fiction, Myth, in: Gerald Moers (ed.), *Definitely: Egyptian Literature, Proceedings of the Symposium "Ancient Egyptian Literature: History and Forms", Los Angeles, March 24–26, 1995*, Lingua Aegyptia – Studia Monographica 2, 17–41.

Bal, Mieke. 1999. Close Reading Today: From Narratology to Cultural Analysis, in: Walter Grünzweig & Andreas Solbach (eds.), *Grenzüberschreitungen: Narratologie im Kontext – Transcending Boundaries: Narratology in Context*, Tübingen, 19–41.

Bal, Mieke. 2002. *Travelling Concepts in the Humanities: A Rough Guide*, Toronto, Buffalo & London.

Bal, Mieke. 2017. *Narratology: Introduction to the Theory of Narrative*, 4th ed., Toronto.

Baroni, Raphaël. 2014. Tellability, in: Peter Hühn et al. (eds.), *The Living Handbook of Narratology*, Hamburg, URL = https://www-archiv.fdm.uni-hamburg.de/lhn/node/30.html [last view date 08 Nov 2022].

Barthes, Roland. 1975 [1966]. An Introduction to the Structural Analysis of Narrative, in: *New Literary History* 6, 237–272.

Blackman, Aylward M. 1932. *Middle Egyptian Stories: Transcription with Textual Notes* 1, Bibliotheca Aegyptiaca 2, Bruxelles.

Bleumer, Hartmut. 2015. Historische Narratologie, in: Christiane Ackermann & Michael Egerding (eds.), *Literatur- und Kulturtheorien in der germanistischen Mediävistik: Ein Handbuch*, Berlin, 213–274.

Bochi, Patricia A., 2003. Time in the Art of Ancient Egypt: From Ideological Concept to Visual Construct, in: *KronoScope: Journal for the Study of Time* 3, 51–82.

Braun, Nadja. 2009. Visual History – Bilder machen Geschichte, in: Martin Fitzenreiter (ed.), *Das Ereignis: Geschichtsschreibung zwischen Vorfall und Befund, Workshop vom 03.10 bis 05.10.08*, IBAES – Internet-Beiträge zur Ägyptologie und Sudanarchäologie / Studies from the Internet on Egyptology and Sudanarchaeology 10, London, 35–50.

Braun, Nadja S. 2015. Narrative, in: Melinda Hartwig (ed.), *A Companion to Ancient Egyptian Art*, Chichester, 344–359.

Braun, Nadja. 2019. Von der Erzählung zum Narrativ, in: Dina Serova et al. (eds.), *Narrative: Geschichte – Mythos – Repräsentation. Beiträge des achten Berliner Arbeitskreises Junge Aegyptologie (BAJA 8) 1.12.–3.12.2017*, Göttinger Orientforschungen IV/65, Wiesbaden, 19–38.

Braun, Nadja S. 2020. *Bilder erzählen: Visuelle Narrativität im alten Ägypten*, Ägyptologische Studien Leipzig 2, Heidelberg.

Breithaupt, Fritz. 2022. *Das narrative Gehirn: Was unsere Neuronen erzählen*, Berlin.

Brockmeier, Jens. 2012. Narrative Scenarios: Toward a Culturally Thick Notion of Narrative, in: Jaan Valsiner (ed.), *The Oxford Handbook of Culture and Psychology*, Oxford & New York, 439–467.

Brockmeier, Jens. 2015. *Beyond the Archive: Memory, Narrative and the Autobiographical Process*, Explorations in Narrative Psychology, Oxford & New York.

Chatman, Seymour. 1990. *Coming to Terms: The Rhetoric of Narrative in Fiction and Film*, Ithaca, N.Y. & London.

Chiesa, Laura. 2016. *Space as Storyteller: Spatial Jumps in Architecture, Critical Theory, and Literature*, Evanston.

Cohn, Neil (ed.). 2016. *The Visual Narrative Reader*, London.

Davies, Whitney. 1992. *Masking the Blow: The Scene of Representation in Late Prehistoric Egyptian Art*, Berkeley, Los Angeles, Oxford.

Davies, Whitney. 1993. Narrativity in the Narmer Palette, in: Peter J. Holliday (ed.), *Narrative and Event in Ancient Art*, Cambridge & New York, 14–54.

De Jong, Irene. 2014a. Diachronic Narratology. (The Example of Ancient Greek narrative), in: Peter Hühn et al. (eds.), *The Living Handbook of Narratology*, Hamburg, URL = https://www-archiv.fdm.uni-hamburg.de/lhn/node/95.html [last view date 08 Nov 2022].

De Jong, Irene. 2014b. *Narratology & Classics: A Practical Guide*, Oxford.

Di Biase-Dyson, Camilla. 2019. Narrative by Ancient Egyptians and of Ancient Egypt: A State of the Art, in: Dina Serova et al. (eds.), *Narrative: Geschichte – Mythos – Repräsentation. Beiträge des achten Berliner Arbeitskreises Junge Aegyptologie (BAJA 8) 1.12.–3.12.2017*, Göttinger Orientforschungen IV/65, Wiesbaden, 39–63.

Dieleman, Jacco. 2005. *Priests, Tongues, and Rites: The London-Leiden Magical Manuscripts and Translation in Egyptian Ritual (100–300 CE)*, Religions in the Graeco-Roman World 153, Leiden & Boston

Eco, Umberto. 1979. *Lector in fabula: la cooperazione interprtativa nei testi narrative*, Milano.

Eco, Umberto. 2006. *Das offene Kunstwerk*, 10. Auflage, stw 222, Frankfurt a. M.

El Hawari, Amr & Tarek Sayed Tawfik 2009. Narrative Elemente der Vignette zum 1. Kapitel des altägyptischen Totenbuchs, in: Stephan Conermann (ed.), *Modi des Erzählens in nicht-abendländischen Gesellschaften,* Narratio Aliena? Studien des Bonner Zentrums für transkulturelle Narratologie 2, Berlin, 41–58.

Enmarch, Roland & Verena Lepper (eds.). 2013. *Ancient Egyptian Literature: Theory and Practice*, Proceedings of the British Academy 188, Oxford.

Erll, Astrid & Simone Roggendorf. 2002. Kulturgeschichtliche Narratologie: Die Historisierung und Kontextualisierung kultureller Narrative, in: Ansgar Nünning & Vera Nünning (eds.), *Neue Ansätze in der Erzähltheorie.* WVT – Handbücher zum literaturwissenschaftlichen Studium 4, Trier, 73–113

Fahrenwald, Claudia. 2011. *Erzählen im Kontext neuer Lernkulturen: Eine bildungstheoretische Analyse im Spannungsfeld von Wissen, Lernen und Subjekt*, Wiesbaden 2011.

Fitzenreiter, Martin (ed.). 2009. *Das Ereignis: Geschichtsschreibung zwischen Vorfall und Befund, Workshop vom 03.10 bis 05.10.08*, IBAES – Internet-Beiträge zur Ägyptologie und Sudanarchäologie / Studies from the Internet on Egyptology and Sudanarchaeology 10, London.

Fitzenreiter, Martin. 2017. Sense and Serendipity: Zur Ambiguität pharaonischer Bildschriftlichkeit, in: Vincent Verschoor, Arnold Jan Stewart & Cocky Demarée (eds.), Imaging and Imagining the Memphite Necropolis: Liber Amicorum René van Walsem, Egyptologische Uitgaven 30, Leuven, 177–199.

Fludernik, Monika. 1996. *Towards a "Natural" Narratology*, London.

Förster, Frank. 2022. A Pretty Happy Hippo: Pictorial Narrativity in the Early Naqada Period, in: Gunnar Sperveslage (ed.), *Early Egyptian Miscellanies: Discussions and Essays on Predynastic and Early Dynastic Egypt*, IBAES – Internet-Beiträge zur Ägyptologie und Sudanarchäologie / Studies from the Internet on Egyptology and Sudanarchaeology 26, Berlin & London, 37–50.

Gaballa, Gaballa Ali. 1976. *Narrative in Egyptian Art*, Mainz.

Genette, Gérard. 2010. *Die Erzählung*, 3., durchgesehene und korrigierte Auflage Aufl., Paderborn.

Giesa, Felix. 2011. Erzählen mit Bildern (Malerei, Comic, *roman-photo*), in: Matías Martínez (ed.), *Handbuch Erzählliteratur: Theorie, Analyse, Geschichte*, Stuttgart, 36–41.

Goebs, Katja. 2002. A Functional Approach of Egyptian Myths and Mythemes, in: *Journal of Ancient Near Eastern Religions*, 27–59.

Groenewegen-Frankfort, Henriette Antonia. 1951. *Arrest and Movement: An Essay on Space and Time in the Representational Art of the Ancient Near East*, London.

Hagen, Frederik, John Johnston, Wendy Monkhouse, Kathryn Piquette, John Tait & Martin Worthington (eds.). 2011. *Narratives of Egypt and the Ancient Near East. Literary and Linguistic Approaches*, Orientalia Lovaniensia Analecta 189, Leuven, Paris & Walpole/MA.

Hausken, Liv. 2004. Coda: Textual Theory and Blind Spots in Media Studies, in: Marie-Laure Ryan (ed.), *Narrative across Media: The Language of Storytelling*, Lincoln & London, 391–403.

Heinz, Susanna Constanze. 2002. Wie wird ein Feldzug erzählt? – Bildrepertoire, Anbringungsschema und Erzählform der Feldzugsreliefs des Neuen Reiches, in: Manfred Bietak & Mario Schwarz (eds.), *Krieg und Sieg: Narrative Wanddarstellungen von Altägypten bis ins Mittelalter. Internationales Kolloquium 29.–39. Juli 1997 in Schloss Haindorf, Langenlois*, Untersuchungen der Zweigstelle Kairo des Österreichischen Archäologischen Instituts 20, Wien, 43–67.

Herman, David. 2013. Cognitive Narratology (revised version; uploaded 22 September 2013), in: Peter Hühn et al. (eds.), *The Living Handbook of Narratology*, Hamburg, URL = https://www-archiv.fdm.uni-hamburg.de/lhn/node/38.html [last view date Nov. 08 2022].

Huber, Martin & Wolf Schmid (eds.). 2018. *Grundthemen der Literaturwissenschaft: Erzählen*, Grundthemen der Literaturwissenschaft, Berlin & Boston.

Hübner, Gert. 2015. Historische Narratologie und mittelalterlich-frühneuzeitliches Erzählen, in: *Literaturwissenschaftliches Jahrbuch, Neue Folge* 56, 11–54.

Hühn, Peter. 2013. Event and Eventfulness, in: Peter Hühn et al. (eds.), *The Living Handbook of Narratology*, Hamburg, URL = https://www-archiv.fdm.uni-hamburg.de/lhn/node/39.html [last view date 08 Nov 2022].

Huwiler, Elke. 2005. Sound erzählt: Ansätze zu einer Narratologie der akustischen Kunst, in: Harro Segeberg & Frank Schätzlein (eds.), *Sound: zur Technologie und Ästhetik des Akustischen in den Medien*, Marburg, 285–305.

Jaeggi, Rahel. 2014. *Alienation*, New York.

Kantor, Helene J. 1957. Narration in Ancient Egypt, in: *Journal of America Archaeology* 61, 44–54.

Kemp, Wolfgang. 2018. Erzählen in Bildern, in: Martin Huber & Wolf Schmid (eds.), *Grundthemen der Literaturwissenschaft: Erzählen*, Grundthemen der Literaturwissenschaft, Berlin & Boston, 172–181.

Klein, Christian. 2017. Comic/Roman-photo, in: Matías Martínez (ed.). 2017. *Erzählen: Ein interdisziplinäres Handbuch*, Stuttgart, 24–32.

Kreiswirth, Martin. 1992. Trusting the Tale: The Narrativist Turn in the Human Sciences, in: *New Literary History* 23, 629–657.

Lashien, Miral. 2011. Narrative in Old Kingdom Wall Scenes: The Progress Through Space and Time, in: *The Bulletin of the Australian Centre for Egyptology* 22, 101–114.

Loprieno, Antonio (ed.). 1996. *Ancient Egyptian Literature: History and Forms*, Probleme der Ägyptologie 10, Leiden, New York & Köln.

Manisali, Alexander. 2015. Rawosers Kleid und Ruddedets Hosenrolle – Struktur und Subtext der fünften Geschichte des pWestcar, in: *Göttinger Miszellen: Beiträge zur ägyptologischen Diskussion* 246, 57–65.

Martínez, Matías. 2011. Erzählen, in: Matías Martínez (ed.), *Handbuch Erzählliteratur: Theorie, Analyse, Geschichte*, Stuttgart, 1–12.

Martínez, Matías (ed.). 2017. *Erzählen: Ein interdisziplinäres Handbuch*, Stuttgart.

Mellmann, Katja. 2017. Anthropologie des Erzählens, in: Matías Martínez (ed.), *Erzählen: Ein interdisziplinäres Handbuch*, Stuttgart, 208–317.

Meister, Jan Christoph. 2014. Narratology, in: Peter Hühn et al. (eds.), *The Living Handbook of Narratology*, Hamburg, URL = https://www-archiv.fdm.uni-hamburg.de/lhn/node/48.html [last view date 08 Nov 2022].

Meister, Jan Christoph. 2018. Erzählen: Eine anthropologische Universalie, in: Martin Huber & Wolf Schmid (eds.), *Grundthemen der Literaturwissenschaft: Erzählen*, Grundthemen der Literaturwissenschaft, Berlin & Boston, 88–112.

Meyers, Elizabeth l. 1985. Component Design as a Narrative Device in Amarna Tomb Art, in: Herbert L. Kessler (ed.) *Pictorial Narrative in Antiquity and the Middle Ages*, Studies in the History of Art 16, Symposium Series / Centre for Advanced Study in the Visual Arts 4, Washington, 35–51.

Moers, Gerald. 2001. *Fingierte Welten in der ägyptischen Literatur des 2. Jahrtausends v. Chr. Grenzüberschreitung, Reismotiv und Fiktionalität*, Probleme der Ägyptologie 19, Leiden, Boston, Köln.

Moers, Gerald. 2011. Broken Icons: the Emplotment of Master-Narratives in the Ancient Egyptian *Tale of Sinuhe*, in: Fredrik Hagen et al. (eds.), *Narratives of Egypt and the Ancient Near East: Literary and Linguistic Approaches*, Orientalia Lovaniensia Analecta 189, Leuven, Paris & Walpole/MA, 165–176.

Moers, Gerald. 2013a. Erzählen, wenn es eng wird: Struktur- und Motivanalogien zwischen dem *Schiffbrüchigen* und dem *Grüffelo*, in: Julia Budka, Roman Gundacker & Gabriele Pieke (eds.), *Florilegium Aegyptiacum: Eine wissenschaftliche Blütenlese von Schülern und Freunden für Helmut Satzinger zum 75. Geburtstag am 21. Jänner 2013*, Göttinger Miszellen: Beihefte 14, Göttingen, 248–254.

Moers, Gerald. 2013b. Von Stimmen und Texten: Pharaonische Metalepsen als mediales Phänomen, in: Ute E. Eisen & Peter von Möllendorff (eds.), *Über die Grenze: Metalepse in Text- und Bildmedien des Altertums*, Narratologia: Contributions to Narrative Theory / Beiträge zur Erzähltheorie 39, Berlin, 29–58.

Moers, Gerald. 2019. Ägyptologie, in: Eva von Contzen & Stefan Tilg (eds.), *Handbuch Historische Narratologie*, Stuttgart, 323–325.

Moreno García, Juan Carlos. 2015. The Cursed Discipline? The Peculiarities of Egyptology at the Turn of the Twenty-First Century, in: William Carruthers (ed.), *Histories of Egyptology: Interdisciplinary Measures*, Routledge Studies in Egyptology 2, New York, 50–63.

Morenz, Ludwig. 2014. *Anfänge der ägyptischen Kunst: Eine problemgeschichtliche Einführung in ägyptologische Bild-Anthropologie*, Orbis Biblicus et Orientalis 264, Fribourg & Göttingen.

Müller-Funk, Wolfgang. 2008. *Die Kultur und ihre Narrative: Eine Einführung*, 2. überarb. u. erw. Aufl., Wien & New York.

Neumann, Sabine & Ansgar Nünning. 2014. Metanarration and Metafiction, in: Peter Hühn et al. (eds.), *The Living Handbook of Narratology*, Hamburg, URL = https://www-archiv.fdm.uni-hamburg.de/lhn/node/50.html [last view date 08 Nov 2022].

Nünning, Vera & Ansgar Nünning (eds.). 2002. *Erzähltheorie transgenerisch, intermedial, interdisziplinär*, WVT – Handbücher zum literaturwissenschaftlichen Studium 5, Trier.

Nünning, Ansgar. 2003. Narratology or Narratologies: Taking Stock of Recent Developments, Critique, and Modest Proposals for Future Usages of the Term, in: Tom Kindt & Hans-Harald Müller (eds.), *What is Narratology? Questions and Answers Regarding the Status of a Theory*, Narratologia: Contributions to Narrative Theory / Beiträge zur Erzähltheorie 1, Berlin & New York, 239–275.

Nünning, Ansgar. 2013. Wie Erzählungen Kulturen erzeugen: Prämissen, Konzepte und Perspektiven für eine kulturwissenschaftliche Narratologie, in: Alexandra Strohmaier (ed.), *Kultur – Wissen – Narration: Perspektiven transdisziplinärer Erzählforschung für die Kulturwissenschaften*, Bielefeld, 15–53.

Parkinson, Richard B. 2002. *Poetry and Culture in Middle Kingdom Egypt: A Dark Side to Perfection*, Athlone Publications in Egyptology and Ancient Near Eastern Studies, London.

Pehal, Martin. 2015. *Interpreting Ancient Egyptian Narratives: A Structural Analysis of the Tale of the Two Brothers, the Anat Myth, The Osirian Cycle, and the Astarte Papyrus*, Nouvelles études orientales, Fernelmont.

Pier, John. 2018. Von der französischen strukturalistischen Erzähltheorie zur nordamerikanischen postklassischen Narratologie, in: Martin Huber & Wolf Schmid (eds.), *Grundthemen der Literaturwissenschaft: Erzählen*, Grundthemen der Literaturwissenschaft, Berlin & Boston, 59–87.

Propp, Vladimir. 1968. *Morphology of the Folktale*, 2nd ed., American Folklore Society Bibliographical and Special Series 9 = Indiana University Research Center in Anthropology, Folklore, and Linguistics 10, Austin.

Richter, Tonio Sebastian. 2005. What's in a story? Cultural Narratology and Coptic Child Donation Papyri, in: *Journal of Juristic Papyrology* 35, 237–264.

Richter, Tonio Sebastian. 2011. „... auch wenn wir nicht an das Maß der seligen Anna heranreichten ...": Kindesschenkungen an ein oberägyptisches Kloster im 8. Jh. nach Chr. und ihr narrativer Horizont, in: Hans-Werner Fischer-Elfert & Tonio Sebastian Richter (eds.), *Literatur und Religion im Alten Ägypten: Ein Symposium zu Ehren von Elke Blumenthal.* ASAW zu Leipzig, philologisch-historische Kl. 81/5, Stuttgart & Leipzig, 164–208.

Ricœur, Paul. 1983. *Temps et récit I*, Paris.

Roeder, Hubert (ed.). 2009. *Das Erzählen in frühen Hochkulturen I: Der Fall Ägypten*, München.

Roeder, Hubert. 2009. Erzählen im Alten Ägypten: Vorüberlegungen zu einer Erzähltheorie zwischen Literaturwissenschaft und Altertumswissenschaften, in: Hubert Roeder (ed.), *Das Erzählen in frühen Hochkulturen I: Der Fall Ägypten*, München, 15–54.

Roeder, Hubert (ed.). 2018. *Das Erzählen in frühen Hochkulturen II: Eine Archäologie der narrativen Sinnbildung*, Paderborn.

Roeder, Hubert. 2018. Narration als Produkt sprachlich visueller Produktion: Eine kognitiv-kommunikative Perspektive auf die altägyptische Sprachkultur, in: Hubert Roeder (ed.), *Das Erzählen in frühen Hochkulturen II: Eine Archäologie der narrativen Sinnbildung*, Paderborn 105–197.

Rogner, Frederik. 2019. Zeit und Zeitlichkeit im ägyptischen Flachbild: Wege zur Analyse bildlicher Narrativität im Alten Ägypten, in: Dina Serova et al. (eds.), *Narrative: Geschichte – Mythos – Repräsentation. Beiträge des achten Berliner Arbeitskreises Junge Aegyptologie (BAJA 8) 1.12.–3.12.2017*, Göttinger Orientforschungen IV/65, Wiesbaden, 93–116.

Rogner, Frederik. 2021. Narrativity – Storytelling – Reference: On Some Fundamental Distinctions in the Discussion of Images (Review of Nadja S. Braun, *Bilder erzählen: Visuelle Narrativität im alten Ägypten*, Ägyptologische Studien Leipzig 2, Heidelberg, 2020), in: *Bibliotheca Orientalis* 78, 568–596.

Rogner, Frederik. 2022. *Bildliche Narrativität – Erzählen mit Bildern: Rezeption und Verwendung figürlicher Darstellungen im ägyptischen Neuen Reich*, Swiss Egyptological Studies 3, Basel & Frankfurt a.M.

Roussin, Philippe. 2017. What is Your Narrative? Lessons from the Narrative Turn, in: Hansen, Per Krogh et al. (eds.), *Emerging Vectors of Narratology*, Narratologia: Contributions to Narrative Theory / Beiträge zur Erzähltheorie 57, Berlin & Boston, 383–404.

Ryan, Marie-Laure. 2004. Introduction, in: Marie-Laure Ryan (ed.), *Narrative across Media: The Language of Storytelling*, Lincoln & London, 1–40.

Ryan, Marie-Laure. 2014. Narration in Various Media, in: Peter Hühn et al. (eds.), *The Living Handbook of Narratology*, Hamburg, URL = https://www-archiv.fdm.uni-hamburg.de/lhn/node/53.html [last view date: 08 Nov 2022].

Schmid, Wolf. 2010. „Fabel" und „Sujet", in: Wolf Schmid (ed.), *Slavische Erzähltheorie: Russische und tschechische Ansätze*, Narratologia: Contributions to Narrative Theory / Beiträge zur Erzähltheorie 21, Berlin & Boston, 1–45.

Schmidt-Haberkamp, Barbara. 2017. Narration, in: Ludger Kühnhardt & Tilman Mayer (eds.), *Bonner Enzyklopädie der Globalität*, Wiesbaden, 985–995.

Schulz, Armin. 2010. Fremde Kohärenz: Narrative Verknüpfungsformen im Nibelungenlied und in der Kaiserchronik, in: Harald Haferland & Matthias Meyer (eds. unter Mitarbeit von Carmen Stange & Markus Greulich), *Historische Narratologie: Mediävistische Perspektiven*, Trends in Medieval Philology 19, Berlin, 339–360.

Serova, Dina, Burkhard Backes, Matthieu W. Götz & Alexandra Verbovsek (eds.). 2019. *Narrative: Geschichte – Mythos – Repräsentation. Beiträge des achten Berliner Arbeitskreises Junge Aegyptologie (BAJA 8) 1.12.–3.12.2017*, Göttinger Orientforschungen IV/65, Wiesbaden.

Simon, Henrike. 2013. *»Textaufgaben«: Kulturwissenschaftliche Konzepte in Anwendung auf die Literatur der Ramessidenzeit*, Studien zur Altägyptischen Kultur, Beihefte 14, Hamburg.

Sommer, Roy. 2012. The Merger of Classical and Postclassical Narratologies and the Consolidated Future of Narrative Theory, in: *Diegesis: Interdisziplinäres E-Journal für Erzählforschung* 1, 143–157.

Sommer, Roy. 2018. Kulturwissenschaftliche Konzepte des Erzählens, in: Martin Huber & Wolf Schmid (eds.), *Grundthemen der Literaturwissenschaft: Erzählen*, Grundthemen der Literaturwissenschaft, Berlin & Boston, 613–622.

Speidel, Klaus. 2013. Can a Single Still Picture Tell a Story? Definitions of Narrative and the Alleged Problem of Time in Single Still Pictures, in: *Diegesis: Interdisziplinäres E-Journal für Erzählforschung* 2, 173–194.

Speidel, Klaus. 2018. What Narrative is: Reconsidering Definitions Based on Experiments with Pictorial Narrative. An Essay in Descriptive Narratology, in: *Frontiers of Narrative Studies* 4, 76–104.

Steiner, Wendy. 2004. Pictorial Narrativity, in: Marie-Laure Ryan (ed.), *Narrative across Media: The Language of Storytelling*, Lincoln & London, 145–177.

Suhr, Claudia. 1999. Zum fiktiven Erzähler in der ägyptischen Literatur, in: Gerald Moers (ed.), *Definitely: Egyptian Literature, Proceedings of the Symposium "Ancient Egyptian Literature: History and Forms", Los Angeles, March 24–26, 1995*, Lingua Aegyptia – Studia Monographica 2, Göttingen, 91–129.

Suhr, Claudia. 2016. *Die ägyptische Ich-Erzählung: Eine narratologische Untersuchung*, Göttinger Orientforschungen IV/61, Wiesbaden.

Tait, John. 2011. 'He Did its Like': Some Use of Repetition in Demotic Narrative Fiction, in: Eszter Bechtold, András Gilyás & Andrea Hasznos (eds.), *From Illahun to Djeme. Papers Presented in Honour of Ulrich Luft*, BAR International Series 2311, Oxford, 279–285.

Tait, John. 2015. May Pharaoh Listen to the Story! Stories-within-Stories in Demotic Fictional Narrative, in: Rune Nyord & Kim Ryholt (eds.), *Lotus and Laurel: Studies in Language and Religion in Honour of Paul John Frandsen,* CNI Publications 39, Copenhagen, 391–401.

Varga, Aron Kibédi. 1990. Visuelle Argumentation und visuelle Narrativität, in: Wolfgang Harms (ed.), *Text und Bild, Bild und Text: DFG Symposium 1988*, Stuttgart, 356–367.

Veits, Andreas. 2020. Narratives (Bild-)Verstehen. Zum narrativen Potential von Einzelbildern, in: Andreas Veits, Lukas R. A. Wilde & Klaus Sachs-Hombach (eds.), *Einzelbild und Narrativität: Theorien, Zugänge, offenen Fragen*, Köln, 124–160.

Verhoeven, Ursula. 2009. Funktionen von Wiederholungen und Abweichungen in ägyptischen Erzähltexten, in: Hubert Roeder (ed.), *Das Erzählen in frühen Hochkulturen I: Der Fall Ägypten*, München, 315–334.

Vinson, Steve. 2008. Through a Woman's Eyes, and in a Woman's Voice: Ihweret as Focalizor in the *First Tale of Setne Khaemwas*, in: Paul McKechnie & Philippe Giullaume (eds.), *Ptolemy II and his World*, Mnemosyne Supplements History and Archaeology of Classical Antiquity 300, Boston & Leiden, 303–351.

Vinson, Steve. 2015. Into the Abyss: The Structure of the 'Tale of the Shipwrecked Sailor' as *mise en abyme*, in: Richard Jasnow & Kathlyn M. Cooney (eds.), *Joyful in Thebes: Egyptological Studies in Honor of Betsy M. Bryan*, Atlanta, 471–482.

Vinson, Steve. 2018. *The Craft of a Good Scribe: History, Narrative, and Meaning in the First Tale of Setna Khaemwas*, Harvard Egyptological Studies 3, Leiden & Boston.

Von Contzen, Eva. 2014. Why we Need a Medieval Narratology: A Manifesto, in: *Diegesis: Interdisziplinäres E-Journal für Erzählforschung* 3/2, *Historische Narratologie*, 1–21.

Von Contzen, Eva & Stefan Tilg. 2019. Einleitung: Was ist historische Narratologie, in: Eva von Contzen & Stefan Tilg (eds.), *Handbuch Historische Narratologie*, Stuttgart, VII–X.

Wellek, Rene & Austin Warren. 2019 [1942]. *Theory of Literature*, New York.

White, Hayden. 1980. The Value of Narrativity in the Representation of Reality, in: *Critical Inquiry* 7, 5–27.

Widmaier, Kai. 2017. *Bilderwelten: Ägyptische Bilder und ägyptologische Kunst: Vorarbeiten für eine bildwissenschaftliche Ägyptologie*, Probleme der Ägyptologie 35, Leiden & Boston.

Wieder, Anja. 2007. *Altägyptische Erzählungen: Form und Funktion einer literarischen Gattung*, Dissertation Heidelberg.

Willems, Harco. 1996. *The Coffin of Heqata (Cairo JdE 36418): A Case Study of Egyptian Funerary Culture of the Early Middle Kingdom*, Orientalia Lovaniensia Analecta 70, Leuven.

Wilson, Thomas. 1553. *The arte of rhetorique; for the use of all suche as are studious of eloquence, sette forth in English*, London, URL = https://quod.lib.umich.edu/e/eebo/A15530.0001.001 (last view date 10 January 2023].

Wolf, Werner. 2002. Das Problem der Narrativität in Literatur, bildender Kunst und Musik: Ein Beitrag zu einer intermedialen Erzähltheorie, in: Vera Nünning & Ansgar Nünning (eds.), *Erzähltheorie transgenerisch, intermedial, interdisziplinär*, WVT – Handbücher zum literaturwissenschaftlichen Studium 5, Trier, 23–104.

Wolf, Werner. 2003. Narrative and Narrativity: A Narratological Reconceptualization and its Applicability to the Visual Arts, in: *Word and Image: A Journal of Verbal/Visual Enquiry*, 180–197.

Wolf, Werner. 2011. Narratology and Media(lity): The Transmedial Expansion of a Literary Discipline and Possible Consequences, in: Greta Olsen (ed.), *Current Trends in Narratology*, Narratologia: Contributions to Narrative Theory / Beiträge zur Erzähltheorie 27, Berlin, 145–180.

Yacoub, Mahmoud. 2009. Die Erzählung von Horus und Seth. Eine narrative Analyse der Handlungssequenzen, in: Stephan Conermann (ed.), *Modi des Erzählens in nicht-abendländischen Gesellschaften*, Narratio Aliena? Studien des Bonner Zentrums für transkulturelle Narratologie 2, Berlin, 59–72.

Žába, Zbyněk. 1956. *Les maxims de Ptaḥḥotep*, Československá Akademie Věd, Praha.

Zeidler, Jürgen. 1993. Zur Frage des Spätentstehung des Mythos in Ägypten, in: *Göttinger Miszellen: Beiträge zur ägyptologischen Diskussion* 132, 85–109.

Zeman, Sonja. 2020. Grammatik der Narration Grammar of Narration, in: *Zeitschrift für germanistische Linguistik* 48/3, 457–494.

What does *sḏd* tell?

Reformulating narratological concepts in Egyptology

Camilla Di Biase-Dyson[1]

Abstract

In the Ancient Egyptian language, narratives can be introduced by two related words: *ḏd* and *sḏd*. Since *sḏd* is used far less than its ubiquitous counterpart, this study undertakes to consider the conditions under which it was used. To do so, it considers all known cases of verbal and nominal iterations of *sḏd/sḏd(.w)* from the perspectives of lexical semantics, grammatical theory and historical syntax. A reconsideration of the meaning span and usage of these words also has implications for text-linguistics and narratological theory, motivating us to reconsider the role of 'tellability' in an ancient Egyptian context.

1 Aims

The verb *sḏd* is generally considered by the Egyptological community to mean 'to tell' or 'narrate' something in its transitive use and 'to speak' in its intransitive use. Such definitions reflect key meanings of the related verb *ḏd*.[2] From a narratological perspective, *sḏd* has been taken as a "metanarrative Einleitung von mindestens hypodiegetischen Binnenerzählungen" (Moers 2019: 323), i.e., what takes place when a narrator is relating a story of theirs within another story, such as in a text bearing one of the most famous cases of *sḏd*, *The Shipwrecked Sailor* (pHermitage 1115), when the sailor attempts to cheer his chief by recounting (*sḏd*) something that had happened to him.[3] Specifically of the nominal usage it has been said that *sḏd(.w)* is "the word in Egyptian which most closely approaches a genre term covering all aspects of popular orality" and "could be regarded as liable to incorporate fantasy and therefore to be untrustworthy" (Redford 2000: 171). Though Redford's perspective on orality enriches our understanding of the meaning of *sḏd*, we will see that the meaning expressing doubt in the veracity of an oral report is not visible in the records until at least the Ramesside Period.[4] Moreover, Redford's

---

1 Macquarie University (<camilla.dibiasedyson@mq.edu.au>).

2 *Wb* V, 618.9–625.2 gives the broad meaning categories: 'sagen', 'vortragen, rezitieren', 'mitteilen, berichten', 'nennen' and 'denken, meinen'. 'Erzählen' is not mentioned.

3 For later examples see also Tait (2015).

4 Indeed, Roeder (2018: 163) goes so far as to produce a definition that is practically the opposite of Redford's: "Beim '*sedjed*' geht es darum, dass dem Rezipienten das für ihn nicht Wahrnehmbare möglichst unverfälscht nahegebracht wird."

Gerald Moers (ed.), *Narrative and Narrativity in Ancient Egypt*, 27–70
DOI: https://doi.org/10.37011/studmon.29.02

understanding of *sḏd* as a technical term for the narrative genre is disputed by a number of scholars before and after him,[5] though here it must be mentioned that—contrary to some of these opinions[6]—the foregoing study highlights an increasing nearness to the category of narrative in Demotic texts.[7]

This study takes all known cases of verbal and nominal iterations of *sḏd* into consideration and reconsiders their usage in context. In so doing, it engages with focal points of synchronic and diachronic lexical semantics (span of meaning(s), change in meaning(s) from Egyptian to Demotic), grammatical theory (the role of the causative prefix *s* and the inflection of the caus. 2.rad. infinitive with *.t*) and historical syntax (transitivity change for verbs and the role of determination in lexicalisation for nouns). The nominal cases also require us to consider the impact of the verb's meaning change over time on the meaning of the noun. Lastly, this study interrogates the relationship between the findings of the lexico-grammatical study and principles of text-linguistics and narratological theory: What kinds of things can be *sḏd* and are they 'tellable' from a narratological perspective? 'Tellability' in narratology is commonly tied to a particular type of 'event', in which something decisive, unpredictable, or unusual happens.[8]

2 The corpus

To begin, we consider the spans of meaning argued for in Adolf Erman and Hermann Grapow's *Wörterbuch der ägyptischen Sprache*, including the source material for the *Wörterbuch* in the *Belegstellen* and the *Digitalisiertes Zettelarchiv* (henceforth *Wb*, *Belegstellen* and *DZA* respectively). We shall also consider Raymond Faulkner's *Concise Dictionary* (*CD*), Dimitri Meeks' *Année Lexicographique* (*AL* I–III) and Rainer Hannig's *Großes Handwörterbuch Ägyptisch–Deutsch – Marburger Edition* (*HWB*), as well as his *Ägyptisches Wörterbuch I: Altes Reich und Erste Zwischenzeit* (*ÄW* I) and *Ägyptisches Wörterbuch II: Mittleres Reich und Zweite Zwischenzeit* (*ÄW* II).

These ideas shall then be tested against the available sources, in other words, all cases of the verb and noun documented not only in the *DZA* (above) but also in both major

5 Redford (2000: 171) mentions Erman as a scholar who doubted its status as a technical term for the narrative genre, but he actually cites Grapow (1936: 59, n. 24). About this should be said that Erman (presumably in his publication from 1911, since it is cited by Caminos 1978: 156) does not explicitly bring up the status of the word as a genre category; Grapow, cited above, on the other hand, does, if we read the more general "Bezeichnung" as Redford's more narrow "technical term". For later studies that follow and develop Grapow's argument, see Simon (2013: 126) and Roeder (2018: 161).

6 Simon 2013: 126: "*sḏd* ist in seiner Bedeutung ‚Wort, Rede (jemds.)' und ‚Erzählung' weder in der 19. und 20. Dynastie noch in einer dieser Zeit vorausgehenden bzw. folgenden Epoche als terminus technicus für verschiedene, merkmalsgleiche Vertreter einer bestimmten literarischen Gattung belegt.'

7 As in Quack (^{2}2009: 17); also Section 6.4.

8 See Hühn (2013) and Baroni (2014). From an Egyptological perspective, consult Fitzenreiter (ed.) (2009).

digital corpora: in the *Thesaurus Linguae Aegyptiae* (*TLA* and *TLA* v.2)[9]—Egyptian and Demotic corpora—and in the *Projet Ramsès* database of Late Egyptian, as well as stray cases mentioned in text editions. Each case has been analysed in relation to the use and semantic span of the lexeme, as well as to the genre, register and text in which it appears and the period in which it is attested. The cases in which there is overlap with the much better attested lexeme *ḏd*[10] will also be investigated, in order, where possible, to explain the use of the one or the other lexeme.[11] Broadly speaking, *sḏd* has throughout its use-life—in comparison with *ḏd*—a very limited number of collocations, which, as we shall see, are significant for determining the meaning of the lexeme.

If we take all cases from the digital corpora into consideration, having accounted for incorrectly lemmatised cases,[12] double-ups of key sources across lexica as well as parallels in various states of repair,[13] the Egyptian corpus currently has a total of 127 (out of 142) reliable (i.e., usable) cases of the verb *sḏd* and 25 (out of 32) reliable cases of the noun *sḏd(.w)*. The Demotic corpus—collected exclusively from the *TLA*[14]—has 83 useable cases out of 95 total cases of the verb and 35 (out of 37) cases of the noun.[15] In sum, there are a total of 270 reliable cases out of 306 found.

3 Orthography

For the verb, the earliest cases (in hieroglyphic and hieratic script) take the spellings  or ,[16] whereas from the 18th Dynasty, there are also the variations  and . In hieratic of the late Ramesside Period and early Third Intermediate Period a series of endings emerge, such as 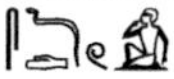 and 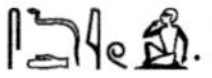. Late Period hieratic texts follow the trend of using S29 (*s*) for the causative *s*, not O34 (the eventual allograph *z*).[17] For the noun, the *Wb* provides the following writings: , 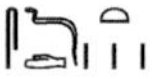 and .[18] New spellings are also attested between the late Ramesside Period and the Late Period, with a

9 This study takes into consideration both the original *TLA* (last updated 2015) as well as the 2nd version (launched in 2022).

10 By means of example, there are 75 attestations of the verb *sḏd* in the Egyptian *TLA* corpus and 4628 of *ḏd*. The *TLA* v.2 has 88 attestations of *sḏd*.

11 For the discursive role of *ḏd*, in other words, its use as a 'quotation index', see Kammerzell & Peust (2002: 197).

12 The first attested case in the *TLA*, the stela of Idu (BM EA 1059, line 5) is actually a case of *ḏd*.

13 These items are included in or excluded from a digital repository in a haphazard manner, some including reconstructed elements, others excluding them. I have decided to exclude all cases in which the passage is too fragmentary or in which *sḏd* or its argument are in a lacuna.

14 The Demotic *TLA* v.2 has no new attestations.

15 This number is a result of my own re-allocation of the sources to these categories, as all but one case in the *TLA* Demotic database (likewise *TLA* v2) were lemmatised as a verb.

16 This reflects the development of the causative prefix (and orthographic practice) in general. In Old Egyptian texts, on the other hand, the causative prefix *s*- is exclusively represented with the folded-cloth sign (S29), see Štubňová (2019: 184).

17 See *Wb* IV, 394–395.12, also *DZA* 29.919.950, *DZA* 29.919.960 and *DZA* 29.919.970.

18 See *Wb* IV, 395.13–18 for the nouns. There are no separate orthographic entries for the nouns in the *DZA*.

new classifier (F18): [19] and .[20] It can be noted that in many cases, the verb and noun are difficult to differentiate orthographically. Even the *.t* (X1) ending of the noun could be mistaken for an infinitive if the plural strokes (Z2 or Z3) are not written. In Demotic texts, the orthographic strategy changes entirely. For the verb, the predominant spelling is  or similar and for the noun predominantly 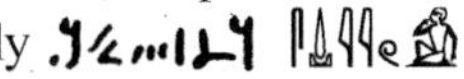 (Erichsen 1954: 482).

4 Definitions: State of the art

The *Wb* proposes a whole range of definitions, or, rather, usages, for both the transitive and the intransitive verb *sḏd*, allegedly attested from the Middle Kingdom (*Wb* IV 394).[21] The sheer detail of the different subcategories not only distracts from the primary distinction between the transitive meaning, 'erzählen', and the intransitive one, 'sprechen', but also, problematically, establishes distinctions that are either false or trivial.

A false distinction can be noted, for instance, between two *transitive* meanings 'etw. erzählen' and 'von etw. erzählen' (*Wb* IV 395.1–2). A cursory look at the *Belegstellen* indicates that the first meaning is tied to cases with different types of direct objects,[22] whereas the second meaning is tied in both cases to people speaking specifically about campaigns abroad. There is nothing in the Egyptian that would imply a distinction, and, strangely, none of these cases would have been translated into German with anything other than 'von etw. erzählen' either. All subsequent groups, in which different direct and indirect objects (via the prepositions *ḥnʿ*, *n* and *ḥr*) of *sḏd* are collected, are important from the perspective of frequent collocations but trivial in respect of the primary definition, which otherwise does not substantially alter: 'erzählen was man erlebt hat', 'von jemds. Macht u.ä. rühmend erzählen', 'in allen Fällen auch mit *n*: jemandem erzählen u.s.w.', 'auch als Aufforderung: [ich erzähle dies] möget ihr es Anderen weitererzählen' (*Wb* IV 395.3–5). The distinction between the different meanings is moreover at times unclear: One of the two *Belegstellen* of the transitive meaning 'seine Wünsche aussprechen' (*Wb* IV 395.6), called *Beleg* Harfner Harr 6.8, fits much better in the main meaning 'von etw. erzählen' (*Wb* IV 395 1–2) since it talks about reporting on one's 'form' (*qd*) and 'condition' (*ḫr.t*), rather than stating a wish. An incorporation of this subcategory into the main one is all the more pertinent, since some *Belegstellen* from the main meaning (such as oCairo 25206) explicitly describe stating wishes.

The intransitive use has one main meaning, namely, 'sprechen' (*Wb* IV 395.7), but, unfortunately, 2/3 of the *Belegstellen* are incorrectly categorised (*Urk.* IV 437, an

19 pMoscow 127, 4.9–10 (Caminos 1977: Pl. 9).

20 tCairo JE 94478, vso 1 (Vittmann 2006: 189–190).

21 This dating disregards, however, a legible case of *sḏd* from the First Intermediate Period, which is unfortunately in a damaged context: the Asyut tomb of *Jt(j)-jb=j* (= *Siut* III 30–31; Griffith 1889; Schenkel 1965: 74–82). This case was known at the time of the *Wörterbuch*'s composition, as it appears as slip DZA 29.921.010.

22 Examples include someone's condition, appearance, or situation, as well as wishes.

inscription of Djehuty, is a passive transitive case and the inscription of Huy Pl. 23/29 is an intransitive case with the direct object marked with *m*, i.e., it is better placed in *Wb* IV 395.11). This group is then followed by three cases, each with a different preposition marking the indirect object (*Wb* IV 395.7–10), which are also at times problematically attested.[23] Other cases using a prepositional phrase either introduce an object with *m* (*Wb* IV 395.11)—such cases we will return to in Section 7.4—or use a specific adverbial *m sḏd.t*, to generate the meaning 'Aussprüche [alter Weiser] gebrauchen' (*Wb* IV 395.12).

The noun *sḏd*, which dates from the New Kingdom (*Wb* IV 395), is depicted as having two predominant meanings, which correspond to nominalised forms of the verbs just discussed: 'Worte, Reden jemds.' (*Wb* IV 395.13) or as 'Erzählung' (*Wb* IV 395.14). The cases for both are well-justified by the *Belege*, though in the case of 'Erzählung' not a single case indicates a personal history in the manner of what we conceive of a 'narrative', but rather is far more closely to be connected to an official 'report', as seen by the *Belegstellen* both of Hatshepsut's Punt expedition inscription (*Urk.* IV 344, 9–10) and the Kuban stela of Ramesses II (K*RI* II, 357.7). Subsequently listed meanings are more problematic. *Wb* IV 395.15 and 395.16 are designated only with the label 'Als Überschrift', representing a report of the *nḫt.w* 'victories' and *bꜣ.w* 'manifestations of power(?)' of a king or god. In other words, it would have been more fitting, if at all, to include both as a sub-category of *Wb* IV 395.14. The other two cases represent (to this day, unfortunately), complete anomalies in the Egyptian record: the source of *Wb* IV 395.17 is the compound *ḥw(j).t sḏd.t* 'figure (lit. flow) of speech' ('sprichwortlich werden') in Merenptah's 'Israel' stela (K*RI* IV, 15.5-7) and the source of *Wb* IV 395.18 is the phrase *m sḫr n sḏd* 'gesprächsweise', i.e., 'conversationally' that is used in the *Tale of the Doomed Prince* (pHarris 500, vso 5.10).

The *TLA* reduces the (as we have seen, often unnecessary) detail of the *Wb* to 'erzählen, sprechen' for the verb (Lemma 150940) and 'Worte, Reden' for the noun (Lemma 150950). The Demotic usage seems to expand to include '(zur Frau) nehmen' (*TLA*; Erichsen 1954: 482) for the verb and 'Erzählung, Angelegenheit, Ereignis' (*TLA*) or 'Rede', 'Ergebnis',[24] 'Erzählung' (Erichsen 1954: 482) for the noun.

Faulkner (*CD*, 260), similarly, gives the transitive definition as 'relate, recount' and the intransitive as 'talk'. The noun *sḏd.t* he renders as 'description' and 'tale' and *sḏd.w* as 'tales'. Hannig (*HWB*, 863) on the other hand, opts for a transitive translation not only of 'erzählen' but also 'zitieren'.[25] 'Zitieren' emerges again as a meaning of the intransitive (s. *Wb* IV 395.12). Regarding the nominal form, Hannig establishes an emphatic distinction

---

23 Of the *Wb Belegstellen* for the meaning *Wb* IV 395.9, '*n* zu jem. sprechen', 2/3 cases are rather passive cases of the transitive *sḏd* (Karn Mar 37b = Cairo CG 583, 8 (in Mariette 1875b: Pl. 37b, right side, 7, also Varille 1968: 46–48, Pl. VIII) and Dend Mar I 31 = Temple of Dendera, Room C, back wall, right, 2nd row (Mariette 1875a: T. 1 Pl. 31; *DZA* 29.920.740).

24 Vittmann (2006: 190) plausibly suggests that this is a *lapsus* and that Erichsen most likely meant 'Erlebnis'.

25 However, the example he cites directly following cannot not feasibly be 'zitieren', as seen by the dictionary entry, but rather 'erzählen': '*sḏd* [kaus] 1. erzählen {31962} (*n* jdm {31963}); zitieren {47852} ≈*y sw n rmw ḥr mtr n ꜣpdw m tꜣ-pt* erzähle (sic) es den Fischen in der Flut und den Vögeln im Himmel {31964}'.

between the allegedly masculine *sḏd* 'Erzählung' and the feminine *sḏd.t* 'Beschreibung'. However, this distinction between the different variants is problematic for several reasons. Firstly, the analysis indicates (see Section 6) that of the 25 pharaonic period cases of the noun in good enough condition, the 'masculine' *sḏd*, the allegedly 'feminine' *sḏd.t* and the plural *sḏd.w* are all used to describe a 'proclamation' or a 'report', which, as mentioned, are definitions not covered by the *Wb*.[26] The fact that 33/35 attested Demotic cases of *sḏj* in the *TLA* are determined, but *not one* by a determiner with feminine inflection (*tꜣ*, *tꜣy⸗*, *wꜥ.t*, etc.), also lends credence to the idea that we are not actually dealing with a masculine or feminine noun *per se*, but rather with a deverbalised nominal form that only becomes standardised in its nominal orthography by the Late Period.[27]

Reflecting the dating of the verb *sḏd* postulated by the *Wb*, no case is attested in Hannig's Old Kingdom dictionary (*ÄW* I). Hannig thus disregards the clear but fragmentary case from a First Intermediate Period tomb in Asyut.[28] The attestations from the Middle Kingdom dictionary (Hannig *ÄW* II, 2414: Lemmata 31962–31967) eschew the translations proposed in the *Marburger Edition* (though both were published in 2006) in favour of the more traditional distinctions of 'erzählen' and 'sprechen' for the verb,[29] with subcategories for specific prepositional phrases marking indirect objects—'zitieren' is here completely avoided. In keeping with the dating proposed by the *Wb*, no attestations of the nominal form predate the New Kingdom.

Meeks in *Année Lexicographique* (*AL* I, 359–360 = 77.4053; *AL* II, 366 = 78.4010 and *AL* III, 282 = 79.2898) opts for 'dire, raconter, relater',[30] and (in *AL* II, 366) describes collocations with objects like *pḥ.tï*, 'proclamer (des hauts faits)'.[31] The noun is regarded as meaning either 'recit' or (in relation to the *Tale of Woe*) 'mensonge' (*AL* I, 360 = 77.4054 and *AL* III, 282 = 79.2899). Meeks is the first lexicographer to highlight, via sources like this from the Third Intermediate Period, a degree of negative polarity in the noun. As we shall discuss below in Section 6.1, a negative meaning (albeit not necessarily the very straightforward 'mengonge/lie') can indeed be attested already in the Ramesside Period, but exclusively in the context of satire, like the *Satirical Letter of Hori*, which tends to contort word meaning for the purpose of making calculated and clever put-downs. Similar cases are the sarcastic use of the term *mtr* 'teaching/instruction' (pAnastasi I, *inter alia* 7.7), or the metaphor *tkꜣ m kk.w* 'torch in the darkness' to describe, via hyperbolic reversal, a putatively incompetent colleague (pAnastasi I, *inter alia* 17.3).

26 See Schott (1990: 365), who translates *sḏdt* as 'Gespräch', 'Bericht'.

27 The four attested pre-Demotic cases with determined noun phrases, as we shall return to in Section 7.5, come from pAnastasi I, from the late 19th Dynasty (two cases) and two cases from the Late Period (*Amenemope* L = pBM EA 10474 and the report on tCairo JE 94478, vso). The first three have the plural possessive *nꜣy⸗* and the last has the article *nꜣ*.

28 Asyut tomb of *Jt(j)-jb⸗j* (= *Siut* III 30–31; Griffith 1889; Schenkel 1965: 74–82).

29 The Tübingen/Stuttgart stela of Sobekhotep is, however, incorrectly grouped with the *Ptahhotep* cases, as it is indeed transitive.

30 The case Meeks (*AL* I, 359–360) groups as a (participial) verb, *sḏdt* «ce qui est raconté», with reference to Zivie (1976: 68.18) I have taken to be a substantive.

31 The late case written 𓋴𓍑𓄿𓂝𓀁 (S29-U28-G1-F18:A2), in Vernus (1978: 211, n. i), is unclear, both in orthography and meaning, and has been excluded from this study.

From a more cognitive-narratological perspective, Hubert Roeder (2018: 162) attempts to take the causal aspect of the word seriously and proposes "sprechen lassen", concretely, a process in which:

> "Man lässt das, was man irgendwo und irgendwann gehört oder wahrgenommen hat, bei einem 'Wiederholen' oder 'Melden/Berichten' gegenüber seinem Adressaten selbst sprechen bzw. eigenhändig zur Sprache kommen. Das ‚Sprechenlassen' beschreibt sozusagen die kognitiv-kommunikative Disposition dieser sprachlichen Aktionen".

What this specifically implies is that "Der Rezipient soll sich selbst ein Bild von dem machen können, was ihm durch den, der *‚sprechen lässt'*, zu Gehör kommt" (Roeder 2018: 163). In other words, there is a high degree of immediacy in the communication: It is "*Präsentieren*", which is only partially compatible with "Erzählen", since other things (e.g., *mdw.t*) can also be communicated thus (Roeder 2018: 163–164).

Gerald Moers (2019: 323) suggests, on the other hand, that a plurality of meanings needs to be taken into consideration, since meanings of *sḏd* range from 'erzählen' to 'berichten' and from 'äußern' to 'sagen'. Nevertheless, the use as 'erzählen' represents a particular narratological function. Specifically, as mentioned in Section 1, *sḏd* can be used, along the lines of Mieke Bal,[32] as a "metanarrative Einleitung von mindestens hypodiegetischen Binnenerzählungen".[33] The extent to which these insights suit the data at hand will be explored in Section 7.6.

The lack of clarity in the semantic scope of the lexeme is an indication of the extent to which the data for *sḏd* needs to be revisited. Most glaringly, the historically dominant connection between the verb *sḏd* and 'erzählen' or 'narrating' requires rethinking, at least for sources of the pharaonic period. In a related fashion, the translation of the noun *sḏd(.w)* as 'Erzählung' or 'narrative' is equally problematic. Instead, a very particular kind of 'reporting' or 'proclaiming' was intended. In this paper, it is argued that a more suitable (if wordier) definition for the transitive verb *sḏd* would be: *A communication of often personal but also culturally significant information that is intended to affect the behaviour of the hearer*. It reflects, more concisely, *transmitting information with purpose*.[34] This naturally also has an impact on the definition of the nominal form in the pharaonic period. An analysis of Demotic sources from the Late Period to the Roman Period rounds out this study and show us that in fact both verb and its derived noun had undergone substantial semantic change. By this time, they had at last come to mean something more like 'to narrate' and 'story' respectively.

---

32 Bal (^{2}1997: 52–66) talks specifically about the relation between 'primary' and 'embedded texts', whereby embedded texts do not perforce need to themselves be narrative.

33 Moers (2019: 323).

34 The role of 'teaching' in the act of 'narrating' has been addressed by Roeder (2009: 103), but not specifically in reference to the meaning of *sḏd*.

5 Findings I: The usage of the verb from a diachronic and generic perspective

In comparison with *ḏd*, which is attested in the corpus from the Old Kingdom at the latest,[35] *sḏd* appears in the record somewhat later. It is unfortunate that the first known case, from a First Intermediate Tomb in Asyut,[36] is in a fragmentary context (*sḏd(.w) n ///=f* 'What was reported (?) to his ///'), as the next dated sources come from the Middle Kingdom (ca. 2055–1650 BCE). Of the 127 useable cases of the verb *sḏd* in Egyptian, only nine cases come from this time. A single case comes from the late Second Intermediate Period (ca. 1650–1550 BCE) and will be counted with the New Kingdom cases. Most examples date to the New Kingdom (ca. 1550–1069 BCE), with 102 useable cases. Additionally, there are eight cases in a clear context from the Third Intermediate Period (ca. 1069–664 BCE), six from the Late Period (ca. 664–332 BCE), one from the Ptolemaic Period (332–30 BCE) and one from the Roman Period (30 BCE–311 CE). These numbers clearly show a skewing of the corpus towards specific time periods and genres, which only the consultation of indices of non-digitised corpora would emend. It also indicates the extent to which later cases are rather to be sought within the Demotic corpus.

5.1 The Middle Kingdom

5.1.1 Sources and genres

Five of the Middle Kingdom examples come from the narrative *The Shipwrecked Sailor* (pPetersburg 1115), two come from *The Teachings of Ptahhotep* (pPrisse), one comes from a private stela (Tübingen Inv. Nr. 458) and one comes from a magical text (pRamesseum XV = pBM EA 10768).

5.1.1 Range of meanings in context

All five cases of *sḏd* from *The Shipwrecked Sailor* are transitive cases, in all of which the meaning is not 'to narrate', but rather 'to relate' something specific about the speaker's own experience (e.g., *sḏd=j r=f n=k mj.t(ï)t-jr.ï ḫpr m-ʿ=j ḏs=j* 'Now, I will tell you (about) something similar that happened to my own self').[37] This relation is specifically intended to influence the outlook and perhaps decision-making process of the hearer, the captain. Moreover, it is shaped and motivated by a transformative experience with a deity, the snake-god,[38] which is also a feature of the usage of *sḏd* in numerous other later sources, not least the *ex-voto* stelae of the New Kingdom (Sections 5.3 and 5.4). Both cases of

35 Giza tomb (G 8090) of Debehen from the reign of Menkaure (ca. BCE), in Hassan (1943: 167–169, Fig. 118, Pl. XLVIII).

36 Asyut tomb of *Jt(j)-jb=j* (= *Siut* III 30–31; Griffith 1889; Schenkel 1965: 74–82). Also slip *DZA* 29.921.010.

37 *The Shipwrecked Sailor*, pPetersburg 1115, line 21.

38 *The Shipwrecked Sailor*, pPetersburg 1115, lines 21 and 125 describe 'something similar' (*mj.t(ï) t-jr.ï*) being related; line 124 shows 'what he experienced (lit. tasted)' (*dp.t.n=f*) and 142 'what happened to him' (*ḫpr.t ḥr=j*). In 139 the sailor tells the snake he will report on his power (*bꜣ.w=k*)

sḏd in *Ptahhotep*,[39] on the other hand, are intransitive,[40] but also here the 'speaking' to (*n* /*ḫr*) children means far more than merely speaking—it is *interacting with purpose.*[41] In the appeal to the living, the usage is transitive, with the direct object being the *mšꜥ.w* 'campaigns' undertaken by the speaker.[42] The fascinating part here is the coda, *mj ḏd⸗ṯn ḥtp-ḏ(j)-nzw* 'like you recite the offering formula', in which the *sḏd* 'relating' (to one's wives) of battles abroad is likened to one's 'recitation' (*ḏd*) of the offering formula for deceased people. One might ponder what is being focalised in this simile. Is it the fact that returning home alive and sharing one's experience should be as natural and as routine as conducting ritual? Or is it rather that the function of the things said, the talk of battles lost and won and ritual recitations, also carries a cultural weight that makes them similar? Lastly, the magical text from pRamesseum XV (= pBM EA 10768), refers to the 'speaking' (or not) of the name of someone.[43]

5.2 The late Second Intermediate Period to the New Kingdom

5.2.1 Sources and genres

Of the 102 useable cases, 28 come from the royal monumental discourse (plus two hieratic versions, making 30) from the time of Kamose to that of Ramesses III. The genres include military narratives, commemorative texts, obelisk inscriptions and boundary stelae.

A similar number, 27/102 attested cases, comes from private monumental discourse, a broad medial categorisation that includes texts of self-presentation, hymns and songs (like mourning songs and harpists' songs). While mourning songs (one case), self-presentation texts (four cases) and texts praising the king (four cases) are less well attested, hymns (19 clear cases, two damaged) and harpist songs (seven well-preserved, four damaged) are comparatively well-attested. Private monumental texts, even more than the royal monumental texts, not only appear in a broad range of monumental contexts (tomb walls,

---

to the king (*MES* 42.7; 45.4; 45.3; 46.1 and 45.14 respectively). See also Roeder (2009: 107–108, 119–123).

39 *The Teachings of Ptahhotep*, pPrisse = pBN 186–194 (P), 17.11 and 17.12 (Žába 1956: 62).

40 The *TLA* (P. Dils) has translated both as a pseudo-transitive form with a dummy subject '(es) mitteilen', but they can be easily rendered as a classic intransitive form 'speak', e.g. 17.12, *sḏd⸗f m-mj.t(ï)t n ḫrd.w⸗f* 'He will speak in a similar fashion to his children'.

41 Perhaps given the meaning overlap between the intransitive, argumentless *sḏd* and *ḏd* proper, the roughly contemporary parallel text of *Ptahhotep* P, 17.11, namely, pBM EA 10371 + 10435 (L1), vso 3-4, uses not *sḏd* but *ḏd: ḏd⸗f mj.t(ï)t ḫr ms.ww* 'He will *say* the same to the children' (Žába 1956: 62).

42 Stela of Sobekhotep, Tübingen Inv. Nr. 458 = Stuttgart stela (Spiegelberg 1902: 3–4 (#4); Sethe ²1928: 88.21–23, Text 28g; *DZA* 29.920.120). Spiegelberg (1902: 3) does not read *mj* as a simile, translating *mj ḏd⸗f* as 'so spricht' in the passage: "dass ihr eure Heldentaten eurer Frauen erzählt, so spricht: 'Möge der Gott Osiris [...] ein Opfer darbringen'", rather than 'and recount your campaigns to your wives, *like* you recite the offering formula'.

43 Gardiner (1955: Pl. XLVII), translation from Popko (*Science in Ancient Egypt* 2022; *TLA* v.2 2022).

stelae and statues), they also have a number of parallels (at least eight) on papyrus and ostraca (particularly hymns and harpists' songs), which brings the total to 35.

Five cases come from wisdom texts, both Middle Egyptian 'classics', like *The Teachings of Amenemhet* and Late Egyptian texts, like *The Teachings of Amunnakht*. All five sources are parallels of two passages, one from each text. The viable examples from *The Teachings of Ani* and *The Teachings of Amenemope*, however, come from manuscripts that date to periods after the New Kingdom and are thus included in Sections 5.5 and 5.6.

11 cases come from scribal texts, three legible cases from the Middle Egyptian *Kemit* and eight cases deriving from four parallel passages of five different Late Egyptian miscellany texts), plus another 12 cases from so-called 'literary letters': one from oBM 50727 and the remaining 11 from three manuscripts of *The Satirical Letter of Hori* (pAnastasi I, pTurin CGT 54011 and oBerlin P 11236), of which there are eight different passages, three of which being parallels.

Of the two reliable cases from the epistolary record, one comes from the corpus of *Late Ramesside Letters* and the other is a contemporaneous letter from the scribe Butehamun to the coffin of his wife Ikhtai. Another three cases come from trial documents.

In stark contrast to the Middle Kingdom, few cases appear in literary genres: two cases come from (parallel) Ramesside copies of the Middle Egyptian *Tale of Sinuhe* and one case comes from the fragmentary 18th Dynasty text *Astarte and the Sea.* There is also a single reliable case from a Middle Egyptian admonition text, *The Admonitions of Ipuwer.*

5.2.2 Range of meanings in context

Most royal monumental cases (23/30) are transitive. Three of the seven remaining intransitive cases come from the time of Hatshepsut and Thutmose III[44] and the other four come from two distinct groups. Two cases on royal stelae, separated by time (Amenhotep II and Ramesses II respectively)[45] use identical structures: *m* + nominal Relative forms *sḏd.t* 'in what is said'). Two others come from a hieratic parallel of the Kadesh inscriptions, pRaifé-Sallier III: the direct objects of the hieroglyphic text are here introduced with *ḥr* and *m*.[46] Of the transitive cases, most direct objects (of which there are 13 types for 23 tokens) relate either to the activities of the king[47] or the words (*mdw.t*) of the kind.[48] In the case of

44 Obelisk inscription of Hatshepsut, northern side, 17 (*Urk.* IV, 365.8–9); Armant stela of Thutmose III (Cairo JE 67377), 3 (*Urk.* IV, 1245.1–2) (*jr sḏd=tw m zp ḥr rn=f*, 'If one reports on the case(s) concerning his reputation...'); Stela fragment from Tell el-Oreima/Kinneret, x+2 (*Urk.* IV, 1347.11).

45 Large Sphinx stela of Amenhotep II, 18 (*Urk.* IV, 1281.3); Quban stela of Ramesses II (Grenoble MG 1937, 1969, 356), 22 (K*RI* II, 357.7).

46 pLouvre E 4892 + pBM 10181 (pRaifé + pSallier III), S 6.7 (§ 191) (K*RI* II, 61.15) (*jw bw.pwy*ᵗ *w*ʿ *m-jm=sn ḥr jy(j) r sḏd ḥr*ʳ *wp.wt*ᵗʷ*=f* 'and none of them came in order to report on his task') and S 7.2 (§ 200) (K*RI* II, 64.10) (*jr(j) ḫ3s.t nb pt{r}j sḏd m rn=j* 'Every foreign land that saw will report on my reputation'). The addition of *ḥr* in § 191 is noted but not commented upon in Spalinger (2002: 49). The presence of *m* in § 200 is not noted.

47 Kamose 2nd stela (Luxor Museum J.43), 28 (Helck ²1995: 94–96): *ḫb(3) ḥʿ.w=f sḏd n=f wp(w).tï=f n3 jr(j).t.n=j* 'His body was destroyed as his messenger reported to him that which I had done'.

48 Great dedicatory inscription of Seti I (Year 1) at the Pachet temple of Speos Artemidos, 12 (K*RI* I, 42.14–15), though *sḏd* is reconstructed: *nn m33.n=tw m zḫ3.ww ḏr.tw nn [sḏd] mdw.t r*ʾ *n r*ʾ *[wpw]-ḥr*

the boundary stelae of Akhenaten at Amarna, it is used more like *ḏd*, to introduce direct speech by the king or the Aten.[49] Other prominent direct objects relate to the attributes (*pḥ.tï* 'might',[50] *bꜣ.w* 'power',[51] *nr.w* 'terror',[52] also, generally, *ꜣb.wt* 'attributes'),[53] reputation (*rn*)[54] or feats (*qnn.w*, 'accomplishments',[55] *nḫt.w* 'victories'[56]) of the king. As for things not directly by or about the king, an implied indirect object relates to what is said (*sḏd.tw*) about the king,[57] or what the ancestors say (*mdw.t* 'words'[58] or *mꜣꜥ.t* 'truth').[59] The *wp.t* 'commission' of soldiers can also be a direct object.[60]

Of private monumental discourse, 9/35 cases are intransitive and 26 are transitive. Five of the intransitive cases are introduced with *m*, of which three come, perhaps unsurprisingly, from hieratic texts, matching a tendency already visible in hieratic copies of royal monumental texts.[61] This being said, two such cases appear in the hieroglyphic

---

ḥm⸗f ḥꜥ[⸗f] 'There was nothing that one could see in the scripts of the ancestors and there was no [recounting] speeches, mouth to mouth, [apart] from (the output of) his majesty [him]self'.

49 Amarna boundary stela K, 2 and 8 (Davies 1908: 29; Murnane & van Siclen 1993: 21.15 and 23.4–7) (*ꜥḥꜥ.n fꜣ(j) ḥm⸗f ꜥ⸗f r p.t n ms(j) sw rꜥ.w-ḥr.w-ꜣḫ.tï-ḥꜥ(j)-m-ꜣḫ.t-m-rn⸗f-[m-šw-n.tï-m-jtn] ḥr sḏd* 'Then His Majesty raised his arm towards heaven to the one who bore him, Re-Horakhty-who-rejoices-in-the-horizon-in-his-name-[of-light/Shu-which-is-in-the-sun-disk], declaring:'); Amarna boundary stela X, 5 (Murnane & van Siclen 1993: 21.16).

50 Three cases occur from inscriptions by or about Ramesside rulers: the rhetorical text over fallen foes from the war inscription of Seti I in Karnak, north wall, east face, east of door, 9–10 (K*RI* I, 8.11–12); the Karnak inscription of Ramesses II, wall between Pylons 3 and 7, western side (K*RI* II, 166.3) and the Libyan war inscription of Merenptah, 40–41 (K*RI* IV, 7.2–3).

51 Both cases come from Medinet Habu, one from the pavillion, above a depiction of captured princes (K*RI* V, 103.10) (*jm(j) n⸗n pꜣ ṯꜣw n ḏd⸗k ꜥnḫ⸗n sḏd⸗n bꜣ.w⸗k* 'Give us the breath out of what you give, that we may live and report of your power'). The other comes from the Syrian war scenes of Ramesses III, series II, scene a, in Medinet Habu II, 94 (K*RI* V, 83.7–8).

52 Medinet Habu, chamber behind terrace, above captured princes (K*RI* V, 317.16–318.1).

53 Medinet Habu, Year 8 inscription of Ramesses III concerning the Sea Peoples (K*RI* V, 38.3).

54 All three are parallels from the Kadesh 'Poem' (§ 200): Karnak temple, hypostyle hall, exterior south wall (K1), 46 (K*RI* II, 64.7); Luxor temple, pylon of Ramesses II (L1), 53 (K*RI* II, 64.8); Luxor temple, court of Ramesses II, exterior east and south walls (L2), 51 (K*RI* II, 64.9).

55 Armant stela of Thutmose III (JE 67377, 2–3) (*Urk.* IV, 1244.17–18).

56 Both cases come from the 'Israel' stela of Merenptah (Cairo CGC 34025), 1–2 (K*RI* IV, 13.8) (*sḏd.t(w) nꜣy⸗f nḫt.w m tꜣ.w nb.w* 'his victories are spoken of in all lands'); 21–22 (K*RI* IV, 18.1).

57 Gebel Barkal stela of Thutmose III, 48–49 (*Urk.* IV, 1242.1–18).

58 Ahmose monument from the chapel of Tetisheri at Abydos, 6–7 (*Urk.* IV, 27.11): *sḏd⸗tw mdw.t tn ḥr-jḫ* 'Why does one recount this speech?'

59 Dedicatory stela of Seti I for Ramesses I, mortuary temple at Abydos, Chapel of Ramesses I, x+13 (K*RI* I, 112.15): *ṯ(ꜣ)z.w jm.ïw-ḥꜣ.t sḏd⸗[sn] mꜣꜥ[.t]* 'The sayings of the ancestors—they convey truth'.

60 Both cases are parallels from the Kadesh 'Poem' (§ 191): Luxor temple, pylon of Ramesses II (L1), 50 (K*RI* II, 61.12); Luxor temple, court of Ramesses II, exterior east and south walls (L2), 49 (K*RI* II, 61.13), cited above.

61 The first case appears in the harpist's song on pHarris 500 = pBM EA 10060, Text A, rto 6.6–7 (Budge 1923: 24, Pl. 45) (*sḏd⸗tj m sḏd.w{t}⸗sn* 'one proclaims with(?) their proclamations'). In the votive text on oCairo/Gurna 12189, rto 1–2 (Luiselli 2011: 326–327) we find *sḏd{y}⸗j m bꜣ.w⸗k* 'I will report on(?) your power'. In the hymn to Thoth on pAnastasi V = pBM EA 10244, 9.8 (*LEM* 60.11; Luiselli 2011: 10–12) we see *ḏ(j)⸗k sḏd{.t}<⸗j> m nꜣy⸗k qn.w* 'May you ensure that <I>

monumental record.[62] The single case in which *sḏd* is followed by *ḥr* matches the case in the monumental record for rarity.[63] Another three cases build adverbial clauses with *ḥnꜥ* (two cases)[64] and *n* (one case).[65] Of the transitive cases, many refer to things the speaker has perceived or wants to perceive: the *qd* 'form' (one case)[66] or *ẖr.t* 'condition' (two cases)[67] of people in the Netherworld, *mꜣꜣ⸗j* 'what I saw' (two cases),[68] *mdw.t* 'speech' (one case),[69] one case refers to 'wishes' (*jm.ïw-jb*).[70] Others refer to properties or actions of the king or a deity: *nfr.w* 'goodness' (three cases),[71] which is not seen in the royal inscriptions, as well as three others that are well-attested there: *nḫt.w* 'victories' (two cases),[72] *bꜣ.w*

---

report on(?) your victories'. Of this group only *bꜣ.w* is recorded also as a direct object amongst the transitive cases.

See the harpist's song on pHarris 500 = pBM EA 10060, Text A, rto 6.6–7 (Budge 1923: 24, Pl. 45).

62 One case is from a harpist song in a monumental context: TT 50 (Neferhotep), Song 2, Text G, line 3 (Kákosy & Fábián 1995: 223, Fig. 3) (*jw sḏm.n(⸗j) [...] sḏd.t⸗sn m sꜥꜣ(j) tp-tꜣ m sꜥnḏ ẖr.t-nṯr* '(I) have heard [...] what they proclaim, glorifying (lit. making great) life on earth (lit. what is on earth) and denouncing (lit. diminishing) death (lit. the necropolis)'). The other comes from TT 40 (Amenhotep Huy), 26 (Davies & Gardiner 1926: Pl. XXIII and XXIX) (*sḏd⸗tw m zp ḥr rn⸗f st ꜥšꜣ r jr(j).t⸗s m zẖꜣ.w* 'If one recounts the case concerning his reputation, it would be too much to put into writing!').

63 The case is from a mourning song in TT 49 (Neferhotep), 7–8. The preposition *ḥr* cannot stand in this manner alone, given that it is followed by another prepositional phrase *ḥnꜥ⸗j*, so it is proposed that the suffix pronoun <*⸗w*> be emended (*pꜣ mr(j) sḏd ḥr<⸗w?> ḥnꜥ⸗j* 'You who loved to speak about <them?> with me'). The problem with the prepositions was not raised in editions of the tomb and text (Davies 1933: Tbl. 24; Lüddeckens 1943: 109–111, #48).

64 See the parallels of TT 41 (Amenemope), Text 196 (Assmann 1991: 137–138) and the door lintel of Userhat-Hatiay, Leiden K 9 (K*RI* I, 361.5–8, *RITA* I, 296) (*n(j) sḏd⸗j ḥnꜥ qꜣ-ḫrw* 'I did not speak with the loudmouth'). A direct parallel for these two is the Late Period door lintel, Louvre C 67, right side (see Frandsen 1998: 995), cited below.

65 Statue E of Amenhotep Son of Hapu, Text 14 (on the back pillar) = Cairo CG 583, 8 (Varille 1968: 46–48, Pl. VIII): *sḏd.tw n⸗j* 'what is recounted about me'.

66 This case comes from a harpist song: pHarris 500 = pBM EA 10060, Text A, rto 6.8 (Budge 1923: 24, Pl. 45).

67 Both cases come from harpist songs: pHarris 500 = pBM EA 10060, Text A, rto 6.8 (Budge 1923: 24, Pl. 45) (*sḏd⸗f ẖ<r>.t⸗sn* 'so that he might report on their condition'), and TT 158 (Tjanefer), Song 1, Text F, lines 5–6 (Wente 1962: 125).

68 Harpist song from TT 194 (Djehutyemhab), Text F, line 10 (Wente 1962: 127), plausibly reconstructed in the parallel TT 364 (Amenemhab), Text F, line 9 (Wente 1962: 127).

69 oLeipzig 23, 8–9 (Černý & Gardiner 1957: Pls 37–37A).

70 oCairo 25206 (Assmann ^{2}1999: 422, #191): *sḏd⸗sn n⸗k jm.ïw-jb⸗sn* 'They report to you their wishes'.

71 Two come from Amarna tombs: AT 6 (Panehesy), east thickness, lower register, line 9 (Davies 1905: 30, Pl. 8) (*sḏd<⸗j> n⸗tn nꜣ nfr.w jr(j) n⸗j [pꜣy⸗j] ḥqꜣ* '<I> will report to you the wonderful things that [my] ruler has done for me') and AT 14 (May), south thickness, line 3 (Davies 1908: 4, Pl. 4). One comes from a hymn to the Nile: oGardiner 28, rto 10 (K*RI* II, 378.12).

72 TT 40 (Amenhotep Huy) (Davies & Gardiner 1926: 29, Pl. XX. However, since the scene is damaged, the text is copied from L*D* III, 115–116a) and a stela of Amenemone, Turin 50045, 5–8 (Luiselli 2011: 368–369).

'power' (five cases)[73] and *pḥ.tï* 'might' (one case).[74] Regarding the pronouns, *=s* (one case) and *=sn* (two cases) refer to the *n.(ï)t-ʿ.w* '(daily) practice' of the sun god in sun hymns.[75] The enclitic pronouns *sj* (one case) and *sw* (three cases) refer to things that happened to them (*ḫpr ḫr=j*)[76] and the power (*bꜣ.w*) of the god respectively.[77] An implied direct object (one case) refers to what is said about the solar barque.[78]

The New Kingdom scribal texts present us currently with 11 cases, of which nine are transitive. The groups that are formed by the direct objects are not particularly informative, as they belong to direct textual parallels. The roughly parallel cases of *Kemit* (§9) can be divided into two groups. The writer seeks to describe either *nn-n mdw.w rḫ.w* 'these words of the colleagues' (two clear cases and one reconstruction)[79] or *nn-n rḫ.w* 'these colleagues' themselves (one clear case and one reconstruction).[80] The scribal miscellany texts are almost all focused on making fun of other professions, so what is being *sḏd* (via the formula *mj sḏd=j n=k* 'Come, let me *sḏd* to you...') concerns *pꜣ sḫr.w n wʿ.w* 'the condition of the soldier',[81] *pꜣy=f šm(j).t* 'his [the soldier's] travels'[82] and the *jꜣw.t gʿb(j).w znn*^{i} 'horrible occupation of the chariot-soldier'.[83] The same can be said of the two intransitive meanings (parallels), which present the *mḥr wʿ.w* 'ills of the soldier',

73 Two stelae of Amenhotep Huy, Turin 1608, 4–6 (Assmann ^{2}1999: #151 = Luiselli 2011: 366–368) and Cairo JE 37463, vso line 2–3 (*Urk.* IV, 2076.1–5; Luiselli 2011: 347–348); the stela of Dydy, Cambridge E.191.1932, 2–3 (Luiselli 2011: 356–357); the stela of Nebre, Berlin 20377, 1–2 (Roeder 1924: 159–160; Assmann ^{2}1999: #147 B) and the stela of Amunnakht, BM EA 374 (Hall 1925: Pl. 29).

74 Sun hymn in TT 194 (Djehutyemhab), 16 (Assmann 1978: 26, col 16).

75 TT 163 (Amenemhat), line 7, Text 161, verse 42–43 (Assmann 1983: 220–221); TT 194 (Djehutyemhab), line 6, Text 186, verse 22–23 (Assmann 1983: 258–259) and TT 23 (Tjay), line 6, Text 17, verse 22–23 (Assmann 1983: 18–19).

76 Stela of Userhat-Hatiay, Leiden V.1 (van Dijk 1995).

77 The stela of Nebre, Berlin 20377, 2 and 3 (Roeder 1924: 159–160; Assmann ^{2}1999: #147 B) with two cases of *sw*, mentions *bꜣ.w* explicitly and the stela of Pay, Turin 50052, lower register 3–4 (Luiselli 2011: 375–377), makes mention of seeing darkness by day.

78 TT 11 (Djehuty), 2nd stela (*Urk.* IV, 437.7).

79 oMMA 35144 + oMMA 36112, rto 5 (Hayes 1948: Pl. II). There is also a clear witness of *sḏd[=j n=t] nn-n mdw.w rḫ.w* '[I] want to report [to you] these words of the colleagues' in oBrussels E.6768, 6–7 (Posener 1951: Pl. 10), but not recorded by the *TLA*. In oBrussels E.3208 + oDeM 1171, 12 the *sḏd* is reconstructed.

80 oCairo JE 56842 + oDeM 1172, x+8 (Posener 1951: Pl. 10). In oIFAO 1114, rto 11 the *sḏd* is reconstructed. All other cases (at least 4 in number but potentially more) have lacunae following *sḏd* (Posener 1951: Pl. 10).

81 pAnastasi III = pBM EA 10246, rto 5.6 (*LEM* 26.4); pChester Beatty V = pBM EA 10685, rto 6.13 (Gardiner 1935: Pls 25–25A); pAnastasi IV = pBM EA 10249, rto 9.4 (*LEM* 44.8).

82 pAnastasi III = pBM EA 10246, rto 5.9 (*LEM* 26.9); pAnastasi IV = pBM EA 10249, rto 9.7–8 (*LEM* 44.12). Both cases use an abbreviated form *mj n=k* 'Come <...> to you', which leaves out the <*sḏd=j*> '<let me relate>' in between. As it is well-attested, it such cases have been included in the corpus.

83 pAnastasi III = pBM EA 10246, rto 6.3 (*LEM* 27.3). At this point it bears mentioning that all transliteration placed in superscript belongs to the orthography of New Kingdom hieratic and is not considered to be meaning bearing.

introduced respectively by the prepositions *m*[84] and *r*.[85] We see that the topics always involve either colleagues or outsiders, for the purpose of in-group reinforcement.

The wisdom texts behave similarly. The parallel cases of *The Teachings of Amenemhet* are the only two intransitive cases in the corpus, both with objects introduced with *m* (*jm⸗j*),[86] all three parallel cases from *The Teachings of Amunnakht* recount *nꜣ sḥnt.w gꜣb(j).wï* 'the horrible commissions' of the fool.[87] All concern 'well-known knowledge' (to the literate community, of course), as do the scribal texts.

The literary letters have no intransitive cases and, like the related genres of scribal texts and wisdom literature, show similarities only where there are parallels. The single case not deriving from *The Satirical Letter of Hori* has indirect speech as its direct object.[88] The other 11 cases, from the *Satirical Letter*, have eight different objects: the *qj* 'form, character' of a person[89] or place,[90] *⸗w*, referring to *tp-rd* 'regulations',[91] *ky tp-rꜣ* 'another saying'[92] as well as nominations of people (perhaps a personal name,[93] certainly a title[94]), a location[95] and *qnw* 'a lot', meaning 'more'.[96] All are things that the receiver of the letter, Amenemope, should know but does not, because, so Hori's implication, he is not sufficiently trained in things of cultural importance.

---

84 pLansing = pBM EA 9994, 9.4 (*LEM* 107.16). This case uses an abbreviated form *mj n⸗k* 'Come <...> to you', which leaves out the *<sḏd⸗j>* '<let me relate>' in between. As it is well-attested, such cases have been included in the corpus.

85 oFlorence 2619, rto 4–5 (Erman 1880: 96–97). This case uses an abbreviated form *mj n⸗k* 'Come <...> to you', which leaves out the *<sḏd⸗j>* '<let me relate>' in between. As it is well-attested, such cases have been included in the corpus.

86 pSallier II = pBM EA 10182, 2.9 and oDeM 1035, 3 (Helck 1969: 74).

87 oTurin CGT 57436 = Suppl. 9598, rto 1; oLacau, rto 14; oDeir el-Medina 01036, 1 (Dorn 2004: 41).

88 oBM 50727, rto 7 (Brose 2009: 59) (*mtw⸗f ꜥḥꜥ r sḏd <r->n.tï bwpw⸗f jr(j).t wp.t nb* 'And he should stand up to recount that he did not make any judgement').

89 pAnastasi I = pBM EA 10247, 9.4 and its parallel pTurin CGT 54011, x+1.4 (Fischer-Elfert 1983: 86) (*mj sḏd⸗j n⸗k qj n zẖꜣ.w rꜣy* 'Come, that I may recount to you the condition of the scribe Ray').

90 pAnastasi I = pBM EA 10247, 27.6 (Fischer-Elfert 1983: 152).

91 pAnastasi I = pBM EA 10247, 28.8 and its parallel pTurin CGT 54011, x+? (Fischer-Elfert 1983: 158).

92 pTurin CGT 54011, x+?, continuing from pAnastasi I, 28.8 (*TLA*, not in Fischer-Elfert 1983: 159): *mj sḏd⸗j n⸗k ky tp-rꜣ* 'Come, let me relate to you another utterance'.

93 The problem with both sources is that neither oBerlin P 11236, 1–2 nor its parallel pAnastasi I = pBM EA 10247, 9.9 actually include *sḏd* (Fischer-Elfert 1983: 90). They may be abbreviating: pAnastasi I has the classic *mj n⸗k* 'Come <...> to you', which probably leaves out the *<sḏd⸗j>* '<let me relate>' in between. However, oBerlin P 11236 has *j.jw(j)⸗j n⸗k r <sḏd> nḫt* 'That I have come to you is <to recount?> about Nakht' could plausibly be read without the reconstruction.

94 oBerlin P 11236, 3 (Fischer-Elfert 1983: 91). The parallel section in pAnastasi I = pBM EA 10247, 10.1, has *ḏd* instead of *sḏd.*

95 pAnastasi I = pBM EA 10247, 20.7 (Fischer-Elfert 1983: 130).

96 pAnastasi I = pBM EA 10247, 27.2 (Fischer-Elfert 1983: 150): *mj sḏd[⸗j] [n]⸗k [q]nw* 'Come, let [me] relate [to] you more'.

Of the narratives, both cases in New Kingdom copies of *Sinuhe* are intransitive with no marked object[97] and the case in *Astarte* is transitive with *nꜣ jr(j).n⸗k* 'what you have done' as its object.[98] The *Admonitions of Ipuwer* has direct speech as its object, which prompts Roland Enmarch to translate *sḏd* as 'exclaim'.[99]

The three cases of trial documents are all intransitive without an object marked prepositionally and convey the meaning of 'speaking',[100] in other words, carrying out a dialogic and not a monologic act, the latter of which is predominant in all other genres.

5.3 The Third Intermediate Period to the Roman Period (Hieroglyphic texts)

5.3.1 Sources and genres

In total there are eight secure verbal cases from the Third Intermediate Period, six from the Late Period, one from the Ptolemaic Period and one from the Roman Period. The cases for the former come from six different genres: royal monumental texts (two cases), a private monumental text, a hymn on papyrus (two cases on the same papyrus), a dialogic narrative, a wisdom text and an oracular amuletic decree. From the Late Period, on the other hand, 4/6 cases come from private monumental texts (tombs and stelae) and the remaining two come from wisdom texts. The two cases of *sḏd* recorded from post-pharaonic hieroglyphic sources comprise a text from the temple of Hathor in Dendera and a stela from the Serapeum.

5.3.2 Range of meanings in context

In the Third Intermediate Period 6/8 meanings are transitive. The case from the victory stela of Piye has as a direct object *wḏ.y<t>⸗f* 'his expedition',[101] the statue of Djed-Djehuty-iuef-ankh has *ꜣḫ.t⸗k mnḫ⸗k* 'your glory and your excellence',[102] two cases from a sun hymn have *sꜣḫ.w* 'ritual recitations',[103] the *Teachings of Ani* has the pronoun *⸗f* 'it', referring to something bad[104] and the direct object following *sḏd* from the *Contendings of*

---

97 oAshmolean Museum 1945.40 (AOS), 26 (Koch 1990: 31.9) and oDeir el Medina 1437 (DM 4), 3 (Koch 1990: 31.16) (*sḏd.n⸗f n⸗j wḏb.n⸗j n⸗f* 'After he had spoken to me, I answered him'). Not surprisingly, given the meaning generated, in the earlier parallel, pBerlin P 3022 (B), 46, *ḏd* is used instead of *sḏd* (Koch 1990: 31.7). Like the *Ptahhotep* case above in Section 7.1, this case suggests the interchangeability of the intransitive *sḏd* without an argument and *ḏd*.

98 pBN 202 + pAmherst 9, 1.3 (Collombert & Coulon 2000: Pl. III).

99 pLeiden I 344, rto 2.9 (Enmarch 2005: 223).

100 pWien 9340, rto 12 (el-Kholi 2006: 24–25) (*jw⸗s ḥr rḏ(j).t sḏd n ky ꜥn* 'she will cause to talk(?) to another (person) again'); pBM 10052, vso 8.9 (*KRI* VI 786.6); pBM 10052, vso 8.12 (*KRI* VI. 786.11).

101 Cairo 48862 (+ JE 47086–JE 47089), 23–24 (Grimal 1981: Pl. VI) (*r sḏd wḏ.y⸗f* 'in order to recount his expedition'). At odds with Grimal's publication, the *TLA* records the line numbers as vso 23–24.

102 Cairo CG 42208, Text c, 2 (*Cachette*).

103 pBerlin P 3050, 3.3–4 and 6.7 (Sauneron 1953: 68 and 69) (*sḏd⸗sn n⸗k sꜣḫ.w* 'May they recite ritual recitations for you').

104 pBoulaq 4, 16.11 (Quack 1994: 287).

the Body and the Head is *qȝj/qj≠w*, which seems to refer to the respective 'character' of the contending parties.[105] Of the intransitive cases, the *Oracular Amuletic Decree* L5 has no argument following,[106] whereas the oracular inscription of Herihor has the preposition *m* followed by *nȝ bjȝ.t*, 'the miracle'.[107]

In the Late Period 3/6 meanings are transitive, all coming from private monumental sources. Kaliut, in the hymn on his stela from Gebel Barkal has *nn* 'this', referring to the proclamation he is about to make to the god[108] and the two cases from private tombs of Harwa and Ibi refer to *bj<ȝ>.t≠j* 'my character'.[109] Of the intransitive cases, the door-lintel text from the Louvre is followed by an adverbial phrase,[110] as is the wisdom text from Brooklyn,[111] whereas the *The Teachings of Amenemope* L[112] has no following argument. The case from the Brooklyn wisdom text is a rare case of *sḏd* potentially (though even here not necessarily) signifying something more mundane than has been common until now. This impacts our discussion of the Demotic cases below.

Both post-pharaonic cases are transitive: the Dendera text has an undefined direct object because *sḏd* is a passive participle, 'what is talked about',[113] and the Serapeum stela has *nfr.w* 'perfection' as its direct object.[114]

5.4 The Late Period to the Roman Period (Demotic texts)

5.4.1 Sources and genres

There are in total 95 cases of the verb *sḏd*, now *sḏj/sḏe,* in Demotic, of which 83 are usable. The genres encompassed include letters, memoranda, literary texts, mythological texts (insofar as they can be separated from literary texts), wisdom texts, dream divination manuals, magical texts and private monuments and cover 21 documents in total.

---

105 tTurin Cat. 6238 = tTurin CGT 58004, 1 (López 1984: Pls 184–184A; Di Biase-Dyson & Stock 2022: 66) (*sḏd q[ȝ]j.w≠w* 'to proclaim their (respective) characters').

106 pBM EA 10321 (L5), vso 22–23 (Edwards 1960: Pls X–XI) (*jw≠j spd r'≠k r sḏd* 'I will make his mouth skilled, in order to speak').

107 Oracular inscription of Herihor, north wall, Khonsu Temple, Karnak, 22 (*LD* III, 248b = Koll. Sethe 4,7, also Epigraphic Survey 1981: 15, Pl. 132).

108 Stela of Kaliut, Gebel Barkal, 24–25 (Reisner 1934: 38ff) (*sḏd.n≠j nn ḫft nb≠j rʿ.w-ḥr.w-ȝḫ.tï* 'It is before my lord, Re-Horachty that I proclaim/say this').

109 TT 37 (Harwa), (unpublished, *DZA* 29.920.470); TT 36 (Ibi) (Kuhlmann & Schenkel 1983: 73, Pl. 24, l. 1; *DZA* 29.920.090) (*sḏd≠j bj<ȝ>.t≠j* 'I will tell (of) my character').

110 Door lintel, Louvre C 67, right side (cited in Frandsen 1998: 995) (*n(j) sḏd≠j ḥnʿ qȝ-ḫrw* 'I did not speak with the loudmouth').

111 pBrooklyn 47.218.135, 4.6 (Jasnow 1992: 75, Fig. 9) (*sḏd≠f n≠k n nȝ j-jr ḫpr j-jr-ḥr≠f* 'that he may recount to you that which happened to him').

112 pBM EA 10474, rto 11.14 (Laisney 2007: 339) (*mtw≠k ḫnḫn≠f r sḏd* 'and do not approach him to talk').

113 Dendera, Room C, back wall, right, 2nd row (Mariette 1875a: T. I, Pl. 31; *DZA* 29.920.740).

114 Louvre Serapeum Apis stela #335 (*DZA* 29.920.230) (*mj sḏ(d)≠tn nfr.w*, 'like your recounting the perfection').

5.4.2 Range of meanings in context

Of the usable cases, 73/83 are intransitive, only 10 are transitive. To review, this means that about 88% of usages are intransitive, compared to around 23% (27/119) in sources dating up until the Late Period. We thus see an inversion of what was happening with the earlier Egyptian documents. This is driven in part by a markedly greater usage of *n* (< *m*) + object, which is first attested in the time of Hatshepsut but is not yet a common strategy in the pharaonic period, being only attested 12 times between the New Kingdom and the Late Period. As will be discussed below (Section 7.4) concerning the intransitive use, it remains unclear if this signals a real change in the valency pattern or if this is the consequence of the spreading of the oblique construction with *n* in various Demotic grammatical patterns (Winand 2015: 533).

In the following discussion, only the nucleus of the argument of the verb is discussed, but it is important to note that all nouns (bar one, *ʿ* 'type') in the Demotic corpus are determined, either with articles, demonstrative or possessive pronouns, or the adjective *nb*. Lastly, in terms of a meaning span in Demotic, it seems that the purely intransitive form is best translated (for the most part) as 'speak' or 'talk'. The intransitive cases with *n* and the transitive cases mostly mean 'recount' or 'report', but can also mean 'narrate', when, for instance (as in *Setne II*), the implied direct object is a *sḏj* 'story', or, as seems to be common in literary texts in general, the teller relates 'what happened to them', or similar. Thus, the Demotic textual record provides us with examples illustrating the telling of 'new' or 'newsworthy' material previously unknown to the hearer and which is not intended to have any edifying or rhetorical function. In other words, we have a decisive shift from the meaning in earlier pharaonic Egyptian texts.

The literary texts present us with features we shall see elsewhere in the corpus, such as the use of the very general and generic object *md.t* 'matter, affair, thing' (introduced by the preposition *n* or not, depending on the definiteness of the object[115]—see Section 7.4). The *Saqqara Demotic Papyri* have two intransitive cases with *n* + *md.t*.[116] *Setne I* has 10 intransitive cases and a single transitive case; apart from a single objectless intransitive case,[117] the object is always *md.t*, either (in one case) as a direct object[118] or introduced with *n*.[119] *Setne II* has six cases, of which four are (surprisingly) transitive, three being anaphoric cases of *sḏj.w* 'stories'[120] and one of which is again *md.t* 'matter'.[121] Both intransitive cases

115 Johnson (1976: 6).

116 Saqqara Demotic Papyri I, Text 01, XIV.35 and XVI.x+3 (Smith & Tait 1984: 9, 41).

117 pCairo CG 30646, III.20, See Vinson (2018: 115), who translates it as a noun, "disquisition", though for the sake of this analysis, I keep it within the group of verbs, as the absence of an article or possessive pronoun makes it likely that this is an infinitive (*tꜣ wnw.t n sḏj r-jr pꜣ wʿb* 'When the priest had recounted (lit. At the moment of the recounting by the priest)').

118 pCairo CG 30646, III.21 (Vinson 2018: 115) (*wꜣḥ=k sḏj j-jr-ḥr=f nꜣï ///* 'You have already recounted to him these ///').

119 pCairo CG 30646, III.20, III.23, IV.10, IV.15, IV.31, IV.32, IV.36, V.3, V.10, V.36, VI.5 (Vinson 2018: 115, 119, 121, 122, 123, 126, 127).

120 pBM EA 10822, III.31, IV.22 and V.24 (Griffith 1900: 172–173, 178–179, 188–189, Pls 3–5).

121 pBM EA 10822, III.23 (Griffith 1900: 170–171, Pl. 3).

involve *n* + *md.t*,[122] as does the single case from the *Setne* story on pCarlsberg 207.[123] The part of the *Inaros/Petubastis* cycle concerning *The Battle for the Benefice of Amun* (pSpiegelberg) has six well-preserved cases, of which five are intransitive, two without an argument,[124] two with *n* + *md.t*[125] and one with *r⸗f*, referring to *tꜣ-mḥ* 'north-country'.[126] The transitive case has as its argument *šn.w* 'inquiries'.[127] The part of the cycle about *The Battle for the Armour of Inaros* (pKrall) has only two truly secure cases, one clearly transitive with *md.t*[128] and one intransitive, without an argument.[129] The poorly preserved story, *Egyptians and Amazons*, has three clear intransitive cases (four are too damaged) with no argument, *n* + *md.t* and *n* + *snt n md.t* 'state of affairs' respectively.[130] The *Petese* cycle (pPetese Tebt. A and C, fragm. C1) has likewise three intransitive cases, one without argument and two involving *n* + *md.t*.[131]

Mythological texts, if they are to be separated from narratives, provide us with six cases from two texts. The *Myth of Horus and Seth* (pBerlin P 15549+15551+23727) may have a case of *n* + *md.t*, but it is reconstructed and thus unreliable. The text also has a transitive case with *md.t* as its argument.[132] The *Myth of the Eye of Ra* (pLeiden I 384) has four cases, two that are intransitive without objects,[133] one that is intransitive with *r* + *md.t* and one that is transitive.[134]

The magical corpus furnishes us with numerous examples, though the cases extend almost exclusively from a single manuscript. The one exception, from pHarkness, is an intransitive case without an argument, implying (as usual) the meaning 'speaking'.[135] The other 30 cases come from the London-Leiden Magical Papyrus, of which 25 are likewise without an argument.[136] Those five with an argument (i.e., an adverbial phrase describing

---

122 pBM EA 10822, V.18, VI.34 (Griffith 1900: 186–187, 202–203, Pls 5–6).

123 Carlsberg 207, x+1.26 (Tait 1991: 23) (*sḏj⸗f n-j-jr-ḥr*^{t}*⸗f n md(.t) nb* 'He recounted to him the whole affair').

124 pSpiegelberg, XV.5 and XVII.14 (Spiegelberg 1910: 30–31 and 34–35).

125 pSpiegelberg, VII.20 and XIV.7 (Spiegelberg 1910: 22–23 and 30–31).

126 pSpiegelberg, XV.7 (Spiegelberg 1910: 30–31) (*bn-pw⸗w ms*^{t}*⸗j ẖn pꜣ tꜣ-mḥ*^{t} *n.tï-jw-jw⸗k sḏj r-r⸗f* 'I was not born in the northern land, of which you speak').

127 pSpiegelberg, XI.7 (Spiegelberg 1910: 26–27).

128 pKrall, VII.4 (Bresciani 1964: 38).

129 pKrall, V.3 (Bresciani 1964: 31) (*sḏj⸗f j-jr-ḥr [nꜣ] [ḥꜣ*^{t}*].w* 'He reported before [the] count'). Fragmentary cases not taken into consideration are pKrall, V.15, VI.5 and VI.26 (Bresciani 1964: 32, 34, 36).

130 pVienna D 6165+6165A, VIII.14, A,2.x+19 and II.20 respectively (Hoffmann 1995: 91–92, 102 and 44).

131 pPetese Tebtunis C., Fragment C1, III.21 (Ryholt, P. Peteese II, 2006, 47 and Plate 4) and A, VIII.20 and VIII.25 respectively (Ryholt 1999: 20 and 21).

132 pBerlin P 15549+15551+23727, 17 and 29 respectively (Zauzisch 1984: 276–277, Taf. 38).

133 pLeiden I 384, II.6 and XI.16 (Spiegelberg 1917: 12 and 32).

134 pLeiden I 384, X.25 and XIV.18 respectively (Spiegelberg 1917: 30 and 38) (*md.t nb.t r-ḏd⸗t ẖr-tw r-hwnnꜣ.w-j-jr<⸗t> sḏj n-jm⸗w* 'Everything that you have said and that <you> have recounted about them').

135 pHarkness, IV.20 (Smith 2005: 75).

136 pLondon-Leiden, III.11, III.22 (two), IV.7–8, V.7, V.15, V.24, VIII.18, IX.27, XI.18 (two), XI.24, XII.6, XV.24, XVII.8, XVII.13, XVII.17, XXIII.22, XXIII.24, XXIII.28, XXVIII.7, XXVIII.11,

what is being talked 'about'), are introduced in 4/5 times with *ḫr* rather than *n*, and all indicate that the meaning of *sḏj* is 'speaking' or 'asking', as the objects are all pertaining to (dialogic) communicative acts expecting an answer, not the more monologic relation of specific contents: *ḫr* + *pꜣ ntï-jw=j šnfw=k* 'what I wanted to ask you',[137] or a nominalised version of the same, *ḫr* + *šn* 'a question',[138] *ḫr* + *pꜣ ntï-j-jr=k wḫꜣ=f* 'what you wish'[139] and lastly, *ḫr* + or *n* + *hb* 'a consignment/matter'.[140]

Of the remaining genres, a dream manual has an intransitive case, also denoting the meaning of 'speaking'.[141] Four cases from four letters have likewise only intransitive cases, either with no object[142] or with *n* +*ʿ* 'type'[143] or *mt*/*md.t* 'matter'.[144] We also find *md.t* a single time (following *n*) in the *Teachings of Ankhsheshonqi*.[145] The four cases from memoranda that we have are all intransitive, two without objects[146] and two with *r* + *tꜣ ḥ.t-md.t*, 'about the matter'.[147] Lastly, the single case we have from a private monument has a different (transitive) usage: *sḏj* has as its argument an enclitic pronoun, *s*, followed by the phrase *tꜣy=f ḥ(j)m.t*, which generates the meaning 'to take her as his wife'.[148]

XXIX.25, vso XXVI.1 and vso XXXIII.5 (Griffith & Thompson 1904: 34–35, 36–37, 40–41, 44–45, 46–47, 48–49, 66–67, 72–73, 84–85, 86–87, 88–89, 108–109, 114–115, 116–117, 146–147, 148–149, 164–165, 168–169, 198–199, 204–205) (*nꜣ.w nb.t-ḥ.t lk=s jw=s sḏj* 'Is Nephthys ceasing to talk?').

137 pLondon-Leiden, vso XVIII.5 (Griffith & Thompson 1904: 190–191).

138 pLondon-Leiden, V.30 (Griffith & Thompson 1904: 48–49) (*mtw=f sḏj wbꜣ=k ḫr pꜣ šn* 'and he will speak to you about the question').

139 pLondon-Leiden, XXVII.19 (Griffith & Thompson 1904: 160–161).

140 pLondon-Leiden, IV.20 and XVIII.2 respectively (Griffith & Thompson 1904: 42–43 and 118–119) (*mtw=k sḏj wbꜣ=f n hb nb* 'and you should talk to him about any matter').

141 pBologna 3173, 3–4 (Bresciani et al. 1978: 95–97) (*tw=j sḏj jrm=s* 'I speak with her').

142 pHamburg D 46, 4 (Wegner 2014: 166) (*pꜣj=s-smt wꜣḥ [nꜣ rmṯ.w] pa-rbs(?) sḏj nꜣj=w-ḥr=j* '[The people] of Pa-rebes(?) reported to me likewise').

143 pBerlin P 13564, 7 (Zauzisch 1993: DPB III P. 13564, 1), though it must be stated that the *sḏj* in this case is reconstructed.

144 pBerlin P 15617, 4 (Zauzisch 1993: DPB III P. 15617, 1) and pLoeb 07, 15–16 (Spiegelberg 1931: 21–22 and Taf. 6) (*sḏj=f j-jr-ḥr=j [n nꜣ] md.wt* 'He told me [about the] things').

145 *Teachings of Ankhsheshonqi*, pBM 10508, III.x+5 (Glanville 1955: 8–9). Glanville (1955: 8) marks it as an error, though as we have seen above with the literary corpus, the use of *n* is common in exactly this construction (*sḏ[j=f m-bꜣḥ] pr-ʿꜣ n md.t nb.t* '[He] recount[ed] every word [before] the Pharaoh').

146 Bresciani, Archivio, Nr. 38, 4 and Bresciani, Archivio, Nr. 39, 13 (Bresciani 1975: 46–47 and 48–49) (*sḏj=n wbꜣ nꜣ wʿb.w* 'We spoke to the priests').

147 Bresciani, Archivio, Nr. 39, 6–7 and 14–15 (Bresciani 1975: 46–47 and 48–49).

148 Stela BM 184, line 9 (= demot. 3) (Brugsch 1891: 937) (*sḏj s pꜣ ḥm-nṯr-n-ptḥ pꜣ-šr-n-jmn tꜣj=f ḥm.t* 'The priest of Ptah, Psenamunis took (lit. declared) her his wife').

6 Findings II: The use of the noun from a diachronic and generic perspective

6.1 The New Kingdom

In the New Kingdom, the noun *sḏd(.w)* has 28 attested cases, of which 20 are useable. Of these, six clearly refer to 'words' (including 'sayings') or 'speech' and 12 indicate what the *Wörterbuch* calls an 'Erzählung'. However, a close analysis of all sources indicates that the word more viably refers— in almost all instances—to a 'report' or 'proclamation' of some kind.[149] Two are unusual, referring to a 'description' in one case[150] and a 'conversation' in another.[151]

In the 18th Dynasty and (for the most part) in the Ramesside Period, the meaning of *sḏd(.w)* is predominantly neutral or positive. From a neutral standpoint, as discussed in Section 4, it is occasionally used to express 'conversation'[152] or in the construction *ḥw(j).t sḏd.t* as a 'figure (lit. flow, or strike) of speech'.[153] Much more frequently, and in line with the meaning of the verb, it implies something of great cultural import that is being transmitted: a 'relaying' of the feats of a king,[154] a 'proclamation' of the *bꜣ.w* of a deity[155] or another aspect of a deity,[156] or the 'proclamation' of a savant.[157] Included in this are 'sayings'.[158] In direct contrast to Redford (2000: 171), and particularly given the royal, monumental context of these proclamations, there is nothing here that smacks of being 'untrustworthy'. I would like to posit that this more negative polarity is indeed something that emerges in *later* usages of the word than those monumental cases of the New Kingdom that Redford cites and that his reading was potentially coloured by them.

149 This meaning seems to be maintained in Copic: ϣⲁϫⲉ in the Gospel of Thomas likewise refers to the 'pronouncements' of Jesus (Vittmann 2006: 190). Also Schott (1990: 365).

150 TT 11 (Djehuty), 2nd stela (*Urk.* IV, 437.7).

151 *The Tale of the Doomed Prince*, pHarris 500, vso 5.10 (*LES* 3.15).

152 *The Tale of the Doomed Prince*, pHarris 500, vso 5.10 (*LES* 3.15) (*jw=sn ḥr ḏd n=f m sḫr n sḏd* 'and they said to him in the manner of a conversation').

153 The 'Israel' stela of Merenptah (K*RI* IV, 15.5-7) (*sw ḫpr m ḥw(j).t sḏd.t* 'He/It has become a saying'); for brief discussions of the term, see Fecht (1983: 128) and Guglielmi (1984: 349, n. 6) on the side of 'flow' and Westendorf (1984: 37–38) on the side of 'strike'.

154 Hatshepsut Punt Expedition Inscription at Deir el-Bahari, 10–11 (*Urk.* IV 344, 9–10); Great Sphinx stela of Amenhotep II, 17 (*Urk.* IV 1281.3); Kuban stela of Ramses II from Year 3, 22 (K*RI* II, 357.7); three parallels from the Kadesh 'Poem' (§ 263): Luxor temple, pylon of Ramesses II (L1), 68 (K*RI* II, 81.1); Luxor temple, court of Ramesses II (L2), 63 (K*RI* II, 81.2) and Karnak temple (K2), 68 (K*RI* II, 81.3); and two parallels of *Praise of the Delta Residence*, pAnastasi II, 1.1 (*LEM* 12.7) and pAnastasi IV, 6.1 (*LEM* 40.12) (*ḥꜣ.t-ꜥ m sḏd [nḫt.w]* 'Beginning of the report of [the victories]').

155 oDeM 1088, 1 = oIFAO 1088 (van Walsem 1982: 242); stela of Neferabu, BM 589 (Luiselli 2011: 361–363) (*ḥꜣ.t-ꜥ m sḏd.t bꜣw n ptḥ* 'Beginning of the report concerning the *bꜣw* (power) of Ptah').

156 Second stela of Djehuty, 18 (*Urk.* IV 437.4–7).

157 See the harpist's song on pHarris 500 = pBM EA 10060, Text A, rto 6.6–7 (Budge 1923: 24, Pl. 45) (*sḏd^w=tj m sḏd.w{t}=sn* 'One proclaims with their proclamations').

158 Letter from the Mayor of Pe to Djehutimesu, pGeneva D 187 = Letter 26, 5-6 (*LRL* 41.14-15) (*n bw-pw=k sḏm /// sḏd* 'Haven't you heard /// the saying').

From the Ramesside Period a single non-monumental source can be cited in which the word is used satirically, in other words, calling the value of these proclamations into question. This source, as mentioned in Section 4, is *The Satirical Letter of Hori*. In one case *sḏd* is modified with *qb(b)*:

(1) 

jst *sḏd.w* *qb(b)* *nꜣy≈k* *tp.(ï)w -rˀ*
jst *sḏd-w* *qbb* *nꜣy-k* *tp-ï-w_rˀ*
PTCL proclamation(M)-PL cool POSS.ART:PL-2SG.M utterance(M)-PL[159]
'Now, your utterances are cool (i.e., trite?) proclamations.'
(oBM EA 65932 = oNash 8, rto 5–6, 19th–20th Dynasty; Fischer-Elfert 1983: 59).[160]

In another two cases, the possessive pronoun is used to convey a negative, ironic sense, as here:

(2) 

nꜣy≈k *sḏd.w* *sḥw(j)* *ḥr* *ns.t≈j*
nꜣy-k *sḏd-w* *sḥw(j)* *ḥr* *ns.t-j*
POSS.ART:PL-2SG.M proclamation(M)-PL collect:RES on tongue:F[SG]-1SG.C

mn *ḥr-tp* *sp.t(ï)≈j*
mn *ḥr=tp* *sp-tï-j*
remain:RES upon lip:F:DU-1SG.C
'Your "proclamations" have collected on my tongue and remain on my lips.'
(pAnastasi I, 28.5, late 19th Dynasty; Fischer-Elfert 1983: 157).[161]

6.2 The Third Intermediate Period

Whether the few satirical cases that emerged in the Ramesside Period presented new nuances of meaning or not, the negatively inflected meaning of *sḏd(.w)* seemed to catch on after this. Two of three nominal cases from the Third Intermediate Period have a negative meaning. In *The Tale of Woe*, a man lies about the harvest, so *sḏd(.w)* takes on the sense of a 'tall story'.[162] In the L1 manuscript of the *Oracular Amuletic Inscriptions*, a female child is promised to be protected from *ḥdb nb bjn m sḏd* 'any evil overthrow via *sḏd*', so *sḏd(.w)*

159 For the glossing of Earlier and Late Egyptian, see Di Biase-Dyson, Kammerzell & Werning (2009).

160 The parallel in pAnastasi I, 5.4, has *mdw* instead of *sḏd* (Fischer-Elfert 1983: 59).

161 The third case is *bw hn(n)≈w nꜣy≈k sḏd.w* 'They did not agree with your "proclamations" ' (pAnastasi I, 26.3, in Fischer-Elfert 1983: 148). The same can be said for the Late Period manuscript of *The Teachings of Amenemope*, pBM EA 10474, rto 14.14 (Laisney 2007: 344).

162 *The Tale of Woe (Wermai)*, pPushkin 127, 4.9–10 (Caminos 1977: Pls 9–10): *mḥ jb≈f sḏd!.w* 'He (the inspector) trusted (lit. heart was full with) the report'.

in this case might mean something like 'slander'.[163] On the other hand, the positive, or rather neutral, meaning remains: in the *Letter to the Dead* of a man to his wife Ikhtay, the dead wife is instructed to give a 'good report' of her husband in the necropolis—thus positive meaning is rather engendered by the modifier *nfr* 'good' than by the positive polarity of the word itself.[164]

6.3 The Late Period (Hieroglyphic texts)

In the Egyptian texts from the Late Period, the neutral meaning of 'report' prevails, both in an official sense (of reporting to superiors) in the Late Egyptian *Teaching of Amenemope*[165] as well as 'reports' or 'pronouncements' (perhaps of a wise man). This latter case may, however, also refer to a 'story',[166] more in line with the meaning visible in the Demotic sources. Unfortunately, there is insufficient context to decide in this case.

6.4 The Late Period to the Roman Period (Demotic texts)

In Demotic texts, all extracted from the *Thesaurus Linguae Aegyptiae* corpus, there are 35 cases (all but one lemmatised as the verb in the corpus) of *sḏj/sḏe*. The noun is commonly used in a neutral manner in the phrase *ḏd sḏj* 'to tell a tale', or 'to make a report'. Considering the potential negative polarity of the term, although at least 2/35 of the Demotic nominal cases recorded in the *TLA* concern 'bad' or 'untrue' stories, the negative aspect is covered not by the lexeme itself, but rather via modifiers, such as *mnḫ* 'excellent' or *mꜣꜥ* 'true'.[167]

As for the meaning of *sḏj* itself, its use in a majority of cases conforms its now predominant meaning as 'story', as derived from the (new) verbal meaning.[168] In this usage, it appears, of course, in literary texts, which make up 16/35 cases,[169] while accounting for a rare case (in direct speech) in which it rather aligns with the more

163 pBM 10083 (L1), 69–70 (Edwards 1960: Pls I–III).

164 Letter to dead wife Ikhtay, oLouvre N 698, vso 18 (Černý & Gardiner 1957: Pls 80–80A): *mntṯ sḏd.t m sḏd nfr* 'You are the one who should recount with(?) a lovely report'.

165 *Teachings of Amenemope* L = pBM EA 10474, rto 14.14 (Laisney 2007: 344) (*jw⸗k wjꜣ<w>jꜣ' m nꜣy⸗k sḏd'* 'You will be unsuccessful with your report').

166 tCairo JE 94478, vso 1 (Vittmann 2006: 189) *nꜣ sḏd ḏd-ḏḥwty-jw⸗f-ꜥnḫ* 'The reports/pronouncements of Djed-Djehuty-iuefankh'. Vittmann (2006: 190) is, understandably, unsure of the translation, suggesting "Worte/Aussprüche/Geschichten". Unfortunately, the lacuna following is such that a disambiguation is not possible, though for the meaning "Aussprüche" Vittmann (2006: 190–191) draws attention to the potential parallel with the 'sayings' of wise men that are cited in the harpist's song on pHarris 500 = pBM EA 10060, Text A, rto 6.6–7 (Budge 1923: 24, Pl. 45). For the meaning "Geschichte" he considers the use in a similar manner at the beginning of *Setne I* (pCairo CG 30646, VI.20, see Vinson 2018: 129).

167 pPetese Tebtunis A, V.9 (Ryholt 1999: 18); pWien D 6920-22, rto x+II.3 (Hoffmann 1996: 172).

168 For a similar view (but without the diachronic dimension of this study), Jasnow (2007: 434).

169 *Die Fabel vom Meer und der Schwalbe*, Krugtexte, Krug A, Text IV, 17 (Spiegelberg 1912: 16); *Amasis und der Schiffer*, pBibl. Nat. 215, vso a.11 (Spiegelberg 1914: 26); *The Tale of Setne I*, pCairo CG 30646, VI.20 (Vinson 2018: 129); pBM 69532, 5 (Tait 2008/9: 115, 117, Taf. 13); *The Tale of Setne II*, pBM EA 10822, III.31, IV.21, V.24 and VI.32 (Griffith 1900: 172, 178, 188, 202,

traditional meaning of 'proclamations'.[170] Another six cases of *sḏj* bearing the meaning of 'story' come from mythological narratives,[171] to which we can add a single (fragmentary) case from the prophetic genre[172] and one (fragmentary) case from a dream manual.[173] On the other hand, the single case in the corpus from an historical archive[174] leans more to the meaning of 'counsel' or 'account'.[175] The two cases from magical texts reflect the meaning of 'word(s)', in terms of 'speech'.[176] Also a satirical text uses its single case of *sḏj* in the sense of 'word(s)', here used plurally, with the modifier 'many', to emphasise it not being worth speaking much about the performance in question.[177] Lastly, the six cases from a legal petition, pRylands IX,[178] seem to reflect a new departure in meaning entirely, namely, 'events',[179] rather than (as would come closer to the meaning in other texts) 'an account of the things that had happened to him'.[180] This is because the *sḏj.w* given are described as being used as evidence in a court case and thus must reflect the contents of the speech act and not the speech act itself.[181]

Like the verb *sḏj*, discussed in Section 5.4.2, what is being said no longer has a high degree of cultural saliency, and it is likely that the term had even developed into a generic term for 'story' by this time.[182] It is also potentially the newsworthiness of the contents of a *sḏj* that make it useable also as something admissible as evidence in a legal dispute.

Pls 3_6); pPetese Tebtunis A, I.9, I.10, V.9, V.10. V.11, VI.x+7 and VIII.4 (Ryholt 1999: 13, 18, 19, 20) (*ḥꜣ.t n nꜣ sḏj* 'The beginning of the stories'). Also pKrall, IX.13 (Bresciani 1964: 48).

170 Saqqara Demotic Papyri I, Text 02, VI.15 (Smith & Tait 1984: 71 and 91): *nꜣj⸗t sḏj.w sr.w bn-pw⸗w ḫpr* 'Your prophetic proclamations: they have not come to pass'.

171 pWien D 6920-22, rto x+II.3 (Hoffmann 1996: 172): *bn-iw-mtw nꜣ sḏj mtr[e]* 'The story is not correct'. Also, *Myth of the Eye of Ra*, pLeiden I 384, II.7, V.12, XII.10, XVI.14 and XVII.8 (Spiegelberg 1917: 12, 20, 34, 42): *sḏm r wꜥ sḏj* 'Listen to a story'.

172 *Das Lamm des Bokchoris*, pWien D 10000, I.21 (Zauzich 1983: 166).

173 pCarlsberg 13, a, II.8 (Volten 1942: 80–81).

174 Ostracon from the Archive of Hor Text 03, 19 (Ray 1976: 21): *nfr nꜣj⸗k sḏj* 'Your counsel/account is good'.

175 Ray (1976: 25).

176 Wien D 12006, rto II.25 (Stadler 2004: 54); pLondon-Leiden, XIX.38 (Griffith & Thompson 1904: 128): *sḏm n pꜣï sḏj ḥr* 'Listen to these words of Horus'.

177 *Der Verkommener Harfenspieler*, pWien KM 3877, 2.11 (Thissen 1992: 70): *bn šw dj.t ꜥšꜣ sḏj* 'It is not worth wasting (lit. giving) many words'.

178 pRylands 9, IV.1, IV.4, V.13, VI.20, XI.17 and XV.12 (Vittmann 1998: 13, 14, 21, 26, 51, 72 and 124, 130, 134, 152, 166): *ḏd⸗f n⸗w sḏj nb* 'He told them every event/incident'.

179 This meaning extends, according to Griffith (1909: 224, n. 2), and echoed by Jasnow (2007: 434), from the fact that the noun is in the plural, but this idea does not account for the many plural usages in the rest of the Demotic corpus and seems to be more of a genre feature. See also Vittmann (1998: 355), who ties this meaning more closely to 'story' in relation to the meanings "Angelegenheit, Begebnis, Ereignis".

180 Jay (2016: 233–234, n. 80). Also Redford (2000: 172), who translates the word as "narratives", presenting the oral account as not trustworthy and as something needing to be written down in order to be taken seriously.

181 Jasnow (2007: 434); also Joey Cross (personal communication).

182 Quack ([2]2009: 17).

7 Discussion

7.1 Ramifications for lexical semantics: Span of meaning and change over time

In sum, from the pharaonic material, it appears that the verb *sḏd* rarely really means 'narrate' in the classical sense, at least in the pharaonic period. It certainly doesn't seem to mean 'racconter une affaire'[183] or similar until Demotic. In this sense, the *Shipwrecked Sailor*, one of our earliest good sources, has led us astray, because though it seems that the narrator is simply 'telling a story', he is also trying to describe a specific encounter with a deity that should influence the actions of the hearer.[184] The focus of *sḏd* is on an oral transmission of some kind, with the causative element perhaps emerging from the position of 'ensuring that something culturally important is properly communicated' (we shall return to this in Section 7.2). This culturally important content could be something the speaker has experienced or something some other person has experienced (in the manner of a 'morality tale'). Both experiences are for the most part closely related to a manifestation of the power of a king or of a god.[185] In this pattern of usage it competes with two partial synonyms: *ḥn* 'acclaim' and, of course, *ḏd* 'say' itself.[186]

Word combination searches within the *TLA* corpus[187] allow us to interrogate the semantic relationship between *ḏd* and *sḏd*. Firstly, we can consider if direct parallels present us with cases of either *ḏd* or *sḏd* and secondly, we can see if co-occurrences of both words together effectuate a disambiguation of the terms from each other. To approach the second case first, we find three rare but interesting cases within the corpus, perhaps tellingly exclusively associated with the earliest attestations of *sḏd*. This may imply that at this time there was a more overt delimitation of their respectively discrete semantic properties. In *The Shipwrecked Sailor*, the sailor says to his superior that he is tired of *ḏd* 'talking' to him but will (despite this) *sḏd* 'relate' something to him.[188] He later says (*ḏd*) to the snake that he wants to report (*sḏd*) to the ruler about him.[189] In *The Teachings of Ptahhotep*, there is an opposition of two consecutive passages: *sḏd⸗f ẖr ms.w* 'he speaks to children', followed by *jḫ ḏd⸗sn <n> ẖrd.w⸗sn* 'that they might speak <to> their

---

183 Winand (2006: 90).

184 See Roeder (2009: 89, 103), though Roeder does not theorise further about the exceptional status of *sḏd* as a narrative marker.

185 For *sḏd bꜣ.w*, see Assmann (1975: 430, n. 5) and Assmann (1980: 6), in the latter of which is said: "Verkunden der (am eigenen Leibe erfahrenen) Machterweise (*sḏd bꜣw*) der Gottheit, dass sich nicht an den Gott selbst, sondern in erster Linie an die 'Öffentlichkeit' richtet." See also Posener (1975: 210): "En effet, *sḏd bꜣw* est un type de glorification bien attesté, une forme de propagande religieuse destinée à faire connaître *urbi et orbi* le terrible pouvoir d'une divinité. C'est un véritable genre hymnique comme l'indique l'existence du titre *ḥꜣ.t-ꜥ n sḏd bꜣw* 'Commencement de l'exposé des *bꜣw*' (du dieu N)." See also Caminos (1978: 156), as well as Roeder (2005 and 2009: 81–90).

186 For *ḥn (pḥ.tï)* 'acclaim might', see the stela of Penbui, Glasgow o.Nr., 5 (Luiselli 2011: 372–373), for *ḏd* (*bꜣ.w*) 'recount power', see the stela of Neferabu, BM 589, 3 (Luiselli 2011: 361–363).

187 This is at present only possible in the original T*LA* corpus, not in *TLA* v.2.

188 pPetersburg 1115, 21 (*MES* 42.7).

189 pPetersburg 1115, 139 (*MES* 45.14).

issue' (pPrisse, 17.12).[190] What makes the differentiation between the two verbs difficult here is that both usages are intransitive, thus both seem to have an identical meaning of 'speaking'.[191] One key difference in *Ptahhotep* may be that the person who does *sḏd* is the teacher, the one with authority, and the one who *ḏd* is the parent. Whether this is significant or not is difficult to judge. In the last case, Sobekhotep on his stela compares the *sḏd* 'relating' of military campaigns to one's wife (i.e., interpersonal) with the *ḏd* of the offering formula (not framed as interpersonal).[192] All three underline the different nuances of *sḏd*-ing something to someone, as compared to *ḏd*-ing something to or for someone.

To return to the idea of *ḏd* and the intransitive *sḏd* having, in some cases, similar meaning, it perhaps bears mentioning that cases of parallels using *ḏd* and *sḏd* interchangeably concern intransitive usages, as seen in *Ptahhotep*[193] and *Sinuhe*.[194] An exception is presented by *The Satirical Letter of Hori*, where the verbs are being used transitively (but in this case both cases are problematic, since the direct object is a person, so generally requires a preposition: '*about* the troop commander').[195]

It is unlikely that diachrony plays a role in this variation: the Middle Kingdom *Ptahhotep* manuscript (P) uses *sḏd* but a roughly contemporary parallel (L1) uses *ḏd*, whereas in *Sinuhe*, the Middle Kingdom manuscript (B) uses *ḏd* and both Ramesside parallels (AOS and DM4) use *sḏd*. Both copies of *Hori*, pAnastasi I (with *ḏd*) and oBerlin P 11236 (with *sḏd*) are Ramesside. The forms thus seem to be interchangeable in a constrained number of usages.

Another way to engage with the *sḏd* vs. *ḏd* debate is via comparable cases of both in which the same direct object is used. One case popular in the Demotic corpus, *sḏd mdw.t*, 'to recount a matter/something', is attested only four times in the pharaonic period.[196] What is fascinating here is that all four use *mdw.t* in its far more specific usage of 'proclamations' of specific individuals, never to vague 'matters', as is attested later. On the other hand,

---

190 pPrisse = pBN 186–194, 17.12 (Žába 1956: 62).

191 As mentioned earlier, P. Dils (*TLA*) has translated it as a pseudo-transitive form with a dummy subject '(es) mitteilen', but no pronoun is included to support this reading.

192 The case of the stela of Sobekhotep (Tübingen Inv. Nr. 458) lies unfortunately outside the *TLA* corpus and it is of course very likely that more such cases exist.

193 *The Teachings of Ptahhotep*, pPrisse = pBN 186–194 (P), 17.11 and pBM EA 10371 + 10435 (L1), vso 3-4 (Žába 1956: 62): *sḏd/ḏd=f m-mj.t(ï)t n ẖrd.w=f* 'he will speak in a similar fashion to his children'.

194 *The Tale of Sinuhe*, pBerlin P 3022 (B), 46, oAshmolean Museum 1945.40 (AOS), 26 and oDeir el Medina 1437 (DM 4), 3 (Koch 1990: 31): *ḏd/sḏd.n=f n=j* 'After he spoke to me'.

195 *The Satirical Letter of Hori*, oBerlin P 11236, 3 = pAnastasi I, 10.1 (Fischer-Elfert 1983: 91): *ḏd/sḏd=j n=k pꜣ-ḫr.ï-pḏ.t* 'I will tell you (about) (or name?) the troop commander'. Compare other very similar cases in the text, where only *ḏd* appears in both cases (presumably only due to a dearth of parallels): pTurin 1889 (s. 62), 5 = pAnastasi I, 13.8 (Fischer-Elfert 1983: 108): *ḏd=j n=k ḥꜣ.w-ḥr j-ḏd.t*^{tw}*=k / ḏd=j n=k* 'I will say to you more than what you said / what I said to you'; pAnastasi I, 22.2–3 (Fischer-Elfert 1983: 135): *ḏd=j n=k ktḫ.wt dmj.wt* 'I will name for you other towns'.

196 The Ahmose monument from the chapel of Tetisheri at Abydos, 6–7 (*Urk.* IV, 27.11); *Kemit*, oMMA 35144 + oMMA 36112, rto 5; oLeipzig 23, 8–9 (Černý & Gardiner 1957: Pl. 37) (an anaphoric case) and the great dedicatory inscription of Seti I (Year 1) at the Pachet temple of Speos Artemidos, 12 (K*RI* I, 42.14–15).

the potentially analogue collocation *ḏd mdw.t* 'to discuss a matter' is substantially more popular in the pharaonic period, with at least 51 cases.[197] Moreover, cases in which *mdw.t* as a direct object of *ḏd* can mean 'matter/s' is attested from at least the Middle Kingdom.[198]

Another more common argument of *sḏd* in the pharaonic period, *bꜣ.w* 'power', can also appear with *ḏd*,[199] but a corpus analysis shows that the collocation is quite rare.[200] The same study of a collocation of *ḏd* with the preferred arguments of *sḏd*, such as *nḫt.w* 'victories', *pḥ.tï* 'might', *mšʿ* 'campaign' and *sḥn* 'commission', brings no results, nor does a study with *sꜣḫ.w* 'ritual recitations'. With *qd* 'form' the study yields only a (fragmentary) case from the Late Period.[201] With *qj* 'form, character', on the other hand, the collocation with *ḏd* is more popular than that with *sḏd* (which boasts only three cases): the cases are seven in number, and, as with the *sḏd* cases, all come from the Ramesside Period. The same can be said of *rn* 'name, reputation', which boasts countless cases with *ḏd* but only three with *sḏd*: a key difference is that in relationship with *ḏd*, it is the 'name' being said, with *sḏd* it is the 'reputation' being proclaimed. These little case studies could be drawn out *ad infinitum*, to cover all comparable cases with direct objects and to consider all cases of *ḏd*, but even this smaller case study indicates clearly that the two words are by no means interchangeable in most cases.

Our last sortie into the relationship between *ḏd* and *sḏd* has to do with the issue of causation, specifically, whether there are attestations of a periphrastic causative *rḏ(j)* + *ḏd* and, if so, whether it is an analogue pattern to *sḏd*, in the manner of other verb forms.[202] In a study of close collocations (1–4 words to the right), 22 clear cases of the periphrastic forms were found in the *TLA*, ranging from the Middle Kingdom[203] to the Late Period.[204] However, none were parallels with cases in the *sḏd* corpus. In any case, what we can see is that the periphrastic construction *rḏ(j)* + *ḏd* provides us with the 'real' causative which *sḏd* cannot be,[205] for reasons discussed in Section 7.2 below. The clear causative meaning of

---

197 This study is based on a combination analysis of cases in which *ḏd* and *mdw.t* co-occur within a span of 1–4 words. This cursory study is merely an indication of the comparative ubiquity of the collocation, not an indication of an actual number of cases. The compound indicating the recitation of a spell or similar, *ḏd-mdw*, was excluded from this analysis.

198 See the fragmentary literary text, *The Story of Hay*, from Lahun, pLondon UC 32157 = pKahun LV.1, vso x+1.1 (Collier & Quirke 2004: 44–47). This being said, the meaning of *mdw.t seemed also to change over time, with the meaning 'matter' becoming more prevalent throughout the New Kingdom.*

199 Stela of Neferabu, BM 589, 3 (Luiselli 2011: 361–363).

200 Following a combination analysis of cases in which *ḏd* and *bꜣ.w* co-occur within a span of 1–4 words, only two parallel cases of *The Praise of Piramesse* emerge: pAnastasi II = pBM EA 10243, 2.2 (*LEM* 13.1) and pAnastasi IV = pBM EA 10249, 6.8 (*LEM* 41.6).

201 pBrooklyn 47.a218.135, 1.13 (Jasnow 1992: 43 and Fig. 3), though the text is fragmentary directly following this point, making the reading uncertain.

202 Štubňová (2019: 193 and 197), though *ḏd* is not mentioned.

203 *Coffin Text* 370 (de Buck 1954: V32.m, versions B2L, B1C and B2P).

204 *Amenemope* L = pBM EA 10474, 22.21 (Laisney 2007: 355), though in this case the <*rḏ(j)*> is not actually present but hypothetically inserted, for which see Laisney (2007: 201).

205 Kuban stela of Ramesses II (Year 3), 24 (K*RI* II, 357.13): *jw=j rḏ(j).t ḏd.y=tw m tꜣ ///* 'I will have it told in the land of ///'.

the periphrastic form is made even clearer by the fact that it can be (in rare cases) precede *sḏd*, as can be seen in Example (3) below.

In any case, what seems to be happening is that although there are semantic overlaps, *sḏd* is used in a far more restricted manner than *ḏd* in relation to a small pool of arguments. What this means, of course, is that contrary to the *communis opinio*, it is *ḏd* that we should call the form that, in addition to many other communicative acts, 'narrates', whereas *sḏd* is the form for purposeful communication (on specific and restricted culturally constrained topics). This finding stands stark contrast to Redford (2000: 176), who sees "the *sḏd* of the people" as something that "stands in disrepute, as something promulgated without reference to a written authority". The very sources of royal victory cited directly thereafter (Redford 2000: 177–279) contradict this reading substantially.

From the Demotic corpus, on the other hand, we see that the meaning of the verb *sḏj* has a different meaning to the Egyptian *sḏd*. Not only can it mean 'speaking' when intransitive and 'relating' when intransitive (with a preposition) or transitive, it can also present more 'tellworthy' material in the manner of 'telling/narrating', moving away from the mere presentation of cultural tropes. This change is likewise reflected in the meaning of the noun, whereby the best attested meaning relates to a 'story', though in more mundane contexts it can also refer to 'events'. It is perhaps significant that the reduction of cultural significance of the noun is crystallised further in the latest stages of the language, whereby the Bohairic ϢⲀⲎⲒ refers simply to a 'Gesprächsthema'.[206]

7.2 Lexicalisation of the 'causative *s*' and ramifications for verbal semantics

Even if the span of meaning and usage of *sḏd* can be more closely interrogated, its meaning as a causative verb in relation to *ḏd* continues to puzzle. Alan Gardiner groups it under those causative verbs "particularly those derived from transitive stems" (though this is not exclusively the case here), which "do not possess full causative force, but have meanings different from that of the simplex", amongst which he groups *jp* 'count' vs. *sjp* 'revise, test, account for', *wḏ* 'command' vs. *swḏ* 'hand over, bequeath', *ḏd* 'say' vs. *sḏd* 'relate' and *nḏm* 'be sweet, be agreeable' vs. *snḏm* 'sit, make oneself comfortable'.[207]

We can reflect on what 'not possessing full causative force' actually means by considering the syntactic constraints on causative derivation, namely, that it "is a valency-increasing operation, which adds a new argument into a clause".[208] Thus it could be considered a process of "transitivisation" for intransitive verbs.[209] In the four 'aberrant' cases above (including *sḏd*) we note that a new argument *per se* (the so-called *causer*, in relation to the old subject, the *causee*)[210] is in this case *not* implied, because active verbs already have as their subject a causative agent.[211] Winand suggests that even though the

---

206 Osing 1976: 237, n. 1041.
207 Gardiner (^{3}1957: 211).
208 Winand (2006: 73), Štubňová (2019: 183).
209 Winand (2006: 73).
210 See for this Schenkel (1999: 318–319).
211 Winand (2006: 90); Štubňová (2019: 190).

subject is the agent in these aberrant transitive cases, "il n'exerce plus nécessairement le contrôle sur l'origine du procès".[212] In those cases where a new agent must be introduced into a cause with a causative transitive verb, the Egyptian language has recourse to a periphrastic causative form with *rḏ(j)*,[213] which engenders indirect causation, rather than direct causation enabled by the prefix *s*.[214]

Concerning the issue that valency doesn't rise when making transitive verbs causative, Štubňová shows, however, that even though the valency "remains the same, it is possible to say which argument is 'missing' in the causative construction". The missing argument could be a subject or an object.[215] However, in the case of *sḏd*, this is also not the case. This is because the object of the 'causative' *sḏd* is *the same object* as would have been of the non-causative *ḏd*. What we end up seeing rather is what occurs to morphological causatives of other transitive verbs when the original subject is omitted: verbs like *jd(j)* 'to cense' as a morphological causative become *sjd(j)* 'cause to be censed'.[216] As we can see, the verb then takes a passive meaning.[217] We might then extrapolate from this that this may also be the case with *sḏd*, which would then mean 'cause to be said'.[218] Such a reading only strengthens the idea that the kinds of concepts being conveyed in this way are (culturally) salient information, something that has already happened, that may impact the hearer and thus may be an indication that the causative force of *sḏd* is more transparent than previously thought.

Though this may be the case, morphological causatives are in general susceptible to lexicalisation, whereby the derivates acquire meanings not able to be predicted.[219] Joan Bybee explains the process in detail: "Because relevant categories [like causatives] produce derived words that are more distinct in meaning from their bases than the ones produced by less relevant categories, the combinations of relevant notions tend to be lexicalized".[220] Lexicalisation is a common process across languages, and is to be seen in various ways in the Egyptian language: "Egyptian stems resulting from the addition of a consonantal phoneme to a root were very soon lexicalized as new autonomous roots, ceasing to be treated as grammatical forms of the basic root".[221]

212 Winand (2006: 73, n. 60). This feature seems to have been shared with other Semitic languages, for which see Lipinski (1997: 387–388).

213 Winand (2006: 73–74); Štubňová (2019: 190).

214 Schenkel (1999: 319).

215 Štubňová (2019: 198).

216 Edel (1955: 194–195, § 440).

217 Štubňová (2019: 202). In Old Egyptian, this process is occasionally assisted by a combination of a detransitivising *n*-affix plus the addition of a causative *s*-affix, which returns the valency of the transitive verb to two (See Štubňová 2019: 204).

218 This is similar, but not identical to, the suggestion by Moers (2011: 167) that the word means something like "vermittelbar machen" ('make sayable'). Roeder (2018: 161–166) also opts for "sprechen lassen".

219 Štubňová (2019: 207), referring to Bybee (1985: 18).

220 Bybee (1985: 17).

221 Loprieno (2001: 1759).

Lexicalisation often leads to the component parts of words no longer being distinguishable from each other. Indeed, it is possible that the causative meaning might not have been recognised in later periods, at least by some speakers/writers. Such an idea fits with the tendencies of Egyptian in general, whereby the causative affix *s.* is already unproductive in Middle Egyptian.[222] A case from the Ramesside Period—a hymn to Thoth from one of the scribal miscellanies—suggests, for instance, that *sḏd* was not (or no longer) seen as a causative form, as it is preceded by the periphrastic causative *rḏ(j)*:

(3) 

ḏ(j)⸗k	*sḏd.t<⸗j>*	*m*	*nꜣy⸗k*	*qn.w*
ḏ(j)-k	*sḏd.t-j*	*m*	*nꜣy-k*	*qn-w*
cause:SBJV	talk:NMLZ:SBJV-1SG	about	POSS.ART:PL-2SG.M	strength(M)-PL

jw⸗j	<*m*>	*tꜣ*	*nb{.t}*
jw-j	*m*	*tꜣ*	*nb*
SBRD-1SG	in	land(M)[SG]	any

'May you ensure that <I> talk about your strengths, when I am <in> any (other) land.' (pAnastasi V = pBM EA 10244, 9.8; *LEM* 60.11; Luiselli 2011: 10–12).

It is important to remember, however, that this one of only two attested cases in the pharaonic period corpus collected so far.[223] Moreover, going from the *TLA* corpus, this combination of both causative forms is not common in Demotic,[224] which can be compared with the substantially larger numbers of cases in which *rḏ(j)/ḏ(j)* + *ḏd* occurs, both in the Egyptian and Demotic corpora in the *TLA*.[225] These tendencies indicate that although the verb was relatively lexicalised, it had not completely lost its 'causative' meaning.

7.3 The inflection of caus. 2rad. in the infinitive and ramifications for morphology

Linked to the previous discussion about the extent to which 'causation' is indicated by the affix *s*, we must also consider the ramifications these ideas have for verbal inflection. Grammatical rules of Egyptian specify that the verbal class *caus. 2rad.* in the infinitive bears the suffix *.t*.[226] This, however, is scarcely borne out by the data collected here.

222 Loprieno (2001: 1759).

223 The other case is from pWien 9340, rto 12 (el-Kholi 2006: 24–25): *jw⸗s ḥr rḏ(j).t sḏd n ky ʿn* 'she will cause to talk(?) to another (person) again'.

224 Two cases of *ti⸗f sḏj* (*ti* being a writing of *ḏ(j)*) can be found in *The Tale of Setne I*, pCairo CG 30646, IV.10 and IV.15 (Vinson 2018: 119). Another single case can be found of *ḏ(j)* plus a periphrastic relative form *jr⸗w sḏ(j)* in the magical papyrus pLondon-Leiden, III.22 (Griffith & Thompson 1904: 36–37).

225 A *TLA* search based on a combination analysis of the lemma *rḏ(j)* (Lemma 851711) and *sḏd* (Lemma 185810). There are 23 cases already in cases in which the lemmata stand within 1–2 words of each other. In the same search in the Demotic corpus there are 16 cases.

226 Gardiner (^{3}1957: 212).

From the data available, there are more cases of the verb in the infinitive do not bear the *.t* than those that do. Of all the cases of a preposition preceding a case of *sḏd*, for which, unfortunately, all cases date to the Ramesside Period, those preceded by *r* are followed in 12 cases by *sḏd* and only 5–7 cases (allowing for two reconstructions) by the more 'grammatically correct' *sḏd.t*. It is perhaps not surprising, though it is noteworthy, that the form without *.t* is predominantly, though not exclusively, in cases written in hieratic. This written form, used predominantly for more mundane texts that reflected more closely the grammar and phonology of the time, took account of the fact that the final *.t* had already begun to be silent during the Middle Kingdom.[227] It is for this reason important to add that all cases with *.t* come from monumental contexts bearing the hieroglyphic script, which maintained a more traditional orthography.[228]

It must be emphasised that the variation within parallel texts negates the possibility that another kind of nominal form of *sḏd* was being implied by leaving off the *.t*, as suggested by Hannig (*HWB*, 863). For instance, two infinitive forms of *sḏd* (following the preposition *r*) in the *Satirical Letter of Hori* have no *.t* (pAnastasi I and Berlin P 11236), whereas the Turin parallel (CGT 54011) has a *.t*.[229] The pRaifé-Sallier III version of the Kadesh 'Poem' §191 has *sḏd* (no *.t*) after the preposition *r* and §200 also has *sḏd* (no *.t*) but also no preposition (though it is present in all other parallels), whereas the two intact monumental cases of §191 and three intact monumental cases of §200 have *sḏd.t*.[230] This trend is followed in other pharaonic monumental (hieroglyphic) contexts: the *sḏd* in Merenptah's Karnak Libyan War text and the one in his 'Israel' stela also have *sḏd.t*. On the other hand, in the private monumental (hieroglyphic) record, all three parallel cases of infinitive *sḏd* in a sun hymn in Theban tombs, TT 163, TT 23 and TT 194, are without *.t* and TT 194 also has another case without a *.t* from a votive hymn.

As for other cases from the late Ramesside Period on, three hieratic texts, a 'literary letter' from London (oBM 50727), an Oracular Amuletic Inscription and a passage from the *Teachings of Amenemope* all have infinitive cases of *sḏd* (no *.t*) after *r*. However, the same can also be said for Third Intermediate Period hieroglyphic monumental texts of Herihor and Piye.

Of the cases preceded by *ḥr*, two cases have *sḏd.t* (Merenptah's 'Israel' stela and the pSallier II copy of the Middle Egyptian *Teachings of Amenemhat*) and two have *sḏd* (a Hymn to the Nile on oGardiner 28 and a text from Medinet Habu, II, 94). It is thus clear that although there are tendencies towards a writing the infinitive *sḏd* with *.t* in monumental sources and without in hieratic ones, there are exceptions to the rule. The forms thus seem to stand in complementary distribution in the Ramesside Period. By the Late Period, however, no more cases with *.t* can be found, indicative that the orthographic tendency preferred in hieratic held out in later cursive iterations.

---

227 Junge (^{2}2005: 35).

228 Junge (^{2}2005: 23).

229 Note, however, that in this case the preposition *r* is reconstructed.

230 For the case of pRaifé-Sallier III, Spalinger (2002: 50) mentions the phenomenon only briefly, and earlier editions and translations by Kuentz (1928) and Gardiner (1960) make no note of it.

7.4 Changes in transitivity and ramifications for syntax

Linguists, amongst others Paul Hopper and Sandra Thompson, have shown based on cross-linguistic research that transitivity and intransitivity in languages are not discrete categories but rather two ends of a continuum.[231] The occasional presentation of the argument via a preposition, in other words, differential object marking (DOM) via *m*/*n* (and others) could be considered a point on this continuum. According to Jean Winand, this gradual introduction of DOM can be seen "as a detransitivizing, detelicising process".[232] It fundamentally involves the use of an oblique construction that is etymologically a partitive construction (*m* 'in, from').[233]

At first glance, it looks like the verb *sḏd* is a good candidate for DOM, since from the New Kingdom on, it seems to be a verb, like *th(j)* 'to transgress', in which the strategies of taking an object as a transitive verb and marking the object with a preposition exist in a relationship of complementary distribution.[234] As mentioned in Section 5.4.2, 11 cases of *m* + argument from the pharaonic period come from a wide range of genres: six from private and royal monumental records, another three from versions of the same texts in hieratic script on papyri and ostraca, a scribal text and a Late Period wisdom text, where the *m* is now an *n*, as we see in Demotic.[235]

By checking the cases marked with prepositions against direct textual parallels or cases with similar objects, we can see some tendencies regarding the interchangeability of marked and unmarked arguments. From the 18th Dynasty onwards, the hieratic oCairo 12189 has as an object of *sḏd* what could be DOM via *m* + *bꜣ.w⸗k*, whereas similarly-themed votive hymns in hieroglyphs on stelae, like that of stela of Amenhotep Huy, Turin 1608 (and a monumental case from Medinet Habu) have *bꜣ.w* as a direct object.[236] The same

231 Hopper and Thompson (1980: 252–253). Transitivity can be measured according to several different factors: number of participants, kinesis, aspect (especially telicity), punctuality, volitionality, affirmation (affirmative/negative), mode (realis/irrealis), agency, affectedness of object and individuation of object.

232 Winand (2015: 533).

233 Jean Winand (personal communication).

234 Winand (2015: 546).

235 The royal monumental records are the obelisk inscription of Hatshepsut, northern side, 17 (*Urk.* IV, 365.8–9); the Armant stela of Thutmose III (Cairo JE 67377), 3 (*Urk.* IV, 1245.1–2) and the oracular inscription of Herihor, Karnak, 22–23 (*LD* III, 248b = Koll. Sethe 4,7, also Epigraphic Survey 1981: 15, Pl. 132). The private monumental records are a text praising the king in TT 40 (Amenhotep Huy), 26 (Davies & Gardiner 1926: Pls XXIII and XXIX) and harpists' songs in TT 50 (Neferhotep), Song 2, Text G, line 3 (Kákosy & Fábián 1995: 223, Fig. 3) and its more damaged parallel in TT 32 (Djehutymes), line 12 (Kákosy & Fábián 1995: 223, Figs. 2–3). The versions on monumental texts on papyrus are pLouvre E 4892 + pBM 10181 (pRaifé + pSallier III), S 7.2 (§ 200) (*KRI* II, 64.10) and the harpist's song on pHarris 500 = pBM EA 10060, Text A, rto 6.6–7 (Budge 1923: 24, Pl. 45). The hymn on an ostracon is oCairo/Gurna 12189, rto 1–2 (Luiselli 2011: 326–327) and the scribal text is pLansing = pBM EA 9994, 9.4 (*LEM* 107.16). The Late Period wisdom text is pBrooklyn 47.218.135, 4.6 (Jasnow 1992: 75, Fig. 9).

236 oCairo 12189, rto 1–2 (Posener 1975: 209, Pl. 21) has *sḏdy⸗j m bꜣ.w⸗k n ḥr-nb* 'I will report *on* your power to everyone...', whereas the stela Turin 1608 (Luiselli 2011: 366–368) has *sḏdt⸗j bꜣ.w⸗k n rm.w* 'I will report your power to the fish...'.

feature is visible in the Kadesh 'Poem' (§ 191 and 200): where the hieratic version pRaifé-Sallier III uses *ḥr* + *wp.t=f* and *m* + *rn=j*, the monumental records use direct objects.[237] In the case of the scribal texts (pLansing and oFlorence 2617), the only two cases concerning 'reporting' the *mḥr wʿ.w*, 'ills of the soldier' introduce this argument using two different prepositions, *m* and *r*.[238] So, for the pharaonic material, marking what is normally a direct object with a preposition is a strategy taken in *hieratic* texts. DOM, a semantic rather than a medial strategy, is not required as a model.

Criteria for DOM are also not really met in the features of *sḏd*. Firstly, the appearance of a preposition does not seem to substantially affect the verb's meaning, as otherwise occurs when transitive verbs are used without direct objects.[239] Secondly, there is no change in affectedness, [240] such as can be seen in other verbs like *th(j)* 'to overstep, go astray', whereby "a conative effect can be observed".[241] This is likely because affectedness cannot really be established in relation to 'transmitted' information (i.e., in relation to a verb of communication), as compared to a more concrete object of an *action* like *th(j)*. Lastly, even though cases in which the direct object of *sḏd* bears a preposition tend to "be used exclusively with the tenses of the *inaccompli*",[242] other factors account for this phenomenon far better.

The first factor to consider is that the transitive form of *sḏd* falls within the category of verbs that Jean Winand calls "objets spécifiques", in other words, that the implied object is inherent to the meaning of the verb. Such cases do not change in meaning when deprived of an object.[243] The second factor draws on this prevalence of the *inaccompli* in the sources in which the direct object carries a preposition. If we consider all 11 cases from the pharaonic era in which the direct object is marked with *m/n*, the last three, dating from the time of Merenptah onwards, only use the preposition if the nominal direct object is *defined* in some way (carrying an article, etc.).[244] These are: the Israel stela,[245] the Hymn to

237 A Kadesh version in Luxor temple (L2), 51 (K*RI* II, 64.9) *has jr(j) ḫ3s.wt pt{r}j (w)j r sḏd.t rn=j* 'The foreign lands that beheld me will report (on) my reputation...', whereas pSallier III 7.1–2 (K*RI* II, 64.10) has *jr(j) ḫ3s.t nb pt{r}j sḏd m rn=j* 'Every foreign land that saw will report on my reputation...'.

238 pLansing = pBM EA 9994, 9.4 (*LEM* 107.16) and oFlorence 2619, rto 4–5 (Erman 1880: 96–97).

239 Winand (2004: 218–219).

240 To quote Beavers (2011: 335), "Affectedness—usually construed as a persistent change in or impingement of an event participant—has been implicated in argument realization, lexical aspect, transitivity, and various syntactic operations. However, it is rarely given a precise, independently motivated definition. Rather, it is often defined intuitively or diacritically, or reduced to the properties it is meant to explain, especially lexical aspect."

241 Winand (2015: 546).

242 Winand (2015: 546). For a similar phenomenon in Lycopolitan Coptic, see Engsheden (2018). The *sḏd* corpus contains: the imperfective relative form, the imperfective emphatic form, the future and the subjunctive. The exception is the infinitive.

243 Winand (2004: 231).

244 This of course does not apply if the direct object is a pronoun.

245 'Israel' stela (Cairo CGC 34025), 21–22 (K*RI* IV, 18.1).

Thoth on pAnastasi V,[246] and the oracular inscription of Herihor.[247] From the Late Period can be added the Brooklyn Wisdom Text.[248]

In fact, this feature turns out to be a predecessor of what is standard in Demotic with "durative tenses", which can be associated with other *inaccompli* verb forms via their representation of ongoing action: "With the durative tenses, a defined object had to follow the preposition *n* (written *n-jm* before a pronoun); an undefined object might, but need not do so."[249] This rule, it turns out, affects a substantial amount of the *sḏj* corpus (Section 5.4.2). Of the 73/83 intransitive cases, there are 34 in which the 'direct object' is marked with a preposition. Only a single case of these has an *undefined* direct object after a preposition and it is indeed not in a durative tense but in the future tense.[250]

The other thing to consider is the type of preposition. The dominant way of marking the argument after *sḏj* is with *n*, but the use of the prepositions *r* and *ẖr*, which in the pharaonic-era material had been limited to a single attestation each,[251] also increases. These various Demotic prepositional phrases are in and of themselves very interesting, as their distribution seems to be bound by genre constraints. Prepositional phrases in which the argument is introduced by *n* appear primarily in literary texts, but also in letters[252] and probably also in a wisdom text.[253] On the other hand, the mythological texts have only a single reliable case with an argument following a preposition, which is *r* + argument, generating the adverbial 'concerning [something]'.[254] This tendency is also followed by memoranda.[255] Finally, the medical texts, excluding a single exception with *n*, use *ẖr* 'about [something]' to introduce arguments, which, as discussed in Section 5.4.2, seems to be due to the fact that these cases, matching the many intransitive cases, convey a meaning

---

246 pAnastasi V = pBM EA 10244, 9.8 (*LEM* 60.11; Luiselli 2011: 10–12).

247 Oracular inscription of Herihor, north wall, Khonsu Temple, Karnak, 22 (*LD* III, 248b = Koll. Sethe 4,7, also Epigraphic Survey 1981: 15, Pl. 132).

248 pBrooklyn 47.218.135, 4.6 (Jasnow 1992: 75, Fig. 9).

249 Johnson (1976: 6). Also Parker (1961: 180) and Engsheden (2018: 159). Engsheden (2018: 158) moreover argues that in non-imperfective tenses, there is an *n*-marking if there is a determiner, but that this occurs late in Coptic.

250 pBerlin P 13564, 7 (Zauzisch 1993: DPB III P. 13564, 1), though it must be stated that the *sḏj* in this case is reconstructed.

251 For the case marked with *ẖr*, see pLouvre E 4892 + pBM 10181 (pRaifé + pSallier III), S 6.7 (§ 191) (K*RI* II, 61.15), cited above. The parallel (Luxor temple from the pylon of Ramesses II (L1), 50 (K*RI* II, 61.12)) has no preposition. The case with *r*, oFlorence 2619, rto 4–5 (Erman 1880: 96–97), uses an abbreviated form *mj n⸗k* 'Come <...> to you', which leaves out the <*sḏd⸗j*> '<let me relate>' in between. The parallel (pLansing = pBM EA 9994, 9.4 (*LEM* 107.16)) uses *m*, which is surprisingly considered by L. Popko (*TLA*) to be an error. The *Wörterbuch* (*Wb* IV 395.11) doesn't record these exceptions, focusing on cases marked with *m*.

252 pLoeb 07, 15 (Spiegelberg 1931: 21–22, Taf. 6).

253 *Teachings of Ankhsheshonqi*, pBM 10508, III.x+5 (Glanville 1955: 8–9). This is of course contingent on this case not being erroneous, as Glanville (1955: 8) suggests.

254 *Myth of the Eye of Ra*, pLeiden I 384, X.25 (Spiegelberg 1917: 30).

255 Bresciani, Archivio, Nr. 39, 6–7 and 14–15 (Bresciani 1975: 46–47 and 48–49).

that is more dialogic ('speaking') than monologic ('relating' or similar). The use of *r* in the abovementioned memoranda and the mythological text is also more dialogic.[256]

In sum, the introduction of a preposition before the direct object, which began in the New Kingdom, was first only visible in hieratic texts, which registered modern vernacular. During the Ramesside Period, the accompaniment of this feature with definiteness establishes the durative direct object rule of Demotic.

7.5 The role of determination in the lexicalisation of nouns and ramifications for historical syntax

The grammatical issue affecting the noun *sḏd* is that of determination, namely, whether an article or another (demonstrative or possessive) pronoun precedes it, and whether this is indicative of a change in word class. This is significant, of course, because the noun is attested so much later than the verb, from which it likely derives. In the New Kingdom, the noun *sḏd* appears mostly in high-register texts, with 15/25 being either high-register monumental texts or versions of these monumental texts on papyrus, and it is thus perhaps not surprising that these cases are not determined.[257] Of the nine remaining, four, coming from lower register texts in Late Egyptian, from the Ramesside Period on, have some form of determination and another two bear adjectives. Two cases of the possessive *nꜣy⸗* appear in the *Satirical Letter of Hori*[258] and another is found in the Late Period manuscript of *The Teachings of Amenemope*.[259] The use of definite articles, however, is attested in hieratic documents only from the Late Period.[260] This trend is continued, as determination in general is prevalent in the Demotic sources, in which 33/35 of *sḏj*-nouns are determined either with an article (definite or indefinite), a possessive pronoun, a demonstrative pronoun or an adjective (including numbers).

The noun, like the verb, seems to be amorphous in terms of orthography, being written both with *.t* and without. However, the closer we look, the more an orthographic logic comes to be apparent. Of the 25 clear cases of the noun *sḏd(.w)* in the Egyptian records, there are 16 cases written in hieratic and 9 cases in hieroglyphic in a monumental context. The nouns in hieratic are, with only a single exception,[261] written as *sḏd*, whereas the nouns in hieroglyphic script are, with only a single—early—exception,[262] written as *sḏd.t*. From this we can draw two conclusions: Firstly, the force borne on the orthography of

256 However, this is not indicated in the *TLA* translation of Leiden I 384, X.25 (G. Vittmann, *TLA*): "indem sie von deinen Dingen (d.h. deinem Wirken?) erzählen". However, because of the use of *r*, perhaps 'talk *about* your matters' is rather more apt.

257 Junge ([2]2005: 57) illustrates that "The earlier form of determination—avoiding articles and demonstratives—is encountered in those texts reflecting the norms of the hierarchically higher and more conservative registers."

258 pAnastasi I, 26.3 and 28.5 (Fischer-Elfert 1983: 148 and 157).

259 pBM EA 10474, rto 14.14 (Laisney 2007: 344).

260 See, for instance, a report of Djed-Djehuty-iuefankh on tCairo JE 94478, vso 1 (Vittmann 2006: 189).

261 Harpist's song on pHarris 500 = pBM EA 10060, Text A, rto 6.6–7 (Budge 1923: 24, Pl. 45).

262 Hatshepsut Punt Expedition Inscription at Deir el-Bahari, 10–11 (*Urk.* IV 344, 9–10).

the noun is not diachronic, but medial, and secondly, the orthographic pattern remains constant along these medial grounds across word classes, since similar tendencies were visible in the writing of the infinitive form of the verb (for which see Section 7.3). Like with the infinitive, the 'hieratic' (i.e., more modern) tendency was carried on in Demotic, where cases with a *.t* ending are nowhere to be found.

7.6 Ramifications of a lexico-grammatical study for narratology

To consider the role of *sḏd* as a 'metanarrative form', as proposed by Gerald Moers,[263] we must consider whether it has a 'narrativising' effect on what is being described. I would like to frame this discussion around two ideas of narrativity. One is that *sḏd* is a narrativising element, which *à la* Hayden White, would take an event and "impose upon it the form of a story".[264] The other is that *sḏd* as a narrativising element marks something with a high degree of 'newsworthiness'[265] or 'tellability',[266] i.e., it highlights aspects that render an event narratologically significant by being new or interesting.

In the former respect, what follows *sḏd* can certainly be *framed* by it as a narrative, even more specifically, as Moers has argued, a metanarrative introduction of hypodiegetic internal narratives: a story within a story. However, I think this only covers the formal aspect, not the functional aspect, of the use of *sḏd*, at least in the pharaonic period. Cases predating the Late Period show considerable cultural constraints on the material and prompt the conclusion that when it comes to the second criterion of 'tellability', this dimension of narrativity is not met. Even cases that seem at first glance to be 'stories' end up being proclamations of some traumatic experience at the hands of kings and gods from which the hearer must learn.[267] They can be summarised as follows:

- Things that are used as a warning: the treatment (via *bꜣ.w*, *pḥ.tï* or the like) of someone by a king or a god in order to influence future behaviour of the hearer.
- Things that happened to the speaker, rarely as a means of self-aggrandisement and more frequently as a means of convincing the hearer about something.
- Things that are customary—and thus important to learn: *tp-rs or n(ï).t-ʿ*.

What *sḏd* introduces is 'tellable' via Ryan's definition only insofar as it might be seen as meeting the vested interests of the hearer, but it seems rather to reflect the interests of the *speaker*, not the hearer. Also, novelty is not a priority. It is the functionality of the experience that is prioritised. Moreover, only in very rare cases is *sḏd* linked to a sequence of events related at great length: here, brevity is key. The fact that many Egyptians knew exactly what the 'power' of the god or the 'victories' of the king entailed meant that superfluous

263 Moers (2019: 323).
264 White (1980: 6).
265 Prince (2008: 23–24), referring to Labov (^{2}1979: 366), though Prince is also critical of the criterion.
266 For a plot-based definition of 'tellability', see Ryan (1986: 319); Ryan (1991: 148–151). Also Moers (2019: 324).
267 This is similar to the proclamatory aspect of Roeder's "sprechen lassen" (2018: 161–166), but I feel that the conditions under which such events occur remain too vague in Roeder's model.

details could be spared in the communication.[268] In the respect of that which is *sḏd* being a complete event, a link can be made to the complementary topic of 'monochronic images', which are also conceptually compact and culturally constrained, whereby one image must be 'legible' to the culture regarding content, scope and significance.[269] There might even be a degree of 'decorum' involved in the brevity of these representations.[270]

As stipulated, the conclusions reached so far conform to the analysis of the pharaonic-era material: cases from the Late Period onwards show *sḏd* to be a complete 'metanarrative form' that can introduce a wide range of narrative structures. On the other hand, in the epochs before this, this function is, in my opinion, squarely represented by *ḏd*.[271] As such, this study supports the general aims of the volume by showing the nuance and historical dimensionality of a lexical item that brings a degree of 'narrative coherence' to a text without necessarily making it conform to a 'narrative' in a traditional sense. This is because, from a narratological perspective, *sḏd* does not foreground event discreteness, a key criterion of narrativity by Gerald Prince,[272] nor do the events it introduces prioritise singularity over banality and specificity over generality, as argued for by Didier Coste.[273] On the other hand, some aspects of events that *sḏd* introduces correlate well with narratological ideas, such as the presence of conflict,[274] causality[275] and also a degree of "conceptual and logical complexity" driven by an "underlying system of purely virtual embedded narratives".[276] The latter aspect is particularly interesting here, because it implies that the 'backstories' and motivations of both speaker and hearer must be taken into consideration when considering what *sḏd* means and what it is supposed to do. Moreover, as regards the idea of conflict as a correlate of narrative, we could establish a link with Frank Ankersmit's idea of the traumatic origins of historical consciousness,[277] whereby "suffering [...] became occasion for thought".[278] Though the traumatic origins of lessons of the past are not metabolised by Egyptian accounts in a theoretical way, Egyptian awareness of such origins seems to be correlated to the fact that that trauma must be put to good use: to teach us for the future.

---

268 Such a communication of course *does* correspond to what Genette (1983: 18–20) calls a "minimal narrative", because even a single event implies a change of state—one can even go so far as to see single words as standing for whole narratives, along the lines of Bal (1999: 25–27). Another idea already introduced to Egyptology by Popko (2009: 213) concerns the idea of the *exemplum*, whereby historical events are reduced to the most salient details in official reports.

269 See Moers, this volume.

270 For a discussion of the term, see Baines (^{2}2001: 277): "the rules which [...] bar certain types of representation from associating freely and occurring freely in different contexts".

271 As suggested already by Moers (2011: 167–168): *ḏd⸗f* at the beginning of autobiographies (as well as some narratives and also wisdom texts) supplies the "narrative macro structure" of the genre(s). See Jurman, this volume, 3.2, who calls it a "quotation statement".

272 Prince (1999: 43–49).

273 Coste (1989: 62).

274 Prince (1999: 43–49).

275 Coste (1989: 62).

276 Ryan (1991: 156).

277 Ankersmit (2002).

278 Ankersmit (2005: 358).

In sum, *sḏd* is a key to culturally important statements, it is thus mostly monologic, rather than dialogic (the latter of which can be better covered by *ḏd*). Also, it usually talks about power but is rarely used by power. If pharaohs themselves *sḏd*, they are doing it to proclaim the deeds of their ancestors, or, though rarely, of gods, as seen in Akhenaten's *sḏd* about the Aten.[279] Given that pharaonic discourse about the kingly self is for the most part focused either on their meeting and surpassing the efforts of kings past or on their personal interaction with deities, this restraint in the use of *sḏd* is notable. It shows us that in the former case, the relating (via *sḏd*) of such great deeds is transferred into the mouths of the public at large and in the second case, other means of depicting the interaction with the divine sphere are chosen.

The 'tellability' of something, in sum, is related to its interest value or 'narrative point'. This factor is in theory driven by its relation to a plot sequence, but it is only measurable by its effect on the reader/hearer (Ryan 1991: 150–151). It is at precisely this conceptual juncture that we find ourselves with the re-definition of *sḏd*. *sḏd*, in its usage prior to the Late Period, presupposes two key ideas: that the idea being communicated is important and that the reader would do well to heed the message.

Bibliography

AL = Meeks, Dimitri. 1977–1979. *Année Lexicographique*, 3 Volumes, Paris.

AW I = Hannig, Rainer. 2003. *Ägyptisches Wörterbuch I: Altes Reich und Erste Zwischenzeit*, Kulturgeschichte der antiken Welt 98, Hannig-Lexica 4, Mainz.

AW II = Hannig, Rainer. 2006. *Ägyptisches Wörterbuch II: Mittleres Reich und Zweite Zwischenzeit*, Kulturgeschichte der antiken Welt 112, Hannig-Lexica 5, Mainz.

Ankersmit, Frank. 2002. Trauma and Suffering: A Forgotten Source of Western Historical Consciousness, in: Jörn Rüsen (ed.), *Western Historical Thinking. An Intercultural Debate*, New York, 72–85.

Ankersmit, Frank. 2005. *Sublime Historical Experience.* Stanford.

Assmann, Jan. 1975. Aretalogien, in: Wolfgang Helck & Eberhard Otto (eds), *Lexikon der Ägyptologie I*, Wiesbaden, 425–434.

Assmann, Jan. 1978. Eine Traumoffenbarung der Göttin Hathor. Zeugnisse 'Persönlicher Frömmigkeit' in thebanischen Privatgräbern der Ramessidenzeit, in: *Revue d'Égyptologie* 30, 22–50.

Assmann, Jan. 1980. Die 'loyalistische Lehre' Echnatons, in: *Studien zur Altägyptischen Kultur* 8, 1–32.

Assmann, Jan. 1983. *Sonnenhymnen in Thebanischen Gräbern, Theben I,* Mainz.

Assmann, Jan. 1991. *Das Grab des Amenemope (TT 41)*, Theben III, Mainz.

Assmann, Jan. ²1999. *Ägyptische Hymnen und Gebete*, 2nd Revised Edition, Orbis Biblicus et Orientalis, Freiburg / Göttingen.

Baines, John. ²2001. *Fecundity Figures: Egyptian Personification and the Iconology of a Genre*, 2nd Edition, Oxford.

Bal, Mieke ²1997. *Narratology. Introduction to the Theory of Narrative*, 2nd Edition, transl. of 1st Edition Christine Van Boheemen, Toronto.

Bal, Mieke 1999. Close Reading Today: From Narratology to Cultural Analysis, in: Walter Grünzweig & Andreas Solbach (eds), *Grenzüberschreitungen: Narratologie im Kontext – Transcending Boundaries: Narratology in Context*, Tübingen, 19–40.

279 Amarna boundary stela K, 8 (Davies 1908: 29; Murnane & van Siclen 1993: 23.4–7).

Baroni, Raphaël. 2014. Tellability, in: Peter Hühn et al. (eds), *the living handbook of narratology*. Hamburg, http://www.lhn.uni-hamburg.de/article/tellability, accessed 05.01.2023.

Beavers, John. 2011. On affectedness. *Natural Language & Linguistic Theory* 29(2), 335–370.

Belegstellen = Erman, Adolf, Wolja Erichsen & Hermann Grapow (eds). 1935–1953. *Wörterbuch der aegyptischen Sprache – Die Belegstellen*, 5 Volumes, Leipzig.

Bresciani, Edda. 1964. *Der Kampf um den Panzer des Inaros (Papyrus Krall)*, Mitteilungen aus der Papyrussammlung der Österreichischen Nationalbibliothek (Papyrus Erzherzog Rainer) 8. Folge, Vienna.

Bresciani, Edda. 1975. *L'archivio demotico del tempio di Soknopaiu Nesos nel Griffith Institute di Oxford. Volume I: P. Ox. Griffith nn. 1–75*, Testi e documenti per lo studio dell'antichità 49, Milano.

Bresciani, Edda, Elsa Bedini, Lucia Paolini & Flora Silvano. 1978. Una rilettura dei papiri demotici Bologna 3173 e 3171, in: *Egitto e Vicino Oriente* 1, 95–104.

Brose, Marc. 2009. Ostrakon BM EA 50727 – "An unknown literary text"?, in: *Studien zur Altägyptischen Kultur* 38, 57–82.

Brugsch, Heinrich K. 1891. *Historisch-biographische Inschriften altaegyptischer Denkmaeler*, Thesaurus inscriptionum Aegyptiacarum: altaegyptische Inschriften 5, Leipzig.

de Buck, Adriaan. 1954. *The Egyptian Coffin Texts*, Oriental Institute Publications 73, Chicago.

Budge, E. A. Wallis. 1923. *Facsimiles of Egyptian Hieratic Papyri in the British Museum, with Descriptions, Summaries of Contents, Etc., Second Series*, London

Bybee, Joan L. 1985. *Morphology: A Study of the Relation Between Meaning and Form*, Typological Studies in Language 9, Amsterdam.

Cachette = *Cachette de Karnak*, https://www.ifao.egnet.net/bases/cachette/ck64, accessed 05.01.2023.

Caminos, Ricardo A. 1977. *A Tale of Woe from a Hieratic Papyrus in the A. S. Pushkin Museum of Fine Arts in Moscow*, Oxford.

Caminos, Ricardo A. 1978. Review, *Egyptian Stelae, Reliefs and Paintings from the Petrie Collection. Part One: The New Kingdom* by Harry Milne Stewart, in: *Journal of Egyptian Archaeology 64, 151–157.*

CD = Faulkner, Raymond O. 1962. *Concise Dictionary of Middle Egyptian*, Oxford.

Černý, Jaroslav & Alan H. Gardiner. 1957. *Hieratic Ostraca I*, Oxford.

Collier, Mark & Stephen Quirke. 2004. *The UCL Lahun Papyri: Religious, Literary, Legal, Mathematical and Medical*, Oxford.

Collombert, Philippe & Laurent Coulon. 2000. Les dieux contre la mer. Le début du "papyrus d'Astarté" (pBN 202), in: *Bulletin de l'Institut Français d'Archéologie Orientale* 100, 193–242.

Coste, Didier. 1989. *Narrative as Communication*, Minneapolis.

Davies, Nina de Garis & Alan H. Gardiner. 1926. *The Tomb of Huy, Viceroy of Nubia in the reign of Tut'ankhamun (No. 40)*, Theban Tomb Series 4, London.

Davies, Norman de Garis. 1905. *The Rock Tombs of El Amarna Part II – The Tombs of Panehesy and Meryra II*, Archaeological Survey of Egypt 14, London.

Davies, Norman de Garis. 1908. *The Rock Tombs of El Amarna Part V – Smaller Tombs and Boundary Stelae*, Archaeological Survey of Egypt 17, London.

Davies, Norman de Garis. 1933. *The Tomb of Neferhotep at Thebes*, 2 Volumes, New York.

Di Biase-Dyson, Camilla, Frank Kammerzell & Daniel A. Werning. 2009. Glossing Ancient Egyptian. Suggestions for Adapting the Leipzig Glossing Rules, in: *Lingua Aegyptia* 17, 243–266.

Di Biase-Dyson, Camilla & Jaqueline Stock. 2022. Einblicke in den Streit zwischen Leib und Kopf—Eine Neuedition und Textanalyse von tTurin CGT 58004 (Cat. 6238), in: *Zeitschrift für Ägyptische Sprache und Altertumskunde* 150(1), 56–73.

van Dijk, Jacobus. 1995. Maya's Chief Sculptor Userhat-Hatiay, in: *Göttinger Miszellen* 148, 29–34.

Dorn, Andreas. 2004. Die Lehre Amunnachts, in: *Zeitschrift für Ägyptische Sprache und Altertumskunde* 131, 38–55.

DZA = *Das digitalisierte Zettelarchiv*, http://aaew.bbaw.de/dza/index.html, accessed 12.01.2020.

Edel, Elmar. 1955. *Altägyptische Grammatik I*, Analecta Orientalia 34, Rome.

Edwards, Iorwerth E. S., 1960. *Hieratic Papyri in the British Museum, Fourth Series: Oracular Amuletic Decrees of the Late New Kingdom*, 2 Volumes, London.

Engsheden, Åke. 2018. Verbal semantics and differential object marking in Lycopolitan Coptic, in: Ilja A. Seržant & Alena Witzlack-Makarevich (eds), *Diachrony of differential argument marking*. Studies in Diversity Linguistics 19, Berlin, 153–182.

Enmarch, Roland. 2005. *The Dialogue of Ipuwer and the Lord of All*, Oxford.

Epigraphic Survey. 1981. *The Temple of Khonsu II: Scenes and Inscriptions in the Court and the First Hypostyle Hall*. Oriental Institute Publications 103, Chicago.

Erichsen, Wolja. 1954. *Demotisches Glossar*, Copenhagen.

Erman, Adolf. 1880. Hieratische Ostraka, in: *Zeitschrift für Ägyptische Sprache und Altertumskunde* 18, 93–99.

Erman, Adolf. 1911. Deksteine aus der thebanischen Gräberstadt, in: *Sitzungsberichte der Königlich Preussischen Akademie der Wissenschaften*. Jahrgang 1911. 2, Halbband. Juli bis Dezember, 1086 –1111.

Fecht, Gerhard. 1983. Die Israelstele, Gestalt und Aussage, in: Manfred Görg (ed.), *Fontes atque pontes. Eine Festgabe für Hellmut Brunner*, Ägypten und Altes Testament 5, Wiesbaden, 106–138.

Fischer-Elfert, Hans-Werner. 1983. *Die satirische Streitschrift des Papyrus Anastasi I. Textzusammenstellung*, Kleine ägyptische Texte 7, Wiesbaden.

Fitzenreiter, Martin (ed.). 2009. *Das Ereignis. Geschichtsschreibung zwischen Vorfall und Befund*. Internet-Beiträge zur Ägyptologie und Sudanarchäologie 10, London, 211–222.

Frandsen, Paul J. 1998. On the avoidance of certain forms of loud voices and access to the sacred, in: Willy Clarysse, Antoon Schoors & Harco Willems (eds), *Egyptian Religion: The Last Thousand Years: Studies dedicated to the memory of Jan Quaegebeur*, Orientalia Lovaniensia Analecta 84–85, Leuven, 975–1000.

Gardiner, Alan H. 1935. *Hieratic Papyri in the British Museum, Third Series: Chester Beatty Gift*, 2 Volumes, London.

Gardiner, Alan H. 1955. *The Ramesseum Papyri*, Oxford.

Gardiner, Alan H. [3]1957. *Egyptian Grammar: Being an Introduction to the Study of Hieroglyphs*, Oxford.

Gardiner, Alan H. 1960. *The Kadesh Inscriptions of Ramesses II*, Oxford.

Genette, Gérard. 1983. *Narrative Discourse Revisited*, transl. Jane E. Lewin, Ithaca.

Glanville, Stephen R. K. 1955. *The Instructions of 'onchsheshonqy Part I: Introduction, transliteration, translation, notes, and plates*, Catalogue of Demotic Papyri in the British Museum II. London.

Grapow, H. 1936. *Sprachliche und schriftliche Formung ägyptischer Texte*. Leipziger Ägyptologische Studien 7. Glückstadt.

Griffith, Francis Ll. 1889. *The inscriptions of Siût and Dêr Rîfeh III*, London.

Griffith, Francis Ll. 1900. *Stories of the High Priests of Memphis. The Sethon of Herodotus and the Demotic Tales of Khamuas*, 2 Volumes, Oxford.

Griffith, Francis Ll. & Herbert Thompson. 1904. *The Demotic Magical Papyrus of London and Leiden*. London.

Griffith, Francis Ll. 1909. *Catalogue of the Demotic Papyri in the John Rylands Library*, 3 Volumes, Manchester.

Grimal, N.-C. 1981. Études sur la propagande royale Égyptienne I. La stèle triomphale de Pi(ʿankh)y au Musée du Caire : JE 48862 et 47086–47089. Les Mémoires publiés par les membres de l'Institut Français d'Archéologie Orientale 105. Cairo: l'Institut Français d'Archéologie Orientale.

Guglielmi, Waltraud. 1984. Zur Adaption und Funktion von Zitaten, in: *Studien zur altägyptischen Kultur* 11, 347–364.

Hall, Harry R. H. 1925. *Hieroglyphic texts from Egyptian stelae, etc., in the British Museum VII*, London.

Hassan, Selim. 1943. *Excavations at Gîza IV*, 1932–1933, Cairo.

Hayes, William C. 1948. A Much-Copied Letter of the Early Middle Kingdom, in: *Journal of Near Eastern Studies* 7: 1–10.

Helck, Wolfgang. 1969. *Der Text der "Lehre Amenemhets I. für seinen Sohn"*, Kleine Ägyptische Texte 1, Wiesbaden.

Helck, Wolfgang. ²1995. *Historisch-biographische Texte der 2. Zwischenzeit*, 2nd Edition, Kleine Ägyptische Texte 6,2, Wiesbaden.

Hoffmann, Friedhelm. 1995. *Ägypter und Amazonen. Neubearbeitung zweier demotischer Papyri P. Vindob. D 6165 und P. Vindob. D 6165 A*, in: Österreichische Nationalbibliothek, Papyrussammlung (eds), Mitteilungen aus der Papyrussammlung der Österreichischen Nationalbibliothek (Papyrus Erzherzog Rainer); Neue Serie, 24. Folge, Vienna.

Hoffmann, Friedhelm. 1996. Der literarische demotische Papyrus Wien D6920–22, in: *Studien zur Altägyptischen Kultur* 23, 167–200.

Hopper, Paul & Sandra Thompson. 1980. Transitivity in Grammar and Discourse, in: *Language* 56, 251–299.

Hühn, Peter. 2013. Event and Eventfulness, in: Peter Hühn et al. (eds), *the living handbook of narratology*. Hamburg, http://www.lhn.uni-hamburg.de/article/event-and-eventfulness, accessed 05.01.2023.

HWB = Hannig, Rainer. ⁶2015. *Die Sprache der Pharaonen. Großes Handwörterbuch Ägyptisch–Deutsch (2800 bis 950 v. Chr.) –Marburger Edition–*, Hannig-Lexica 1, Kulturgeschichte der antiken Welt 64, Mainz.

Jansen-Winkeln, Karl. 2007–2016. *Inschriften der Spätzeit*, 4 Volumes, Wiesbaden.

Jasnow, Richard. 1992. *A Late Period Hieratic Wisdom Text (P. Brooklyn 47.218.135)*, Studies in Ancient Oriental Civilization 52, Chicago.

Jasnow, Richard. 2007. 'Through Demotic Eyes': On Style and Description in Demotic Narratives, in: Zahi A. Hawass & Janet Richards (eds), *The Archaeology and Art of Ancient Egypt: Essays in Honor of David B. O'Connor*, Annales du Service des antiquités de l'Égypte, Cahier No. 36, Cairo, 433–448.

Jay, Jacqueline. 2016. *Orality and Literacy in the Demotic Tales*, Culture and History of the Ancient Near East 81, Leiden & Boston.

Johnson, Janet H. 1976. *The Demotic Verbal System*, Studies in Ancient Oriental Civilization 38, Chicago.

Junge, Friedrich. ²2005. *Late Egyptian Grammar: An Introduction*, 2nd English Edition, transl. David Warburton, Oxford.

Kákosy, László & Zoltán I. Fábián. 1995. Harper's Song in the Tomb of Djehutimes (TT 32), in: *Studien zur altägyptischen Kultur* 22, 211–225.

Kamerzell, Frank & Carsten Peust. 2002. Reported speech in Egyptian. Forms, types and history, in: Tom Güldemann & Manfred von Roncador (eds), *Reported Discourse. A meeting ground for different linguistic domains*, Amsterdam & Philadelphia, 289–322.

el-Kholi, Mohamed Salah. 2006. *Papyri und Ostraka aus der Ramessidenzeit mit Übersetzung und Kommentar*. Monografie del Museo del Papiro 5, Siracusa.

Koch, Roland. 1990. *Die Erzählung des Sinuhe*, Bibliotheca Aegyptiaca XVII, Brussels.

K*RI* = Kitchen, Kenneth A. 1969–1990. *Ramesside Inscriptions: Historical and Biographical*, 8 Volumes, Oxford.

Kuentz, Charles. 1928–1934. *La Bataille de Qadesh*, Mémoires de l'Institut Français d'Archéologie Orientale 55, Cairo.

Kuhlmann, Klaus P. & Wolfgang Schenkel. 1983. *Das Grab des Ibi, Obergutsverwalters der Gottesgemahlin des Amun (Thebanisches Grab Nr. 36)*, 2 Volumes, Archäologische Veröffentlichungen, Mainz.

Labov, William. ²1979. *Language in the Inner City: Studies in the Black English Vernacular*, 2nd Edition, Philadelphia.

Laisney, Vincent P.-M. 2007. *L'Enseignement d'Aménémopé*, Studia Pohl: Series Maior 19, Rome.

LD = Lepsius, Carl Richard. 1849–1859. *Denkmäler aus Ägypten und Äthiopien*, 12 Volumes, Berlin, http://edoc3.bibliothek.uni-halle.de/lepsius/tafelw.html, accessed 06.06.2021.

LEM = Gardiner, Alan H. 1937. *Late Egyptian Miscellanies*, Bibliotheca Aegyptiaca VII, Brussels.

LES = Gardiner, Alan H. 1932. *Late-Egyptian Stories*, Bibliotheca Aegyptiaca I, Brussels.

Lipinski, Edward. 1997. *Semitic Languages. Outline of a Comparative Grammar*, Orientalia Lovaniensia Analecta 80, Leuven.

López, Jesús. 1984. *Ostraca ieratici N. 57450–57568. Tabelle lignée N. 58001–58007*, Catalogo del Museo Egizio di Torino, Serie Seconda Collezioni III.4, Milan.

Loprieno, Antonio. 2001. Late Egyptian to Coptic, in: Martin Haspelmath (ed.), *Language Typology and Language Universals: An International Handbook*, Handbücher zur Sprach- und Kommunikationswissenschaft 20, Berlin, 1742–1761.

LRL = Černý, Jaroslav. 1939. *Late Ramesside Letters*, Bibliotheca Aegyptiaca IX, Brussels.

Lüddeckens, Erich. 1943. *Untersuchungen über religiösen Gehalt, Sprache und Form der ägyptischen Totenklagen*, Mitteilungen des Deutschen Instituts für Ägyptische Altertumskunde in Kairo 11, Berlin.

Luiselli, Maria Michaela. 2011. *Die Suche nach Gottesnähe. Untersuchungen zur Persönlichen Frömmigkeit in Ägypten von der Ersten Zwischenzeit bis zum Ende des Neuen Reiches*, Ägypten und Altes Testament 73. Wiesbaden.

Mariette, Auguste. 1875a. *Denderah : description générale du grand temple de cette ville*, Paris.

Mariette, Auguste. 1875b. *Karnak : étude topographique et archéologique avec un appendice comprenant les principaux textes hiéroglyphiques découverts ou recueillis pendant les fouilles exécutées à Karnak*, Leipzig.

MES = Blackman, Aylward M. 1932. *Middle Egyptian Stories*, Bibliotheca Aegyptiaca II.1, Brussels.

Moers, Gerald. 2011. Broken Icons: The Emplotting of Master-Narratives in the Ancient Egyptian *Tale of Sinuhe*, in: Fredrik Hagen, John Johnston, Wendy Monkhouse, Kathryn Piquette, John Tait & Martin Worthington (eds), *Narratives of Egypt and the Ancient Near East: Literary and Linguistic Approaches*, Orientala Lovaniensia Analecta 189, Leuven, 165–176.

Moers, Gerald. 2019. 33 Ägyptologie, in: Eva von Contzen & Stefan Tilg (eds), *Handbuch Historische Narratologie*, Stuttgart, 323–324.

Murnane, William J. & Charles C. van Siclen III. 1993. *The Boundary Stelae of Akhenaten*, London & New York.

Osing, Jürgen. 1976. *Die Nominalbildung des Ägyptischen I. Textband.* Sonderschrift des Deutschen Archäologischen Instituts Abteilung Kairo, Mainz.

Parker, Richard A. 1961. The Durative Tenses in P. Rylands IX, in: *Journal of Near Eastern Studies* 20(3), 180–187.

Popko, Lutz. 2009. Exemplarisches Erzählen im Neuen Reich? – Eine Struktur der Ereignisgeschichte, in: Martin Fitzenreiter (ed.). *Das Ereignis. Geschichtsschreibung zwischen Vorfall und Befund.* Internet-Beiträge zur Ägyptologie und Sudanarchäologie 10, London, 211–222.

Popko, Lutz. 2022. Papyrus Ramesseum XV, in: *Science in Ancient Egypt*, https://sae.saw-leipzig.de/de/dokumente/papyrus-ramesseum-xv?version=20, accessed 05.01.2022.

Posener, Georges. 1951. *Catalogue des ostraca hiératiques littéraires de Deir el Médineh, Tome II (Nos 1109 à 1167)*, Cairo.

Posener, Georges. 1975. La piété personelle avant l'âge Armanien, in: *Revue d'Égyptologie* 27, 195–210.

Prince, Gerald. 1999. Revisiting Narrativity, in: Walter Grünzweig & Andreas Solbach (eds), *Grenzüberschreitungen: Narratologie im Kontext – Transcending Boundaries: Narratology in Context*, Tübingen, 43–51.

Prince, Gerald. 2008. Narrativehood, Narrativeness, Narrativity, in: John Pier & José Angel García Landa (eds), *Theorizing Narrativity*, Narratologia 12, Berlin, 19–28.

Quack, Joachim F. 1994. *Die Lehren des Ani. Ein neuägyptischer Weisheitstext in seinem kulturellen Umfeld.* Orbis Biblicus et Orientalis 141. Fribourg / Göttingen.

Quack, Joachim F. ²2009. *Einführung in die altägyptische Literaturgeschichte III. Die demotische und gräko-ägyptische Literatur*, Einführungen und Quellentexte zur Ägyptologie 3, Münster.
Ramsès Online, http://ramses.ulg.ac.be/, accessed 14.01.2020.
Ray, John D. 1974. *The Archive of Ḥor*, Texts from Excavations, Second Memoir, London.
Redford, Donald B. 2000. Scribe and Speaker, in: Ehud Ben Zvi & Michael H. Floyd (eds), *Writings and Speech in Israelite and Ancient Near Eastern Prophecy*, Atlanta, 145–218.
Reisner, Mary B. 1934. Inscribed Monuments from Gebel Barkal, in: *Zeitschrift für Ägyptische Sprache und Altertumskunde* 70 (1934), 35–46.
RITA = Kitchen, Kenneth A. 1993–2014. *Ramesside Inscriptions, Translated and Annotated: Translations*, 7 Volumes, Oxford & Chichester.
Roeder, Günther. 1924. *Aegyptische Inschriften aus den staatlichen Museen zu Berlin. Zweiter Band – Inschriften des Neuen Reichs, Indizes zu Band 1 und 2*, Leipzig.
Roeder, Hubert. 2005. Das „Erzählen der Ba-u". Der *Ba-u*-Diskurs und das altägyptische Erzählen zwischen Ritual und Literatur im Mittleren Reich, in: Burckhard Dücker & Hubert Roeder (eds), *Text und Ritual. Kulturwissenschaftliche Essays und Analysen von Sesostris bis Dada*, Heidelberg, 187–239.
Roeder, Hubert. 2009. Die Erfahrung von *Ba'u* „Sinuhe" und „Schiffbrüchiger" zwischen dem Erzählen und Lehren der 12. Dynastie, in: Hubert Roeder (ed.), *Das Erzählen in frühen Hochkulturen I*, Ägyptologie und Kulturwissenschaft 1, München, 75–157.
Roeder, Hubert. 2018. *Das Erzählen in frühen Hochkulturen: II. Eine Archäologie der narrativen Sinnbildung*, Ägyptologie und Kulturwissenschaft 2, Paderborn.
Ryan, Marie-Laure. 1986. Embedded Narratives and Tellability, *Narrative Poetics* 20(3), 319–340.
Ryan, Marie-Laure. 1991. *Possible Worlds, Artificial Intelligence, and Narrative Theory*, Bloomington.
Ryholt, Kim. 1999. *The Story of Petese Son of Petetum*, The Carlsberg Papyri 4, Copenhagen.
Sauneron, Serge. 1953. L'hymne au soleil levant des papyrus de Berlin 3050, 3056 et 3048, in: *Bulletin de l'Institut Français d'Archeologie Orientale* 53, 65–90.
Schenkel, Wolfgang. 1965. *Memphis, Herakleopolis, Theben: die epigraphischen Zeugnisse der 7.–11. Dynastie Ägyptens*, Ägyptische Abhandlungen 12, Wiesbaden.
Schenkel, Wolfgang. 1999. c-Kausativa, t-Kausativa und "innere" Kausativa: die c-Kausativa der Verben I.c in den Sargtexten, in: *Studien zur Altägyptischen Kultur* 27, 313–352.
Schott, Siegfried. 1990. *Bücher und Bibliotheken im alten Ägypten. Verzeichnis der Buch- und Spruchtitel und der Termini technici.* Wiesbaden.
Sethe, Kurt. ²1928. *Aegyptische Lesestücke zum Gebrauch im akademischen Unterricht zusammengestellt – Texte des mittleren Reiches*, Leipzig.
Simon, Henrike. 2013. *„Textaufgaben". Kulturwissenschaftliche Konzepte in Anwendung auf die Literatur der Ramessidenzeit*, Studien zur altägyptischen Kultur, Beihefte 14, Hamburg.
Smith, Henry Sidney & W. John Tait. 1984. *Saqqara Demotic Papyri I*, London.
Smith, Mark. 2005. *Papyrus Harkness (MMA 31.9.7)*, Oxford.
Spalinger, Anthony. 2002. *The Transformation of an Ancient Egyptian Narrative. P. Sallier III and the Battle of Kadesh*, Göttinger Orientforschungen, IV. Reihe: Ägypten 40, Wiesbaden.
Spiegelberg, Wilhelm. 1902. *Grabsteine und Denksteine aus süddeutschen Sammlungen I: Karlsruhe, Mühlhausen, Straßburg, Stuttgart*, Strassburg.
Spiegelberg, Wilhelm. 1910. *Der Sagenkreis des Königs Petubastis nach dem Strassburger demotischen Papyrus sowie den Wiener und Pariser Bruchstücken*, Demotische Studien 3, Leipzig.
Spiegelberg, Wilhelm. 1912. *Demotische Texte auf Krügen*. Leipzig.
Spiegelberg, Wilhelm. 1914. *Die sogenannte demotische Chronik des Pap. 215 der Bibliothèque Nationale zu Paris nebst den auf der Rückseite des Papyrus stehenden Texten*, Leipzig.
Spiegelberg, Wilhelm. 1917. *Der ägyptische Mythus vom Sonnenauge (der Papyrus der Tierfabeln – „Kufi") nach dem Leidener demotischen Papyrus I 384*. Strassburg.
Spiegelberg, Wilhelm. 1931. *Die demotischen Papyri Loeb der Universität München*, Munich.

Stadler, Martin A. 2004. *Isis, das göttliche Kind und die Weltordnung. Neue religiöse Texte aus dem Fayum nach dem Papyrus Wien D. 12006 Recto*, Mitteilungen aus der Papyrussammlung der österreichischen Nationalbibliothek (Papyrus Erzherzog Rainer), Neue Serie 23, Wien.

Štubňová, Silvia 2019. Where syntax and semantics meet: a typological investigation of Old Egyptian causatives, in: *Lingua Aegyptia* 27, 184–213.

Tait, W. John. 1991. P. Carlsberg 207: Two columns of a Setna-text, in: Paul J. Frandsen (ed.), *Demotic Texts from the Collection*, The Carlsberg Papyri 1, Copenhagen: Copenhagen, 19–46, Pls 1–3.

Tait, W. John. 2008/9. Pa-di-pep tells Pharaoh the Story of the Condemnation of Djed-her: Fragments of Demotic Narrative in the British Museum, in: *Enchoria* 31, 113–143.

Tait, W. John. 2015. May Pharaoh listen to the story! Stories-within-stories in Demotic fictional narrative, in: Rune Nyord & Kim Ryholt (eds), *Lotus and Laurel: Studies on Egyptian language and religion in honour of Paul John Frandsen*, CNI Publications 39, Copenhagen, 391–401.

Thissen, Heinz J. 1984. *Die Lehre des Anchscheschonqi (P. BM 10508)*, Bonn.

Thissen, Heinz J. 1992. *Der Verkommener Harfenspieler. Eine altägyptische Invektive (pWien KM 3877)*. Sommerhausen.

TLA = *Thesaurus Linguae Aegyptiae*, http://aaew.bbaw.de/tla/, accessed 14.01.2020.

TLA v.2 = *Thesaurus Linguae Aegyptiae*, Version 2, https://thesaurus-linguae-aegyptiae.de/, accessed 05.01.2022.

Urk. IV = Sethe, Kurt. 1906–9. *Urkunden der 18. Dynastie. Urkunden des ägyptischen Altertums IV*, 4 Volumes, Leipzig: Hinrichs; Helck, Wolfgang. 1955–8. *Urkunden der 18. Dynastie*. Urkunden des ägyptischen Altertums IV, 6 Volumes, Berlin.

Varille, Alexandre. 1968. *Inscriptions concernant l'architecte Amenhotep Fils de Hapou*, Bibliothèque d'Étude 44, Cairo.

Vernus, Pascal. 1978. *Athribis. Textes et documents relatifs à la géographie, aux cultes et à l'histoire d'une ville du Delta égyptien à l'époque pharaonique*, Bibliothèque d'étude 74, Cairo.

van Walsem, René. 1982. Month-Names and Feasts at Deir el-Medina, in: Rob J. Demarée & Jac J. Janssen (eds), *Gleanings from Deir el-Medina*, Egyptologische Uitgaven I, Leiden, 215–244.

Vinson, Steve. 2018. *The Craft of a Good Scribe: History, Narrative and Meaning in the First Tale of Setne Khaemwas*, Harvard Egyptological Studies 3, Leiden.

Vittmann, Günter. 1998. *Der demotische Papyrus Rylands 9*, 2 Volumes, Ägypten und Altes Testament 38, Wiesbaden.

Vittmann, Günter. 2006. Eine spätzeitliche Schülertafel aus dem Asasif, in: *Ägypten und Levante* 16, 187–193.

Volten, Aksel. 1942. *Demotische Traumdeutung (Pap. Carlsberg XIII und XIV Verso)*, Analecta Aegyptiaca 3, Copenhagen.

Wb = Erman, Adolf & Hermann Grapow (eds). 1971 [1926–1971]. *Das Wörterbuch der aegyptischen Sprache*, 7 Volumes, Reprint Edition, Berlin.

Wegner, Wolfgang. 2014. Eine demotische Abrechnung und ein demotischer Brief aus Tebtynis (P. Hamburg D 45 und 46), in: Sandra L. Lippert & Martin A. Stadler (eds) *Gehilfe des Thot. Festschrift für Karl-Theodor Zauzich zu seinem 75. Geburtstag*, Wiesbaden, 155–183.

Wente, Edward F. 1962. Egyptian "Make Merry" Songs Reconsidered, in: *Journal of Near Eastern Studies* 21, 118–128.

Westendorf, Wolfhart. 1984. *Ḥwj.t-sḏd.t* "das Schlag-Wort", in: *Göttinger Miszellen* 72, 37–38.

White, Hayden. 1980. The Value of Narrativity in the Representation of Reality, in: *Critical Inquiry* 7(1) – *On Narrative*, 5–27.

Winand, Jean. 2004. La non-expression de l'objet direct en égyptien ancien (Études Valentielles, I), in: *Lingua Aegyptia* 12, 205–234.

Winand, Jean. 2006. *Temps et aspect en égyptien. Une approche sémantique*, Probleme der Ägyptologie 25, Leiden.

Winand, Jean. 2015. The oblique expression of the object in Ancient Egyptian, in: Eitan Grossman, Martin Haspelmath & Tonio Sebastian Richter (eds), *Egyptian-Coptic Linguistics in Typological Perspective*, Empirical Approaches to Language Typology 55, Berlin, 533–560.

Žába, Zbyněk. 1956. *Les Maximes de Ptahhotep*, Académie Tchécoslovaque des Sciences. Section de la linguistique et de la littérature, Prague.

Zauzich, Karl-Theodor. 1983. Das Lamm des Bokchoris, in: Österreichische Nationalbibliothek, Papyrussammlung (eds), *Festschrift zum 100-jährigen Bestehen der Papyrussammlung der Österreichischen Nationalbibliothek – Papyrus Erzherzog Rainer (P. Rainer Cent.)*, Wien, 165–174.

Zauzich, Karl-Theodor. 1984. Der Streit zwischen Horus und Seth in einer demotischen Fassung (Pap. Berlin P 15549 + 15551 + 23727), in: Karl-Theodor Zauzich & Heinz J. Thissen (eds), *Grammata Demotika: Festschrift für Eric Lüddeckens*, Würzburg, 275–281, Taf. 38.

Zauzich, Karl-Theodor. 1993. *Papyri von der Insel Elephantine*, Demotische Papyri aus den Staatlichen Museen zu Berlin III, Berlin.

Zivie, Christiane M. 1976. *Giza au deuxième millénaire*, Bibliothèque d'Étude 70, Cairo.

Non, je ne regrette rien !

A narratological essay on life writing, life telling, and life reading in Old Kingdom Egypt

Claus Jurman

Abstractum

Origo omnium et vitae regina est narratio. Cum videmus quod in parietibus sepulcri scriptum et depictum est, non possumus quin e fragmentis orationis mutae fingamus fabula. Homo vescitur fabellis. Ea de causa esse est narrari, in vitam atque in mortem, olim et nunc.

Table of contents

Gerald Moers (ed.), *Narrative and Narrativity in Ancient Egypt*, 71–216
DOI: https://doi.org/10.37011/studmon.29.03

0 Introductory remarks

The only way to make sense of life is to tell it, whether to oneself or to others. Wanting life to make sense is natural. Telling it is cultural. So is sense itself.

This is by necessity the axiological starting point of any narratological approach to life writing from ancient Egypt and basically any human society past or present. But these tenets also lie at the heart of many problems related to the application of narratology to ancient societies. With the exception of natural language in the broadest sense, there is perhaps no other creation of human culture serving as much as a battleground for advocates of the antagonistic concepts of universalism on the one hand and of cultural relativism on the other hand than "narrative". Debates already start at the level of the epistemic framework, thus, whether we are dealing with an observable phenomenon of human communication, a theoretical concept reified through literary analysis or a conventionalised (and clichéd) technical term put to (too) many different uses in (too) many different contexts.[1] Irrespective of the individual understandings of its essence, most scholars would agree that "narrative" is interconnected with the human inclination to derive meaning from lived experience through retrospective structuring.[2] Because such efforts at structuring become most tangible in the form of carefully laid out stories – whether told orally or put down in writing – it is no wonder that literary criticism provided the breeding ground for discussions on the topic. It even held a sort of monopoly on them for quite some time and spawned the establishment of "narratology" as a subdiscipline of literary criticism devoted to studying the workings of "narrative" and "narrativity".[3] The ubiquity of "narrative" as a concept in today's scholarly discourse was therefore not inherent in its original institutional framing.

1 Already in 2009 Arnauld bemoaned that a "pan-narrativism" had taken root, in which the term "narrative" was used metaphorically to serve as a synonym for practically any form of generation of meaning. "Das »Narrativ« wird in metaphorischer Verwendung zum Synonym jeglicher kultureller Sinnproduktion; der Pan-Narrativismus droht an die Stelle eines vordem modischen Pan-Fiktionalismus zu treten." Arnauld (2009: 47). See also Georgakopoulou & Goutsos (2000: 65); Bal (2019: 243).

2 Exemplary is Ricœur's (1983: 17) claim that "le temps devient temps humain dans la mesure où il est articulé de manière narrative".

3 For different narratological concepts and definitions of key terms, see below, Chapter 2.1.

Rather, the growing allure of narratology for disciplines beyond the field of literary studies may relate to the fact that the Western literary tradition simply provides particularly "telling" manifestations of much more general properties of human behaviour and interaction. But it took decades of scholarly discussions on sophisticated narrative strategies within the literary sphere before one thought about abstracting from them the underlying narrative structures at work in other, more mundane spheres of communication. Once this basic relation had been realised (usually not by literary critics), the analytical toolkit developed by literary criticism could be readily adopted, adapted or transformed to serve the needs of a host of quite diverse disciplines.[4] It is thus easily understandable why "narrative" and "narrativity" have turned into household names enjoying wide currency in almost every field of the humanities and the social sciences (occasionally even foraying into the natural sciences[5]). Still, the success of the analytical concept of "narrative", which is often acknowledged by speaking of the "narrative turn" in XYZ,[6] cannot conceal the fundamental disagreements among those who have made the study of narratives their preoccupation. Lively, and sometimes also very isolated, debates dwell not only on the question of how narrativity may manifest itself in myriad ways within different cultural spheres but on the very essence of the object of investigation. If narrativity is construed as an exclusively textual or language-bound phenomenon, then non-textual cultural products are necessarily excluded from consideration. If, on the other hand, narrativity is thought of as a universal, evolutionarily conditioned overarching cognitive principle permeating the entirety of human life, one faces the problem of demarcating and justifying a meaningful area of enquiry and an appropriate methodology. Even the simple assertion that, in some form, narrative or narrativity are human universals[7] begs the question of precisely which dimensions and manifestations of narrativity are universal and which are determined by temporal and cultural alterity. In a society such as ours, in which – despite all the formalistic and media-specific developments of the past centuries – the canonical 19th century novel still constitutes the epitome of a narrative, applying the "duck test" to the medium of an ancient culture may not lead to a satisfactory result: "If it looks like a (modern Western) narrative and can be analysed as a narrative and is treated by scholars and the wider public as a narrative, then it probably *is* a narrative." But what if it does not? And what if something not bearing resemblance to "our" way of telling stories nevertheless serves all the major functions we generally tend to associate with narratives? Mutatis mutandis, these issues also apply to the concepts of (auto)biography and of life writing more gener-

4 See Nünning & Nünning (2002: 2–4); Fludernik (2005: 46–48).

5 Damasio offers a particularly interesting case in point for neuroscience when stating that "[m]ental experiences are [...] narratives of several micro events in the body proper and the brain." Damasio (2018: 121). Similarly: "Equipped with language, organisms can generate continuous translations of nonverbal to verbal items and build dual-track narratives of such items." Damasio (2018: 63).

6 A critical appraisal of the different "narrative turns" having occurred in literary studies, historiography, social sciences and humanities in general is found in Hyvärinen (2010) and particularly in Dawson (2017).

7 Cf. White (1987: 1); Wolf (2017b: 257).

ally.[8] If this is accepted as a dilemma worthwhile exploring then there is hope that efforts to probe the foundations of ancient Egyptian narrativity have something to add to more general narratological discourses. It may be precisely the "unfamiliarity" of the Egyptian material (from a non-Egyptological perspective) that lays bare some components of the transcultural essence of narrativity itself. At the same time, however, there is an undeniable risk that such endeavours result in nothing more than a fruitless dissection of terms and concepts forcefully applied to cultural phenomena that are far removed from the modern tradition for which they were originally designed. Perhaps, therefore, it is advisable to steer towards a middle ground, where ambition is seasoned with a good deal of open-ended curiosity and pragmatism.

As this volume's introductory chapter by Gerald Moers demonstrates, narratology has already been enjoying an extended and, at times, nuanced reception within Egyptology. So far, however, there have been only very limited attempts to direct narratological questions at cultural products beyond the narrowly defined "literary" sphere (e.g. those one may call in a generalising manner non-fictional texts) or even at non-textual semiotic entities such as pictorial compositions.[9] For this reason the multimodal *iconotexts*[10] centred on the tomb owner in Egyptian elite tombs of the Old Kingdom promise to provide interesting test-cases for the application of contemporary narratological theories. While one should not take for granted that any of the strands of narratology in vogue today offers a tailored toolkit for analysing Egyptian funerary culture of the 3rd millennium BCE, the field's richness and diversity render it a real possibility that aspects of Old Kingdom tomb decoration can indeed be meaningfully conceptualised from a narratological perspective.

That said, the aims of the present contribution remain very modest. Its theoretical footing will likely appear as unnecessarily eclectic and hybrid to many proponents of mainstream narratology. It is also not meant to be a comprehensive narratological take on the emergence and early development of life writing in ancient Egypt. The past two decades have seen a sizeable number of important monographs, collected volumes and individual papers come out, which have laid the ground for a better understanding of the "biographical genre" in ancient Egypt, not least of the Old Kingdom.[11] Many publications have highlighted the complex interaction between a number of different oral and written traditions of discourse and the wealth of sources to consider. Thanks to these seminal studies I feel entitled to restrict my considerations to a discussion of some particularly intriguing narratological issues such as "voice", "tellability" and "narrative coherence".

---

8 On these and associated terms, see Chapter 3.1.

9 Di Biase-Dyson (2019) makes a case for the broad and flexible application of narratological concepts within Egyptology. For narratological approaches towards ancient Egyptian imagery, see Braun (2019; 2020).

10 In the tradition of postmodernist art history, "iconotext" is here understood as the amalgam of interdependent textual and pictorial elements to form one overarching unit of meaning. See esp. Nerlich (1990: 268); also Wagner (1995: 23; 1996: 15). In relation to the Egyptian monumental discourse, iconotexts can be situated at different levels, ranging from that of a single scene with textual and pictorial elements to that of the entire tomb with all its carved or painted components.

11 Baines (1999a; 1999b); Kloth (2002); Baud (2003; 2005); Frood (2007); Bassir (2014; 2019); Stauder-Porchet (2017); Stauder-Porchet et al. (2020).

They shall be investigated on the basis of an eclectic but not haphazardly chosen mix of better and lesser-known "biographical assemblages" taken from the repertoire of the preserved archaeological record. As the subtitle of my paper suggests, this will be done with three major avenues of enquiry in mind: *life writing* as a shorthand for the composition of (auto)biographical narration and its media-related multimodal instantiation, *life telling* as a shorthand for the mesh of relations between voice, authorship and agency, and finally, *life reading* as a shorthand for the recipient's role in the concrete enactment of narrativity. Rather than purporting to provide a comprehensive and well-balanced discussion of these topics, I shall be content if this text passes for an essay in the original French meaning of the word,[12] being a personal epistemic *attempt* at coming to terms with emanations of irreducible otherness.[13]

1 *For sale: baby shoes, never worn* – micro-stories from "Hemingway's" baby to Hekenu's son

What is a story? What are its core elements and how long does it have to be? Before attempting to define *narrative* and *narrativity* for the purposes of this study (see the following chapter), let us consider the following line of text consisting of just six words:

For sale: baby shoes, never worn.

Without additional contextual information we will most likely infer from the tag phrase "for sale" that we are dealing with a conventional sale advertisement published in an unspecified medium. Accordingly, we will classify the line as a very simple functional text, which is written in a nominal note-style and does neither contain a finite verb nor identifiable human protagonists. One could argue that by all standards of literary fiction these six words are as far from representing a coherent storyline as a text can be. But is this really the way we process the line in our minds? Does it really appear to us as a piece of purely technical information without relevance or emotive power? If we are not in the middle of bargain hunting for our little one and thereby blessed (or cursed) with selective perception we will inevitably feel an urge to wonder about the circumstances of this sale. Who is the unidentified seller, whose presence in the text is but an implied one? What could have possibly made this person sell baby shoes in mint condition? Through association, the compound "baby shoes" introduces "the baby" as another protagonist, even though it is not explicitly mentioned. As there is not much else one can do with baby shoes than to put them on baby feet, and as babies are normally not very particular about their looks the act of offering the shoes for sale implies a significant change of circumstances. What these circumstances might be is not subject of the text, but I would be surprised if not the overwhelming majority of readers surmised that something tragic had happened. The

12 Montaigne (1617: 333).

13 For the anthropological pitfalls connected with wanting to counter "othering" with well-inteded "saming", see Viveiros de Castro (2015: 42).

baby's sudden death is by no means the only possible explanation for the act of sale, but it certainly provides the greatest degree of *tellability*[14] or narrative salience. Such inferences transcending the immediate textual coherence are usually referred to as *elaborative inferences*[15] (as opposed to *necessary inferences* such as the assumption that the participal clause "never worn" refers to the baby shoes). Regardless of the exact path our hypothesising takes, it is incontestable that most of this processing happens without a conscious effort of our own. The chain of potential events conforms to the mental representations of patterns already present in our memory and seems to be triggered or induced by the text rather than constructed anew.[16] This may at first appear counterintuitive but is not really surprising. Cognitive science and evolutionary psychology have conclusively shown that we as a species are almost "hardwired" to structure incomplete or inconclusive information and extrapolate from it an explanatory model which makes sense to us.[17] In this specific context, the most basic meaning of "sense" is simple recognisability, in turn leading to (felt) predictability and an activation of the human reward system, which are all key assets in the struggle to survive the vicissitudes of our environment and even thrive therein.[18] Recognition first and foremost applies to *schemata*, which can be conceptualised as forms of structured world knowledge that help us to orientate ourselves in factual and fictional environments.[19] In psychology, linguistics and cognitive narratology these schemata are often divided into *frames* or *scenarios* (mental representations of persons, things, environments and actions in stereotypical situations/contexts) and the temporarily-ordered *scripts* (patterns of stereotypical events),[20] both of which are addressed, for example, by Scenario Mapping Theory.[21] The underlying processes of such structuring involve inferences of temporalities, agents, causalities and "relative normativity" (e.g. to what degree the phenomena are perceived as "standard, stereotypical, new, unusual, indeterminate or persis-

---

14 For the narratological concept of *tellability*, see Chapter 2.4.

15 For the respective terminology and the psycho-linguistic understanding of processing narrativity in texts, see Sanford & Emmott (2012: 9–44).

16 Cf. Hoey (2001: 119–141).

17 For a recent and accessible presentation of current scholarship on this topic, see Breithaupt (2022). The development of the "narrative sense" seems indeed to predate the evolution of verbal language. See Abbott (2000; esp. 249); Boyd (2009: 159–176); Breithaupt (2022: 263–290); cf. also Brockmeier (2012: 443).

18 For the role of pattern recognition in the evolution of the human cognitive system, see Boyd (2009: esp. 137, 166); Jordan (2013: 193–201); Mattson (2014). For its link to the reward system, see Blain & Sharot (2021). One could draw a line back to Aristotle, who in his *Poetics* draws a connection between the mimetic representation of reality, recognition and the pleasure of learning. Aristot. Poet. 1448b, 12–19.

19 As a matter of fact, many more or less diverging concepts of schema theory are used in the different disciplines and subdisciplines related to human cognition. Influential were especially those developed in psychology by Mandler (1984) and others. For a concise general overview on schema theories, see Dasgupta (2019: 61–64). For its impact on narratology, see Fludernik (1996: 12–14).

20 Minsky (1974: 24–50); Emmott (2014: [2]). For the impact of scripts on the formation of narrativity, see especially Herman (1997).

21 Sanford & Garrod (1981); Sanford & Emmott (2012).

tently ambiguous"[22]), which also happen to be the most basic components of narrative.[23] In my understanding, this structuring activity is not simply a primordial ancestor of modern storytelling, it constitutes the very core of narrativity, and the prototypical 19th/20th century novel is but one of its highly particular manifestations.[24] While our mind provides us by default with an apparently universal set of cognitive tools to construe temporal and causal relationships,[25] the exact ways in which narratives are derived therefrom and are made to conform to internalised patterns are unquestionably culturally quite specific.[26] Thus, in the case of the advertisement, culturally conditioned expectations shape our elaborative inference that the sale of as good as new baby shoes likely indicates the baby's premature death. In Fludernik's diction, what we have done is recuperate a story from incomplete/elusive information through the process of *narrativisation*, i.e. imposing *narrativity* on the material.[27] While we as readers are therefore the true creators of the story, our freedom and creativity is necessarily predicated on subconsciously operating frames. That the death of a baby is a bad thing of high significance and emotive force relates to value judgements equally dependent on societal norms. We do not need to know anything about the particular seller or the baby to come to these conclusions, because the generic scripts with their generic protagonists already exist in our minds. These cultural codes are precisely what the author of the ad has sought to exploit. By now it will have dawned upon those originally unfamiliar with the text that they are not simply facing a chance find taken from the classifieds section of a newspaper but a conscious attempt to create a micro-story (in the particular case, micro-fiction) through mimicking a non-literary genre.[28] In literary criticism, "Baby shoes" counts as the epitome of condensed story-telling and is commonly associated with the uncontested master of the short story, Ernest Hemingway.[29] According to legend, the text was the outcome of a wager between Hemingway and fellow writers he was meeting at a restaurant. In showing off his skills of taking terseness to the extreme, Hemingway is said to have simply written down the six words on a napkin and passed

22 As expressed by Jahn (2005: 69) in relation to the preference rule system of human cognition (cf. Jackendoff 1983: 128–158; 1987: 252–253).

23 Cf. Herman (2013: 232–251).

24 That is not to say that there are no significant differences between "reading" footprints of a wild animal in the snow and reading James Joyce's *Ulysses*. But as prolonged exposure to *Finnegan's Wake* may remind us, any knowledgeable reception of literary narratives may be just one step away from simple inferences and searching for clues.

25 Edwards et al. (2011).

26 For the role of socialisation in constructing narratives and making sense of them, see De Fina & Georgakopoulou (2012: 12–15). Even so, there is certain evidence of similarities in higher-level semantic processing of narratives across languages and cultures. See Dheghani et al. (2017: 6104). Of course, the study's neuroscientific setup targets basic cognitive functions and does not address the issue that in the modern world many story patterns and scenarios are shared across language traditions.

27 See Fludernik (1996: 25).

28 In Broich's and Pfister's classification of intertextuality this would be a case of system-referential intertextuality. See Pfister (1985: 52–58).

29 Nelles (2012: 91); Gair (2012: 11); Fishelov (2019: 31–32); Eckardt (2020: 509, n. 6).

it around in triumph.[30] While the story as such as well as Hemingway's original authorship can now be relegated to urban myth[31] – in fact, very similarly phrased micro-stories were already circulating in the early 20th century – the apocryphal tradition that the author considered "Baby shoes" his finest piece of work[32] seems to be an irony worthy of Hemingway. If nothing else, "Baby shoes" would certainly have done him credit. Irrespective of the origins of the story, reading it as a short piece of fiction rather than a functional text mobilises a range of genre-specific interpretative frames and expectations (e.g. the one that stories put in writing usually tell us something of a certain poignancy).[33] Even though modern genre conventions of short story fiction demand that the text provoke a personal emotional response, the (intended) interpretative frames are intersubjective and culturally encoded. In a way, the text *emplots* schemata whose decoding does not require additional information for those sharing a specific socialisation. In the terminology of classical Genettian narratology, it is shaped by the implicit, abstract *histoire/fabula* (≈ content of the story) embedded in the text, while the *récit* (≈ its mode of telling) merely provides a generic structure to be filled with content. Now let us consider the following variation:

For sale: English harpsichord, never played.

By changing two of the text's constituents while leaving its structure untouched, the tragic storyline becomes suddenly opaque to anyone lacking very specific contextual information about the author. One might still suspect strong poignancy couched in the line, but the preconditions for decoding it are too particular to make the personal narrative resonate as a cultural one.

As will be discussed in slightly more detail in the following chapter, narrativity is therefore a quality which does not hinge on individualised protagonists or the signposting of particularity. A culturally meaningful narrative can be largely devoid of specifics and still function as a story of sorts.[34] In the case of "Baby shoes" the "storyline" only emerges because the text draws on narrative schemata that have long been internalised. What is "individual" about it is not the implied sad story of one human's particular fate but merely the striving for originality in telling it.[35] At the same time, however, "Baby shoes" cannot be said to communicate culturally important master narratives relating to death, since its schemata are more geared towards triggering emotional responses than towards showcasing social salience.

---

30 Miller (1991: 27).

31 See Wood (2013: 160–161), Wright (2014), and the recommendable article in Wikipedia (2022).

32 Gair (2012: 11).

33 These relate particularly to Level III of Fludernik's model of *natural* narratology. Fludernik (1996: 32).

34 This is in marked contrast to most narratological traditions which hold the quality of particularity to represent a core criterion of narrativity. Cf., e.g., Doležel (1999: 265), who equals "fictional worlds" with "worlds of individualized particulars". Herman (2009: 92) at least concedes that particularity is "a scalar, more-or-less notion, with context determining whether a text or a discourse counts as more or less particularistic."

35 This is itself a culturally mediated requirement of the respective genre and thus intersubjective.

Similar and yet slightly different is the situation with another short and, at first sight, non-narrative text, which was composed more than 2000 years earlier. The archaic Attic epigram in question[36] is inscribed on the base of a *kore* statue of Parian marble dating from the second half of the 6th century BCE (Athens, National Archaeological Museum, NM 4889).[37] The ensemble was dedicated as a grave monument to the memory of a prematurely deceased girl of noble descent. As is common with Greek *mnemata* of that period, the lines of the inscription[38] were carved and positioned in such a way as to be easily visible for people passing by the tomb.[39] The complementary inscription containing the artisan's signature is almost as prominently placed on the left side of the base.

Front side

|1 ΣΕΜΑΦΡΑΣΙΚΛΕΙΑΣ
|2 ΚΟΡΕΚΕΚΛΕΣΟΜΑΙ
|3 ΑΙΕΙΑΝΤΙΓΑΜΟ
|4 ΠΑΡΑΘΕΟΝΤΟΥΤΟ
|5 ΛΑΧΟΣΟΝΟΜΑ

|1 σε̄̃μα Φρασικλείας· |2 κόρε̄ κεκλέ̄σομαι |3 αἰεί,
ἀντὶ γάμο̄ παρὰ θεο̃̄ν τοῦτο |4 λαχο̃̄σ' ὄνομα.

The funerary monument of Phrasikleia (Ø/is this/am I).[a] "'Maiden' shall I always be called, who instead of a wedding was allotted this name by the gods."

Left side

ΑΡΙΣΤΙΟΝ⌜Π⌝Α⌜ΡΙ⌝[ΟΣΜ?ΕΠ]Ο[ΙΕ]⌜Σ⌝Ε

Ἀριστίο̄ν Πάρι[ός μ'? ἐπ]ο[ίε̄]σ̣ε.
Aristion of Par[os] [mad]e [me?]/(it?).[b]

a) The first line's ambiguity in relation to voice has led to diverging interpretations. Svenbro (1988: 23: "Moi, sèma de Phrasikleia [...]") takes the line as an autoreferential designation of the statue explaining itself (similarly also Stieber 2004: 146) and considers the entire inscription as representing the statue's voice as a "speaking object". In contrast, Sourvinou-Inwood (1995: 281) sees a change of voice from that of the statue to that of the deceased girl after line 1, with the inscription of the left side taking up the initial voice. Wachter (2010: 254–255) and others (e.g. Vestrheim 2010: 73; *IG* I³ 1261), on the other hand, consider line 1 an abridged third person nominal sentence distinct from the following utterance in the 1st person. The question is further complicated by the incomplete preservation of the artist's signature, which may or may not share the voice of line 1 at the front (certainly, it is not metrically integrated into the elegiac distich). Only if the signature did include "made *me*" (see the following note), the monument can

36 *IG* I³ 1261; *DNO* I, 348.

37 A comprehensive study of the statue and its art historical context is provided by Stieber (2004: 141–178). The dating is still conjectural (550/40 BCE or, as Stieber argues, slightly later), but the archaeological evidence suggests that the monument was deliberately buried before the end of the 6th century BCE (thus its excellent preservation). While the base has been known since the 18th century, the statue was excavated only in 1972. See Svenbro (1988: 16); Michaud (1973: 265; 269–272, figs. 33–38).

38 Among the earliest ones in the *stoichedon* arrangement with evenly spaced letters. Cf. Jeffery (1962: 139, cat. 46).

39 Cf. Baumbach et al. (2010: 11). For a comprehensive discussion of the relation between image and inscription on archaic funerary monuments, see Reinhardt (2020: esp. 87–96).

be confidently attributed to the "speaking object" type. For "speaking objects", see also below, p. 171.

b) On epigraphic grounds (> spacing of the letters between the preserved parts of the line) the restitution of the enclitic first-person pronoun μ' is by no means certain, even though the majority of editors (exception: Jeffrey 1962: 138, cat. 46) has not called its presence into question. Admittedly, the pronoun is found on two other signature inscriptions of Aristion. Cf. *DNO* I, 347 & 350. The question of whether Phrasikleia's statue is to be classified as a "speaking object" must therefore remain open. I am indebted to Prof. Thomas Corsten from the Department of Ancient History at the University of Vienna for sharing with me his view on the epigraphic evidence.

The distichal verses allude to the maiden's untimely death, which most likely foiled the plans for her marriage. While the inscription thus clarifies the context, it is only in conjunction with Phrasikleia's once brightly-painted, life-like figural representation[40] showing her in a richly adorned dress (*like* or *as* a bride), crowned by a floral *stephane* and holding a closed lotus flower in the left hand (Fig. 1) that the monument gains its immediacy and emotional force. Yet, one should be wary of taking the statue as Phrasikleia's individualised portrait in any meaningful sense of the word.[41] Likewise, one should keep in mind that the epigram – though voiced in the first person singular from line 2 onwards[42] – is far from evoking a particular personal experience. What establishes Phrasikleia's personhood are first and foremost the existence of the monument itself and the act of naming her in the inscription. The latter creates a multivalent bond between the entities of inscribed (and voiced) name, beheld representation and remembered/imagined deceased,[43] which each visitor of the tomb activates anew. He or she will also realise (or subconsciously experience) that at least three distinct narratives are interwoven in Phrasikleia's memorial: the maiden's premature death, the mythological architext of Kore/Persephone's[44] entering of Hades, and the glorious history of Phrasikleia's lineage. This is achieved by activating schemata through allusion (= semantic priming), through the monument's impressive materiality, and through the social practices associated with it (erection, burial, commemoration rituals etc.). While we have no definite proof of the assumption that the memorial was commissioned by members of the Alcmaeonid clan,[45] Phrasikleia's family must have been of preeminent importance in late 6th century Athens and surely did not forego staging a stately funeral for their deceased relative. As Svenbro (1988: 17–30) convincingly argued,

40 With a height of 176 cm the statue seems to be slightly over life-size. For a recent reconstruction of the kore's original polychrome paint and partial gilding, see Brinkmann & Koch-Brinkmann (2020: 71–73, figs. 79–85; 156–157, cat. 14).

41 *Pace* Stieber, who points to what she sees as tokens of realism and individualisation and concludes (2004: 177) that "[...] the whole image constitutes a coherent synthetic visual identity of one particular Archaic Greek woman." Stieber's methodological approach has been heavily criticised by Gray (2005: 368–369) and Tanner (2006: 213) but also found partial endorsement by Brown (2019: 37).

42 For the use of first-person voices in archaic Greek epigrams, see particularly Vestrheim (2010) and Wachter (2010).

43 Similarly Brown (2019: 36–38).

44 *Kore*, "maiden", acts as a common mythological cover-name for the chthonic female deity Persephone. For the link in the present case, see Svenbro (1988: 25); Brown (2019: 38–39).

45 See Svenbro (1988: 17–18); Stieber (2004: 147).

Fig. 1 Reconstruction of original polychromy of Phrasikleia's monument (after Brinkmann) © Liebighaus Skulpturensammlung/ Norbert Miguletz

it is not least through showcasing Phrasikleia's name with its etymological (and through the *-kleia* name pattern, potentially also genealogical) connotations that the monument serves to communicate notions of familial renown (κλέος). It will not have escaped ancient visitors of the tomb that by virtue of her eternalised name Phrasikleia's σῆμα is literally charged with pointing out (> φράζειν) her family's κλέος,[46] whose very essence is the commemoration of exemplary virtue in socially sanctioned narrative.[47] Viewed from this perspective then, the statue, the inscription, and the topographical setting jointly evoke a *meta-* or *hyper*narrative in the mind of the onlooker. Because this narrative is at the same time particular *and* generic[48] it is ideally suited to define and affirm individual roles within the societal fabric and thus to become socially meaningful.

But what on earth have Hemingwayesque short stories and Greek epigrams to do with the narrativity of ancient Egyptian biographical texts, the dear reader of these lines might ask. A lot, I would answer. As I aim to show below in my last example of micro-storytelling, similar principles of evoking and utilising narrativity are indeed at work in most Egyptian funerary monuments of the 3rd millennium BCE. This can be demonstrated best with highly conventional, unassuming iconotexts that do not appear to contain straightforward narratives at all.

A case in point is the limestone stela Louvre E 26904 of transverse rectangular shape, which has been tentatively dated to the late Old Kingdom or the First Intermediate Period and allegedly originates from Mo'alla (Fig. 2).[49]

---

46 In Svenbro's (1988: 29–30) words, "Phrasikleia veille à la survie de sa famille dans la mémoire collective."

47 Cf. Lavigne (2018: 270): "[...] the aim is to produce authentic memories of the past, which in Greek can be expressed succinctly as *kleos*." That Phrasikleia's monument was dismantled and buried soon after its erection (possibly for political reasons; cf. Knigge 2006: 157) only to be elevated due to its excellent preservation to the status of an archaeological icon more than 2000 years later constitutes yet another narrative of κλέος.

48 "Particular" also in the sense that the ensuing narratives are heavily dependent on the contextual knowledge of the respective onlooker (including modern scholars). Deconstructivism is always afoot, and even *topos* and *mimesis* (cf. Loprieno 1988: esp. 10–13 vs. Buchberger 1989/90: esp. 32) can change places.

49 Ziegler (1990: 204–206, cat. 34). Cf. Fischer (1992: 145); Kloth (2002: 26, cat. 32); Postel (2004: 101, n. 457); Strudwick (2005: 345, no. 248); Shubert (2007: 93, FIP.30); Manassa (2011: 5). The dating of the stela is problematic. While Ziegler (1990: 204) gives the date as "sans doute VIe dynastie", referring (1990: 206) to an unpublished study by Henry Fischer, a First Intermediate

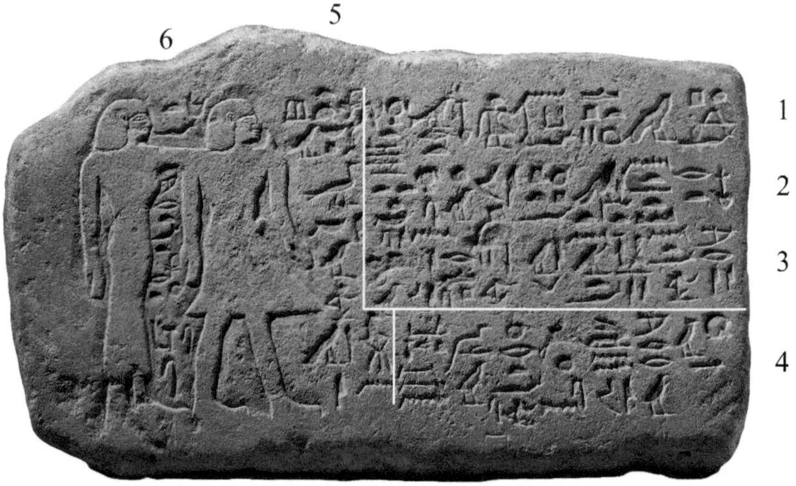

Fig. 2 Limestone stela of Iku and his wife Sabes, Louvre E 26904, Adapted from an image at https://collections.louvre.fr/en/ark:/53355/cl010004207, © 2016 Musée du Louvre / Hervé Lewandowski

The stela features on the left two figures carved in crudely executed raised relief, depicting Iku, son of Hekenu, and his wife Sabes embracing her husband. An inscription in sunk relief arranged as a slightly garbled mix of lines and columns takes up two thirds of the surface. The vertical lines 5 and 6 immediately preceding each of the figures can be seen as a continuation of the main text but also as identifying captions linking the figures to the text.

The inscription reads:

[1]| ← *ḫpj=f m ḥtp zp sn.nw n kꜣ=f jꜣw(.w) nfr wr.t ḥr wꜣ.wt* [2]| *nfr.(w)t nj.(w)t zmj.t jmnt.t ḫpp.(w)t jmꜣḫw(.w) ḥr=sn (n-)ntj.t jnk js jmꜣḫw* [3]| *mrjj n jtj=f ḥzjj n mw.t=f jw wp<.n>(=j)* [a] *sn.wj r ḥtp=s<n>* [4]| ↓ *tpj.w tꜣ mrr.w wnn jmꜣḫ=sn ḫr jtj(.w)=sn (j)ḏd.w ḥnk* (or *rdj.t*) *(m) tʾ ḥnḳ.t mw (n)* [5]| *ḫrj-tp nswt Ḥknw zꜣ Jkw msj.n Ḥmj* [6]| *ḥm.t=f mrj.t=f rḫ.t-nswt Sꜣb=s*	[1]| May he proceed in good peace to his ka, having attained very old age, on the [2]| perfect [1]| ways [2]| of the Western Desert on which the *imakhuu* proceed. For I am/was indeed an *imakhu*, [3]| one beloved by his father, favoured by his mother. (I) <have> judged between two litigants to th<eir> satisfaction. [4]| (O), you on earth who desire that your (lit.: their) *imakh* status be in the presence of your (lit.: their) father(s), say an offering (of) bread, beer and water (for) [b] [5]| the royal subordinate, Hekenu's son Iku [c], whom Hemi has borne, [6]| (and to) his wife, his beloved, the royal acquaintance Sabes.

Period date is considered by Kloth (2002: 26) and Shubert (2007: 93). Postel (2004: 101, n. 457) extends the period to be considered even to the 12th Dynasty, perhaps in light of the presence of the filiation formula *msj.n*, for which see Obsomer (1993: 172–180; 195–196).

a) For the (most likely) erroneous omission of the tense marker *n* see Kloth (2002: 80). The perfective tense *jw sḏm.n=f* usually serves to express a past event's continuing relevance to the present (cf. Stauder-Porchet 2017: 185–186) which ties in with the potential of the Old Egyptian *sḏm.n=f* form to express resultative meaning (cf. Werning 2008: 286).
b) The relation between the vocal offering and the two beneficiaries named in lines 5 and 6 is left undefined, unless the lowest wavy line of water within the logogram for *mw* (𓈗) is consciously differentiated from the two lines above in order to denote also the preposition *n*.[50]
c) As was already remarked by Fischer (1992: 145) in correcting Ziegler's (1990: 204) original translation of the inscription, the conventions of indicating filiation in the Old Kingdom[51] (→ B A / B *zꜣ=f* A / B *zꜣ* A ≡ B's son A) require that Iku be identified with the beneficiary of the stela, not Hekenu. The only moot point is whether the preceding title refers to Hekenu alone, to father as well as son, or only to Iku (separated from the name by the inserted apposition "Hekenu's son").[52]

As is apparent to anyone familiar with Old Kingdom funerary inscriptions, the text on Iku's stela is cobbled together using conventional textual building blocks and more or less exchangeable stock phrases, which were drawn from an already sizeable corpus.[53] But despite its pasticcio-like composition the text offers a condensed and therefore remarkably transparent version of the Egyptian biographical discourse within the funerary sphere. It starts with a so-called *Gnadenbitte*[54] from the offering formula repertoire, which refers to the deceased in the third person. This *Gnadenbitte* identifies *pars pro toto* the deceased's desired outcome of the funerary rituals and, in a way, sets the goal for the act of communication with those visiting the tomb. The following nominal sentence with the particle *js* in modal use[55] abruptly switches to the first person. It communicates the reason why the wish expressed above should be applicable: the deceased has achieved the *imakh* status. While the concept of *imakh* – an elevated status closely connected with the process of erecting a tomb and implying social and ritual bonds in this world and beyond – is still not easy to grasp for modern scholars,[56] we have good reasons to believe that it carried significance both for the *imakhu* himself and for any person socially interacting with him (also in his state of being deceased). Quite fittingly, therefore, line 3 expands on the assertion by providing epithets and a verbal statement that illustrate and at the same time justify Iku's

---

50 For similar phenomena of graphemic disambiguation, see Jurman (in press: 178).

51 Cf. Sethe (1911: 98–99); Ranke (1952: 9); Berlev (1962a); Olabarria (2020: 131). I am grateful to Roman Gundacker and Annik Wüthrich from the Austrian Academy of Sciences for their insights when discussing this matter with me.

52 In Old Kingdom texts containing filiations of such a type it is sometimes the case that each name is preceded by a title or string of titles. Cf. Vandekerckhove & Müller-Wollermann (2001: 183–186, O 74); Gundacker (2006: 304). More frequently, only one title preceding the name of the father is indicated. Cf., e.g., Sethe (1933: 298, 7); Posener-Kriéger (1985: 196–197).

53 The most important studies on biographical phraseology are Edel (1944); Coulon (1997); Kloth (2002); Coulon (2020). For the so-called *appeals to the living* in the Old Kingdom, see the classical, if partially outdated, studies by Sainte Fare Garnot (1938), the aforementioned one by Edel (1944: 3–30), and Berlev's (1962b) focussing on the MK. More recent studies of the appeals with different emphases are Lichtheim (1992: 155–159 for the OK); Shubert (2007: 16–60 for the OK).

54 Barta (1968: 28, Bitte 12).

55 See Oréal (2011: 131–132).

56 For the ongoing discussions, see *pars pro toto* Fischer (1991: 22); Jansen-Winkeln (1996); Kuraszkiewicz (2009); Troche (2021: 54–57).

entitlement to being an *imakhu*. These conventional phrases belong to the tradition of the so-called ideal biography and are unquestionably generic in both their argument and their scope. But it is not difficult to realise that the stereotypical phrase describing Iku as someone who has successfully settled a dispute between two litigants serves as an exemplification of the attributions of ethical qualities implied by the two preceding epithets. The point here is not that Iku's inscription would offer an original account of a particular achievement or ethical quality. Quite obviously, it does not. The important point is that the argument is structured through a narrative frame whose functionality does not depend on the particularity of any of its constituent elements. In other words, whether or not the "slots" in the structure are filled with concrete events or personal experiences is negligible, since the schemata triggered by the clichés suffice to evoke the narrative's *histoire* (a Genettian term here used more or less synonymously with *fabula*). And this *histoire* is primarily an intersubjective, cultural one, not an individual's "personal story".[57] Two additional textual components complete the temporal and causal structure inherent in the iconotext. The first is the call to action addressed to potential tomb visitors (the *address to the living* of line 4). They are urged to act on behalf of the deceased and his wife (namely, to say an offering prayer) on the basis of the information provided in the preceding lines. The impact of the past, if only alluded to, is thus projected into the future. The last and perhaps crucial textual component is the only truly individualised element of the stela, the identification of the owner and his wife via names, filiation and titles. It provides the nexus that links the pictorial representation of the couple with the narrative schemata and the ritual action asked from the passers-by.

Commemorating titles, filiation and family members is not merely a non-temporal function geared towards identification and display of status but possesses an implicit diachronic dimension as well. There are in fact good reasons to assume that title strings are important forerunners of (and also potential substitutes for) the developed genre of *event/career biography*,[58] even if they should not be seen as completely analogous. While there is no direct genetic derivation of the latter from the former, as Stauder-Porchet has convincingly argued,[59] the royal praise staged in early event biographies can be regarded as an *exemplification* (see p. 54) of the qualities necessary to follow through the stages of an exemplary elite existence. These stages are indexed by the title strings. Through putting real or purported claims to offices into a linear order they presuppose an already completed *cursus honorum* and thereby connote all the typical achievements and instances of recognition that in the corresponding frame of elite life go hand in hand with it.[60] This

57 *Pace* Assmann (1983: 68), who maintains that the tomb is an "Ort der Selbst-Thematisierung nicht der Gesellschaft, sondern des Individuums;" On the complex question of what constitutes a persona within the monumental discourse of the funerary sphere, see Chapters 2.4 and 3.4.

58 Gnirs (1996: 220; 226); Baines (1999a: esp. 36–37); Baud (2005: 110–111); cf. Stauder-Porchet (2017: 18–19).

59 Stauder-Porchet (2017: 19; 165).

60 Otherwise it would be difficult to understand a particular topos well-attested in biographical inscriptions of the First Intermediate Period, namely, that the tomb owner has not engaged in a "discourse about offices of the necropolis" (*ḏd m jꜣ.wt ẖr.t-nṯr* and similarly), i.e. the fictional

does not mean, however, that title strings within a tomb are fixed entities that represent a coherent chronological or hierarchical sequence. In fact, they turn out to be quite sensitive to respective spatial/iconographic contexts and often seem to index a career rather than portraying it. Similar processes are at work when it comes to showcasing both synchronic and diachronic social integration through the presentation of family ties and kinship. Arguably, both dimensions are only touched upon in Iku's case. We simply learn that he has obtained the office of a *royal subordinate*[61] and presumably started a nuclear family with his wife Sabes, herself bearing the (ranking?) title of *royal acquaintance*.[62] Taking together all the individual components of Iku's monument, the story (*histoire* or *fabula*) abstracted from its informational structure goes more or less like this: Iku's personal qualities and his meeting of societal norms and expectations (e.g. taking a wife) have enabled him to achieve favours and recognition within the settings of officialdom as well as his familial environment. This is exemplified by his role in judging between litigants. As a logical consequence, Iku has obtained the *imakh* status, which in turn serves as his main justification for being entitled to lead a blessed existence in the hereafter. His privileged status – backed up by his personal yet highly generic "history", of which the creation of the respective funerary monument itself forms an integral part – is then communicated to visitors of the tomb as an incentive to act in Iku's and Sabes' favour. If the addressees of Iku's inscription meet his request they at the same time validate his narrative and become part of the narrative discourse (this aspect is discussed in Chapter 7.3). Put differently, the past is only evoked in order to explain and justify the status quo, which is itself presented as the prerequisite for achieving a goal in the future.

Even though this formula admittedly bears the risk of being an oversimplification – for example, the temporal relations between the Genetteian categories[63] of *histoire*, *récit*, and *narration* are often not well defined – and does not account for all the peculiarities of the texts considered in this contribution, I would argue that it nevertheless forms one of the most important, if not *the* most important, structural principle of funerary iconotexts in Old Kingdom monumental tombs. For this reason it is essential to consider "biographical" inscriptions not in isolation but in the wider context of a tomb's architectural and visual programme as well as its social embeddedness.[64] What is commonly referred to as the

---

claim to offices presented in the tomb inscriptions which do not correspond to actual functions accumulated during one's lifetime. For this topos see Assmann (1996a: 118–119); Coulon (1997: 113–114, n. k).

61 For the role and status of the *ḫrj-tp nswt* in the provincial administration, see most recently Martinet (2019: 340–354).

62 For the reading and understanding of this title in the late Old Kingdom, see again Martinet (2019: 330–339); cf., however, Leprohon (1994: 46).

63 Genette (1972: 71–76). On p. 72 of his *Discours du récit* (1972) Genette defines the three categories as follows: "Je propose, sans insister sur les raisons d'ailleurs évidentes du choix des termes, de nommer *histoire* le signifié ou contenu narratif (même si ce contenu se trouve être, en l'occurrence, d'une faible intensité dramatique ou teneur événementielle), *récit* proprement dit le signifiant, énoncé, discours ou texte narratif lui-même, et *narration* l'acte narratif producteur et, par extension, l'ensemble de la situation réelle ou fictive dans laquelle il prend place".

64 Cf. Baines (1999a: 34–37); Baines (2020); Walsem (2020: 118).

genres of *ideal biography* on the one hand and of the narratively more elaborated *event biography* on the other hand[65] merely occupy two particular slots within the basic structure mentioned above. While both are aimed at presenting the socially validated essence of the deceased's (past) existence, one could say that the former is primarily concerned with the *telling* mode (fast-paced, "objective", declarative, large distance) while the latter features in addition also aspects of *showing* (slow-paced, detailed, mimetic, small distance), to use a classical, if somewhat problematic, narratological distinction.[66]

But if the essence of biographical discourse in the Egyptian Old Kingdom could be summarised by the phrase "How I became what I have always been", where does narrativity start and where does it end? After all, most specialists would agree that there are indeed marked differences between the Egyptian biographical subgenres in evidence in the latter part of the Old Kingdom and that these differences also have to do with degrees of relative narrativity. The following chapter will consider the narratological underpinnings of such assessments in greater detail.

2 Narrativity and genre: what it takes to tell a life

2.1 The problems with defining *narrative* and *narrativity* – historical viewpoints

Over the past 150 years scholars from many different backgrounds have arrived at quite diverging answers to the question of what constitutes a narrative at the most basic level.[67] In contrast to the relatively broad definitions of narrative/narrativity (for the differentiation see the following chapter) employed by many contemporary narratologists, the proponents of classical narratology favoured for a long time a rather narrow understanding of their subject, which followed almost naturally from narratology's institutional and epistemological origins.[68] As a consequence, focus lay primarily on verbally related stories communicated in an environment that was shaped by the literary discourse. Even in some narratological traditions more attuned to the fact that abstract narrative structures transcend the Western literary canon, the traditional genres of literary "narrative" such as novel, epic, short story etc. still formed the basis from which general theories were deduced.[69] In recent decades discussions on narrative have certainly diversified,[70] and it would be misleading to postulate a dichotomic opposition between classical (primarily structuralist) and postclassical schools. The differences in framing and the offered definitions depend

65 The main tenets of the bipartite classification of biographical texts are already found *in nuce* in Junker (1949: 67; 1955: 91–94). For the *locus classicus* see Gnirs (1996: 203–204).

66 Cf. Klauk & Köppe (2014). Depending on one's understanding of what constitutes prototypical *showing* and *telling* one might also arrive at a different partition.

67 See the overview of historical positions in Ryan (2007: 22–24); Kuhn (2011: 47–56).

68 Cf., e.g., the *locus classicus* of Forster (1927: 30; 86).

69 Even the concept of "narrator" owes its centrality in narratology more to the prototypes of the common literary canon than to its indispensability within narrative theory (*pace* standard narratological views such as Margolin 2014: § 2). Cf. Almén (2008: 32–35; 234, n. 10).

70 See the overviews in Nünning & Nünning (2002: 5–17, esp. 7); Hyvärinen (2006a: 5–9; 2006b); Ritivoi (2013); Fludernik & Ryan (2020: 7–15). Cf. also the contributions in Hansen et al. (2017).

first and foremost on different choices as to where the focus is placed: on narrative content or on the experiential quality; on informational micro-structure or on genre conventions; on language and style or on performative aspects; on traditional textual and oral forms of transmission or on multi/cross-mediality; on abstract functioning or on social embeddedness; on a fixed set of familiar cultural creations or on a global perspective taking into account the potential otherness of non-Western, non-modern narrativity. These oppositions sometimes represent just both ends of a more or less continuous scale, and particular foci often cut across the boundaries of narratological "schools".[71] While many concepts of classical narratology may today appear as not completely fit for purpose in the context of a transdisciplinary outlook, it would be unwise to dismiss them wholeheartedly. Structuralist toolkits such as those found in Genette's studies,[72] which were honed on European literary classics, still have a lot to offer when applied with circumspection. But it is important to make oneself aware of the significant differences and sometimes outright contradictions between the numerous concepts of narrative circulating in many humanist subjects. Before setting out the concrete understanding of narrative and narrativity underlying this contribution, I shall briefly review some influential conceptions of narrative that have played a role in Egyptological debates.

If narrative – in accordance with narratological theories in the tradition of Chatman – is first and foremost conceived of as a text type or "master genre",[73] the theoretical reasoning will be primarily based on works of narrative fiction conforming most closely to the genre prototype. This way of thinking is still a common attitude in Egyptology,[74] where narratological analysis has usually been directed towards fictional tales such as the *Shipwrecked Sailor* or the *First Tale of Setne*.[75] In many cases of "applied philology" the – often intuitive and implicit – working definition of "narrative" comprises a story of a certain length and complexity with several protagonists and memorable events portrayed in sequential order, possessing in Aristotelian fashion a beginning, a middle and an end.[76] If, in contrast, one considers "narrative" more as a general mode of discourse distinct from or even opposed to other modes,[77] one will find instances of narrative in many different genres

71 As a matter of fact, many recent contributions to postclassical narratology show a decisively structuralist slant (e.g. Zeman 2016; cf. Sommer 2017).

72 Particularly Genette (1972; 1979; 1991).

73 Chatman (1978: 19–31; 1990: 6–21). Chatman (1990: 10) characterises the "Narrative text-type" as a sort of master genre comprising several "generic subclasses".

74 Cf., e.g., Loprieno (1996: *passim*); Moers (2001: *passim*); Parkinson (2002: *passim*, e.g. 63); Simpson (2003: 4–5). This does not mean, of course, that these scholars view "narrative" exclusively as a literary genre. But they do not always differentiate very clearly between "narrative" as a mode of discourse and "narrative" as a genre label. The terminological grey area is acknowledged, although not conceptualised in terms of modern narratological theory, by Assmann (2009: 222).

75 For a convenient recent overview of narratological approaches in Egyptology, see Moers (2019); cf. further Roeder (2009; 2018a; 2018b); Vinson (2018: 11–17); Braun (2019); Di Biase-Dyson (2019); Rogner (2022: 16–37).

76 Thus, Assmann (2009: 222). Cf. Aristot. Poet. 1450b, 26–27.

77 This conceptualisation has its roots in 19th century rhetoric, although the criteria for the distinctions were at the beginning still very much genre- and content-driven. See Hewett (2020: 113) = Newman

beyond the sphere usually associated with "literature" or "belles-lettres".[78] By this token, passages of "narrative" – however defined in detail[79] – are to be identified in text types and genre settings as diverse as eulogistic royal inscriptions, expedition reports, juridical stipulations or private letters.[80] Of course, one can construe the relationship between text type and discourse mode also the other way round and regard "narrative" as a certain text type that may be used within different discourse types (e.g. "one can put forth an argument by telling a story, but the opposite does not apply;"[81]). In Egyptology, similar approaches informed by text linguistics go back at least to Hintze, who in his influential study on Late Egyptian stories makes a general distinction between the grammatically and stylistically salient modes of "narrative" ("Erzählung") and of "speech" ("Rede"). The two modes are distinguished by the different tenses employed and the respective levels of subjectivity or personal involvement.[82] In the following decades the study of the linguistic dimensions of narrative text gained momentum, and grammatical criteria focussing on the use of specific tense patterns were employed as heuristic tools to identify narrative discourse.[83] Even though Hintze himself devised his model exclusively for the study of works of fiction, later scholars developed more general versions, which they brought to bear on different parts of the Egyptian text corpus. In his study on text types of the Third Intermediate Period, Jansen-Winkeln, for example, employs a combination of formal, functional and contextual criteria to divide continuous texts ("satzhafte Texte") at the most basic level of textual form into "report" ("Bericht") on the one hand and into "speech" ("Rede") on the other hand.[84] Whereas reports present an action as unrelated to the moment of communication, speeches are always directly or indirectly tied to the communicative act (the respective "Sprech-/Handlungssituation"). Other criteria for differentiation according to Jansen-Winkeln include specificity (situatedness in space and time), representation of speaker and audience, chronological sequencing, relative functional autonomy, and the potential for permanent efficacy.[85] This analytical matrix leads to some interesting results, as biographical texts of

---

(1862 [1839]: 28–29). In a certain way, Benveniste's (1966 [1959]: 238–239) classical distinction between *énonciation de l'historique* and *du discours* can be seen as a late offshoot of the rhetorical modes of discourse.

78 In fact, in Chatman's theoretical framework "narrative" becomes a strange hybrid between genre and discourse type, since he (1978: 22–27) acknowledges that at the bottom of things it is but an abstract semiotic structure. Cf. Grünzweig & Solbach (1999: 4–6).

79 The categories of tense and voice usually play a decisive part in such categorisations. Cf., e.g., Junge (1989: 97; 107).

80 Cf. Roeder (2009).

81 De Fina & Georgakopoulou (2012: 12).

82 Hintze (1952: 3–4). For this categorisation see Satzinger (2008: 40).

83 See, e.g., Polotsky (1965: [17], § 35); Depuydt (1998: 21–27), making reference to Hintze, Polotsky and Weinrich; Malaise & Winand (1999: 654–666, §§ 1032–1046); Winand (2006: 371–372); Borghouts (2010, vol. I: 433, § 118); cf. also Vinson (2018: 14).

84 Jansen-Winkeln (1994: 12–14). Jansen-Winkeln's term "Bericht" more or less corresponds to Hintze's "Erzählung".

85 This general distinction is complemented by the categories "lists" ("Listen") and "notations" ("Vermerke") for non-verbal non-continuous texts. These four "Textformen" then constitute the basic ingredients of the different classes of genre, the "Textsorten". Jansen-Winkeln (1994: 26–27).

the Third Intermediate Period, in contrast to those of earlier periods, are classified exclusively as speeches. "Die biographischen Geschehnisse werden nicht erkennbar chronologisch und auf jeden Fall nicht als aufeinander bezogen dargestellt, sondern als mehr oder weniger beziehungslose Einzelfakten ohne zeitliche und örtliche Festlegung."[86] Thus, the perceived degree of chronological and thematic coherence is singled out as a significant factor in the attribution of narrativity. In general, Jansen-Winkeln relates his overarching distinction between "'aktualisierenden'" (= "speeches") and "'nichtaktualisierenden' Texten" (= "reports") to Weinrich's tense-based dichotomy of "besprochene" versus "erzählte Welt",[87] but although both concepts bear some resemblance to the *telling–showing* (or, in this case, *showing–telling*) opposition of classical narratology,[88] they should certainly not be taken as congruous. While the latter is usually thought[89] to focus on the degree of experiential distance between the events related and the narrating authority (the less distance, the more mimetic and the more opaque in terms of narrating voice), the former is primarily aimed at the degree of relevance of the related events to the communicative act.

The basic tenet of a dichotomous system is also shared by another Egyptological conceptualisation of narrativity, even though the distinctions are not made along exactly the same lines. In his study of the narrative verbal system of Old and Middle Egyptian, Doret devotes a few paragraphs to the theoretical foundations of his approach, in which he considers narrativity primarily in relation to tense and verbal aspect (not unlike Weinrich, whom he mentions only passingly[90]). Reviewing the semantic contexts of particular tense–person patterns, he comes to the conclusion that "narrative texts relate a succession of events set in the past", whereas "texts in non-narrative discourse [...] describe past events from the point of view of the present."[91] In both cases, the grammatical category of person may but need not be indicative of the discursive mode. "Although narrative sequences in (auto)biographical texts dating from the Old and Middle Kingdoms were generally written in the first person, i.e., discourse[92], examples are attested in the third person, and even once in the second person."[93] When reading Jansen-Winkeln's critique of Doret's diverging use of terminology, which culminates in the remark "Vielleicht sollte man auf den Begriff 'narrativ' lieber ganz verzichten. Er wird – in Sprach- und Literaturwissenschaft ebenso wie in der Ägyptologie – so unterschiedlich und oft verschwommen verwendet, daß er

86 Jansen-Winkeln (1994: 17).

87 Jansen-Winkeln (1994: 15). See Weinrich (2001: 29–33).

88 Cf., e.g., Booth (1983: 3–20); Klauk & Köppe (2014: § 3).

89 As Klauk & Köppe (2014: § 2) highlight, the concept lacks a clear and universally accepted definition in narratology despite its widespread use. Genette (1972: 75) was the first one to reframe *telling vs. showing* by explicitly referring to the differing narrative "distance" of the two modes, but the notion as such can be traced back at least to Friedrich Schiller's letter to Goethe of 26 December 1797, which is quoted in this context by Weinrich (2001: 34). Cf. Gräf & Leitzmann (1955: 455–457); Goethe- und Schiller-Archiv (2022: Bl. 7, file 13 = digitised autograph).

90 Thus, Doret (1986: 14, n. 20; 97; 183).

91 Doret (1986: 14; similarly, 183).

92 This use of "discourse" for speech mode is indebted to Benveniste's description of *discours* as consisting "d'abord dans la relation de personne *je : tu*." Benveniste (1966 [1959]: 239).

93 Doret (1986: 14). N.B.: The footnote markers and references have been omitted from the quote.

eigentlich nur noch Mißverständnisse hervorrufen kann",[94] one cannot help but feel that the baby is being thrown out with the bath water. The deeper problem might be related to the fact that discourse modes characterised by certain prevalent *tense–person* combinations are not easily aligned with contemporary concepts of narrativity (see also Chapter 2.2 below), which regard narrative structure is an emergent meta-textual phenomenon not tied to particular syntax. But Jansen-Winkeln certainly has a point when he calls for a more appropriate and rigorous discussion of the narratological key terms and their scope of validity.

In this context it is interesting to note that Egyptology's tendency to place particular emphasis on the tense system when ascribing narrativity to textual discourse does not find many parallels within the current narratological mainstream.[95] It seems as if many Egyptologists have never fully warmed to the notion that the narrative potential of a textual composition does not primarily hinge on whether so-called "narrative" grammatical constructions are employed or not.[96] To equate narrativity with the presence of "narrative" grammatical constructions would be as if speech act theory did not differentiate between a locutionary act and its illocutionary force.[97] Like a grammatically unambiguous interrogative clause can, from a pragmatic point of view, represent an order, a textual composition featuring resultative present perfect or imperfective verbal clauses can indeed tell a story, even if that story will possess different characteristics compared with one comprising, for example, primarily past anterior constructions. At any rate, one should bear in mind that in relation to the syntax–semantics interface most verb forms already come with a temporal/causal structure embedded *in nuce*.[98] Thus, to have killed an enemy presupposes that one has entered a conflict and engaged in physical violence in the first place. This is all implied in phrases of the kind found in the biographical inscription of Amenemhat at Beni Hasan (BH 2, reign of Senwosret I): *ꜥḥꜥ.n* $\overset{10}{|}$ *ḥm=f wḏꜣ(.w) m ḥtp sḫr.n=f ḫftj.w=f m kꜣš ẖsj.t*; "And then His Majesty proceeded calmly (and) cast down his enemies in vile Kush."[99] In ancient Egyptian as in many other languages the basic building blocks of narrativity are already ingrained in the aspect, tense and modal relations of the verbal system through

94 Jansen-Winkeln (1994: 16, n. 5).

95 For example, in an edited volume on the relation between narration and time, which was published seven years ago in the *Narratologia* series (Weixler & Werner 2015), "tense" and "verbal aspect" are almost completely absent from the analytical agenda.

96 Of course, highlighting the existence of temporal constructions preferably used for relating events of the past in sequential order is not the same as claiming that narrative content can only be delivered by such constructions (cf. Doret 1986: 13–17).

97 Cf. Searle (1979: vii–ix).

98 Cf. Lehmann (2012). For Herman (1997: 1053) such grammatical properties are cues that help to form narrative structure.

99 See Kanawati & Evans (2016: 26, Pl. 84b, l. 9–10); Lichtheim (1988: 138; translating *sḫr.n=f* without justification as "having overthrown" with anterior meaning). The allusion to the mythological meta-narrative (which would constitute Assmann's [1977: 39] genotext) of the killing of Osiris in PT 580 (P) is another case in point: *ḥwj jtj(=j) smꜣ wr jr=f ḥwj.n=k jtj(=j) smꜣ.n=k wr jr=k*; "(Oh, you), who has slain (my) father and killed the one greater than him. You have slain (my) father. You have killed the one greater than you." Sethe (1910: 329, § 1543a–b).

the complex interplay between lexical semantics, event time, duration, reference time and evaluative position.[100] Following Zeman, one could situate these building blocks at the level of narrative micro-structure, which does not form stories by itself but provides the basis for narrative inferences.[101]

As I will argue below (Excursus, p. 104), this is also the reason why bare infinitives are so effective in transmitting narrative content. Even if the temporal structure of a finite clause focusses on the speaker and the relevance of past events to reference time – as is the case with many phrases of the Egyptian genre of ideal biography[102] – a narrowly construed *narrative/récit–speech/discours* opposition does not necessarily reflect the degree of narrativity at a composition's macro-level (see Chapter 5.1). The limits of many traditional approaches to narrative also become apparent in regard to the subjective nature of speech mode. Personal affective involvement of the speaker/narrator is indeed seen as one of the main characteristics of speech mode and is contrasted with the "objective" claim asserted by third-person narrative discourse. To cite a somewhat dated but still representative example, which was formulated by Junge in 1989: "*Although (E 78)a and (E 78)d* [i.e. two passages from the *Shipwrecked Sailor* using *jw sḏm.n=f* constructions, CJ] *are used to complete the narrative frame (in the last case cooperating with ꜥḥꜥ.n), I think they are "less narrative" than the forms treated above* [such as *sḏm.jn*- and *ꜥḥꜥ.n*-forms, CJ] *insofar as they more heavily involve speaker/hearer as a person while "narrative" in its narrower sense is supposed to express a more distant attitude towards the subject talked about: narration lays a claim to objectivity;*"[103] This clearly echoes the *telling–showing* opposition viewed through a Genettian lens. To be fair, Junge qualifies his statement as relating only to a narrow definition of narrative (presupposing a high degree of narrativity) and does not imply that all levels of the production of narrative meaning are affected in the same way. Indeed, the opposition between two major discourse types in many ancient Egyptian text genres is more than a mere figment of philological analysis. As Hintze and others have demonstrated, it often plays out quite well at the level of individual phrases or sections.[104] What it does not do, however, is tell us much about the narrative valence of a composition as a whole. In fact, the presence of subjective, even emotive, colouring in a text could also be seen as an index of its pronounced experiential quality,[105] which in Fludernik's view is an essential component of narrativity. She argues that "*narrativity is a function of narrative texts and centres on experientiality of an anthropomorphic nature* [original emphasis]."[106] Accordingly, she does not count historiographical writ-

100 See particularly Junge (1989: 29–30); Winand (2006: 418–440); Werning (2008).

101 Zeman (2016: 22–25).

102 Cf. *prj.n=j m nꜣw.t=j hꜣj.n=j m spꜣ.t=j jrj.n=j mꜣꜥ.t n nb=s*, "When I have left my town and descended from my region, (then only after) having done maat for her lord." For the phraseology see Kloth (2002: 54–60); Stauder-Porchet (2017: 110–111; 169–176). See also Chapter 2.4.

103 Junge (1989: 107).

104 Hintze (1952).

105 Cf. Sinuhe's desperate exclamation in his darkest hour during his "flight": *ḏd.n=j dp.t mw.t nn*, "... I said to myself: 'This is the taste of death'." Koch (1990: 20, B23).

106 Fludernik (1996: 19).

ing as a manifestation of prototypical narrativity, because in her view it consists merely of reporting calibrated sequences of events as facts and lacks experiential anchoring.[107] But irrespective of the question of how far experientiality contributes to narrativity, it is clear that Fludernik follows a broad definition of narrative, seeing it as a "deep structural concept"[108] rather than a specific type of text or concrete form of discourse. In addition, she rightly stresses that a narrative comes into being only in a person's mind. Whether the process of narrativisation (see above, Chapter 1) always coincides with a naturalisation of the Genettian tandem *discours–narration* (i.e. the mode and the implementation of telling) is another matter. At least as far as ancient Egyptian tomb biographies are concerned, *discours* and *narration* are intricately linked to the monumental three-dimensional medium incorporating (usually) multiple texts, imagery and the spatial relation between the two categories. Multimodal telling cannot be easily tied back to a "natural" oral discourse (see Chapter 4). Therefore, naturalisation appears to be a problematic concept when defining narrativity in Egyptological contexts.

2.2 Minimal criteria for *narrativity* and *narrative*

But what then are the core characteristics of narrative applicable to modern as well as to ancient cultures? And does this question really matter that much? For, as Mieke Bal has fittingly remarked, there is no point in demonstrating the narrative nature of an object while engaging in circular arguments and losing sight of the function of narrativity as a "cultural mode of expression".[109] If *narrative* is an abstract, transgeneric and transmedial structure defining the relations between protagonists, events and time (for more detail, see the end of this section), and if *narrativity* describes the potential of cultural entities or parts thereof to become (a) narrative in both an absolute and a scalar sense (the *narrativeness* of narrative, so to speak),[110] then narrativity is indeed everywhere, but not every instance of narrativity has the same cultural impact and significance.[111] Perhaps one should be more precise and add that narrativity is not an inalienable quality of a cultural object as such. It is always an attribution by a participant (creator, reader, viewer, listener, experiencer) in the communicative process that Fludernik referred to as *narrativisation*.[112] While classical narratology has for a long time focussed on identifying and analysing *narrative structure in the text*, the ultimate goal of transmedial and transcultural narratology should be to look at *narrative structure in the mind* and elucidate its cultural use.[113] But in the absence of readable (ancient) minds we must make do with the instantiations of narrative structures in

107 Fludernik (1996: 19).

108 Fludernik (1996: 19).

109 Bal (1999: 21).

110 Abbott (2014: § 1).

111 Alluding to Bal's (1999: 19) subheading "*Monday: Narrative is everywhere ... but it isn't always so important.*"

112 "It is on the basis of this reinterpretation that Culler's strategy of naturalization will be redeployed and redefined as *narrativization,* i.e. as the reading of texts *as narrative,* as constituting narrativity in the reading process." Fludernik (1996: 14).

113 For transmedial narratology see Ryan & Thon (2014); Alber & Hansen (2014); Wolf (2017b).

their physical form and see whether we can take it further from there. Viewing narrativity as a gradual or scalar concept has become quite fashionable in the past few decades[114] and reflects narratology's move away from the canonical literary discourse towards embracing a multiplicity of textual genres and non-textual media.[115] The quantification of narrativity usually relates to specific sets of criteria selected according to the narratological tradition one feels indebted, whether it be the quantity of "narrative" grammatical constructions, the level of experiential engagement, the degree of *eventfulness* and *tellability*, or the relative potential of an object to become narrativised. By this token, the narrativity embodied in a cultural entity is usually conceived of as a linear spectrum. A prominent example of such an approach is Wolf's categorisation of media according to their potential to provide the recipient with *indices* of their narrativity. His scale ranges from full-blown prototypical narration epitomised in the Western novel and epic (highest degree of explicit narrativity) to merely quasi-narrative analogues such as those one may find in western instrumental music (lowest degree of explicit narrativity).[116] But the latter example also highlights the pitfalls of such an approach. Wolf himself does not fail to remark that music can indeed meet important requirements of narrativity, e.g. chronology, teleology, and eventfulness as well as creating temporally structured experientiality.[117] He even states that music renders experientiality in a particularly persuasive fashion because the content of this 'staging of experience' (Wolf's emphasis) remains necessarily vague due to music's referential indeterminacy. "Damit öffnet die Musik Projektionsflächen, die jeder Hörer nach Maßgabe seiner eigenen Erfahrungswelt narrativ ausfüllen kann."[118] While I would argue that this potential of narrativisation comes already close to the essence of transmedial narrativity (see below), Wolf apparently does not feel inclined to embrace the logical consequences of his own assessment, namely the possibility of the existence of narratives that are not primarily representational. Despite its transmedial scope and high-level abstraction, Wolf's theoretical framework operates with the novel as the prototypical embodiment of a narrative medium, necessarily leading to the conclusion that instrumental music offers but 'quasi-narrativity' (Wolf's emphasis) which "can best be likened not to novels but to drama".[119] He also stresses that many features of music appearing homologue to narrativity can also be interpreted in different terms (the "Other of narrative").[120] As recent musicological contributions have pointed out,[121] however, the notion that instrumental music,

114 Cf. Brütsch (2017), who also highlights some problems related to this approach. Often implicitly, this scalar concept of narrativity takes a prominent position within Egyptological writing, e.g. when Vernus (2020: 166) refers to a "trend to move from narrative discourse to narration" in 2nd millennium BCE autobiography.

115 Herman (1997: 1052); Abbott (2014: § 3.2). See also the convenient overview in Kuhn (2011: 47–49).

116 Wolf (2002: 96, Schema 3), which seems to have "inspired" Braun (2020: 21, Fig. 2).

117 Wolf (2002: 82–83).

118 Wolf (2002. 83).

119 Wolf (2017a: 488).

120 Wolf (2017a: 496 w. n. 19).

121 See Almén (2008: esp. 38–54); Pinto (2020: §§ 2–5); Lock (2020).

in lacking apparent hetero-referentiality,[122] displays at best second-rate analogues to narrativity is somewhat misconceived. The decisive question relates to the parameters used for such an evaluation. Music is certainly not a unified global metalanguage to be narratively decoded through instinct without prior knowledge.[123] Even the basic concept of music as an autonomous mode of cultural expression well-demarcated from other modes cannot be regarded as a human universal but needs to be historicised and contextualised.[124] Yet, most traditions of (instrumental) music are embedded in human culture at an individual as well as an intersubjective level in such a way that their repertoire of system-internal signification will always carry the potential to reference temporally structured emotional states or voice-like entities. While these indexical features may, according to some, not amount to more than the *showing* dimension of narrative discourse,[125] the way these features are often made part of a temporally evolving meta-structure has many similarities (I would maintain, all the important ones) with textual narrative. The main problem with many discussions on narrativity in music seems to be that language-based narrativity is always taken as the only imaginable point of departure.[126] If, however, the temporal and causal integration of experientially salient system-internal events and the manipulation of perceived time through the mediation of a prescient diegetic voice (imagined as the composer's or not) count as important indices of narrative, then many forms of music must score high on the narrativity scale.[127] Examples such as the Scherzo of Mahler's Seventh Symphony with its "shadowy" integration of distorted waltz tunes[128] or the dramaturgy of Kalitzke's piece "Story Teller" for cello and orchestra[129] make abundantly clear that music is very well capable of creating the impression that several "diegetic" levels are implemented and interwoven with one another in a single composition.[130] In addition to these structural characteristics, one should also not forget that agentive emotional forces commonly attributed to musical motifs and phrases share some important similarities with how human or humanised protagonists of textual narratives are construed.[131] In this re-

---

122 For scholars such as Wolf the potential to provide precise hetero-reference to a reality beyond the medium is a hallmark of narrativity. See Wolf (2002: 78).

123 Cf. Kopiez (2004: 20–21); Mirelman (2010), or, as Mehr et al. (2019: 15) put it: "Music is universal but clearly takes on different forms in different cultures."

124 For the difficulties of applying the concept of "music" to ancient sonorous performance, see e.g. Kolltveit (2010: 105–106); Emerit (2015: 119).

125 As Klein (2004: 24) rightly points out, there lies a certain irony in the fact that music is often considered either a mimetic art form incapable of providing a diegetic voice, or a medium confined to pure diegesis through the lack of real representational potential.

126 This attitude is made explicit by Wolf (2017a: 481): "Nonetheless, if we consider the wide-spread feeling that verbal narratives can give a fairly good idea of what is typical about narratives in general and if we also take into account the advanced state of literary narratology, provisionally approaching the question of musical narrativity from a literary angle is perhaps not altogether unjustifiable."

127 Accordingly even Wolf (2005: 327).

128 Cf. Stoll Knecht (2019: 210–216); Adorno (1971: 219–220).

129 See Drees (2018: 6–7/10–11).

130 Cf., e.g., Almén (115–117); with certain reservations: Holtsträter (2012–2014: 233–234).

131 Cf. Micznik (2001: 211–212); Lock (2020: 342–343).

spect one is reminded of the well-known psychological experiments in which test persons (usually of WEIRD extraction[132]) are shown dynamically moving abstract objects such as triangles, squares, circles or blocks on a screen. As questionnaires completed by the participants after the viewing reveal, the majority of them attributed human-like intentionality to these objects and engaged in (sub)conscious narrativisation of their movements, typically referring to the semantic fields of "fight", "escape", "innocence" etc.[133]

My digression on music and abstract visuals serves merely as a reminder that in human existence almost anything can be narrativised. That said, it is also apparent that narrativisation is not triggered completely randomly. In fact, a substantial portion of the creations of human culture seems to be consciously fashioned in such a way as to provide nuclei or *Kristallisationspunkte* for narrativisation. It is certainly a valid observation that irrespective of basic human conditioning towards recognising narrativity, a recipient's cognitive *effort* in narrativisation[134] will differ from medium to medium and from genre to genre. But it will also differ from recipient to recipient, from social context to social context, and from culture to culture.[135] In contrast, the *degree* of narrativisation does not show such a fluctuation across media because stories are construed in the recipient's mind almost regardless of the effort it takes. What is at least partly media-specific are the constraints put on the recipient's freedom of how to narrativise the raw material. While some instances of narrative communication may provide more elaborate guidance than others, even the most explicit forms of narrative literature (following the scheme "then ... and then ... and therefore that...") cannot prevent a person's mental representation of *histoire* and *récit* to transcend the linear sequence of sentences and pages.[136] Thus, even with a 19th century novel the narrativisation will go beyond the signposts provided by the text itself. Stories in our minds are always less and more than the stories that provide the analytical target of standard narratology and literary criticism. In the course of processing a narrative the recipient is constantly occupied with making simple as well as elaborate inferences and carrying out pattern-matching operations. These multiple and concomitant processes create a fuzzy set of open-ended, non-linear narratives not yet conforming closely to the narrative structure and content of the source.[137] Once the medially translated narrative has been fully processed, however, it has already become a "different story", having been semantically enriched by personal connotations as well as a recipient's idiosyncratic way of

---

132 WEIRD stands for "Western, Educated, Industrialised, Rich, and Democratic". Cf. Henrich et al. 2010.

133 Heider & Simmel (1944); Bloom & Veres (1999); Visch & Tan (2009). See also Boyd (2009: 137).

134 Wolf's (2002: 95–97) "Anteil rezipientenseitig nötiger Narrativierung".

135 In that respect, Ryan (2014: § 3.3.2) overestimates the peculiarity of music and downplays the fact that also the narrativisation of textual compositions is to a significant degree dependent on social and cultural conventions. Otherwise, micro-fiction such as the one presented in Chapter 1 or many works of modernist literature would not be successfully decoded as narratives.

136 As Herrnstein Smith (1980: 226) rightly states: "In other words, by virtue of the very nature of discourse, nonlinearity is the rule rather than the exception in narrative accounts."

137 Thus, through being mentally processed in associative networks every text potentially becomes a non-linear hypertext at some stage during its reception. Cf. Hess-Lüttich 1999 (215–217).

linking temporal, causal and associative clues.[138] This process does not differ in principle between media and genres.

Viewing narrativity only in terms of a linear scale has another drawback, for it does not take into account that several levels of narrativity situated at different positions within the spectrum may operate concurrently. "Descriptive" mode is almost as powerful in inducing narrativity than "narrative" mode, but it operates at different levels of specificity. If a text states "The valiant king smote the enemy", the sentence's narrative essence does not just lie in the spelled out event of killing a foe but encompasses via the qualifying adjective also the potentially numerous but unspecified previous instances of the king's giving proof of his braveness. At the same time every narrative entity, be it a text, a wall painting, or a complex monument, has semiotic dimensions not connected to narrativity.[139] This leads directly to the question of what one regards as the core criteria of narrativity and the minimal conditions under which it can unfold. Different to what many narratologists claim, the answer to this question seems to be more arbitrary and more determined by the cultural repertoire informing the discussion than one would assume. This can be illustrated by two well-known yet quite differing narratological perspectives. The first one is closely associated with the English novelist E. M. Forster, who in his collection of lectures published under the title *Aspects of the Novel* made the significant distinction between a story – featuring change of circumstances and sequentiality – and a plot – involving in addition also a causal link between the events. Forster gave a famous example of minimal units to illustrate his point:

> "'The king died and then the queen died' is a story. 'The king died, and then the queen died of grief' is a plot."[140]

While according to some contemporary narratological positions, "the king died", on its own, would already constitute a minimal narrative through the indication of a change of circumstances,[141] Forster's distinction clearly aims at signalling a gradation of narrative sophistication. Though not spelled out in detail and couched in the poetic language of his time, his understanding of the core criteria for meaningful narrative presupposes human protagonists, a temporarily ordered sequence of *tellable* events and a mediating entity providing causal structure as well as emotional guidance. The interesting thing about Forster's example is that a quite significant aspect of his narrative is usually[142] overlooked or at

138 This notion is not identical with the idea of the "death of the author" as an authority of signification (for the latter see Nehamas 1981 rather than the usual suspect Barthes 1968). It simply stresses that narrativisation happens irrespective of authorial intent.

139 Cf. Bal (1990: 730).

140 Forster (1927: 86). The necessity for a causal link between events is already stressed by Tomashevsky in his discussion of *fabula* and *sûzhet* (1925: 136).

141 Cf. Schmid (2014a: 3–4). This position highlights the temporary structure already inherent in verb forms such as "died" through the aspect and tense system. See above, Chapter 2.1.

142 One of the few exceptions in a non-narratological context: Constantinou (2019: 296–297).

least left uncommented.[143] By arranging the sequence of events in that particular order and by attributing the cause of the queen's death to the (excessive) grieving for her husband Forster activates a meta-narrative of gender-specific marital devotion and dependency. This level of narrative relates to a schema that describes the socially approved emotional relation between wife and husband, and constitutes a typical component of the societal fabric in 19th and 20th century Europe. Not unlike the *Baby Shoes* example of Chapter 1, the temporal structure of the schema transcends the level of simple cliché; it represents in essence a "narrativised bias" which exerts its force on the recipient even without the presence of particular components scoring high on the narrativity scale. At the same time, the schema is highly context-sensitive. If one associated Forster's queen dying of grief with e.g. the Daḫamunzu Affair[144] at the end of the Amarna Period, it would probably yield a completely different plot, which was shaped more by the frustration over foiled plans than by a strong marital bond.

In contrast to the tradition represented by Forster, a position advocated among others by Marie-Laure Ryan places particular emphasis on the web of relational signification which characterises narrative. Before venturing to provide a "fuzzy-set definition" herself, she points out that any attempt at defining the concept needs to acknowledge that

> "Narrative is about problem solving.
> Narrative is about conflict.
> Narrative is about interpersonal relations.
> Narrative is about human experience.
> Narrative is about the temporality of existence."[145]

Accordingly, Ryan's criteria hover around several dimensions:

> "**Spatial dimension**
> (1) Narrative must be about a world populated by individuated existents.
> **Temporal dimension**
> (2) This world must be situated in time and undergo significant transformations.
> (3) The transformations must be caused by non-habitual physical events.
> **Mental dimension**
> (4) Some of the participants in the events must be intelligent agents who have a mental life and react emotionally to the states of the world.
> (5) Some of the events must be purposeful actions by these agents.
> **Formal and pragmatic dimension**
> (6) The sequence of events must form a unified causal chain and lead to closure.

143 In contrast to the meticulous assessment of the different states represented by the sentence and their temporal relationships. See, for example, Davis (1992: 237–239) within an Egyptological context.

144 For a handy overview of the widely diverging "stories" told by historians about the fate of the Egyptian widowed queen who sought to marry a Hittite prince, see Ridley (2019: 220–224).

145 Ryan (2007: 24).

(7) The occurrence of at least some of the events must be asserted as fact for the storyworld.
(8) The story must communicate something meaningful to the audience."[146]

According to Ryan's conception, narrativity is a textual property whose multiple dimensions can each take a different value not restricted to just 0 and 1.[147] In acknowledging thus the fluidity of most narratological parameters she foregrounds the social signification *within* and *of* narrative, which is not just predicated on a temporary sequence of events. At the same time, however, she restricts the application of her concept to textual media and calibrates her criteria in such a way that Western literary narrative discourse still provides the implicit prototype against which all other communication of narrative purport is measured. This is especially true for her criterion no. 6, which is meant to eliminate "lists of causally unconnected events, such as chronicles and diaries, as well as reports of problem-solving actions that stop before an outcome is reached."[148] Yet, what constitutes an acceptable conception of causation (e.g. as opposed to providing reasons or drawing associative connections) is determined by how social groups or individuals derive meaning from the world that surrounds them.[149] One may wonder whether a list of "causally" unconnected events such as those found within the ancient Egyptian annalistic tradition or in relief programmes on temple walls could not indeed form a macro-narrative circling around, for example, royal and divine agency in the cyclical maintaining of cosmic order. What may appear to modern viewers as a haphazard accumulation of isolated and partially repetitive events may from an emic perspective represent a temporarily ordered string of preconditions for the successful stabilisation of the present status quo.[150] The true narrative then would not lie in the explicit wording of the text itself, it would emerge from the combination of the text *and* its social *con*text. In fact, many conceptions of narrative seem to presuppose a teleological structure entailing a disruptive (i.e. non-standard, not predictable) event and a linear progression: *A causes B, B causes C*, where C is significantly different from B and at most homologue to A.[151] An *histoire* not conforming to this pattern such as *A leads to B, B leads to A'* is usually not deemed a worthwhile subject of narrato-

146 Ryan (2007: 29).

147 Ryan (2007: 28).

148 Ryan (2007: 29).

149 For the multiple dimensions of causality, which may relate to both predictable/regular and unpredictable/extraordinary events, see Grishakova (2011: 129–130). Physical laws and scientific explanation do certainly not represent the only imaginable framework for discussing causality. Causality may be construed based on post-hoc efforts to rationalise what in modern scientific perspective would be nothing but physically unconnected events. In this regard Brockmeier (2016: 160) speaks of "socially plausible arguments and culturally acceptable storylines".

150 Well beyond sequential representations of rituals such as the Daily Temple Ritual. Cf. Lurson (2021: 180–181). For a more detailed consideration of multi-stage narrativity in the visual domain, see Rogner (2022).

151 Paradigmatic is Brook's (1992: 11–12) emphasis on the teleological, goal-oriented forces of plot. The fairy tale pattern offers a basic prototype: *Initial equilibrium – disruptive event caused by negative forces – hero's/heroine's struggle to overcome disruption – return to an equilibrium slightly differing from the one at the beginning*. Cf. Propp (1968: 92–116).

logical enquiry, especially if *B* does not constitute a major disruption of the equilibrium.[152] Narratives in which the disruption of an equilibrium is only presented as an implicit, contrastive possibility would stand at odds with modern understandings of tellability, i.e. the noteworthiness of an event or a whole plot.[153] Yet, it is precisely this pattern (e.g. "Starting from *A*, I did *B* (in order to avoid *C*), resulting in *A'*.") which seems to inform a substantial amount of ancient Egyptian biographical texts. Denying them a narrative status because they would lack sufficient tellability would be a rather problematic choice, since the materiality of these monumental inscriptions alone already serves as an index of tellability. One does not have to look to ancient Egypt to realise that the linear temporal progression of particularised events linked through causal chains is not a narrative universal but the expectation of a modern audience.[154] As has been pointed out in historical narratology, medieval epics and romances tend to exhibit a structuring of spacetime (Bakhtin's *chronotope*)[155] that is much more defined by cyclical repetition/revisiting and non-mimetic contractions than one would typically find in (early) modern narrative literature.[156]

Even though Ryan's multidimensional narratological approach has a lot to offer, it does not seem to be flexible enough to cover the phenomenon of narrative in its transcultural totality. For the purposes of this study I will therefore adopt a still broader perspective:

At the most basic level, narrative provides nothing more and nothing less than a meaningful structural connection between human or humanised agentive/patientive[157] *entities, temporality (i.e. the notion of time-sensitive changeability) and general relevance within the framework of culturally specific communicative conventions (since even disruptive communication presupposes such conventions).*

This definition has certain affinities with Herman's demand that anything called a narrative must meet the core conditions of possessing particularity, temporality, tellability, and experientiality.[158] Unlike Herman, however, I consider particularity and experientiality as secondary features, since they may emerge only in the process of *re*-cognising narrative schemata. While every narrative is anthropocentric or humanised and thus anchored in

---

152 There is, however, a growing awareness in narratology that beyond the "aesthetics of opposition", the "aesthetics of identification", aiming at recognisability and predictability, play an important role in many narrative cultures. See Schmid (2017: 241–243).

153 According to Herman (2007: 10), "an event-sequence must therefore involve some kind of noteworthy (hence 'tellable') disruption of an initial state of equilibrium by an unanticipated and often untoward event or chain of events" in order to qualify as a narrative.

154 For a good example of this, see Di Biase-Dyson (2015). For the role attributed to causality and expectation within narratological discussions, see Rossholm (2017).

155 Bakhtin (1981: 84–85). It was Assmann (1996: 25) who first – and that quite fittingly – applied Bakhtin's term to pharaonic Egypt, even if he targets not just textual discourse but the culture as a whole.

156 See Störmer-Caysa (2010).

157 This is not meant in a grammatical sense, but simply signals that the protagonists are taken into view either as agents or as patients of actions/circumstances, no matter how this is expressed grammatically in any potential verbalisation.

158 Herman (2007: 10–11).

human experience, not every narrative can be tied back to conventional human communication and be "re-naturalised" in terms of oral speech acts. The concrete medium adds a component to the narrative that is irreducible and non-translatable. In this regard one may think of a typical dream, which most often meets all the basic criteria for forming a narrative (temporally structured events of high salience and experientiality featuring human or humanised protagonists), but usually defies attempts at translating all its ambiguities into spoken language. When waking up, there is the impression of having just experienced a story of sorts, but one would be hard-pressed to retell it in a consistent fashion.[159] In a similar way, multimodal narrative compositions such as an ancient Egyptian elite tomb cannot simply be reduced to a verbal text and/or a sequence of pictorial scenes. When a tomb inscription mentions the rightful construction of the tomb in accordance with the tomb owner's ethical self-conceptualisation and social status, the visitor's experience of the physical space of the tomb and the material manifestations of what the owner claims to be entitled to acts as an integral component of the overarching biographical meta-narrative. Looking just at the textual component misses part of the story, so to speak (see Chapters 4, 5.1, and 7.1 for an exploration of this topic).

2.3 Narrating versus inducing narrativity

At this point it seems advisable to offer some further clarifications on terminology. As will have become apparent, in the view adopted in this contribution *narrative* is first and foremost not a type of text or a genre of any sorts. One may still speak of, for example, *The Story of Sinuhe* as belonging to a narrative genre, but such a classification pertains to a subordinated level of analysis, which I do not have in mind here. Narrative can be conceptualised as a mental structure meeting the conditions outlined in the previous paragraphs. If we speak about a specific realisation of such a structure, we may call it *a* narrative. If we consider the phenomenon of narrative structure in human culture as such, we may refer to *narrative* without article.[160] Even a specific narrative structure is an abstraction and must not be reified as a tangible object or a concrete text. It is not tied to a particular medium and can manifest itself in many different ways. At the same time, however, medial specificity has an important influence on the the possible manifestations of narrativity and thus on the way narratives can be represented through *narration*.[161] To give a banal example, the split screen technique of classical cinema is able to represent

159 As Moers (personal communication) suggests, this notion is perhaps already expressed in Sinuhe's assertion that the causes of his flight were as intangible as the shape of a dream (*jw mj sšm rsw.t mj mꜣꜣ sw jdḥy m ꜣbw zj nj ẖꜣ.t m tꜣ-ztj*; "It was like the shape of a dream, like a dweller of the Delta seeing himself in Elephantine, a man of the (northern) marshes in the South." Koch 1990: 67, B 225–226). Sinuhe's words can also be read as the "author's" metaleptic commentary on the poorly defined motivation for the story's cardinal plot point.

160 This distinction is also found in Abbott (2014: § 1) and corresponds roughly to Wolf's (2002: 42) differentiation between narrative ("das Narrative") as a multifactorial cognitive (macro-)schema and story/ies ("Geschichte(n)") as abstract realisations of the schema of narrative in specific mental representations ("Vorstellungsinhalten").

161 Cf. Ryan (2014).

temporal concomitance with an immediacy that purely textual media cannot faithfully replicate. The same holds true for the concept of monumental portfolio or assemblage biography, which I will introduce in Chapter 5.1 (p. 158).

No single medium or object *is* a narrative, but it may be fair to state that a given cultural object may *represent* or *instantiate* an abstract narrative. This said, a narrative can only be represented in a given medium through the act of *narrativisation* (see above, p. 77), which is a normally unconscious social practice undertaken by all participants in narrative communication. From a historical and transcultural perspective it is therefore not ideal to investigate a narrative one has deduced from a decontextualised medium while disregarding its original physical and social context. This holds especially true for studying narrative cultures far removed from our own embodied practices of dealing with narrativity.[162] If the social context in which one abstracts (= produces) a narrative from a given stimulus forms an integral part of the process of narrativisation then the definition of the unit of analysis and the demarcation of the narrative entity become a pertinent issue. While this problem has most pointedly been discussed in regard to non-fictional texts and social media,[163] it also pertains to other contexts including literary fiction.[164] As a consequence, investigations targeting narrative phenomena in unfamiliar cultural environments have to acknowledge the possibility that entities of narrative signification are polymorphous and not so easy to delimit. We have to ask ourselves, for example, whether we are dealing with a narrative section within a lengthy text, whether we are to take the entirety of a continuous inscription as a narration, or whether we are indeed faced with a group of texts and images producing a carefully calibrated meta-narration. Like it needs text linguistics to assess the temporal significations of a set of sentences and utterances forming a text,[165] it needs postclassical transmedial narratology to assess the narrative signification of (a) cultural object(s) in which text(s), non-textual media, space, and social performance intersect.[166] As will be shown in the following chapters, the perspective on ancient Egyptian biographical narratives changes significantly if "biographical" texts are not considered in isolation but related to the tomb's general iconotextual programme

162 The reason we can readily abstract from the socially conditioned practice of reading western fictional literature is that we all share implicit knowledge about the appropriate epistemological strategies to decode it.

163 See Page (2015).

164 E.g. Vladimir Nabokov's hypertextual meta-fiction *Pale Fire* (1962) consisting of a narrative poem and its academic paratextual framing attributed to a different author, which would constitute a less clear case in that respect if the author had chosen to publish the components separately (as is illustrated by the 2011 "facsimile" edition including the "original" index cards; Boyd [2011]). One may also think of Marlene Streeruwitz' fictional tandem *Nachkommen* (2014; a novel about a young female writer receiving the *Deutsche Buchpreis*) and *Die Reise einer jungen Anarchistin in Griechenland* (2015; the novel for which the fictional character of the previous book is said to have been awarded the prize), which may or may not be viewed as constituting an autofictional, polydiegetic meta-narrative transcending one single text (cf. Goggio 2021: 212–214).

165 Cf. Weinrich 2001: 19–21.

166 For a perspective on the potentials of postclassical narratology in its diverse manifestations, see Sommer (2012: esp. 152).

as well as to its spatial structure and its embeddedness in social practice (see especially Chapter 7.1).

Identifying the narrative entity is a necessary first step in narrativisation, and in certain cases probably represents the most important one. But narrativisation cannot succeed without the attribution of *narrativity*, i.e. ascribing a stimulus the potential to contribute to the forming of a narrative in the recipient's mind. As outlined above, narrativity is often viewed as an inalienable property of a cultural creation relating to the criteria of relative "narrativeness". Thus,

> 1: *After the truck driver had abused the girl, he jumped out of the trunk of the truck and ran away through the mist, abhorred by his own deed.*[167]

will typically be attributed a much higher degree of narrativity than the string of words

> 2: *Girl's face – blood stains – fog.*[168]

Even though (1) undeniably contains significantly more factual and temporal data than (2), both texts succeed to a certain extent in triggering non-explicit narrative structures elaborated from (but not identical with) pre-existing schemata and scripts – with the results for (2) probably primed by the previous reading of (1). In the case of (1) the narration is relatively elaborate while in (2) it merely consists of the juxtaposition of potentially narrativisable nominal nuclei. One could therefore say that the attribution of narrativity to (2) is based on less cues than to (1), but this does not necessarily mean that the effectiveness of narrativisation is reduced in equal measure in the second case. For this reason I would not like to speak of narrativity being *indexed* by certain characteristics and qualities of the medium as Wolff maintains.[169] Rather, it seems to me that narrativity can be *induced*[170] in the mind of a recipient by individual units of signification (regardless of whether it concerns a single word/image, or a temporally complex hypotactic compound/visual sequence) *and* the interplay of these units with the overall context during the effort of narrativisation. In this sense, individual units may act as *Kristallisationspunkte* (see above, p. 95) for narrative, but it depends on the context and the recipient's attitude whether the potential is realised or not. In certain cases, a single word such as "rape"[171] or the less generic "Rosebud" (figuring as keyword in Orson Welles' *Citizen Kane*) may indeed induce an entire narrative through triggering cultural pre-knowledge and

---

167 Modelled upon the rape scene of Theo Angelopoulos' feature film *Landscape in the Mist/Τοπίο στην ομίχλη* of 1988.

168 For a detailed analysis of similar examples, see Herman (1997).

169 Wolf (2002: 96).

170 Not unlike an electric current is induced in a conductor by a changing magnetic field. Of course, I do not want to insinuate that the induction of narrativity in a person's mind happens with the predictability of a law of physics.

171 Bal (1999: 25–26) has drawn attention to the fact that the use of a *nomen actionis* such as "rape" is inextricably linked to a story: "Rape implies an event, if not an entire story with a number of episodes." Bal (1999: 26).

associative mental networks.[172] Already Genette pointedly remarked that at the most basic level any *récit* can be understood as an expansion of a single verb: "*Je marche, Pierre est venu,* sont pour moi des formes minimales de récit, et inversement *l'Odyssée* ou la *Recherche* ne font d'une certaine manière qu'amplifier (au sens rhétorique) des énoncés tels qu'*Ulysse rentre à Ithaque* ou *Marcel devient écrivain.*"[173] The force of narrative nuclei is often overlooked or underrated when considering highly salient religious texts that feature limited emplotment such as the Egyptian Pyramid Texts (see also Hutter & Serova in this volume).[174]

Whereas the concept of *narrativisation* highlights the active contribution of a recipient to create a narrative, one could characterise *narration* as its passive flipside, namely, a recipient's impression (or illusion) that, in the course of his/her reading/viewing/listening/ experiencing, a story is being told. Therefore, narration is always an emergent phenomenon created during and through the act of reception. Since the impression of narration is always tied to a point in space and time, Genette is inclined to extend the meaning of narration also to the concrete (real of fictitious) situation in which it occurs.[175] It goes without saying that single-word "narratives" or similarly basic cultural objects are not able to create the impression of narration as convincingly as more elaborate narrative compositions. In that sense, they could indeed be said to induce narrativity rather than to narrate a story. But one may also look at it in a different way and simply state that the narration of communication that merely induces narrativity relies more heavily on a network of inter- and transtextual relations to accomplish the task. This is why parodies and mythological discourse work so well via simple allusions. As the mastertext can be considered common knowledge, only minor narrative clues are required in order to create a tweaked yet seemingly complete storyline.

Even if the spectrum of narrativity seems to aggregate around two oppositional poles – merely inducing narrativity versus properly narrating – one should bear in mind that the induction of narrativity at the micro level pervades any large-scale narrative as well. One should also not fall into the trap of equating proper narration with the simulation or evocation of a natural speech situation and thus try to re-naturalise instances of highly medialised narratives. As will again be shown later in this contribution (Chapter 6), the narrating voices of an ancient Egyptian funerary iconotext can only be realised in the medium of a monumental tomb itself and are not fully translatable into oral retelling.

To round up my considerations of narratological key terms I would like to point to a consequence for the study of non-western historical narrativity such as the one found in ancient Egyptian funerary complexes. From speech act theory we know that it is advisable to differentiate between locutionary and illocutionary acts, since, depending on

172 Which does not mean, of course, that the narrative meaning of a single expression is a fixed, unambiguous parameter. For example, there are lively discussions in film studies about precisely which narrative "Rosebud" is associated with. See Carringer (1976).

173 Genette (1972: 75).

174 See also Volokhine (2018) and Di Biase-Dyson (2019: 43–45) for the current state of debate on myth and narrative within Egyptology.

175 Genette (1972: 72).

the pragmatic context of a speech act, a question may well represent an order, and a mere statement a question. By analogy, there needs in my opinion to be more awareness that the essence of narrativity lies in the combination of the information structure provided by a given stimulus *and* the context of its reception. This is the reason why in certain cases a simple infinitival statement or a single noun can trigger a complex narrativisation and thus indeed "tell a story".

Excursus: the "narrative" infinitive

This phenomenon can be illustrated with the use of bare – narrative – infinitives within the Egyptian monumental discourse. Before taking a look at an infinitival statement within the funerary sphere let us have a look at an inscription located far from a necropolis but sharing phraseological elements with biographical statements known from later tomb contexts. The text in question is an expedition inscription located near Khor el-Aquiba in Lower Nubia and was created or commissioned by an official named Khaibaubata probably at some point during the 4th Dynasty.[176]

[1] ← *rḫ-nswt Jnpw.t Ḫꜥj-bꜣ.w-B(ꜣ)t(ꜣ) jw.t=f* [2] *ḥnꜥ mšꜥ zj 20,000 ḫbs Wꜣwꜣ.t*	[1] The royal acquaintance of the Anubis nome Khaibaubata: His coming [2] with an expedition force of 20,000 men (and) the hacking up of Wawat.

Structurally, the two-line text is divided into the naming of the protagonist and a chain of two infinitival statements which represent two consecutive events linked through an implicit causal nexus. The fact that this inscription is situated on a rock surface north of Khor el-Aquiba suggests that it presents its content as a *fait accompli* rather than a threat directed at the local population. While Strudwick and Martinet render the last part of the inscription as a final clause ("to hack up Wawat"/"pour raser Ouaouat"),[177] implying that the devastation of Wawat is a goal yet to be achieved, *ḫbs* is not preceded by the preposition *r*. There is also no reason to assume that at the time of writing *jw.t* should have happened but not *ḫbs*. In fact, the roughly contemporary inscription Khor el-Aquiba No. 1[178] mentions the capturing of 17,000 Nubians in an infinitival statement (*nḏrj.t Nḥsj.w 17,000*), which must, again, have communicated the (purported) result of the expedition rather than its envisaged target. Thus, we end up with the basic ingredients of a "proper" narrative: a main (human) protagonist (Khaibaubata) and two tellable events of great significance (coming *to* and hacking up *of* Wawat), which are temporarily and causally linked by implication and represent a momentous change of fortune for the local

176 Khor el-Aquiba No. 2. See López (1966: 25–28, no. 27, Pl. XVI; 1967: 52, d); Helck (1974a: 215–217); Eichler (1993: 113, no. 261); Strudwick (2005: 150, no. 76, A); Moreno García (2009/10: 41, n. 103); Hsieh (2012: 123, n. 44); Martinet (2019: 338, with misreading of *ḫbs*). The two lines are superimposed over a carving of three ships of an earlier date.

177 Strudwick (2005: 150, no. 76, A); Martinet (2019: 338).

178 López (1966: 28–30, no. 28, Pl. XVII, 1; 1967: 51, 1); Helck (1974a: 215–217); Eichler (1993: 112, no. 260); Strudwick (2005: 150, no. 76, B); Martinet (2019: 338, with misreading of *nḏrj.t*).

inhabitants. The reasons for the intervention are not mentioned, nor the status quo before Egyptian officials felt a need to act (or, to be more precise, to communicate the necessity of acting). However, the network of events and social practices within which the expedition was embedded were certainly known to the potential addressees (including members of other Egyptian expeditionary forces) and could be readily interpolated by them. One therefore arrives at the tentative temporal structure $[A^{\text{status quo}} – B^{\text{disruption 1}}] – C^{\text{disruption 2 = Eg. intervention}} – \ulcorner A'^{\text{new status quo}} \urcorner$, where the initial status quo and the events leading to the Egyptian intervention are not addressed at all whereas the new status quo is but represented through the inscription's very existence. In attesting its coming-into-being – the physical incising as well as the deliberations preceding it – the text gains historicity at the moment of its reception. As Mieke Bal has so fittingly remarked when commenting on the impact of a contemporary love-letter graffito on the reader, the assertion of presence is often "loaded with 'pastness'".[179] Also the inscription's location adds to the narrative dimension, since it testifies to the factual veracity of the message and, at the same time, supplies the physical details for imagining the setting of the events, which were not fleshed out in writing. The process of imagination is aided by the presence of representations of boats over which Khor el-Aquiba No. 2 has been intentionally superimposed.[180] Through experiencing the scenery and the palimpsestic textual surface, the reader/viewer gets drawn into a story created by himself out of the multimodal building blocks at hand, no matter how rudimentary the skeleton of textual narrative representation may seem at first. It is also apparent that in this case *histoire* and *récit* emerge only through the active engagement with the narrative nuclei.[181] As a consequence, the reader/experiencer of the original rock graffito is the ultimate source of *narration* and becomes the narrator at the highest diegetic level of the expedition "report" (see also Chapter 7.3).

Such infinitival statements within inscriptional expedition reports are also attested during later periods and can be said to constitute one of the grammatical manifestations of the genre.[182] As Darnell and Manassa have pointed out in relation to the Middle Kingdom texts from the Gebel el-Asr region, the type of expedition report with multiple infinitival statements exhibits striking similarities with the so-called daybook entries known primarily from New Kingdom sources.[183] In these entries, consecutive dates are linked to particular noteworthy events related in the terse nominal style that mainly comprises infinitives, participles and lists as core elements.[184] Whatever the origins of this style, there can be no doubt that it possesses considerable narrative potential and was employed over centuries to present in a concise fashion protagonists as well as plot anchored in space and time by context.

179 Bal (1999: 38).

180 It would not have been difficult to avoid this section of the rock surface.

181 This, in turn, means that a narrativised reading is not the only possible way to perceive the text in its environment.

182 Cf. Doret (1986: 173–174), although his evaluation of the chronological extension is no longer valid. See Hsieh (2012).

183 Darnell & Manassa (2013: esp. 86–89).

184 See also Redford (1986: 97–126, esp. 121–122); Hsieh (2012: esp. 123).

In the funerary sphere too, infinitives may form the nucleus of a *récit*, even though the anchoring follows different principles there. As the infinitive is not anchored in time by itself, it points out temporal position only in conjunction with the scenic context with which it is associated. Infinitival statements in monumental tombs of the Old Kingdom are thus usually context-sensitive and tend to require non-textual complements as 'adjuncts' to complete the narrative arc. It would be misleading, however, to assume that in the autobiographical discourse infinitives are used as framing devices or for complementing background information only.[185] There are indeed cases where they form the narrative's core.

One of the best examples for this is provided by the decoration of the right thickness of the entrance leading to the tomb chapel of Akhtihotep's mastaba in central Saqqara (mid/late 5th Dynasty; now Louvre E 10958 A, Fig. 3).[186] There, a large representation of the tomb owner and two smaller representations of his sons face three registers with scenes related to funerary rituals. Whereas Akhtihotep's sons are each provided with a conventional hieroglyphic caption, indicating chief titles and the protagonist's name, Akhtihotep's title string is preceded by a single column that runs the entire height of the scene and contains information on a remarkable event in the life of his eldest son Seankhuptah, namely, the bestowal of special diadems for his father at the behest of the king.

A) Inscription in front of and above the figure of Akhtihotep:

[1] ↓ *rḏj.t*[a] *ḥm=f šdj n=f zꜣ=f smr wꜥtj jmꜣ-ꜥ Sꜥnḫw-Ptḥ wꜣḏ šmꜥw ḫsbḏ wsḫ 1 šnw 1 ꜥnḫ.t jzn n wꜣḏ šmꜥw ḫbs? r ḫḫ=f ḥnꜥ jwꜣ 2 m š(j) m ḥzw.t sbꜣ=f sw r ḥzj.t sw*[b] *nswt* [2–5] *smr wꜥtj jmꜣ-ꜥ* (etc.) [6] *ḥrj wr.w smr ꜣḫ(tj)-ḥtp(.w)*	[1] The king's granting that his (i.e. Akhtihotep's) son, the sole companion, with gracious arm Seankhuptah take for him a *wesekh* and a *shenu* collar both of Upper Egyptian malachite and of lapis lazuli, furthermore an *ankhet*-pendant and a *izen*-necklace of quarried (?) Upper Egyptian malachite to (place) around his neck together with two pieces of cattle from the #? as a favour, since he (i.e. Akhtihotep) taught him (i.e. Seankhuptah) in such a way that the king praises him, [2–5] the sole companion, with gracious arm (etc.), [6] the superior of the great ones and courtier Akhtihotep.

a) Although other grammatical interpretations of *rḏj.t* have been brought forward,[187] I can see no compelling reason to challenge the identification as infinitive. Introducing the nominal agent of the infinitive through direct genitive instead of *jn* was certainly a viable choice in formal texts of the Old Kingdom and is found in other tomb contexts as well.[188]

b) Grammatically, the referent of the dependent pronoun *sw* is ambiguous, but the context speaks in favour of identifying the object of the king's praise with Seankhuptah.

---

185 *Pace* Vernus (2020: 165 w. n. 12).

186 See Ziegler (1993: 106–114); Stauder-Porchet (2017: 153–154). For a different understanding of the pronominal referents, see Strudwick (2005: 261, no. 194).

187 E.g. as a perfective relative form. Brovarski (1997: 137 w. n. 3). See also Baud (2005: 121–122, n. 81).

188 See Edel (1955–1964: 352, § 697).

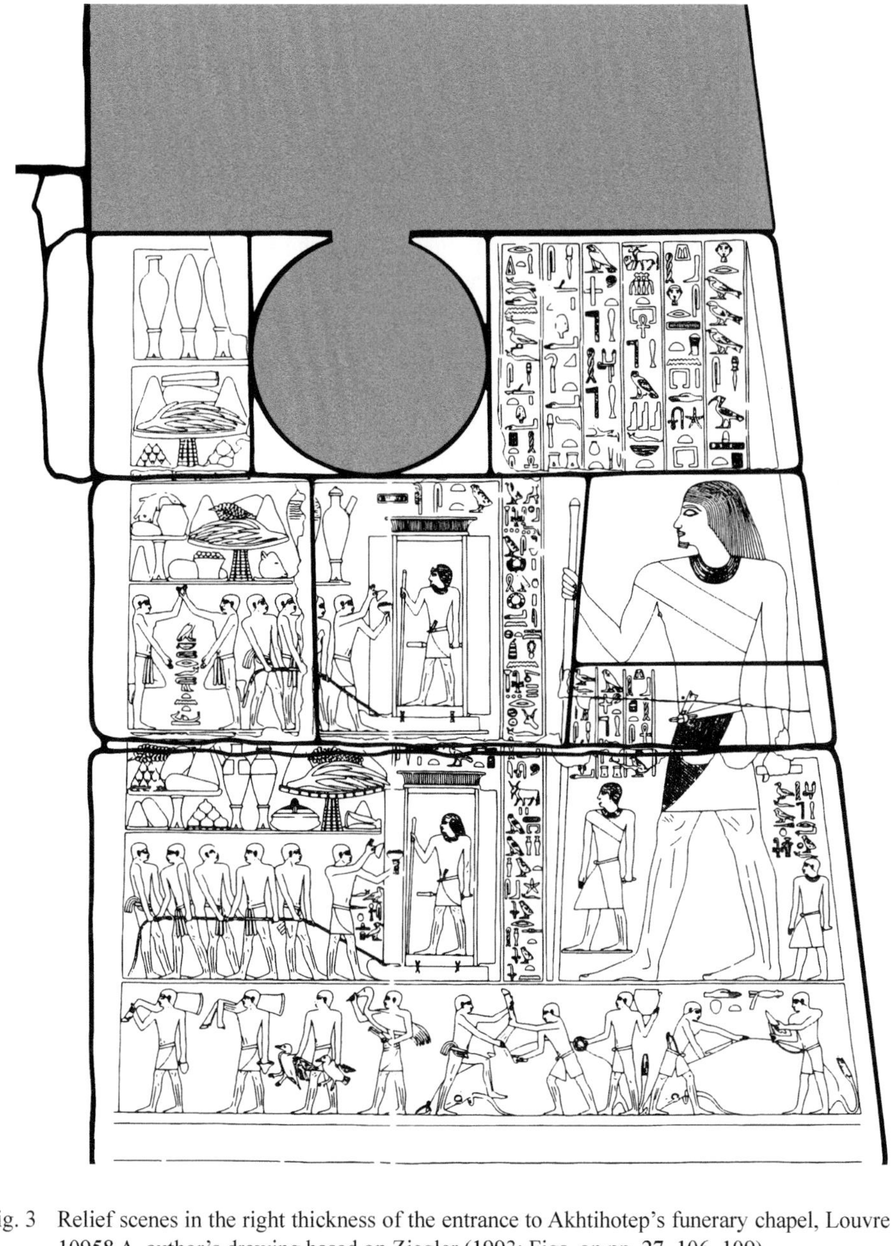

Fig. 3 Relief scenes in the right thickness of the entrance to Akhtihotep's funerary chapel, Louvre E 10958 A, author's drawing based on Ziegler (1993: Figs. on pp. 27, 106–109)

B) Inscription above the figure of Seankhuptah:

1–2 ↓ *zꜣ=f smsw smr wꜥtj jmꜣ-ꜥ* (etc.) 3 *ḫrj-ḥꜣb(.t) Sꜥnḫw-Ptḥ*	1–2 His (i.e. Akhtihotep's) eldest son, the sole companion, with gracious arm (etc.), 3 the lector priest Seankhuptah.

While Text A features two finite verb forms in addition to its two infinitives, it is the initial infinitive *rḏj.t* that forms the story's grammatical as well as narrative nucleus.[189] The two name-title captions of Akhtihotep and his son Seankhuptah (complemented by that of Akhtihotep's younger son Rakhuiefui) together with the respective figures belong to this narrative network as well and can be taken into view as an integrated image-text unit. They serve to characterise the protagonists, whose exemplariness is narratively encoded through relating the act of royal largesse towards Seankhuptah and Akhtihotep in Text A. The temporal relation between the mentioned reward ceremony and the actions depicted to the left of the tomb owner and his two sons (preparations connected with Akhtihotep's burial) are left unspecified. However, the divergence of topic and focal point between them suggests that they cover a certain temporal depth or represent at least different temporal layers, as is the case with the different components of Senedjemib Inti's portfolio biography (see Chapter 5).

On a more general level, it has to be kept in mind that infinitival captions or nominal identifications in tomb decoration and elsewhere always imply a higher, extradiegetic plane, in which an unidentified narrator makes statements about the nature and identity of certain agents and actions. Whether this narrator is to be equated with the tomb owner or one of his heirs is not always easy to ascertain. It seems, however, that for the Egyptians, infinitives could be conceptualised as representing the tomb owner's voice and agency much like in a third-person homodiegetic narration. In the tomb of Pepyankh-Herib at Meir (late 6th Dynasty) this is ingenuously expressed through a scene (Fig. 4) in which the tomb owner, seated on a sedan chair, is shown touching with his reed brush a hieroglyphic inscription with infinitival caption that relates to the five registers of agricultural scenes to its right. It reads: *mꜣꜣ ꜣzḫ jt bd.t ḥwj(.t) mḥꜥj* ("watching the harvesting of barely and emmer wheat and the beating of flax").[190] In this way, Pepyankh is represented in a metalepsis[191] as painting his own tomb decoration,[192] while at the same time being part of the painted scene in which he is watching the labourers. Thus, the figure of the tomb owner can be understood as both an extradiegetic narrator and an intradiegetic character, which also means that the act of narrating and the narrated action are compressed into one focal plane of infinitival simultaneity (for such *mꜣꜣ*-scenes see also p. 149).

189 Already pointed out by Stauder-Porchet (2017: 154). See also Kloth (2002: 169, n. 593).

190 Blackman (1924: Pl. XIV).

191 For similar phenomena in Egyptian imagery, see Rogner (2021: 238–245). Cf. also Moers (2013: 29–30, n. 6) and Widmaier (2017: 497–504), who call for caution regarding the application of the term 'metalepsis' regarding ancient Egyptian iconotexts.

192 Quite fittingly, Pepyankh-Herib bears among others the titles of *zšw pr-mḏꜣ.t pr-ꜥꜣ* and of *zšw-ḳdw.t*. See Lashien (2018: 254).

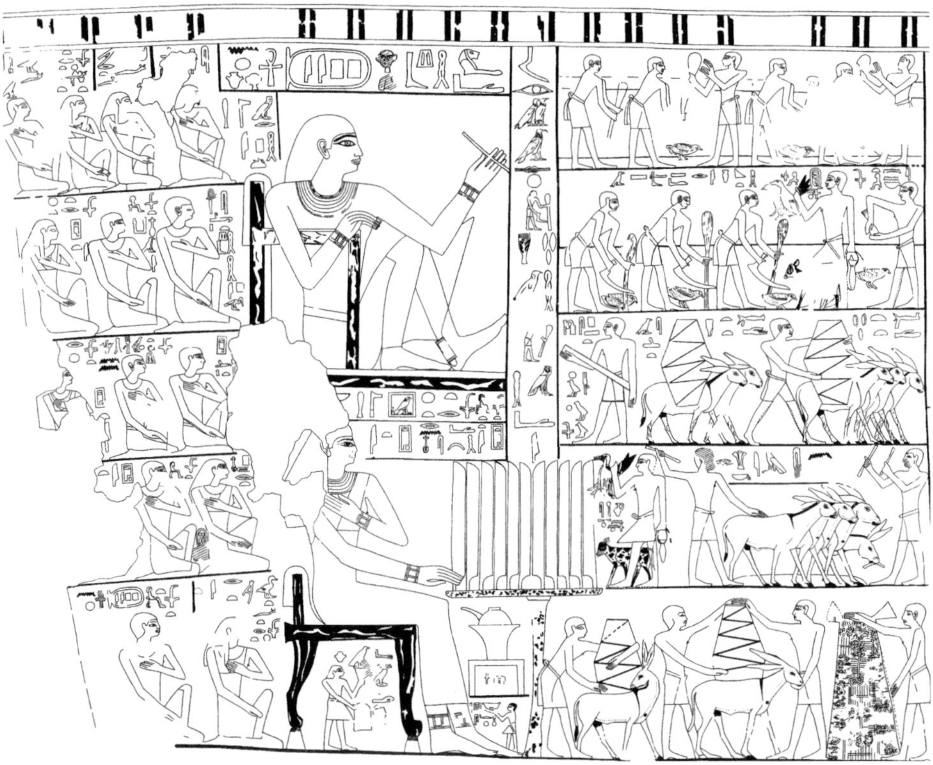

Fig. 4 Scenes on the west wall (excerpt) of the tomb chapel of Pepyankh-Herib at Meir, after Blackman (1924: Pl. XIV)

The use of infinitives to narrate or to evoke narrative content is certainly no invention for non-royal funerary chapels. Already in King Snofru's valley temple the infinitive is employed to communicate that the king has taken notice of the arrival of foreign trees, implying the reception of an expedition and everything that went before. The statement *mꜣꜣ jrd ꜥš wꜣḏ ꜥntj.w wꜣḏ(.w)* ("watching as the fresh fir tree and the fresh incense trees grow")[193] acts as a narrative cue for a whole set of more or less conventionalised plot elements that are later found in more elaborate form in the decoration of the causeway of Sahure.[194]

2.4 *How I became what I have always been* – exemplification as narrative encoding of societal norms and values

As has been explained above (p. 99), when tellability as one of the potential criteria of narrativity is applied to different forms of communication, it is often linked with relating the disruption of an equilibrium and with extraordinary events experienced by an individu-

193 For this scene on one of the temple's pillars, see Fakhry (1961: 80–85 w. Figs. 63 and 67); Edel (1996: 200–204 w. Fig. 1); El Awady (2009: 70–71 w. Fig. 45).

194 El Awady (2006; 2009: 70–71; 155–186).

al.[195] The criteria by which extraordinariness is judged, however, are usually rooted within modern Western notions of value, significance and novelty. In conversations of daily life, the fact that tellability tends to be created and recognised in a highly dynamic process of discursive interaction by the interlocutors is relatively transparent[196] (anyone having ever been made to pay attention to someone's telling of holiday "adventures" can testify to it). In written or pictorial communication, on the other hand, tellability – although in principle still a malleable property – is posited as a given by the author, and it requires a certain effort by the recipient to challenge it.[197] That such challenging of claims of tellability occurs rather infrequently[198] should probably be attributed to a basic common understanding among the members of the potential audience of what constitutes significance enshrined in permanent form (via text, image, etc.). It is thus based to a significant degree on convention. We tend to conceive of tellable events and/or actor(s) as standing out from the background plane of societal norms and ordinary life with its daily routines. This is even more true of texts attributed to the biographical discourse, since the whole point of writing about someone's life in a modern context is to create an individual persona through showcasing *extra*-ordinariness (see also chapter 3.1). But following Baroni and others, tellability refers in essence to nothing more and nothing less than those "features that make a story worth telling, its 'noteworthiness'."[199] If noteworthiness is a relative concept highly dependent on societal norms, conventions, and cultural context, then any understanding of narrativity relating to the notion of tellability has to accommodate a wide range of cultural manifestations. While a low level of tellability may not necessarily impact on the level of relative narrativity,[200] a high degree of tellability often correlates with narrative salience and suggests the consideration of a certain cultural creation from a narratological perspective. As Prince highlights, however, even high degrees of tellability are subject to contextual inferences and no absolute givens. Any judgement on tellability/narratability does not solely consider textual characteristics but takes into account a potentially "inexhaustible" context encompassing mediality, identity of sender and recipient and many other factors.[201] Indeed, the material features of a cultural creation and the general parameters of its medialisation may alone suffice to indicate a high degree of intended tellability, even if we struggle to grasp its point at times. Decorated Egyptian tomb chapels of Old Kingdom elite necropoleis can be considered prime examples of this phenomenon. Designed to exhibit monumentality, visibility and durability of the encoded content (decoration usually carved into durable limestone), the iconotexts they contain serve to stress the relevance of their messages, which circle around tomb and tomb owner. That he is predominantly pre-

195 See Fludernik (1996: 18); Herman (2007: 10). Cf. n. 153 above.

196 Cf. Ochs & Capps (2001: 33–36).

197 Cf. Prince (2008: 23).

198 Communication in social media, which is more akin to conversations of daily life, shall not be considered here.

199 Baroni (2014: 1). Similarly, Prince's concept of *narratability*, which he differentiates from *narrativity*. Prince (2008: 23–26).

200 Questioning the point of a story presupposes that one is dealing with a story in the first place.

201 Prince (2008: 25).

sented as going about the daily business of his elite existence (which includes caring for his funerary estate) demonstrates that this "ordinariness" was clearly deemed worthy of communication (irrespective of any potential deeper symbolic/religious meanings). While this basic fact has never been disputed, the interesting question is whether one could view the showcasing of ordinariness as an effort to narrativise societal norms and values in the mode of "telling through showing". As Assmann has pointedly remarked, the tomb owner appears in his tomb as though he were the editor of his "Collected Works".[202] More often than not, however, these lifetime achievements set in stone seem to adhere to parameters we would not necessarily consider as encompassing novelty and individuality in a narrow sense. Instead of focussing on transgression of norms and conventions, they bring to the attention of visitors how an official has excelled in leading a life of unsurpassed conformity.[203] Exceptionality is negotiated within the framework of societal norms and expectations, and its presentation obeys the rules of non-contingent generalisability. This does not mean that individualised elements and showcasing of contingency are completely absent from elite self-presentations, but they manifest themselves solely within the limits of a rhetorically constituted projection of personhood. The voice of the tomb owner in his tomb chapel (see Chapter 6) speaks about himself and his experience only insofar as his life can be aligned with the repertoire of phraseology[204] and plot elements that are available for the biographical discourse at a given time in pharaonic history. This repertoire is of course not an unchangeable monolith but was modified and expanded over time in accordance with the principle of the "Erweiterung des Bestehenden"[205]. Thus, the phraseology characteristic of the so-called ideal biography saw a significant enrichment from the late Old Kingdom into the First Intermediate Period[206] while retaining its slot within the overall structure of the biographical discourse, that of the *generic exemplification* of lived and embodied virtue (see also below).

A good example of this is provided by the ideal biography found on the false-door of the vizier Sekhemankhptah in his mastaba tomb G 7152 located in the East Field of Giza (probably early 6th Dynasty).[207] There the innermost panel of the false-door on the west side of the tomb chapel is covered by two columns of hieroglyphic text comprising conventional phraseology of the developed ideal biography sub-genre.[208]

202 "In Gestalt seines monumentalen Grabes tritt der vornehme Ägypter sozusagen als Herausgeber seiner 'Gesammelten Werke' auf." Assmann (1996b: 103).

203 Thus already Stauder-Porchet (2011: 750) with her insightful remark: "En accord avec les règles qui régissent la société égyptienne de l'Ancien Empire, le propriétaire de la tombe exprime donc sa singularité dans l'exceptionnalité de sa conformité." Cf. also Chauvet (2013: 57): "'Evidence' from life experience was selectively chosen and organized in a narrative self-presentation intended to project an image of social conformity (a typical property of premodern autobiographies), and at the same time to single out aspects of uniqueness (that which is deemed worth telling)."

204 Cf. Coulon (2020).

205 For this concept see Hornung (1971).

206 Cf. Moreno García (1998: 158–160); Stauder-Porchet (2017: 169–178; 297).

207 See Badawy (1976: 16–17, Fig. 19, Pl. 18); Kloth (2002: 33, no. 70).

208 Kloth (2002: 278–279); Stauder-Porchet (2017: 169–170).

[1] ↓ *[jj.n(=j) m] nꜣw.t(=j) prj.n(=j)*
m spꜣ.t(=j) hꜣj.n(=j) m [a] *jz pn*
ḏd.n(=j) mꜣꜥ.t jrj.n(=j) mꜣꜥ.t mrr.t
nṯr wḏꜥ.n(=j) mdw [2] *[mꜣr ḫ]f[t]*
nḫt r bw mꜣꜥ n rḏj.n(=j) jṯj n=f
šps (j)ḫ.t nj.t šwꜣ(w) (j)r=f
jrj.n(=j) jz pn r jmꜣḫ(=j) n
jrj.t(=j) mꜣꜥ.t [1a] *ẖrj-tp nswt*
[2a] *smr wꜥtj* [3] *Sḫm-ꜥnḫ-Ptḥ*

[1] [When I have come from] (my) town, left (my) region and descended in this tomb, (then after) having spoken *maat*, done *maat*, which the god appreciates, and having judged the matter [2] [of a miserable one in rela]tion to a mighty one in a just way. I did not tolerate that a noble seized for him the possessions of someone who was poorer than him. I have made this tomb for (my) *imakh* status on the grounds of (my) having done *maat*. [1a] The royal subordinate and [2a] sole companion [3] Sekhemankhptah.

a) The combination of a verb of motion and the locative preposition *m* with allative instead of ablative meaning continues to puzzle (see Stauder-Porchet 2009: 199–200; 2017: 187). Nevertheless, context dictates that the meaning cannot be "descended *from* my tomb".

The position of the text at the focal point of the funerary offering cult corresponds to its information structure and primary message, which does not expand on lived experience but presents the listing of generic deeds (summarised by the expression *jrj.t(=j) mꜣꜥ.t*) as prerequisite for being entitled to the *imakh* status. Sekhemankhptah's achievements are thus invoked as an argument to explain the status quo and to justify his elevated position in the hereafter, which is meant to be partly facilitated through an ongoing funerary cult (cf. Chapter 1, p. 83). While this justification could have been presented as a purely descriptive enumeration of adjectival ethical attributes, the Egyptians chose to exemplify the tomb owner's adherence to societal norms and values via generic micro-narratives usually expressed through emphatic constructions employing the perfective *sḏm.n=f* form. The effect is an increase in salience and tellability, which in turn enhances the rhetorical efficacy of the justification within the communicative constellation (> tomb owner addressing visitors to his tomb chapel). The complexity of the *narration* (in the Genettian sense) is further increased by the fact that the tomb functions both as a medium and an object of narrative communication, since its erection counts among the essential achievements of an official during the Old Kingdom.[209] Therefore, its material presence figures not only as a non-verbal indicator of a particular set of events in a person's biography (e.g. the reception of royal permission and support, the commissioning, the actual building phase, any subsequent alterations, the staging of the funeral, etc.). Through the justificatory discourse it acts also as an index of ethical behaviour – the theoretical precondition of receiving a monumental tomb in the first place. This is the essence of the concluding sentence *jrj.n(=j) jz pn r jmꜣḫ(=j) n jrj.t(=j) mꜣꜥ.t*. What precedes it constitutes nothing but the exemplification of the word *mꜣꜥ.t*; in this case a highly conventionalised rhetoric of conformity that eschews particularity and detail because the ideal (i.e. the epitomised norm) is attributed greater communicative reliability (thus the ubiquity of stock phrases in funerary biogra-

209 Cf. Alexanian (2006).

phies). A similar structure can even be found in statue inscriptions such as the one on the seated statue of Memi (Leipzig, no. 2560) from Giza mastaba D 32A (5th or 6th Dynasty).[210]

Side A

[1]| → *wꜥb-nswt Mmj* [2]| ↓ *ḏd=f rḏj.n(=j) jrj.t(j)* [3]| *(ḥmtw) (j)pw twt(w).w* [a] *jn ḳstj* [4]| *ḥtp(.w) ḥr jsw jrj.t.n(=j) n=f*	[1]| The royal wab-priest Memi, [2]| he says: "That (I) have had [3]| these (three) likenesses made by the sculptor was (to ensure) that he was [4]| satisfied with the reward that (I) had made for him.

Side B

[1]| ← *wꜥb-nswt Mmj* [2]| ↓ *ḫpj=f ḥr wꜣ.wt nfr.(w)t* [3]| *ḫpp.(w)t jmꜣḫw(.w)* [4]| *ḥr=sn*	[1]| The royal wab-priest Memi, [2]| may he proceed on the perfect ways [4]| on which [3]| the *imakhuu* proceed.

a) The writing  suggests that the inscriptions refers to three particular statues of Memi. One of them might be Roemer- und Pelizaeus-Museum Hildesheim no. 2, which shows Memi standing and likewise comes from Mastaba D 32A.[211] Alternatively, the phrase could be understood as a simple plural, in which case it would read *twt(w).w (j)pw*. For the "tabular" notation of cardinal number phrases in Old Egyptian see Edel (1955-1964: 174, §401) and Vernus (2004: 281, § 7).

Here the material presence of the statue on its own testifies to the veracity of the statements in its inscriptions, because in the context of the ethical standards of the Old Kingdom elite its very existence is preconditioned on exemplary behaviour. The just compensation of workers is a topos usually situated on the margin of the biographical discourse, since it is regarded as focussing on the tomb and funerary equipment rather than on the life of the deceased. Structurally, however, it occupies a slot that is similar to the ideal biography on Sekhemankhptah's false-door, even though the link between the past-oriented statement of Side A and the wish expressed on Side B is only implicit. In both Sekhemankhptah's and Memi's case, the exemplification of ethical behaviour as affirmation of noteworthiness is dialectically related to an overarching event, which could even be considered as the *actual event: the fact, that the narrativisation takes place as such.* This narrativisation assumes a particular material form and is actualised in the moment of its reception.[212] But the individual components constituting the narrative schema do not need to possess any particularised identities.[213] Instead, their manifestation is often shaped by the generic repertoire of a context-specific rhetorical mode. As Moers has shown, ancient Egyptian

---

210 Sethe (1933: 225, no. 1); Krauspe (1997: 51–53, no. 100, Pl. 40,3–41,4).

211 See Krauspe (1997: 52); Martin-Pardey (1977) 9–15.

212 This is made explicit in the biographical inscription of Werre, which autoreferentially comments on its own coming-into-being through an order of the king. See Stauder-Porchet (2017: 47–48).

213 Which does not mean that no mimesis was intended. Following Coulon (2020), it is necessary to differentiate between the conventionality of phrases and linguistic images (clichés) on the one hand, and the concrete actualisation of social norms within a narratively presented life on the other hand. To put it differently: If your repertoire of expression is limited by (non-linguistic) constraints, even the most extraordinary life story will be cast in familiar imagery.

discourses of elite self-presentation – with the biographical discourse constituting one of the largest subsets thereof – dwell on the "amplification of likeness" as the basic aim of societal rhetoric.[214] While asserting the equivalence between self and ideal in a highly conventionalised manner, the rhetorical nature of the meta-discourse still opens up a plethora of ways to furnish one's tomb with *exempla virtutis*. These *exempla* too may be more or less generic, but they bear the potential of enabling subtle manipulations of conventions and expectations belonging to the realm of Vernus' *appogiature*[215]. Rather than representing the tomb owner's past life as a linearly structured portrait of reality they furnish the rhetorical mode of discourse with an "effet de réel", to use an expression by Roland Barthes.[216] While generic *exempla* such as those found in the ideal biography tend to put greater emphasis on conformity, the more or less elaborate *exempla* of the event biography are more suited to let the tomb owner stand out in regard to his peers and subordinates alike without compromising the overarching framework of decorum. But even they communicate within the narrow limits of societal normativity. This is well illustrated by the famous biographical inscription from the 5th Dynasty mastaba of Shepsesptah at Saqqara, which counts among the few biographical texts of the Old Kingdom providing explicit chrono-biographical information (see Chapter 5.3).[217] The inscription is found on a monumental panelled false door niche, which occupies four fifths of the western wall in the mastaba's cult chapel (now BM EA 682 + Chicago ISAC E 11048). With the exception of the false door and a monumental architrave over the entrance to the main corridor (bearing elaborate, if conventional, offering formulae), the mastaba's decoration does not seem to have ever been completed. Mariette reports faded paintings depicting the transportation of funerary statues as the only surviving pictorial features apart from the representation of offerings framing the chapel niche.[218] The central section of the false door in the chapel carries several inscriptions with Shepsesptah's titularies, whereas the biographical text of concern to us here is distributed over eight individual columns to the left and the right of the central false door (reading progresses from right to left), each found on one of the panels of the palace façade.[219] Shepsesptah's biographical inscription is without doubt a carefully crafted piece of writing, whose poetics extend both to the auditive and to the visual spheres (Fig. 5).[220]

---

214 Moers (in press).

215 See Vernus (2009/2010: 95–115; 2012: 109–111).

216 Barthes (1984: 167–174; esp. 172–174). Cf. Genette (1972: 186). For the reception of this concept within Egyptological narratology, see Coulon (1997: 130–131 w. n. 116); Rogner (2022: 27).

217 Assmann (1983: 72–73); Baud (1999: Vol. II, 452–454); Kloth (2002: 15–16); Dorman (2002); Gundacker (2015a); Stauder-Porchet (2017: 85–98).

218 Mariette (1889: 114, C.1).

219 James (1961: 17, Pl. XVII).

220 For the inscription's word play on *špss* and the iterative positioning of names at the top and the bottom of the columns cf. Stauder-Porchet (2017: 97).

1 ↓ *[ẖrd msj.n mw.t=f n jtj=f m]* [a] *rk (Mn-kꜣ.w-Rꜥ) šdjw=f m-m msj.w-nswt m pr-ꜥꜣ nj nswt m ẖnw-ꜥ m jpꜣ.t špss ḫr nswt r ẖrd nb Špss-Ptḥ*	1 [A child that his mother bore his father in] the time of (Menkaure). He was raised among the royal children in the king's palace, in the inner sector, in the private chamber, one more highly estimeed before the king than any (other) child, Shepsesptah.
2 *[jdw ṯꜣz mḏḥ m] rk (Špss-kꜣ=f) šdjw=f m-m msj.w-nswt m pr-ꜥꜣ nj nswt m ẖnw-ꜥ m jpꜣ.t špss ḫr nswt r jdw nb Špss-Ptḥ*	2 [A boy who tied the fillet in] the time of (Shepseskaf). He was raised among the royal children in the king's palace, in the inner sector, in the private chamber, one more highly esteemed before the king than any (other) youth, Shepsesptah.
3 *[wn m ḥwnw ḫr ḥ]m nj (Wsr-kꜣ=f) rḏj n=f ḥm=f zꜣ.t-nswt smsw.t Ḫꜥj-mꜣꜥ.t m ḥm.t=f mrj.n ḥm=f wnn=s ḥnꜥ=f r zj nb Špss-Ptḥ*	3 [One who became a youth under the maj]esty of (Userkaf). His majesty gave him the eldest king's daughter Khaimaat as wife, because His Majesty wished that she should be with him more than (with) any (other) man, Shepsesptah.
4 *[d(jj) m wr ḫrp ḥmw.t m pr.]wj nj (Sꜣḥ-wj-Rꜥ) špss ḫr nswt r bꜣk nb hꜣj=f r wjꜣ nb stp-zꜣ ꜥḳ=f ḥr wꜣ.wt ꜥḥ-nṯr šmꜥw m ḥꜣb.w nb.w nj.w ḫꜥw Špss-Ptḥ*	4 [One who was installed as Great one and Leader of the artisans in the two hous]es of (Sahure). One more highly esteemed before the king than any (other) servant, he used to descend to every ceremonial bark, being in palatial service, he used to enter the ways of the divine palace of Upper Egypt at all the festivals of the appearance, Shepsesptah.
5 *[wr ḫrp ḥmw.t m pr.wj nj (Nfr-jrw-kꜣ-Rꜥ) špss ḫr nswt r bꜣ]k nb m ḥrj-sštꜣ nj kꜣ.t nb.t mrrw.t ḥm=f jrj.tj=s snfr jb nj nb=f rꜥ nb Špss-Ptḥ*	5 [The Great one and Leader of the artisans in the two houses of (Neferirkare). One more highly esteemed before the king than] any (other) [ser-]vant officiated as master of the secret of every work, of which His Majesty wished that it be done, he who gladdens the heart of his lord every day, Shepsesptah.
6 *[wr ḫrp ḥmw.t m pr.wj nj (Rꜥ-nfr=f) špss ḫr nswt r bꜣ]k nb jḫr ḥzj sw ḥm=f ḥr jḫ.t rḏj ḥm=f sn=f rd=f n rḏj.n ḥm=f sn=f tꜣ Špss-Ptḥ*	6 [The Great one and Leader of the artisans in the two houses of (Raneferef). One more highly esteemed before the king than] any (other) [ser-]vant: As His Majesty (once) praised him for a matter, he let him kiss his (i.e. the king's) foot, (for) His Majesty did not let him kiss the earth, Shepsesptah.

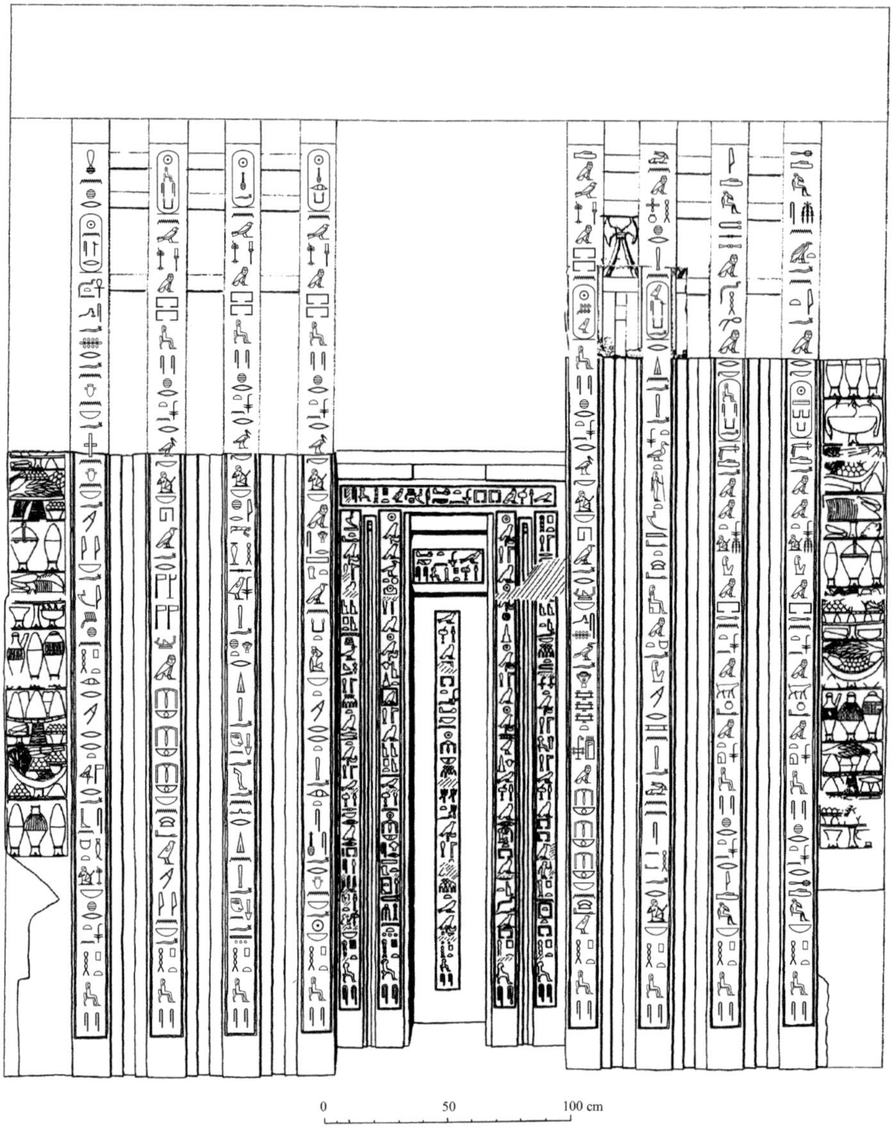

Fig. 5 Reconstruction of false door of Shespesptah with inscriptions after Gundacker (2015: 96–97, Fig. 1)

7 *[wr ḫrp ḥmw.t m pr.wj nj (Špss-kꜣ-Rꜥ)] špss ḫr nswt r bꜣ]k nb hꜣj=f r (wjꜣ) Wṯs-nṯr.w m ḥꜣb.w nb.w nj.w ḫꜥw mrjj nj nb=f Špss-Ptḥ*

7 [The Great one and Leader of the artisans in the two houses of (Shepseskare)]. One more highly esteemed before the king than] any (other) [ser-]vant: He used to descend towards (the ceremonial bark) “Lifted are the Gods” during all the festivals of the appearance, beloved of his lord, Shepsesptah.

8 *[mrn*[b] *ḫr (Nj-Rʿ-wsr) ʿnḫ.j ḏ.t stp=f zꜣ r=f jnj-jb nj nb=f jm]j-jb n nb=f mrjj*[c] *nb=f jmꜣḫ.n Ptḥ jrr mrrw.t nṯr=f sbnj ḥmwtj nb ḫr nswt Špss-Ptḥ*

8 [The favoured of (Niuserre), may he live forever, he used to do palatial service for him, one belonging to his lord's heart, one within] his lord's heart, beloved of his lord, whom Ptah has furnished, who keeps doing what his god desires, who lets every artisan be pleasant to the king, Shepsesptah.

a) The reconstruction of the missing portions of the text at the upper edge of the false door follows Gundacker (2015a). The understanding of the rest of the text and the translation are equally indebted to him.
b) For the still problematic interpretation of  within biographical texts of the Old Kingdom see Gundacker (2015a: 79–80, n. a; 81–85). What is clear is that the word can hardly be understood as the adverb *mrn/mjn* "today". Rather, one may be faced with a nominalised derivation of a verb *mrn* used in a fashion similar to *jmꜣḫw ḫr* and *špss ḫr*.
c) In contrast to Gundacker (2015a: 80, n. g), I see no reason to doubt that *mrjj* of col. 8 represents the passive perfective participle form followed by a direct genitive in analogy to that of col. 7, where it is followed by an indirect genitive.

The stages of Shepsesptah's career mentioned in the inscription are specific and generic at the same time; specific insofar as they anchor Shepsesptah's life to a sequence of reigning kings and communicate – among other things – the highly significant facts of his becoming married to the daughter of King Userkaf or his being singled out by the king during a ceremony by granting permission to kiss the royal foot instead of the earth.[221] These two pieces of information each relating to a single, if vaguely particularised, event are provided with narrative frames that exhibit high degrees of tellability through showcasing royal intervention. In accordance with the conventions characterising the early development of the biographical genre, Shepsesptah's exceptionality is reflected not in his own actions, but in that of the king. Within the general structure of the biographical discourse, however, the evocation of both royal and non-royal agency serves as historicising exemplification of the tomb owner's a-temporal status and his claims to the existence of an *akh*. While events such as Shepsesptah's royal marriage indeed index his identity and are as inseparable from his persona as is his name, the represented *cursus honorum* as a whole merely provides a stage to assert that Shepsesptah has shown exemplary skill in conforming to the norms and meeting the expectations of court society, thus his receiving honours by the king. Therefore, the passage mentioning the marriage to the king's eldest daughter in col. 3 occupies a structural slot similar to the one referring to being "raised among the royal children in the palace of the king." (cols 1–2). Likewise, the phrase *ṯꜣz mḏḥ m rk* KN, which has become conventionalised in slightly later biographical inscriptions,[222] may not primarily be seen as a reference to an extraordinary event during Shepsesptah's youth but relates to a common rite of passage, whose completion seems to have been obligatory

221 For the latter motif and its significance within the development of the biographical genre, see Stauder-Porchet (2011: 759–760; 2017: 94–96; 2021a: 147–148).
222 Feucht (1995: 238–245, esp. 239–240); Kloth (2002: 128–131).

for being allowed to enter into official service.[223] Its evocation acts as a reminder that Shepsesptah's whole earthly existence was geared towards meriting praise and favours from the king and his entourage (which is indeed spelled out in vague terms in the episode of kissing the royal foot in col. 6). One could speak in this regard of a slightly twisted teleology of broad temporal scope (from birth to advanced age) but with reduced temporal resolution (the individual phases of life only cursorily hinted at as vignettes), where the starting point exemplifies the outcome on which it is predicated. In their specific selection and arrangement within the tomb context (one could also speak of material "emplotment"), the six columns produce a second-order meaning[224] aligned but not identical with the contents of the respective utterances, namely, that Shepsesptah became what he has always been. This meta-statement forms an argument within the wider context of communication tied to the maintaining of his funerary cult.[225] The *exempla*, however, are only effective as justification because they can be easily related to pre-existing scripts and schemata associated with normative life at court. In such a way, they not only provide narrative nuclei for imaging the idealised life of the tomb owner but succeed in narratively encoding the very norms and values of the society he forms part of.

At this point it is important to stress that the narrative encoding of an elite existence does not require explicit verbalisation. In the case of Shepsesptah's panel inscription, the iterative juxtaposition of cartouches of successive kings close to the top, and the name of the tomb owner at the bottom of the individual columns (see Fig. 5) is already an iconic representation of a life led in constant royal favour.[226] It is evident that this visual level of narrative encoding cannot be re-naturalised in a straightforward oral speech act (cf. p. 100). The concrete verbalisation within the columns merely adds to this meta-narrative by providing exemplifications. Viewed from the perspective of postclassical transmedial narratology, ancient Egyptian life writing is thus clearly a transmedial phenomenon not exclusively based on biographical texts in the narrow sense. In this vein, Baines has convincingly demonstrated that in ancient Egypt and Nubia, biographical narration without resorting to writing did not only exist but was commonly practised from the earliest times of pharaonic civilisation.[227] This was possible because the nucleus around which the Egyptian biographical discourse in the wider sense formed focussed on the *assertion of existence*, not its explanation or dwelling on its historical derivation. This assertion may manifest itself in nothing but the very existence of the funerary structure or the presence of a name inscription (cf. the inscriptions with the bare name of Shepsesptah on the door rolls

223 See Feucht (1995: 239).

224 For the differentiation between first-order and second-order meaning in textual discourse, see Polkinghorne (1988: 61).

225 One should not forget that the columns frame the focus of Shepsesptah's offering cult and are flanked by depictions of food offerings. For the nexus between the biographical discourse and the funerary cult, see Jansen-Winkeln (2004: 61).

226 Cf. Dorman (2002: 105); Stauder-Porchet (2017: 97).

227 Baines (2020: 48–52). I would go even further than Baines and maintain that the display of values via interventions in the funerary ensemble relates to a narrative core, even if not made explicit in terms familiar to us. For the Egyptian tomb as biographical artefact, see also Walsem (2020: 125–126).

of the two false door niches in the northern half of the mastaba's eastern façade[228]).[229] It may, however, also take the form of an elaborate three-dimensional multimodal iconotext (see Chapter 4), to which the individual textual and non-textual components contribute. In this iconotext, explanation plays a role insofar as the existential status of a person in this world as well as in the hereafter needs to be justified and, if possible, maintained or even enhanced. Through explanation, assertions of existence, identity, and status are endowed with a sense of logical necessity, which can be (and often explicitly *is*) projected into the future. At its simplest, however, explanation may appear as bare claim to excellence such as expressed in epithets and eulogies composed in a nominal style, which are usually not firmly anchored in time and space. Another way to strengthen the power of one's assertion of existence is to "enact" explanation through *exemplification*, as shown above. In its most elaborate form, the *exemplification principle* comes close to giving the impression that a unique and individualised life story is being presented. For the Old Kingdom, this is probably true of a number of late biographical inscriptions such as the ones of Herkhuf, Sabni and Weni the Elder, all dating to the later 6th Dynasty.[230] Notwithstanding the stress on narrative particularity (cf., e.g., the death of Sabni's father abroad), whose level, according to our standards, by far exceeds that of Shepsesptah's inscription, the seemingly individualised narrative is still part of a rhetorical matrix, in which it occupies the slot of *explanans* within the overarching communicative frame.[231] The point is not that there would be no correspondence whatsoever between monumentalised life stories and factual events, but that they function primarily as Barthesian "effets de réel"[232] within the rhetorically constituted meta-discourse of living an elite existence during the third millennium BCE. As such, the tomb is constituted by a *built rhetoric* and the associated reciprocal practice during the funerary cult.[233]

If we then look at the wider picture and adopt a structuralist perspective, we will come to the conclusion that the only indispensable and truly individual element of a funerary biography is the tomb owner's name. It lies at the heart of the communicative frame within which the cultic functionality of Egyptian elite tombs unfolds.[234] All other dimensions of narrative signification are arranged around it as a *cascade of exemplifications* within a

---

228 See Mariette (1889: 110, C.1).

229 Cf. Assmann (1983: 64).

230 Cf. Stauder-Porchet (2017: 275–283)

231 In this connection, Jansen-Winkeln (2004: 61) rightly remarks: "Daher ist ein biographischer Text ohne seine situative Einbettung (und ohne die andersartigen, nichtbiographischen Textsorten, mit denen zusammen er meist vorkommt) zwar verständlich und sinnvoll, sein eigentlicher Zweck würde so aber nicht recht deutlich."

232 See above, n. 216. For a different conception of such details in pictorial scenes, see Kanawati (2009).

233 In respect to the monumental Late Period tombs of the Asasif necropolis, Einaudi states: "On peut ainsi parler de « rhétorique de la tombe », où le mot « rhétorique » évoque une méthode de pensée et de communication comportant des aspects stylistiques et personnels : c'est l'art du discours ou de l'éloquence." Einaudi (2020: 25); cf. also Einaudi (2021: 319–321).

234 Cf. Assmann (1983: 67; 1987: 215). Assmann sees "tomb" and "name" as the two roots of the Egyptian funerary biography. In my understanding, however, the tomb as a built entity is itself also an exemplification of the owner's name, i.e. identity.

non-narrative matrix. Thus, the basic structure within which the biographical discourse is embedded may be imagined like this:

Statement	**Expressed through (e.g.)**
I am.	tomb/burial
I am X.	name inscription (with or without titles)
I am X, therefore Y.	typically an offering formula, addresses to the living etc.
I am X, therefore Y, because I have done Z.	biographical discourse in the widest sense
I am X, therefore Y, because I have done Z^1, Z^2, Z^3 etc.	generic and more particular exemplifications
I am X, therefore Y, because I have done Z^1, Z^2, Z^3 etc.	exemplification cascade

Z^a Z^b Z^c

What is commonly taken to be the evolution of the biographical textual formats/genres[235] in ancient Egypt (the Z in the table above) could also be considered as the formation of different exemplification strategies, pertaining equally to textual units as to the diverse repertoire of iconotexts. For example, the tomb owner's watching of his subordinates as they engage in activities of accounting or the like is an appropriate instantiation of narrative exemplification, even if the activities do not transcend the realm of (idealised) daily routine. What such scenes do is encode societal norms and values in more or less particularised vignettes of life, which may be narratively enriched through contextual information during the reception process. Biographical texts in a narrower sense play a very similar structural role, even if their topics do not regularly overlap with the rest of the tomb's iconotext. While the structural configuration as such is remarkably stable across the centuries, the linearly construed typology of exemplification strategies does not imply an equally linear pattern in the development of modes of biographical discourse that would have seen a constant sophistication from simple title strings via generic ideal biographies to elaborate event biographies. As in-depth studies by Stauder-Porchet and others have shown,[236] the formation of the biographical text genres in non-royal tombs was a complex and multi-faceted process which cannot be attributed solely to a desire to elaborate exemplification strategies. That said, however, if narrative or narrativity-inducing features occur, they fulfil the structural role of exemplifying a person's socially conceived grounds for entitlement to a permanent existence within the general communicative framework of the tomb: "I have excelled in amplifying my conforming to existing norms of elite society for the specified reasons (*exempla virtutis*). Therefore I am entitled to attaining the

235 For this distinction see Vernus (2020: 163–164).

236 Stauder-Porchet (2010; 2016; 2017; 2020a); Eyre (2019); Baud (2005); Kloth (2002); Gnirs (1996).

status of an *imakhu* (and that of an *akh*), and my funerary cult ought to be maintained." In certain biographical texts dating to the late Old Kingdom the *exemplification principle* is made transparent, e.g., where narrative episodes attributable to the event biography genre interchange with phraseology typical of the ideal biography.[237] The reason is that both text types occupy similar structural slots within the meta-discourse.

In my opinion, the link between exemplification and justification is inscribed in the discourse of life writing in ancient Egypt from earliest times. Therefore, I do not take it as a late aberration when – like in the case of the architrave inscription of Mehu from Saqqara (Teti cemetery, 6th Dynasty)[238] – phraseology of the ideal biography repertoire is embedded in an offering formula also incorporating a reference to the addressees of the tomb inscription. This configuration simply lays bare the underlying argumentative structure of the communication. A similar situation can be observed for the pillar inscription of Hetepherniptah (Cairo JE 15048), whose dating on stylistic grounds is somewhat debated (late 3rd to mid–late 5th Dynasty; the latter seems more likely).[239] In the inscription of four columns, each ending with Hetepherniptah's name, a long sequence of titles is followed by a narrative vignette in which the royal favour of granting the tomb owner a sedan chair with carriers is mentioned.[240] This short passage, which may be a condensed version of a lengthier narrative account, clearly has a structural relation to the preceding strings of titles and offices, acting as a narrative exemplification of Hetepherniptah's position at the royal court.[241] On the other hand, this bricolage of direct and indirect narrative components suggests an active modulation of the conventions governing the biographical meta-discourse.[242] In this regard it is interesting to observe that by the end of the Old Kingdom at the latest the biographical discourse had indeed become self-reflective. Not only was the veracity of genre conventions commented upon (cf. the evocation of "the discourse on offices of the necropolis"; see n. 60). As Vernus has pointed out,[243] also particular phraseology of the *ideal biography* genre could be made the subject of a meta-discourse seemingly infused with parodistic intent. In the 6th Dynasty rock-cut tomb of Ibi at Deir el-Gebrawi a four-part scene in the northern half of the west wall devoted to the accoun-

---

237 For example in the inscription of Sabni II at Qubbet el-Hawa (QH 35e), where the account of an expedition to Nubia is interspersed with more generic phraseology of the ideal biography repertoire, with a compact ideal biography following suit. See Edel (2008b: 817–818, Text 55); Strudwick (2005: 339–340, no. 244); Roccati (1982: 214–215, § 204).

238 Hawass (2002); Stauder-Porchet (2017: 195–196).

239 Sethe (1933: 231, no. 6 [146]); Helck (1954: 111–112); Baud & Farout (2001: 47–48; 56, Fig. 2); Kloth (2003); Stauder-Porchet (2017: 37 w. n. 5).

240 *Pace* Stauder-Portchet (2017: 37, n. 5) one should note that the inscription does not contain an offering formula. Rather, the signs 𓇓𓏙 denote a perfective relative form construction dependent on the preceding sequence of name and titles, as was already pointed out by Sethe (1933: 231, n. f-f) and Baud & Farout (2001: 47, n. 25). Later, Baud (2005: 109 w. n. 57) opted to interpret *(r)dj* rather as a perfective *sḏm=f*.

241 See also Baud (2005: 107–110).

242 At least if the monument indeed dates from the 5th Dynasty, as Stauder-Porchet (2017: 37) argues.

243 Vernus (2015).

tability topic depicts a man being beaten by officials for some misdemeanour.[244] While such scenes occur in other tombs as well, the particular speech caption attributed to the offender, an overseer of the herds named Rensi, deserves attention. The words put in his mouth read as follows:[245]

[1]| ← *jnk mr(jj) ḫꜣ(w)* [a] ? [2]| ↓ *ḫb[ḏ n] nb=f* [3]| *kn.t n ḥnw.t=f* [4]| *msḏḏ zꜣ.w-pr nb=f*	[1]| I am one beloved of the measurer (?), [2]| one loath[some to] his lord, [3]| a displeasure to his mistress, [4]| whom the watchmen (lit.: "sons of the house") of his lord detest.

a) While Vernus' (2015: 312–313, n. a) arguments for reading the sign  as *ḫꜣw* are robust, I would not rule out the possibility that the passage should be understood as *mrj ḫꜣ*, "one who loves a thousand (i.e. great quantity)" with active perfective participle and the numeral 1,000. It could ironically hint at an act of misappropriation by Rensi. Alternatively, 1,000 could refer to the number of blows with the baton that Rensi has to endure. For the latter interpretation see Grunert (2022).

Vernus regards Rensi's "confession" as a sort of sketch playing with the conventions of the biographical genre for parodistic effect.[246] Working at two levels simultaneously, it not only presents the appropriation of the (auto)biographic discourse by a subordinate figure[247] but also conveys deliberately distorted versions of this discourse by turning common elite values upside down. In so doing, the "intervention of *appogiature*" in Ibi's tomb also communicates on a third level. It points to the fact that what is being narrated in biographical texts (not restricted to the genre of ideal biography) relates primarily to a social role model rather than to a human being endowed with irreducible individuality.[248] Tellability is conditioned upon the plane of a rhetorically constituted genre. What provides Rensi with personhood (irrespective of whether factual or fictional) is not his self-characterisation but his name and filiation.

3 Biography, memoir, autofiction: genres and modes of life writing from different narratological perspectives

3.1 The terminological maze

Having looked at the basic structural framework of the ancient Egyptian biographical discourse, it now seems in place to undertake some forays into the terminological maze

---

244 Davies (1902: Pl. VIII); Kanawati (2007: Pl. 50).

245 Based on Vernus' (2015: 312–315) rendering. See also Yoyotte (1953: 144–145, no. 7); Fischer (1976: 9; 11–12 w. Fig. 3).

246 Vernus (2015: 316–318). He also provides further examples from Old Kingdom tomb scenes.

247 A case of a system-referential intertextuality. Cf. n. 28 above.

248 Cf. Luhmann (2008: 156): "Die Höherwertigkeit [i.e. of the amplified communication; C.J.] war in der allgemeineren Form aufgehoben, weil nur so, nur durch sachlich-zeitlich-soziale Generalisierungen, die Kommunikation verstärkt werden konnte, und das Individuelle des Einzelfalls, des Einzelobjekts, der Situation, der Biographie blieb bloß akzidentieller Anlaß der Kommunikation."

connected with narrating the life of a factual human being. Let us thus briefly consider the theoretical context of the use of terms such as "biography", "autobiography", "life writing", and others within the different strands of narratology. As will be no surprise, such terms and the concepts they represent are far from being unequivocal or unproblematic and are consequently not unanimously agreed upon within the discipline. Nevertheless, they help to stake out the field of discussion and provide invaluable signposts for the honing of the terminological toolkit.

In this regard, "biography" is certainly the best-known and most widely used word. As a technical term, "biography", the "writing of *a* life", – designating both the process and the finished product – goes back to late antique Greek *βιογραφία*, whereas in classical antiquity the meaning "(written) history of a life" was encompassed in the words for "life" itself, thus *βίος* in Greek and *vita* in Latin.[249]

In modern days, the common-language definition found in the *Oxford English Dictionary* identifies biography as a "written account of the life of an individual, esp. a historical or public figure".[250] More specifically, the tenets of classical narratology maintain that a biography is a specific (predominantly) nonfictional literary genre taking the form of a self-contained unit of oral or (more often) written text.[251] It usually portrays a particular person's life in a comprehensive and multi-faceted fashion, providing insight not only into the what, when, and where of that life but also into the how and why. Personal attitudes, thoughts, aspirations, and illusions often figure prominently in such accounts, since it is the aim of the biographer also to shed light on the psychological disposition of the biographed as a token of their irreducible individuality.[252] At the same time, biographers seek to tame the alterity and complexity of their subject matter by imposing a(n often chronological) sense of order and enhance the potential of the account's main protagonist to appear as a relatable character. In the words of Fludernik, "[t]elling other people's lives (...) works by constructing uniformity and consistency on the basis of a mass of recalcitrant material."[253] Similar considerations apply to the genre of *auto*biography, where biographer and biographed are usually taken to be identical (see below). But there exist many other, perhaps less salient, terms associated with the biographical discourse;[254] among them *life narrative*, *life (his)story*, *biofiction*, *autofiction*, *memoir*, *res gestae*, and *life writing*. In their current, quite variable usages, these terms fall short of providing a neat typological framework for studying texts centred on specific factual persons regardless of a composition's geographical origin and time of creation. Rather, the terms referred to tend to reflect the historical development of the biographical genre in Western literary culture and are not always easy to apply when dealing with non-European traditions of

249 See Temmerman (2020: 7–8). Probably best exemplified through Plutarch's *Βίοι παράλληλοι* and Sueton's *De vita caesarum*.

250 OED (2022a).

251 Cf. Hoberman (2001).

252 Mutatis mutandum for the autobiography. Lejeune (1975: 14).

253 Fludernik (2007: 262).

254 In 2001, Smith and Watson (2001: 183–207) presented a list of 52 terms referring in their view to different genres and sub-genres of what they call "life narrative".

text production. Notwithstanding these limitations, some of the terms can be usefully ordered using four axes of differentiation:[255] the *fictional–factual* spectrum, the *literary–non-literary* spectrum, the opposition *heterodiegetic–homodiegetic* (with all its caveats) and the differentiation between *holistic* and *selective* (Fig. 6).

Thus, while autobiography, in its normal conceptualisation, bears the attributes "factual", "auto/homodiegetic"[256] and "holistic", the term autofiction usually refers to texts that are more selective in the material they present and where the pendulum swings overtly in the direction of fictionality. Memoires and res gestae are equally selective in that they deal primarily or even exclusively with a person's official role in society, but they differ in terms of their potential diegetic configuration. While memoirs are by convention homodiegetic (at least as long as one disregards any role of ghostwriters or posthumous editors), res gestae may but need not be authored by the very subject of the account (Augustus' *Res gestae* are a prime example for the identity of implied author and narrated protagonist). In certain strands of literary criticism and narratology, the whole range of the biographical discourse is subsumed under the umbrella term *life writing*,[257] which in its openness and versatility fosters interdisciplinary dialogue and will therefore also be adopted here (more or less synonymously with the "biographical discourse"). In its broadest sense, *life writing* also encompasses *ego-documents* of a purely non-literary nature such as letters, personal diaries, contracts etc.[258] The reader should bear in mind, however, that in other schools of thought, *life writing* is used exclusively for autodiegetic life accounts such as autobiography and memoir, and has thus a much narrower scope of meaning.[259]

Another important term, which has gained wide currency within Egyptology after its introduction there by Morenz in 2003[260] and independently by Baines in 2004,[261] is *self-presentation*.[262] It designates ego-documents created for public display within the monumental discourse and relates to textual as well as to visual modes of communication. For Baines, the term *self-presentation* has many advantages over the conventional designations *biography* and *autobiography*, because self-presentations "encompassed visual media at least as much as textual ones and because the visual and the textual existed in a social context that must have included ceremonies and performances in which a person's self was presented."[263] Baines' integrational view has the merit of working against isolating texts from images/iconotexts, and against separating both groups from the performative context which imbued them with concrete meaning. However, when the narrative

255 Cf. the less complex model found at Jeannelle (2008: 13).

256 For the differentiation between *auto-* and *homo-*, see Chapter 3.3.

257 E.g. Jolly (2001: ix); Besemeres & Perkins (2004).

258 Cf. Fludernik & Ryan (2020: 13).

259 Cf., e.g., Eakin (2020: 41; 66–67).

260 Morenz (2003: 186–187).

261 Baines (2004: 34–36). For a discussion see Jurman (2020, Vol. I: 11–12). The concept as such is of course much older. For its significance within narratology cf. De Fina & Georgakopoulou (2012: 168).

262 Cf., e.g., the subtitle of Bassir's (2019) edited volume "Living Forever: Self-Presentation in Ancient Egypt".

263 Baines (2004: 34–35). See also Baines (2020: 76–77).

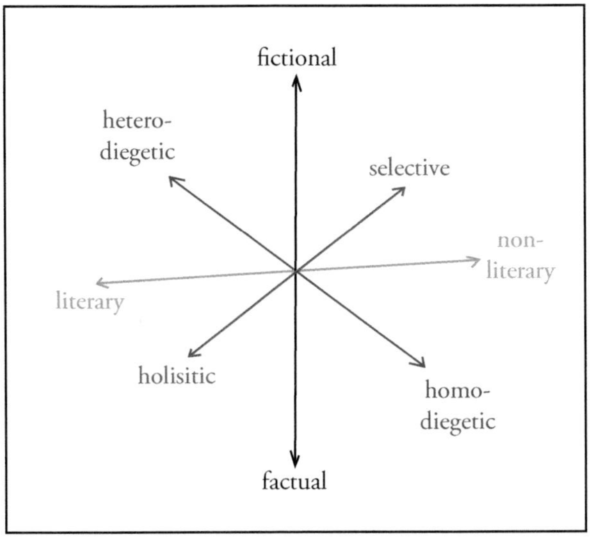

Fig. 6 Four-dimensional axis of life writing in classical narratology

dimension of a *self-presentation* is taken into view, the terms *life writing* and *biographical discourse* are to be preferred, since they better convey that a certain spatial configuration of textual and visual signs succeeds in creating a storyworld centred on a single individual (in our case, usually the tomb owner).

3.2 Demarcations of life writing

While "biographical discourse" is a conveniently vague expression which can easily extend to the entirety of a funerary ensemble, the pertinent question in Egyptology is whether it makes sense also to use more concrete terms such as *biography* or *autobiography*, and if yes, to what units of analysis they respectively apply. Do they represent particular text genres sharply delineated from other genres present in the tomb? Or are they to be equated with the tomb's biographical meta-narrative to which a host of different communicative elements contribute (among them the text genres *ideal biography* and *event biography*)? This closely correlates with the question of whether *biography*, within the context of an Egyptian tomb, is primarily a self-contained unit of inscription placed in a particular part of the funerary ensemble, or whether "text" has to be understood in a much wider sense to incorporate all forms of communication mediated by the materiality of the tomb and its decoration (thus semiotic *text*).[264] In a second step one has to ask what precisely is *auto-* in the autobiographical discourse of Egyptian tombs and how biographical authorship can be conceptualised. Finally, one should consider where autobiographical narratives of the Old Kingdom are positioned in relation to the fictional–factual axis. Before addressing these

264 For this semiotic understanding of *text*, see Lotman (1977: 50–56). Within Egyptology, a comparable use of the term "text" is adopted by Davis (1992: 236 and *passim*) and Kutscher (2020: 84). The latter chooses to designate this usage by small capitals as TEXT.

question in a number of case studies, let us first briefly consider classical and postclassical narratological approaches to *autobiography*.

In light of its epistemic evolution it comes as little surprise that classical narratology considers autobiography predominantly as a literary text genre. In her survey of narratological approaches to autobiography, Schwalm represents the orthodox view as follows:

> "More specifically, autobiography as a literary genre signifies a retrospective narrative that undertakes to tell the author's own life, or a substantial part of it, seeking (at least in its classic version) to reconstruct his/her personal development within a given historical, social and cultural framework. While autobiography on the one hand claims to be non-fictional (factual) in that it proposes to tell the story of a 'real' person, it is inevitably constructive, or imaginative, in nature and as a form of textual 'self-fashioning' ultimately resists a clear distinction from its fictional relatives (autofiction, autobiographical novel), leaving the generic borderlines blurred."[265]

Acknowledging that the coherence of autobiographical storytelling is by nature constructive and no faithful rendition of the ontological reality of a lived life opens up the perspective to regard all attempts at making sense of one's existence and at creating a stable identity as forms of *life writing*.[266] This approach is probably best represented by the work of Bruner[267] and finds also reflection in more recent contributions to cognitive narratology. In Brockmeier's words,

> "[w]e start with a story, or more precisely, with a number of stories, or fragments or traces of stories because we are born into, grow up, and live in the midst of a world of narratives that—a point noted before—for the most part are not our own. In this world, an event, experience, memory, or a fact can only be understood as a segment cut out of a narrative web, a web that would exist even without my actively being involved in weaving it."[268]

If the narrative web surrounding one's self is all-encompassing, then one may ask where the autobiographical persona begins and where it ends, and by extension, where the "writing" of the persona has its demarcation. This seemingly abstract question is filled with concrete meaning when taking the autobiographical discourse of the ancient Egyptian funerary sphere into view. Depending on one's conception of an (auto)biographical text, the units of analysis will differ accordingly and will affect the analytical result. While the conventional philological approach to ancient Egyptian life writing was developed with self-contained, continuous[269] texts featuring third- or first-person narratives in mind, the

---

265 Schwalm (2014: § 1).

266 After all, identity is according to Hall (1992: 277) nothing but a narratively constituted construct.

267 E.g. Bruner (1990). Cf. De Fina & Georgakopoulou (2012: 160). For a critique of the "life is life writing" theory, which dwells on the level of conscious decision making, see Strawson (2015).

268 Brockmeier (2015: 181).

269 In the definition of Stauder-Porchet (2021b: 442), continuous texts are those "that display cohesion, integration, and hierarchies between clauses. (Under this definition, the difference between non-

archaeological record preserves many instances of text and image compositions where the units of narrative signification cannot be identified so easily. A broader understanding of "life writing" will often lead to a new evaluation of what constitutes an element of (auto)biographical narration in the second order. The crucial task in this regard is to identify syntactic and semantic *coherence* while bearing in mind that modern European modes of creating and maintaining coherence (e.g. signalled through paratextual markers such as genre specifications on book covers, formatting decisions, etc.[270]) may not apply to premodern and/or non-Western text production. Especially when it comes to assessing the potential integration/interaction of "pure" text (i.e. a seemingly isolated inscription) and iconotext in a complex spatial disposition, the concept of *coherence* as a culturally conditioned, potentially complex ordering principle has its merits.[271] In a multimodal composition such as an ancient Egyptian elite tomb (see Chapter 4), visual/spatial syntactic coherence often has implications for potential narrative coherence, since phenomena such as juxtaposition and spatial association of elements may imply a narrative connection not immediately apparent to modern viewers. But the more complex the semantic and syntactic relations become, the more they are open to variant ways of reading. The mere identification of a reasonable sequence in which different elements are to be viewed/read is often a frustrating task and cannot have been devoid of ambiguity in ancient times either. This does not mean, however, that narrativity requires linear sequentiality in order to emerge. Indeed, medieval studies and related philologically oriented disciplines have time and again drawn attention to the way in which premodern texts may create narrative coherence and use temporal referencing in unexpected ways.[272] A strict understanding of temporal sequentiality, according to which an element of narration cannot be generic and specific at the same time, may thus fall short of providing a suitable analytical framework to study Egyptian iconotexts from the funerary sphere.[273] If the perceived *récit* is a shape-shifting entity, then higher-order narrative constellations involving biographical inscriptions of any sort assume the character of "flip images", where a narrative reading is just one among several, not mutually exclusive options. This also means that multimodal life writing almost always transcends the strict sequentiality of spoken language and cannot simply be translated back to linear text.[274] Instead, it creates a narrative world of its own.[275] Such is the case with the Great Inscription on the west wall of the pillared hall in

continuous and continuous texts is one of degree: an additively patterned sequence of sentences, as for instance in Netjerikhet's Heliopolis shrine, does not qualify as fully continuous.)." She acknowledges, however (Stauder-Porchet 2017: 10), that there are other forms of coherence such as visual parataxis in decrees and non-royal legal texts.

270 Cf. Genette (1987).

271 For an Egyptological application, see Backes (2020: 541–560).

272 Cf., e.g., Schulz (2010), who has coined the term "fremde Kohärenz" (unfamiliar coherence) in connection with medieval storytelling; in a similar vein, Glauch (2010); see also Knape (2013: 153).

273 Cf. Baines's (2015a: 40) comment on earlier judgements on coherence of biographical texts.

274 For similar conclusions, see also Stauder-Porchet (2021b: 451).

275 This ties in with the notion that writing as well as imagery constitute particular ways of "speaking" and "seeing" not reducible to experiences of daily life. See Fitzenreiter (2017: 185–190).

the mastaba tomb of Akhtihotep Hemi/Nebkauhor Idu at Saqqara (time of Unas or early 6th Dynasty).[276] The unfortunately badly preserved inscription comprises two juxtaposed texts facing each other. While the text on the left-hand side is a legal deed with stipulations for the funerary priests, the text to the right has more similarities with a composition of the ideal biography genre; a composition, however, with a highly unusual textual layout featuring horizontal "headings" and split columns much like the facing legal text.[277] Both texts are thus referring to each other via proximity and inscriptional design. They are also thematically linked inasmuch as the biographical text names those ethical qualities and official comportment that are the theoretical prerequisite for the public acknowledgement of the stipulations recorded to the left. The "ideal biography" and the legal text are thus interdependent and, together, form a meta-narrative of which provisioning for the hereafter and taking care of the continuation of the funerary cult are integral parts. The biographical text captures this relation quite well when the tomb owner states: [12]| *jnk ḏd jnk jrj jnk sḫꜣ(w)* [...] [13]| *jn ꜥšꜣ.t*, "I was one who spoke, I was one who acted, I was one who was remembered [...] by the multitude."[278] Utterance, action, and remembrance are precisely evidenced by the act of drafting and recording the stipulations to the left. That is not to say that the latter had no signification outside the narrative frame. Rather to the contrary, their long-term significance as a testimony of juridical obligations imbues them with the power also to perpetuate a part of the tomb owner's life story. Should the fragmentary inscription found by Hassan in the debris close to the tomb's façade,[279] which preserves part of an event biography, belong to the same official as does the Great Inscription,[280] the mastaba's narrative discourse would become even more complex.

Let us look at one further example, this time without any outrightly biographical text. A well-known scene in the rock-cut mastaba complex of Wepemneferet and his relatives (Giza, Central Field, G 8882, second half of 5th Dynasty) represents the juridical act of transferring funerary property to Wepemneferet's eldest son Ibi.[281] This is done through showing proprietor and beneficiary in the moment of concluding the legal act as well as through providing a monumental copy of what must have originally been a decree on

---

276 The date and ownership of the inscription have been debated. Whereas Hassan (1975: 5) and Kloth (2002: 22, no. 42) maintain that it commemorates Nebkauhor Idu, who would have reused the mastaba of Akhtihotep Hemi during the early 6th Dynasty, Strudwick (2005: 261–262, no. 195) and Stauder-Porchet (2017: 214; 2021b: 443, n. 4) are more cautious in their assessments and consider the possibility that the carving of the Great Inscription took place still under Akhtihotep Hemi.

277 Hassan (1975: 38–44 w. Figs. 17–18, Pls. XXVI–XXX).

278 One should note that the absolute time reference of the perfective participle is unspecific. Therefore, the phrases could also be translated in present simple tense.

279 Hassan (1975: 60–61, Pl. LI A). See also Kloth (2002: 4, no. 03); Strudwick (2005: 262, no. 195 B).

280 According to Hassan (1975: 61), the inscription was originally carved for Akhtihotep and was later reused by Nebkauhor.

281 For a detailed analysis of this scene in terms of its multimodal signification, see Kutscher (2020: 93–105).

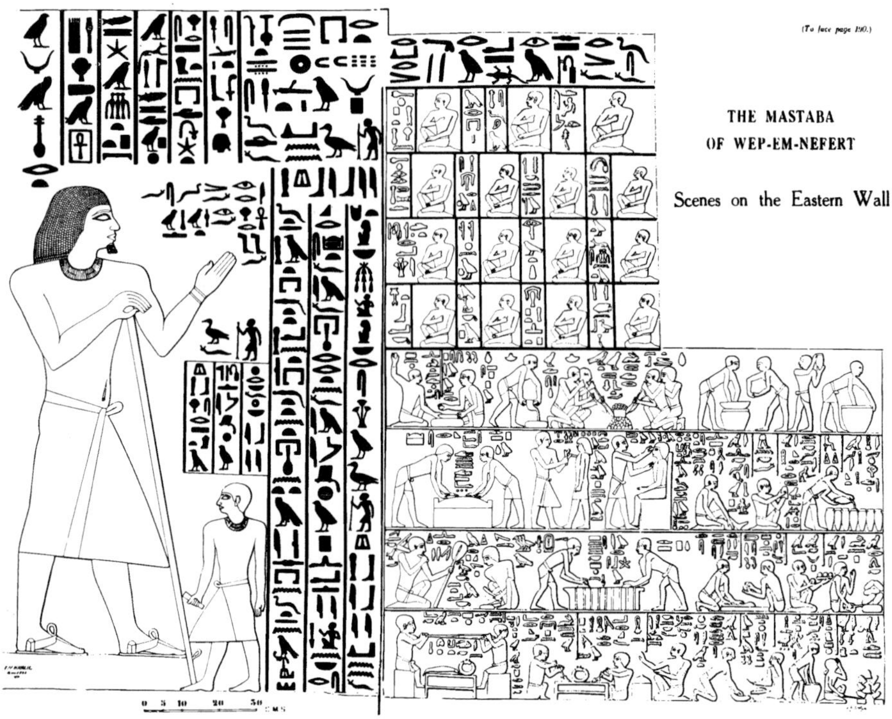

Fig. 7 Scenes on the eastern wall of the tomb chapel of Wepemneferet at Giza (G 8882), after Hassan (1936: foldout facing p. 190).

papyrus (Fig. 7).[282] The scene is found on the east wall of the funerary chapel of Ibi, which in contrast to his father's was clad with fine limestone blocks. The composition in raised relief comprises a large-scale depiction of Wepemneferet facing right and standing on what must be a mat,[283] his right hand resting on a staff while his left arm is positioned in a speech or presentation gesture.[284] On a much smaller scale and on a level below him, one finds the depiction of his eldest son Ibi facing his father. Both figures are each provided with an identifying caption in sunk relief:

|[1] ↓ *smr wꜥtj ḥrj-tp Nḫb* |[2] *ḥrj-sštꜣ nj pr dwꜣ.t* |[3] *ḥm-nṯr Ḥr Jnpw ꜥḏ-mr Dpw* |[4] *ꜥḏ-mr sbꜣ Ḥr ḫntj p.t* |[5] *ḫrp ꜥḥ ḥrj-wḏb m pr-ꜥnḫ* |[6] *Wp-m-nfr.t*

|[1] Sole companion, leader of Nekheb, |[2] master of secrets of the morning house, |[3] prophet of Horus and Anubis, administrator of Buto, administrator of "Star of Horus, foremost of heaven", director of the palace, overseer of the distribution of food in the house of life, Wepemneferet.

282 Hassan (1936: 190–199 w. Fig. 219; Pls. LXXIV–LXXVI); Goedicke (1970: 31–43; esp. 32–33); Fitzenreiter (2004: 19–21).

283 The front end of the mat seems to be rolled in. I am grateful to Ľubica Hudáková for discussing the iconography with me.

284 For this standard gesture, see Dominicus (1994: 77–80).

|[1] ↓ *zꜣ=f smsw* |[2] *ẖrj-hꜣb ḥrj-sštꜣ* |[3] *zšw mḏꜣ.t-nṯr jmꜣḫw* |[4] *ḫr nb=f rꜥ nb Jbjj*	|[1] His eldest son, |[2] the lector priest and master of secrets, |[3] scribe of the divine book, an *imakhu* before his lord daily, Ibi.

As a hieroglyphic note positioned above Wepemneferet's left hand explicates, the tomb owner is depicted in the moment of putting into force the legal document, a *wḏ.t-mdw*, whose more or less faithful copy in hieroglyphs in sunk relief is represented opposite the two figures. The text[285] reads:

|[1] ← *jr(jj) r gs=f ḏs=f* |[2] *ꜥnḫ(.w) ḥr rd.wj=f(j)* |[3] *jrj=f wḏ.t-mdw*	|[1] Made in his own presence, |[2] while he was (still) living on his two feet. |[3] He made the decree.

The document itself is introduced by a dating formula (cf. Chapter 5.3) and the obligatory quotation statement *ḏd=f*:

|[1] ↓ *rnp.t smꜣ-tꜣ.wj ꜣbd 3 pr.t sw 29* |[2] → *smr-wꜥtj Wp* |[3] *ḏd=f dj.n(=j) n zꜣ(=j) smsw* |[3] *ẖrj-ḥꜣb Jbjj* |[4] ↓ *ḏ.t(=j) ḥꜣ.t mḥtj.t ḥnꜥ jz.t mḥtj.t nj.t prj.t-ḫrw ntj.t m jz nj ḏ.t(=j) nj ẖr.t-nṯr* |[5] *ḳrs.t(j)=f jm=f prr.t ḫrw n=f jm jmꜣḫw pw n ꜥjj sn(=j) nb (j)r=s* |[6] *ḥm.t(=j) nb(.t) ms.w(=j) nb (j)r=s ḥꜣw zꜣ(=j) smsw ẖrj-ḥꜣb Jbjj dj.n(=j) n=f*	|[1] Year of the unification of the two lands, third month of Peret, day 29: |[2] The sole companion Wep, |[3] he said: "(I) am (herewith) giving to (my) eldest son, |[3] the lector priest Ibi, |[4] my funerary estate, (more precisely,) the northern burial shaft together with the northern funerary chapel, which are in the tomb of (my) funerary estate of the necropolis. |[5] That he shall be buried therein and that the funerary offering shall be taking place for him is because he is an *imakhu*. No brother (collateral relative) (of mine), no wife (of mine) and no children (of mine) shall have any claim to it with the exception of (my) eldest son, the lector priest Ibi, for *to him* I have given it.

A table of witnesses, in which each one is represented by his name and a figural icon, follows further to the right. The 15 figures are headed by the following label:

→ *rḏj r gs mtr.w ꜥšꜣ(.w) jrj m zš r gs=f ḏs=f*	(Statement) given in the presence of many witnesses. Put in writing in his (i.e. Wepemneferet's) own presence.

Below the table of witnesses we see a separate scene in four registers showing craftsmen engaged in the production of funerary equipment and offerings. These figures and their captions are again executed in raised relief, as are the witnesses above them.

The whole composition is remarkable for a number of reasons. First, it represents a particular and significant event in the "life" (see below) of both Wepemneferet and Ibi, whose high level of tellability is underlined by the size of the composition as well as the fact that it directly quotes from a legal ego-document.[286] The scene's ontological status

285 Statements such as this are quite common within decrees and posthumous authorisation notes. See, e.g., the similar case in the funerary decree of Kaemneferet: Goedicke (1970: 44, Pl. V).

286 By their nature, quotations always have a signalling function.

could be called hybrid, since the list of witnesses included in the original papyrus document is metalepticly represented on the wall through images of the participants in order to suggest that the men are indeed present in the scene's storyworld. The scene is also interrelated with its environment. While the four registers depicting the production of funerary equipment belong to a different point in space and time than the rest of the composition, they are inextricably linked with the legal act through a semantic connection.[287] The transfer of funerary property and Ibi's *imakh* status imply his provision with appropriate quantities of funerary goods, so that their production is the logical consequence of Wepemneferet's deed. Finally, the scene's placement within the very funerary chapel mentioned in the document ties the depicted event to the physical reality of the tomb complex and acts like a comment on the stages preceding and following upon the actual burial.[288] Whereas the composition's individual texts and images on their own bear only limited narrative potential, they become charged with narrative meaning when being integrated into a holistic view. Then, the wall develops its full narrative potential and tells about the transfer of property and its protagonists, the act's implications and its consequences. From this point of view, we are indeed entitled to speak of a biographical episode or narrative vignette, where narration – the act of telling – is not only alluded to but explicitly staged. Of course, the telling of the legal act has an objective transcending the storyworld, namely, to present the stipulations as fait accompli following from a natural course of events.

3.3 The *auto-* in autobiography

Since it was not the norm to reinforce an heir's claim to his father's burial complex through the reproduction of legal documents within the tomb, we can only speculate about Wepemneferet's and/or Ibi's motivation. Wepemneferet together with his son may have ordered the artisans working on the tomb to commemorate this important moment of the past in order to serve as an unchallengeable testimony in the face of family strife or comparable problems. In the case of a premature death of Ibi, as suggested by Perepelkin,[289] the scene's status as a factual representation of a real event in the lives of the two main protagonists would become dubious, however. It may also be that it was Wepemneferet who died prematurely. In that case Ibi might have wanted to secure his rights to the tomb against potential other claimants.[290] Wepemneferet's speech act would then have been transmitted (or fabricated) posthumously under the auspices of his son. Since Wepemneferet is clearly the main protagonist of the composition, we would be facing a biographical rather than an *auto*biographical vignette. But the matter is more complex, for even if Wepemneferet had still been alive at the time the relief was created, the lack of a first-person pronoun outside of the decree would not necessarily indicate that the scene's narrator has to be differentiated from the main protagonist. One should bear

---

287 This would also apply in the case that the four registers had been carved prior to the creation of the scene with the decree, as maintained by Perepelkin (1986: 155–156).

288 While the built tomb *jz nj ḏ.t(=j)* implies past actions, the future is represented through the wish (= legal stipulation) that Ibi may be buried therein and receive his funerary cult.

289 Perepelkin (1986: 148–157, esp. 156).

290 Cf. Goedicke (1970: 32).

in mind in this regard that Wepemneferet's recitation of the content of the legal document features an introductory *ḏd=f* in the third person before the text switches to the first person. Through these means Wepemneferet impersonates on an intradiegetic level an unspecified hypodiegetic narrator typical of formal ego-documents such as letters and decrees.[291] This acts as a reminder that a similar complexity could be governing the textualisation at the highest diegetic level. As will be further discussed in Chapter 6.1, voice is indeed not the most reliable indicator when trying to identify autodiegetic narration within the ancient Egyptian textual universe and differentiate between biographical, autobiographical, and allobiographical[292] discourse. Is it then appropriate to use the term "autobiography" at all for ancient Egyptian life writing? And if so, only for those texts voiced in the first person? To address this question, let us briefly look at the wider narratological context.

According to Genette's classification of narrative configurations, a typical autobiography would be autodiegetic (implying the asserted identity between author, narrator and narrated main protagonist[293]) as well as extradiegetic (implying that the main narrative level and the act of narration lie outside the narrated story).[294] The first criterion seems to presuppose that autobiographical discourse is linked to first-person narratives, where narrating "I" and narrated "I" intersect and overlap. However, Genette himself acknowledges that autobiographical narration is not thus restricted and can equally be represented by non-first-person voices. One of the best known examples of the latter is probably Caesar's autobiographical account of the wars in Gaule (*Commentarii de bello Gallico*), where the transparent and consistent use of third-person voice may be nothing but an *énallage*,[295] a mere conventionalised stand-in for a first person voice chosen perhaps to reconcile the claim to objectivity with "subjective authenticity".[296] One may therefore be entitled, thus Genette,[297] to regard the text as purely homodiegetic (i.e. presupposing the identity between narrator and narrated protagonist) and ultimately as autodiegetic (presupposing also the identity between author and narrated protagonist). This example shows that there is a wide field for interpretation opening up when analysing narrative voicing. The traditional claim that in a first-person autobiographical narrative author, narrator, and narrated protagonist coincide[298] whereas they cannot do the same in a third-person narrative is nowadays hard to defend. Indeed, Genette's foundational distinction between autodiegetic, homodiegetic, and heterodiegetic narration, which is based on the triadic relation between author, narrator, and narrated subject, has been problematised in light of contemporary literary practice and the insights of unnatural narratology.[299] It is not surprising then that its explanatory

291 Cf. Strudwick (2005: 175–207); Goedicke (1970: *passim*); Helck (1974b: 117–123).

292 Gnirs (1996: 196). With reference to Genette (1991: 80), Gnirs uses the term allobiography to designate ancient Egyptian biographical texts that are voiced in the first person but were certainly not authored by their main protagonists. See now also the comprehensive discussion in Vernus (2020).

293 Cf. also Lejeune (1975: 15–19).

294 Genette (1972: 254–259; 1991: 82–83).

295 For this term see Genette (1991: 87).

296 Riggsby (2006: 149); Schmid (2011: 133).

297 Genette (1991: 81).

298 Lejeune (1975: 19–21).

299 Richardson (2006: 10).

power has equal limitations as far as non-Western or premodern textual traditions are concerned.[300] As pointed out by Vernus, there are numerous cases where Egyptian autobiographical discourse in the nominal style (classifying predication) switches grammatical reference from first-person subject to third-person subject without implying a switch in the logical referent.[301] From here it is only a small step to assume that a switch of grammatical reference could have been implemented from a text's very beginning without resorting to the initial first-person anchoring of *jnk* or *jrj.n=j*.[302] Another problem with Genette's model is that it does not factor in the potentially important distinction between the actual author of a composition and the *implied author*, an "author-image evoked by a work and constituted by the stylistic, ideological, and aesthetic properties for which indexical signs can be found in the text."[303] In general, the majority of texts/iconotexts belonging to the Egyptian monumental discourse give the impression that their conception and design, though not necessarily their material execution, originated with the tomb owner, whether this be actually the case or not (see also the following Chapter 3.4). As has already been mentioned, a scene where the tomb owner is represented painting a part of his own tomb decoration (see p. 108) can hardly be understood in any other way. On the other hand, we have ample evidence for the practice that a descendant/relative of the tomb owner was responsible for finishing a tomb and/or its decoration and made sure to commemorate this intervention in hieroglyphic writing.[304] A representative case of this practice is found on the inner frame of the false door niche of Kainefer (now BM EA 1324, probably late 5th Dynasty) from his mastaba tomb in Dahshur.[305] There, his lengthy titulary, divided into two parts to cover the upper sections of each of the jambs, is followed by the statement: *jr nw jn zꜣ=f smsw rḫ-nswt Kꜣ-wꜥb jrj* [*n jtj=f*] *sk sw m jmnt.t ḫpj n kꜣ=f*, "What regards this (i.e. the tomb or the false door), it is his eldest son, the royal acquaintance Kawab who acted [for his father], because he is now in the West, having joined his ka."[306] Kawab is indeed depicted on the middle panels of the false door as a subordinate figure standing in front of his father's legs, but the statement about his involvement in the tomb's completion is put in the mouth of an unspecified narrator, who may or may not be equated with either of the false door's two main protagonists. As already observed by Lejeune,[307] grammatical person on its own is no reliable indicator of narratorial identity, nor of authorship. Lacking intimate knowledge of the original context and the *Sitz im Leben* of these texts,[308] we are thus struggling to provide an authoritative narratological model of their diegetic configuration and the opera-

300 Cf., e.g., Balmes (2018: esp. 29); Glauch (2010).

301 Vernus (2020: 166).

302 This is probably what Vernus (2020: 189) refers to as "overcoding", "transgressing the basic tenet of the code", although he restricts this analytical approach to the third-person (auto)biography of Samut son of Kyky.

303 Schmid (2014b: 1).

304 See Alexanian (2006: 2).

305 See Morgan (1903: 22–23, Pl. XXVI); James (1961: 10, Pl. X, 1); Gundacker (2006: 153–158; 455, Fig. 36a).

306 This phraseology is well-known from inscriptions relating to the construction of the tomb. Cf. Strudwick (2005: 239–250); Alexanian (2006: 2).

307 Lejeune (1975: 17; 19).

308 For some forays into a better understanding, see Gnirs (1996: 220–223); Baines (1999a: 36–37; 2020: 53–55); cf. also Kloth (2018: 7–13).

tions necessary to decode it. Out of pragmatic considerations, it is usually assumed that the tomb owner's heir had a significant influence on the final configuration of the tomb, including its biographical iconotext. Thus, Baines writes:

> "Since the dead do not bury themselves, the deceased's heirs contribute decisively to a biography's final realization, both in the funerary ceremonies and often in the composition and inscription of tomb decoration (it cannot be known what proportion of biographies was commissioned during a protagonist's lifetime or after his death—the latter was probably the more frequent case)."[309]

Baines and others also consider it likely that the Old Kingdom biographical discourse in the traditional, narrow sense (e.g. the event biographies voiced in the third or the first person) derives from oral performances during the funerary rituals,[310] where the son or a descendant would lend his voice to a posthumously drawn up text commemorating the deceased. Such a scenario reminds of the tradition of *miroloi* (*μοιρολόι* or *μοιρολόγια*), biographical ballads sung in certain parts of (pre-)modern Greece at funerals.[311] According to this view, the switch from third-person narrative to first-person narrative, which took place around the middle of the 5th Dynasty, could represent a strategy aiming at the literalisation of the biographical genre and a wish to detach it from a recourse to lived practice,[312] thus resulting in a *de-mimetisation*, so to speak. But there remain problems with this model. As of yet, we do not possess any unequivocal evidence pointing to the existence of a "biographical performance" conducted at a person's funeral, which would later have been rephrased, condensed and adapted to a monumental inscriptional layout. In contrast, thanks to the research of Stauder-Porchet it has become clearer in recent years that a different kind of discourse made itself felt when life writing entered the phase of being cast in lengthy inscriptions with continuous text.[313] Official events, declarations and performances at court, where royal speech acts formed the single most important component, are likely to have played an important part in the formation of the event biography genre during the first half of the 5th Dynasty. After all, it is the staging of royal speech that takes so much room in texts such as those of Niankhsakhmet or Werre.[314] Over time, the focus would shift to how officials received formalised royal praise for their accomplishments. This *ḥzj*-logos was put into writing at the behest of the king and often features explicitly or implicitly his voice, while the tomb owner as the receiver of the praise remains largely passive. Accordingly, these early "biographical" texts (Stauder-Porchet refers to them as royal texts within non-royal tombs) do not represent a first-person narrative, even though royal and non-royal speech (probably via recourse to official

---

309 Baines (1999a: 25).

310 Gnirs (1996: 220); Baines (1999a: 36; 1999b: 29; 2013: 239–241; 2020: 76); Reintges (2011: 29); for critical remarks see Dorman (2002: 105); Jansen-Winkeln (2004: 72); Eyre (2013: 122–123 w. n. 74); Vernus (2020: 180 w. n. 70).

311 Cf. Kosoglou et al. (2016).

312 See Gnirs (1996: 220); Reintges (2011: 29).

313 Stauder-Porchet (2011; 2016: 585–586; 2017: 71–73; 225–226; 2021a).

314 Stauder-Porchet (2017: 72–73; 157–165; 2020a: 110–111: 2021a; 2021c).

documents) may be quoted directly.[315] But even if substantial parts of the wording of these texts should have been taken over from court performances or royal documents, the mere fact that they were included in the tomb and afforded a prominent position within its decorative programme implies a second-order narrativisation which constitutes the actual (auto)biographical discourse. Selecting and presenting narrative or narrativisable elements within the funerary context becomes the domain of the highest-level narrator, and the option always exists to equate this narrator with the tomb owner himself if no other person is explicitly labelled as originator (= "implied author") of the structure and its iconotext. For this reason, the fact that early biographical discourse stages royal action and is literally built upon royal input (via royal donations of funerary equipment etc.) does not remove the question of who narrates the tomb owner's tomb at the highest diegetic level. Stauder-Porchet's tenet that the "advent of the event autobiography implies a change in voice"[316] is certainly correct as far as the surface level of the biographical discourse is concerned but may not reflect the entire diegetic complexity of the tombs concerned.

This shift to first-person narrative while maintaining an introductory third-person speech formula poses another challenge when tracing the biographical discourse preserved in Egyptian tombs back to oral performances during funerals. In inscriptions of the later 5th and 6th Dynasties, biographical statements in the first person are consistently (though not without exceptions[317]) introduced by the designation *ḏd=f*, implying that there exists a higher-level narrator who quotes an auto-referential speech by the tomb owner in an unspecified narrative setting. If that speech had been composed by the tomb owner during his lifetime, we would be dealing with an autodiegetic narration mediated through a heterodiegetic framing, whether the latter was performed by the deceased's descendant at a funeral[318] or only entextualised in its monumental setting. If, however, the text had been drawn up posthumously, the imagined performance at the funeral would resemble a complex role-playing game involving several diegetic levels and voices, and its subsequent remodelling for the monumental record would amount to partly fictionalised pseudepigraphy.[319] Given the evidence from contemporaneous funerary texts[320] and the example of Wepemneferet's "reading" of his funerary decree, such a scenario is not at all impossible. One may ask, however, why it should be the most likely one. In order not to be mistaken I should stress that I too consider recitation a crucial component of

---

315 One of the best examples for this practice is the monumental false door stela of Niankhsakhmet, which quotes speech by both the king and Niankhsakhmet within an apparently heterodiegetic narrative frame. See Baines (1999b: 22–23); Strudwick (2005: 302–303, no. 225); Stauder-Porchet (2017: 58–62; 2021a: 139; 142).

316 Stauder-Porchet (2020a: 110). See also Baines (1999b: 21–24); Baud (2005).

317 See, e.g., the tomb of Pepyankh-Herib at Meir (Blackman 1924: Pl. IV) or that of Sabni at Qubbet el-Hawa (Edel 2008a: 50–51; 243–244, Figs. 32–34, Pl. IX). For these reference cf. also Baines (2015a: 21, n. 7).

318 Comparable to a conference paper read out by a colleague because the original author could for whatever reason not attend the event and deliver the talk in person.

319 Cf. Vernus (2020: 179; 189–192), who cautions against any excessive use of the label "pseudepigraphic".

320 See Reintges (2011); Quack (2012); Eyre (2013: 122–123, n. 74); Willems (2019).

biographical narration in ancient Egypt (see Chapter 7.2). But in my opinion, recitation does not precede the entextualisation but follows it. Two further arguments can be put forward against a performance having been the master-text of the biographical texts preserved in the epigraphic record. As will have become apparent from the preceding sections, my definition of what constitutes the monumental biographical discourse in Egypt is a broad one.[321] Consequently, many of those elements I take to be integral parts of the narrative framework do not have a clear-cut equivalent in linear speech and can thus not be re-naturalised within the context of an oral performance.[322] It requires the tomb's built materiality to derive narrative meaning from them. An even stronger argument relates to the biographical discourse preserved in certain rock inscriptions that follow the conventions of contemporaneous tomb biographies by introducing first-person narrative through *ḏd=f*. Compare the following quite well-known example by the scribe Anusu from Wadi Umm Hoda in the Eastern Desert:[323]

[1] ↓ *nswt-bj.t* (*Nfr-kꜣ-Rꜥ*) *ꜥnḫ(.w)*	[1] The Double King (Neferkare), may he live
ḏ.t [2] *zšw ꜥnw-s(w) ḏd=f* [3] *jrj.n(=j)*	forever. [2] The scribe Anusu, he says: [3] "That (I)
šd(.t) ẖnw.wt jptn [4] *rḏj.n(=j)*[a] *mw*	made the well of these cisterns is [4] in order to
n jb [5] *rḏj⟨.n⟩(=j) tꜣ n ḥḳr n rḏj(=j)*	give water to the thirsty [5] and bread to the hungry.
[6] *ḫpr gbb nb jm* [7] *sk w(j) sꜣj.k(j)*	I did not let [6] occur any tiring therefrom, [7] for I
ḫr nb(=j)	am satiated in (my) lord's presence.

a) *Pace* Eichler,[324] I take the grammatical structure to be similar to the common introductory formula of the ideal biography genre with a nominal *sḏm.n=f* acting as the subject of an adverbial sentence.

In cases such as this, the identity of factual author, implied author, narrator and narrated protagonist can be presupposed with high probability,[325] while the option of an oral performance preceding the text's carving appears to be rather unlikely, even if it may have held cultic significance.[326]

3.4 "Authorising" *auto*biography – the question of fact and fiction

The preceding section has drawn attention to the fact that we have little explicit information on Egyptian conceptualisations of authorship within the monumental discourse.[327] Whether the difference between author and implied author was acknowledged or even

321 In line with Baines (1999a: 34–36); Walsem (2020: 118; 124–125); *pace* Lieven (2010: 59).

322 This is also acknowledged by Baines (1999b: 22–23), who points to the intrinsic differences between oral and written/visual discourses.

323 Eichler (1998: 263–265, Pl. 34d); Kloth (2002: 9–10, no. 17; 238–239); Strudwick (2005: 149, no. 75).

324 Eichler (1998; 263, n. 31).

325 Cf. Kloth (2002: 239).

326 As suggested by Eichler (1994), some rock inscriptions and expedition graffiti may have been tied to ritual action such as offerings, and addresses to the living are attested from the First Intermediate Period onward. There is no hint to suggest, however, that the majority of commemorative texts of this genre were somehow acted out before the actual carving.

327 For a discussion of Egyptian concepts of authorship primarily during the Ramesside period, see Simon (2013: 227–281); Fischer-Elfert (2014: 333–334).

reflected upon remains an open question. That said, examples such as Pepyankh-Herib's depiction as a creator of his own tomb decoration (see p. 108) suggest that it was part of the self-conceptualisation of the Egyptian elite to claim a certain degree of agency regarding the design and iconotextual content of their funerary structure, at least during the latter part of the Old Kingdom.[328] Relief compositions where biographical narrative is associated with the depiction of the tomb owner in speech/presentation gesture (e.g. in the tomb of Kagemni[329] or, in a slightly different context, in that of Qar[330]; see also p. 150) provide further arguments for the view that the tomb's discourse was meant to originate, entirely or partially, from its patron and primary beneficiary, regardless of whether the latter was actually involved in its design or not.[331] The auctorial force[332] of the tomb's iconotext and that of the whole act of funerary communication certainly derived from the tomb owner, turning biographical discourse in the wider sense into an autobiographical one.[333] A potentially illuminating piece of evidence in this regard is an inconspicuously looking inscription on the eastern face of the mastaba tomb of Niuty in Giza's West Field (G 4611 = LG 50, late 5th or 6th Dynasty).[334] Niuty's tomb comprises a number of unremarkable scenes selected from the standard repertoire of contemporaneous funerary iconotextual programmes, among them a decorated architrave over the entrance featuring a conventional offering text. What stands out, however, is a curious little hieroglyphic text inscribed on the recess north of the entrance to the tomb chapel. It is circumscribed by an incised rectangle, which gives it the appearance of a label or some sort of *mode d'emploi* for the rest of the tomb: .[335]

→ *sḥḏ jbꜣ(.w) Nʿwtjj* ← *ḏd=f* [a] → *ʿnḫ(.w) ḥr rd.wj=f(j)*	The superintendent of the dancers Niuty, saying while (still) alive on his two feet:

---

328 Arguing for the active involvement of the tomb owner in the tomb design: Walsem (2013: 129; 136; 2020: 155, n. 105; 156, n. 108). For further conclusive evidence for the active participation of the tomb owner in design decisions during the Old Kingdom and later periods, see Vernus (2020: 173–180). Certainly, distinguished artisans and sacerdotal scribes will still have played a crucial role in the design process. Cf. Laboury (2012: 201–202); Lashien (2018: 265–266). Cf. also Vischak (2006); Jurman (2020, Vol. II: 1214–1221).

329 Firth & Gunn (1926, Vol. II: Pl. 59, no. 2); Kloth (2018: 8–9 w. fig.).

330 Simpson (1976: 8–9, Fig. 28). In Qar's case, the text (in my opinion to be read from right to left) is not biographical in the narrow sense but features an offering formula introduced by *ḏd=f* that provides a list of Qar's priestly titles associated with different kings of the 4th and 6th Dynasties.

331 As noted by Baines (2015a: 21), the mere spatial association between an autobiographical inscription and the depiction of the tomb owner suffices to indicate a speech act, even in the absence of *ḏd=f* or *ḏd*. Indeed, of the 96 biographical inscriptions listed in Kloth (2002), 38 are introduced neither through *ḏd=f* nor through *ḏd*. Kloth (2002: 52–54).

332 This role roughly corresponds with what Silverstein (2020: 16), following Goffman's model of the "sender" role (1979: 16–18), defines as the "principal" of the biographical communicative events.

333 For a similar view see Stauder-Porchet (2021a: 146). Cf. also Vernus (2020: 169–172), although I would not see the first-person voicing as a major factor in this classification. For differing views see Baines (1999a: 23; 1999b: 37); Frood (2007: 3); Landgráfová (2011: XIX); Chauvet (2013: 57); Bassir (2014: 8).

334 Lepsius (1897: 73); Lepsius (1849–1859, II: Pl. 89a; 1913: Pls. Xc; XXX–XXXI); Porter & Moss (1974: 133).

335 Fischer (1977: 54, no. 14 w. n. 134; 55, Fig. 57); Digital Giza (2022: Photo PDM_1993.098.19).

a) The reversal of *ḏd=f* is a common way to indicate that the speech act emanates directly from the mouth of a depicted tomb owner, which is why Fischer calls this sort of hieroglyphic arrangement "vocative reversal".[336] In our case, the spatial reference is not so straightforward to decode, since there is no tomb owner represented in the inscription's immediate vicinity.

The inscription was likely added to the tomb's entrance some time after the completion of the relief programme in order to reflect Niuty's promotion to the office of "superintendent of the dancers", which is not mentioned elsewhere there. Although Fischer ponders whether a statement was meant to follow but did not reach the state of completion, the inscription in its present form seems self-contained and is positioned close to the visitor's eyelevel. I therefore propose to regard it as an introductory statement to the tomb's iconotext in its entirety. Niuty is presented as the authority standing behind everything the visitor is about to behold and can thus be said to encourage an "autobiographical" reading of the narrativisable raw material to follow. Niuty's assertion to have been still alive when creating his self-presentation (a statement found quite often in connection with the construction of tombs or the provision of funerary equipment[337]) can be taken as a rhetorical "factualisation device".[338] Irrespective of whether the statement is actually true or was fabricated posthumously by one of Niuty's descendants, it is unquestionably suited to strengthen what Lejeune has referred to as the "pacte autobiographique".[339] This expression refers to an implicit understanding shared by the author and the reader of an autobiography that in the latter, subject, narrator, and authorship coincide. Whether the text under consideration is also an authentic and truthful account of the former's life is of little consequence in this regard. What matters is the "suspension of suspicion for the moment", to rephrase Coleridge.[340] From the perspective of cognitive narratology, the distinction between *fictional* and *factual* is indeed of minor importance, since it does not represent a primary mental category. Narratives are by default processed mimetically, as long as there is no compelling reason to do otherwise.[341]

Yet, factuality can become a topic of the autobiographical discourse itself and may be of great importance for historiographical research.[342] If Egyptian funerary iconotexts were meant to be read, or rather, reassembled, as an autobiographical discourse, the pertinent

336 See Fischer (1977: 49–57).

337 E.g. in the false door inscription of Ankhkhufu likewise from Giza (Boston, MFA 21.3081). See Stauder-Porchet (2017: 39).

338 For similar phenomena in the medieval European *historia* discourse, see Schulz & Hübner (2011: 198).

339 Lejeune (1975: 25–26).

340 Cf. Coleridge's (2014: 208) "willing suspension of disbelief for the moment, which constitutes poetic faith", commonly cited as "temporary suspension of disbelief".

341 See Gerrig & Gagnon (2020: 134); Caracciolo (2020). One may also point to Roeder's (2018b: 160) clarification regarding the status of ancient Egyptian fictional texts: "So haben wir es bei den fiktionalen Erzählungen vielmehr mit Erzählungen von als faktisch erachteten politischen, sozialen und religiösen Ideologien und damit von ideologischen Realitäten zu tun."

342 For historiographical interpretations of particular Old Kingdom biographies and iconotexts more generally, see, e.g., Richards (2002); McFarlane (2003: 33); Walsem (2005: 71–83); Mourad (2011: 147–149); Baines (2015a: 32–33); Begon (2016).

question arises, in what way they map onto our conventional distinction between factual and fictional narratives. Certainly, the messages conveyed by funerary ensembles were meant to be taken seriously. After all, a person's status as evidenced by an exemplary elite biography was the precondition for being able to grant favours to benevolent passers-by and to communicate credible threats to those poised to violate the tomb. This applies in equal measure to those tombs lacking biographical texts in the narrow sense. On the other hand, the dialectic relation between rhetoric hyperbole of exceptionality ("never has the like been done..."[343]) and equally hyperbolic assertions of truthfulness ("I say this as someone who speaks truthfully"[344]), including the comparatively late trope of avoiding a discourse on "offices of the necropolis" (see n. 60), point to certain frictions within the reception of the autobiographical mode. Yet, the potential lack in veracity of statements does not turn an autobiographical account into homodiegetic fiction. As remarked by Genette, the demarcation between fictionality and factuality may be drawn not on the basis of fictional content (the level of *histoire*) but of the fictionality of the presented narration as such.[345]

The difference can be exemplified by looking at the remarkable but partly damaged autobiography of Debehni in his rock-cut tomb at Giza (LG 90, 5th Dynasty[346]), which is often taken to be one of the earliest preserved autobiographies phrased in the first person[347] and has been cited as a case where outright content-related fictionality did indeed enter the (auto)biographical discourse. The first part of Debehni's inscription relates events connected with a royal visit to the pyramid complex. At this occasion King Menkaure also seems to be taking care that Debehni is provided with a proper location for his tomb in the vicinity and has access to the man-power required to carry out the necessary construction work. Towards the end of the text we find the reference to a tomb built according to royal decree and measuring 100×50 cubits. Since these values cannot be satisfactorily reconciled with the extension of Debehni's rock-cut structure in the Giza necropolis,[348] they have been taken to indicate that the inscription's author used a fair amount of poetic licence when composing Debehni's life writing.[349] Some years ago, M. Müller offered a different and, in my opinion, more convincing explanation for the seeming discrepancy between biographical statement and reality: in all probability, the passage simply refers to the tomb Debehni had erected for his late father somewhere in the Delta.[350] But even if

343 Cf. Kloth (2002: 173–175).

344 Kloth (2002: 103–104). See generally Coulon (1997).

345 Genette (1991: 81), drawing on Herrnstein Smith (1978: 29). Cf. also Suhr (2016: 33) for an Egyptological perspective. For the wider narratological context, see Rajewsky (2020).

346 The date of the tomb's architecture and that of its main iconotext(s) have been hotly debated. See Kloth (2002: 38–39, no. 84). There are certain hints that the tomb has a complex history involving more than one stage of decoration. See Jánosi (2005: 386–393). For a mid-5th Dynasty date, see most recently Dulíková et al. (2021: 62).

347 Cf., e.g., Baud (2005: 122–123).

348 Alexanian's (2006: 3–5) attempt to explain the indicated measurements in terms of the parcel of land allocated to Debehni seems a bit forced. See also Chauvet (2013: 70–71).

349 Cf. Reisner (1931: 258); Hassan (1943: 163).

350 Müller (2006).

the inscription's author had given erroneous information regarding the size of Debehni's tomb, the text would not automatically become a fictional narrative, since it does not breach the *pacte autobiographique* and its implications. A slightly different question, which equally continues to puzzle commentators, is the one of who actually tells Debehni's life in the first place, implying also the question at what point in time he does so.[351] Is the text consistently voiced in the first person or does it feature additional narrative voices? Is it even Debehni's voice represented posthumously by his son as Helck assumed?[352] What unquestionably complicates the interpretation of the entire inscription is its bad state of preservation and the fact that certain columns do not seem to have ever been completely carved. Consequently, the presence of the term *jtj*, "father", has been tentatively interpreted as an indication that the inscription features two voices, that of Debehni and that of his son, and may therefore be considered a heterodiegetic biography or even pseudepigraphy. Stauder-Porchet remarks in regard to the inscription's seeming incongruities:

> « La 1ère personne dans la partie principale de Debeheni est posthume, potentiellement de plusieurs décennies. C'est en effet le fils qui, non seulement parle à la fin (col. 16–...), mais encore, en faisant l'inscription, fait parler son père (col. 2–16). […] Par un dispositif de voix complexe, le fils fait parler son père avec des éléments textuels qui, au temps de l'existence terrestre de ce dernier, ne s'étaient pas encore développés."[353]

Should Stauder-Porchet be correct in her assessment of the chronological position of the text in relation to the evolution of the biographic genres, the problems surrounding its voicing and factual veracity would grow even larger, for no filial voice can be discerned with any degree of certainty. As Müller has shown, there exists a different solution to account for the mention of *jtj*, *mw.t* and the *jmꜣḫ* status within the last section of the inscription. Furthermore, there is also no "father" mentioned in the first column (i.e. line 2 if we consider the partly preserved introductory horizontal line above the columns as line 1, which must have contained Debehni's name and titles[354]). As correctly recorded by Hassan[355] (*pace* Lepsius[356] and Sethe[357]), the contentious passage must read *jn nswt-bj.t* (*Mn-kꜣ.w-Rꜥ*) [… *r*]*ḏj n*(=*j*) *s.t*=*f*, "It was the Double King (Menkaure) [...] who gave me its (= the tomb's) location." The  preceding  is clearly visible on archival photographs of the Boston-Expedition.[358] As a consequence, we would be dealing with a first-person

351 See Stauder-Porchet (2017: 84–85).

352 Helck (1972: 11). Similarly, Gnirs (1996: 220, n. 148).

353 Stauder-Porchet (2017: 85).

354 *Pace* Sethe (1933; 18, 8 w. n. a). The horizontal line with the preserved *nb* is not only reproduced by Sethe but also recorded in the preliminary drawing (BBAW 1842–1845: Z.285) to Plate 37b of Lepsius' (1849–1859: Abth. II, Pl. 37) Denkmäler. I am very grateful to Silke Grallert of the Berlin-Brandenburgische Akademie der Wissenschaften for sending me scans of the drawings relating to LG 90.

355 Hassan (1943: 168, Fig. 118, l. 2).

356 Lepsius (1849–1859: Abth. II, Pl. 37b).

357 Sethe (1933: 18, 10).

358 E.g. Digital Giza (2022: Photo AAW1399). See also Edel (1955–1964: 442) and Alexanian (2006: 3, n. 10).

"auto"biography that could have been composed some time after the main character's death.[359] That said, however, Debehni's tomb is still surrounded by too many open question as to safely draw any wider-ranging conclusions from the preserved material.

Also beyond Debehni, Egyptological debates about the veracity of the autobiographical discourse have often dwelled on potential pseudepigraphy and the questions of whether the tomb owner could have been still alive at the moment an (auto)biographical statement was created. For example, in the case of Washptah's mid-5th Dynasty tomb (blocks now in Cairo and Aberdeen)[360] the wording of the partially preserved third-person narrative was interpreted in such a way that Washptah had died of an accident prior to the incident's formal emplotment.[361] As a consequence, the whole textual composition would of necessity have been composed under the aegis of his son Merinetjernisut, who is indeed mentioned in the introductory formula as the one responsible for creating the monumental record (or the entire tomb?) after his father's death: [...? *jn zꜣ*]*=f smsw jrj n=f ḫrj-tp nswt mdw rḫy.t Mrj-nṯr-nswt sk sw m jz=f nj ḫr.t-nṯr*, [... It is] his eldest son who has acted for him, the royal subordinate and baton of the Rekhyt Merinetjernisut, since he (i.e. Washptah) was in his tomb of the necropolis.[362] While Merinetjernisut was thus apparently responsible for the *entextualisation* of the biography, it is by no means self-evident that he was also presented as the authority of the account of his father's life, and not just as its mediator. In any event, a careful textual analysis by Stauder-Porchet has shown that Washptah's *histoire* must have featured his recovery, since the *récit* later represents him as being invited to eat with the king.[363] A posthumous composition of the text is therefore not without alternative. But irrespective of the concrete case, it may well be that the distinction between contemporaneous and posthumous biographical accounts has in general only limited value for the discussion on autobiographical *auctoritas*, for the tomb owner remains a member of his social network beyond death[364] and does not lose all of his agency once his corpse has been interred in the burial chamber. Therefore, depictions of funerary rituals may become part of a tomb's autobiographical iconotext, even though they would in our modern view be considered fictional if they had been created during a person's lifetime before the referenced event took place. This topic is of course too complex to be treated here in due fashion, as it relates to the significance and ontological status of ritual or "religious" scenes within a tomb more generally.[365] Suffice it to say that the autobiographical vantage point is often extremely difficult to locate in the funerary discourse, and opinions on the life-status of the depicted tomb owner vary. Fitzenreiter, for example, points to a seeming paradox: "Der (tote) Grabherr berichtet bzw. wird beim

---

359 For similar cases, see Vernus (2020: 176).

360 See Kloth (2002: 14, no. 26; 330–333, Figs. 4a–d, Pls. IIa–c); Stauder-Porchet (2017: 48–53).

361 E.g. Kloth (2002: 14, no. 26); Baines (1999b: 23–24); Picardo (2010: 94).

362 After Kloth (2002: 330. Fig. 4a); Stauder-Porchet (2017: 49).

363 Stauder-Porchet (2017. 48–58, esp. 53–54.

364 See most recently Siffert (2022).

365 Cf. Fitzenreiter (2001) and the individual contributions in Fitzenreiter & Herb (2006) as well as the convenient short overview of opinions in Kloth (2018: 7–13).

'Schauen'/*mꜣꜣ* von Ereignissen gezeigt, die sich zu seinen Lebzeiten zugetragen haben."[366] Since the deceased is still bound in a web of social relations, and his aspirations for the hereafter as well as the continuous performance of the funerary cult are part of his life story,[367] one could say that an Egyptian autobiographical iconotext is as much prospective as it is retrospective. This becomes especially clear with statements of the ideal biography discourse relating the tomb owner's descendance into his tomb (see p. 112) and thus alluding to his death. In such cases the (likely) time of composition and the reference time (sort of a *praeterito in futuro*) can only be reconciled *sub specie aeternitatis*.[368] At the same time, during its reception, the tomb's multimodal iconotext tends to assert a perpetual presence that puts the visitor in the role of a contemporary (see also Chapter 7.1). His or her "host" is always a "living" being, and the act of narration takes place *hic et nunc*. In addition, one needs to bear in mind that a particular group of autobiographical narrative schemes is inherent in any tomb irrespective of its concrete configuration, namely, those relating to the erection, the burial, and the continuation of the funerary cult. While these schemes are not always expressed directly, they are always implicitly present and may, from time to time, be given tangible form through a specific manifestation in the iconotext (such as in the case of the scenes in Chapel F of the tomb of Pepyankh/Heny the Black in Meir depicting funerary rituals[369]), even if the latter should be only generic in nature. Thus, the elite tomb becomes a lapidary *exemplum* that binds the autobiographical discourse to an a-temporal or, more precisely, a poly-temporal reality. As a consequence, there is only a small playground for the potential introduction of "fictionality", because the *pacte autobiographique* exerts its influence on a larger portion of the monumental discourse than it would in our own culture.

4 Presenting life: The Old Kingdom tomb as a multimodal iconotext

In the preceding chapters I have repeatedly referred to the ancient Egyptian monumental tomb – the preferred place for staging life writing during the Old Kingdom – as a multimodal iconotext. Here I shall finally contextualise this designation and relate it to the scope and aims of postclassical transmedial narratology.

Roughly concomitant with technology-driven discussions on communication via multimedia, the interest in the study of multimodality has seen a sharp increase in the past few decades.[370] Basis for this approach, which draws from social semiotics, textual linguistics, communication theory and cognitive sciences alike, is the conviction that intentional human communication does never happen in unimodal form, i.e. activating only one semiotic resource through one sensory channel. Thus, a speech is not only delivered through segmented sounds but also communicates through facial expressions, gestures, the space chosen for the communicative act, and other potential factors. Written text has always a

366 Fitzenreiter (2001: 87).
367 Fitzenreiter (2001: 67–68).
368 Cf. Baines (2020: 47).
369 See Blackman & Apted (1953: 50–56, Pl. XLII–XLIII).
370 Cf. Jewitt (2009); Pinar Sanz (2015); Bateman et al. (2017); Wildfeuer et al. (2019a).

material, perceptive form and an environment that co-communicates and impacts on the process of semiosis, etc. Unlike the term multimedia, which is related primarily to the employed technology and the material means of communication,[371] multimodality focusses on the transmission and reception of information in a human cultural environment, where different strands of semiotic resources interact and converge to form a complex unit of meaning transcending its individual components. According to an often-cited definition by Kress, a mode can thus be conceived as "a socially shaped and culturally given resource for making meaning. *Image, writing, layout, music, gesture, speech, moving image, soundtrack* are examples of modes used in representation and communication."[372] More specifically, *mode* is here taken to encompass the materiality and form of a perceptive stimulus/sign *and* its socially conditioned semiotic attributions.[373] While different modes may be perceived through different sensory channels (such as seeing and hearing in cinema), a sensory channel such as vision can be related to different modes (such as in a comic strip or an Egyptian iconotext). Studies in multimodality focus on identifying different semiotic modes and exploring how they interrelate and contribute to forming meaning in a given social, cultural, and historical context. As has been pointed out before, research on multimodality in its current form is a theoretically informed approach to complex human communication but neither a unified theory nor (or, not yet) a fully-fledged academic discipline.[374] As a multifaceted concept, which is, like *narrativity*, used by many different agents in different scholarly contexts, it still lacks an authoritative set of commonly accepted axioms and definitions.[375] This fluidity may entail the risk that boundaries of analytical concepts become blurred, but at the same time it provides enquiries into multimodality also with the flexibility to be adapted to many different cultural contexts and communicative situations. Offering by its origins and very nature a transdisciplinary framework, the concept of multimodality lends itself to being utilised within the scope of a transmedial narratological study of ancient Egyptian funerary monuments.[376]

That said, there is no question that multimodality has already become a well-established concept within Egyptology thanks to the pioneering contributions by Lapčić, Kutscher, and Kammerzell.[377] One may go even further and state that generations of Egyptologists have intuitively been analysing ancient Egyptian artefacts in terms of multimodal communication without explicitly resorting to the terminological and methodological toolkit of contemporary multimodality research. There is thus no need to offer a lengthy introduction or to demonstrate the concept's usefulness for Egyptological research. What

371 For the relation between modes and media, see Bateman et al. (2017: 123–128).

372 Kress (2014: 60).

373 For this understanding of mode, see Bateman et al. (2017: 113–114).

374 Cf. Wildfeuer et al. (2019b: 3–38).

375 Björkvall 2012: 18. For the achievements of the last decade, see Wildfeuer et al. (2019b: 21–27).

376 For the impact of multimodality research on postclassical narratology, see Ryan & Thon (2014).

377 Lapčić (2014), Kutscher (2020), Kammerzell (2021). One may equally refer to the conference on "Multimodal Artefact Analysis in Ancient Studies" held at the LMU Munich in March 2021, which featured many Egyptological contributions and was co-organised by the Egyptologist Patricia Heindl. See https://multimodality.hcommons.org/ (last accessed on 22 December 2022).

I would like to do instead is to set out how a multimodal understanding of monumental tombs of the Old Kingdom can be aligned with concepts of complex higher-order narratives formed in the recipient's mind through the amalgamation of a host of different narrative cues in image, text, sound, and space.

4.1 How many modes in a tomb?

An ancient Egyptian monumental elite tomb of the Old Kingdom can be considered a prime example of a semiotic product communicating multimodally by default. With its ordered architectural space, its tangible materiality, its often rich and complex pictorial and textual programmes, and its being used during cultic performances such as the burial or regular offering rituals, the mastaba or rock-cut tomb resorts to a host of different modes within the scope of what can be termed a cultural "hyper-genre". The "hyper-genre" of the Egyptian elite tomb encompasses all the permissible patterns and conventions related to architectural design, textual formats or genres and iconographic themes.[378] Like every genre, it aims at recognisability without limiting its potential to manifest itself in diverse and often unpredictable ways.

The ancient addressee or experiencer (let us refer to him/her as visitor) of the tomb as a multimodal artefact is first and foremost faced with a wealth of sensory input related to the complex interplay of global and local semiotic modes. If we take the well-known tomb complex of Senedjemib Inti (G 2370, 5th Dynasty, time of Djedkare Izezi) in Giza's *Cemetery en Échelon*[379] as an example, we will get an idea of the many dimensions of signification operating almost simultaneously during the communicative experience. Visiting the tomb means first approaching it and realising its proximity to the royal pyramid of King Khufu, but also the space's crowdedness with other funerary structures. It means beholding the monumentality of the portico façade, recognising, perhaps touching, the grey nummulitic limestone used to build up the tomb's visible surfaces and apprehend its difference to the few architectural elements carved of white high-quality limestone (presumably from Tura).[380] It means that one's attention is being guided by architectural hints and colour schemes, that one feels (i.e. sees and hears) the space enclosed by the walls of the rooms, noticing the dimensions and distances while striding through the complex, including the undecorated pillared hall. It means appreciating the tomb's original statuary programme, of which today not even remnants are preserved.[381] Furthermore, it means realising the

---

378 Perhaps inspired by Assmann (1996b: 103), van Walsem (2020: 156, n. 108) has likened the Egyptian elite tomb to the personal "library" of the tomb owner. As attractive as this simile may seem, one should probably add the qualification that a tomb owner might have been free to choose individual book titles, but the library's range of authors and subjects as well as its general arrangement was governed by conventions transcending individual agency.

379 See Brovarski (2001).

380 See Brovarksi (2001: 19–21). In the end, most of the relief surface was covered with a coating of white plaster so as to mimic the appearance of fine white limestone.

381 The statue fragment found by Reisner in serdab II is intrusive. Brovarski (2001: 66; 82). Like in the case of Seshemnefer IV, obelisks could have lined the path to the entrance of G 2370, but, again, no traces thereof have been preserved. Brovarski (2001: 12).

richness of the iconotextual programme and demarcating individual semiotic units based on pre-knowledge of the "grammaire de la tombe". It means identifying visual clues to separate individual scenes and texts, and experiencing colour as a way to highlight features of layout and general composition.[382] It means singling out salient figures and relate them to textual captions that provide information on the tomb owner's identity and the ritual significance of the icons. It equally means valuing the textual and pictorial arrangements, and drawing connections between different units and sub-units based on layout clues and global spatial configuration. It means recognising motifs and genres represented within the tomb's iconotext (e.g. the reproduction of royal letters or the spear fishing motif) and relating them to known conventions while realising more or less subtle differences in respect to previously visited funerary ensembles. Finally, it means audibly reading out the texts in order to grasp their meaning (see Chapter 7.2), hearing one's own voice resonating when striding through the structure, perhaps while performing an offering or a different ritual activity in the company of other participants. This enumeration of a visitor's potential experiences and perceptive actions when visiting the superstructure of Senedjemib Inti's mastaba during the 5th Dynasty is nothing but a rough sketch and could be elaborated almost ad libitum. It shall simply draw attention to the fact that the semiotic modes at work in a given communicative situation are numerous and often difficult to disentangle already at a global level of analysis. More detailed and sophisticated studies such as Kutscher's multi-step analysis of the relief panel of Wepemneferet[383] can add considerably to our understanding of ancient Egyptian multimodal communication, but they are difficult to implement on the scale of an entire tomb complex. For the purposes of the current essay, this level of detail is not even necessary, as it would only distract from the broader units of narrative signification building up what I would like to call the "portfolio biography" (see the Chapter 5.1).

The important issue to bear in mind is that within the context of a funerary structure, (auto)biographical texts produce their meaning not as simple, isolated units of text but signify together with their co- and context, which includes among other things the materiality of their "Textträger". Lapidary texts that reflect upon their own coming into being and/or mention the very object they have been inscribed on (such as the inscription on the slab of Werre,[384] the biographical false door inscription of Niankhsakhmet[385] or that of Ankhkhufu[386]) would have a much reduced narrative impact, had they been carved on a random part of the tomb surface and deprived of their auto-referentiality. In these cases it becomes particularly obvious that the slab or false door is not simply the carrier of the message, it is an integral and irreplaceable part of the story, namely the events, actions, and preconditions leading to the creation, erection and cultic use of the respective

382 For the few traces of colour within the tomb, see Brovarski (2001: 21).

383 Kutscher (2020: 93–105).

384 Hassan (1932: 15; 18–19, Fig. 13, Pl. XVIII); Sethe (1933: 232, no. 7 [147]); Kloth (2002: 23, no. 47); Strudwick (2005: 305–306, no. 227); Stauder-Porchet (2017: 45–46).

385 Mariette (1889: 202–205, no. D 11 [sic = 12]); Sethe (1933: 38–40, no. 26); Kloth (2002: 21, no. 40); Strudwick (2005: 302–303, no. 225); Chauvet (2013: 62–64); Stauder-Porchet (2017: 58–62).

386 Kloth (2002: 27, no. 56); Strudwick (2005: 262–263, no. 196); Stauder-Porchet (2017: 39).

monument. The particular layout and "visual poetics" of biographical texts too have a significant impact on their meaning and narrative salience, as demonstrated by Stauder-Porchet in a number of case studies (cf. also the example of Shepsesptah above, p. 53).[387] The same holds true for the location of the tomb within the necropolis and its general architectural design. A large part of the biographical discourse during the 4th and early 5th Dynasties dwells on issues connected with the construction of the tomb. But in the almost complete absence of descriptive passages about the latter (even generic ones) the built reality becomes an instantiation of deictic expressions such as *jz pn* or *nw*. Physical tomb and textual anaphora are thus multimodally linked within a second-order narrative, since each component contains complementing information on the way the tomb is tied to a particular person's life. In the case of Ankhkhufu, for example, it is the inscription that connects the false door to royal agency and thereby stresses Ankhkhufu's high esteem at court. But at the same time, it is the physical false door that lends credibility to this claim and provides the counterpart of *telling* in the *telling – showing* opposition. Within the mind of the beholder, textual and non-textual information are amalgamated to form one multidimensional narrative unit within the framework of the *exemplification cascade* introduced above (p. 119).

Another aspect where a multimodal approach can lead to new insights concerns *narrating through space*, meaning at the same time *via space* and *across space*.[388] As has often been remarked, inscriptions of a biographical nature are predominantly found in areas of the tomb affording particular attention.[389] This can be the tomb's façade, the entrance doorway with its thicknesses, a false door inserted into the façade or the cult focus of the inner offering chamber. The hieroglyphic texts and associated depictions of the tomb owner are usually oriented towards the entrance of the tomb so as to invite the visitor to enter the cult chapel and engage in offering activity.[390] Accordingly, in tombs where (auto)biographical texts in the narrow sense are present, they are often the first major component of the tomb decoration that a visitor beholds and have the potential to significantly shape the latter's experience of the three-dimensionally distributed iconotext that is to follow. Thus, Herkhuf's account of his expeditions and the reproduced royal letter on the façade of his tomb open up a narrative canvas of specified exemplifications which as a whole provide an argument for his *imakh* status and the maintenance of the familial funerary cult. These concerns are focussed on within the funerary chapel, in whose decorative programme not only Herkhuf but also other members of his family occupy a prominent position.[391] But it is interesting to observe that Herkhuf's textual characterisation in the scenes on the pillars seems to hark back to the similarly phrased introduction of his expedition report on the northern entrance niche as if these two units were not intertextually but hypertextually linked. Embedded within offering formulae and

387 Stauder-Porchet (2020b; 2020c; 2021b).

388 Cf. the case study of Meyers (1985) on Amarna tombs. For the interrelation between architecture and narrative more generally, see Psarra (2009); Rashid (2010).

389 See the overview in Kloth (2002: 248–251).

390 Kloth (2002: 248 w. fig.; 2018: 26–27 w. fig.).

391 For the tomb's iconotext, see Edel (2008a: 620–636); Vischak (2015: 97–102).

following title strings, we find epithets inspired by the phraseology of the ideal biography genre, which stress Herkhuf's ties with the king as well as his effectiveness when on foreign mission. On the eastern side of Pillar IV one reads for example:[392]

$\overset{3}{\vert}$ ↓ (...) *jmj-jb nj nb=f* $\overset{4}{\vert}$ *jrr ḥzz.t nb=f ḏd nrw Ḥr m ḫ3s.wt* $\overset{5}{\vert}$ *jnn jnw n ḫkr nswt m ḫ3s.wt jm3ḫw ḫr nṯr ꜥ3* (...)[a]	$\overset{3}{\vert}$ (...) confidant of his lord, $\overset{4}{\vert}$ who does what his lord praises, who puts the terror of Horus in the foreign lands, $\overset{5}{\vert}$ who brings the produce for the king's ornament from the foreign lands, an *imakhu* with the Great God, (...)

a) To be compared to $\overset{2}{\vert}$ (...) *jnn jnw n ḫkr nswt jmj-r' ḫ3s.t nb.t nj.t tp-rsj ḏd nrw* $\overset{3}{\vert}$ *[Ḥr] m ḫ3s.wt jrr ḥzz.t nb=f* (...) in the introduction of the expedition report. See Edel (2008a: 623–624, Text 2, Pl. XXVII). For a detailed analysis of Herkhuf's inscribed façade, see Stauder-Porchet (2020c).

A similar text is found on the east side of Pillar III. Both Pillars III and IV lie close to Herkhuf's false door inserted into the northern half of the tomb chapel's western wall, and the orientation of their iconotexts guides the visitor to the primary offering space. In this sense, the tomb's architectural configuration and the positioning of its individual iconotextual elements determine to a significant degree the structure of the higher-order *récit*, even though the actual *narration* in the visitor's mind is not strictly pre-defined and open to variability (see also the following chapter). In actually walking through Herkhuf's life writing, the visitor may mentally combine specific and generic exemplification strategies into a single global narrative mapped onto space (as memory maintains a link between narrativisable cues and physical space), which culminates at the place of offering.

Conversely, in those cases where the biographical text is located close to the tomb chapel's primary cult space, it can only be understood in view of the iconotextual programme that went before. That is not to say that (auto)biographical texts and scenes from the iconotextual repertoire are so closely integrated that they can be considered illustrations of one another. Such cases are rather rare and isolated (cf. Inscription D in the tomb of Senedjemib Inti, p. 157). Rather, they belong to different exemplification strategies with different evolutionary trajectories but may nevertheless be taken to belong to one single communicative framework outlined on p. 119.

In cases where (auto)biographical texts are found in spaces not normally accessible after the burial such as serdab[393] or burial chamber,[394] one may feel entitled to question the concept of *narrating through space* during visits of the tomb and ask whether these iconotexts were actually addressing living human beings.[395] This objection can be countered in two ways. First, the efficacy of a tomb's global narrative framework is not

392 Edel (2008a: 631, Text 14, Pl. XXXI).

393 E.g. the tomb of Werre. See Hassan (1932: 17–18). In Werre's case, the principal serdab was closed by a wooden door and was probably accessible during the posthumous funerary cult.

394 Cf. the case of the late 5th or 6th Dynasty tomb of Kaikherptah at Giza, where the burial chamber contains not only ideal biographical phraseology but also an address to lector priests. See Sethe (1933: 186, no. 26 [117]); Junker (1947: 118–120, Fig. 56, Pl. XXI); Kanawati (2010: 59–60, no. 2, Fig. 16). For the context of decorated burial chambers in general, see Kanawati (2010).

395 See Fitzenreiter (2015). For later periods see also Lieven (2010: 57–60).

affected by the ontological nature of the potential recipient, be it a living person, an *akh*, or a god. Second, the telling of one's life within the funerary discourse does not start with the burial but with the actual construction of the tomb. Consequently, the production of funerary equipment and the creation of the tomb's iconotext did find its audience already well before the start of the post-burial funerary cult. In fact, the biographical inscription on the slab found by Hassan within the principal serdab of Werre[396] makes this abundantly clear when it states that the inscription was designed (and carved?) under the king's eyes at the royal palace, thus, in an environment ideally suited for gaining attention among the highest elite:

[8] ↓ (...) *rḏj ḥm=f* [*jrj.t(j) n=f*] [9] *ꜥ jm zšw r-gs nswt ḏs*[*=f*] [10] *ḥr š(j) nj pr-ꜥꜣ* [a] *r zš ḫft* [*ḏdd.t*] [11] *m jz=f* [b] *ntj m ḫr.t-nṯr*	[8] (...) His Majesty had [made for him] [9] a document concerning this matter, drawn up in the presence of the king [him]self [10] on the *šj*-grounds of the palace in order to write (it) according to that [which had been said] [11] in his tomb which is in the necropolis.

a) *Š(j) nj pr-ꜥꜣ* is a recurring term in 5th Dynasty inscriptions used to designate a locality within the palace area where royal activity such as rewarding of officials took place.[397] On the other hand, *š(j)* may also (or specifically?) refer to a place of production (cf. Stauder-Porchet 2017: 59, n. 50 w. further references), for which reason Stauder-Porchet (2017: 40; 46) chooses the translation "atelier du Palais". In any case, one can easily imagine that King Neferirkare inspected the progress of the carving of Werre's slab in a similar fashion as Sahure is said to have done for two false doors in the slightly earlier inscription of Niankhsakhmet.[398]

b) Note that *m jz=f...* qualifies *r zš*, not *ḫft* [*ḏdd.t*]. The restorations follow Sethe (1933: 232, 14-16).

But *narrating through space* can have yet another meaning. We know that certain high officials gradually enlarged their tombs in accordance with their successes in climbing the career ladder.[399] Werre is probably one of the best examples for this practice. His tomb underwent several building phases at the end of which the structure had become one of the largest private funerary complexes in Giza at the time.[400] In this sense, a visitor striding through the structure would indeed be confronted with a built autobiography, in which architecture indexes advancement of wealth and status. While space does not necessarily tell a story by itself, in combination with the totality of the iconotext it becomes a means to induce narrativity.

396 Hassan (1932: 17, Fig. 12; 18).
397 See Brovarski (2001: 98, n. b).
398 See Sethe (1933: 38, 16–17); Stauder-Porchet (2017: 59).
399 For this phenomenon see Jánosi (2020: 734).
400 Hassan (1932: 1–61).

4.2 Key characteristics of narrating in the multimodal environment of a funerary structure

As the present contribution is not meant to be a comprehensive account of how to analyse an Old Kingdom tomb in terms of multimodality, I shall single out only two aspects that play a role for narratological approaches.

The first aspect relates to the concrete narrative mode (to be distinguished from the *mode* in multimodality research) that communicates the tomb's narrative content. In the previous chapters we have seen that a typical Old Kingdom elite tomb can be considered the brainchild of the tomb owner in his role of implied author. His "authorship" thus pertains to a multimodal configuration that comprises among other things purely textual and purely pictorial elements as well as complex combinations of the two. While both groups partake in the higher-order narrative signification of the tomb complex, they differ in terms of their relation to the *telling – showing* opposition. As most (auto)biographical texts of the Old Kingdom, including the event biographies, and the majority of the other text genres present in the tomb exhibit a relatively low level of mimetic representation, they are at the highest diegetic level associated with the role of a "master teller". The slot of "master teller" is necessarily occupied by the tomb owner himself (safe posthumous statements to the contrary). But the tomb owner is also the lens through which we view the tomb's pictorial dimension. He is focaliser and focalised at the same time, for no image within the tomb relates to an event outside his own experience (which includes his continued post-mortem existence). The common *mꜢꜢ*-scenes,[401] explicitly labelled as depicting the tomb owner "watching"/"inspecting" diverse activities in his environment, make this double role apparent. For what is represented to the right or left of the tomb owner's large-scale figure (see Fig. 8) indeed constitutes a part of *his* imaginary field of vision that he wishes to communicate to the onlooker as if through passing binoculars.[402] It might not be a coincidence that *mꜢꜢ* can also have a meaning approaching *rḏj mꜢꜢ*, namely "showing", "letting someone see" (see also p. 185).[403] In this respect it is of no consequence that the sight presents a generic, idealised extract of his self-image within the context of common occupations/ritual activities, (usually) not a true snapshot of a concrete autobiographical episode. As a note of caution I need to stress here that this observation pertains to the abstract narrative structure of the scenes and does not imply that we are dealing with simple illustrations of daily life detached from the ritual funerary context.[404]

---

401 See Fitzenreiter (2001: 83–88); Harpur (1987: 139–172).

402 In those cases where the figure of the tomb owner is absent (cf., e.g., Harpur 1987: 102), the narrative mechanism becomes even more direct.

403 Fitzenreiter (2001: 84). In certain cases where the word *mꜢꜢ* is oriented facing the tomb owner (usually in connection with the presentation of the offering list), the meaning "showing", "letting see" seems to be primary. Cf., e.g., Junker (1934: 128: Fig. 11, Mastaba of Merib). One is reminded in this context of the double meaning of *ḥr*, which represents not only "face", thus, a part of the body only visible to other people, but also "sight", "regard", "attention", i.e. the perceptive faculty originating in the respective person's visual system. Cf. Hannig (2003: 858, nos. 21118 & 21119).

404 See again Fitzenreiter (2001) for a different analytical focus.

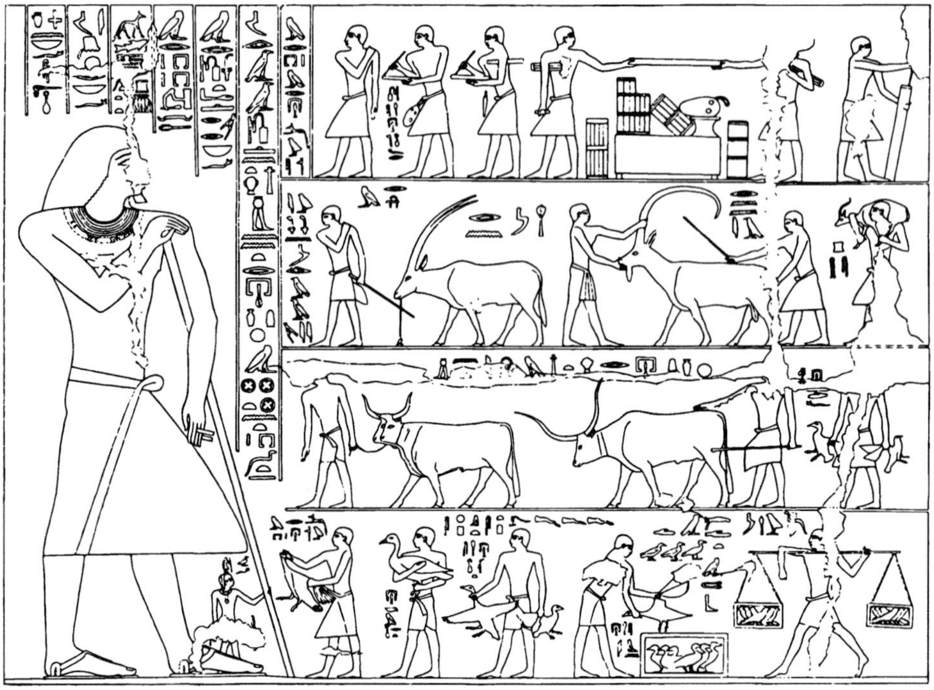

Fig. 8 *mꜢꜢ*-scene on the east wall of the tomb chapel of Seshemnefer III at Giza (G 5170), after Junker (1938: 73, Fig. 8b)

Since the level of mimesis in the pictorial semiotic mode is relatively high, the tomb owner as implied author becomes not so much a *teller* of his pictorial self-image but a *shower*. In a narratological context, these two complementary terms were coined by Chatman in 1990 in order better to describe the narrative mode and narrative potential of cinema.[405] Notwithstanding some qualifications within film studies brought forward since then,[406] the terms continue to prove particularly useful for a multimodal configuration such as ancient Egyptian monumental tombs. As a superordinate narratological entity Chatman suggests to introduce the term *presenter*, who may be conceived of as a narrator in the broad sense, having at his/her/its disposal the modes of both *telling* and *showing*: "Thus we can say that the implied author presents the story through a tell-er or a show-er or some combination of both."[407] Quite interestingly, the terms of *teller*, *shower*, and *presenter* are echoed in Roeder's approach to the ancient Egyptian narrative discourse, although he argues from a different, primarily text-based narratological perspective.[408] He too regards the presenting mode as the core of narrative communication in Egypt and associates

405 Chatman (1990: 113; 116).

406 See Horstkotte (2009) for some critical remarks concerning the proper analytical framework for the "cinematic mode" of narration. While the concept of "implied author" may be problematic for cinema, it suits the evidence within the context of ancient Egyptian funerary culture quite well.

407 Chatman (1990: 113).

408 See Roeder (2018b: 159–168, esp. 163).

it with the two sub-modes of "letting speak" and "letting see". If the semantic field of visuality can thus be shown to feature so prominently within the Egyptian textual narrative discourse, then the narrative mode of "letting see" through visually salient iconotexts must have played an important role in this culture as well. As a multimodal autobiographical monument, the funerary complex seems therefore predestined to be *presented* by the tomb owner as *implied author* equalling *narrator* equalling *presenter*. The position of his raised arm on many tomb façades or entrance thicknesses can accordingly be understood not only as speech gesture but also as a more general presentation/welcoming gesture[409] pointing to the entirety of the iconotextual content.

If we adopt a broad definition of *life writing* as outlined above (p. 124), a typical Old Kingdom elite tomb conveys the idea that the tomb's semiotic *text* is *presented* by the tomb owner or a close relative through an intricate combination of the *telling* and *showing* modes. But this presenting of life does not happen in a uniform or linear fashion. That brings me to the second topic of this chapter, the significance of non-linearity in multimodal narration within an architectural setting.

Since narrativity implies a world situated in time (see Chapter 2.2) and since time is conceived of as linearly progressing, linearity and sequentiality usually figure quite prominently in narratological analyses.[410] Of course, it has long been realised that the linearly progressing *histoire* or *fabula* is but a construct in the addressee's (and author's) mind(s), which is abstracted from a narrative's *récit*.[411] The *récit* itself may jump back and forth between distant points in time and show little consideration for the chronological sequence of events as they unfolded "in reality". What is often taken for granted, however, is that the *récit* is perceived and narrativised in a linear fashion, like a literary book – the prime model for traditional narratological theorising – is meant to be read from cover to cover. While postmodernist literature such as the fiction by Mark Z. Danielewski[412] has demonstrated that even within the book-centred literary discourse narrativity without predefined sequentiality is possible, the challenges to the linearity-concept of classical narratology reach much deeper.[413] Indeed, for the complex processing of narrative information within human minds, sequential linearity is not the most important category.[414] During the reception process, narrative inferences are constantly made, linked, and relinked with prior knowledge to create a dynamically evolving image of the composition's global narrative content. Following Pier,[415] Caracciolo maintains that narrative sequences, no matter how simple they might seem, are thus never devoid of complexity. Individual narrative se-

---

409 See Harpur (1987: 53); Kloth (2002: 248; 2018: 26–27). Cf. also Dominicus (1994: 77–80).

410 Grabes (2014). See also Branigan's (1992: 19–20) focus on sequences and temporal/causal chains within film narrative, or Martínez' (2011: 11) definition of story as a "chronologisch geordneten Sequenz von konkreten Zuständen und/oder Ereignissen, die kausal miteinander vernetzt sind und tendenziell in Handlungsschemata gefasst werden können."

411 Cf. Genette (1972: 74).

412 See the contributions in Pöhlmann (2012).

413 Cf. Hayles (2001).

414 Cf. Brockmeier (2015: 298).

415 Pier (2017: 558). Quoted by Caracciolo (2021: 34).

quences and global story do not share the relation of mutual deductibility, which means that "all narratives can be said to be nonlinear to the extent that the reader cannot determine their outcome from the outset."[416] This intrinsic nonlinearity is especially well developed in higher-order narratives[417] of the kind we come across in ancient Egyptian monumental tombs, where narrativisation by necessity takes place in a complex and nonlinear fashion. Although architectural design, the orientation of pictorial and textual elements, and visual signposting have an impact on the way visitors progress through the tomb chapel and direct their fields of vision,[418] there is (usually) no single correct or logical sequence in which the individual elements of the iconotext should be perceived.[419] The sequence and intensity of the receptive engagement will also have depended on the concrete purpose of one's visit and the potentially accompanying ritual/performative actions. In this respect it seems rather unlikely that – apart perhaps from the situation during the burial ritual – visitors were expected to read a tomb "from cover to cover" (see Chapter 7.1). This explains the great pains taken by many tomb owners to catch the passers-by's attention and engage them in the respective funerary cult.

Nonlinearity also means that individual elements of the iconotext may attain higher-order narrative meaning only in combination with other elements. This principle also lies at the heart of the concept of "portfolio biography", which I shall discuss in the following chapter.

5 Life writing: instantiation of (auto)biographical narratives in 3D+

Whereas the focus of the previous chapters lay on theoretical considerations, the remainder of this essay will illustrate select issues through case studies taken primarily from the tomb of Senedjemib Inti at Giza. A transcription and translation of the most important texts is found in Chapter 5.2.

5.1 The portfolio biography

Senedjemib Inti attained among many other offices those of vizier as well as overseer of all royal works. As such he belonged to the highest stratum of society apart from the royal house itself.[420] As we learn from his autobiographical inscription (A1, see below), he held these duties under King Djedkare Izezi towards the end of the 5th Dynasty and probably

416 Caracciolo (2021: 34).

417 Communication in contemporary digital media offers another field for the study of multimodal nonlinear narration. See Skains (2019: 139).

418 Cf. the illuminating psychological studies by Rosenberg and his colleagues where the complex visual perceptions of beholders of works of art are analysed. E.g. Sancarlo et al. (2020); Commare et al. (2018).

419 Of course, individual texts may signpost reading direction and ensure cohesion across spatial breaks so that the reader is guided through a complex textual composition. Examples of this include the already mentioned inscription of Shepsesptah (see p. 118) or the autobiography of Hezy. For the latter see Baines (2015b: 521); Stauder-Porchet (2015: 192).

420 Strudwick (1985: 132–133, no. 120).

also died under that king. At some point in his life, when he had already accumulated considerable wealth and social prestige, he must have decided to commission a funerary structure that would adequately represent his high status and position at court. Despite the fact that Giza had long ceased to be the site of the royal necropolis, officials throughout the 5th Dynasty continued to use the cemeteries surrounding the pyramids of the kings of the previous dynasty to erect their own tombs or repurpose already existing mastabas for their personal funerary needs. Senedjemib Inti too chose to be buried at Giza but did not adopt one of the already existing mastaba cores of the Western Field. Instead, his tomb constitutes a newly built structure located close to the north-western corner of the pyramid of King Khufu within a space commonly referred to as *Cemetery en Échelon*. As pointed out by Brovarski and Jánosi, the site was far from being virgin soil and generally not well suited to a monumental tomb with subterranean burial chamber due to the local geological and hydraulic conditions.[421] The question therefore remains why the tomb was not constructed elsewhere in Giza. Should the Senedjemib Inti of G 2370 be identical with the Senedjemib Inti whose name features in the small, unfinished rock-cut chamber of LG 10 (west of the pyramid of Khafre),[422] then we can at least surmise that the building project at the *Cemetery en Échelon* reflected a change of plan and a step towards a grander scheme. In any event, G 2370 was completed at the location and later provided the nucleus for subsequent tombs erected by family members and later descendants. In its final layout the rectangular tomb measures 22.8×20.9 m[423] and comprises eight rooms, namely, a two-columned portico, an anteroom, a supplementary offering room (?), the main offering chapel, two serdabs, a pillared hall, and an inaccessible "magazine" to the south, which could have housed funerary equipment, even a small ritual boat.[424] Like other high-profile non-royal tombs of the late 5th Dynasty, Senedjemib Inti's structure features several architectural characteristics that are indebted to the vocabulary of royal funerary complexes, and reflect on his status as a high official. Not to this group of features belong the two burial shafts positioned behind the magazine (G 2370 A) and behind the main false door of the offering chapel (G 2373 A). The latter shaft originally belonged to the already existing mastaba G 2373. G 2370 A and G 2373 A were evidently not used for Inti's burial and would not have been large enough to receive his voluminous limestone sarcophagus. Instead, a burial chamber with a sloping passage (intentionally citing royal paradigms?[425]) was constructed c. 30 m to the east of the mastaba tomb (G 2370 B), resulting in a separation of burial place and offering cult that can be considered unique for Old Kingdom non-royal funerary monuments.[426] As convincingly argued by Jánosi,[427] this particular arrangement was probably due to the fact that Inti's son Mehi had managed to procure by royal decree a

---

421 Brovarski (2001: 1–2); Jánosi (2020: 737). The present paragraph draws primarily from Jánosi (2020).

422 Jánosi (2020: 737). Cf. Porter & Moss (1974: 229, LG 10); Baud (1999: 573, no. 215).

423 Brovarski (2001: 37).

424 For such spaces within non-royal tombs, see Altenmüller (2002: 271–272).

425 After all, both Inti and his son Mehi were overseers of all royal works.

426 Brovarski (2001: 22; 79–81); Jánosi (2020: 736–737).

427 Jánosi (2020: 737–740).

limestone sarcophagus for his recently deceased father (deducible from Inscriptions C and D, see below) and was forced to "outsource" the burial site because it would not have been possible to insert the sarcophagus into the burial chamber of either of the tomb's two shafts without dismantling a large part of the superstructure. The 15 months mentioned at the end of inscription C as the period of time needed to complete the building work then relates in all probability to the construction of G 2370 B[428] and not to that of the entire mastaba as Strudwick surmised.[429]

As to be expected from a mastaba of the size and architectural complexity of Senedjemib Inti's, the tomb chapel's iconotextual programme is quantitatively rich and diverse in content.[430] While a comprehensive analysis of it is complicated by its relatively bad state of preservation, the documentation produced by Lepsius[431] during the Prussian Expedition enables us in large parts to identify at least the original themes and motifs on the walls. Originally, every accessible room of the tomb chapel with the exception of the pillared hall bore decoration in low relief, whereas the inscriptions on the façade and the decoration of the outermost parts of the portico's lateral walls were executed in sunk relief. The greatest density of textual and pictorial elements is certainly found in the portico (I) and the immediately adjacent parts of the façade. At the outer corners of the portico (see Fig. 9) we find altogether six lengthy texts, which are, apart from a few horizontal headings, inscribed in vertical columns: A1 and A2 at the façade north of the portico, B1 and B2 on the portico's northern wall, D on the portico's southern wall, and C at the façade south of the portico.[432] They make up the primary textual component of Senedjemib Inti's life writing and were clearly visible from the mastaba's paved forecourt. The inscriptions feature the first securely dated event autobiography phrased in the first person (A1), the copies of three royal letters by King Izezi (A2, B1, and B2), and finally, two first-person texts (featuring a quotation from a royal decree), which describe the efforts of Senedjemib Inti's son Senedjemib Mehi regarding the burial of his father (C and D). While this amassment of diverse biographical material is exceptional, Senedjemib Inti's tomb is not the only one where the autobiographical discourse was focussed on the tomb's entrance.[433] Around the same time, the façades/front parts of the tombs of Shespsesre[434] and Kaemtjenenet[435] were respectively inscribed with copies of a royal letter (again by Izezi)[436] and a long event autobiography, thus marking the entrance of the tomb chapel as a preferred place to showcase one's achievements and recognition at court.

---

428 Jánosi (2020: 740). Cf. also Reisner (1942: 151; 163). As a matter of fact, the burial apartment does not seem to have been finished. Brovarski (2001: 22; 79).

429 Strudwick (1985: 133 w. n. 2).

430 See Brovarski (2001: 37–88).

431 Lepsius (1849–1859: Abth. II, Pls. 76–78; 1897: 56; 1913: Pls. XVII–XXIII).

432 Sethe (1933: 59–67, no. 42); Brovarski (2001: 89–110).

433 Brovarski (2001: 15).

434 Quibell (1909: 23–24); Spiegelberg (1909: 79–82, Pl. LXI, 2); Sethe (1933: 179–180, no. 24 [115]); Eichler (1991a: 149–152); Chauvet (2011: 299).

435 Spiegelberg (1909: 82–88, Pl. LXI, 3–5); Sethe (1933: 180–186, no. 25 [116]); Schott (1977: 443–444).

436 See also Stauder-Porchet (2017: 135–136).

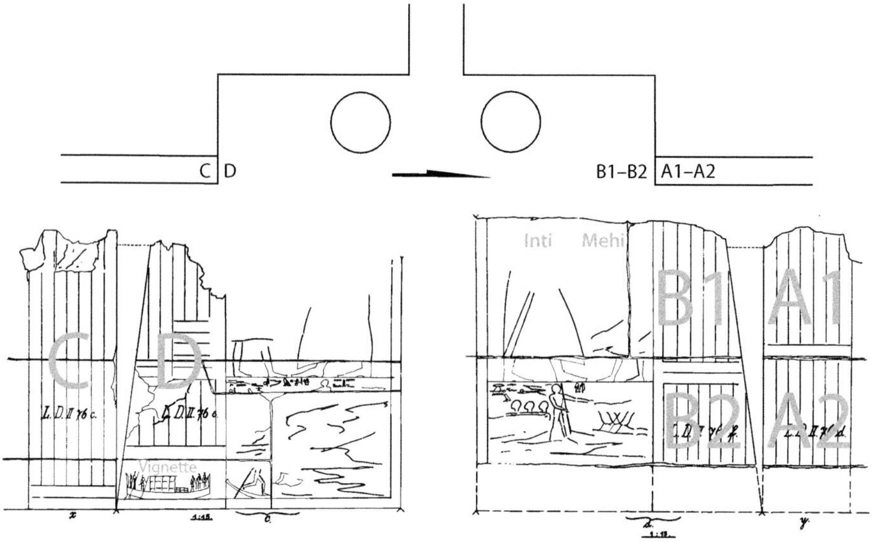

Fig. 9 Configuration of the biographical iconotext on the façade and portico of the mastaba of Senedjemib Inti at Giza (G 2370), using Lepsius (1897: Figs. on p. 56)

In Inti's tomb, the portico's side walls are further decorated with depictions of the tomb owner before his son (similarly, the thicknesses of the entrance) as well as marsh scenes and a vignette of the transport of Inti's sarcophagus associated with Inscription D. The rear wall is covered by a monumental antithetical composition showing the tomb owner spear hunting and fowling in the marshes. The following anteroom (II) bears a rich decorative programme of scenes relating to "daily life" and preparations for the funerary rituals. Of these the return journey of three ships on the lower registers of the east wall and the scene with the tomb owner being borne on a sedan chair on the upper register of the south wall are particularly noteworthy. The north-south oriented Room III comprised personifications of funerary domains as well as agricultural scenes. Finally, in the offering chapel (IV), we find to the south and north of the central false door the usual rows of offering bearers approaching a figure of the tomb owner seated before an offering table. While the pillared hall (V) was left undecorated, its entrance thicknesses were covered with reliefs each showing the tomb owner and his wife Tjefi being received by their eldest son Senedjemib Mehi. Since we know from Inscriptions C and D, executed at the behest of his son, that Senedjemib Inti had died before he could make the final preparations for his burial, it is little wonder that some of the reliefs in the tomb's outer parts were created or at least adapted posthumously under the supervision of Mehi. This is certainly true of Inscriptions C and D as well as the associated vignette on the portico's south wall. Since the final layout of the tomb's façade is symmetrical, Mehi will also have been responsible for the present configuration of the northern half. He[437] is indeed depicted on the upper register of the portico's northern wall, where he is addressing his father. The inscription in low relief (as opposed

437 The figure and the inscription are now partly destroyed, but the context and the parallel scenes in the tomb make the identification as good as certain.

to the sunk relief of the adjacent text B1) seems to represent a direct speech,[438] in which Mehi apparently elaborates on a royal favour regarding Inti's embalming equipment granted to him on account of his and his father's excellence.[439] Interestingly, the fourth and last column of the inscription was reworked at a later stage in poorer quality, indicating some changes to the final wording or text configuration. Stauder-Porchet rightly stresses the similarities of the text with that of Akhtihotep (cf. p. 73), where a son is likewise granted a royal favour for the sake of his father. Like Inscriptions C and D (see below), the current text represents Mehi's agency in relation to his father's burial, if only indirectly. What is presented is not so much Mehi's petitioning but its result and the reasons for its success: the excellence of father and son. The inscription thus belongs to the biographical discourse of both individuals and stands in spatial and semantic relation to the representation of two royal letters immediately to the right (B1 and B2). These two inscriptions were carved in a significantly smaller hieroglyphic module in sunk relief and replicate the general layout of royal decrees/papyrus documents with an introductory horizontal line. We can well imagine that B1 and B2 reproduce actual letters received from Izezi that were integrated into the iconotextual programme of the portico-façade as elements of a higher-order (auto) biographical narrative. The same holds true for Inscription A2, the copy of another letter from Izezi, which is positioned around the corner at the northern façade immediately below Inti's autobiography A1. In selecting these ego-documents, relating them to the neighbouring texts with biographical content, and presenting them for visitor's to see and read, Senedjemib Inti and/or Mehi become the actual, if implicit, higher-order narrator(s) of the royal discourse represented therein. As a result we arrive at an interesting narrative constellation: In these three letters Senedjemib Inti is not only the addressee but also the main object of the king's focalisation as narrator *qua* letter writer. At the next higher level of diegesis, however, the tomb owner himself becomes the one who takes on both the roles of focaliser and of the one who is being focalised by proxy.[440] The narratological complexity is further enhanced by the fact that A2 and B1 report the content of previous exchanges of letters and thus open up the reader's imagination to another level of intradiegetic narration (see Chapter 6.2).[441] In that sense the letters contribute a second person voice to Inti's autobiographic meta-narration.[442]

At the southern, opposite end of the portico we find a badly preserved depiction of two figures that are likely to represent again Mehi and his father. One may assume that the scene was once associated with a text comparable to the one on the portico's opposite

438 See the restauration of Edel (1955–1964: 339–340, § 676) and Brovarski (2001: 41).

439 Sethe (1933: 67, no. 43); Brovarski (2001: 41–42); Stauder-Porchet (2017: 154–155). Stauder-Porchet (2017: 154, n. 64) restores an initial narrative infinitive (*rḏj.t*) in analogy to the inscription of Akhtihotep, but Brovarski's restoration with a finite verb seems equally possible.

440 See Genette's (1972: 206–211) explication of narrative modalities.

441 That level of diegesis would of course only be a virtual one, since the previous letters' content is not quoted verbatim.

442 Cf. Stauder-Porchet (2021a: 154): "Mises en regard avec l'autobiographie événementielle en constitution, les lettres font ainsi une « biographie » du dignitaire à la 2ᵉ personne, dite par le roi lui-même."

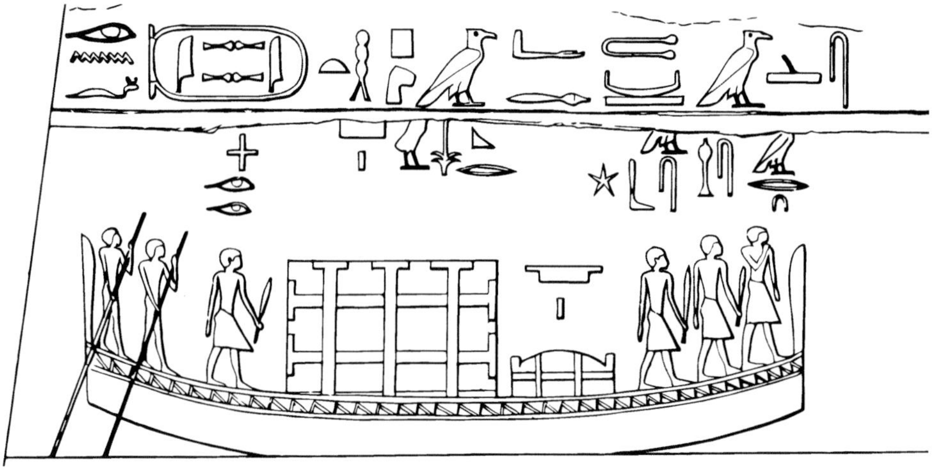

Fig. 10 Detail of the vignette below Inscription D on the southern wall of the portico of Senedjemib Inti (G 2370), after Lepsius (1849–1859, II: Pl. 76e)

wall. Further to the left and bordering the wall's edge is Inscription D, an unfortunately badly preserved first-person narrative text dealing with Mehi's handling of the transport of Inti's sarcophagus and the royal support he has received. The text also restates in terms different to Inscription C the royal favour of granting Mehi the means to procure the funerary object. At the bottom is a carefully carved little vignette in sunk relief (Fig. 10), which depicts the sarcophagus and its lid firmly tied to the deck of a transport barge, surrounded by mariners who are provided with captions. The barge itself is labelled as *ꜥꜣ pḥtj* (*Jzzj*), "Great is the strength of (Izezi)".[443] This scene belongs to the *showing domain* of Inti's meta-narrative and has no direct equivalent in the wording of either Inscription C or D, although it is clear from content and spatial association that it is meant as an illustration of the above text. However, the vignette provides descriptive information that goes beyond the data deducible from Inscriptions C and D (as far as they are preserved) and significantly increases the episode's experientiality. Inscription C at the northern corner of the southern half of the façade is Mehi's first-person account of his arrangements for his father's funerary cult approved by the king. These arrangements included successfully petitioning the king for a limestone sarcophagus from Tura, whose procurement and installation in the tomb took according to the inscription a year and three months. During this period Inti's body rested in his *wabet* erected somewhere within the necropolis associated with the pyramid complex of Izezi.

All these six inscriptions are centred on a single individual (with Mehi as a second major protagonist), but they do not build that sort of narrative unity one would commonly associate with an autobiography consisting of continuous running text. Rather, they form an assemblage of material where each piece retains its autonomy while at the same time complementing the others and thus contributing to narrative meaning at a higher level. It is a *combined* reading of these texts in the given *context* that allows, actually demands, a

443 Brovarski (2001: 38; Fig. 4 between pp. 104 & 105).

biographical narrativisation. How a *récit* is formed out of the "narrativisation offer" and how the generational jump is processed which occurs in the switch from Inti's perspective to that of his son lies more or less at the discretion of the visitor. What counts is that these texts by their semantic and spatial relatedness invite a holistic reading. This phenomenon I would like to call *portfolio* or *assemblage biography/life writing*.

By definition, a portfolio is "a collection of samples of a person's work, typically intended to convey the quality and breadth of his or her achievement in a particular field."[444] Its individual elements may be filed according to a certain order, e.g. chronological or alphabetical, but there is a common understanding that following this order is of less importance than knowing the totality of the work output. This output is then related to a specific person and judged according to criteria appropriate for the given context. It is important to stress that a portfolio such as a bundle of artwork submitted to an art school prior to admission fluctuates between presence and history. In a certain way it has the capacity to be narrativised as a life story, but this potential does not have to be made use of. Even if it is used, that story covers only a very limited slice of one's life, pertaining predominantly to a person's professional training or output. In a similar sense, an ancient Egyptian *portfolio biography* can be said to represent a collection of material (continuous text, iconotext, statuary etc.) authorised by and centred on one particular person that carries a significant potential to become narrativised as a group. While close spatial proximity between group elements can enhance this potential, it is no precondition for successful narrativisation, since in the reception process the unit of assessment can easily be extended to an entire tomb (cf. also the case of Herkhuf, p. 146). In that sense, scenes such as the sedan chair-episode and the riverine journey in Room II are equally components of Inti's life writing, even if they signify differently compared with Inscriptions A–D. The widely practiced Egyptian principle of "distributed (self-)representation", where a person's self-image is projected onto several iconotextual elements or entire monuments erected more or less apart from one another[445] also means that the highest biographical unit of signification can theoretically encompass much more than a single tomb. But, of course, the greater the spatial distance, the more difficult a holistic reading of distributed life writing will become. While it is not the main strength of portfolio biography to convey temporal sequentiality across portfolio elements, circumstantial hints may indeed establish a temporal framework wherein the different elements are to be inserted. In the case of Inti's portfolio biography, a certain chronological depth (and sequence?) is communicated by the inclusion of chrono-biographical data (see Chapter 5.3). From this we can surmise that the events represented within the tomb unfold within the latter part of Izezi's reign.

Another characteristic of the *portfolio biography* is that it represents a complex multimodal narrative which can be described but not plainly translated into linear linguistic text. Its signification will always go beyond the merely textual. While a recitation of the purely textual elements appears possible, the higher-order narrative deriving from all its components cannot easily be re-naturalised in spoken language. The pictorial vignette

444 OED (2022b).
445 Jurman (2020: Vol. II, 1183). See also Chauvet (2013: 58 w. n. 9); Baines (2020: 66).

showing the transport of Inti's sarcophagus below Inscription D demonstrates that the modelling of biographical content is always modally specific. The portfolio principle further implies a certain freedom on the part of the recipient. Juxtaposed textual and pictorial elements may be inserted into an overarching narrative framework, but they are equally decodable as self-sufficient semiotic entities.

5.2 Senedjemib Inti (G 2370): the texts[446]

Northern half of façade, south end, top, Inscription A1

$\overset{1}{|}$ → [*(j)r(j)-pꜥ.t ḥꜣtj-ꜥ tꜣytj zꜣb ṯꜣtj (j)m(j)-rʾ zš(w.w)-ꜥ nj nswt* $\overset{2}{|}$ *(j)m(j)-rʾ kꜣ.t nb.t nj.t nswt (j)m(j)-rʾ ḥw.t-wr.t 6*] $\overset{3}{|}$ *(j)m(j)-rʾ šnw.tj (j)m(j)-rʾ pr.wj-ḥḏ* $\overset{4}{|}$ *(j)m(j)-*[*rʾ*] *jz.wj* ⌜*ḫkr*⌝ *nswt (j)m(j)-rʾ pr-ꜥḥꜣw* $\overset{5}{|}$ *(j)m(j)-rʾ s.t nb.t nj.t ẖnw (j)m(j)-rʾ pr.w* ⌜*ms.w-nswt*⌝ $\overset{6}{|}$ *rnp.t 5 ꜣbd 4 sw 3 mrn(=j) ḫr (Jzzj)*[a]

$\overset{1}{|}$ [The *iri-pat*, *hati-a*, chief justice and vizier, overseer of the royal documents, $\overset{2}{|}$ overseer of all royal works, overseer of the six great courts,] $\overset{3}{|}$ overseer of the double granary, overseer of the double treasury, $\overset{4}{|}$ over[seer] of the two chambers of royal ⌜adornments⌝, overseer of the armoury, $\overset{5}{|}$ overseer of every office of the residence, overseer of the houses of the ⌜royal children⌝: $\overset{6}{|}$ Five years, four months and three days are (my) favour with (Izezi).

$\overset{7}{|}$ ↓ *sk w(j) špss.k(j) ḫr (Jzzj)* [*r mrtj(=j) nb*] *m ḥrj-sštꜣ nj ḥm=f m jmj-jb nj ḥm=f m (j)ḫ.t nb.t* $\overset{8}{|}$ *mrr.t ḥm=f jrj.t(j) sk ḥm=f ḥz(.w) w(j) ḥr kꜣ.t nb(.t) wḏ.t.n ḥm=f jrj.t(j) wn(=j) jrj(=j) mr s.t-jb nj.t ḥm=f (j)r=s* $\overset{9}{|}$ *jw rḏj.n n(=j) (Jzzj) wꜣḏ šmꜥw jzn n* [*ḫ*]*ḫ*[*=j*[b] …] *ḥm=f sk sw m s.t-ꜥ sk ḫpr* $\overset{10}{|}$ *ꜥḥꜥ(=j) ḥr š(j) rḏj ḥm=f tz.t(j)=f r ḫḫ*[*(=j)* ...] *rḏj ḥm=f wrḥ.t(j=j) m ꜥnd* $\overset{11}{|}$ *smꜥr.t(j) jwf(=j) r-gs ḥm=f jn sḥḏ* [*jrw šn*] *pr-ꜥꜣ ḥrj-tp* [*Nḫb jrj-nfr-ḥꜣ.t*] *n zp jrj.t(j) mrt.t r-gs nswt n rmṯ nb* $\overset{12}{|}$ *n špss | mnḫ | mrj w(j) ḫr (Jzzj) r mrtj(=j) nb* $\overset{13}{|}$ *jw jrj.n n(=j)* [*(Jzzj) wḏ*] *zš ḥm=f ḏs=f m ḏbꜥ.wj=f(j) r ḥzj.t(=j)*

$\overset{7}{|}$ Since I was esteemed before (Izezi) [more than any companion (of mine)] as master of secrets of His Majesty and as confidant of His Majesty in every matter $\overset{8}{|}$ that His Majesty wished to be carried out, and since His Majesty praised me for every work that His Majesty had commanded to be carried out, I used to act according to the desire of His Majesty in this regard. $\overset{9}{|}$ (Izezi) gave me an *izen* necklace of Upper Egyptian malachite for [my] ne[ck …] His Majesty. Since he was in the records office and since it came to pass that $\overset{10}{|}$ (I) stood on duty at the *šj*-grounds His Majesty had it (i.e. the necklace) tied around (my) neck […] His Majesty saw to it that (I) was anointed with *aned* unguent $\overset{11}{|}$ and that (my) flesh was purified beside His Majesty by the inspector of [hairdressers] of the palace, the governor of [Nekheb and the keeper of the *nfr-hat* diadem]. Never before was something similar done in the presence of the king for any person, $\overset{12}{|}$ because I was esteemed, diligent and beloved

446 My translations are indebted to Brovarski's (2001: 89–110) and Stauder-Porchet's (2017: 139–152) previous editions. Thanks to their comprehensive treatments commentary can be kept to a minimum. Only restored text not included in Lepsius' and Reisner's copies is put between square brackets.

[14] *ḥr (j)ḫ.t nb(.t) jrj.t.n(=j) [r špss] r nfr r mnḫ ḫft s.t-jb nj.t ḥm=f (j)r=s*

before (Izezi) more than any companion (of mine). [13] [(Izezi)] made a [decree] for (me), which His Majesty himself wrote with his two fingers in order to praise (me) [14] for everything that (I) had made [estimably], perfectly and diligently according to His Majesty's desire in that respect.

a) Here ends the introductory section in horizontal lines. A comparable configuration with just one horizontal line is found in the 6th Dynasty autobiography of Nekhebu (right jamb: Boston MFA 13.4331),[447] which was originally located close to the tomb of Senedjemib Inti.[448]
b) Cf. the inscription of Akhtihotep, p. 73.

Northern half of façade, south end, bottom, Inscription A2

[1] ← *wḏ-nswt* → *ṯꜣjtj zꜣb ṯꜣtj (j)m(j)-rʾ zš(w.w)-ʿ nj nswt* [2] *(j)m(j)-rʾ kꜣ.t nb.t nj.t nswt Snḏm-jb*

[1] Royal Command (to) the chief justice and vizier, the overseer of the royal document scribes, [2] the overseer of every royal work Senedjemib.

[3] ↓ *jw mꜣꜣ.n ḥm(=j) mḏꜣ.t=k tn jrj.t.n=k r rḏj.t rḫ ḥm(=j) (j)ḫ.t nb.t ntj.t jrj.⌜t⌝.n=k m ⌜ḳd⌝ zš* [4] *nj mr.t (Jzzj) ntj.t ḥr š(j) nj pr-ʿꜣ jn rr jw wnn mꜣʿ snḏm jb(=j) jm* [c] *n wnn ḏd (j)ḫ.t js pw* [5] *m snḏm jb* [d] *nj (Jzzj) (r)dj rḫ ḥm(=j) bw mꜣʿ (j)r(j) ḥr ʿw jn ḥm wn r ḫpr ṯwt* [6] *ḏd mrr.t (Jzzj) r sʿḥ nb ḫpr m tꜣ pn rḫ.n(=j) ṯwt šps wrt n(=j) m jšs.t* [7] *sk ḥm ḥm(=j) rḫ wnt ḥʿw nb ḥr nfrw=f ⌜twt⌝ n(=j) ḏd (j)m(j)-rʾ kꜣ.t nb(.t) n(j.t) nswt* [8] *snḏm jb pw nj (Jzzj) mꜣʿ.t mꜣʿ.t ḥꜣ ⌜jw.t⌝[=k] ḥr(=j) [n?] jrr?=k (j)ḫ.t pw ḥr⌜=s⌝* [9] *jḳr jḳr jw jrj.n(=k) ḥḥ.w nj.w zp mrj ṯw [ḥm(=j)] sk ḥm rḫ.t(j) mrr(=j) ṯw*

[3] (My) Majesty has seen (≈ read) this letter of yours, which you wrote in order to inform (My) Majesty about everything that you have done in terms of designing the decoration [4] of the *meret* of (Izezi), which is on the *šj* grounds of the palace. Does it really exist about which my heart rejoices? Is it not rather saying things [5] as a consolation of the heart of (Izezi)? Let (My) Majesty immediately know its veracity! If (it) comes to pass thus, it will be you who will [6] speak what (Izezi) loves more than (what) any (other) dignitary having appeared on this earth (says). In what way do (I) know that you are very precious to me? Inasmuch as (My) Majesty evidently knows that every ship is on its bottom. The speech of the overseer of every royal work suits (me). [8] It is truthfully rejoicing of the heart of (Izezi). May [you] come before (me), since you act in this respect very excellently! You have made millions of actions for which (My) Majesty loves you. Therefore it is generally known that (I) love you.

c) I follow here the grammatical analysis of Stauder-Porchet (2017: 146).
d) This is most likely a wordplay on Senedjemib's own name. Whether it was devised by the king or edited into the letter at a later stage is anybody's guess.

---

447 See Dunham (1935: Pl. II).
448 Brovarski (2001: 3).

Northern wall of portico, east end, top, Inscription B1

[|1 ← *wḏ-nswt* |2 → *ṯꜣtj zꜣb ṯꜣtj* |3 *(j)m(j)-rꜣ zš(w.w)-ꜥ nj nswt* |4 *(j)m(j)-rꜣ kꜣ.t nb.t nj.t nswt* |5 *Snḏm-jb smsw*] [e]
|6 ↓ [*jw sjꜣ.n(=j) md.t nj.t mḏꜣ.t=k tn jrj.t*].*n=k ḫr* ⸢*nswt*⸣ *r jz.t r rḏj.t rḫ ḥm(=j) wnt jnj n=k wḏ n nswt r* [...] *sk ṯw ḏd=k ḫr ḥm(=j) wnt=k r jrj.t š(j)* [f] *ḫft ḏdd.t m* [*stp*]*-zꜣ* |7 [... *k*]*ꜣ.t m stp-z*[*ꜣ*] *m-ḫmt=k sk ṯw ḏd=k ḫr ḥm(=j) wnt=k r* [...] *ḥꜣb-sd jw mrj.n ḥm(=j) sḏm mdw=k pn w*[*r*].*t*
|8 [... *n d*]*jj(=j) ṯw* [*ḥ*]*r gs=k n rḏj ṯw kꜣ nj* (*Jzzj*) *n (j)ḫ.t nb(.t) m ꜥ ḫftj=k* [...] *ṯwt jrj n=f ḥm(=j) (j)ḫ.t nb(.t) srḫ.t ḥm(=j) ḏr-ntj.t ḏd.t(j) (j)m(j)-rꜣ kꜣ.t nb(.t) n(j.t) nswt* |9 *ḥr-ꜥw mꜣꜣ(=j) kꜣ.t m stp-zꜣ sk ṯw m* [...] *ḥr rs-tp jrj.n=f m grḥ mr hrw r jrj.t wḏ*[*.t*]*.n* |10 *nb(.t) ḥm(=j) jm rꜥ nb rḫ.n(=j) ḥm mrr w(j) Rꜥ ḥr* |11 *rḏj.t=f n(=j) ṯw*

|1 Royal Command |2 (to) the chief justice and vizier, |3 the overseer of the royal document scribes, |4 the overseer of every royal work |5 Senedjemib the Elder].
|6 [I have taken notice of the matter of this your letter which you mad]e for the king (and sent) to the council chamber in order to inform (My) Majesty that a royal command was brought to you in order [...] So you tell (therein) to (My) Majesty that you will make the *šj* in accordance with what was said in the [court] council. |7 [... wo]rk in the court coun[cil] without you. So you (likewise) tell (therein) (My) Majesty that you will [...] *heb-sed*. It pleased (My) Majesty gr[eat]ly to hear this concern of yours.
|8 [... (I)] will [not put] you at your side (i.e. discomfit you?). The *ka* of (Izezi) will not deliver you to the hand of your enemy on account of any matter [...] You are someone for whom (My) Majesty does everything one informs (My) Majesty about, for the overseer of every royal work is mentioned |9 immediately when (I) inspect the work in the court council, while you are in [...] due to the vigilance he has exercised night and day in order to do |10 everything (My) Majesty |9 has commanded |10 to that effect daily. It is because |11 he has given you to (me) |10 that (I) know (how much) Re really loves me.

e) The restoration, which is determined by the available space, follows Brovarski (2001: 94).
f) Stauder-Porchet (2017: 59, n. 50; 140) translates this instance of *š(j)* as "fabrication". See also above, p. 148, n. a.

Northern wall of portico, east end, bottom, Inscription B2

|1 ← *wḏ-nswt* → *ṯꜣtj zꜣb ṯꜣtj (j)m(j)-rꜣ kꜣ.t nb.t nj.t* ⸢*nswt*⸣ |2 *(j)m(j)-rꜣ zš(w.w)-ꜥ nj nswt Snḏm-jb* [*smsw*]
|3 ↓ *jw mꜣꜣ.n ḥm(=j) snṯw pn rḏj.n=k* [*jnj*].*t(j)=f r sjꜣ m stp-zꜣ n š(j) nj* ⸢*sḫ.t*⸣ [g] |4 *nj ꜥḥ nj* (*Jzzj*) *nj ḥꜣb-sd* [h] *sk ṯw ḏd=k ḫr ḥm(=j) wnt jrj.n=k sw* |5 *r* [*ꜣw*] ⸢*mḥ*

|1 Royal Command (to) the chief justice and vizier, |3 the overseer of every ⸢royal⸣ work, |2 the overseer of the royal document scribes Senedjemib [the Elder].

|3 (My) Majesty has seen this ground plan that you had brought to be considered in the court council for the ground of the *sekhet*-hall |4 of (Izezi's) *heb-sed* palace. Thus, you say (therein) to (My) Majesty that you have made it |5 to a [length] of 1,000 cubits

1000⌝ [*sḫw*] ⌜*mḥ 440*⌝ *ḫft wḏḏ.t n=k m stp-zꜣ rḫ w(j)* ⌜*ṯ*⌝*w tr ḏd mrr.t* (*Jzzj*) *r (j)ḫ.t nb(.t)* [6]| *jrj.n ṯw ḥm nṯr r s.t-jb nj.t* (*Jzzj*) *jw ḥm(=j) rḫ(.w) ḥmw=k r (j) m(j)-rʾ kꜣ.t nb(.t)* [7]| *ḫpr m tꜣ pn r* ⌜*ḏr*⌝*=f jw jrj ḫr=k wrt jrj.*[*t*] *(j)* ⌜*mrj.t(=j)*⌝ *r (j)ḫ.t nb(.t) jw ḥm jrj.n=k* [8]| *ḫrp ḥḥ.w nj.w zp jw*[*=k*] *r (j)m(j)-rʾ kꜣ.t nb(.t) nj.t nswt*[i] [9]| *j Snḏm-jb smsw mrr ṯw* ⌜*ḥm*⌝ *sk ḥm rḫ.t(j) mrr(=j) ṯw* [10]| *rnp.t-zp* [*1*]⌜*6*⌝ *ꜣbd 4 šmw sw 28*

and a [width] of 440 cubits in accordance with what was commanded to you in the court council. How well you indeed know to say what (Izezi) loves more than anything! [6]| God has really made you according to the wish of (Izezi). (My) Majesty knows that you possess more expertise than any overseer of every work [7]| who has appeared in this entire land. A lot has been done through you so that what I desire more than anything is done. You have indeed assumed [8]| control on a million of occasions. (Therefore) you will be overseer of every royal work. [9]| O Senedjemib the Elder! I really love you that much that it is basically known (I) love you. [10]| Year of the [1]⌜6⌝th occasion, 4th month of shemu, day 28.

g) Or to be read *wsḫ.t*. See Brovarski (2001: 98–99, n. c).
h) The date of the letter probably lies within the time Djedkare Izezi was preparing to celebrate his first *heb-sed* festival. Cf. Brovarski (2001: 97, n. d).
i) This remark turns the royal letter into a promotion decree. Thus its inclusion in Inti's portfolio biography.

Northern wall of portico, west end, top, inscription over the figure of Inti

[1]| ↓ [*(j)r(j)-pꜥ.t ḥꜣtj-ꜥ tꜣjtj zꜣb ṯꜣtj (j)m(j)-rʾ*] *kꜣ.t nb.t nj.t nswt* [2]| [*(j)m(j)-rʾ zš(w.w)-ꜥ nj nswt ḥrj-sštꜣ wḏ.t mdw nb.t nj.t*] *nswt (j)m(j)-rʾ pr-ꜥḥꜣ* [3]| [... *mḏḥ*] *ḳd* [*nswt*] *m pr.wj* [4]| ← *Snḏm-jb rn=f ꜥꜣ* [5]| *Jntj rn=f nfr*

[1]| [The *iri-pat* and *hati-a*, chief justice and vizier, overseer of] every royal work, [2]| [the overseer of the royal document scribes, master of the secret of every command] of the king, overseer of the armoury, [3]| [... royal master] builder in the two houses, [4]| Senedjemib is his great name, [5]| Inti is his beautiful name.

Northern wall of portico, west end, top, inscription over the figure of Mehi[449]

[1]| ↓ [*rḏj.t*[j] *ḥm nj nb(=j) šdj n(=j)* ...]⌜*w*⌝ *nb štꜣ wn.n(=j) dbḥ(=j) n jtj(=j) tꜣjtj zꜣb ṯꜣtj* [*mꜣꜥ*] [2]| [*Snḏm-jb* ...]*w n špss=f ḫr nswt r šps=f nb n wr*[*r=f*] [3]| [*ḫr nswt r wr=f nb ... sk w(j)*] *mnḫ.k(j) ḫr ḥm nj nb(=j) sḏm.t(j)(=j) r (j)ḫ.t nb(.t) ḏd(=j) ḫ*[*r ḥm=f*] [4]| [... *ḥꜣtj-*]*ꜥ mꜣꜥ (j)m(j)-rʾ kꜣ.t nb.t nj.t nswt Sn*[*ḏm-jb*]

[1]| [The Majesty of (my) lord's granting that there be taken for (me) every ...] secret which (I) had asked for my father, the [true] chief justice and vizier [2]| [Senedjemib ...] because he was more highly esteemed before the king than any of his esteemed ones, because [he was] greater [3]| [before the king than any of his great ones ... while I] was diligent before the Majesty of (my) lord and was heard more than anything when I was talking be[fore His Majesty] [4]| [...] the true [*hati-*]*a*, overseer of every royal work Sene[djemib].

j) For the restoration see Stauder-Porchet (2017: 155 w. n. 64).

449 See Brovarski (2001: 41–42, Pls. 29–30).

Southern half of façade, north end, Inscription C

|1 ← *[(j)r(j)-pʿ.t ḥꜣtj-ʿ] ⸢mꜣʿ (j)m(j)-rʾ kꜣ.t⸣ [nb.t nj.t nswt]* |2 *⸢smr wʿtj⸣ ẖrj-⸢tp nsw⸣t [mḏḥ] ⸢ḳd nswt⸣ [m pr.wj]* |3 *⸢Snḏm-jb⸣ [Mḥ]⸢j ḏ⸣d[=f jrj.n(=j) nw]* |4 *[n jtj(=j)] tꜣjtj zꜣb ṯꜣtj (j)m(j)-rʾ kꜣ.t nb[.t nj.t]* |5 *n[swt] (j)m(j)[-rʾ] zš(w.w)-ʿ nj nswt (j)m(j)[-rʾ] pr[.wj-ḥḏ (j)m(j)-rʾ]* |6 *[ẖkr nswt (j)m(j)-rʾ] šnw.tj [Snḏm-jb]*

|7 ↓ *[...] m swꜣš=f* |8–12 *[...] ḥr* |13 *[...] m ⸢stp-zꜣ⸣* |14 ← *jrj.t n=f [ʿjm rḏj.n ḥm] nj nb(=j) jrj.t(j)* |15 ↓ *wḏ.w r dmḏ sr(.w) ⸢ḥnʿ⸣ [6].t [jz.wt] ntj.w m [wpj.t] ḥtp.t-nṯr nj.t Ḏr*[k] |16 *r jrj.[t(j) n=f] ⸢jdr wnw.t⸣ ntj m mdw n=f jtj(=j) ḏr-bꜣḥ jnj ꜣzḫ m wpj.t ḥtp.t-nṯr m tꜣ mḥw šmʿw m jdr wnw.t* |17 *[...]* |18 *[...]* |19 *[...] Nfr-(Jzzj) ḥr[=s]* |20 *tpj[.t ...] ḥw.t-kꜣ [tn] jrjj[.t(=j)]* [l] *...]* |21 *[...] ꜣḫ [n=f] ḫr=f m sšr [nb] n n[t]j.t[=f]* |22 ← *[ẖ]r ʿn nʾw.wt (j)ptn r ⸢jrj⸣.t ⸢n(jj)⸣* |23 ↓ *mrn mr mꜣw.t jw rḏj ḥm=f ḫtm wḏ.w (j)r=s m sḏꜣ.t nj.t ⸢ʿ⸣* |24 *jw jrj n=f ḥm.w-kꜣ jw rḏj.n(=j) (w)d.t(j) m zš* |25 *m zš-ḳd.t m jz pn sḥr=sn jn ḳstj* |26 *dd m ḥr(=j) tpj.t-rd jm mr psš m stp-zꜣ ḫr dbḥ(=j)* |27 *ḥr nb(=j) jnj.t(j) n=f ḳrsw m Rʾ-ꜣw* |28 ← *r jz{n}=f pn jrj.n(=j) n=f n rnp.t 1 ꜣbd 3 sk sw m wʿb.t* |29 *nj.t ʿḥʿw m pr-ḏ.t=f ntj m Nfr-(Jzzj)*

|1 [The iri-pat and] ⸢true⸣ [*hati-a*], ⸢overseer of⸣ [every royal] ⸢work⸣, |2 sole companion, royal chamberlain, royal [master] builder [in the two houses] |3 Senedjemib [Meh]i, saying: "(I) have made this] |4 [for (my) father], the chief justice and vizier, the overseer of every work [of] |5 the ki[ng], the over[seer] of the royal document scribes, the over[seer] of the [two] trea[suries, overseer of] |6 [the king's adornment, overseer of] the two granaries [Senedjemib]."

|7 [...] in his honouring |8–12 [...] |13 [...] in the ⸢court council⸣. |14 Making for him [of a document in this respect. The Majesty] of (my) lord [has granted] that |15 decrees |14 be made |15 in order to assemble the officials ⸢together with⸣ [the six] crews who are concerned with the [apportionment] of the divine offerings of "The Wall" so that there be ma[de for him] the ⸢share of the hour-service⸣ which (my) father had formerly claimed, once the harvest had been brought, from the apportionment of the divine offerings from Lower and Upper Egypt as share of the hour-service |17–18 [...] |19 [...] (the pyramid complex) '(Izezi) is perfect' on account of [it] |20 [this] *ka*-house, [which] (I) will make? |21 [...] beneficial [to him] in [every] issue since [he] |22 [had] a title to these estates so that it might be ⸢done⸣ ⸢for him⸣ |23 anew today. And so His Majesty has had the respective decrees sealed with the ⸢document⸣ seal. |24 Funerary priests were appointed for him, and (I) have had (them) put in writing |25 as drawing in this tomb to be engraved? by a sculptor. |26 The stipulations therein were pronounced in (my) presence in accordance with the apportioning in the court council. Then (I) asked |27 from (my) lord that a sarcophagus be brought for him from Tura |28 to this tomb of his, which (I) have made (= made ready) for him within one year and three months, while he was in the *purification house* |29 *of the duration* within his funerary estate which is in the (necropolis of the pyramid complex) '(Izezi) is perfect'.[m]

k) Brovarski (2001: 103, n. h) regards *Ḏr* as a synonym of *Jnb.w-ḥḏ.w* (equally, Strudwick 2005: 325, n. 37). The arrangement of the individual signs is curious in any event and may point to scribal inattention prior to carving.

l) The rendering of this passage is very tentative, and other interpretations of the traces of signs are possible. See Brovarski (2001: 105-106, n. p).
m) For a different interpretation of this passage, see Frandsen (1992: 59).

Southern wall of portico, east end, top, Inscription D

|1 ↓ [... *dbḥ.k(j) ḫr nb*](=*j*) *jnj.t(j)* [*n=f*] *ḳrsw* |2 [*m Rꜣ-ꜣw*] *rḏj ḥm nj nb*(=*j*) *ḏꜣj* [(*j*)*m*(*j*)-*rꜣ mšꜥ ḥnꜥ* (*j*)*m*(*j*)-*rꜣ sr.w r jnj.t ḳrsw pn m Rꜣ-ꜣw m m*] *sꜣṯ* [*ꜥꜣ*] *nj ḫnw* |3 [...[(*j*)*m*(*j*)-*rꜣ mšꜥ*] (*j*)*m*(*j*)-*rꜣ sr*⸢.*w*⸣ |4 ← *ḥr ḏꜣj.t jrj* (*j*)*ḫ.t nb*(.*t*) *n* |5 *mšꜥ* |6 *pn* |7 *mr wn.*[*t*].*n* [*wḏ.t*(*j*)] |8 *jm m ḫnw* |9 ↓ [...] *jnj*[.*t*(*j*)] *ḳr*[*sw*] *pn ḥn*⸢*ꜥ ꜥꜣ*⸣=*f r ꜣḫ.t-*(*Ḫwj=f-w*(*j*)) |10 [...] (*w*)*djj m jz=f ḫnj*(.*w*) *m Rꜣ-ꜣw* |11 (*w*)*djj m* ⸢*ḥnk.t*⸣[=*f*] |12 ← *n* |13 *hrw* [5?] |14 *m* [*šmj*(.*t*) *jj*(.*t*)] |15 ↓ *jw jrj.n n=sn ḥm=f* |16 *wḏ.wt r ḥzj.t=sn* |17 [*r* (*j*)*ḫ.t nb*(.*t*)] *sk gr wn=sn jrj=sn* |18 [*mḏꜣ.wt m ḫrj.t-hrw*] *rꜥ nb r rḏj.t rḫ* |19 [*ḥm=f wn.t*] *ḳrsw pn* |20 [*spr*(.*j*) *r ḥtp*]=*f m s.t=f*

|1 [... I asked from (my) lord] that a sarcophagus be brought [for him] |2 [from Tura]. The Majesty of (my) lord had the [overseer of troops together with the overseer of officials] traverse (the river) [in order to bring this sarcophagus from Tura on] a [great] transport vessel of the residence. |3 [... the overseer of the troops] and the overseer of the officials |4 were traversing (the river). There was done everything for |6 these |5 troops |7 like that which [had been commanded] |8 in this respect in the residence. |9 [...] This sarco[phagus was] brought together ⸢with⸣ its ⸢lid⸣ to the (necropolis of the pyramid complex) 'Horizon of (Khufu)'. |10 [...] placed in his tomb, after having been ferried from Tura, |11 and placed in [its] ⸢bed⸣ |12 during |13 [five?] days |14 in [a round-trip]. |15 So His Majesty made for them |16 decrees in order to reward them |17 [more than anything], while they were making |18 [messages in the course of] every day in order to infrom |19 [His Majesty that] this sarcophagus |20 had arrived to safely rest at its location.

Southern wall of portico, east end, bottom, captions[450]

|1 ← *sꜣṯ ꜥꜣ pḥtj* (*Jzzj*) *rn=f*	|1 The transport vessel, whose name is 'Great is the strength of (Izezi)'.
|2 ↓ (*j*)*m*(*j*)-*rꜣ mḏw*	|2 Overseer of the ten.
|3 ↓ *sḥḏ* (*wjꜣ*)	|3 Inspector (of the barge).
|4 ↓ (*j*)*m*(*j*)[-*rꜣ*] *sbꜣ*	|4 Over[seer] of the navigation.
|5 ← *ꜥꜣ*	|5 Lid.
|6 ← *ḳrsw*	|6 Sarcophagus.
|7 ↓ *jmj-jr.tj*	|7 Captain.

450 See Brovarski (2001: 38, Pls. 22–23).

5.3. Felt time: chronobiographical anchoring

As explained in Chapter 5.1, the adherence to a strict chronological order is not one of the hallmarks of the portfolio biography (or single biographical texts, for that matter). Nevertheless, composers of such assemblages sought time and again to enrich their material with chronological information of different kinds, ranging from the presumptive chronological ordering of title strings to the inclusion of explicit dates. The motivation for this practice should probably be situated within the exemplification cascade (see p. 119) as a means to increase the specificity of the biographical discourse and thereby enhance its rhetorical force.

The explicit or implicit chronological ordering of career steps seems to have enjoyed some popularity in the latter part of the Old Kingdom, but it becomes really tangible only in those event/career biographies where the individual steps are associated with the reigns of successive kings.[451] An early and particularly prominent example for this is the already mentioned biographical inscription of Shepsesptah at Saqqara (see p. 114), wherein the tomb owner traces his career across the reigns of eight kings of the 4th and 5th Dynasties. However, the famous event biography of Weni the Elder also ties the autobiographical narrative to specific reigns of the early–mid 6th Dynasty.[452] Other event biographies, especially those of the 5th Dynasty, may mention a king but neither indicate a royal succession nor stress chronological sequentiality (in contrast to temporal sequentiality, the succession of events).[453] Occasionally, inscriptions specify the duration of an engagement under a certain king. Thus, Nekhebu, possibly the grandson of Senedjemib Inti,[454] relates that he spent six years directing building work for Pepy I at Heliopolis: [*jrj.n(=j)*] *rnp.t* 6 *jm ḥr ḫrp kꜣ.t*, “[I spent] six years there directing the work.”[455]

In this context, Senedjemib Inti’s textual programme offers some peculiarities. On the one hand it is firmly associated with just one king, namely Djedkare Izezi. On the other hand it stands out through the presence of chronological anchoring in the form of the repeated inclusion of specific time references. The first such case is encountered in the last horizontal line of Inscription A1, Inti’s main autobiographical text. After Inti’s initial title string we find there the following statement: [6] *rnp.t 5 ꜣbd 4 sw 3 mrn(=j) ḫr (Jzzj)*, “Five years, four months and three days are (my) favour with (Izezi)”,[456] immediately followed by [7] *sk w(j) špss.k(j) ḫr (Jzzj)* [*r mrtj(=j) nb*] (...), “Since I was esteemed before Izezi

451 See Kloth (2002: 128–129).

452 Sethe (1933: 98–110, no. 17); Strudwick (2005: 352–357, no. 256). See also Richards (2002: 84).

453 The inscriptions of Debehni and of Kaemtjenenet being cases in point. For the latter, wherein Shespsesre, a vizier of Izezi, is mentioned, see Sethe (1933: 180–186, esp. 182, 10); Kloth (2002: 35, no. 76); Stauder-Porchet (2017: 121–126).

454 Brovarski (2001: 3).

455 On block Cairo JE 44608. Sethe (1933: 215, 13); Dunham (1938: 4); Stauder-Porchet (2017: 250–251). Later in the text, Nekhebu provides another piece of chronological information, namely that he stood in the service of his brother for 20 years. See Sethe (1933: 217, 3); Dunham (1938: 5).

456 The interpretation and translation follow Edel (1953: 215–216, no. 7). See also above, p. 117, n. b.

[more than any companion (of mine)] (...)." Despite the exceptionality of this phrasing the passage can only mean that at the time Inscription A1 was devised Inti's favour with Izezi had already lasted the said amount of time. The likely starting date of this period is not Izezi's enthronement, as Grdseloff thought,[457] but Inti's entering service under Izezi (probably equalling the start of his vizierate).[458] The end point could theoretically coincide with the act of inscribing A1 onto the mastaba's façade, although this is merely speculation, and a much later date of entextualisation seems possible.[459]

The second chronological information stems from the explicit dating of Inti's third letter from Izezi (Inscription B2), which is given in the last column as *rnp.t-zp [1]⌜6⌝ ꜣbd 4 šmw sw 28*.[460] Even though we cannot presuppose a regular biannual cycle for the cattle counts under Izezi,[461] the date is likely to lie relatively late in the king's reign.[462] In any event, it is remarkable that the person responsible for adapting the letter's layout to the monumental textual format bothered to include the date into the composition at all. No other copy of a royal letter in Inti's tomb is thus provided with a chronological reference, and a date is also absent from the copies of a letter from Izezi in Shespsesre's tomb.[463] The only other Old Kingdom copy of a royal letter provided with a date formula is the one inscribed on the façade of the tomb of Herkhuf, which dates to the year of the second occasion under Pepy II.[464] Interestingly, in Inti's case the date formula seems to follow the letter's main text, whereas the document format for official letters would normally demand that it precede the header.[465] Given, however, that the date is squeezed into the space between the last column of the main body of text and the inclined outer edge of the portico wall, one may ponder whether it should not actually be read first. Whatever the correct sequence, the date's inclusion was a deliberate choice which should probably lend more weight to the textual element by indexing authenticity. Remains the question why this was not deemed desirable for the other letters.

The third piece of chronological information derives from Mehi's account in Inscription C (cols./l. 26–29).[466] At the end of the text Mehi explains that it took him one year and three months to have a sarcophagus for his father granted and transported from the quarries

457 Grdseloff (1943: 59). This interpretation is still followed by Eichler (1991a: 148, n. f).

458 Cf. Smith (1952: 123); Brovarski (2001: 91, n. e).

459 If Senedjemib Inti started G 2370 when he became vizier under Izezi, a period of five years and four months could have been just enough time to erect the mastaba's superstructure and start with its decoration. However, Senedjemib Mehi may have ultimately been responsible for finishing the tomb's façade including Inscriptions A1 and A2.

460 The ten is today destroyed, but Reisner thought that he could make out the remnants of a single number sign in that position without completely ruling out the reading [2]⌜6⌝. See Brovarski (2001: 101, n. m).

461 See Gundacker (2015b: 94).

462 The highest secure date attested for Djedkare Izezi is 21 (or 22). See Verner (2006: 141). A year of the 28th occurrence may also be attributed to him. See Spalinger (1994: 301).

463 Sethe (1933: 179, 12).

464 Cf. Eichler (1991a: 160–161).

465 See Helck (1974b: 15).

466 See Wilson (1947: 239); Smith (1952: 123); Brovarski (2001: 102; Fig. 3 between pp. 104 & 105).

of Tura to the tomb during which time his father's corpse was housed in the embalming workshop close to Izezi's pyramid complex:

[26] ↓ (...) *ḫr dbḥ(=j)* [27] *ḫr nb(=j) jnj.t(j) n=f ḳrsw m R'-ꜣw* [28] ← *r jz{n}=f pn jrj.n(=j) n=f n rnp.t 1 ꜣbd 3 sk sw m wꜥb.t* [29] *nj.t ꜥḥꜥw m pr-ḏ.t=f ntj m nfr-(Jzzj)*	[26] (...) Then (I) asked [27] from (my) lord that a sarcophagus be brought for him from Tura [28] to this tomb of his, which I have made (= made ready) for him within one year and three months, while he was in the *purification house* [29] *of the duration* within his funerary estate which is in the (necropolis of the pyramid complex) '(Izezi) is perfect'.

Like with the first chronological statement, we are dealing here with an indication of a duration of time and not with an absolute chronological anchor. In the wider context of the tomb's life writing the indicated duration could simply express "effort" on the part of Mehi, although we do not know whether the stated period of time is particularly short or long for the completion of a funerary structure.[467]

Finally, another indication of duration is found in Inscription D (lines 12–14), where Mehi specifies the time it took to transfer the sarcophagus from Tura to Giza. Viewed together, the four chronobiographical details in G 2370 unquestionably serve to increase the specificity of the chosen exemplifications via creating *effets de réel*. This is particularly apparent with the handling of the ego-document (or, to be more precise, the *emulation* of an ego-document) in Inscription B2. Through this strategy the composer(s) may have hoped to heighten the narrative salience of the respective elements within the portfolio.

While concrete references to a person's date of birth and lifespan is lacking for the Old Kingdom,[468] the archaeological record has preserved occasional references to the date of death or burial.[469] While in the case of Nikauizezi the reference to the date of his burial seems to be a secondary addition to the original decorative programme,[470] the two vertical façade inscriptions flanking the entrance to the tomb of Queen Meresankh III at Giza appear as part of the primary iconotext, even if they were necessarily carried out after the queen's death:[471]

467 It certainly goes way beyond the 70 day period usually assigned for the stay in the embalming workshop, but one should bear in mind that in the case of Meresankh III, 273/4 days lay between her death and her interment. Spalinger (1994: 289); Alexanian (2006: 9); Vernus (2020: 186 w. n. 83). See also below.

468 Such information has been preserved from the Middle Kingdom onwards (see Vernus 2020: 163, n. 4) and gains popularity during the Late Period (see Jurman 2010: 248–256).

469 Smith (1952: 126); Spalinger (1994: 286–287); Vernus (2020: 186).

470 Kanawati & Abder-Raziq (2000: 41, Pl. 50); Vernus (2020: 186–187).

471 Smith (1952: 116, Fig. 4; 126); Dunham & Simpson (1974: 202 w. Pl. IIa; Fig. 2); Spalinger (1994: 288); Alexanian (2006: 9); Vernus (2020: 186–187).

On left jamb: ↓ *ḥm.t-nswt Mrj-s(j)-ꜥnḫ rnp.t (m)-ḫt zp tpj ꜣbd 2 pr.t sw 18 ḫpj.t=s r jz=s nfr*	The royal wife Meresankh. The year after the first occasion, second month of Peret, day 18: Her translocating to her accomplished tomb.
On door roll: ← *mꜣꜣ.t Ḥr Stḫ wr.t jꜣm.t ḥm.t-nswt Mrj-s(j)-ꜥnḫ*	The one who sees Horus and Seth, great of pleasantness, the royal wife Meresankh.
On right jamb: ↓ *zꜣ.t-nswt Mrj-s(j)-ꜥnḫ rnp.t zp 1 ꜣbd 1 šmw sw 21 ḥtp kꜣ=s ḫpj.t=s r wꜥb.t*	The royal daughter Meresankh. Year of the first occasion, first month of Shemu, day 21: The resting of her ka, her translocating to the *purification house*.

In Vernus' view, Meresankh III's inscriptions, whose terse style reminds of contemporary building graffiti,[472] "might be a case of sacralization of notations that elsewhere belonged to merely casual, mundane, and trivial domains (…)" and where only exceptionally extended "to elite self-thematizing monuments."[473] This is certainly a valid remark, and yet, these short, obituary-like texts with their narrative infinitives demonstrate that such posthumous narrative vignettes could be fully integrated into a person's life writing and fulfil a function beyond the administrative or documentary. On the other hand, the tomb owner's permanent connection to his/her tomb asserted an a-temporal presence that might have made the concrete starting point of this relation a minor concern. Be that as it may, we can state that concrete chronobiographical anchoring belonged to the repertoire of Old Kingdom life writing but was usually not exploited to its full potential.

The same holds true for the representation of different stages of life and aging. While the developed career biography may refer to events in the tomb owner's youth such as the *ṯꜣz mḏḥ* rite, such episodes are to the best of my knowledge never represented in a tomb's two-dimensional pictorial programme. The circumcision scene in the tomb of Ankhmahor relates to youth in general but does not represent the tomb owner's lived experience.[474] Slightly different may be the case of a comparable scene from the pyramid complex of Djedkare Izezi, where the context suggests that we are indeed dealing with a representation of the king as a child; this, however, within a mythologised ritual reminiscent of the birth legend known from later periods.[475]

As far as the three-dimensional sculptural iconotexts are concerned, funerary statues sometimes give the impression that they represent the tomb owner at different stages of his life.[476] In relation to the different statues made of wood and limestone that were found in Weni's serdab at Abydos, Richards remarks: "This circumstance suggests that originally there may have been at least one more small limestone statue, perhaps produced locally,

472 Cf. Smith (1952: 126–128).

473 Vernus (2020: 187).

474 Cf. Spigelman (1997), who argues for interpreting the scene as depicting an exceptional case of surgery, not the common rite as such.

475 Megahed & Vymazalová (2015).

476 Cf. Smith (1949: 49); Hawass (1999); Hill (1999). For the assumed age difference noticeable in the reliefs of Hezire, see Baines (2020: 53), although doubts as to the significance of the 'age' features have been voiced. See Davis (2003: 58).

with these two forming perhaps part of a group of three statues of Weni in the most important stages of life: adolescence, young manhood, and middle aged prosperity."[477] Richards relates these three statues to the three life stages mentioned in Weni's autobiography, namely his youth under King Teti, the starting of his career under Pepy I, and the rise to prominence under King Merenre.[478] Should this interpretation be correct, we would have here another example of how different strands of multimodal communication converge to form an assemblage which conveys an overarching narrative meaning. That statues could usually not be appreciated by the visitors after they had been installed in the serdab need not speak against this hypothesis. After all, not every non-royal funerary statue was placed in a serdab.[479] As will be discussed in more detail in Chapter 7, the process of narrating did also not start only with the interment of the deceased, and the living were not the only addressees of the narrative communication.

That said, one should equally not overestimate the significance of chronobiographical details within the Egyptian biographical discourse. Where they occur they are often not used to provide a chronological framework for a linearly told story. Rather, they seem to serve two main functions: increasing the specificity and thus authenticity of the exempla, and representing life's timely progression via multiplying the representation of social roles.[480]

6 Life telling: of voices and narrators

Since the Russian formalists and Genette, "voice" has been a topic extensively treated within narratology,[481] and yet it constitutes one of the most elusive and controversial concepts of the discipline.[482] Part of the problem lies in the fact that narratological usages of "voice" fluctuate between an abstract and merely technical function of text to bring about the effect of narration (synonymous or closely related to the concept of narrator) and an understanding that presupposes an anthropomorphised speech situation encoded in every textual communication. Given that textual objects do not (normally) produce sound, the term "voice" in its narratological application is by definition a metaphor.[483] But it is a powerful one indeed, as it invites conceptualisations that see a speaking human voice permeating narrative discourse and emphasise the latter's dependency on the paradigm of "natural

477 Richards (2002: 94).

478 Richards (2002: 94). Cf. Sethe (1933: 98, 12–105, 12).

479 See Arnold (1999).

480 Cf. Baines (2020: 52–53).

481 Aumüller (2006); Genette (1972: 225–267). As pointed out by Patron (2011: 15–21), Genette's conceptualisation of "voix" is actually quite vague and moves between an answer to the question "qui parle ?" (e.g. Genette 1972: 203), an analytical category (e.g. Genette 1972: 260), and an umbrella term for the very act of narrative enunciation (e.g. Genette 1972: 226). See also Segal (2012: 495).

482 Cf. Aczel (1998: 467).

483 For the genealogy of this conceptualisation and its implications, see Blödorn & Langer (2006). As shown by Meyer-Dietrich (2010: 2–3), the semantic field of human voice also figured as a repository for ancient Egyptian metaphor production.

communication".[484] Such conceptualisations have proved influential also in Egyptology, where epigraphic voices are often related to human bodies speaking them in concrete performances.[485] However, in the wake of the rise of postclassical narratology and the concomitant focus on *unnatural* voices[486] the ontological status of voice within the scope of Egyptological narratological endeavours seems in need of a slight recalibration.[487] The comprehensive and systematic study necessary for such an undertaking is way beyond the scope of the following paragraphs. Instead, they shall be confined to a few pertinent observations loosely related to the topic of epigraphic voice.

6.1 Epigraphic voices

By the time the most relevant sounds of speech of the ancient Egyptian language could be encoded in standardised writing and used to record utterances – whether it be during the 1st or during the 2nd Dynasty[488] – the question posed itself in what relation the written speech act stood to its producer/commissioner and the object (*Textträger*) on which it was recorded. In the beginning, text production could hardly have been a trivial enterprise, and the question of who or what speaks (on) an epigraphic monument will not have been considered trivial either. Today, we are so completely immersed in our ubiquitous textual universe that we sometimes fail to realise what conceptional effort it takes to transpose an oral act of speech or a verbal thought into a medialised written form. To be able to give a visual and tangible physical shape to audible communication must have been deemed remarkable and accompanied by extensive speculations as to the ontological status of written discourse. In this context one is reminded of the "biographical" remark on the original façade of the niche chapel of Itet at Meidum (time of Snofru), where Prince Nefermaat is said to have created imperishable written signs referred to as *nṯr.w=f*.[489] While the full meaning of this term may continue to elude us, Fitzenreiter has suggested to understand *nṯr* here as an entity capable of projecting agency.[490] Whether this agency was also tied to an "auto-enunciative" force is the topic of much Egyptological speculation[491] but difficult to substantiate in the absence of contemporaneous theoretical accounts. We are therefore left with the simple fact that every inscribed artefact is *some*thing that seems

484 See Jongeneel (2006: 11–12).

485 See, e.g., Meyer-Dietrich (2010: 2–3); Simon (2013: 186); Weiss (2014: 297).

486 See, e.g., Richardson (2006); Hansen et al. (2011).

487 Some recent contributions in this vein: Reintges (2011); Quack (2012); Weiss (2014); Willems (2019).

488 For what might be the earliest attestations of verbal sentences, see Kammerzell (2021: 22–23).

489 The passage reads: *swt jrr nṯr.w=f m zšw n zjn=f*, "It is he who made his *netjeru* in a writing that cannot be erased." See Petrie (1892: Pl. XXIV); Sethe (1933: 7, 11). As an aside, I would like to draw attention to the fact that the incompletely preserved counterpart inscription left of the false door niche seems to comprise another phrase attributable to the biographical discourse: [...] *sr mḏd*(*w*) *jb=f m ꜥnḫ*, "[...] an official who followed his heart in life." See Mariette & Maspero (1872–1892: Pl. 17); Petrie (1892: Pl. XXIII); Sethe (1933: 7, 12); despite Harpur's (2001: 82–83) qualification.

490 Fitzenreiter (2017: 192–193).

491 E.g. Quack (2012: 134–135); Weiss (2014: 297); Willems (2019: 247).

to speak (even if we may not understand what it says) and at the same time seems to be made to speak by something beyond the material signs, the imagination of an uttering entity. This entity is not to be equated with the *Textträger* itself, not even if Egypt were to have produced, like ancient Greece, "speaking objects" which use the first person singular to refer to the inscribed textual artefact.[492] The closest we come to this type of utterance are autoreferential impersonal statements such as the one found on the false door stela of Ankhkhufu (see above, p. 146), where we read: B 1 | ↓ *jr(w) r-gs nswt ḏs=f ḥr pgꜣ n ḏꜣdw* B 2 | *sk ḥm=f mꜣꜣ=f ẖr.t-hrw rꜥ nb* B 3 | ← *ꜥnḫ-⸢Ḫwj=f-w(j)⸣*, "B 1 | Made (i.e. the false door) in the presence of the king himself at the gate of the portico, B 2 | while His Majesty inspected it on a daily basis – B 3 | Ankhkhufu."[493] A wording such as "I was made (...)" would introduce another diegetic level in the first person but would not remove the problem that it is not the stone itself that makes the stone speak. Epigraphic text (and viewed from a particular angle, every text) always refers to a shapeless enunciative entity "behind" the text, which may be called the (highest-level) narrator and is not to be confused with the actual author of a textual composition nor with its material producer. Whether this narrator is actually situated within the text or stands outside of it is difficult to decide and of minor concern in the present context. What counts are the characteristics attributable to the role of narrator. To cite Margolin,

> "[t]he position occupied by this presumed inner-textual originator of the discourse functions as a logico-linguistic center for all spatio-temporal and personal references occurring in the discourse, i.e. as highest-level center of the discourse. An inner-textual narrator can in principle be assigned to any narrative text, not just a fictional one, and such ascription does not require any knowledge about the actual world producer of the words of the text, be it a human being or a computer program."[494]

In my understanding, any text has a narrating entity at the highest-level of discourse that is bound to the text's entextualisation in a given medium. An *epigraphic* voice is therefore one projected onto the medium by a recipient/reader without the necessity to provide it with an anthropomorphic identity. It is an identity beyond mimesis. The specific mediality of language conveyed through epigraphic text results in a particular constellation of voice and enunciative act that cannot be fully replicated with human speech acts, no matter how much resemblance one might be willing to see. For this reason alone biographical inscriptions can hardly be conceptualised as precise written records of oral speech acts taking place in the course of the funerary rites.[495] The consequence of this thought is that even a straightforward first-person narrative is ultimately embedded in a higher-order

492 For ancient Greek "speaking objects", see Svenbro (1988: 33–52); Wachter (2010); Kaczko (2016: 24–26). For an anti-animistic interpretation, see Dietrich (2020: 192, n. 522).

493 Reisner (1942: 504, Pl. 65b), Stauder-Porchet (2017: 39).

494 Margolin (2014: § 2).

495 Baines (1999a: 30; 1999b: 36) does not go as far as to postulate a complete correspondence between the two types of discourse but sees some potential overlaps.

narrative level constituted by the text's mediality and its paratextual setting. This applies also to texts lacking enunciative formulae such as *ḏd=f* or *ḏd*.[496]

The argument may be illustrated by taking epistolary discourse as an example.[497] In preserved actual letters from the late 3rd millennium BCE, the voice of the sender is almost always mediated by a genre-specific header "enveloping" the main text.[498] In the case of pBerlin 8869, found in Saqqara and probably dating to the 8th Dynasty,[499] the header includes the names and titles of sender (Iru) and addressee (Merernakht) but no explicit enunciative formula that would introduce the ego-perspective.[500] Grammatically, the latter is consistently phrased in the third person, with *sn=k*, "your brother", being a circumlocution for "I", and *zš w=k*, "your scribe", for "you".[501] While the epistolary header may actually have been written by Iru himself and may have been read out by a messenger before the addressee upon delivery, it does not belong to the same diegetic level as the main text. It also does not belong to the voice of a third party who would somehow oversee the communication process and act as a guarantor for its succeeding. Instead, the voice framing the communication via giving information about sender and recipient must be imagined as embedded in the medium itself. In the case of the letter written on clay tablet no. 3686 from Balat (6th Dynasty),[502] the embedding of the first-person voice is accomplished through a simple verbal sentence: *ḏd bꜣk jm*, "The servant there said:".[503] Since *bꜣk jm*, as a signifier of modesty and subordination, is a common substitute for the first-person suffix pronoun *=j*, one might be tempted to paraphrase the sentence as *ḏd=j*. In that case we would be dealing with a first-person voice embedded in a diegeticly differentiated and yet identical first-person voice. But even then, "I say/said" is subordinated to a higher-level narration which is bound to the communicative constellation constituted by the medium of the letter. Only mediated by and through it a first-person voice can manifest itself. This perspective is somewhat indebted to Banfield's notion of "unspeakable sentences" which

---

496 This is not the place to discuss in detail the grammatical identity of these verbal forms, which have been analysed in many different ways over the last decades. Cf., e.g., Edel (1955–1964: 216, § 473: perfective *sḏm=f*); Fischer (1977: 55: infinitive); Borghouts (2010: 216: circumstantial *sḏm=f* with nominal antecedent); Reintges (2011: 29, n. 15: part of a relative clause with finite verb or participle). Even if *ḏd=f* should represent a "normal" perfective *sḏm=f*, its unspecific time reference is necessarily difficult to pin down in English translation. Cf. Fitzenreiter (2017: 181, n. 12).

497 For the structural similarities between letter writing and the (auto)biographical discourse, see already Morenz (2003: 186).

498 See Eichler (1991b).

499 Edel (1970: 117).

500 Möller & Gardiner (1911: Pls. II–III); Smither (1942); Wente (1991: 58, no. 67); Strudwick (2005: 178–179, no. 96). Strudwick's reading of the names and the identification of sender and recipient differs from that of previous editors.

501 This serves as a reminder that grammatical person can give misleading hints when assessing questions of narrative voice or authorship.

502 Pantalacci (1998: 306–311 w. Fig. 1).

503 In pCairo 49623, which may be a letter or an aide-mémoire (cf. Balanda 2000: 26–27), the enunciative formula follows the reference to the sender. In this case, *ḏd* could represent an active participle. Gunn (1925: 247), however, regarded occurrences such as this as pseudoparticiples.

oppose a naturalised reading of the communicative situation and may well be conceived of as "autonomous text".[504] In a different context, Kammerzell and Peust have argued along the same lines when they interpreted the enunciative formula *ḏd-mdw(.w)*, "saying of words" (originally just *mdw*, "utterance"?) introducing divine speech as a "quotation mark" not corresponding with an element of the spoken language.[505]

With this in mind let us now consider the handling of voices in Senedjemib Inti's life writing. Inti's autobiography A1 is introduced by a horizontal heading consisting of his titles and the reference to the period of time spent in royal favour. As already remarked by Stauder-Porchet, this layout alludes to the royal document format (= in this case an epistolary format) also used for the royal letters A2, B1, and B2,[506] and may be seen as a rhetorical device to present autobiographical information along the lines of an ego-document. On another level, the use of this format in non-royal contexts is probably generally meant to signal heightened significance and tellability of a given textual content.[507] The heading is phrased in a purely nominal style and does not showcase any particular voicing. As such it is attributable to the unspecified extradiegetic narrator who appears as the originator of the tomb's complete iconotextual programme and may be imagined as "telling" also the other textual genres and scene captions present in G 2370. Inti's first-person narrative is not preceded by an enunciative formula such as *ḏd=f* or *ḏd* but rather starts with subordinate clauses introduced by *sk* (cols. 7–8), which depend on the main clause *wn(=j) jrj(=j) mr s.t-jb nj.t ḥm=f (j)r=s*, "I used to act according to the wish of His Majesty in that matter."[508] The absence of *ḏd=f/ḏd* before a first-person narrative is not the norm but also not exceptional in the latter part of the 5th and the 6th Dynasties.[509] Unfortunately, we do not know whether Inscriptions C, D, or the address to the living (?) partly preserved over the figure of Senedjemib Mehi on the southern thickness of the entrance[510] ever contained enunciative formulae.[511] If not, G 2370's biographical corpus would show itself indebted to the earlier tradition of biographical texts in the third person lacking such devices.[512] However that may be, a knowledgeable ancient visitor would soon have realised that the inscriptional ensemble of the tomb's façade/portico featured three distinct first-person voices within the continuous texts:[513] that of Senedjemib Inti (A1), that of his son Senedjemib Mehi (C, D), and that of the king represented in the three royal letters (A2, B1, B2).

---

504 Banfield (1982: esp. 8–11).
505 Kammerzell & Peust (2002: 295).
506 Stauder-Porchet (2021a: 154).
507 Cf. Baud (2003: 286–288).
508 For the grammatical analysis of this passage, see Stauder-Porchet (2017: 148, n. 55).
509 Cf., e.g., the case of the unintroduced first-person texts in the tomb of Pepyankh-Herib. Blackman (1924: Pl. IV). See also Kloth (2002: 52 w. n. 7).
510 Brovarski (2001: 43, Fig. 35).
511 For threat formulae and addresses to the living, the enunciative embedding is often only implicit. Cf. Sainte Fare Garnot (1938). For some cases of *ḏd=f* before appeals to the living, see Shubert (2007: 456, n. 30).
512 E.g. Werre. Cf. Stauder-Porchet (2017: 45).
513 This does not include the first-person direct speech captions included in the marsh scenes. For these see Brovarski (2001: 38; 42).

From a structural point of view, however, these three voices are not all situated at the same diegetic level. The voice of the king is subordinated to that of Inti, who is implicitly presented as citing the three letters in the context of his portfolio biography. This is borne out by the fact that the letters complement and corroborate Inti's first-person autobiography. Their textual design and relative position towards A1 likewise suggest a *syn*diegetic (see the following chapter) link between the two levels of narration. What the king has to say about Inti's qualities is hypodiegeticly embedded in Inti's auto-referential meta-story, of which A1 forms a part. That this embedding is not an explicit but an implicit one has to do with the nature of the portfolio biography and the way it creates narrative meaning through juxtaposition and spatial association.

But what about Mehi's first-person narratives that presuppose a deceased Inti and are thus necessarily removed in time from the perspective expressed in A1–B2? In what way do they relate to the complex narrative composed of A1–B2? There are actually (at least) two ways of addressing this question. One option would be to postulate another hypodiegetic relationship, this time between A1–B2 and C/D. In such a scenario, Mehi's voice expressed in C/D and other iconotexts from the portico-area (see. p. 156) would implicitly also narrate his father's life story through "ego-documents" focussed on the latter. The result would be an implicit nesting of hypodiegeticly related narratives: C/D > A1 > A2–B2. According to the second view, the connection between the two groups of texts is much looser and resembles that one would find in posthumously published memoires provided with a lengthy editorial preface or, rather, epilogue. In that case one would be dealing with two hierarchically differentiated yet not nested diegetic levels. Irrespective of which option one may favour, both scenarios have in common that the superordinate unit of narrative meaning is constituted by the tomb itself. The medialisation of the narrative levels becoming manifest in the materiality of writing represents the shapeless extradiegetic narrative entity that makes both Mehi and Senedjemib Inti speak. This conclusion does not contradict my earlier statement that the tomb's auctorial force derives from the tomb owner (see Chapter 3.4). It simply relates to a different analytical category. In a somewhat simplified take on the issue one could state that the *source* of the biographical *récit* is to be identified with the *medium* of the tomb (a non-narrator, so to speak), while the *originator* of the autobiographical *fabula* has to be imagined as the tomb owner (and/or his heir). In terms of agency, on the other hand, the tomb together with its *récit* has been authorised by the tomb owner (if only theoretically), which ties the diegetic levels back to a human originator. In that sense the historical change from third-person narrative to first-person narrative does not affect the overarching diegetic structure, as was already observed by Reintges.[514]

514 Reintges (2011: 29): "This shift in narrative perspective does, however, not mark a transition from *histoire* to *discours*. Rather, the introduction of the speaker-oriented point of view is a literary construct." While one could debate the usefulness of the categories of *histoire* and *discours* in this context (see above, Chapter 2.1), Reintges' point is further corroborated by observations on biographies of a later date, e.g. that of Ahmose son of Ibana, where we encounter a triple framing involving both *ḏd=f* and *ḏd=j*. See Baines (2020: 61).

Diegesis, however, does not end at the level of the monumental text. As I will try to show in Chapter 7.2, it encompasses likewise the process of narrativisation of the *récit* undertaken by the recipient as the ultimate source of narrative meaning. From a certain point of view then the reader takes on the role of an actual narrator.

6.2 Extradiegetic – intradiegetic – syndiegetic

In his classical account on diegesis, Genette posited two types of narrator.[515] Firstly, an extradiegetic narrator whose perspective is positioned outside the narration's diegesis and who recounts what happened at the first diegetic level. Secondly, a story may comprise also an intradiegetic narrator, i.e. a character of the first diegetic level who, in turn, recounts a story at the second level (metadiegesis), which is in a hypodiegetic relation to that of the first level.[516] This constellation can be multiplied several times, resulting in potentially complicated nested diegetic configurations. According to this way of thinking, the narrative level of a portfolio biography can be classified as extradiegetic, because it provides an overarching synthesis of the different iconotextual elements. The latter are linked to intradiegetic narrative units such as individual autobiographical texts or letters, which may likewise comprise metadiegetic phrases or episodes (e.g. in the form of quotations or paraphrasing like in Inscriptions A2 or B1; see p. 156). But if we try to consider the mutual relationship between the different iconotextual elements, the picture becomes slightly blurred and the categories of "extra-" and "intradiegetic" lose their fixed boundaries. As outlined in the previous chapter, I regard the royal letters of A2, B1, and B2 to be hypodiegetic in relation to Inti's autobiographical account of A1. This structural relationship, however, is not made explicit in A1 and suggests itself only when taking the thematic and spatial context into view. The positioning of A2, B1, and B2 around A1 develops a narrative momentum of its own that contributes to narrative meaning making without being firmly attributable to a specific narrative level. This principle can be extended to the micro- as well as the macrolevel. At the microlevel of text design, for example, the conventional layout of the header of a royal letter already tells a story of sorts: The way the hieroglyphic signs of the "royal command"[517] and the addressee's title string face each other ()[518] is not just an index of the text's identity as a royal missive, it actually "tells" about this communication process through purely eugraphic means.[519] From this disposition we learn of the micro-story's two protagonists, the king and Senedjemib Inti, and the way they are related to each other by a highly tellable event, namely the act of communication initiated by the king through his letter.[520] Similarly, Werre's biographical inscription is formatted as to mimic a royal de-

515 Genette (1969: 202–203; 1972: 238–241).

516 Cf. Pier (2016: § 1).

517 For the understanding of *wḏ-nswt*, see Vernus (2013).

518 Brovarski (2001: Fig. 33, Pl. 60).

519 For this type of reversal, see Fischer (1977: 57–60); Vernus (2013: 281–282).

520 In this context Farout (2013: 17 w. n. 17) points to the later verbalisation of the hieroglyphic configuration in the Middle Kingdom autobiography of Ameniseneb: *wḏ rdj.t m ḥr nj mtj-n-zꜣ nj*

cree while telling about its own creation at a royal workshop.[521] Thus, the text's form does not only illustrate this relationship, it literally *inscribes* the narrative nexus between the object and the past event. As far as the macrolevel is concerned, I would like to stress once again that the tomb tells first and foremost of its own coming into being and the very act of narration. In this sense the iconotextual and architectural components of the structure become narratively meaningful beyond their potential integration into intradiegetic levels of narration. They constitute part of a web of narrative meaning whose exact diegetic position is difficult to pin down. The ways in which materiality and form contribute to diegesis I would like to call *syndiegetic*. This term was coined by Bunia in connection with the narrative "voice" of typography in E. T. A. Hoffmann's *Lebens-Ansichten des Katers Murr*. There, typography and orthography have a share in telling the story of how the text ended up in the book the reader is currently reading. Consequently, Bunia maintains, "das Schriftbild des Romans ist, will man einen Begriff dafür wählen, *syndiegetisch*: es ist Teil der Diegese."[522] Likewise, text/iconotext of the Egyptian funerary discourse may be linked through *syndiegesis* to the tomb's coming into being and its functioning as a narrativisable entity. The already mentioned label at the entrance of the mastaba of Niuty (see p. 137) provides a convenient example for this. It is the inscription's position next to the entrance of the tomb that showcases diegesis and makes explicit the very process of higher-order narration comprising the entirety of the iconotextual programme. Thus, like with Senedjemib Inti's Inscriptions A1–B2, the spatial relation of the part towards the whole influences to a significant degree the outcome of efforts to narrativise the entire assemblage. "Syndiegetic" therefore means that the reader/viewer/recipient is provided with cues that invite and suggest narrative connections without completely determining the narrative pathway. This freedom turns the reader/viewer/recipient into the ultimate authority in deriving narrative meaning from Egyptian funerary iconotexts. And what's more, this authority, too, has a voice, as will be seen in the next chapters.

7 Life reading: who reads narrates

7.1 Reception as social and ritual performance

The first recipient of a narrative is by necessity its narrator. This insight might seem at first paradoxical but soon starts to make sense if we consider the enormous role autonarratives play in the construction and maintenance of our own identity and personhood.[523] As personal life experience and culture as a whole are narratively constituted,[524] narration about oneself is a powerful means to create coherence and self-awareness over the course of a human existence. The reception of life writing thus starts in the mind of the "author" or

ꜣbḏw Jmny-snb(.w) mꜣꜥ ḫrw m ḏd, "Command put before the controller of the phyle of Abydos Ameniseneb, true of voice, saying:". See Sethe (1924: 76, 18–19).

521 See Stauder-Porchet (2021b: 455).

522 Bunia (2005: 375).

523 Brockmeier & Carbaugh (2001); Bruner (2001).

524 Brockmeier (2012).

commissioning authority already before the finished work has been prepared for anyone to see and digest. But since life writing within the context of Egyptian monumental funerary culture is a complex and time-consuming undertaking, no stage of the reception happens outside of the social fabric.[525] For high officials, the planning as well as the construction of a tomb and its iconotext involved significant economic resources and manpower, ranging from the lector priests responsible for the ritual functionality of the design to the construction workers.[526] In many cases it will also have involved dealing with royal authorities or even with the king himself, since the distribution of resources or even the furnishing with certain funerary items was often regulated by the palace (cf. Inscriptions C and D in Senedjemib Inti's mastaba). From time to time, the tomb owner will have visited the construction site and the workshops where his burial equipment was being produced. In this latter role he is quite often represented on the walls of tomb chapels (cf. the depiction next to the deed in the tomb of Wepemneferet). We have to imagine that such visits were undertaken not alone but in the company of a retinue. This retinue may have also included superiors or peers whom the progress of the project was shown. Accordingly, texts such as the false door inscriptions of Niankhsakhmet (see p. 145) or of Ankhkhufu (see p. 146) put stress on the fact that the *Textträger* were the object of royal attention and interest already before they were placed inside the tomb. When we try to consider the different stages during which the reception of the tomb as a narrative entity played a part, then the initial conception and building phase, which might already have involved certain ritual acts, will have to feature prominently. What about the other situations and contexts that provided opportunities for an audience to engage with the tomb's iconotext?

Certainly one of the most important occasions was the burial of the deceased, which took place some weeks or months after his or her death (cf. p. 167) upon the execution of all rituals related to the physical and spiritual preparation of the dead body.[527] The burial was preceded by a procession from the place of purification to the location of the tomb, and it is not difficult to imagine that the funeral of prominent officials drew large crowds of people who might have gathered along the way. How many people participated in the actual rites performed at and inside the tomb is difficult to assess but will have varied greatly. One needs to bear in mind in this connection that the often narrow access ways and the limited space available in many tomb chapels put considerable constraints on the gathering of a large party of family members, priests, and mourners. Certain activities had to be carried out by specialists, e.g. lowering the prepared body into the burial chamber and closing any potential stone sarcophagus (see below). During all of these procedures the tomb's iconotextual programme was accessible to at least some of the participants, even if bad lighting conditions may have formed an obstacle to the comprehensive appreciation of what today is conveniently presented between the book covers of archaeological publications. In the context of the burial, reception was likely a

---

525 See also the fundamental considerations on reception and accessibility in Fitzenreiter (2015).

526 This is of course an idealised scenario.

527 For a recent overview of the social implications of burial and subsequent activities around the tomb, see Baines (2022).

social activity. It incorporated a whole range of sensory experiences and went beyond the mere lapidary "canvas" that today constitutes the main focus of Egyptological research. Whether on this occasion the deceased's son or designated heir indeed recited a text commemorating his father/mother is impossible to say in the absence of concrete evidence. According to Baines, such as recital may have included a eulogy of the deceased[528] or an unabridged version of the latter's (auto)biographical discourse enacted by the son's voice.[529] In another suggested scenario, the performances incorporated a declamation of the biographical texts as they appeared inscribed on the tomb walls.[530] What this meant in concrete practice, however, and where the line was drawn between texts that were recited and those that were not is usually left unexplored (see Chapter 7.2).[531]

Subsequent to the burial, the deceased's relatives may from time to time have gathered in the tomb's vicinity to commemorate their departed family member and maintain social ties between him/her and the community of the living. Such gatherings certainly involved eating and drinking as well as specific ritual performances including the dedication of offerings.[532] In the course of the event, the tomb chapel will have been turned into a ritual stage that provided a truly multimodal experience for the participants. Apart from these special occasions, members of the elite will also have set up a permanent funerary cult which received resources from the deceased's funerary estate. This cult was carried out by dedicated priests who paid visits to the tomb at (regular?) intervals in order to recite religious formulae and lay down offerings. Whether this service focussed solely on the primary offering place within the cult chapel or involved also other areas of the accessible parts of the tomb remains in most cases an open question.

Finally, we need to factor in occasionally visiting family members as well as unrelated professionals who passed by funerary monuments when frequenting the necropoleis mainly as priests or on other duty.[533] During these visits, particular tombs will for one reason or another have attracted their attention and motivated them to engage with parts of the iconotext. It is this engagement and potential subsequent ritual performance for the benefit of the deceased (e.g. pronouncing a *ḥtp-dj-nswt* formula or providing a libation) that the common addresses to the living seek to instigate.[534] In order to promote their cause they usually make promises of compensation for desired behaviour as well as voicing

528 Baines (1999a: 36; 1999b: 30). See also Reintges (2011: 29).

529 Baines (1999b: 22 [stressing the partial incommensurability of oral and written forms); 2020: 76 [for a later period]); Kloth (2002: 253 [with the restriction of texts in the third person]); Willems (2019: 220–221).

530 Baines (2013: 239–241).

531 Willems (2019: 220) suggests that the common association of offering formulae and ideal biography near the cult place could be an indicator that at least these groups of the texts "were part of cultic recitation".

532 For the significance of these activities, see Fitzenreiter (2001: 85–86). While the spatio-temporal location of such feasts during the 3rd millennium BCE is difficult to ascertain, we have clear evidence of this practice for the Theban necropolis during the New Kingdom. See Baines (2014: 7–14).

533 Cf. Kloth (2002: 251–253).

534 Cf. Gnirs (1996: 199).

threats against those who might violate the tomb's integrity and purity.[535] But for the addresses to the living to succeed, the process of reception needs already to have started. Therefore many components of the funerary iconotext that show a strong visual appeal and engage directly with the onlooker are positioned on the tomb's façade or in close proximity to the entrance.

While gods and *akhu* may equally have been on the tomb owner's mind as a potential audience for his autobiographical discourse, they are not found among the groups of visitors directly addressed in the tomb inscriptions. Either they were of secondary importance in this regard or their participation in the process of reception was so obvious that it did not bear mentioning.[536]

The information contained in the addresses to the living does not only touch upon the "who" of tomb visits, it also provides some insight into the "what" and "how", i.e. the way in which the visitors were meant to engage with the tomb's iconotext. Revealing are addresses such as the one of Kaihersetef inscribed on a panel incorporating a serdab opening (Cairo CG 1566, probably 6th Dynasty),[537] where the visitors are encouraged to look at the tomb and appreciate its visual contents: *rmṯ nb mꜣꜣ.t(j)=sn nw dwꜣ=sn n(=j) nṯr m nw*, "As to all the people who shall see this, they should praise god for me therein." This statement clearly conveys the ideal of a thorough appreciation as it would be facilitated through a careful "reading" of the textual and pictorial elements in the tomb chapel.[538] An address in the tomb of Iti-ibi at Assiut (Siut II) from the First Intermediate Period is even more explicit in its concern:[539]

[1] | ← *j ꜥnḫ.w j tpj.w-tꜣ ms.w ntj.w r msj.t ḫdw.t(j)=sn ḫntj.t(j)=sn wṯsn m šms nj Wp-wꜣ.wt nb Zꜣwtj jrj.t(j)=sn swꜣw ḥr wꜥr.t tn ꜥḳ.t(j)=sn jz pn mꜣꜣ.t(j)=sn ntj.t jm=f ꜥnḫ n=ṯn Wp-wꜣ.wt nb Zꜣwtj Jnpw nb rʾ jw=ṯn r dwꜣ nṯr r prj.t ḫrw n ḥꜣtj-ꜥ Jtj-jb=j*

[1] | O living ones, o you who are on earth, already born or yet to be born, travelling down- and upstream, who shall come in the retinue of Wepwaut, the lord of Assiut, who shall make a stroll to this district, who shall enter this tomb and shall see/appreciate that which is in it: As Wepwaut, lord of Assiut, and Anubis, lord of the Entrance, live for you, you should praise god and present an offering for the *hati-a* Iti-ibi.

Here the visitors are expected to praise god and present (a verbal) offering after they have seen "that which is in it", i.e. the iconotextual programme of the cult chapel. What precisely this seeing/appreciating implied is not so easy to assess, but we can imagine that

535 For the spectrum of phraseology, see Sainte Fare Garnot (1938); Edel (1944: 3–30) Morschauser (1991: 145–157); Shubert (2007: 16–60).

536 It may also be that decorum during the Old Kingdom prohibited direct addresses to the gods, the king, and the blessed dead.

537 Sethe (1933: 10, 6 7); Sainte Faire Garnot (1938: 2); Borchardt (1964: 35, Pl. 66); Strudwick (2005: 243, no. 161).

538 Alas, Kaihersetef's tomb is known only from a handful of blocks dispersed over several collections.

539 Griffith (1889: Pl. 11, 1); Schenkel (1965: 76, no. 60); Chauvet (2013: 68).

Iti-ibi reckoned with a prolonged engagement that also involved the reading (= *mꜣꜣ* ?) of his autobiography following directly below.

Another interesting case is the inscription on the earlier lintel of the vizier Mehu from his tomb at Saqqara (probably early 6th Dynasty),[540] where ideal-biographical phrases are embedded in offering formulae and combined with statements regarding the provision for the tomb as well as the *akh* status of the tomb owner. In such cases the addressive and instrumentalist nature of the biographical discourse is laid bare. This is particularly apparent with the genre of ideal biography but equally applies to other biographical statements and the whole remainder of the tomb's iconotext; the main difference being that the individual elements belong to different slots within the communicative framework of the exemplification cascade (see p. 119). In the inscription of Djau from Abydos (Cairo CG 1431, 6th Dynasty),[541] an explicit connection is drawn between the reception of Djau's *cursus honorum* and the actions desired from the visitors of his monument. Thus, we read in the address to the living:

[4]| ↓ (…) *j ꜥnḫ.w* (…) [5]| *ꜥnḫ n=ṯn nswt jw=ṯn r šdj.t n(=j) prj.t-ḫrw m wḏb nj ḥw.t-nṯr tn m jrj.t=<ṯ>n n wḏ m jrj.t=ṯn n ḏs=ṯn ḏr mꜣꜣ=ṯn jꜣ.wt(=j) ḫr nswt n špss(=j) ḫr ḥm nj nb(=j)*

[4]| (…) O living ones, (…). [5]| As the king lives for you, you shall recite for me a voice offering from the reversion offering of this temple (or) from that which <you> offer by obligation (or) from that which you offer by your own desire, when you see (read about) (my) offices with the king on account of (my) being esteemed before the Majesty of (my) lord.

It remains the question whether the totality of the tomb formed the desired unit of reception or only the most important (and salient) of its parts such as the façade, the entrance area, or the cult place. If we conceive of the tomb as the tomb owner's "Collected works", as Assmann would have it (see above, p. 111),[542] then we may ask whether it was ever read "from cover to cover". And if so, by whom?

At least in certain cases it seems that the addressive function extended even to texts inscribed in parts of the tomb that were not normally accessible to visitors or priests performing the normal funerary cult. Thus, we know sarcophagi from the Teti Pyramid cemetery bearing inscriptions that give the impression of being directed at the specialists responsible for lowering the lid onto the base and closing the sarcophagus. The version on the lid of the sarcophagus of Ankhmahor Zezi reads, for example:[543]

540 Hawass (2002); Strudwick (2005: 294–295, no. 220 A). Cf. also Kloth (2021: 281–285).

541 Sethe 1933 (119, 6–12); Junker (1955: 89).

542 Assmann (1996b: 103).

543 Sethe (1933: 204–205, no. 41 [132]); Sainte Fare Garnot (1938: 41–42 w. texte VIII, b); Kanawati & Hassan (1997: Pl. 69); Strudwick (2005: 424, no. 322 A).

[1] ← *(j)m(j)-rʾ kꜣ.t nb.t nswt m tꜣ r-ḏr=f Zzj ḏd=f j rmṯ 80 wtj ḥḳꜣ ẖr.t-nṯr jꜣ.t nb.t hꜣw.t(j)=sn r s.t tn (j)n-jw mrjj=ṯn ḥzjj=ṯn nswt prj=ṯn ḫrw m ẖr.t-nṯr* [2] *wnn jmꜣḫ=ṯn nfr ḫr nṯr ꜥꜣ ḏḏ=ṯn n(=j) ꜥꜣ pn nj ḳrs pn ḥr mw.t=f m bw mnḫ nj rḫ.t=ṯn mr jrj.t(j) {ṯ} n ꜣḫ jḳr jrj ḥzz.t nb=f jnk Zzj n mrw.t(=j)*	[1] The overseer of every royal work in the entire land, Zezi, he says: "O eighty men, embalmer, ruler of the necropolis and any office holder that shall descend into this tomb: Do you wish that the king praises you and that the voice-offering will be made for you in the necropolis, that you become an *imakhu* in perfection before the Great God? Then you should place this lid of this sarcophagus for me upon its base according to the excellence of which you are capable, as is done for an excellent *akh* who does what his lord praises (or: doing what his [i.e. the sarcophagus'] owner praises). I am Zezi on account of (my) popularity."

The first-person statement on the sarcophagus of Queen Meresankh III (KM JE 54935a–b, GEM 45475), according to which it was Hetepheres II who provided her with the item, may be understood along roughly similar lines: *(r)ḏj.n(=j)* (*nw*?) *n zꜣ.t-nswt ḥm.t-nswt Mrj-s(j)-ꜥnḫ*, "(I) (i.e. Hetepheres II) gave (this) to the royal daughter and wife Meresankh."[544]

While these texts do not contain a lot of biographical information, they relate to the wider discourse of life writing inasmuch as the latter provides arguments for the conscientious observance of funerary customs. In this respect the texts are important for the deceased's transformation process and were likely expected to be read by knowledgeable people before and during the burial. But does this mean that the same also applied for the less conspicuous elements of the tomb's iconotextual programme below and above ground? It is commonly assumed that at least the outrightly ritual texts (e.g. offering formulae or offering lists) were at some point recited in the course of funerary ceremonies. But in many tombs there is very little in terms of placement, textual configuration and size that would differentiate "ritual texts" intended for recitation from all the other texts present in the tomb. If the names and titles of the deceased inscribed on many false doors were pronounced, did the same apply to the names and titles of family members or of subsidiary figures associated with the bringing of offerings? As difficult as these questions are to tackle, we can at least state that certain subtle features of inscriptional design and textual layout can only be appreciated when carefully working through the text in its inscribed manifestation. In this context Stauder-Porchet writes:

> "Many other features of inscriptional layout take time to reveal themselves to the viewer—at least to the modern viewer trained in privileging the sequence of words in a text. Could these features of inscriptional layout in continuous texts of the Old Kingdom have been more immediately apparent to the differently trained eye of their

---

544 Dunham & Simpson (1974: 21, Fig. 14).

original audiences? Thus, inscriptional layout raises some basic questions about how inscriptions were seen, read, and more generally experienced in ancient times."[545]

At this point in time we have to stress that we do not know particularly much about the way Egyptian life writing from the funerary sphere was engaged with in ancient times. What we can state with reasonable confidence, however, is that the life stories conveyed by the monuments were not all spelled out in meticulous detail but emerged in the minds of the recipients, whether they were the intended ones or not – whether the stories were the intended ones or not. For this reason the recipient should be regarded as the ultimate narrative authority of a tomb owner's (auto)biographical discourse. In drawing on the diverse material offered to him by the multimodal iconotext he decides about the *récit*'s structure and imagines a storyworld which may or may not coincide with the originally desired outcome. In that sense the reader becomes indeed the narrator at the highest diegetic level. As Zymner reflects,

> "Es ist der Lesende selbst, der – einer Textstruktur folgend – die Erzählung im eigentlichen Sinn erzählt (nämlich die Schriftzeichen in verstandene Sprache überführt) und durch eben diese Versinnlichung der Textstruktur zugleich den Eindruck gewinnen kann, er habe es bei der ‚Stimme des Erzählers' mit derjenigen einer anderen, von ihm selbst unterschiedenen Person zu tun."[546]

Another reason why the ancient reader turns into a narrator lies in the fact that he is also the one who lends his audible voice to the texts. As shall be explored in the following chapter, we have to assume that under normal circumstances reading in ancient Egypt took the form of reciting or reading aloud.

7.2 What it means to "read" a hieroglyphic inscription

Without doubt, Egyptian text culture was not only a manuscript culture but also an oral text culture. As research of the past few decades has been able to show, non-administrative texts written on papyrus were usually intended to be recited and performed before an audience.[547] A large part of the ritual text corpus can be considered scripts put down in writing for the main reason to receive an actualisation through a performative recitation,[548] and discussions continue whether the same applied also to the funerary corpora of Pyramid Texts and Coffin Texts.[549] Even in narrative texts related to court culture, which are conventionally labelled "literary" in Egyptology, oral speech acts form a cornerstone of the textualisation strategy. In these manuscripts, the textual staging of a story presented

545 Stauder-Porchet (2021b: 463).
546 Zymner (2006: 337).
547 Cf. Morenz (1996: 20–57); Parkinson (2009: 30–40).
548 Whether by real-life human performers or other entities. Weiss (2014) argues that ritual texts are fixed as speech and not as writing. Thus, orality is a constitutive component of these texts.
549 Cf. Reintges (2011); Hays (2012, Vol. I: 17–78); Quack (2012); Weiss (2014); Willems (2019).

as being orally narrated is often the starting point of the entire discourse.[550] Beyond elaborate framing devices that play with the fluctuating boundaries between written and oral spheres, Egyptian culture developed early on[551] two (en)textualisation formulae that are firmly linked to oral discourse: *ḏd-mdw(.w)*, "saying of utterances", as an introduction for religious and magico-medical texts, and *ḏd=f*, "he says/said", for other contexts. Thus, Sinuhe's fictional account of his life phrased in the first person is framed like a conventional autobiography by *ḏd=f* and not by *zš=f*, "he writes/wrote".[552]

It is therefore little wonder that oral performance and aural reception have also been considered for (auto)biographical texts (see already above, p. 134). One of the most outspoken advocates of this scenario is Baines, who not only favours the idea that biographical texts were orally performed at funerals ("Biographies from all periods presumably relate to oral practices."[553]) but also that any true engagement with tomb inscriptions in general took the form of reading aloud. While conceding the incommensurability between oral and written discourse, he stresses that "virtually all writing was pronounced both when read and when written down".[554] Considering the case of the copied royal letters in Senedjemib Inti's tomb he further remarks that

> "the exchange in these slightly later cases is not something that would naturally be pronounced and enacted in oral form and subsequently acquire a written memorialization, but rather something that had full meaning only as action at a certain distance and required the use of writing, even if, as with all writing of the time, its full realization was through being spoken aloud (...)."[555]

While disagreeing with Baines over the status of first-person voices,[556] Eyre too considers oral performance crucial for the efficacy of biographical narratives:

> "(...) it seems to me that these texts have a structure appropriate for recitation, were composed with a view to performance, and in a social context where the eulogy as a form of praise poetry is a social norm, and that they are not a purely written construct, composed only for inscription."[557]

The question then arises whether a reading reception of these texts always equalled reading them aloud and thus, in a certain way, performing them.[558] Whether silent reading was known and commonly practiced in ancient Egypt is a contested issue and

550 For this strategy of "fictionalised" orality, see Goetsch (1985); Parkinson (2009: 35); Moers (2013: 36).
551 The first securely datable use of the *ḏd-mdw* formula occurs on the relief blocks from a Heliopolitan shrine of Djoser, where they introduce divine speech. See Smith (1949: 135, Fig. 50).
552 See Koch (1990: 2, R2).
553 Baines (1999b: 29).
554 Baines (1999b: 23).
555 Baines (1999b: 25).
556 Eyre (2013: 122–123, n. 74).
557 Eyre (2013: 122).
558 Cf. Assmann (1987: 213).

relates partly to the wider discussion about the status of silent reading in Graeco-Roman antiquity.[559] A number of ancient authors allude to the competence of silently processing and comprehending written text, but this is usually contrasted with the normative practice of reading aloud. Whether silent reading enjoyed wider popularity among the *literati* of the time is still not entirely clear, but there is little to suggest that reading habits were similar to our modern customs.[560] According to a theory promoted by Saenger, the *scriptio continua* characterising ancient written discourse made it difficult to segment verbal units of meaning and comprehend continuous writing without the concomitant pronunciation of the deciphered sounds. Only when the insertion of spaces between sentences and individual words was introduced to European manuscript culture starting from the 7th century CE the medial environment more and more supported silent engagement with text.[561] Given that Egyptian hieroglyphic inscriptions were likewise written in unsegmented *scriptio continua*, one may be tempted to conclude that they too had to be pronounced by ancient readers in order to grasp their meaning. But there are some caveats. First, the Egyptian writing system with its many logograms, classifiers and all the metalinguistic information it provides is not directly comparable with alphabetic text in *scriptio continua*. Second, even in antiquity and early medieval Europe the contrast was not solely between loud declamation and silent reading. The spectrum of text reception included murmuring,[562] which basically constituted a method of reading out text to oneself for better comprehension. There is much reason to believe that murmuring while reading was practiced in ancient Egypt as well, although definite proof is lacking. Following the *Wörterbuch*,[563] Morenz argues that the verb *šdj* could mean both loud recitation and reading in a low voice or murmuring.[564] In concrete cases, however, the differentiation is extremely difficult to make, since it hinges on our own conception of what would be the best form of receptive engagement in a given situation. As far as we can say from an etymological and a contextual analysis, *šdj* implied an action performed with one's mouth that usually projected agency for a real or an imagined audience through raising one's voice.[565] Certain texts do indeed indicate that biographical discourse on tomb walls and other monuments was intended to be engaged with through the act of *šdj*. An address to the living in the 18th Dynasty autobiographical inscription of Khaiemhat[566] is quite explicit in this regard:

559 Weiss (2014: 300).
560 See Busch (2002).
561 Saenger (1989; 1997).
562 Saenger (1997: 397, n. 8).
563 Erman & Grapow (1926–1931, Vol. IV: 563).
564 Morenz (1996: 51). This is not necessarily contradicted by the statement of pLansing 1,4: ⸢*sš*⸣ *m ḏr.t=k šdj m* ⸢*r*ʾ⸣[*=k*] *jrj mj j.ḏdw.t=j*, "Write with your hand, read with your mouth, act according to what I have said." Gardiner (1937: 100, 5–6). For this passage see Morenz (1996: 51); Ragazzoli (2010: 160).
565 Cf. Loret (1889: 127–129); Meyer-Dietrich (2010: 6).
566 Helck (1958: 1845, 9–14).

|1 (...) *Ḫʿj-m-ḥꜣ.t mꜣʿ ḫrw ḏd=f ḫr rmṯ ḫpr.tj=sn ḥrj.w tꜣ m wr.w kttj.w sš(.w) nb wḥʿ.w ḏrf spd.w ḥr m* |2 *mdw.w-nṯr wnfj.w jb ʿḳ(ꜣ).w m rḫ ḥtp.w ḥr zp.w n ꜣḫ.t swꜣ.tj=sn ḥr ḥw.t tn jrj(.t).n(=j) r ḫn ꜣḫ.w gm{t}ḥ.<tj>=sn r sꜣ.wt=j šdj.tj=sn m ṯz.w=j*	|1 (...) Khaiemhat, true of voice, saying to the people who will come into being (or) who are on earth as great ones or small ones, all scribes who are able to explain the writing, perspicacious in relation to the |2 divine words, who rejoice when they are correct in knowing, who are content with occasions of usefulness, who will pass by this monument, which I have made to serve as a resting place of the *akhu*, who will look at my walls and will recite from my phrases (...).

The partitive use of the preposition *m* suggests that Khaiemhat did not have in mind a complete recitation of very single inscription found inside his tomb but rather a selective engagement with salient elements of the iconotext. Dating to an earlier epoch, the Abydene stela of Montuwoser (New York, MMA 12.184, 12th Dynasty)[567] suggests a similar approach:

|16 ↓ (...) *jr gr.t rmṯ* |17 *nb.t sḏm<.t>(j){r}=sn ʿbꜣ pn ntj.w m-m rmṯ ʿnḫ(.wt) jw=sn r ḏd mꜣʿ.t pw* (...)	|16 (...) As for every person |17 who shall hear this stela, being among the living people, they will say, "It is the truth!" (...)
|18 (...) *jr gr.t zšw nb šdj.t(j)=f(j) ʿbꜣ pn rmṯ nb.t spr<.tj>=sn jr=f* (...)	|18 (...) As for every scribe who shall read this stela and all the people who shall reach it (...)

In this case we have a direct correspondence between two forms of reception. On the one hand there are those who are not capable of reading hieroglyphic texts themselves and have to listen to other people reciting the inscriptions' wording. On the other hand there are the fully literate scribes whose task is to recite/read aloud the text for everyone to hear. Unfortunately, we lack similar statements from the Old Kingdom, but we have little reason to believe that there was a fundamental difference in the reception process compared with later periods. This is not to say that *šdj* was the only way for literate contemporaries to engage with written text. When audible voicing was not the main concern, the process of reading text could probably be expressed through the verb *mꜣꜣ*, lit. "to see", in the sense of visually "ingesting" and comprehending the content of a piece of writing. In captions to the so-called "scenes of presenting the scroll"[568] the collocation *mꜣꜣ zš* is often encountered as an analogue to *rdj.t zš*. As already discussed (see above, n. 403), in these cases the verb may have the meaning of "letting see/showing the document" to the tomb owner, who is usually depicted as the addressee.[569] But there are attestations where *mꜣꜣ* must refer to the act of "viewing" and, in a wider sense, to "checking", "(proof-)reading",

567 Sethe (1924: 100, 1–4); Landgráfová (2011: 132–133).
568 See Der Manuelian (1996: 581–585).
569 In one case, the tomb of Ankhmahor Zezi, the caption states that the document listing the funerary equipment is recited before the tomb owner: \|1 *šdj.t n=f zš* \|2 *n ḳrstj.t=f ḏjj.t* \|3 *n=f m ḥtp-ḏj-nswt*, "\|1 Reciting to him the document \|2 for his burial equipment which was given \|3 to him as a *ḥtp-ḏj-nswt*." Der Manuelian (1996: 585); Kanawati & Hassan (1997: 41, Pl. 45).

e.g. in a scene caption in the mastaba of Meresankh III, where it says: [1] *rḏj.t zš nj ḥm.w-kꜣ* [2] *r mꜣꜣ jn* [3] *(j)m(j)-r(ꜣ) ḥm(.w)-kꜣ Ḫmtn(w)*, "[1] Presenting the document of the *ka*-priests [2] in order to be viewed/checked/read by [3] the overseer of the *ka*-priests Khemetenu."[570] In another case from a different context the meaning of *mꜣꜣ* seems to come even closer to our notion of non-declamatory reading. It is the first royal letter represented in the tomb of Senedjemib Inti (Inscription A2), wherein the king states that he has "seen" Inti's last letter (*jw mꜣꜣ.n ḥm(=j) mḏꜣ.t=k tn*). While we could render this passage simply by "(My) Majesty has taken notice of this letter of yours", a straightforward translation as "read" may not be completely off the mark,[571] even though in the letter of Inscription B2 (l. 7) the king mentions being pleased to hear (*sḏm*) about Inti's concern.

However this may be in the concrete case, there can be no doubt that certain features of an inscriptional layout such as spatial relations between specific words or lines (for the widespread partial reversals of hieroglyphs and their semiotic significance, see p. 175), visual anaphora etc. cannot be replicated by oral recitation. But the two dimensions of text reception should not be conceived of as mutually exclusive. Rather, they could complement each other within the process of engaging with a multimodal iconotext. This notwithstanding, we still have to assume that the most common way of processing linguistic information from hieroglyphic inscriptions in ancient times was to pronounce them in an audible voice. This is certainly to be expected for lengthy compositions of continuous text such as those belonging to the genres of event and ideal biography. Whether the literal voicing or audible enactment of narrativisable text presents in narratological terms a significant difference to silent modes of reception has to the best of my knowledge not been widely considered within narratology, probably, because its research agenda has for such a long time been linked to modern Western book culture.[572] While one may opt to regard a reader's inner voice totally analogous to his/her audible voice, there will be few to deny that a loud reading provides the entity of the narrator (which every narrative possesses) and the Genettian *narration*, the actual act of narrating, with an immediacy not easily achieved through other means. The questions thus becomes whether the reader/recipient acts merely as an external mediator of a narrative or becomes himself part of the diegesis through his oral performance of someone else's voice. In connection with ancient Greek "speaking objects", Svenbro considered the extreme view that the epigrams on such monuments could be said to hijack the visitor's voice and turn it into a reproducing machine in order to make themselves heard.[573] Even though this interpretation has not gained universal acceptance in Classical Studies,[574] one may ponder whether the

---

570 Dunham & Simpson (1974: 9, Fig. 3b, Pl. 2c); Der Manuelian (1996: 583).

571 After all, there must have been confidential correspondence a literate king would rather not have everyone in the palace know about.

572 Still, Forster (1927: 39), in an attitude of deliberate naivety, conceptualises "the story as the repository of a voice. It is the aspect of the novelist's work which asks to be read out loud, which appeals not to the eye, like most prose, but to the ear;" For a historical contextualisation of this statement, see Bal (2004: 36).

573 Svenbro (1988: 56; 117–118).

574 Cf. Rösler (1992: 2–3); Mackie (1995: 289–290); Lavinge (2018: 178–179).

extradiegetic narrator of the Egyptian biographical discourse was meant to be represented by the concrete recipient of the text and not, or not just, by a narrative entity embedded in the iconotext. In such a way, the receptive mode of voicing the texts would already have become part of the narrative equation.[575] In the absence of conclusive evidence such thoughts need to be marked as mere speculation. But if we consider the tomb as an entity that was designed to become narrativised as a totality, the act of reception should form part of the narrative emerging from it. One needs to stress here that the notions of the narrator as impersonal text function and as an entity embodied by the reader are not contradictory but may represent merely two ways of looking at the same phenomenon. Certainly, the tomb's multimodal complexity and nonlinearity transcend any single act of voicing. They also work against a universally binding *récit* only waiting to be followed through by each and every visitor. This lack of fixedness in funerary portfolio biographies gives the visitor *qua* narrator undoubtedly a much larger role to play during the act of narration compared with the reader of a modern Western novel. I would therefore maintain that orality and (per) formative exploration followed upon the entextualisation of life writing (in the broadest sense) and not the other way round.[576]

7.3 Édith Piaf in Giza, or: reception as a narrative perpetuum mobile

When Édith Piaf visited Egypt at the end of February 1949 to give a few concerts in Alexandria and Cairo, she was at the height of her career. Having escaped poverty and the other hardships of her childhood and youth she had by the end of the war become a treasured French national icon whose charisma and golden voice with its special timbre had the power to move millions of devotees. Accordingly, reviewers from the French diaspora in Cairo were enthusiastic about the concerts and praised the emotional range of her performance.[577] Before she continued her triumphal tour of the "French Orient" by travelling to Beirut, however, Piaf took a day off in order to pay a visit to the pyramids of Giza. This event has been transmitted to posterity thanks to the efforts of accordionist and amateur filmmaker Marc Bonel – at that time a constant member of Piaf's entourage – who produced colour footage that shows Piaf riding a camel across the Giza necropolis.[578] We will probably never know whether she had on that occasion the opportunity to visit any of the non-royal tombs open at the time and make acquaintance with their iconotexts. In any event, Piaf's short exposure to ancient Egyptian funerary culture and, possibly, life writing, provides a welcome opportunity to engage in the context of this essay with her own special contribution to life writing. I am not referring here to her autobiography of

575 Cf. a related notion in Svenbro (1988: 53): "si le *sêma* est incomplet sans la *nóēsis* ou l'*anágnōsis*, cela veut dire que la *nóēsis* ou l'*anágnōsis* fait partie du *sêma*. En d'autres mots : la lecture fait partie du texte."

576 Of course, written discourse may have contained textual elements that were originally part of courtly performances or formalised recitations.

577 Burke (2011: 136–137).

578 Burke (2011: 137); Rosteck (2013: 238). See https://www.youtube.com/watch?v=r_H8htkDVxk (last accessed on 22 December 2022).

1958[579] but to *Non, je ne regrette rien*, probably one of her most famous chansons, which she recorded two years later. The song had been written by Charles Dumont to lyrics by Michel Vaucaire already in 1956, but it was not until four years later that the two were able to convince Piaf of its qualities.[580] With the song's positive message as a booster, Piaf apparently managed to (temporarily) turn the tide in terms of her deteriorating health and endeavoured to perform to great acclaim a string of concerts at Paris' Olympia venue.[581] Unsurprisingly, the song became the shows' highlight and from that time on determined to a large degree the perception of Piaf's public persona. While *Non, je ne regrette rien* had originally been composed for the singer Rosalie Dubois,[582] after its premiere in 1960 it became an emblem of Piaf's personal identity. As a consequence, it was difficult not to interpret it as an autobiographical statement reflecting on Piaf's attitude towards her past and life in general. Nevertheless, it should be noted here that despite its obvious autobiographical overtones, the song also acquired political meaning in conservative to rightist contexts. At its initial release Piaf had chosen to dedicate it to the French Foreign Legion, who adopted it as a sort of anthem subsequent to their defeat in the attempted putsch of 1961. In 1962 Piaf performed it on the platform of the Eiffel Tower to mark the premiere of the American war film epic *The Longest Day*.[583] But the tolerated political and ideological appropriation of *Non, je ne regrette rien* did little to change its common perception among the wider public as an autobiographical micro-story told by Piaf as the *implied author*. The precondition for such a development was the fact that Piaf had long ago become a public figure whose private tragedies attracted at least as much attention in the media as her achievements as a singer. The affirmative statement "Non, je ne regrette rien" then provides a narrative nucleus to which prior knowledge of Piaf's life story can be anchored. The sentence evokes an autobiographical narrative, even though it does not narrate in the narrow sense of the term. Yet, its semantics imply a temporal structure, a marked retrospective viewpoint on personal experience and a causal link between the past and the moment of utterance (re-experience leading to affirmation). What is crucial for my present point is the way in which narrative valence is heightened through the receptive context (e.g. through attending a concert or listening to a record). This context is already inscribed in the transmitted plot: a famous chanteuse at the height of her popularity, marked by personal tragedies and a lifestyle full of wasting engages in defiant introspection. To the degree to which reception forms an integral part of Piaf's career, the plot gets actualised and perpetuated in the very act of reception, which equals the narrativisation of the narrative nucleus. In this particular way reception is also in-built in ancient Egyptian life writing of the funerary sphere. While the physical space of the elite tomb figures as the material manifestation of biographical content and thereby structures reception, reception also forms a constitutive component of the tomb's plot and becomes a factor in the exemplification cascade. Through repeated engagement with the tomb's iconotext visitors

579 Piaf (1958).

580 Marchois (1995: 98–99; 252–253).

581 Looseley (2015: 9); Rosteck (2013: 372–375).

582 Marchois (1995: 99).

583 Looseley (2015: 115).

affirm and thereby actualise the narrative about the tomb owner's entitlement to the *akh* status. Whereas Piaf's narrative identity is shaped by the individuality dogma of Western modernity (a dogma anything but free from cultural normativity and genre conventions), ancient Egyptian representations of life narratives instead focus on the exceptionality of a person's achievement in conforming to societal norms. This achievement extends to the capacity to attract visitors actively engaged in the reception process (a part of which is performing ritual speech acts to the benefit of the deceased).

For this reason a large part of the secondary inscriptions and graffiti we find in the funerary sphere may be regarded as part of the tomb owner's self-perpetuating life writing and not just as elements of the tomb's *object biography*. A particularly interesting case in this regard is offered by a relief panel on a pillar in the 6th Dynasty rock-cut tomb chapel of Khuiui at the Qubbet el-Hawa (QeH 34e). As already highlighted by Vischak and Baines,[584] the panel stands out for containing below the main offering scene a sequence of images depicting Khuiui's subordinate Khnumhotep and the latter's family members engaged in different actions relating to the offering ritual.[585] Exceptional is not only the fact that Khnumhotep has been depicted four times in what appear to be successive actions, but that his images are accompanied by a one-line autobiographical inscription in which he points out his connection to the tomb owner Khuiui, the latter's colleague Tjetji (buried in QeH 103, which features likewise a depiction of Khnumhotep as funerary officiant[586]), as well as his professional achievements connected with the two:

<table>
<tr><td>← ḫrp zḥ Ḫnmw-ḥtp(.w) ḏd
jw prj.k(j) ḥnꜥ nb(.wj=j) ḥꜣtj-ꜥ
ḫtmw-nṯr Ṯtj [a] | Ḫ(wj)-wj r Kbn |
Pwn.t r Rṯnw n zp jw jj.k(j) m ḥtp
jrj.n(=j) ḫꜣs.wt (j)ptn</td><td>The director of the booth Khnumhotep (is it who) says: "I went out together with (my two) lord(s), the hati-a and god's treasurer Tjetji and Khuiui to Byblos, Punt, and Retjenu together. I returned in peace after I had travelled (lit. 'done') these foreign lands."</td></tr>
</table>

a) Tjetji is also attested in Graffiti C-M 35 and C-M 64 in Wadi Hammamat.[587]

Equally noteworthy is that the same Khnumhotep appears to have been buried next to his superior in QeH 34e and to have received a false door there.[588] According to Edel and Kokina, this constellation could suggest that Khuiui died without leaving an heir and Khnumhotep took over to provide for his funerary cult.[589] However this may be, the interweaving of two biographical narratives in QeH 34e brings to the fore the potential of reception to enter diegesis. While acts of commemoration require a commemorated plot, however basic it may be, they at the same time inscribe themselves into the trajectory of a life not ended by death. This could be said to constitute the narrative perpetuum mobile of ancient Egyptian life writing.

---

584 Vischak (2015: 85–86); Baines (2020: 56–57).

585 Edel (2008a: 466–471 w. Fig. 1a).

586 Edel (2008c: 1509–1511; 1528–1529).

587 Eichler (1993: 68–69, no. 116; 71, no. 126).

588 Edel (2008a: 471–473 w. Fig. 2).

589 Edel (2008a: 502); Kokina (2017: 167).

8 Conclusions and caveats: challenges of Egyptological narratology

If the goal of historical narratology is to describe and elucidate the parameters of narrating in their historical setting and practice,[590] then this task presupposes a firm preunderstanding of the phenomena one endeavours to look out for. Seeing narrative coherence in textual and pictorial assemblages not previously thought of as being narrative may be a step towards a better understanding of narrativity in ancient Egypt. It could, however, also mean taking one step too far and eventually ending up on a path where everything one touches becomes a narrative (a cruel divine punishment not mentioned by Ovid). Human pattern recognition is a powerful if often indiscriminate tool indeed, and patterns do not only reside in *fabulae* but also in analyses of purported *fabulae*. One thing that can be learned from Rorschach tests is that narratives as well as their narratological explanations are ultimately located in the recipient's mind. Is the Egyptian elite tomb thus a Rorschach test for Egyptological narratologists, or Egyptologists more widely? Such a risk is not to be underestimated, and yet it is in the hope to find intersubjectively meaningful patterns that one sets out to engage with historical narratology in the first place. As a consolation we can always refer to the old wisdom that it is not only the result that counts but the fact that there is a result at all. *Se non è vero, è ben trovato.* With this in mind I would like to present in a nutshell (in this case more telling than showing) my conclusions from the previous chapters.

With a broad understanding of narrativity as the point of departure, one can understand and analyse ancient Egyptian life writing not only in terms of lengthy narrative texts but equally in terms of multimodal nuclei of narrative signification, which may be experienced to relate overarching narratives through modular enrichment (addition, juxtaposition, complementation, etc.). This is not to say that there is no difference in narrative valence between, let's say, a title string and the biographical text of Weni the Elder. My point is merely that the two show a correspondence in narrative structure at a more abstract level. Even though I have constantly been referring to biographical text genres (foremost, event and ideal biography), one would be hard-pressed to define the characteristics of the ancient Egyptian autobiography as an overarching genre. Essentially, it does not exist as such, for the function it would serve had structurally taken shape in the material totality of the tomb long before explicit autobiographical text was first recorded in stone. From a purely structural point of view, funerary biography is nothing more than a slot in the discourse of justification within the context of a socio-cultic claim: "I am because of XYZ, therefore tomb, therefore offering, therefore the right to continued existence…" As explained at the end of Chapter 2.4, the function manifests itself in the form of modular exemplifications. This fundamental link is implicit in the entirety of the monumental discourse, but early tombs as well as the majority of the elite tombs of the 5th and 6th Dynasties do not dwell on it within a coherent textual whole. Even in tombs featuring distinct autobiographical exemplifications, they most commonly extend to several textual and pictorial units within a configuration I have termed "portfolio biography" (see p. 158). In its totality, the Egyptian tomb as the physical manifestation of an elite existence constitutes

590 See Contzen & Tilg (2019: VII).

at the same time the object, medium, and subject of narration. It requires, however, the active engagement of an external recipient to exploit its narrative potential and turn narrative *Kristallisationspunkte* into a narration. While the Egyptian tomb can thus be conceived of as a narrative of sorts, it is always also something else: a cultic stage, a ritual device, a self-presentation, a commemorative monument, a communal space, etc. After all, representation, cultic functionality, and narrativity should not be considered as mutually exclusive modes of signification. These spheres may overlap, become intertwined, and produce a surplus of meaning not easily boiled down to a simple technical term or catch phrase. But that is another story…

Acknowledgments

I would like to thank the co-contributors to this volume, especially Gerald Moers, for their extremely valuable feedback and the fruitful discussions on a number of issues. Further thanks are due to Vinzenz Brinkmann, Martin Fitzenreiter, Roman Gundacker, Ľubica Hudáková, Peter Jánosi, Elisabeth Kruck, Uta Siffert, and Annik Wüthrich for reproduction permissions, references and for sharing with me their insights regarding a number of topics.

Bibliography

Ancient Sources

Aristotle, *Poetics*
Immanuel Bekker (ed.). 1831. *Aristoteles Graece* [Opera], Volumen alterum, Berlin.
Caesar, *Commentarii de bello Gallico*
Wolfgang Hering (ed.). 1987. *Gaius Iulius Caesar, Volumen I: Bellum Gallicum*, Bibliotheca scriptorum Graecorum et Romanorum Teubneriana 1127, Berlin/New York.

Unpublished Sources

BBAW (1842–1845) = Original drawings of the *Preußische Expedition an den Nil von 1842–1845*, Berlin-Brandenburgische Akademie der Wissenschaften, Akademienvorhaben *Strukturen und Transformationen des Wortschatzes der ägyptischen Sprache*, Berlin.

Published Sources

Abbott, H. Porter. 2000. The Evolutionary Origins of the Storied Mind: Modeling the Prehistory of Narrative Consciousness and its Discontents, in: *Narrative* 8(3), 247–256.
Abbott, H. Porter. 2014. Narrativity, in: Peter Hühn, Jan Christoph Meister, John Pier & Wolf Schmid (eds.), *The Living Handbook of Narratology*, Hamburg (https://www-archiv.fdm.uni-hamburg.de/lhn/printpdf/article/narrativity, last accessed on 22 December 2022).
Aczel, Richard. 1997. Hearing Voices in Narrative Texts, in: *New Literary History* 29(3), 467–500.
Adorno, Theodor W. 1971. *Die musikalischen Monographien. Versuch über Wagner | Mahler. Eine muikalische Physiognomik | Berg, der Meister des kleinsten Übergangs*, Theodor W. Adorno Gesammelte Schriften 13, suhrkamp taschenbuch wissenchaft 1713, Frankfurt am Main.

Alber, Jan & Per Krogh Hansen. 2014. Introduction: Transmedial and Unnatural Narratology, in: Jan Alber & Per Krogh Hansen (eds.), *Beyond Classical Narration: Transmedial and Unnatural Challenges*, Narratologia 42, Berlin/Boston, 1–14.

Alexanian, Nicole. 2006. Tomb and social status. The textual evidence, in: Miroslav Bárta (ed.), *The Old Kingdom Art and Archaeology. Proceedings of the Conference Held in Prague, May 31–June 4*, 2004, Prague, 1–8.

Almén, Byron. 2008. *A Theory of Musical Narrative*, Bloomington/Indianapolis.

Altenmüller, Hartwig. 2002. Funerary Boats and Boat Pits of the Old Kingdom, in: *Archiv Orientální* 70(3), 269–290.

Arnauld, Andreas von. 2009. Was war, was ist – und was sein soll. Erzählen im juristischen Diskurs, in: Christian Klein & Matías Martínez (eds.), *Wirklichkeitserzählungen. Felder, Formen und Funktionen nicht-literarischen Erzählens*, Stuttgart/Weimar, 14–50.

Arnold, Dieter. 1999. Old Kingdom Statues in Their Architectural Setting, in: Dorothea Arnold & Christine Ziegler (eds.), *Egyptian Art in the Age of the Pyramids*, The Metropolitan Museum of Art, New York, 41–49.

Assmann, Jan. 1977. Die Verborgenheit des Mythos in Ägypten, in: *Göttinger Miszellen* 25, 7–43.

Assmann, Jan. 1983. Schrift, Tod und Identität. Das Grab als Vorschule der Literatur im alten Ägypten, in: Aleida Assmann & Jan Assmann (eds.), *Schrift und Gedächtnis*, Beiträge zur Archäologie der literarischen Kommunikation, Archäologie der literarischen Kommunikation I, Munich, 64–93.

Assmann, Jan. 1987. Sepulkrale Selbstthematisierung im Alten Ägypten, in: Alois Hahn & Volker Kapp (eds.), *Selbstthematisierung und Selbstzeugnis. Bekenntnis und Geständnis*, Frankfurt a. M., 208–232.

Assmann, Jan. 1996a. *Ägypten. Eine Sinngeschichte*, Munich.

Assmann, Jan. 1996b. Der literarische Aspekt des ägyptischen Grabes und seine Funktion im Rahmen des "Monumentalen Diskurses", in: Antonio Loprieno (ed.), *Ancient Egyptian Literature: History and Forms*, Probleme der Ägyptologie 10, Leiden/New York/Cologne, 97–104.

Assmann, Jan. 2009. Die Piye(Pianchi)Stele: Erzählung als Medium politischer Repräsentation, in: Hubert Roeder (ed.), *Das Erzählen in frühen Hochkulturen, I. Der Fall Ägypten*, Ägyptologie und Kulturwissenschaft 1, Munich, 221–236.

Aumüller, Matthias. 2006. Die Stimme des Formalismus. Die Entwicklung des Stimmenbegriffs im russischen Formalismus, in: Andreas Blödorn, Daniela Langer & Michael Scheffel (eds.), *Stimme(n) im Text. Narratologische Positionsbestimmungen*, Narratologia 10, Berlin/New York, 31–52.

El Awady, Tarek. 2006. King Sahura with the precious trees from Punt in a unique scene!, in: Miroslav Bárta (ed.), *The Old Kingdom Art and Archaeology. Proceedings of the Conference Held in Prague, May 31–June 4, 2004*, Prague, 37–44.

El Awady, Tarek. 2009. *Sahure – The Pyramid Causeway: History and Decoration Program in the Old Kingdom*, Abusir XVI, Prague.

Backes, Burkhard. 2020. *Sarg und Sarkophag der Aaschyt (Kairo JE 47355 und 47267)*, Vols. I–II, Studien zum altägyptischen Totenbuch 21,1–2, Wiesbaden.

Badawy, Alexander. 1976. *The Tombs of Iteti, Sekhemꜥnkh-Ptah, and Kaemnofert at Giza*, Berkeley/Los Angeles/London.

Baines, John. 1999a. Forerunners of Narrative Biographies, in: Anthony Leahy & John Tait (eds.), *Studies on Ancient Egypt in Honour of H. S. Smith*, Egypt Exploration Society, Occasional Publications 13, London, 23–37.

Baines, John. 1999b. Prehistories of Literature: Performance, Fiction, Myth, in: Gerald Moers (ed.), *Definitely: Egyptian Literature. Proceedings of the Symposium "Ancient Egyptian Literature: History and Forms", Los Angeles, March 24–26, 1995*, Lingua Aegyptia – Studia Monographica 2, Göttingen, 17–41.

Baines, John. 2004. Egyptian Elite Self-presentation in the Context of Ptolemaic Rule, in: William V. Harris & Giovanni Ruffini (eds.), *Ancient Alexandria between Egypt and Greece*, Columbia Studies in the Classical Tradition 26, Leiden, 33–61.

Baines, John. 2013. *High Culture and Experience in Ancient Egypt*, Sheffield/Bristol.

Baines, John. 2014. Not only with the dead: banqueting in ancient Egypt, *Studia Universitatis "Babeş-Bolyai", Historia* 59 (1), 1–35.

Baines, John. 2015a. The Self-presentation of Pepyankh the Middle at Meir: Scandal, Religious Institutions and Participation, the Next World, in: Rune Nyord & Kim Ryholt (eds.), *Lotus and Laurel. Studies on Egyptian Language and Religion in Honour of Paul John Frandsen*, Carsten Niebuhr Institute Publications 39, Copenhagen, 19–43.

Baines, John. 2015b. On the Old Kingdom inscriptions of Hezy. Purity of Person and Mind; Court Hierarchy, in: Hans Amstutz, Andreas Dorn, Matthias Müller, Miriam V. Ronsdorf & Sami Uljas (eds.), *Fuzzy Boundaries. Festschrift für Antonio Loprieno*, Vol. II, Hamburg, 519–536.

Baines, John. 2020. From Living a Life to Creating a Fit Memorial, in: Julie Stauder-Porchet, Elizabeth Frood & Andréas Stauder (eds.), *Ancient Egyptian Biographies: Contexts, Forms, Functions*, Wilbour Studies in Egyptology and Assyriology 6, Atlanta, GA, 47–83.

Baines, John. 2022. Taking the dead to the cemetery, communicating with them, and managing their presence, in: Lara Weiss, Nico Staring & Hugh Twiston Davies (eds.), *Perspectives on Lived Religion II. The Making of a Cultural Geography*, Papers on Archaeology of the Leiden Museum of Antiquities 28, Leiden, 15–28.

Bakhtin, Michail Michailovich. 1981. Forms of time and of the chronotope in the novel. Notes toward a Historical Poetics, in: Michail Bakhtin, *The Dialogic Imagination. Four Essays by M. M. Bakhtin* (Edited by Michael Holquist, translated by Caryl Emerson & Michael Holquist), University of Texas Press Slavic Series 1, Austin.

Bal, Mieke. 1990. The Point of Narratology, in: *Poetics Today* 11(4), 727–753.

Bal, Mieke. 1999. Close Reading Today: From Narratology to Cultural Analysis, in: Walter Grünzweig & Andreas Solbach (eds.), *Grenzüberschreitungen: Narratologie im Kontext/Transcending Boundaries: Narratology in Context*, Tübingen, 19–40.

Bal, Mieke. 2004. Critique of Voice: The Open Score of Her Face, in: Lazar Fleishman, Christine Gölz & Aage A. Hansen-Löve (eds.), *Analysieren als Deuten. Wolf Schmid zum 60. Geburtstag*, Hamburg, 31–51.

Bal, Mieke. 2019. The point of narratology: part 2, in: *Interdisciplinary Description of Complex Systems* 17(2-A), 242–258.

Balanda, Stanley Z. 2000. Yet Another Look at a Sixth Dynasty "Letter" from Saqqara, in: *Discussions in Egyptology* 47, 9–27.

Balmes, Sebastian. 2018. Sprachliche Grundbedingungen der klassischen Tagebuchliteratur Japans und Probleme von Erzählstimme und Perspektive im ‚Tosa nikki', in: Eva von Contzen & Florian Kragl (eds.), *Narratologie und mittelalterliches Erzählen*, Das Mittelalter, Beiheft 7, Berlin/Boston, 9–41.

Banfield, Ann. 1982. *Unspeakable Sentences: Narration and Representation in the Language of Fiction*, Abingdon/New York.

Baroni, Raphaël. 2014. Tellability, in: Peter Hühn, Jan Christoph Meister, John Pier & Wolf Schmid (eds.), *The Living Handbook of Narratology*, Hamburg (https:/www-archiv.fdm.uni-hamburg.de/lhn/printpdf/article/schemata, last accessed on 22 December 2022).

Barta, W. 1968. *Aufbau und Bedeutung der altägyptischen Opferformel*, Ägyptologische Forschungen 24, Glückstadt.

Barthes, Roland. 1968. La mort de l'auteur, in: *Mantéia* 5, 12–17.

Barthes, Roland. 1984. *Le bruissement de la langue*, Essais critiques IV, Paris.

Bassir, Hussein. 2014. *Image & Voice in Saite Egypt: Self-Presentation of Neshor Named Psamtikmenkhib and Payeftjauemawyneith*, Wilkinson Egyptology Series 2, Tuscon, AZ.

Bassir, Hussein (ed.). 2019. *Living Forever: Self-Presentation in Ancient Egypt*, Cairo.

Bateman, John, Janina Wildfeuer & Tuomo Hiippala. 2017. *Multimodality: Foundations, Research and Analysis – A Problem-Oriented Introduction*, Berlin/Boston.

Baud, Michel. 1999. *Famille royal et pouvoir sous l'Ancien Empire égyptien*, Vol. I–II, Bibliothèque d'étude 126, Cairo.

Baud, Michel. 2003. Le format de l'histoire. Annales royales et biographies de particuliers dans l'Égypte du IIIe millénaire, in: Nicolas Grimal & Michel Baud (eds.), *Événement, récit, histoire officielle. L'écriture de l'histoire dans les monarchies antiques. Colloque du Collège de France, amphithéâtre Marguerite-de-Navarre 24–25 juin 2002*, Paris, 271–302.

Baud, Michel. 2005. The Birth of Biography in Ancient Egypt: Text Format and Content in the IVth Dynasty, in: Stephan Johannes Seidlmayer (ed.), *Texte und Denkmäler des ägyptischen Alten Reiches*, Berlin, 91–124.

Baud, Michel & Dominique Farout. 2001. Trois biographies d'Ancien Empire revisitées, in: *Bulletin de l'Institut français d'archéologie orientale* 101, 43–57.

Baumbach, Manuel, Andrej Petrovic & Ivana Petrovic, Archaic and classical Greek epigram: an introduction, in: Manuel Baumbach, Andrej Petrovic & Ivana Petrovic (eds.), *Archaic and Classical Greek Epigram*, Cambridge, 1–19.

Begon, Matthieu. 2016. Nédia, Dia ou bien plutôt Ida ? La « campagne asiatique » d'Inti de Deshasha (fin de la Ve dynastie) et le littoral sud de la Palestine durant la seconde moitié du IIIe millénaire (Bronze Ancien III), in: *NeHeT* 4, 1–24.

Benveniste, Émile. 1966. Les relations de temps dans le verbe français, in: *Problèmes de linguistique générale* I, Bibliothèque de sciences humaines, Paris, 237–250 (originally published in *Bulletin de la Société de Linguistique* 54, 1959, 69–82).

Berlev, Oleg Dmitrievich [Берлев, Олег Дмитриевич]. 1962a. Способы указания филиации в письменности Среднего царства [Sposoby ukazaniya filiatsii v pis'mennosti Srednego tsarstva], in: *Палестинский Сборник [Palestinskiy sbornik]* 9, 13–42.

Berlev, Oleg Dmitrievich [Берлев, Олег Дмитриевич]. 1962b. Один из способов датировки стел Среднего царства [Odin iz sposobov datirovki stel Srednego tsarstva], in: *Краткие сообщения Института народов Азии [Kratkie soobščenija Instituta narodov Asii]* 46, 45–87.

Besemeres, Mary & Maureen Perkins. 2004. Editorial, in: *Life Writing* 1(1), vii–xii (doi: https://doi-org/10.1080/10408340308518239).

Björkvall, Anders. 2012. Multimodality, in: Jan-Ola Östmann & Jeff Verschueren (eds.), *Handbook of Pragmatics*, Amsterdam/Philadelphia, 1–20.

Blackman, Aylward M. 1924. *The Rock Tombs of Meir, Part IV: The Tomb-Chapel of Pepiʿonkh the Middle Son of Sebkḥotpe and Pekhernefert (D, No. 2)*, Archaeological Survey of Egypt 25, London.

Blackman, Aylward M. & Michael R. Apted. 1953. *The Rock Tombs of Meir. Part V: the tomb-chapels A, No. 1 (that of Ni-ʿAnkh-Pepi the Black), A, No. 2 (that of Pepiʿonkh with the "good name" of Ḥeny the Black), A, No. 4 (that of Ḥepi the Black), D, No. 1 (that of Pepi), and E, Nos. 1–4 (those of Meniu, Nenki, Pepiʿonkh and Tjetu)*, Archaeological Survey of Egypt 28. London.

Blain, Bastien & Tali Sharot. 2021. Intrinsic reward: potential cognitive and neural mechanisms, in: *Current Opinion in Behavioral Sciences* 39, 113–118 (doi: https://doi.org/10.1016/j.cobeha.2021.03.008).

Bloom, Paul & Csaba Veres. 1999. The perceived intentionality of groups, in: *Cognition* 71, B1–B9.

Blödorn, Andreas & Daniela Langer. 2006. Implikationen eines metaphorischen Stimmenbegriffs: Derrida – Bachtin – Genette, in: Andreas Blödorn, Daniela Langer & Michael Scheffel (eds.), *Stimme(n) im Text. Narratologische Positionsbestimmungen*, Narratologia 10, Berlin/New York, 53–82.

Booth, Wayne C. 1983. *The Rhetoric of Fiction*, Second Edition, Chicago/London.

Borchardt, Ludwig †. 1964. *Denkmäler des Alten Reiches (außer den Statuen) im Museum von Kairo Nr. 1295–1808. Teil II: Text und Tafeln zu Nr. 1542–1808 (Manuskript abgeschlossen 1899)*, Catalogue général des antiquités égyptiennes du Musée du Caire, Cairo.

Borghouts, Joris F. 2010. *Egyptian. An Introduction to the Writing and Language of the Middle Kingdom*, Egyptologische Uitgaven 24, Leiden/Leuven.

Boyd, Brian. 2009. *On the Origin of Stories: Evolution, Cognition, and Fiction*, Cambridge, MA/London.

Boyd, Brian (ed.). 2011. *Vladimir Nabokov, Pale Fire. A Poem in Four Cantos by John Shade*, Berkeley, CA.

Branigan, Edward. 1992. *Narrative Comprehension and Film*, London et al.

Braun, Nadja. 2019. Von der Erzählung zum Narrativ, in: Dina Serova, Burkhard Backes, Matthieu W. Götz & Alexandra Verbovsek (eds.), *Narrative: Geschichte – Mythos – Repräsentation. Beiträge des achten Berliner Arbeitskreises Junge Ägyptologie (BAJA 8), 1.12–3.12.2017*, Göttinger Orientforschungen IV. Reihe Ägypten 65, Wiesbaden, 19–38.

Braun, Nadja S. 2020. *Bilder erzählen. Visuelle Narrativität im alten Ägypten*, Ägyptologische Studien Leipzig 2, Heidelberg.

Breithaupt, Fritz. 2022. *Das narrative Gehirn. Was unsere Neuronen erzählen*, Berlin.

Brinkmann, Vinzenz & Ulrike Koch-Brinkmann (eds.). 2020. *Bunte Götter – Golden Edition. Die Farben der Antike*, exhibition catalogue Liebieghaus Skulpturensammlung, Frankfurt am Main, Munich/London/New York.

Brockmeier, Jens. 2012. Narrative Scenarios: Toward a Culturally Thick Notion of Narrative, in: Jaan Valsiner (ed.), *The Oxford Handbook of Culture and Psychology*, Oxford/New York, 439–467.

Brockmeier, Jens. 2015. *Beyond the Archive: Memory, Narrative, and the Autobiographical Process*, Oxford.

Brockmeier, Jens. 2016. A Picture Is Worth a Thousand Words: On Causes, Reasons, and Images, in: Rom Harré & Fathali M. Moghaddam (eds.), *Questioning Causality. Scientific Explorations of Cause and Consequence across Social Contexts*, Santa Barbara, CA, 157–166.

Brockmeier, Jens & Donal Carbaugh. 2001. Introduction, in: Jens Brockmeier & Donal Carbaugh (eds.), *Narrative and Identity*, Studies in Narrative 1, Amsterdam/Philadelphia, 1–22.

Brook, Peter. 1992. *Reading for the Plot. Design and Intention in Narrative*, Cambridge, MA/London.

Brovarski, Edward. 1997. Old Kingdom Beaded Collars, in: Jacke Philipps (ed.), *Ancient Egypt, the Aegean, and the Near East: Studies in Honour of Martha Rhoads Bell, Volume I*, San Antonio, TX, 137–162.

Brovarski, Edward. 2001. *The Senedjemib Complex, Part I: The Mastabas of Senedjemib Inti (G 2370), Khnumenti (G 2374), and Senedjemib Mehi (G 2378)*, Giza Mastabas 7, Boston.

Brown, Nick. 2019. Phrasikleia. Playing with signs, in: Juliette Harrisson (ed.), *Imagining the Afterlife in the Ancient World*, Abingdon, 33–48.

Bruner, Jerome. 1990. *Acts of Meaning*, Cambridge, MA/London.

Bruner, Jerome. 2001. Self-making and world-making, in: Jens Brockmeier & Donal Carbaugh (eds.), *Narrative and Identity*, Studies in Narrative 1, Amsterdam/Philadelphia, 25–37.

Brütsch, Matthias. 2017. How to Measure Narrativity? Notes on Some Problems with Comparing Degrees of Narrativity Across Different Media, in: Per Krogh Hansen, John Pier, Philippe Roussin & Wolf Schmid (eds.), *Emerging Vectors of Narratology*, Narratologia 57, Berlin/Boston, 315–334.

Buchberger, Hannes. 1989/90. Zum Ausländer in der altägyptischen Literatur – Eine Kritik, in: *Die Welt des Orients* 20/21, 5–34.

Bunia, Remigius. 2005. Die Stimme der Typographie. Überlegungen zu den Begriffen ‚Erzähler' und ‚Paratext', angestoßen durch die *Lebens-Ansichten des Katers Murr* von E. T. A. Hoffmann, in: *Poetica* 37, 373–392.

Burke, Carolyn. 2011. *No Regrets: The Life of Edith Piaf*, London et al.

Busch, Stephan. 2002. Lautes und leises Lesen in der Antike, in: *Rheinisches Museum für Philologie Neue Folge* 145, 1–45.

Caracciolo, Marco. 2020. Is Factuality the Norm? A Perspective from Cognitive Narratology, in: Monika Fludernik & Marie-Laure Ryan (eds.), *Narrative Factuality. A Handbook*, Revisionen 6, Berlin/Boston, 149–156.

Caracciolo, Marco. 2021. *Narrating the Mesh: Form and Story in the Anthropocene*, Charlottesville/London.

Carringer, Robert L. 1976. Rosebud, Dead or Alive: Narrative and Symbolic Structure in *Citizen Kane*, in: *Publications of the Modern Language Association* 91(2), 185–193.

Chatman, Seymour. 1978. *Story and Discourse: Narrative Structure in Fiction and Film*, Ithaca/London.

Chatman, Seymour. 1990. *Coming to Terms. The Rhetoric of Narrative in Fiction and Film*, Ithaca/London.

Chauvet, Violaine. 2011. Entrance-porticoes and Portico-chapels: The Creation of an Outside Ritual Stage in Private Tombs of the Old Kingdom, in: Miroslav Bárta, Filip Coppens & Jaromír Krejčí (eds.), *Abusir and Saqqara in the Year 2010*, Vol. I, Prague, 261–311.

Chauvet, Violaine. 2013. Between a Tomb and a Hard Place: Tomb Inscriptions as a Source of Historical Information, in: *Journal of the American Research Center in Egypt* 49, 57–71.

Coleridge, Samuel Taylor. 2014. *Biographia Literaria*, edited by Adam Roberts, Cambridge.

Commare, Laura, Raphael Rosenberg & Helmut Leder. 2018. More Than the Sum of Its Parts: Perceiving Complexity in Painting, in: *Psychology of Aesthetics, Creativity, and the Arts* 12(4), 380–391 (doi: https://doi.org/10.1037/aca0000186).

Constantinou, Stavroula. 2019. Gendered Emotions and Affective Genders: A Response, in: Stavroula Constantinou & Mati Meyer (eds.), *Emotions and Gender in Byzantine Culture*, New Approaches to Byzantine History and Culture, Cham, 283–315.

Contzen, Eva von & Stefan Tilg. 2019. Einleitung, in: Eva von Contzen & Stefan Tilg (eds.), *Handbuch Historische Narratologie*, Berlin, VII–X.

Coulon, Laurent. 1997. Véracité et rhétorique dans les autobiographies égyptiennes de la Première Période Intermédiaire, in: *Bulletin de l'Institut français d'archéologie orientale* 97, 109–138.

Coulon, Laurent. 2020. Clichés in Ancient Egyptian Autobiographies, in: Julie Stauder-Porchet, Elizabeth Frood & Andréas Stauder (eds.), *Ancient Egyptian Biographies: Contexts, Forms, Functions*, Wilbour Studies in Egyptology and Assyriology 6, Atlanta, GA, 205–223.

Damasio, Antonio R. 2018. *The Strange Order of Things. Life, Feeling and the Making of Cultures*, New York.

Darnell, John C. & Colleen Manassa. 2013. A Trustworthy Sealbearer on a Mission: The Monuments of Sabastet from the Khephren Diorite Quarries, in: Hans-Werner Fischer-Elfert & Richard B. Parkinson (eds.), *Studies on the Middle Kingdom. In memory of Detlef Franke*, Philippika 41, Wiesbaden, 55–92.

Dasgupta, Subrata. 2019. *A Cognitive Historical Approach to Creativity*, Abingdon/New York.

Davies, Norman de Garis. 1902. *The Rock Tombs of Deir el-Gebrâwi, Part I.–Tomb of Aba and Smaller Tombs of the Southern Group*, Archaeological Survey of Egypt 11, London.

Davis, Whitney. 1992. *Masking the Blow. The Scene of Representation in Late Prehistoric Egyptian Art*, Berkeley/Los Angeles.

Davis, Whitney 2003. Archaism and Modernism in the Reliefs of Hesy-Ra. in: John Tait (ed.), *'Never had the like occurred': Egypt's view of its past*, London, 31–60.

Dawson, Paul. 2017. How Many 'Turns' Does it Take to Change a Discipline? Narratology and the Interdisciplinary Rhetoric of the Narrative Turn, in: Per Krogh Hansen, John Pier, Philippe Roussin & Wolf Schmid (eds.), *Emerging Vectors of Narratology*, Narratologia 57, Berlin/Boston, 405–433.

De Fina, Anna & Alexandra Georgakopoulou. 2012. *Analyzing Narrative. Discourse and Sociolinguistic Perspectives*, Cambridge.

Depuydt, Leo. 1998. The Meaning of Old and Middle Egyptian 𓇋𓅱 *Jw* in light of the Distinction between Narration and Discussion, in: Irene Shirun-Grumach (ed.), *Jerusalem Studies in Egyptology*, Ägypten und Altes Testament 40, Wiesbaden, 19–36.

Der Manuelian, Peter. 1996. Presenting the Scroll: Papyrus Documents in Tomb Scenes of the Old Kingdom, in: Peter Der Manuelian (ed.), *Studies in Honor of William Kelly Simpson, Volume 2*, Boston, 561–588.

Dheghani, Morteza, Reihane Boghrati, Kingson Man, Joe Hoover, Sarah I. Gimbel, Ashish Vaswani, Jason D. Zevin, Mary Helen Immordino-Yang, Andrew S. Gordon, Antonio Damasio & Jonas T. Kaplan. 2017. Decoding the neural representation of story meanings across languages, in: *Human Brain Mapping* 38(12), 6096–6106 (doi: https://doi.org/10.1002/hbm.23814).

Di Biase-Dyson, Camilla. 2015. Amenemheb's Excellent Adventure in Syria: New Insights from Discourse Analysis and Toponymics, in: Gregor Neunert, Henrike Simon, Alexandra Verbovsek, Kathrin Gabler, Catherine Jones & Burkhard Backes (eds.), *Text: Wissen – Wirkung – Wahrnehmung: Beiträge des vierten Münchner Arbeitskreises Junge Aegyptologie (MAJA 4), 29.11. bis 1.12.2013*, Göttinger Orientforschungen IV. Reihe Ägypten 59, Wiesbaden, 121–150.

Di Biase-Dyson, Camilla. 2019. Narratives by Ancient Egyptians and of Ancient Egypt. A State of the Art, in: Dina Serova, Burkhard Backes, Matthieu W. Götz & Alexandra Verbovsek (eds.), *Narrative: Geschichte – Mythos – Repräsentation. Beiträge des achten Berliner Arbeitskreises Junge Ägyptologie (BAJA 8), 1.12–3.12.2017*, Göttinger Orientforschungen IV. Reihe Ägypten 65, Wiesbaden, 39–63.

Dietrich, Nikolaus. 2020. Überlegungen zum Layout griechischer Statueninschriften ausgehend von der Nikandre-Weihung, in: Nikolaus Dietrich, Johannes Fouquet & Corinna Reinhardt (eds.), *Schreiben auf statuarischen Monumenten. Aspekte materialer Textkultur in archaischer und frühklassischer Zeit*, Materiale Textkulturen 29, Berlin/Boston, 147–193.

Digital Giza. 2022. The Giza Project at Harvard University, Cambridge, MA (http://giza.fas.harvard.edu, last accessed on 22 December 2022).

DNO I, 348 = Hallof, Klaus & Sascha Kansteiner. 2014. Aristion (Ἀριστίων) von Paros, in: Kansteiner, Sascha, Klaus Hallof, Lauri Lehmann, Bernd Seidensticker & Klaus Stemmer (eds.), *Der Neue Overbeck. Die antiken Schriftquellen zu den bildenden Künsten der Griechen*, Berlin/Boston (https://www.degruyter.com/database/OVERBECK/entry/ov.0057.b1/html, last accessed on 22 December 2022).

Doležel, Lubomír. 1999. Fictional and Historical Narrative: Meeting the Postmodernist Challenge, in: David Herman (ed.), *Narratologies: New Perspectives on Narrative Analysis*, Columbus, 247–273.

Dominicus, Brigitte. 1994. *Gesten und Gebärden in Darstellungen des Alten und Mittleren Reiches*, Studien zur Archäologie und Geschichte Altägyptens 10, Heidelberg.

Doret, Éric. 1986. *The Narrative Verbal System of Old and Middle Egyptian*, Cahiers d'Orientalisme 12, Geneva.

Dorman, Peter. 2002. The Biographical Inscription of Ptahshepses from Saqqara: A Newly Identified Fragment, in: *Journal of Egyptian Archaeology* 88, 85–109.

Drees, Stefan. 2018. Image — Sound — Memory/ Bild — Klang — Erinnerung, in accompanying booklet: *Johannes Kalitzke: Story Teller . Figuren am Horizont*, performed by Johannes Moser (cello), Ivana Pristašová (piano), Deutsches Symphonie-Orchester Berlin and the oenm . österreichisches ensemble für neue musik conducted by Johannes Kalitzke, Kairos 0015038KAI, compact disc, 6–9/10–13.

Dulíková, Veronika, Lucie Jirásková & Martin Odler. 2021. Ptahshepses, vizier and king's son-in-law as reflected in his unpublished tomb equipment, in: Miroslav Bárta, Filip Coppens & Jaromír Krejčí (eds.), *Abusir and Saqqara in the Year 2020*, Prague, 47–69.

Dunham, Dows. 1938. The Biographical Inscriptions of Nekhebu in Boston and Cairo, *Journal of Egyptian Archaeology* 24, 1–8.

Dunham, Dows & William Kelly Simpson. 1974. *The Mastaba of Queen Mersyankh III (G 7530–7540)*, Giza Mastabas 1, Boston.

Eakin, Paul John. 2020. *Writing Life Writing: Narrative, History, Autobiography*, New York/Abingdon.

Eckardt, Regine. 2020. Narrative Mikrostruktur, in: *Zeitschrift für germanistische Linguistik* 48(3), 495–528.

Edel, Elmar. 1944. Untersuchungen zur Phraseologie der ägyptischen Inschriften des Alten Reiches, in: *Mitteilungen des Deutschen Instituts für ägyptische Altertumskunde in Kairo* 13, 1–90.

Edel, Elmar. 1953. Inschriften des Alten Reiches. II. Die Biographie des *Kȝj-gmjnj* (Kagemni), in: *Mitteilungen des Instituts für Orientforschung* 1, 210–226.

Edel, Elmar. 1955–1964. *Altägyptische Grammatik*, Vols. I–II, Analecta Orientalia 34/39, Rome.

Edel, Elmar. 1970. *Die Felsengräber der Qubbet el Hawa bei Assuan. II. Abteilung. Die althieratischen Topfaufschriften. 1. Band. Die Topfaufschriften aus den Grabungsjahren 1960, 1961, 1962, 1963 und 1965. 2. Teil. Text (Fortsetzung)*, Wiesbaden.

Edel, Elmar. 1996. Studien zu den Reliefffragmenten aus dem Taltempel des Königs Snofru, in: Peter Der Manuelian (ed.), *Studies in Honor of William Kelly Simpson, Volume I*, Boston, 199–208.

Edel, Elmar †. 2008a. *Die Felsgräbernekropole der Qubbet el-Hawa bei Assuan. I. Abteilung, Band 1: Architektur, Darstellungen, Texte, archäologischer Befund und Funde der Gräber QH 24–QH 34p. Aus dem Nachlaß verfaßt und herausgegeben von Karl-J. Seyfried (Leipzig) und Gerd Vieler (Saarbrücken)*, Paderborn et al.

Edel, Elmar †. 2008b. *Die Felsgräbernekropole der Qubbet el-Hawa bei Assuan. I. Abteilung, Band 2: Architektur, Darstellungen, Texte, archäologischer Befund und Funde der Gräber QH 35–QH 102. Aus dem Nachlaß verfaßt und herausgegeben von Karl-J. Seyfried (Leipzig) und Gerd Vieler (Saarbrücken)*, Paderborn et al.

Edel, Elmar †. 2008c. *Die Felsgräbernekropole der Qubbet el-Hawa bei Assuan. I. Abteilung, Band 3: Architektur, Darstellungen, Texte, archäologischer Befund und Funde der Gräber QH 103–QH 209. Aus dem Nachlaß verfaßt und herausgegeben von Karl-J. Seyfried (Leipzig) und Gerd Vieler (Saarbrücken)*, Paderborn et al.

Edwards, Brian J., Benjamin M. Rottman & Laurie R. Santos. 2011. The Evolutionary Origins of Causal Cognition: Learning and Using Causal Structures, in: Teresa McCormack, Christoph Hoerl & Stephen Butterfill (eds.), *Tool Use and Causal Cognition*, Oxford, 111–128.

Eichler, Eckhard. 1991a. Untersuchungen zu den Königsbriefen des Alten Reiches, in: *Studien zur altägyptischen Kultur* 18, 141–171.

Eichler, Eckhard. 1991b. Zwei Bemerkungen zu den hieratischen Briefen des Alten Reiches, in: *Göttinger Miszellen* 123, 21–26.

Eichler, Eckhard. 1993. *Untersuchungen zum Expeditionswesen des ägyptischen Alten Reiches*, Göttinger Orientforschungen IV. Reihe Ägypten 26, Wiesbaden.

Eichler, Eckhard. 1994. Zur kultischen Bedeutung von Expeditionsinschriften, in: Betsy M. Bryan & David Lorton (eds.), *Essays in Egyptology in Honor of Hans Goedicke*, San Antonio, TX, 69–80.

Eichler, Eckhard. 1998. Neue Expeditionsinschriften aus der Ostwüste Oberägyptens, Teil II: Die Inschriften, in: *Mitteilungen des Deutschen Archäologischen Institutes, Abteilung Kairo* 54, 250–266.

Einaudi, Silvia. 2020. Le programme décoratif des tombes tardives de l'Assassif : reflet de croyances, pratiques cultuelles et savoir, in: *Bulletin de la Société française d'égyptologie* 203, 25–35.

Einaudi, Silvia. 2021. *La rhétorique des tombes monumentales tardives (XXVe–XXVIe dynasties). Une vue d'ensemble de leur architecture et de leur programme décoratif*, Cahiers « Égypte Nilotique et Méditerranéenne » 28, Drémil-Lafage.

Emerit, Sybille. 2015. Autour de l'ouïe, de la voix et des sons. Approche anthropologique des « paysages sonores » de l'Égypte ancienne, in: Sybille Emerit, Sylvain Perrot & Alexandre Vincent (eds.), *Le paysage sonore de l'Antiquité. Méthodologie, historiographie et perspectives. Actes de la journée d'études tenue à l'École française de Rome, le 7 janvier 2013*, Recherches d'archéologie, de philologie et d'histoire 40, Cairo, 115–154.

Emmott, Catherine. 2014. Schemata, in: Peter Hühn, Jan Christoph Meister, John Pier & Wolf Schmid (eds.), *The Living Handbook of Narratology*, Hamburg (https://www-archiv.fdm.uni-hamburg.de/lhn/printpdf/article/schemata, last accessed on 22 December 2022).

Erman, Adolf & Hermann Grapow (eds.). 1926–1931. *Wörterbuch der aegyptischen Sprache im Auftrage der Deutschen Akademien, Erster bis fünfter Band*, Leipzig.

Eyre, Christopher. 2013. The practice of literature: the relationship between content, form, audience, and performance, in: Roland Enmarch & Verena M. Lepper (eds.), *Ancient Egyptian Literature: Theory and Practice*, Proceedings of the British Academy 188, Oxford, 101–142.

Eyre, Christopher. 2019. Egyptian Self-Presentation Dynamics and Strategies, in: Hussein Bassir (ed.), *Living Forever: Self-Presentation in Ancient Egypt*, Cairo, 9–23.

Fakhry, Ahmed. 1961. *The Monuments of Sneferu at Dahshur, Volume II. – The Valley Temple, Part I. – The Temple Reliefs*, Cairo.
Farout, Dominique. 2013. Naissance du dialogue de cour sur les monuments d'Ancien Empire, in: *Revue d'Égyptologie* 64, 15–23.
Feucht, Erika. 1995. *Das Kind im Alten Ägypten*, Frankfurt/New York.
Firth, Cecil M. & Battiscombe Gunn. 1926. *Teti Pyramid Cemeteries*, Vol. I–II, Excavations at Saqqara, Cairo.
Fischer, Henry George. 1976. Notes, Mostly Textual, on Davies' *Deir el Gebrâwi*, in: *Journal of the American Research Center in Egypt* 13, 9–20.
Fischer, Henry George. 1977. *Egyptian Studies II. The Orientation of Hieroglyphs, Part 1: Reversals*, New York.
Fischer, Henry George. 1991. Marginalia, in: *Göttinger Miszellen* 122, 21–30.
Fischer, Henry George. 1992. Review of Christiane Ziegler, Stèles, peintures et reliefs égyptiens de l'Ancien Empire, 1990, in: *Orientalia* 61, 142–146.
Fischer-Elfert, Hans Werner. 2014. Review of Simon, Henrike. 2013. »Textaufgaben«. Kulturwissenschaftliche Konzepte in Anwendung auf die Literatur der Ramessidenzeit, Studien zur Altägyptischen Kultur, Beihefte 14, Hamburg, in: *Lingua Aegyptia* 22, 327–336.
Fishelov, David. 2019. The Poetics of Six-Word Stories, in: *Narrative* 27(1), 30–46.
Fitzenreiter, Martin. 2001. Grabdekoration und die Interpretation funerärer Rituale im Alten Reich, in: Harco Willems (ed.), *Social Aspects of Funerary Culture in the Egyptian Old and Middle Kingdoms*, Orientalia Analecta Lovaniensia 103, Leuven et al., 67–140.
Fitzenreiter, Martin. 2004. *Zum Toteneigentum im Alten Reich*, Achet A 4, Berlin.
Fitzenreiter, Martin. 2015. (Un)Zugänglichkeit. Über Performanz und Emergenz von Schrift und Bild, in: in Annette Kehnel & Diamantis Panagiotopoulos (eds.), *Schriftträger – Textträger. Zur materialen Präsenz des Geschriebenen in frühen Gesellschaften*, Materiale Textkulturen 6, Berlin/Munich/Boston, 179–208.
Fitzenreiter, Martin. 2017. Sense and Serendipity: Zur Ambiguität pharaonischer Bildschriftlichkeit, in: Vincent Verschoor, Arnold Jan Stuart & Cocky Demarée (eds.), *Imaging and Imagining the Memphite Necropolis. Liber amicorum Renée van Walsem*, Egyptologische Uitgaven 30, Leiden/Leuven, 177–199.
Fitzenreiter, Martin & Michael Herb (eds.). 2006. *Dekorierte Grabanlagen im Alten Reich. Methodik und Interpretation*, Internet-Beiträge zur Ägyptologie und Sudanarchäologie 6, London.
Fludernik, Monika. 1996. *Towards a 'Natural' Narratology*, London/New York.
Fludernik, Monika. 2005. Histories of Narrative Theory (II): From Structuralism to the Present, in: James Phelan & Peter J. Rabinowitz (eds.), *A Companion to Narrative Theory*, Malden, 36–59.
Fludernik, Monika. 2007. Identity/alterity, in: David Herman (ed.), *The Cambridge Companion to Narrative*, Cambridge et al., 260–273.
Fludernik, Monika & Marie-Laure Ryan. 2020. Introduction, in: Monika Fludernik & Marie-Laure Ryan (eds.), *Narrative Factuality. A Handbook*, Revisionen 6, Berlin/Boston, 1–26.
Forster, Edward Morgan. 1927. *Aspects of the Novel*, New York.
Frandsen, Paul John. 1992. On the Root *nfr* and a 'Clever' Remark on Embalming, in: Jürgen Osing & Erland Kolding Nielsen (eds.), *The Heritage of Ancient Egypt. Studies in Honour of Erik Iversen*, Carsten Niebuhr Institute Publications 13, Copenhagen, 49–62.
Frood, Elizabeth. 2007. *Biographical Texts from Ramesside Egypt, edited by John Baines*, SBL Writings from the Ancient World 26, Atlanta, GA.
Gair, Christopher. 2012. "Perhaps the Words Remember Me": Richard Brautigan's Very Short Stories, in: *Western American Literature* 47(1), 4–21.
Gardiner, Alan H. 1937. *Late-Egyptian Miscellanies*, Bibliotheca Aegyptiaca 7, Brussels.
Genette, Gérard. 1969. *Figures II*, Paris.
Genette, Gérard. 1972. Discours du récit : essai de méthode, in: *Figures III*, Paris, 65–267.
Genette, Gérard. 1979. *Introduction à l'architexte*, Paris.

Genette, Gérard. 1987. *Seuils*, Paris.

Genette, Gérard. 1991. *Fiction et diction*, Paris.

Georgakopoulou, Alexandra & Dionysis Goutsos. 2000. Revisiting discourse boundaries: The narrative and non-narrative modes, *Text* 20(1), 63–82.

Gerrig, Richard J. & Janelle M. Gagnon. 2020. The Factual in Psychology, in: Monika Fludernik & Marie-Laure Ryan (eds.), *Narrative Factuality. A Handbook*, Revisionen 6, Berlin/Boston, 133–147.

Glauch, Sonja. 2010. Ich-Erzähler ohne Stimme. Zur Andersartigkeit mittelalterlichen Erzählens zwischen Narratologie und Mediengeschichte, in: Harald Haferland & Matthias Meyer (eds.), *Historische Narratologie – Mediävistische Perspektiven*, Trends in Medieval Philology 19, Berlin/New York, 149–185.

Gnirs, Andrea M. 1996. Die ägyptische Autobiographie, in: Antonio Loprieno (ed.), *Ancient Egyptian Literature. History and Forms*, Probleme der Ägyptologie 10, Leiden/New York/Cologne, 191–241.

Goedicke, Hans. 1970. *Die privaten Rechtsinschriften aus dem Alten Reich*, Wiener Zeitschrift für die Kunde des Morgenlandes, Beiheft 5, Vienna.

Goethe- und Schiller-Archiv. 2022. Signatur GSA 25/W 2991 (date of processing: 21 May 2015), in: *Archivdatenbank des Goethe- und Schiller-Archivs* (https://ores.klassik-stiftung.de/ords/f?p=401:2:::::P2_ID:5760, last accessed on 22 December 2022).

Goetsch, Paul. 1985. Fingierte Mündlichkeit in der Erzählkunst entwickelter Schriftkulturen, in: *Poetica* 17, 202–218.

Goffman, Erving. 1979. Footing, in: *Semiotica* 25(1), 1–29.

Goggio, Alessandra. 2021. Der Verleger als literarische Figur. Narrative Konstruktionen in der deutschsprachigen Gegenwartsliteratur, Gegenwartsliteratur 9, Bielefeld.

Grabes, Herbert. 2014. Sequentiality, in: Peter Hühn, Jan Christoph Meister, John Pier & Wolf Schmid (eds.), *The Living Handbook of Narratology*, Hamburg (https://www-archiv.fdm.uni-hamburg.de/lhn/printpdf/article/sequentiality, last accessed on 22 December 2022).

Gräf, Hans Gerhard & Albert Leitzmann (eds.), *Der Briefwechsel zwischen Schiller und Goethe in drei Bänden*, Band I: 1794–1797, Leipzig.

Gray, Celina. 2004. Review of Mary Stieber, The Poetics of Appearance in the Attic Korai, in: *Mouseion* 4(3), 365–369.

Grdseloff, Bernhard. 1943. Deux inscriptions juridique de l'Ancien Empire, in: *Annales du Service des antiquites égyptiennes* 42, 25–70.

Griffith, Francis Llewellyn. 1889. *The Inscriptions of Siûṭ and Dêr Rîfeh*, London.

Grishakova, Marina. 2011. Narrative Causality Denaturalized, in: Jan Alber & Rüdiger Heinze (eds.), *Unnatural Narratives – Unnatural Narratology*, linguae & litterae 9, Berlin/Boston.

Grunert, Stefan. 2022. *Thesaurus Linguae Aegyptiae*, Deir el-Gebrawi, Grab des Ibi, Opferkapelle, Westwand, nördlicher Teil, zentrales Bildfeld, 2. Register v.o., Beischriften (https://aaew.bbaw.de/tla/servlet/GetTextDetails?u=guest&f=0&l=0&tc=10803&db=0, last accessed on 22 December 2022).

Grünzweig, Walter & Andreas Solbach. 1999. Einführung: »Narratologie und interdisziplinare Forschung«, in: Walter Grünzweig & Andreas Solbach (eds.), *Grenzüberschreitungen: Narratologie im Kontext/Transcending Boundaries: Narratology in Context*, Tübingen, 1–15.

Gundacker, Roman. 2006. *Untersuchungen zur Chronologie der Herrschaft Snofrus*, Beiträge zur Ägyptologie 22 (= Veröffentlichungen der Institute für Afrikanistik und Ägyptologie der Universität Wien 104), Vienna.

Gundacker, Roman. 2015a. Die (Auto)Biographie des Schepsesptah von Saqqarah. Ein neuer Versuch zur Rekonstruktion der Inschrift und ein Beitrag zur stilistischen Grundlegung des wiederhergestellten Textes, in: *Lingua Aegyptia* 23, 61–105.

Gundacker, Roman. 2015b. The Chronology of the Third and Fourth Dynasties according to Manetho's *Aegyptiaca*, in: Peter Der Manuelian & Thomas Schneider (eds.), *Towards a New History for the*

Egyptian Old Kingdom: Perspectives on the Pyramid Age, Harvard Egyptological Studies 1, Leiden/Boston, 76–199.

Gunn, Battiscombe. 1925. A Sixth Dynasty Letter from Saqqara, in: *Annales du Service des antiquités égyptiennes* 25, 242–255.

Hall, Stuart. 1992. The Question of Cultural Identity, in: Stuart Hall, David Held & Tony McGrew (eds.), *Modernity and Its Futures*, Understanding Modern Societies: An Introduction, Book 4, Cambridge, 273–316.

Hannig, Rainer. 2003. *Ägyptisches Wörterbuch I. Altes Reich und Erste Zwischenzeit*, Hannig-Lexica 4, Kulturgeschichte der antiken Welt 98, Mainz.

Hansen, Per Krogh, Stefan Iversen, Henrik Skov Nielsen & Rolf Reitan (eds.). 2011. *Strange Voices in Narrative Fiction*, Narratologia 30, Berlin/Boston.

Hansen, Per Krogh, John Pier, Philippe Roussin & Wolf Schmid (eds.). 2017. *Emerging Vectors of Narratology*, Narratologia 57, Berlin/Boston.

Harpur, Yvonne. 1987. *Decoration in Egyptian Tombs of the Old Kingdom: Studies in Orientation and Scene Content*, London/New York.

Harpur, Yvonne. 2001. *The Tombs of Nefermaat and Rahotep at Maidum: Discovery, Destruction and Reconstruction*, Egyptian Tombs of the Old Kingdom 1, Cheltenham.

Hassan, Selim. 1932. *Excavations at Gîza* [I], *1929–1930*, Cairo.

Hassan, Selim. 1936. *Excavations at Gîza* [II], *1930–1931*, Cairo.

Hassan, Selim. 1943. *Excavations at Gîza* [IV], *1932–1933*, Cairo.

Hassan, Selim. 1975. *The Mastaba of Neb-Kaw-Her*. Re-Edited by Zaky Iskander, Excavations at Saqqara, 1937–1938—Volume I, Cairo.

Hawass, Zahi. 1999. Four Statues of the Artisan Inti-Shedu, in: Dorothea Arnold & Christine Ziegler (eds.), *Egyptian Art in the Age of the Pyramids*, The Metropolitan Museum of Art, New York, 300, no. 89–92.

Hawass, Zahi. 2002. An Inscribed Lintel in the Tomb of the Vizier Mehu at Saqqara, in: *Lingua Aegyptia* 10, 219–224.

Hayles, N. Katherine. 2001. The Transformation of Narrative and the Materiality of Hypertext, in: *Narrative* 9(1), 21–39.

Hays, Harold M. 2012. *The Organization of the Pyramid Texts: Typology and Disposition*, Vols. I–II, Probleme der Ägyptologie 31, Leiden/Boston.

Heider, Fritz & Marianne Simmel. 1944. An experimental study of apparent behavior, in: *The American Journal of Psychology* 57(2), 243–259.

Helck, Wolfgang. 1954. *Untersuchungen zu den Beamtentiteln des ägyptischen Alten Reiches*, Ägyptologische Forschungen 18, Glückstein.

Helck, Wolfgang. 1958. *Urkunden der 18. Dynastie. Heft 21: Inschriften von Zeitgenossen Amenophis' III.*, Berlin.

Helck, Wolfgang. 1972. Zur Frage der Entstehung der ägyptischen Literatur, in: *Wiener Zeitschrift für die Kunde des Morgenlandes* 63/64, 6–26.

Helck, Wolfgang. 1974a. Die Bedeutung der Felsinschriften J. Lopez, *Inscriciones rupestres* Nr. 27 und 28, in: *Studien zur altägyptischen Kultur* 1, 215–225.

Helck, Wolfgang. 1974b. *Altägyptische Aktenkunde des 3. und 2. Jahrtausends v. Chr.*, Münchner Ägyptologische Studien 31, Munich/Berlin.

Henrich, Joseph, Steven J. Heine & Ara Norenzayan. 2010. The weirdest people in the world?, in: *Behavioral and Brain Sciences* 33(2–3), 1–75 (doi: https://doi.org/10.1017/S0140525X0999152X).

Herman, David. 1997. Scripts, Sequences, and Stories: Elements of a Postclassical Narratology, in: *Publications of the Modern Language Association* 112(5), 1046–1059.

Herman, David. 2007. Introduction, in: David Herman (ed.), *The Cambridge Companion to Narrative*, Cambridge et al., 3–21.

Herman, David. 2009. *Basic Elements of Narrative*, Chichester.

Herman, David. 2013. *Storytelling and the Sciences of Mind*, Cambridge, MA/London.

Herrnstein Smith, Barbara. 1978. *On the Margins of Discourse: The Relation of Literature to Language*, Chicago/London.

Herrnstein Smith, Barbara. 1980. Narrative Versions, Narrative Theories, in: *Critical Inquiry* 7(1), 213–236.

Hess-Lüttich, Ernest W. B. 1999. Im Irrgarten der Texte. Zur Narratologie holistischer Textualität, in: Walter Grünzweig & Andreas Solbach (eds.), *Grenzüberschreitungen: Narratologie im Kontext/ Transcending Boundaries: Narratology in Context*, Tübingen, 209–230.

Hewett, Beth L. 2020. *A Scholarly Edition of Samuel P. Newman's* A Practical System of Rhetoric, International Studies in the History of Rhetoric 13, Leiden/Boston.

Hill, Marsha. 1999. Head of an Older Man, in: Dorothea Arnold & Christine Ziegler (eds.), *Egyptian Art in the Age of the Pyramids*, The Metropolitan Museum of Art, New York, 289, no. 81.

Hintze, Fritz. 1952. *Untersuchungen zu Stil und Sprache neuägyptischer Erzählungen*, Deutsche Akademie der Wissenschaften zu Berlin, Institut für Orientforschung, Veröffentlichung Nr. 6, Berlin.

Hoberman, Ruth, Biography: General Survey, in: Margaretta Jolly (ed.), *Encyclopaedia of Life Writing: Autobiographical and Biographical Forms*, Vol. II, London, 109–112.

Hoey, Michael. 2001. *Textual Interaction. An introduction to written discourse analysis*, London/New York.

Holtsträter, Knut. 2012–2014. "So pocht das Schicksal an die Pforte": Some Remarks on Narrativity in Music, in: *Amsterdam International Electronic Journal for Cultural Narratology* 7/8, 219–236 (https://cf.hum.uva.nl/narratology/issue/7/a12_Knut_Holtstrater.html, last accessed on 22 December 2022).

Hornung, Erik. 1971. Politische Planung und Realitäten im alten Ägypten, in: *Saeculum* 22, 48–58.

Horstkotte, Silke. 2009. Seeing or Speaking: Visual Narratology and Focalization, Literature to Film, in: Sandra Heinen & Roy Sommer (eds.), *Narratology in the Age of Cross-Disciplinary Narrative*, Narratologia 20, Berlin/New York, 170–192.

Hsieh, Julia. 2012. Discussions on the Daybook Style and the Formulae of Malediction and Benediction Stemming from Five Middle Kingdom Rock-Cut Stelae from Gebel el-Girgawi, in: *Zeitschrift für ägyptische Sprache und Altertumskunde* 139, 116–135.

Hyvärinen, Matti. 2006a. An Introduction to Narrative Travels, in: Matti Hyvärinen, Anu Korhonen & Juri Mykkänen (eds.), *The Travelling Concept of Narrative*, Helsinki, 3–9.

Hyvärinen, Matti. 2006b. Towards a Conceptual History of Narrative, in: Matti Hyvärinen, Anu Korhonen & Juri Mykkänen (eds.), *The Travelling Concept of Narrative*, Helsinki, 20–41.

Hyvärinen, Matti. 2010. Revisiting the Narrative Turns, in: *Life Writing* 7(1), 69–82.

IG I^3 = Lewis, David & Lilian Jeffrey (eds.). 1994. *Iscriptiones Graecae, Vol. I: Inscriptiones Atticae Euclidis anno anteriores. Editio tertia. Fasc. 2: Dedicationes, catalogi, termini, tituli sepulcrales, varia, tituli Attici extra Atticam reperti, addenda*, Berlin (http://telota.bbaw.de/ig/digitale-edition/liste/40, last accessed on 22 December 2022).

Jackendoff, Ray. 1983. *Semantics and Cognition*, Current Studies in Linguistics Series 8, Cambridge, MA.

Jackendoff, Ray. 1987. *Consciousness and the Computational Mind*, Explorations in Cognitive Science 3, Cambridge, MA.

Jahn, Manfred. 2005. Cognitive Narratology, in: David Herman, Manfred Jahn & Marie-Laure Ryan (eds.), *Routledge Encyclopedia of Narrative Theory*, London/New York, 67–71.

James, Thomas G. H. 1961. *Hieroglyphic Texts from Egyptian Stelae etc., Part I, Second Edition*, London.

Jánosi, Peter. 2005. *Giza in der 4. Dynastie. Die Baugeschichte und Belegung einer Nekropole des Alten Reiches, Band I: Die Mastabas der Kernfriedhöfe und die Felsgräber*, Untersuchungen der Zweigstelle Kairo des Österreichischen Archäologischen Institutes 24 (= Österreichische Akademie der Wissenschaften, Denkschriften der Gesamtakademie 30), Vienna.

Jánosi, Peter. 2020. Some Thoughts on Monumental Non-royal Tombs at Giza in the Second Half of the 5th Dynasty and the Burial of Senedjemib-Inti, in: Janice Kamrin, Miroslav Bárta, Salima Ikram, Mark Lehner & Mohamed Megahed (eds.), *Guardian of Ancient Egypt: Studies in Honor of Zahi Hawass, Volume II*, Prague, 733–743.

Jansen-Winkeln, Karl. 1994. *Text und Sprache in der 3. Zwischenzeit. Vorarbeiten zu einer spätmittelägyptischen Grammatik*, Ägypten und Altes Testament 26, Wiesbaden.

Jansen-Winkeln, Karl. 1996. Zur Bedeutung von *jmꜣḫ*, in: *Bulletin de la Société d'égyptologie de Genève* 20, 29–36.

Jansen-Winkeln, Karl. 2004. Lebenslehre und Biographie, in: *Zeitschrift für ägyptische Sprache und Altertumskunde* 131, 59–72.

Jeannelle, Jean-Luis. 2008. *Écrire ses Mémoires au XXe siècle : Déclin et renouveau*, Paris.

Jeffrey, Lilian Hamilton. 1962. The Inscribed Gravestones of Archaic Attica, in: *The Annual of the British School at Athens* 57, 115–153.

Jewitt, Carey (ed.). 2009. *The Routledge Handbook of Multimodal Analysis*, Abingdon/New York.

Jolly, Margaretta, Editor's Note, in: Margaretta Jolly (ed.), *Encyclopaedia of Life Writing: Autobiographical and Biographical Forms*, Vol. I, London, ix–xii.

Jongeneel, Els. 2006. Silencing the Voice in Narratology? A Synopsis, in: Andreas Blödorn, Daniela Langer & Michael Scheffel (eds.), *Stimme(n) im Text. Narratologische Positionsbestimmungen*, Narratologia 10, Berlin/New York, 9–30.

Jordan, Brigitte. 2013. Pattern Recognition in Human Evolution and Why It Matters for Ethnography, Anthropology, and Society, in: Brigitte Jordan (ed.), *Advancing Ethnography in Corporate Environments: Challenges and Emerging Opportunities*, Walnut Creek, 193–213.

Junge, Friedrich. 1989. *"Emphasis" and Sentential Meaning in Middle Egyptian*, Göttinger Orientforschungen IV. Reihe Ägypten 20, Wiesbaden.

Junker, Hermann. 1934. *Gîza II. Bericht über die von der Akademie der Wissenschaften in Wien auf gemeinsame Kosten mit Dr. Wilhelm Pelizaeus † unternommenen Grabungen auf dem Friedhof des Alten Reiches bei den Pyramiden von Gîza, Band II. Die Maṣṭabas der beginnenden V. Dynastie auf dem Westfriedhof*, Vienna.

Junker, Hermann. 1938. *Gîza III. Bericht über die von der Akademie der Wissenschaften in Wien auf gemeinsame Kosten mit Dr. Wilhelm Pelizaeus † unternommenen Grabungen auf dem Friedhof des Alten Reiches bei den Pyramiden von Gîza, Band III. Die Maṣṭabas der fortgeschrittenen V. Dynastie auf dem Westfriedhof*, Vienna.

Junker, Hermann. 1947. *Gîza VIII. Bericht über die von der Akademie der Wissenschaften in Wien auf gemeinsame Kosten mit Dr. Wilhelm Pelizaeus † unternommenen Grabungen auf dem Friedhof des Alten Reiches bei den Pyramiden von Gîza, Band VIII. Der Ostabschnitt des Westfriedhofs, Zweiter Teil*, Denkschriften der Österreichischen Akademie der Wissenschaften, Philosophisch-historische Klasse 73/1, Vienna.

Junker, Hermann. 1949. *Pyramidenzeit. Das Wesen der altägyptischen Religion*, Einsiedeln.

Junker, Hermann. 1955. *Gîza XII. Bericht über die von der Akademie der Wissenschaften in Wien auf gemeinsame Kosten mit Dr. Wilhelm Pelizaeus † unternommenen Grabungen auf dem Friedhof des Alten Reiches bei den Pyramiden von Gîza, Band XII. Schlußband mit Zusammenfassungen und Gesamt-Verzeichnissen von Band I–XII*, Denkschriften der Österreichischen Akademie der Wissenschaften, Philosophisch-historische Klasse 75/2, Vienna.

Jurman, Claus. 2010. Running with Apis. The Memphite Apis Cult as a Point of Reference for Social and Religious Practice in Late Period Elite Culture, in: Ladislav Bareš, Filip Coppens & Květa Smoláriková (eds.), *Egypt in Transition. Social and Religious Development of Egypt in the First Millennium BCE. Proceedings of an International Conference, Prague, September 1–4, 2009*, Prague, 224–267.

Jurman, Claus. 2020. *Memphis in der Dritten Zwischenzeit. Eine Studie zur (Selbst-)Repräsentation von Eliten in der 21. und 22. Dynastie*, Vols. I–II, Hamburg.

Jurman, Claus. In press. From hieroglyphs to cognition and back again (with a few detours and dead ends...), in: Gaëlle Chantrain (ed.), *Language, Semantics and Cognition in Ancient Egypt and Beyond*, Yale Egyptological Studies 14, New Haven, CT, 159–194.

Kaczko, Sara. 2016. *Archaic and Classical Attic Dedicatory Epigrams: An Epigraphic, Literary, and Linguistic Commentary*, Trends in Classics Supplementary Volume 33, Berlin.

Kammerzell, Frank. 2021. Reading Multimodal Compositions from Early Dynastic Egypt (with an Appendix on Previously Unlisted, Reinterpreted or Otherwise Noteworthy Signs), in: Eva-Maria Engel, Anke Ilona Blöbaum & Frank Kammerzell (eds.), *Keep out! Early Dynastic and Old Kingdom Seals and Sealings in Context*, Menes 7, Wiesbaden, 1–98.

Kammerzell, Frank & Carsten Peust. 2002. Reported Speech in Egyptian: Forms, types and history, in: Tom Güldemann & Manfred von Roncador (eds.), *Reported Discourse: A Meeting Ground for Different Linguistic Domains*, Typological Studies in Language 52, Amsterdam/Philadelphia, 289–323.

Kanawati, Naguib. 2007. *Deir el-Gebrawi, Volume II: The Southern Cliff, The Tomb of Ibi and Others*, The Australian Centre for Egyptology: Reports 25, Oxford.

Kanawati, Naguib. 2009. Specificity in Old Kingdom Tomb Scenes, in: *Annales du Service des antiquités de l'Égypte* 83, 261–278.

Kanawati, Naguib. 2010. *Decorated Burial Chambers of the Old Kingdom*, Cairo.

Kanawati, Naguib & Linda Evans. 2016. *Beni Hassan, Volume III: The Tomb of Amenemhat*, The Australian Centre for Egyptology: Reports 40, Oxford.

Kanawati, Naguib & Mahmoud Abder-Raziq. 2000. *The Teti Cemetery at Saqqara, Volume VI: The Tomb of Nikauisesi*, Australian Centre for Egyptology: Reports 14, Warminster.

Kanawati, Naguib & Ali Hassan. 1997. *The Teti Cemetery at Saqqara, Volume II: The Tomb of Ankhmahor*, Australian Centre for Egyptology: Reports 9, Warminster.

Klauk, Tobias & Tilmann Köppe. 2014. Telling vs. Showing, in: Peter Hühn, Jan Christoph Meister, John Pier & Wolf Schmid (eds.), *The Living Handbook of Narratology*, Hamburg (https://www-archiv.fdm.uni-hamburg.de/lhn/printpdf/article/telling-vs-showing, last accessed on 22 December 2022).

Klein, Michael. 2004. Chopin's Fourth Ballade as Musical Narrative, in: *Music Theory Spectrum* 26(1), 23–56.

Kloth, Nicole. 2002. *Die (auto-) biographischen Inschriften des ägyptischen Alten Reiches: Untersuchungen zu Phraseologie und Entwicklung*, Studien zur Altägyptischen Kultur, Beihefte 8, Hamburg.

Kloth, Nicole. 2003. Die Inschrift des *Ḥtp-ḥr-n(j)-Ptḥ* aus dem Alten Reich: Eine phraseologische Betrachtung, in: Nicole Kloth, Karl Martin & Eva Pardey (eds.), *„Es werde niedergelegt als Schriftstück". Festschrift für Hartwig Altenmüller zum 65. Geburtstag*, Studien zur Altägyptischen Kultur, Beihefte 9, Hamburg, 225–230.

Kloth, Nicole. 2018. *Quellentexte zur ägyptischen Sozialgeschichte I. Autobiographien des Alten Reichs und der Ersten Zwischenzeit*, second edition, Einführungen und Quellentexte zur Ägyptologie 12, Berlin.

Kloth, Nicole. 2021. Zum Ausdruck *m sḫm.t.n(=j)* „mit dem, worüber ich Macht hatte" in den autobiographischen Inschriften des Alten Reichs, in: *Lingua Aegyptia* 29, 281–289.

Knape, Joachim. 2013. Textleistung. Eine moderne rhetorische Kategorie, erprobt am Beispiel mittelalterlicher Chronistik, in: Klaus Ridder & Steffen Patzold (eds.), *Die Aktualität der Vormoderne. Epochenentwürfe zwischen Alterität und Kontinuität*, Berlin, 135–159.

Knigge, Ursula. 2006. Ein Grabmonument der Alkmeoniden im Kerameikos, in: *Mitteilungen des Deutschen Archäologischen Instituts, Athenische Abteilung* 121, 127–163.

Koch, Roland. *Die Erzählung des Sinuhe*, Bibliotheca Aegyptiaca 17, Brussels.

Kokina, Evgeniia. 2017. Alone or together: for whom were the private tombs of the Old Kingdom built?, in: Miroslav Bárta, Filip Coppens & Jaromír Krejčí (eds.), *Abusir and Saqqara in the Year 2015*, Prague, 163–172.

Kolltveit, Gjermund. 2010. The Problem of Ethnocentricity in Music Archaeology, in: Ricardo Eichmann, Ellen Hickmann & Lars-Christian Koch (eds.), *Studien zur Musikarchäologie VII. Musikalische Wahrnehmung in Vergangenheit und Gegenwart. Ethnographische Analogien in der Musikarchäologie/Musical Perceptions – Past and Present. On Ethnographic Analogy in Music Archaeology. Vorträge des 6. Symposiums der Internationalen Studiengruppe Musikarchäologie im Ethnologischen Museum der Staatlichen Museen zu Berlin, 09.–13. September 2008/Papers from the 6th Symposium of the International Study Group on Music Archaeology at the Ethnological Museum, State Museums Berlin, 09–13 September, 2008*, Orient-Archäologie 25, Rahden, 103–113.

Kopiez, Reinhard. 2004. From Toddler's Headturn to Tchaikovsky and Haydn. A Review of Studies on Preferences for So-called Natural Musical Intervals, in: Ellen Hickmann & Ricardo Eichmann (eds.), *Studien zur Musikarchäologie IV. Musikarchäologische Quellengruppen: Bodenurkunden, mündliche Überlieferung, Aufzeichnung, Vorträge des 3. Symposiums der Internationalen Studiengruppe Musikarchäologie im Kloster Michaelstein, 9.–16. Juni 2002*, Orient-Archäologie 15, Rahden, 11–28.

Kosoglou, Siphis, Christos Makris & Odysseas Tsangarakis [Κοσόγλου, Σήφης, Χρίστος Μακρής & Οδυσσέας Τσαγκαράκης]. 2016. *Ta kritika moirologia [Τα κρητικά μοιρολόγια]*, Anogeia.

Krauspe, Renate. 1997. *Statuen und Statuetten*, Katalog Ägyptischer Sammlungen in Leipzig 1, Mainz.

Kress, Gunther. 2014. What is mode?, in: Carey Jewitt (ed.), *The Routledge Handbook of Multimodal Analysis, Second Edition*, London/New York, 60–75.

Kuhn, Markus. 2011. *Filmnarratologie. Ein erzähltheoretisches Analysemodell*, Narratologia 26, Berlin/New York.

Kuraszkiewicz, Kamil Omar. 2009. Remarks on the Meaning of the Word *jmꜣḫw*, in: Joanna Popielska-Grzybowska, Olga Białostocka & Jadwiga Iwaszczuk (eds.), *Proceedings of the Third Central European Conference of Young Egyptologists. Egypt 2004: Perspectives of Research. Warsaw 12–14 May 2004*, Pułtusk, 117–118.

Kutscher, Silvia. 2020. Multimodale graphische Kommunikation im pharaonischen Ägypten. Entwurf einer Analysemethode, in: *Lingua Aegyptia* 28, 81–116.

Laboury, Dimitri. 2012. Tracking Ancient Egyptian Artists, a Problem of Methodology. The Case of the Painters of Private Tombs in the Theban Necropolis during the Eighteenth Dynasty, in: Katalin Anna Kóthay (ed.), *Art and Society. Ancient and Modern Contexts of Egyptian Art. Proceedings of the International Conference held at the Museum of Fine Arts, Budapest, 13–15 May 2010*, Budapest, 199–208.

Landgráfová, Renata. 2011. *It Is My Good Name that You Should Remember. Egyptian Biographical Texts on Middle Kingdom Stelae, with contribution by Hana Navrátilová*, Prague.

Lapčić, Aleksandra. 2014. Bild-Schrift-Gestalten des Göttlichen. Multimodale Informationsverarbeitung im Amduat Thutmosis' III., in: Gregor Neunert, Alexandra Verbovsek & Kathrin Gabler (eds.), *Bild – Ästhetik – Medium – Kommunikation. Beiträge des dritten Münchner Arbeitskreises Junge Aegyptologie (MAJA 3) 7. bis 9.12.2012*, Göttinger Orientforschungen IV. Reihe Ägypten 58, Wiesbaden, 169–192.

Lashien, Miral. 2018. The art in the tomb of Pepyankh the Middle. Innovation or copying?, in: Kamil O. Kurasziewicz, Edyta Kopp & Dániel Takács (eds.), *'The Perfection That Endures...' Studies in Old Kingdom Art and Archaeology*, Warsaw, 253–266.

Lavigne, Donald E. 2018. The Authority of Archaic Greek Epigram, in: Andrej Petrovic, Ivana Petrovic & Edmund Thomas (eds.), *The Materiality of Text – Placement, Perception, and Presence of Inscribed Texts in Classical Antiquity*, Brill Studies in Greek and Roman Epigraphy 11, Leiden/Bosto, 169–186.

Lehmann, Volkmar. 2012. Narrativität aus linguistischer Sicht, in: Matthias Aumüller (ed.), *Narrativität als Begriff. Analysen und Anwendungsbeispiele zwischen philologischer und anthropologischer Orientierung*, Narratologia 31, Berlin/Boston, 169–183.

Lejeune, Philippe. 1975. *Le pacte autobiographique*, Paris.

Leprohon, Ronald J. 1994. The Sixth Dynasty False Door of the Priestess of Hathor Irti, in: *Journal of the American Research Center in Egypt* 31, 41–47.

Lepsius, Carl Richard. 1849–1859. *Denkmäler aus Aegypten und Aethiopien, nach den Zeichnungen der von Seiner Majestät dem Könige von Preussen Friedrich Wilhelm IV. nach diesen Ländern gesendeten und in den Jahren 1842–1845 ausgeführten wissenschaftlichen Expedition*, Abth. I–VI, Berlin.

Lepsius, Carl Richard †. 1897. *Denkmäler aus Aegypten und Aethiopien, Text, herausgegeben von Eduard Naville unter Mitwirkung von Ludwig Borchardt bearbeitet von Kurt Sethe, Erster Band: Unteraegypten und Memphis*, Leipzig.

Lepsius, Carl Richard †. 1913. *Denkmäler aus Aegypten und Aethiopien, Ergänzungsband, herausgegeben von Eduard Naville unter Mitwirkung von Ludwig Borchardt bearbeitet von Kurt Sethe*, Leipzig.

Lichtheim, Miriam. 1988. *Ancient Egyptian Autobiographies Chiefly of the Middle Kingdom. A Study and an Anthology*, Orbo Biblicus et Orientalis 84, Fribourg/Göttingen.

Lichtheim, Miriam. 1992. *Maat in Egyptian Autobiographies and Related Studies*, Orbis Biblicus et Orientalis 120, Fribourg/Göttingen.

Lieven, Alexandra von. 2010. Zur Funktion der ägyptischen Autobiographie, in: *Die Welt des Orients* 40, 54–69.

Lock, Gerhard. 2020. Salienz, Narrativität und die Rolle musikalischer Parameter bei der Analyse musikalischer Spannung von post-tonaler Orchestermusik, in: *Zeitschrift der Gesellschaft für Musiktheorie* 17(2), 311–349.

Looseley, David. 2015. *Édith Piaf: A Cultural History*, Liverpool.

López, Jesús. 1966. *Las inscripciones rupestres faraonicas entre Korosko y Kasr Ibrim (orilla oriental del Nilo)*, Memorias de la Misión Arqueológico Española en Nubia 9, Madrid.

López, Jesús. 1967. Inscriptions de l'Ancien Empire à Khor el-Aquiba, in: *Revue d'égyptologie* 19, 51–66.

Loprieno, Antonio. 1988. *Topos und Mimesis. Zum Ausländer in der ägyptischen Literatur*, Ägyptologische Abhandlungen 48, Wiesbaden.

Loprieno, Antonio. 1996. Defining Egyptian Literature: Ancient Texts and Modern Theories, in: Antonio Loprieno (ed.), *Ancient Egyptian Literature. History and Forms*, Probleme der Ägyptologie 10, Leiden/New York/Cologne, 39–58.

Loret, Victor. 1889. Le verbe  et ses dérivés, in: *Recueil de travaux relatifs à la philologie et à l'archéologie égyptiennes et assyriennes* 11, 117–131.

Lotman, Jurij. 1977. *The Structure of the Artistic Text* (translated from the Russian by Ronald Vroon), Michigan Slavic Contributions 7, Ann Arbor.

Luhmann, Niklas. 2008. *Schriften zu Kunst und Literatur*, stw 1872, Frankfurt a. M.

Lurson, Benoît. 2021. Fonction d'ancrage, fonction de relais et diégèse de l'action royale dans les textes articulés à l'image, in: Horst Beinlich (ed.), *12. Ägyptologische Tempeltagung: Synergie und Divergenz. Zum Zusammenwirken von Bild und Text in ägyptischen Tempeln, Würzburg, 2020*, Königtum, Staat und Gesellschaft früher Hochkulturen 3,7, Wiesbaden, 175–206.

Mackie, Hilary. 1995. Review of Jesper Svenbro, Phrasikleia: An anthropology of reading in Ancient Greece. Translated from the French by Janet Lloyd. Ithaca, NY, in: *Language in Society* 24(2), 288–291.

Malaise, Michel & Jean Winand. 1999. *Grammaire raisonnée de l'égyptien classique*, Ægyptiaca Leodiensia 6, Liège.

Mandler, Jean Matter. 1984. *Stories, Scripts, and Scenes. Aspects of Schema Theory*, Hillsdale.

Manassa, Colleen. 2011, El-Moalla to El-Deir, in: Willeke Wendrich (ed.), *UCLA Encyclopedia of Egyptology*, Los Angeles, 1–16 (http://digital2.library.ucla.edu/viewItem.do?ark=21198/zz00293crv, last accessed on 22 December 2022).

Marchois, Bernard. 1995. *Édith Piaf : « Opinions publiques », Paris.*

Margolin, Uri. 2014. Narrator, in: Peter Hühn, Jan Christoph Meister, John Pier & Wolf Schmid (eds.), *The Living Handbook of Narratology*, Hamburg (https://www-archiv.fdm.uni-hamburg.de/lhn/printpdf/article/narrator, last accessed on 22 December 2022).

Mariette, Auguste †. 1889. *Les mastabas de l'Ancien Empire. Fragment du dernier ouvrage de A. Mariette, publié d'après le manuscrit de l'auteur par G. Maspero*, Paris.

Mariette, Auguste & Gaston Maspero. 1872–1892. *Monuments divers recueillis en Égypte et en Nubie*, Paris.

Martin-Pardey, Eva. 1977. *Die Plastik des Alten Reiches, Teil 1*, Corpus Antiquitatum Aegyptiacarum, Pelizaeus-Museum Hildesheim, Lieferung 1, Mainz.

Martinet, Émilie. 2019. *L'Administration provinciale sous l'Ancien Empire égyptien*, Vols. 1–2, Probleme der Ägyptologie 38/1–2, Leiden/Boston.

Martínez, Matías. 2011. Erzählung, in: Matías Martínez (ed.), *Handbuch Erzählliteratur – Theorie, Analyse, Geschichte*, Stuttgart/Weimar, 1–12.

Mattson, Mark P. 2014. Superior pattern processing is the essence of the evolved human brain, in: *Frontiers in Neuroscience* 8, 1–17 (doi: https://doi.org/10.3389/fnins.2014.00265).

McFarlane, Ann. 2003. *Mastabas at Saqqara: Kaiemheset, Kaipunesut, Kaiemsenu, Sehetepu and Others*, The Australian Centre for Egyptology: Reports 20, Oxford.

Megahed, Mohamed & Hana Vymazalová. 2015. The South-Saqqara Circumcision Scene: a Fragment of an Old Kingdom Birth-legend, in: Filip Coppens, Jiří Janák & Hana Vymazalová (eds.), *Royal versus Divine Authority. Acquisition, Legitimization and Renewal of Power, 7. Symposium zur ägyptischen Königsideologie/7th Symposium on Egyptian Royal Ideology*, Königtum, Staat und Gesellschaft Früher Hochkulturen 4,4, Wiesbaden, 275–287.

Mehr, Samuel A., Manvir Singh, Dean Knox, Daniel M. Ketter, Daniel Pickens-Jones, S. Atwood, Christopher Lucas, Nori Jacoby, Alena A. Egner, Erin J. Hopkins, Rhea M. Howard, Joshua K. Hartshorne, Mariela V. Jennings, Jan Simson, Constance M. Bainbridge, Steven Pinker, Timothy J. O'Donnell, Max M. Krasnow, Luke Glowacki. 2019. Universality and diversity in human song, in: Science 366(971), 1–17 (doi: https://doi.org/10.1126/science.aax0868).

Meyer-Dietrich, Erika. 2010. Recitation, Speech Acts, and Declamation, in: Willeke Wendrich, Jacco Dieleman, Elizabeth Frood & John Baines (eds.), *UCLA Encyclopedia of Egyptology* (https://escholarship.org/content/qt1gh1q0md/qt1gh1q0md.pdf, last accessed on 22 December 2022).

Meyers, Elizabeth L. Component Design as a Narrative Device in Amarna Tomb Art, in: *Studies in the History of Art* 16, 35–51.

Michaud, Jean-Pierre. 1973. Chronique des fouilles et découvertes archéologiques en Grèce en 1972, in: *Bulletin de correspondance hellénique* 97, 253–412.

Micznik, Vera. 2001. Music and Narrative Revisited: Degrees of Narrativity in Beethoven and Mahler, in: *Journal of the Royal Musical Association* 126(2), 193–249.

Miller, Peter. 1991. *Get Published! Get Produced! A Literary Agent's Tips on How to Sell Your Writing*, New York.

Minsky, Marvin. 1974. *A Framework for Representing Knowledge*, Massachusetts Institute of Technology Artificial Intelligence Laboratory Memo 306, Cambridge, MA (see https://dspace.mit.edu/bitstream/handle/1721.1/6089/AIM-306.pdf, last accessed on 22 December 2022).

Mirelman, Sam. 2010. The Definition of 'Music' in Music Archaeology. The Contribution of Historical Ethnomusicology, in: *Studien zur Musikarchäologie VII. Musikalische Wahrnehmung in Vergangenheit und Gegenwart. Ethnographische Analogien in der Musikarchäologie. Vorträge des 6. Symposiums der Internationalen Studiengruppe Musikarchäologie im Ethnologischen Museum der Staatlichen Museen zu Berlin, 09.–13. September 2008*, Orient-Archäologie 25, Rahden, 115–118.

Moers, Gerald. 2001. *Fingierte Welten in der ägyptischen Literatur des 2. Jahrtausends v. Chr. Grenzüberschreitung, Reisemotiv und Fiktionalität*, Probleme der Ägyptologie 19, Leiden/Boston/Cologne.

Moers, Gerald. 2013. Von Stimmen und Texten. Pharaonische Metalepsen als mediales Phänomen, in: Ute E. Eisen & Peter von Möllendorff (eds.), *Über die Grenze. Metalepse in Text- und Bildmedien des Altertums*, Narratologia 39, Berlin/Boston, 29–58.

Moers, Gerald. 2019. Ägyptologie, in: Eva von Contzen & Stefan Tilg (eds.), *Handbuch Historische Narratologie*, Berlin, 323–325.

Moers, Gerald. In press. Strategic Discourse in the Ancient Near East and Egypt: Egypt, in: Henriette van der Blom & Harvey Yunis (eds.), *The Cambridge History of Rhetoric, Vol. I: Rhetoric of the Ancient World (to 250 CE)*, Cambridge.

Möller, Georg & Alan H. Gardiner. 1911. *Hieratische Papyrus aus den Königlichen Museen zu Berlin, Dritter Band, Schriftstücke der VI. Dynastie aus Elephantine, Zaubersprüche für Mutter und Kind, Ostraka*, Leipzig.

Montaigne, Michel de †. 1617. *Essais*, revised posthumous edition, Paris.

Moreno García, Juan Carlos. 1998. De l'Ancien Empire à la Première Période Intermédiaire: l'autobiographie de *Qꜣr* d'Edfou, entre tradition et innovation, in: *Revue d'Égyptologie* 49, 151–160.

Moreno García, Juan Carlos. 2009/10. Introduction. Élites et états tributaires : le cas de l'Égypte pharaonique, in: Juan Carlos Moreno García (ed.), *Élites et pouvoir en Égypte ancienne : actes du colloque Université Charles-de-Gaulle – Lille 3, 7 et 8 juillet 2006*, Cahiers de recherches de l'Institut de papyrologie et d'égyptologie de Lille 28, Lille, 11–50.

Morenz, Ludwig. 1996. *Beiträge zur Schriftlichkeitskultur im Mittleren Reich und in der Zweiten Zwischenzeit*, Ägypten und Altes Testament 29, Wiesbaden.

Morenz, Ludwig. 2003. Tomb Inscriptions: The Case of the I Versus Autobiography in Ancient Egypt, in: *Human Affairs* 13, 179–196.

Morgan, Jacques de. 1903. *Fouilles à Dahchour en 1894–1895*, Vienna.

Morschauser, Scott. 1991. *Threat-Formulae in Ancient Egypt: A Study of the History, Structure and Use of Threats and Curses in Ancient Egypt*, Baltimore.

Mourad, Anna-Latifa. 2011. Siege Scenes of the Old Kingdom, in: *The Bulletin of the Australian Centre for Egyptology* 22, 135–158.

Müller, Matthias. 2006. Falsche Maße? Oder falsches Grab? Anmerkungen zu einer Inschrift im Grab des Debeheni (LG 90), in: *Göttinger Miszellen* 209, 59–62.

Nabokov, Vladimir. 1962. *Pale Fire*, New York.

Nehamas, Alexander. 1981. The Postulated Author: Critical Monism as a Regulative Ideal, in: *Critical Inquiry* 8(1), 133–149.

Nelles, William. 2012. Microfiction: What Makes a Very Short Story Very Short?, in: *Narrative* 20(1), 87–104.

Nerlich, Michael. 1990. Qu'est-ce qu'un iconotexte ? Réflexions sur le rapport texte-image photographique dans *La Femme se découvre* d'Évelyne Sinnassamy, in: Alain Montandon (ed.), *Iconotextes*, Paris, 255–302.

Newman, Samuel P. 1862. *A Practical System to of Rhetoric or the Principles & Rules of Style, Inferred from Examples of Writing; to Which is Added a Historical Dissertation on English Style*, London [reprint of 7th edition of 1839].

Nünning, Vera & Ansgar Nünning. 2002. Produktive Grenzüberschreitungen: Transgenerische, intermediale und interdisziplinäre Ansätze in der Erzähltheorie, in: Vera Nünning & Ansgar Nünning (eds.), *Erzähltheorie transgenerisch, intermedial, interdisziplinär*, WVT-Handbücher zum literaturwissenschaftlichen Studium 5, Trier, 1–22.

Obsomer, Claude. 1993. *Di.f prt-ḫrw* et la filiation *ms(t).n* / *ir(t).n* comme critères de datation dans les textes du Moyen Empire, in: Christian Cannuyer & Jean-Marie Kruchten (eds.), *Individu, société et spiritualité dans l'Égypte pharaonique et copte. Mélanges égyptologiques offerts au Professeur Aristide Théodoridès*, Ath/Brussels/Mons, 163–200.

Ochs, Elinor & Lisa Capps. 2001. *Living Narrative: Creating Lives in Everyday Storytelling*, Cambridge, MA/London.

OED 2022a = biography, n., *Oxford English Dictionary Online*, Oxford University Press, September 2022 (https://www.oed.com/view/Entry/19219, last accessed on 22 December 2022).

OED 2022b = portfolio, n., Oxford English Dictionary Online, Oxford University Press, September 2022 (https://www.oed.com/view/Entry/148175, last accessed on 22 December 2022).

Olabarria, Leire. 2020. *Kinship and Family in Ancient Egypt*, Cambridge.

Oréal, Elsa. 2011. *Les particules en égyptien ancien : de l'ancien égyptien à l'égyptien classique*, Bibliothèque d'étude 152, Cairo.

Page, Ruth. 2015. The Narrative Dimensions of Social Media Storytelling. Options for Linearity and Tellership, in: Anna De Fina & Alexandra Georgakopoulou (eds.), *The Handbook of Narrative Analysis*, Chichester, 329–347.

Pantalacci, Laure. 1998. La documentation épistolaire du palais des gouverneurs à Balat-ʿAyn Aṣīl, in: *Bulletin de l'Institut français d'archéologie orientale* 98, 303–315.

Parkinson, Richard Bruce. 2002. *Poetry and Culture in Middle Kingdom Egypt. A Dark Side to Perfection*, London/New York.

Parkinson, Richard Bruce. 2009. *Reading Ancient Egyptian Poetry: Among Other Histories*, Chichester.

Patron, Sylvie. 2011. Homonymy, Polysemy and Synonymy: Reflection on the Notion of Voice, in: Per Krogh Hansen, Stefan Iversen, Henrik Skov Nielsen & Rolf Reitan (eds.), *Strange Voices in Narrative Fiction*, Narratologia 30, Berlin/Boston, 13–36.

Perepelkin, Jurij Jakovlevič. 1986. *Privateigentum in der Vorstellung der Ägypter des Alten Reichs, herausgegeben und übersetzt von Renate Müller-Wollermann*, Tübingen.

Petrie, William Mathew Flinders. 1892. *Medum*, London.

Pfister, Manfred. 1985. Zur Systemreferenz, in: Ulrich Broich & Manfred Pfister (eds.), *Intertextualität. Formen, Funktionen, anglistische Fallstudien*, Tübingen, 52–58.

Piaf, Édith. *Au bal de la chance*, Paris.

Picardo, Nicholas S. 2010. (Ad)dressing Washptah: Illness or Injury in the Vizier's Death, as Related in His Tomb Biography, in: Zahi Hawass & Jennifer Houser Wegner (eds.), *Millions of Jubilees: Studies in Honor of David O. Silverman*, Supplément aux Annales du Service des antiquités de l'Égypte, Cahier 39, Cairo, 93–104.

Pier, John. 2016. Narrative Levels (revised version; uploaded 23 April 2014), in: Peter Hühn, Jan Christoph Meister, John Pier & Wolf Schmid (eds.), *The Living Handbook of Narratology*, Hamburg (https://www-archiv.fdm.uni-hamburg.de/lhn/printpdf/article/narrative-levels-revised-version-uploaded-23-april-2014, last accessed on 22 December 2022).

Pier, John. 2017. Complexity: A Paradigm for Narrative?, in: Per Krogh Hansen, John Pier, Philippe Roussin & Wolf Schmid (eds.), *Emerging Vectors of Narratology*, Narratologia 57, Berlin/Boston, 534–565.

Pinar Sanz, María Jesús. 2015. *Multimodality and Cognitive Linguistics*, Benjamins Current Topics 78, Philadelphia.

Pinto, Angelo. 2020. "The Hand that Writes": The Scriptorial Unfinishedness of the First Movement of Mahler's Tenth, in: *Musicologica Austriaca: Journal for Austrian Music Studies* (version of 22 October 2020; https://www.musau.org//parts/neue-article-page/pdf/89, last accessed on 22 December 2022).

Pöhlmann, Sascha (ed.), *Revolutionary Leaves: The Fiction of Mark Z. Danielewski*, Newcastle upon Tyne.

Polkinghorne, David. 1988. *Narrative Knowing and the Human Sciences*, New York.

Polotsky, Hans Jakob. 1965. *Egyptian Tenses*, Publications of the Israel Academy of Sciences and Humanities, section of Humanities 2 (5). Jerusalem.

Porter, Bertha & Rosalind L. B. Moss. 1974. *Topographical Bibliography of Ancient Egyptian Hieroglyphic Texts, Reliefs, and Paintings, Volume III/1: Memphis, Abû Rawâsh to Abûṣir*, second edition revised and augmented by Jaromír Málek, Oxford.

Posener-Kriéger, Paule. 1985. Décrets envoyés au temple funéraire de Rêneferef, in: Paule Posener-Kriéger (ed.), *Mélanges Gamal Eddin Mokhtar, Volume II*, Bibliothèque d'étude 97/2, Cairo, 195–210.

Postel, Lilian. 2004. *Protocole des souverains égyptiens et dogme monarchique au début du Moyen Empire. Des premiers Antef au début du règne d'Amenemhat Ier*, Monographies Reine Élisabeth 10, Brussels.

Prince, Gerald. 2008. Narrativehood, Narrativeness, Narrativity, Narratability, in: John Pier & José Ángel García Landa (eds.), *Theorizing Narrativity*, Narratologia 12, Berlin/New York, 19–27.

Propp, Vladimir. 1968. *Morphology of the Folktale*, Second Edition Revised and Edited with a Preface by Louis A. Wagner/New Introduction by Alan Dundes, Austin.

Psarra, Sophia. 2009. *Architecture and Narrative: The structure of space and cultural meaning in buildings*, London/New York.

Quack, Joachim Friedrich. 2012. Wenn die Götter zuhören. Zur Rolle der Rezitationssprüche im Tempelritual, in: Amr El Hawary (ed.), *Wenn die Götter und Propheten reden. Erzählen für die Ewigkeit*, Narratio Aliena? Studien des Bonner Zentrums für Transkulturelle Narratologie (BZTN) 3, Berlin, 124–152.

Quibell, James Edward. 1909. *Excavations at Saqqara (1907–1908), with sections by Sir Herbert Thompson, bart. and Prof. W. Spiegelberg*, Cairo.

Ragazzoli, Chloé. 2010. Weak Hands and Soft Mouths. Elements of a Scribal Identity in the New Kingdom, in: *Zeitschrift für ägyptische Sprache und Altertumskunde* 137, 157–170.

Rajewsky, Irina. 2020. Theories of Fictionality and Their Real Other, in: Monika Fludernik & Marie-Laure Ryan (eds.), *Narrative Factuality. A Handbook*, Revisionen 6, Berlin/Boston, 29–50.

Ranke, Hermann. 1952. *Die ägyptischen Personennamen. Band II: Einleitung. Form und Inhalt der Namen. Geschichte der Namen. Vergleiche mit andren Namen. Nachträge und Zusätze zu Band I. Umschreibungslisten*, Glückstadt/Hamburg.

Rashid, Mahbub. 2010. Review of: Sophia Psarra, Architecture and Narrative: The Formation of Space and Cultural Meaning, in: *The Journal of Architecture* 15(4), 543–549. (doi: https://doi.org/10.1080/13602365.2010.486570).

Redford, Donald B. 1986. *Pharaonic King-Lists, Annals, and Day-Books: A Contribution to the Study of the Egyptian Sense of History*, SSEA Publication 4, Mississauga.

Reinhardt, Corinna. 2020. Schrift am Grabmal. Zur Materialität der Inschriften an archaischen Grabmälern aus Athen und Attika, in: Nikolaus Dietrich, Johannes Fouquet & Corinna Reinhardt (eds.), *Schreiben auf statuarischen Monumenten. Aspekte materialer Textkultur in archaischer und frühklassischer Zeit*, Materiale Textkulturen 29, Berlin/Boston, 31–102.

Reintges, Chris. 2011. The Oral-Compositional Form of Pyramid Text Discourse, in: Fredrik Hagen, John Johnston, Wendy Monkhouse, Kathryn Piquette, John Tait & Martin Worthington (eds.), *Narratives of Egypt and the Ancient Near East. Literary and Linguistic Approaches*, Orientalia Lovaniensia Analecta 189, Leuven/Paris/Walpole, MA, 3–54.

Reisner, George A. 1931. *Mycerinus: The Temples of the Third Pyramid at Giza*, Cambridge, MA.

Reisner, George Andrew. 1942. *A History of the Giza Necropolis: Volume I*, Cambridge, MA.

Richards, Janet. 2002. Text and Context in late Old Kingdom Egypt: The Archaeology and Historiography of Weni the Elder, in: *Journal of the American Research Center in Egypt* 39, 75–102.

Richardson, Brian. 2006. *Unnatural Voices: Extreme Narration in Modern and Contemporary Fiction*, Columbus.

Ricœur, Paul. 1983. *Temps et récit, Tome I*, Paris.

Ridley, Ronald T. 2019. *Akhenaten. A Historian's View*, The AUC History of Ancient Egypt 1. Cairo/New York.

Riggsby, Andrew M. 2006. Caesar in Gaul and Rome: War in Words, Austin.

Ritivoi, Andreea Deciu. 2013. Twists and turns. The circulation of narrative concepts across disciplines and cultures, in: Matti Hyvärinen, Mari Hatavara & Lars-Christer Hydén (eds.), *The Travelling Concepts of Narrative*, Studies in Narrative 18, Amsterdam/Philadelphia, 287–301.

Roccati, Alessandro. 1982. *La littérature historique sous l'Ancien Empire égyptien*, Paris.

Roeder, Hubert. 2009. Erzählen im Alten Ägypten. Vorüberlegungen zu einer Erzähltheorie zwischen Literaturwissenschaft und Altertumswissenschaft, in: Hubert Roeder (ed.), *Das Erzählen in frühen Hochkulturen, I. Der Fall Ägypten*, Ägyptologie und Kulturwissenschaft 1, Munich, 15–54.

Roeder, Hubert. 2018a. Eine Archäologie der narrativen Sinnbildung, in: Hubert Roeder (ed.), *Das Erzählen in frühen Hochkulturen, II. Eine Archäologie der narrativen Sinnbildung*, Ägyptologie und Kulturwissenschaft 2, Munich, 17–27.

Roeder, Hubert. 2018b. Narration als Produkt sprachlich-visueller Präsentation. Eine kognitiv-kommunikative Perspektive auf die altägyptische Sprachkultur, in: Hubert Roeder (ed.), *Das Erzählen in frühen Hochkulturen, II. Eine Archäologie der narrativen Sinnbildung*, Ägyptologie und Kulturwissenschaft 2, Munich, 105–196.

Rogner, Frederik. 2021. Gottheiten, die den König führen und auf Wänden schreiben: Akteure und Inschriften in Tempeln des Neuen Reiches zwischen Bildraum und Realraum, in: Horst Beinlich (ed.), *12. Ägyptologische Tempeltagung: Synergie und Divergenz. Zum Zusammenwirken von Bild und Text in ägyptischen Tempeln, Würzburg 2020*, Königtum, Staat und Gesellschaft Früher Hochkulturen 3,7, Wiesbaden, 221–254.

Rogner, Frederik. 2022. *Bildliche Narrativität – Erzählen mit Bildern. Rezeption und Verwendung figürlicher Darstellungen im ägyptischen Neuen Reich*, Swiss Egyptological Studies 3, Basel/ Frankfurt am Main.

Rösler, Wolfgang. 1992. Review of Jesper Svenbro, Phrasikleia, Anthropologie de la lecture en Grèce ancienne, in: *Gnomon* 64, 1–3.

Rossholm, Göran. 2017. Causal Expectation, in: Per Krogh Hansen, John Pier, Philippe Roussin & Wolf Schmid (eds.), *Emerging Vectors of Narratology*, Narratologia 57, Berlin/Boston, 207–227.

Rosteck, Jens. 2013. *Édith Piaf. Hymne an das Leben*, Berlin.

Ryan, Marie-Laure. 2007. Toward a definition of narrative, in: David Herman (ed.), *The Cambridge Companion to Narrative*, Cambridge et al., 22–35.

Ryan, Marie-Laure. 2014. Narration in Various Media, in: Peter Hühn, Jan Christoph Meister, John Pier & Wolf Schmid (eds.), *The Living Handbook of Narratology*, Hamburg (https://www-archiv.fdm.uni-hamburg.de/lhn/printpdf/article/narration-various-media, last accessed on 22 December 2022).

Ryan, Marie-Laure & Jan-Noël Thon. 2014. Storyworlds across Media: Introduction, in: Marie-Laure Ryan & Jan-Noël Thon (eds.), *Storyworlds across Media: Toward a Media-Conscious Narratology*, Lincoln/London, 1–21.

Saenger, Paul. 1989. Physiologie de la lecture et séparations des mots, in: *Annales. Histoire, Sciences Sociales* 44(4), 939–952.

Saenger, Paul. 1997. *Space Between Words: The Origins of Silent Reading*, Standford.

Sainte Fare Garnot, Jean. 1938. *L'appel aux vivants dans les textes funéraires égyptiens des origines à la fin de l'Ancien Empire*, Recherches d'archéologie, de philologie et d'histoire 9, Cairo.

Sancarlo, Rosa, Zoya Dare, Jozsef Arato & Raphael Rosenberg. 2020. Does Pictorial Composition Guide the Eye? Investigating Four Centuries of Last Supper Pictures, *Journal of Eye Movement Research* 13(2)/7, 1–13 (doi: https://doi.org/10.16910/jemr.13.2.7).

Sanford, Anthony J. & Catherine Emmott. 2012. *Mind, Brain and Narrative*, Cambridge.

Sanford, Anthony J. & Simon C. Garrod. 1981. *Understanding Written Language. Explorations of Comprehension Beyond the Sentence*, Chichester.

Satzinger, Helmut. 2008. Hintzes Kategorie der Erzählung im Neuägyptischen – zwischen Stil und Grammatik, in: *Der antike Sudan* 19, 39–45.

Schenkel, Wolfgang. 1965. *Memphis · Herakleopolis · Theben. Die epigraphischen Zeugnisse der 7.–11. Dynastie Ägyptens*, Ägyptologische Abhandlungen 12, Wiesbaden.

Schmid, Wolf. 2011. Erzählstimme, in: Matías Martínez (ed.), *Handbuch Erzählliteratur – Theorie, Analyse, Geschichte*, Stuttgart/Weimar, 131–138.

Schmid, Wolf. 2014a. *Elemente der Narratologie*, 3rd, augmented and revised edition, Berlin/Boston.

Schmid, Wolf. 2014b. Implied Author (revised version; uploaded 26 January 2013), in: Peter Hühn, Jan Christoph Meister, John Pier & Wolf Schmid (eds.), *The Living Handbook of Narratology*, Hamburg (https://www-archiv.fdm.uni-hamburg.de/lhn/printpdf/article/implied-author-revised-version-uploaded-26-january-2013, last accessed on 22 December 2022).

Schmid, Wolf. 2017. Eventfulness and Repetitiveness: Two Aesthetics of Storytelling, in: Per Krogh Hansen, John Pier, Philippe Roussin & Wolf Schmid (eds.), *Emerging Vectors of Narratology*, Narratologia 57, Berlin/Boston, 229–245.

Schott, Erika. 1977. Die Biographie des Ka-em-tenenet, in: Jan Assmann, Erika Feucht & Reinhard Grieshammer (eds.), *Fragen an die altägyptische Literatur. Studien zum Gedenken an Eberhard Otto*, Wiesbaden, 443–461.

Schulz, Armin. 2010. Fremde Kohärenz. Narrative Verknüpfungsformen im Nibelungenlied und in der Kaiserchronik, in: Harald Haferland & Matthias Meyer (eds.), *Historische Narratologie – Mediävistische Perspektiven*, Trends in Medieval Philology 19, Berlin/New York, 339–360.

Schulz, Armin & Gert Hübner. 2011. Mittelalter, in: Matías Martínez (ed.), *Handbuch Erzählliteratur – Theorie, Analyse, Geschichte*, Stuttgart/Weimar, 184–205.

Schwalm, Helga. 2014. Autobiography, in: Peter Hühn, Jan Christoph Meister, John Pier & Wolf Schmid (eds.), *The Living Handbook of Narratology*, Hamburg (https://www-archiv.fdm.uni-hamburg.de/lhn/printpdf/article/autobiography, last accessed on 22 December 2022).

Searle, John R. 1979. *Expression and Meaning. Studies in the Theory of Speech Acts*, Cambridge.

Segal, Eyal. 2012. Review of Per Krogh Hansen et al. (eds.). 2011. Strange Voices in Narrative Fiction, Narratologia 30, Berlin/Boston, in: *Poetics Today* 33(3–4), 495–499.

Sethe, Kurt. 1910. *Die altaegyptischen Pyramidentexte nach den Papierabdrücken und Photographien des Berliner Museums. Zweiter Band: Text, zweite Hälfte: Spruch 469–714 (Pyr. 906–2217)*, Leipzig.

Sethe, Kurt. 1911. Der Name »Merui-tensi« und die Entwicklung der Filiationsangabe bei den Ägyptern, in: *Zeitschrift für ägyptische Sprache und Altertumskunde* 49, 95–99.

Sethe, Kurt. 1924. *Aegyptische Lesestücke zum Gebrauch im akademischen Unterricht. Texte des Mittleren Reiches*, Leipzig.

Sethe, Kurt. 1933. *Urkunden des Alten Reichs. Erster Band*, Leipzig.

Shubert, Steven Blake. 2007. *Those Who (Still) Live on Earth: A Study of the Ancient Egyptian Appeal to the Living Texts*, PhD thesis, University of Toronto.

Siffert, Uta. 2022. 'Death ends a Life, not a Relationship'. Some Thoughts on Designating the Deceased *ꜣḫ* and *Wsir* NN in the Middle Kingdom, in: Gianluca Miniaci & Wolfram Grajetzki (eds.), *The World of Middle Kingdom Egypt III: Contributions on Archaeology, Art, Religion, and Written Sources*, Middle Kingdom Studies 12, London, 313–334.

Silverstein, Michael. 2020. Narrating Biography versus Biographical Indexicality, in: Julie Stauder-Porchet, Elizabeth Frood & Andréas Stauder (eds.), *Ancient Egyptian Biographies: Contexts, Forms, Functions*, Wilbour Studies in Egyptology and Assyriology 6, Atlanta, GA, 9–28.

Simon, Henrike. 2013. *»Textaufgaben«. Kulturwissenschaftliche Konzepte in Anwendung auf die Literatur der Ramessidenzeit*, Studien zur Altägyptischen Kultur, Beihefte 14, Hamburg.

Simpson, William Kelly. 1976. *The Mastabas of Qar and Idu, G 7101 and 7102*, Giza Mastabas 2, Boston.

Simpson, William Kelly. 2003. Introduction, in: William Kelly Simpson (ed.), *The Literature of Ancient Egypt. An Anthology of Stories, Instructions, Stelae, Autobiographies, and Poetry*, third edition, New Haven/London, 1–10.

Skains, R. Lyle. 2019. The materiality of the intangible: Literary metaphor in multimodal texts, in: *Convergence* 25(1), 133–147 (https://doi.org/10.1177/1354856517703965).

Smith, Sidonie & Julia Watson. 2001. *Reading Autobiography: A Guide for Interpreting Life Narratives*, Minneapolis/London.

Smith, William S. 1949. *A History of Egyptian Sculpture and Painting in the Old Kingdom*, second edition, London.

Smith, William S. 1952. Inscriptional Evidence for the History of the Fourth Dynasty, in: *Journal of Near Eastern Studies* 11, 113–128.

Smither, Paul C. 1942. An Old Kingdom Letter Concerning the Crimes of Count Sabni, in: *Journal of Egyptian Archaeology* 28, 16–19.

Sommer, Roy. 2012. The Merger of Classical and Postclassical Narratologies and the Consolidated Future of Narrative Theory, in: *Diegesis* 1(1), 143–157.

Sommer, Roy. 2017. The Future of Narratology's Past: A Contribution to Metanarratology, in: Per Krogh Hansen, John Pier, Philippe Roussin & Wolf Schmid (eds.), *Emerging Vectors of Narratology*, Narratologia 57, Berlin/Boston, 593–608.

Sourvinou-Inwood, Christiane. 1995. *'Reading' Greek Death – to the End of the Classical Period*, Oxford.

Spalinger, Anthony. 1994. Dates Texts of the Old Kingdom, in: *Studien zur altägyptischen Kultur* 21, 275–319.

Spiegelberg, Wilhelm. 1909. Egyptian Texts, in: James Edward Quibell. 1909. *Excavations at Saqqara (1907–1908), with sections by Sir Herbert Thompson, bart. and Prof. W. Spiegelberg*, Cairo, 79–93.

Spigelman, Mark. 1997. The Circumcision Scene in the Tomb of Akhmahor: The First Record of Emergency Surgery?, in: *The Bulletin of the Australian Centre for Egyptology* 8, 91–100.

Stauder-Porchet, Julie. 2009. *La préposition en égyptien de la première phase. Approche sémantique*, Aegyptiaca Helvetica 21, Basel.

Stauder-Porchet, Julie. 2011. Les autobiographies événementielles de la Ve dynastie: premier ensemble de textes continus en Égypte, in: Miroslav Bárta, Filip Coppens & Jaromír Krejčí (eds.), *Abusir and Saqqara in the Year 2010*, Volume 2, Prague, 747–766.

Stauder-Porchet, Julie. 2015. Hezi's Autobiographical Inscription: Philological Study and Interpretation, in: *Zeitschrift für ägyptische Sprache und Altertumskunde* 142, 191–204.

Stauder-Porchet, Julie. 2016. Les actants des autobiographies événementielles de la Ve et de la VIe dynastie, in: Philippe Collombert, Dominique Lefèvre, Stéphane Polis & Jean Winand (eds.), *Aere perennius. Mélanges égyptologiques en l'honneur de Pascal Vernus*, Orientalia Lovaniensia Analecta 242, Leuven, 579–591.

Stauder-Porchet, Julie. 2017. *Les autobiographies de l'Ancien Empire. Étude sur la naissance d'un genre*, Orientalia Lovaniensia Analecta 255, Leuven/Paris/Bristol, CT.

Stauder-Porchet, Julie. 2020a. Genres and Textual Prehistories of the Egyptian Autobiography in the Old Kingdom, in: Julie Stauder-Porchet, Elizabeth Frood & Andréas Stauder (eds.), *Ancient Egyptian Biographies: Contexts, Forms, Functions*, Wilbour Studies in Egyptology and Assyriology 6, Atlanta, GA, 87–116.

Stauder-Porchet, Julie. 2020b. Harkhuf's Autobiographical Inscriptions. A study in Old Kingdom Monumental Rhetoric, Part I. Texts, Genres, Forms, in: *Zeitschrift für ägyptische Sprache und Altertumskunde* 147, 57–91.

Stauder-Porchet, Julie. 2020c. Harkhuf's Autobiographical Inscriptions. A study in Old Kingdom Monumental Rhetoric, Part II. The Inscribed Facade, in: *Zeitschrift für ägyptische Sprache und Altertumskunde* 147, 197–222.

Stauder-Porchet, Julie. 2021a. L'inscriptions lapidaire de la parole royale chez les particuliers à la Ve dynastie, in: Philippe Collombert, Laurent Coulon, Ivan Guermeur & Christophe Thiers (eds.), *Questionner le Sphinx. Mélanges offerts à Christiane Zivie-Coche*, Bibliothèque d'Étude 178, Cairo, 137–164.

Stauder-Porchet, Julie. 2021b. Inscriptional Layout in Continuous Texts of the Old Kingdom, in: *Bulletin de l'Institut français d'archéologie orientale* 121, 442–474.

Stauder-Porchet, Julie. 2021c. Appropriation of Royal Forms and the Early Development of Textual Narrative During the Fifth Dynasty, in: Bárta, Miroslav, Filip Coppens & Jaromír Krejčí (eds.), *Abusir and Saqqara in the Year 2020*, Prague, 199–212.

Stauder-Porchet, Julie, Elizabeth Frood & Andréas Stauder (eds.) 2020. *Ancient Egyptian Biographies: Contexts, Forms, Functions*, Wilbour Studies in Egyptology and Assyriology 6, Atlanta, GA.

Stieber, Mary. 2004. *The Poetics of Appearance in the Attic Korai*, Austin.
Stoll Knecht, Anna. 2019. *Mahler's Seventh Symphony*, New York.
Störmer-Caysa, Uta. 2010. Kausalität, Wiederkehr und Wiederholung. Über die zyklische Raumzeitstruktur vormoderner Erzählungen mit biographischem Schema, in: Harald Haferland & Matthias Meyer (eds.): *Historische Narratologie – Mediävistische Perspektiven*, Trends in Medieval Philology 19, Berlin/New York, 361–383.
Strawson, Galen. 2015. The Unstoried Life, in: Zachary Leader (ed.), *On Life-Writing*, Oxford.
Streeruwitz, Marlene. 2014. *Nachkommen*, Frankfurt am Main.
Streeruwitz, Marlene (as Nelia Fehn). 2015. *Die Reise einer jungen Anarchistin in Griechenland*, Frankfurt am Main.
Strudwick, Nigel. 1985. *The Administration of Egypt in the Old Kingdom: The Highest Titles and Their Holders*, London et al.
Strudwick, Nigel C. 2005. *Texts from the Pyramid Age, edited by Ronald J. Leprohon*, SBL Writings from the Ancient World 16, Leiden/Boston.
Suhr, Claudia. 2016. *Die ägyptische „Ich-Erzählung". Eine narratologische Untersuchung*, Göttinger Orientforschungen IV. Reihe Ägypten 61, Wiesbaden.
Svenbro, Jesper. 1988. *Phrasikleia : anthropologie de la lecture en grèce ancienne*, Paris.
Tanner, Jeremy. 2006. Statues and societies in the ancient world, in: *Antiquity* 80, 210–214.
Temmerman, Koen de. 2020. Writing (about) Ancient Lives: Scholarship, Definitions, and Concepts, in: Koen de Temmerman (ed.), *The Oxford Handbook of Ancient Biography*, Oxford, 3–18.
Tomashevsky, Boris Viktorovich [Томашéвский, Борис Викторович]. 1925. *Теория литературы. Поэтика [Teoriya literatury. Poėtika]*, Leningrad.
Troche, Julia. 2021. *Death, Power, and Apotheosis in Egypt: The Old and Middle Kingdoms*, Ithaca/London.
Vandekerckhove, Hans & Renate Müller-Wollermann, *Die Felsinschriften des Wadi Hilâl. 1. Text/2. Tafeln*, Elkab VI, Turnhout.
Verner, Miroslav. 2006. Contemporaneous Evidence for the Relative Chronology of Dyns. 4 and 5, in: Erik Hornung, Rolf Krauss & David A. Warburton (eds.), *Ancient Egyptian Chronology*, Handbuch der Orientalistik/Handbook of Oriental Studies, Section One: The Near and Middle East 83, Leiden/Boston, 124–143.
Vernus, Pascal. 2004. Le syntagme de quantification en égyptien de la première phase : sure les relations entre Textes des Pyramides et Textes des Sarcophages, in: Susanne Bickel & Bernard Mathieu (eds.), *D'un monde à l'autre. Textes des Pyramides & Textes des Sarcophages. Actes de la table ronde internationale « Textes des Pyramides versus Textes des Sarcophages » Ifao – 24–26 septembre 2001*, Bibliothèque d'étude 139, Cairo, 279–311.
Vernus, Pascal. 2009/2010. Comment l'élite se donne à voir dans le programme décoratif de ses chapelles funéraires. Stratégie d'épure, stratégie d'appogiature et le frémissement du littéraire, in: Juan Carlos Moreno García (ed.), *Élites et pouvoir en Égypte ancienne*, Cahiers de recherches de l'Institut de papyrologie et d'égyptologie de Lille, Lille, 67–115.
Vernus, Pascal. 2012. Stratégie d'épure et stratégie d'appogiature dans les productions dites « artistiques » à l'usage des dominants. Le papyrus dit « érotique » de Turin et la mise à distance des dominés, in: Katalin Anna Kóthay (ed.), *Art and Society: Ancient and Modern Contexts of Egyptian Art. Proceedings of the International Conference held at the Museum of Fine Arts, Budapest, 13–15 May 2010*, Budapest, 109–121.
Vernus, Pascal. 2013. The Royal Command (*wḏ-nsw*): A Basic Deed of Executive Power, in: Juan Carlos Moreno García (ed.), Ancient Egyptian Administration, Handbuch der Orientalistik/Handbook of Oriental Studies, Section One: The Near and Middle East 104, Leiden/Boston, 259–340.
Vernus, Pascal. 2015. Autobiographie et scènes dites « de la vie quotidienne », in: Rémi Legros (ed.), *Cinquante ans d'éternité. Jubilé de la Mission archéologique française de Saqqâra*, Mission archéologique française de Saqqâra 5, Bibliothèque d'étude 162, Cairo, 309–321.

Vernus, Pascal. 2020. Autobiography versus Biography in the Second Person and Biography in the Third Person: Textual Formats, Authorship, and Apocryphal/Pseudepigraphic Works, in: Julie Stauder-Porchet, Elizabeth Frood & Andréas Stauder (eds.), *Ancient Egyptian Biographies: Contexts, Forms, Functions*, Wilbour Studies in Egyptology and Assyriology 6, Atlanta, GA, 163–203.

Vestrheim, Gjert. 2010. Voice in sepulchral epigram: some remarks on the use of first and second person in sepulchral epigrams, and a comparison with lyric poetry, in: Manuel Baumbach, Andrej Petrovic & Ivana Petrovic (eds.), *Archaic and Classical Greek Epigram*, Cambridge, 61–78.

Vinson, Steve. 2018. *The Craft of a Good Scribe. History, Narrative and Meaning in the* First Tale of Setne Khaemwas, Harvard Egyptological Studies 3, Leiden/Boston.

Visch, Valentijn T. & Ed S. Tan. 2009. Categorizing moving objects into film genres: The effect of animacy attribution, emotional response, and the deviation from non-fiction, in: *Cognition* 110, 265–272 (doi: https://doi.org/10.1016/j.cognition.2008.10.018).

Vischak, Deborah. 2006. Agency in Old Kingdom elite tomb programs: traditions, locations, and variable meanings, in: Martin Fitzenreiter & Michael Herb (eds.), *Dekorierte Grabanlagen im Alten Reich. Methodik und Interpretation*, Internet-Beiträge zur Ägyptologie und Sudanarchäologie 6, London, 255–276.

Vischak, Deborah. 2015. *Community and Identity in Ancient Egypt: The Old Kingdom Cemetery at Qubbet el-Hawa*, New York.

Viveiros de Castro, Eduardo. 2015. *The Relative Native: Essays on Indigenuous Conceptual Worlds*, Chicago.

Volokhine, Youri. 2018. À propos de la construction d'un débat sur les mythes égyptiens, in: *Revue de l'histoire des religions* 235(4), 619–644 (doi: https://doi.org/10.4000/rhr.9328).

Wachter, Rudolf. 2010. The origin of epigrams on 'speaking objects', in: Manuel Baumbach, Andrej Petrovic & Ivana Petrovic (eds.), *Archaic and Classical Greek Epigram*, Cambridge, 250–260.

Wagner, Peter. 1995. *Reading Iconotexts. From Swift to the French Revolution*, London.

Wagner, Peter. 1996. Introduction: Ekphrasis, Iconotexts, and Intermediality – the State(s) of the Art(s), in: Peter Wagner (ed.), *Icons – Texts – Iconotexts: Essays on Ekphrasis and Intermediality*, European Cultures 6, Berlin/New York, 1–40.

Walsem, René van. 2005. *Iconography of Old Kingdom Elite Tombs: Analysis and Interpretation, Theoretical and Methodological Aspects*, Mededelingen en Verhandelingen Ex Oriente Lux 35, Leiden/Leuven.

Walsem, René van. 2013. Diversification and variation in Old Kingdom funerary iconography as the expression of a need for "individuality", in: *Jaarbericht van het Vooraziatisch-Egyptisch Genootschap Ex Oriente Lux* 44, 117–139.

Walsem, René van. 2020. (Auto-)"Bioconographies" versus (Auto-)Biographies in Old Kingdom Elite Tombs: Complexity Expansion of Image and Word Reflecting Personality Traits by Competitive Individuality, in: Julie Stauder-Porchet, Elizabeth Frood & Andréas Stauder (eds.), *Ancient Egyptian Biographies: Contexts, Forms, Functions*, Wilbour Studies in Egyptology and Assyriology 6, Atlanta, GA, 117–159.

Weinrich, Harald. 2001. *Tempus. Besprochene und erzählte Welt*, 6th, revised edition, Munich.

Weiss, Lara. 2014. The Power of the Voice, in: Ben J. J. Haring, Olaf E. Kaper & René von Walsem (eds.), *The Workman's Progress: Studies in the Village of Deir el-Medina and Other Documents from Western Thebes in Honour of Rob Demarée*, Egyptologische Uitgaven 28, Leiden/Leuven, 291–303.

Weixler, Antonius & Lukas Werner (eds.). 2015. *Zeiten erzählen. Ansätze – Aspekte – Analysen*, Narratologia 48, Berlin/Boston.

Wente, Edward. 1991. *Letters from Ancient Egypt*, SBL Writings from the Ancient World 1, Atlanta, GA.

Werning, Daniel. 2008. Aspect vs. relative tense, and the typological classification of the Ancient Egyptian *sḏm.n=f*, in: *Lingua Aegyptia* 16, 261–292.

White, Hayden. 1987. *The Content of the Form. Narrative Discourse and Historical Representation*, Baltimore/London.

Widmaier, Kai. 2017. *Bilderwelten: Ägyptische Bilder und ägyptologische Kunst. Vorarbeiten für eine bildwissenschaftliche Ägyptologie*, Probleme der Ägyptologie 35, Leiden/Boston.

Wikipedia. 2022. For sale: baby shoes, never worn (https://en.wikipedia.org/w/index.php?title=For_sale:_baby_shoes,_never_worn&oldid=1066235231, last revised on 17 January 2022, last accessed on 22 December 2022).

Wildfeuer, Janina, Jana Pflaeging, John Bateman, Ognyan Seizov & Chiao-I Tseng (eds.). 2019a. *Multimodality: Disciplinary Thoughts and the Challenge of Diversity*, Berlin/Boston.

Wildfeuer, Janina, Jana Pflaeging, John Bateman, Ognyan Seizov & Chiao-I Tseng. 2019b. *Multimodality: Disciplinary Thoughts and the Challenge of Diversity – Introduction*, in: Janina Wildfeuer, Jana Pflaeging, John Bateman, Ognyan Seizov & Chiao-I Tseng (eds.), *Multimodality: Disciplinary Thoughts and the Challenge of Diversity*, Berlin/Boston, 3–38.

Willems, Harco. 2019. Who Am I? An Emic Approach to the So-Called 'Personal Texts' in Egyptian 'Funerary Literature', in: Rune Nyord (ed.), *Concepts in Middle Kingdom Funerary Culture. Proceedings of the Lady Wallis Budge Anniversary Symposium Held at Christ's College, Cambridge, 22 January 2016*, Culture and History of the Ancient Near East 102, Leiden/Boston, 204–247.

Wilson, John A. 1947. The Artist of the Egyptian Old Kingdom, in: *Journal of Near Eastern Studies* 6, 231–249.

Winand, Jean. 2006. *Temps et aspect en égyptien : une approche sémantique*, Probleme der Ägyptologie 25, Leiden/Boston.

Wolf, Werner. 2002. Das Problem der Narrativität in Literatur, bildender Kunst und Musik: Ein Beitrag zu einer intermedialen Erzähltheorie, in: Vera Nünning & Ansgar Nünning (eds.), *Erzähltheorie transgenerisch, intermedial, interdisziplinär*, WVT-Handbücher zum literaturwissenschaftlichen Studium 5, Trier, 23–104.

Wolf, Werner. 2005. Music and Narrative, in: David Herman, Manfred Jahn & Marie-Laure Ryan (eds.), *Routledge Encyclopedia of Narrative Theory*, London/New York, 324–329.

Wolf, Werner. 2017a. Narrativity in Instrumental Music? A Prototypical Narratological Approach to a Vexed Question [2008], in: Walter Bernhart (ed.), *Selected Essays on Intermediality by Werner Wolf (1992–2014). Theory and Typology, Literature-Music Relations, Transmedial Narratology, Miscellaneous Transmedial Phenomena*, Studies in Intermediality 10, Leiden/Boston, 480–500.

Wolf, Werner. 2017b. Transmedial Narratology: Theoretical Foundations and Some Applications (Fiction, Single Pictures, Instrumental Music), in: *Narrative* 25(3), 256–285.

Wood, Daniel Davis. 2013. *For Argument's Sake: Essays on Literature and Culture*, New York et al.

Wright, Frederick A. 2014. The Short Story Just Got Shorter: Hemingway, Narrative, and the Six-Word Urban Legend, in: *The Journal of Popular Culture* 47(2) 327–340.

Yoyotte, Jean. 1953. Un corps de police dans l'Égypte pharaonique, in: *Revue d'Égyptologie* 9, 1953, 139–151.

Zeman, Sonja. 2016. Perspectivization as a link between narrative micro- and macro-structure, in: Natalia Igl & Sonja Zeman (eds.), *Perspectives on Narrativity and Narrative Perspectivization*, Linguistic Approaches to Literature 21, Amsterdam/Philadelphia, 17–42.

Ziegler, Christiane. 1990. *Catalogue des stèles, peintures et reliefs égyptiens de l'Ancien Empire et de la Première Période Intermédiaire vers 2686–2040 avant J.-C.*, Musée du Louvre, département des antiquités égyptiennes, Paris.

Ziegler, Christiane. 1993. *Le mastaba d'Akhethetep : Une chapelle funéraire de l'Ancien Empire*, Musée du Louvre, département des antiquités égyptiennes, Paris.

Zymner, Rüdiger. 2006. ‚Stimme(n)' als Text und Stimme(n) als Ereignis, in: Andreas Blödorn, Daniela Langer & Michael Scheffel (eds.), *Stimme(n) im Text. Narratologische Positionsbestimmungen*, Narratologia 10, Berlin/New York, 321–347.

Ägyptische monochrone Einzelbilder als Erzählungen

Eine Fallstudie

Gerald Moers[1]

Abstract

The contribution examines the potential of so-called *monochronic single still pictures* to constitute autonomous narratives. Their ability to do so has been explicitly contested in *classical narratology* (section 1) as well in transmedially oriented *postclassical narratology* (section 2). Allegedly, images in general and especially those which show only one moment in time do not possess a clearly-structured temporal program in the same way as textual narratives do, which progress, on the discourse-level of narrative presentation, in a linear and sequential manner. *Monochronic* pictures thus cannot, by definition, show *events* in their *temporal-causal contiguity*, which would be one common set of criteria that would define *a narrative*. Although this view has also been imported into Egyptology (section 4.1), it must be questioned from a cognitive perspective that is combined with a serious reflection on the medial specificities of representing time in images (section 3). The final part of this contribution (section 4) is devoted to the case study of an ostracon that shows an image which belongs to the so-called Egyptian genre-scenes – a variety of images that, according to Egyptological preconceptions, lacks any form of newsworthiness or *tellability* (section 4). First of all, it is argued for the need to alter the transcultural and transhistorical conception of the narrative criterion of *tellability* in a way that it is sensible enough to also suit Egyptian conceptions of events that are worth being told. It then can be shown that the chosen example of *monochronic* images can very well present an autonomous story by the way in which recognisable objects and movement-patterns are arranged across the pictorial space. Beholders are not only triggered to narrativize the image according to mentally stored cognitive schemes and scripts, but their reception of the image is also guided by the clearly defined temporal succession of the tellable event on the discourse-level of the image.

1 Mein Dank gilt Camilla di Biase-Dyson, Claus Jurman, und Frederik Rogner, die die Studie durch ihre Diskussionsbereitschaft und eine Vielzahl von Hinweisen immer wieder befördert haben. Ferner danke ich Orly Goldwasser und Elisabeth Kruck für Einzelhinweise sowie Bernard Mathieu für die Übersendung eines mir in Wien nicht zugänglichen Manuskriptes. Danken möchte ich auch dem/der Autor*in eines anonymen Peer-Reviews, von dem die Studie ebenfalls profitiert hat.

Gerald Moers (ed.), *Narrative and Narrativity in Ancient Egypt*, 217–262
DOI: https://doi.org/10.37011/studmon.29.04

1 Können Einzelbilder erzählen? Die bildnarratologische Ausgangslage

Nicht erst seit dem/n oft bemühten *narrative turn/s*[2] und der Weiterentwicklung der *klassischen* zur *postklassischen Narratologie*[3], die sich unter anderem der Untersuchung des Erzählens in anderen als verbalen Medien widmet,[4] wird die Erzählfähigkeit von unbewegten Einzelbildern („a picture contained in one frame“)[5] behauptet[6] und vielfältig – und vor allem kontrovers – diskutiert[7]. Während, wie Antonius Weixler ausführt, „die Vorstellung, Malerei und Poesie könnten beide gleichwertig dieselben Stoffe erzählen, historisch gesehen der dominante Konsens war“,[8] hat sich dies seit und mit Rekurs auf Gotthold Ephraim Lessings *Laokoon* recht fundamental geändert. Unter Verweis auf dessen berühmte Diktum, dass „die Mahlerey zu ihren Nachahmungen ganz andere Mittel, oder Zeichen gebrauchet, als die Poesie; jene nehmlich Figuren und Farben in dem Raume, diese aber artikulirte Töne in der Zeit“[9] ist die Differenzierung von ‚Raumkünsten‘ und ‚Zeitküsten‘ in der *klassischen Narratologie* zwischenzeitlich nachgerade naturalisiert worden.[10] Ausgehend von transhistorisch und transmedial generalisierten Definitionen von ‚Narrativität‘, die die textzentrierte strukturalistische *klassische Narratologie* aus ihrer Beschäftigung mit Standardformen des fiktionalen literarischen Erzählens alteuropäischer Prägung und dort vor allem dem Roman des 19. Jahrhunderts gewonnen hatte,[11] wurde nun einerseits

---

2 Vgl. Kreiswirth 1992; Fahrenwald 2011: 82–96; Roussin 2017.

3 Zum Unterschied zwischen diesen narratologischen Spielarten vgl. etwa Nünning 2003, bes. 243–244; Alber & Fludernik 2010; Sommer 2012; Pier 2018.

4 Vgl. etwa Nünning & Nünning (Hgg.) 2002; Ryan (Hg.) 2004; Ryan 2005; Ryan 2014; s.a. die Abschnitte „Erzählen jenseits der Literatur“ in Huber & Schmid (Hgg.) 2018: 441–565 und „Medien des Erzählens“ in Martínez (Hg.) 2017: 24–114.

5 Speidel 2018b: 7 mit Diskussion.

6 Vgl. z.B. Barthes 1975 [1966]: 237. Weitere Literatur bei Ryan 2005: 1; Speidel 2018a: 77; Speidel 2018b: 3; Speidel 2020: 176.

7 Konzise Zusammenfassungen mit der wesentlichen relevanten Literatur(geschichte) finden sich u.a. bei Wolf 2002: 53–75, Speidel 2018a: 80–87, Speidel 2018b und Speidel 2020: 172–177.

8 Weixler 2020: 58–61 (Zitat: 59); s.a. Wolf 2003: 180 und Speidel 2020: 162–163 mit weiteren Belegen.

9 Lessing 1839 [1766]: 95; Lessing 1839 [1766]: 95–96 setzt fort: „wenn unstreitig die Zeichen ein bequemes Verhältnis zu dem Bezeichneten haben müssen: So können neben einander geordnete Zeichen, auch nur Gegenstände, die neben einander, oder deren Theile neben einander existieren, auf einander folgende Zeichen aber, auch nur Gegenstände ausdrücken, die auf einander, oder deren Theile auf einander folgen. Gegenstände, die neben einander, oder deren Theile neben einander existieren, heissen Körper. Folglich sind Körper, mit ihren sichtbaren Eigenschaften, die eigentlichen Gegenstände der Mahlery. Gegenstände, die auf einander, oder deren Theile auf einander folgen, heissen überhaupt Handlungen. Folglich sind Handlungen der eigentliche Gegenstand der Poesie.“ S.a. „Die Mahlerey braucht Figuren und Farben in dem Raume. Die Dichtkunst artikulirte Töne in der Zeit“ (Lessing 1839 [1766]: 195) und „die Zeitfolge ist das Gebiete des Dichters, so wie der Raum das Gebiete des Mahlers.“ (Lessing 1839 [1766]: 108).

10 Vgl. Chatman 1990: 7; Veits, Wilde & Sachs-Hombach 2020: 10–11; Weixler 2020: 59–60; zur Kritik dieser Unterscheidung vgl. v.a. Speidel 2013: 187; Speidel 2018b: 41–53; Speidel 2020: 170.

11 Vgl. Steiner 1988: 9; Hausken 2004: 393–397; Ryan 2005: 1–3; Huck 2009: 204; Speidel 2018a: 77; Speidel 2018b: 3, 9; Brockmeier 2012: 454; Veits 2020: 125–126 m. Anm. 1. So verbleiben selbst

den Kunst- und Bildwissenschaften, die die Erzählfähigkeit von Bildern aus ihrer eigenen disziplinären Tradition heraus nach wie vor unhinterfragt voraussetzten, mangelndes narratologisches Theoriebewusstsein vorgeworfen.[12] Andererseits wird unter impliziter oder expliziter Bezugnahme auf Lessing argumentiert, dass die narrative Kohärenz[13] von Bildern oder zumindest einiger Typen von Bildern im Vergleich zum linear-sequentiellen textuellen Erzählen von zumindest anderer Art und womöglich auch defizitär[14] sei. So wurde, entlang der Dichotomie zwischen ‚fabula' und ‚sujet' bzw. ‚histoire' und ‚récit' (bzw. ‚discours'),[15] u.a. von Seymor Chatman, darauf verwiesen, dass es Bildern gegenüber Texten auf der Diskurs- bzw. Präsentationsebene (=> ‚Erzählzeit'[16]) an der geordneten Steuerung des rezipierendenseitigen Zugangs zu den dargestellten Bildelementen und damit an ‚doppelter Zeitlichkeit' fehle: „By ‚text' I shall mean any communication that *temporally* [Kursive S.C.] controls its reception by the audience. Thus texts differ from [...] (non-narrative) paintings [...], which do not regulate the temporal flow or spatial direction of the audience's perception".[17]

Tatsächlich war und ist bei der Frage, ob und wie[18] welche Art (s.u. Abschnitt 2) von unbewegten Einzelbildern ‚narrativ' sein können und unter welchen Voraussetzungen sie

---

intermedial ausgerichtete Ansätze mit Transzendierungsabsicht wie der von Werner Wolf (2003: 181) dem zu transzendierenden „exclusively literary view" zumindest als Startpunkt verbunden. Wolf 2011: 174 beharrt zudem auf dem prototypischen „*par excellence* [Kursive W.W.]" Status verbaler Narrative und der literarischen Narratologie, während Ryan 2004a: 11 von Sprache als „the native tongue of storytelling" spricht. Zur Kritik s.u. Abschnitt 3.

12 Gern zitiert wird Wendy Steiner 1988: 2: „the general art-historical use of the term ‚narrative' seems incomprehensible to literary scholars"; ähnlich Steiner 1988: 8–9 und Steiner 2004: 146. Zur Diskussion vgl. Speidel 2013: 174–175; Speidel 2018a: 95; Speidel 2018b: 23; Speidel 2020: 161–165; Weixler 2020: 60, jeweils mit weiteren Belegen.

13 Im Sinne des als ‚Kontiguität' bekannten Narrativitätskriteriums einer inhaltlichen Geschlossenheit, vgl. etwa Martínez 2017: 2–3; s.a. Weixler 2020: 66–68 sowie Abschnitt 2 unten.

14 Vgl. etwa Wolf 2003: 189: „lack of narrative precision" bzw. 192: „natural incompleteness" zum *monochronen* Einzelbild (zur Terminologie s.u. Abschnitt 2).

15 Zusammenfassend mit Wellek & Warren 2019 [1942]: 194 der Unterschied zwischen „the temporal-causal sequence which is, however it may be told, the ‚story' or story-stuff [...,] an abstraction from the ‚raw materials'" und „the ‚narrative structure' [of] the artistically ordered presentation"; vgl. zur Terminologie dieser Unterscheidungen den Überblick bei Gerald Moers, Egyptological narratology as *historical narratology*, in diesem Band: Abschnitt 1.

16 Im Gegensatz zur ‚erzählten Zeit', vgl. erstmals Müller 1974 [1946]: 247–268; s.a. Chatman 1978: 62–63 („discourse-time" vs. „story-time") und Weixler 2020: 70–75.

17 Chatman 1990: 7 mit Bezug auf Lessing 1839 [1766]; s.a. Rimmon-Kenan 2006: passim, bes. 16 oder Kafalenos 2006: 159; zur eingehenden Kritik vgl. Speidel 2013: bes. 179–189; s.a. Speidel 2018b: 34–37, 41–53, 62–64, jeweils mit relevanter weiterer Literatur. In seiner Basisdefinition „Was ist Erzählen" reflektiert Matías Martínez (2017: 3) die geöffnete Diskussion folgendermaßen: „Wenn man aber auch Einzelbildern, Skulpturen u.a. narratives Potential zubilligen möchte, dann ist Geschehensdarstellung auch ohne doppelte Zeitlichkeit möglich." Obwohl Martínez also das Kriterium der ‚doppelten Zeitlichkeit' als nicht Bild-sensitiv ausscheidet, verbleibt er mit seinem Ansatz im Rahmen der Standardwahrnehmung.

18 Zur Unterscheidung von *ob* und *wie* vgl. bes. Speidel 2020: 169–177.

sogar als vollwertige und „autonome“[19] ‚Erzählungen‘ – „*the representation of a story proper* [Kursive W.W.]“[20] – klassifiziert werden können,[21] die Diskussion der Fähigkeit von Bildwerken zur gesteuerten Präsentation und Repräsentation von *Zeitlichkeit* als einem wesentlichen Narrativitätskriterium („vital narrative element of time“) zentral.[22] Ausgangspunkt der meisten diesbezüglichen Diskussionen ist die medial bedingte Differenz von Zeichen und Zeichenorganisation zwischen verbalen und bildlichen Artefakten (s.o.). Auch noch nach *postklassischen* und transmedial ausgerichteten Neubestimmungsversuchen der narrativen Vermittlungsinstanz (originär der/die ‚Erzähler*in‘) z.B. als „transmitting agency“[23] wird diese Differenz gern auf den Unterschied zwischen zwei Formen der narrativen Vermittlung abgebildet: dem diegetisch-verbalen ‚Erzählen‘ und dem mimetisch-bildlichen ‚Zeigen‘.[24] Daran gekoppelt bleiben – neben dem Hinweis auf die mangelnde Steuerung der Bildrezeption durch eine „ontologisch“[25] von der im Bild repräsentierten Zeit zu unterscheidenden Präsentationszeit (s.o.) – vielfach die Wahrnehmungen einer „weitgehenden A-Temporalität“ von Bildern,[26] insofern diese entweder Zeit „nicht eigentlich“ (re-)präsentieren, sondern nur „suggerieren“ können,[27] oder sie nicht in der Zeit wahrgenommen werden, da sie Betrachtenden all ihre Informationen gleichzeitig und auf einmal[28] – analog und im Raum[29] – präsentieren, und folgerichtig das Präsentierte auch nur als Gleichzeitiges präsentieren.[30] Bilder offerieren somit nur „synchrone Zustandshaftigkeit“, nicht aber eine „diachrone Zustandsfolge“,[31] sodass zumindest manche Arten von Einzelbildern keine Erzählungen sein können, sondern nur „narrative Implikationen“[32] haben oder bestenfalls „narrationsindizierende“[33] Eigenschaften aufweisen. Ferner können,

19 Vgl. etwa Ryan 2004a: 14 und Hühn 2015: 354–356 im Rahmen der Unterscheidung zwischen eigenständigen und „illustrativen“ Bildern, s.u. Abschnitt 2.

20 Wolf 2003: 180.

21 Vgl. auch die Unterscheidung von „being a narrative“ und „possessing narrativity“ bzw. „having narrativity“ bei Ryan 2004a: 9–10 und Ryan 2005: 6–7.

22 Vgl. u.a. Wolf 2003: passim, bes. 180, 189–193 (Zitat: 189) sowie Steiner 2004: 149: „[T]emporal sequence […] is the single most essential narrative trait. […] The insistence on temporality is part of every definition of narrative, regardless of its philosophical orientation“; s.a. Speidel 2013; Speidel 2018b: esp. 24–31, 41–54.

23 Rimmon-Kenan 2006: 16; s.a. Speidel 2013 und Speidel 2018b: 21–22 mit weiterer Literatur sowie Weixler 2020: 69 mit anderer Perspektivierung.

24 Hühn 2015: 349–350. Zum Gegensatz von ‚telling‘ und ‚showing’ vgl. Klauk & Köppe 2014. S.a. Rogner 2022: 34 m. Anm. 239.

25 Rimmon-Kenan 2006: 16.

26 So etwa Wolf 2002: 54.

27 Wolf 2003: 192.

28 Kafalenos 2006: 230: „The information a painting offers is presented in its entirety all at once“.

29 Schaeffer 2001: 13: „L’image fixe ne peut […] représenter [séquences événementelles] qu’un ‘donnant à voir’ comme un ensemble d’états de fait à cooccurrence spatiale“.

30 Zur Diskussion des letztgenannten Aspekts vgl. Speidel 2018b: 41–44 mit weiterer Literatur.

31 So die einschlägige Formulierung bei Titzmann 1990: 379.

32 Kafalenos 1996: 56.

33 Wolf 2002: 96.

so heißt es, manche Typen von Bildern, anders als Texterzählungen, auch keine Spannung erzeugen.[34]

2 Typen von Einzelbildern und ihre Narrativität: Das *monochrone* Einzelbild als Problemfall in der klassischen transmedialen Bildnarratologie

Unter Rückgriff auf eine kürzlich von Klaus Speidel vorgeschlagene Terminologie lassen sich in Hinsicht auf die über ihre interne Ordnung vermittelte (Re-)Präsentation von Temporalität grundsätzlich vier Typen unbewegter Einzelbilder unterscheiden. Dabei bedarf es zur eindeutigen Ansprache eines Einzelbildes als Vertreter eines der vier Typen im konkreten Kontext in der Regel eines zusätzlichen, historisch und kulturell präfigurierten Vorwissens über die im Bild impliziten Darstellungs- und Wahrnehmungskonventionen.[35] (1) *Achrone* Einzelbilder wie z.B. Piktogramme[36] sind in keinerlei Hinsicht mit Zeit befasst, sie zeigen keinen Moment in der Zeit. (2) Die in dieser Studie thematischen *monochronen* Einzelbilder zeigen genau einen Moment in der Zeit.[37] (3) *Polychrone* Einzelbilder zeigen mehrere Momente in der Zeit, die diskret über die Bildfläche verteilt, synthetisch verdichtet, oder überlagernd oder zyklisch angeordnet sein können.[38] (4) *Äonochrone* Einzelbilder zeigen einen stetig wiederkehrenden oder auf Dauer gestellten Moment in (und wohl auch jenseits) der Zeit, der synthetisch verdichtet oder zyklisch dargestellt sein kann. Dazu kommen Bildreihen bzw. Bildserien, die für den hiesigen Diskussionszusammenhang nur

34 So etwa Werner Wolfs Ansicht zur „deficiency of teleology" auf der Diskursebene monochroner Einzelbilder, vgl. Wolf 2003: 187–188, 192 (Zitat); s.a. Wolf 2002: 55.

35 Speidel 2018b: 24–31 mit Verweis auf ältere Terminologien. Zu einer ägyptologischen Kurzkritik an diesem Modell vgl. Rogner 2022: 30 m. Anm. 204. Die dort von Frederik Rogner angebotene Lesart von Reuter 2003, dass dieser die kunstwissenschaftliche Diskussion von der Dichotomie zwischen *monochronen* und *polychronen* Bildern für überdeterminiert halte, kann ich nicht teilen. Reuter verweist lediglich auf die generelle kunstwissenschaftliche Diskussion der sich seit der Renaissance verändernden Darstellungskonventionen von Zeitlichkeit, vgl. Reuter 2003: 65–69, bes. 66: „Zeit gehörte nicht mehr zum Wesen der bildenden Kunst"; s.a. Abschnitt 3 unten.

36 Speidel 2018b: 26; s.a. Wilde 2020: 106–110 zur Rolle von selbstreferentiellen Piktogrammen als nunmehr „äußerste Position visueller Narrativität" (so die klassische Formulierung von Kibédi Varga 1990: 363, allerdings zum monochronen Einzelbild). Wildes Einschätzung basiert auf seinem Konzept von „Basisnarrativität", welche Bildern, die nicht Piktogramme sind, grundsätzlich eigne, s.u. Abschnitt 3.

37 Weitere Bezeichnungen jenseits der bei Speidel 2018b: 24–31 diskutierten sind ‚monoszenisches (Einzel)Bild' (Kibédi Varga 1990: 360, 361, 363), ‚image fixe unique à scène unique' (Schaeffer 2001: 21), ‚Monophaseneinzelbild' (Wolf 2002: 55, 96 mit weiterer Literatur), ‚single still picture' (Speidel 2013) oder ‚single-phase picture' (Schöttler 2016: 167); s.a. Speidel 2018a: 81 m. Anm. 4.

38 Weitere Bezeichnungen jenseits der bei Speidel 2018b: 24–31 diskutierten sind ‚(integriertes) pluriszenisches (Einzel)Bild' (Kibédi Varga 1990: 360, 361, Schaeffer 2001: passim: ‚image à scènes multiples'), ‚Mehrphasenbild' bzw. ‚Polyphaseneinzelbild' (Wolf 2002: 55, 96 mit weiterer Literatur), oder, wie generell in der Kunstgeschichte ‚Simultanbild' (vgl. etwa Blümel 2013: bes. 40). s.a. Speidel 2018a: 81 m. Anm. 4.

bedingt relevant sind und daher, von einzelnen Bemerkungen abgesehen, weitestgehend außer Acht gelassen werden.

Diesen Temporalität auf je unterschiedliche Weise repräsentierenden Typen von Einzelbildern wird nun endsprechende ‚Narrativität' in je unterschiedlichem Ausmaß zugestanden. Dies geschieht in der Regel einerseits in Abhängigkeit von der jeweilig in Anschlag gebrachten Definition von ‚Erzählung' auf Basis von als ‚Narratemen' oder ‚Narremen' bezeichneten notwendigen und fakultativen Narrativitätskriterien.[39] Matías Martínez etwa definiert eine Erzählung als „Geschehensdarstellung + x". Notwendige Kriterien für die Geschehensdarstellung sind *Konkretheit* (ein *singuläres* Geschehen), *Temporalität* (das Geschehen besteht aus Ereignissen, die eine *chronologische Ordnung* mit ‚vorher' und ‚nachher' darstellen) und *Kontiguität* (neben der chronologischen Ordnung besteht auch ein temporaler, räumlicher und kausaler *Zusammenhang* zwischen den dargestellten Ereignissen).[40] Diese von Martínez genannten notwendigen Kriterien decken sich weitestgehend mit einer Definition von Erzählung von Marie-Laure Ryan, die besonders in transmedial orientierten narratologischen Diskussionen häufig zitiert wird: eine Erzählung ist die Präsentation (1) einer Welt mit Charakteren und Objekten (=> Martínez: Konkretheit), in der es (2) zu Veränderungen mit Ereignischarakter kommt (=> Martínez: Temporalität), die sich (3) u.a. kausal relationieren und erklären lassen (=> Martínez: Kontiguität).[41] Je nach Vorhandensein dieser als ‚Narrateme' oder ‚Narreme' bezeichneten Narrativitätskriterien wird andererseits mit Referenz auf ein weithin akzeptiertes Diktum von Gerald Prince auf die generellen „Skalierbarkeit"[42] von ‚Narrativität' zwischen den Polen von „being a narrative" und „possessing narrativity"[43] verwiesen. Dabei wird das jeweilige Potential der unterschiedlichen Typen von Einzelbildern, selbständig, autonom und daher „werkseitig"[44] eine bisher unbekannte ‚Geschichte' erzählen zu können, bestenfalls kontrovers diskutiert. Während, von wenigen Ausnahmen abgesehen,[45] Serialität als hinreichende Bedingung für die Fähigkeit von Bildern angesetzt wird, eine autonome Geschichte erzählen zu können,[46] ist der Kreis derer, die diese Fähigkeit auch für die hier mit

39 Prinzipiell gibt es nach wie vor keine allseitig anerkannte kriterienbasierte Definition von ‚Erzählung', vgl. Speidel 2018b: 16: „It would take a book-length text to enumerate and comment the definitions of narrative on the market, but [...] scholarly appreciation of the narrative potential of pictures often depends more on (the kinds of) definitions embraced than on the pictures themselves and the way they were traditionally experienced".

40 Martínez 2017: 2–6. Dazu kommen als fakultative „Narrateme" u.a. *doppelte* Zeitlichkeit, Vermittlungsinstanz, Kausalität, Intentionalität, Ganzheit, Ereignishaftigkeit, Experientiality, Tellability, und konversationelle Zugzwänge.

41 Vgl. z.B. Ryan 2004a: 8–9 u. Ryan 2005: 4; s.a. Ryan 2014: Abschnitt 17 in Kap. 3.3; zur Rezeption dieser Definition vgl. etwa Prince 1999: 46; Hühn 2015: 349; Wilde 2020: 100–101.

42 Zum „scalar view of narrativity" vgl. Prince 1999: bes. 46, mit weiterer Literatur; vgl. dazu auch Wolf 2003: 181; Speidel 2018a: 88; Speidel 2018b: 5.

43 Vgl. nochmals Ryan 2004a: 9–10 und Ryan 2005: 6–7.

44 So die deutsche Formulierung u.a. bei Wolf 2002: 96.

45 Referenzen bei Speidel 2018a: 81–82; zur weiteren Diskussion vgl. auch Ryan 2005: 2–3.

46 Klassisch etwa Titzmann 1990: 379: „Wo Bildpropositionen nur synchrone Zustandshaftigkeit abbilden können und somit dem Bild (*außer in der Bildserie* [Kursive G.M.]) keine Temporalisierung und deshalb auch keine Narrativisierung möglich ist, können Textpropositionen auch diachrone

Klaus Speidel als *polychron* angesprochenen Einzelbilder ansetzen, schon kleiner.[47] Und nur die wenigsten Forschenden sind der Ansicht, dass die in der vorliegenden Studie thematischen *monochronen* Einzelbilder selbständig bzw. ‚werkseitig' eine unbekannte Geschichte erzählen können[48] und begründen dies in der Regel mit der mangelnden Fähigkeit dieses Bildtyps, Zeit und insbesondere Veränderung in der Zeit darstellen zu können (s.o. Abschnitt 1). Die jeweilige Anzahl an Forschenden, die den genannten Bildtypen selbständige Erzählfähigkeit zubilligen oder eben nicht, ist dabei wiederum verhältnismäßig gut abbildbar auf das bereits oben angesprochene Diktum einer prinzipiellen ‚Skalierbarkeit werkseitiger Narrativität', wie sie z.B. von Werner Wolf im Rahmen seiner Überlegungen zum narrativen Potential verschiedener Medien vorgeschlagen worden ist. Dort findet sich der in hiesigem Beitrag thematische Typ des *monochronen* Einzelbildes (Wolf: „Monophaseneinzelbild"), den die wenigsten Forschenden für potentiell selbständig narrativ halten, zwischen „narrationsindizierend" und „quasinarrativ" am rechten, kaum noch als ‚werkseitig' narrativ eingestuften Rand der Skala.

Wenn nun oben wie auch in Abb. 1 vom Konzept ‚werkseitiger Narrativität' die Rede war, welches an der von der *klassischen* Narratologie gepflegten und vor allem am Kriterium der ‚doppelten Zeitlichkeit' hängenden textzentrierten Idealvorstellung von ‚Narrativität' orientiert ist, kommt mit dem Stichwort der „rezipientenseitig nötigen Narrativierung" ein Komplex an Parametern ins Spiel, welcher sich der Kontrolle von rein kriteriologisch ausgerichteten Standardefinitionen wie denen der *klassischen* Textnarratologie weitestgehend entzieht und die Menge potentiell ‚narrativer' Artefakte ebenso potentiell unendlich erweitern kann.

Dieser Komplex speist sich einerseits aus der kunstwissenschaftlichen Perspektivierung der literaturwissenschaftlichen Wirkungs- und Rezeptionsästhetik (‚reader-response criticism'). Diese untersucht und rekonstruiert in Hinsicht auf die vom jeweiligen Artefakt präsentierte und gesteuerte Auswahl an dargestellten und nicht dargestellten Informationen, wie die aus der Auswahl des Präsentierten resultierenden ‚Leer-' oder ‚Unbestimmtheitsstellen' durch die dafür unabdingbare Rezipierendenbeteiligung im Rahmen der Sinnkonstitution künstlerischer Artefakte aufgefüllt werden und wie ein solcher

---

Zustandsfolgen abbilden". In Bezug auf Bildserien v.a. im bewegten cinematographischen Modus vgl. etwa Chatman 1990, Rimmon-Kenan 2006: 10–11, 16 sowie Schaeffer 2001: 13 (obgleich er ebd. 14 den Terminus Technicus ‚Erzählung' (‚narration') für verbale Artefakte reserviert) u. 27: „il faut partir du principe que l'image fixe ne peut montrer la sucession temporelle que sous la forme d'une coprésence ou d'une contiguïté spatiales[sic]: contiguïté spatiale dans le cas de la série, coprésence spatiale dans le cas de l'image à scènes multiples".

47 Vgl. etwa Kibédi Varga 1990: 363, der mit seiner klassischen Formulierung zum „monoszenischen Einzelbild [als] die äußerste Position visueller Narrativität" für diesen Bildtypus in Frage stellt, „ob in diesen Fällen noch immer eine vom Betrachter perzipierbare *narratio* dargestellt wird [Kursive A.K.V]"; s.a. Wolf 2002: 55–57, 73, 92; Wolf 2003: passim, bes. 193; Wolf 2011: 150; Steiner 2004; Schöttler 2016: 178–179.

48 Neben Ranta 2013: 10–11 (ähnlich, aber weniger pointiert und aus kognitiv-rezeptionsorientierter Perspektive auch schon Ranta 2011: letzter Absatz) und Hühn 2015 ist dies vor allem Klaus Speidel, vgl. Speidel 2013; Speidel 2018a; Speidel 2018b; Speidel 2020.

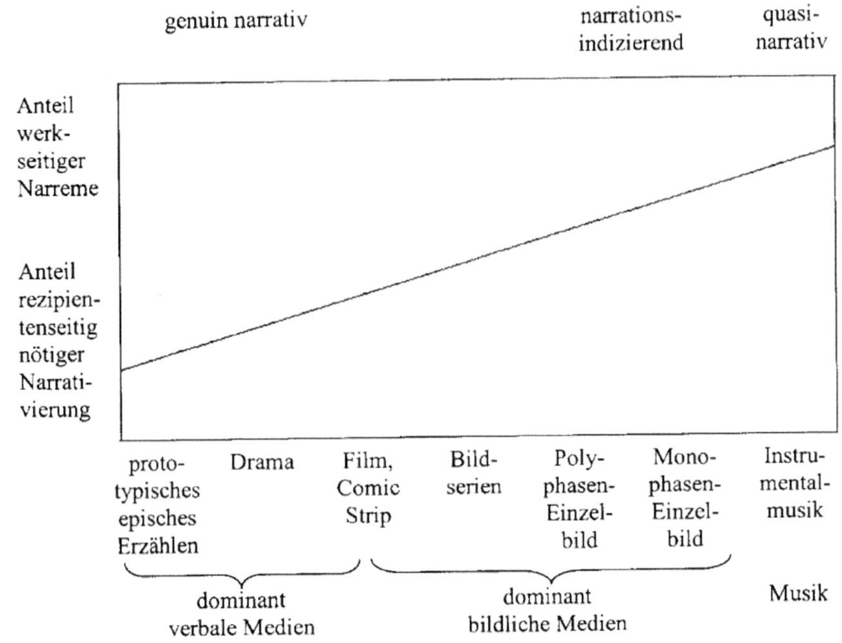

Abb. 1 | „Abnahme von Narrativität in Abhängigkeit vom werkseitigen Potential unterschiedlicher Medien" (Wolf 2002: 96)

Rezeptionsvorgang artefaktseitig gesteuert wird.[49] In diesem Zusammenhang wird in der kunstwissenschaftlichen Bildnarratologie in erster Linie die Frage der Nutzung von *monochronen* Einzelbildern als *Illustrationen* diskutiert. In dieser „kulturphilologischen" Wahrnehmung von Bildern als „bloßes Vehikel […] dominante[r] Erzähltexte"[50] sind bildliche Illustrationen nichts außer (Teil-)Visualisierungen von vorgängigen verbalen Erzählungen bzw. Prätexten wie z.B. religiösen und mythologischen Geschichten, welche den kontextspezifisch kompetenten Bildbetrachtenden bekannt sind. Als Illustrationen oder, wie Werner Wolf formuliert, „intermedial transposition of (a part of) a verbal story"[51] verwendete Bilder fordern die Betrachtenden zur rezipierendenseitigen Narrativierung des niemals die gesamte Geschichte (‚fabula'/‚histoire') zeigenden Bildobjektes auf. Sie sind aus dieser Perspektive aber keine eigenständigen Erzählungen, deren Narrativität ausschließlich werkseitig angelegt wäre.[52]

49 Für die literaturwissenschaftliche Ausgangssituation vgl. etwa die Klassiker von Umberto Eco (1979) und Wolfgang Iser (1994 [1976]). Für die kunstwissenschaftliche Adaption vgl. vor allem die Pionierarbeit von Wolfgang Kemp (1987; 1989; 1992; 1996); s.a. Weixler 2019: 91–93, 99–101, und Wilde 2020: 95–96, jeweils mit weiterer Literatur.

50 So Frank & Frank 1999: 44.

51 Wolf 2011: 152.

52 Kibédi Varga 1990: 364 spricht diesbezüglich etwa von der „Sekundarität dieser visuellen *narratio* [Kursive: A.K.V.]"; Ryan 2004b: 139 beschreibt dies als den „illustrative mode"; vgl. auch Schaeffer 2001: 12–13; zur Kritik vgl. Frank & Frank 1999: 42–45 oder Speidel 2018b: 22–23 und

Wenn es bei der Frage der Rezipierendenbeteiligung nicht nur, wie bei der Verwendung von Bildern als *Illustrationen* im gerade erläuterten Verständnis, um bekannte konkrete Prätexte geht, ist die text- und bildwissenschaftliche Rezeptionsästhetik zudem grundsätzlich anschlussfähig an die *kognitive* Narratologie. Diese untersucht das wechselseitige Verhältnis von Kognition und Erzählen im weitesten möglichen Sinn und fragt unter anderem vereinfacht formuliert, ob „wir narrative Lebewesen [sind]?",[53] d.h. also ob und wie mentale Prozesse als Ermöglichungsbedingung narrativer Erfahrung oder ob und wie die narrative Struktur mentaler Prozesse als eine Grundbedingung menschlichen Weltverstehens verstanden werden können.[54] Ein prominenterer Zweig der kognitiven Narratologie befasst sich mit der auch evolutionsbiologisch[55] herleitbaren menschlichen Fähigkeit zur Informationsverarbeitung auf Basis von schematisch strukturierten und konventionalisierten (individuellen wie kollektiven und historisch differenten) Wissensbeständen, die bei Aktivierung allgemeiner menschlicher Erfahrungen als ‚Schemata', bei stereotypisierten Situationswahrnehmungen als ‚Frames' sowie bei vorab festgelegten stereotypen Handlungssequenzen als ‚Skripte' bezeichnet werden.[56] Diese je kulturspezifisch erwartungsbesetzten Weltwissensbestände (z.B. über Menschen, Objekte, Artefaktgattungen wie literarische Genres samt spezifischen Plotstrukturen, Handlungssituationen, u.v.m., darunter auch die im Folgenden besonders relevanten Bewegungs- oder Motorschemata,[57] s.u. Abschnitt 4.2.3) werden im Rezeptionsprozess aus dem Gedächtnis aktiviert und steuern die Integration der artefaktseitig präsentierten Informationen zu einer mentalen Simulation, dem sog. „Situationsmodell". Bei diesem Situationsmodell handelt es sich um den rezipierendenseitigen Entwurf einer aktuell und situativ validen Artefaktbedeutung, in welchem die ‚Leerstellen' der vom Artefakt nicht präsentierten Informationen durch Inferenz mit konventionalisiertem Weltwissen aufgefüllt werden.[58]

Eine derartig kognitionsnarratologisch erweiterte und damit rezeptionsbasierte Bestimmung von Narrativität hat weitreichende Implikationen für die Frage, ob und unter welchen Bedingungen Objekte wie z.B. *monochrone* Einzelbilder ihre Rezeption als eigenständige Erzählung artefaktseitig steuern oder ob sie als nur narrationsindizierend interpretiert werden können. Grundsätzlich besteht die Möglichkeit, das solche Bilder

---

37–41; interessant ist der Hinweis von Kurt Weitzmann 1957: 83 („thus the art of storytelling in pictures is inextrinsically linked with the history of book-illumination") auf die möglicherweise mediengeschichtliche Bedingung dieser Wahrnehmung in der direkten Nähe von visueller Narration und Buchillumination, s. dazu auch Steiner 2004: 153.

53 Breithaupt 2022: 11.

54 Vgl. etwa Herman 2013, Wege 2017 oder Schneider 2018 mit jeweils weiterer Literatur auch zu den Binnendifferenzierungen des weiten Feldes.

55 Wege 2017: bes. 346–347, 350; Schneider 2018: 583–584.

56 Wege 2017: 350–351; Hühn 2015: 352; Schneider 2018: 586–587. In Monika Fluderniks *Natural Narratology* ist Erzählen selbst bereits ein kognitiver (Meta-)Frame: „the entire frame of storytelling itself operates as a cognitively grounded frame" (Fludernik 1996: 11); vgl. auch Wolf 2002: 28–29; Wolf 2003: 181; Herman 2013, Abschnitt 18.

57 Vgl. dazu Veits 2020: 134–142.

58 Vgl., besonders zum „Situationsmodell", konzise Wege 2017: 349–350 und Schneider 2018: 587, beide mit weiterführender relevanter Literatur.

von Betrachtenden unter Rückgriff auf kulturell präfigurierte Schemata, Frames oder Story-Skripts selbst dann als Geschichten aufgefasst werden, wenn die Bilder nicht als Illustrationen zu vorgängig bekannten Geschichten dienen und sie stattdessen auf einen einzigen, besonders relevanten Moment eines kognitiv gespeicherten Schemas, Frames oder Skripts referieren.[59] Im extremsten Fall sind es dann übereifrige Rezipierende, die, sofern historisch und kulturell je unterschiedlich konventionalisierte Praxen bestehen, Bilder als Geschichten interpretieren zu *können*, jederzeit in der Lage sind, eine Geschichte zu erfinden auf Basis eines Bildes, welches werkseitig selbst eigentlich keine Geschichte vorhält.[60] Und auch ganz grundsätzlich ist bei Einnahme einer kognitiv-narratalogischen Perspektive die Menge von Artefakten, die als Erzählungen wahrgenommen werden können, kaum mehr kriteriologisch zu kontrollieren und potenziert sich ins Unbestimmbare. So treten neben Bilderzählungen auch Objekterzählungen nichtbildlicher Artefakte und sogar natürlicher Objekte, die unter konventionalisierten kulturellen Bedingungen narrative Strukturen repräsentieren können und auf der Basis der durch sie bei den Rezipierenden aktivierten Schemata, Frames und Skripte (s.o.) als Geschichten interpretierbar werden.[61]

Dieser kognitionsnarratologisch bedingte Zuwachs an Möglichkeiten wird nun selbst in transmedial ausgerichteten Zugängen der postklassischen Narratologie als problematisch wahrgenommen, da er die Gefahr eines Verlusts der definitorischen Kontrolle darüber impliziert, unter welchen Bedingungen ein Artefakt nicht nur als narrationsindizierend eingestuft werden kann, sondern auch selbständig bzw. ‚werkseitig' eine autonome Geschichte vorhält. Deswegen wird, in der Regel wiederum unter Hinweis auf das textnarratologisch basierte Kriterium der ‚doppelten Zeitlichkeit' (s.o. Abschnitt 1) auf engeren und implizit nach wie vor textzentrierten Definitionen von Narrativität beharrt: „By narrowing the scope of ‚narrative', I am trying to defend the term against being emptied of all semantic content: if everthing is narrative, nothing is".[62]

3 Eine bildtheoretische Alternativperspektive zur klassischen transmedialen Bildnarratologie

Klaus Speidel hat nun in jüngster Zeit mehrfach auf die inhärente Problematik solcher *strikt* theorie- und kriteriengeleiteter Definitionen von ‚Erzählung' und ‚Narrativität' hingewiesen.[63] So konstatiert er, dass selbst transmedial orientierte Ansätze noch häufig in

59 Wolf 2003: 191; Speidel 2018a: 97; Speidel 2018b: 39–40; Speidel 2020: 174–175.

60 Vgl. etwa Speidel 2018b: 22–24.

61 Vgl. etwa Ranta 2011: Abschnitt 3 Ende.

62 Rimmon-Kenan 2006: 17. Im Kontext bezeichnet „narrative" die Eigenschaft „Erzählung sein" im Unterschied zu dem, was Rimmon-Kenan als „narrative elements in[..] formations that I would not call ‚a narrative'" nennt. S.a. Speidel 2018a: 79; Speidel 2018b: 71; Speidel 2020: 161–162, jeweils mit weiteren Referenzen.

63 Speidel 2018a: 96: „rather than the criteria themselves, it is particulary narrow ways of interpreting them that narratology has to give up".

einer Form von „Medienblindheit“[64] operieren, insofern sie implizit an aus verbalen und textuellen Artefakten gewonnenen und für paradigmatisch gehaltenen Kriterien wie z.B. dem der ‚doppelten Zeitlichkeit‘ festhalten und diese „revisionär“ und „präskriptiv“[65] zur Definition von ‚Erzählung‘ und ‚Narrativität‘ auch in anderen als verbalen Medien einsetzen. Er konnte z.B. zeigen, dass es sich bei der auf Lessing zurückgehenden Unterscheidung zwischen ‚Zeit-‘ und ‚Raumkünsten‘ (und dem daraus narratologisch abgeleiteten, für notwendig gehaltenen Narrativitätskriterium der ‚doppelten Zeitlichkeit‘, s.o.) schon bei deren Einführung um ein normativ konventionalisiertes Geschmacksurteil handelte, dass sich auf die frühneuzeitlicher Veränderung der Darstellungs- und Wahrnehmungsgewohnheiten von Zeitlichkeit in Einzelbildern zurückführen lässt.[66] So kamen die u.a. im Mittelalter noch sehr geläufigen *polychronen* Einzelbilder, die *mehrere* Zeitmomente in *einem* Bild darstellen, durch die Einführung der Zentralperspektive und der damit verbundenen realistischen Illusion in der Renaissance zunehmend außer Mode.[67] Dementsprechend wurden nun die keinesfalls natürlicheren *monochronen* Einzelbilder favorisiert, und deren Beschränkung auf die Darstellung nur *eines* Momentes in der Zeit wurde in der Folge von narratologischer Seite dahingehend verallgemeinert und naturalisiert, dass Einzelbilder Zeitlichkeit grundsätzlich nicht darstellen und sie deswegen auch nicht erzählen können (s.o. Abschnitte 1 u. 2). Im wissenschaftlichen Experiment mit Laien, die viel häufiger als Narratolg*innen geneigt sind, Artefakten den Status einer ‚Geschichte‘ zuzuerkennen, konnte Klaus Speidel das aus klassisch-narratologischer Perspektive als notwendig erachtete Narrativitätskriterium der ‚doppelten Zeitlichkeit‘ tatsächlich als ausschließlich theoriegeleitet und somit überflüssig ausscheiden: „If all goes well, it will soon be little more than a reminder of the kind of revisionary narratology that media-blindness can lead to“.[68]

So, wie sich die heutige Präferenz für die „photographische Konvention“[69] der Darstellung nur eines einzigen Moments im *monochronen* Einzelbild als eine zementierte historische Zufälligkeit analysieren lässt, aus der durch narratologische Theoriebildung durchaus fragwürdige Grundannahmen zur Narrativität von Bildern generalisiert und naturalisiert

64 Speidel 2018a: 77 und Speidel 2020: 176 mit Verweis auf Liv Hausken 2004: 392–393, die zwischen „totaler“ und „nonchalanter“ Medienblindheit unterscheidet. Totale Medienblindheit wird dadurch definiert, dass die Tatsache, „that the medium itself matters is simply neglected, but at the same time a particular medium is silently presumed. In short, theories that are seemingly independent of the medium are usually implicitly tied to a particular medium […]. Nonchalant blindness is most readily apparent in those approaches that uncritically borrow ideas from medium-specific or medium-sensitive studies of media other than the medium under consideration“. Vgl. dazu auch Veits 2020: 125. Weixler 2020: 68 spricht diesbezüglich von einem „medialen Bias“.

65 Speidel 2018a: 77.

66 Speidel 2013: 179–186, bes. 182–183. Weitere Alternativinterpretationen dessen, worum es Lessing bei seiner Unterscheidung ging, finden sich in Weixler 2020: 60–61.

67 Speidel 2013: 181–182; Speidel 2018b: 49–50 u. 64; Steiner 1988: 2 spricht von der „Renaissance proscription against temporal disunity“; ähnlich auch Reuter 2003: 65–69, bes. 66: „Zeit gehörte nicht mehr zum Wesen der bildenden Kunst“, vgl. ferner Wolf 2002: 56, Wolf 2003: 190; zuletzt Boehm 2018: 40–41.

68 Speidel 2013; Speidel 2018a: 89–97 (Zitat: 96); Speidel 2020: 177–194.

69 Speidel 2013: 181.

wurden, muss auch das immer wieder aus der Idee der ‚Skalierbarkeit' von Narrativität (s.o. Abschnitt 2) hergeleitete Primat des *verbalen* Erzählens in Frage gestellt werden. Weder sind oral-mündliches Erzählen oder, häufig daran gekoppelt, fiktives schriftliches Erzählen „prototypisch" für das Erzählen schlechthin,[70] noch ist Sprache notwendigerweise „the native tongue of storytelling".[71] So sieht etwa H. Porter Abbot den evolutionären Grund des Erzählens bei frühe Hominiden im „mimetic narrative" einer „prelinguistic" „‚language' of enactment" [Anführungszeichen H.P.A.] mit einer eigenen „flexibility in the understanding and the management of time".[72]

Es ist also sinnvoll, Erzählen als eine grundsätzlich vom Medium der erzählenden Vermittlung unabhängige Praxis zu verstehen und deswegen z.B. mit Alexander Honold und Ralf Simon „die dem Erzählen zugewiesene Vorstellung linearer Sukzession", auf der die oben (Abschnitte 1 u. 2) diskutierte Negativeinschätzung beruht, (besonders monochrone) Bilder seien nur ‚mimetisch' und könnten daher im Gegensatz zu Texten keine ‚diachrone Zustandsfolge', sondern nur ‚synchrone Zustandshaftigkeit' präsentieren, „grundsätzlich zu hinterfragen".[73] Dies lässt sich sinnfällig anschließen an die Forderung von Gottfried Boehm, strikt zwischen den medialen Spezifika der simultanen ‚Bildzeit' und der Erzählzeit literarischer Texte zu unterscheiden[74] und stattdessen gegen Lessing von einer „Einsicht in die *Gleichursprünglichkeit* [Kursive G.B.] von Raum und Zeit im Bild" auszugehen, welche sich eben nicht dem Import „methodische[r] Modelle aus dem Bereich der procedierenden Sprache" verdankt.[75] In ähnlicher Art ist in Max Imdahls ‚Ikonik' die potentielle „Sinndichte" einer Bildstruktur „außerhalb der Malerei als unmittelbare Evidenzerfahrung unvorstellbar" und deswegen auch „sprachlich narrativ nicht sinnfällig zu formulieren".[76] Antonius Weixler spricht in diesem Zusammenhang vom *„piktorial erzählte[n] Mehr* [Kursive A.W.] von Bildern", welches „aus der Rückbindung dieser angereicherten Temporalität in die Simultanität des Bildes" resultiert.[77] Diese Aspekte lassen

70 So z. B. Wolf 2002: 34–37; s.o. Abb. 1, links.

71 So Ryan 2004a: 11; s.a. Ryan 2014: Kap. 3.3 und Hühn 2015: 350: „language can claim primacy as a mode of mediating narrative".

72 Abbott 2000: 248–250 (Zitate: 255, 249, 250); Mellmann 2017: 308 spricht in diesem Zusammenhang von einer „erfahrungsmimetischen Basisstruktur des Erzählens", die sie „(Proto-)Narration" nennt; zur Diskussion s.a. Brockmeier 2012: 443 („performed story worlds") und Meister 2018: 105; ethnographisches Material aus dem Paläolithikum scheint diese Ansicht zu bestätigen, vgl. Speidel 2018b: 8–11, bes. 10: „the first narratives may still have been based on pictures […] or on enactments or on hand gestures or something else".

73 Honold & Simon 2010: 9.

74 Boehm 1987.

75 Boehm 2018: 41. Eine im weitesten Sinn vergleichbare Wahrnehmung wurde ägyptologisch in aller Kürze in Hinsicht auf die ‚narrativen' Qualitäten von Grabmalereien der Amarna-Zeit formuliert, vgl. Meyers 1985: bes. 49–50: „Instead of the sequential development of a narrative, the theme is generated by the meaningful juxtaposition of images. And pictorial narrative, instead as being presented as a sequence of images, is derived from the interplay of relationships in which the underlying narrative process aspires to the space-logic rather than a time-logic alone and a structure of juxtaposition rather than linear sequences".

76 Imdahl 1996 [1980]: 93, 95.

77 Weixler 2020: 79 u. 82.

sich schließlich wiederum narratologisch perspektivieren in Hinsicht auf das von Lukas R. A. Wilde vorgeschlagene und kognitionspsychologisch hinterfütterte Konzept einer „Basisnarrativität", welche Bildern, die nicht Piktogramme sind, nach seiner Argumentation grundsätzlich eignet. Aufgrund der unhintergehbaren ‚ikonischen Differenz' zwischen Bildträger (dem materiellen Bild), Bildobjekt (der kognitiven Refiguration des Bildträgers durch Betrachtende) und Bildsujet (der kognitiven Konstruktion einer historisch, kulturell und intersubjektiv anschlussfähigen Bildbedeutung im Sinne des kognitionsnarratologischen Begriffs des ‚Situationsmodells' (s.o. Abschnitt 2) ist zur „piktorialen Kontextbildung" auf Rezipierendenseite notwendigerweise eine „dreidimensionale Rekonfiguration von Sinnesdaten zweidimensionaler Flächen" zu vollziehen. Diese konstituiert einerseits das Bildobjekt und führt andererseits zum Entwurf des Bildsujets als dem „Diegetisierungsrahmen einer möglichen Welt". In diesem Zusammenhang wird ein „diegetischer Kontext" erzeugt, der notwendigerweise narrative Grundeigenschaften besitzt, insofern Rezipierende durch Inferenz zwischen den im Bildraum dargestellten Charakteren und/oder Objekten „raumzeitliche, kausale und ontologische Relationen" konstruieren und damit Basiskriterien für das Vorliegen einer Erzählung in den z.B. von Martínes oder Ryan vorgeschlagenen Definitionen (‚Konkretheit', ‚ereignishafte Temporalität', ‚Kontiguität', s.o. Abschnitt 2) realisieren.[78] Alexander Honold und Ralf Simon haben in ähnlichem Kontext eine mögliche Schlussfolgerung aus Argumenten abgeleitet, die den hier kurz dargebrachten vergleichbar sind:

> „Der Grundansatz […] der strukturalistischen Narratologie [muss] neu überdacht werden […]. Die Erzählung trägt nach dieser Theorie eine semantische Opposition temporal aus. Sie *ist* die Temporalisierung eines basalen *a versus b* [Kursive A.H. & R.S.]. Aber es scheint, dass man […] eine andere These stark machen kann: in der genotextuellen Tiefe der Erzählung liegen nicht semantische Oppositionsbündel, sondern Bilder. Und die Erzählung ist nicht eine Vermittlung von Semantik, sondern eine Exegese von Bildlichkeit."[79]

Wichtig an dieser Einschätzung für die hier vorgelegte Fallstudie ist nun nicht die Ersetzung des Primats eines für die ‚Erzählung' für originär gehaltenen Mediums durch ein anderes, sondern das aus dieser Denkbewegung resultierende Plädoyer für eine umfassende transmediale Offenheit der narratologischen Diskussion. Denn aus kognitiver Perspektive ist es mit Jens Brockmeier tatsächlich wenig sinnvoll, definitions- und kriteriengeleitet davon auszugehen, „that there are universal components of […] ‚narrative' that exist prior to and independent from a culturally situated event" oder davon, dass es medienunabhängig

78 Wilde 2020: bes. 98–105 (Zitate: 104, 110, 100, 109). Vergleichbar wäre eine Position von Brigitte Scheer, die davon ausgeht, dass im Bild „der Zeithorizont mitgestaltet [wird], nicht nur das in ihm Erscheinende", und folgert: „das Präsentische, das durch die Gleichgegenwärtigkeit aller Bildelemente der herrschende Zeitmodus zu sein scheint, das Bild-*Sein* also, wird immer schon konterkariert von dem Bild-*Werden*, das heißt dem innerbildlichen Verweisungsgeschehen, durch das sich überhaupt erst das Bedeutungshafte des Bildlichen vollzieht", vgl. Scheer 2001/2002: 265 u. 266.

79 Honold & Simon 2010: 23.

so etwas geben könnte wie eine „abstract entity called ‚story'". Vielmehr ist Ausschau zu halten nach „concrete contexts of action and interaction in which a *linguistic or otherwise performed action sequence* [Kursive G.M.] is perceived as a story".[80]

4 Ein ägyptisches monochrones Einzelbild als Erzählung: eine Fallstudie

4.1 Die jüngste ägyptologische Ausgangslage

Auf Basis des in Abschnitt 3 diskutierten, grundsätzlich transmedial offenen, kognitionsnarratologisch angereicherten und angemessen kriteriengeleiteten Verständnisses von ‚Erzählung' soll im Folgenden dargelegt werden, dass es auch im pharaonischen Ägypten *monochrone* Einzelbilder gegeben hat, die aus ägyptischer Perspektive *selbständige Erzählungen* sind, als solche intendiert waren und als solche verstanden wurden, ohne dass es sich bei ihnen um Bilder handeln würde, die als ‚Illustrationen' zu bekannten historischen Ereignissen oder vorgängigen Texterzählungen fungieren.

Nadja Braun hat die Existenz solcher Bilder aus Ägypten in ihrer jüngst erschienenen Studie *Bilder erzählen: visuelle Narrativität im alten Ägypten*[81] aus grundsätzlichen Erwägungen prinzipiell ausgeschlossen: „monoszenische Einzelbilder [enthalten] streng genommen nicht einmal narrative Aussagen" und „können keine Erzählung zeigen, sondern nur eine Handlung".[82] Grund dieser Einschätzung ist das für ihre Studie aus der transmedial erweiterten klassischen Narratologie importierte Rahmenmodell (s.o. Abschnitt 2). Darin geht Braun auch für transmediale Kontexte vom prototypischen Primat des „komplexere[n] verbale[n] und episch-literarische[n] Erzählens" aus,[83] perpetuiert die Auffassung von der vermeintlichen – auch spannungslosen[84] –‚A-Temporalität' von Bildern (s.o. Abschnitt 1)[85] und übernimmt vor dem Hintergrund des Diktums von der ‚Ska-

80 Brockmeier 2012: 458.

81 Braun 2020. Kritische Auseinandersetzungen mit Brauns Studie finden sich bei Moers, Egyptological narratology as *historical narratology*, in diesem Band: Abschnitt 3 und v.a. bei Rogner 2021 und Rogner 2022: 19–21. Nadja Braun bietet in ihrer bedeutsamen Studie eine umfassende Diskussion sowohl der *klassisch-narratologische* Ausgangslage als auch der *transmedial* erweiterten Spielart der *klassischen Narratologie* (s.o. Abschnitt 2) und perspektiviert damit auch die gesamte bisherige ägyptologische Auseinandersetzung mit dem Gegenstand Bilderzählung. Aus diesem Grund muss Letztgenanntes im Kontext des hiesigen Beitrags nicht mehr systematisch aufgearbeitet werden (s. dazu auch Moers, Egyptological narratology as *historical narratology*, in diesem Band: Abschnitt 3), es bleibt bei sporadischen Erwähnungen, wo solche angemessen sind. Auch die umfangreiche, grundsätzlich rezeptionsorientierte und kognitionsnarratologisch anschlussfähige Studie von Frederik Rogner 2022 kann in der folgenden Diskussion weitgehend unberücksichtigt bleiben, insofern das *monochrone* Einzelbild an sich und als narratologischer Problemfall dort keine besondere Rolle spielt, da Rogner die ‚Narrativität' ägyptischer Bilder grundsätzlich definiert als deren „narrative Wirkung" bzw. „deren Potential, bei Rezipienten einen narrativen Eindruck zu hervorzurufen" (Rogner 2022: 33, s.a. Rogner 2021: 574–575).

82 Braun 2020: 50, 51.

83 Braun 2020: 14–17.

84 Braun 2020: 37.

85 Braun 2020: 31, 50, 392.

lierbarkeit von Narrativität' (s.o. Abschnitt 2) die Annahme, dass monoszenische Einzelbilder notwendigerweise rezipierendenseitig *narrativiert* werden *müssen*, um als ‚narrativ' angesprochen werden zu können.[86] Zwar kann sich laut Braun „das narrative[...] Potenzial eines monoszenischen Einzelbildes [...] durch die rezipientenseitige Narrativierung selbst dann entfalten, wenn der Betrachter die dazugehörende Erzählung nicht kennt", z.B. durch „Vorkenntnisse über die Gattung",[87] andererseits aber „kann m. E. [N.B.] nie mit Sicherheit gesagt werden, dass der Betrachter ein Bild als narrativ auffasst und der Narrativierungsprozess in Gang gesetzt wird, selbst wenn der Sender dies intendiert".[88] Ägyptische *monochrone* Einzelbilder sind für Nadja Braun also nur dann ‚narrativ', wenn sie von Betrachter*innen als ‚Illustrationen' zu vorgängigen Erzählungen interpretiert werden – sie bespricht solche Fälle in extenso bei ihrer Diskussion ägyptischer Bildnarrationen *zu* bekannten Ereignissen sowie *zu* bekannten oder noch unbekannten (s.o. „Vorkenntnisse über die Gattung"[89]) Tierfabeln.[90] Eigenständige Erzählungen, die den Rezeptionsprozess von Betrachter*innen durch das Arrangement der im Bildträger präsentierten Bildobjekte zielgerichtet steuern und sich damit aus sich selbst heraus als autonome Erzählungen anbieten, können Bilder dieses Typs im von Nadja Braun konzipierten methodischen Rahmen aber per definitionem nicht sein.

Hinzu kommt, dass Nadja Braun auch jegliche Form von Alltags- und Ritualdarstellungen aus Ägypten als Erzählungen ausschließt, wenn sie für ihr Modell die standardnarratologischen Definition des Narratems ‚tellability' („a notion referring to features that make a story worth telling"[91]) als notwendigerweise devianz-, komplikations- oder außergewöhnlichkeitsdeterminiert übernimmt:

> „Auch bei ägyptischen Alltags- bzw. Genrebilder[sic] geht es nicht um außergewöhnliche Handlungen bestimmter Personen, sodass sie m.E. *keine Bilderzählungen* [Kursive G.M.] sind. Zwar können gezeigte Bewegungen diesen Bildern Dynamik und Lebendigkeit verleihen, das Kriterium *tellability* [Kursive N.B.] erfüllen sie jedoch nicht, da im Vordergrund die Wiedergabe typischer wiederkehrender Situationen und Handlungen als Grundmuster menschlichen Verhaltens und Zusammenlebens stehen".[92]

Sie schreibt damit nicht nur ägyptologische Standardpositionen trotz der daran bereits geäußerten Kritik fort,[93] sondern ignoriert auch die implizite Problematik der Anwendung einer solchen Definition von ‚tellability' in kulturvergleichender Perspektive, auf die sie andererseits selbst hinweist: „Dieser entscheidende Punkt kann zum Problem werden, wenn

---

86 Braun 2020: 30, 50, passim.
87 Braun 2020: 30.
88 Braun 2020: 53.
89 Nochmals Braun 2020: 30.
90 Braun 2020: 79–338.
91 Vgl. Baroni 2014.
92 Braun 2020: 27 (Zitat), s.a. 12–13, 17, 84, 97–101, 108–109, 133, 137, passim; zum Problem der Verabsolutierung dieses Kriteriums s.a. Rogner 2022: 21.
93 Braun 2020: 106–115 und bes. 84 gegen Davis 1992; zur Kritik s. Rogner 2022: 20 und Moers, Egyptological narratology as *historical narratology*, in diesem Band: Abschnitt 3.

Informationen darüber fehlen, ob das Bild ein außergewöhnliches Ereignis präsentiert. Was aus unserer Sicht als besonders oder von der Norm abweichend erscheint, kann von den alten Ägyptern anders empfunden worden sein – und umgekehrt".[94]

Abgesehen von der Tatsache, dass es gerade im Bereich der konversationellen Alltagserzählung – in welchem Medium auch immer – auch langweilige oder schlechte Geschichten gibt,[95] dürfte das eigentliche Problem aber weniger im ägyptologischen Informationsdefizit begründet liegen als vielmehr in der modelltheoretischen Modellierung von Erwartbarkeiten in Hinsicht auf eine Kultur, in der die weitestgehend rhetorisch organisierte Produktion von Gleichheit und Kopie in allen Medien (Sprache, Texte, Bilder, Architektur, materielle Kultur, menschliche Körper) als eine, wenn nicht als *die* zentrale kulturelle Leistung galt.[96] Möchte man, in Übertragung des von Nadja Braun formulierten Arguments mangelnder ‚tellability' bildlicher ägyptischer Alltagsdarstellungen auf die textuellen Zeugnisse ägyptischer Identitätsdiskurse (vulgo ‚Auto-Biographien') und in Hinsicht auf die wissenschaftlich akzeptierte, wenngleich vieldiskutierte Wahrnehmung personaler Identität als grundsätzlich ‚narrativ' strukturiert[97] tatsächlich annehmen, dass ägyptische Personen im Rahmen ihrer phraseologisch konventionalisierten Selbstrepräsentation z.B. in Texten nichts zu erzählen gehabt haben? Wohl besser nicht. Versteht man demgegenüber personale Identität für das pharaonische Ägypten als eine auf rhetorischem Wege hergestellte „amplifizierte Gleichheit",[98] dann bietet nicht nur der ägyptologisch mittlerweile vielfältig differenzierte Begriff von „Idealbiographie" eine zwar historische,[99] im Kern aber zutreffende Wahrnehmung des Vorhandenseins eines kulturell präfigurierten *Schemas* (s.o. Abschnitt 2) zur Herstellung und Wahrnehmung von konventionalisierten Lebensbeschreibungen, sondern dann sind selbst die simpelsten, nur aus phraseologischen Versatzstücken zusammengesetzten Präsentationen eines solchen idealen ägyptischen Lebens nichts anderes als *Lebens-Erzählungen* voller ‚tellability':

> „Ich war [Titelreihe], einer, der Aufgaben im Herrscherhaus zuwies, ein seiner Stadt Loyaler. Ich war jemand mit schönen Teichen und schlanken Sykomorenbäumen. Ich war jemand, der ein geräumiges Haus in seiner Stadt gebaut und ein Grab auf seinem Friedhof gegraben hat. Ich habe eine Wasserstelle für meine Stadt eingerichtet und sie [G.M. die Stadt] in meinem Boot übergesetzt. Ich war einer, der seine Leute aufmerksam angeleitet hat, bis zum Eintritt des Tages, an dem es mir gut erging und ich sie [G.M.: die Leute] meinem Sohn testamentarisch überantwortete."[100]

94 Braun 2020: 13, 133 (Zitat), 137. Zum ‚Ereignis' und dessen potentielle Verbindung zur ‚Erzählung' aus ägyptologischer Perspektive vgl. die ägyptologischen Beiträge in Fitzenreiter (Hg.) 2009.

95 Vgl. Wolf 2003: 188, Brockmeyer 2012: 456–458 oder Speidel 2018b: 59.

96 Das Argument der rhetorischen Determination sämtlicher Ausdrucksformen der ägyptischen Elite-Kultur wird entfaltet in Moers im Druck.

97 Vgl. etwa Bamberg 2013; Römer 2017.

98 Vgl. nochmals Moers im Druck: Abschnitt „Rhetoric on Display".

99 Nach wie vor zielführend Gnirs 1996.

100 Stele Florenz 1774, vgl. Landgràfovà 2011: 268–269.

Der Mediävist Gert Hübner hat in seinem Beitrag *Historische Narratologie und mittelalterlich frühneuzeitliches Erzählen* ein zur hier vertretenen Perspektive passendes vormodernes Verständnis von ‚tellability' skizziert, vor dessen Hintergrund die von Nadja Braun kriteriologisch für Ägypten definierte Differenz zwischen ‚narrativen' und ‚nichtnarrativen' Bildern tatsächlich in sich zusammenfallen würde:

> „Als Aktualisierung kulturellen Regularitäten- und Situationsdeutungswissens war vormoderne Handlungsdarstellung immer exemplarisch, insofern der kulturelle Sinn konkreten Handelns in den Relationen zwischen den Spezifika der einzelnen Handlungssituationen und dem Allgemeinen des kulturellen Regularitäten- und Situationsdeutungswissens bestand, wenn es das kulturelle Handlungswissen war, das dargestelltes ebenso wie tatsächliches Handeln sinnhaft machte. Aus diesem Grund hatte auch die Darstellung exorbitanten Handelns einen exemplarischen Sinn, während exemplarisches dargestelltes Handeln umgekehrt nicht exorbitant zu sein brauchte." [101]

Von der potentiellen Komplexität solcher um spezifisch ägyptische Formen von ‚tellability' angereicherter narrativer Identitätsentwürfe gibt Claus Jurmans Interpretation der Ikono-Texte aus Gräbern des Alten Reiches als multimodal und multimedial integrierte *Portefolio-Biographien* einen guten Eindruck.[102]

4.2 Die Fallstudie

Während also Nadja Brauns Studie – zumindest aus der hier vertretenen Perspektive – ein konkretes ägyptologisches Beispiel für eine mit Klaus Speidel immer noch „medienblinde", „revisionäre" und „präskriptive" Definition von (Bild)-Erzählung (s.o. Abschnitt 3) darstellt, wird im Folgenden am gezielt gewählten Beispiel eines gemeinhin als *Alltagsszene* oder *Genrebild* eingestuften *monochronen Einzelbildes* auf einem Ostrakon[103], welches eine spezifische Interaktion zwischen einem Stier und einem Menschen darstellt,[104] exemplifiziert, dass dieser Typus von Bildern aus Ägypten durchaus ‚Erzählungen' *sein*[105]

101 Hübner 2015: 54. In eine ähnliche Richtung dürfte nun auch Förster 2022: 43 gehen, wenn er ohne weitere Begründung „the sequential representation" von „typical behavior" als ‚narrativ' ansieht.

102 Claus Jurman, *Je ne regrette rien!*, in diesem Band.

103 Die meisten Ostraka sind im Gegensatz zu kompositorisch komplexeren Grabdarstellungen leicht als Einzelbild – „a picture contained in one frame" (vgl. Speidel 2018b: 7) – ansprechbar.

104 Vgl. nochmals Braun 2020: 257: „diese Szenen mit Stier und Mann [sind] keine Bilderzählung, sondern Genrebilder". Eine differenziertere Wahrnehmung findet sich bei Dorn 2011: 107, der zwischen einem „Einstiegs-" bzw. „Basismotiv ‚schreitender Stier'" zu Übungszecken und „Gelegenheitsbildern" unterscheidet, die „zur Unterhaltung und Belustigung" dienen. Das offensichtliche Unterscheidungskriterium ist Einmaligkeit, insofern die Mehrfachbelegung eines Motivs die entsprechenden Bilder zu Übungsstücken macht (ebd.). Andreas Dorn führt nicht weiter aus, ob die von ihm postulierte „Unterhaltung und Belustigung" durch Gelegenheitsbilder einen narrativen Charakter besäße, grundsätzlich ist seine Perspektive im Sinne der unten durchgeführten Analyse aber narratologisch anschlussfähig.

105 „Sein" selbstverständlich nur im Rahmen eines medienspezifische Kompetenzen involvierenden Vorgangs der Bildrezeption (s.o. Abschnitt 2), welches zur Entwicklung eines konkreten narrativen „Situationsmodells" (s.o. Abschnitt 3) führt. Auch intuitiv für natürlicher gehaltenen

können, obwohl sie nur einen einzigen, in der Regel ‚fruchtbaren' und damit einen für eine temporalisierte Auffassung des Bildes besonders relevanten Moment in der Zeit zeigen.[106] Es wird damit jedoch keinesfalls behauptet, dass jedes monochrone Bild in jedem Fall eine Geschichte *ist*, auch wenn übereifrige Rezipierende grundsätzlich jedes solches Bild ‚narrativieren' könnten (s.o. Abschnitt 2).[107]

4.2.1 Der Versuchsaufbau

Die Fallstudie verbleibt als konkretes Bild-Beispiel dabei diesseits der von Lukas R. A. Wilde als Hauptargument aus kognitionsnarratologischer Perspektive postulierten abstrakten „Basisnarrativität" von Bildern, die aus der im Rahmen der rezipierendenseitigen Konstitution des Bildsujets notwendigen Erzeugung eines intersubjektiv belastbaren diegetischen ‚Situationsmodells' resultiert (s.o. Abschnitte 2 u. 3). Festgehalten wird stattdessen, kognitionsnarratologisch unnötig (s.o. Abschnitt 3), aber in Hinsicht auf eine klassisch-narratologische Anschlussfähigkeit der hier vorgelegten Analyse sinnvoll, am Kriterium der ‚doppelten Temporalität' (s.o. Abschnitte 1 u. 2). Obwohl das Bild also nur einen einzigen ‚prägnanten' oder ‚fruchtbaren' Moment in der Zeit zeigt, bringt es nicht nur eine ‚Geschichte' im Sinne einer ‚fabula' (‚histoire'; ‚story') zur Anschauung, in der ein konkretes singuläres Ereignis in einer klaren chronologischen Ordnung von ‚vorher' und ‚nachher' sowie räumlich und kausal verknüpft entfaltet wird (s.o. Abschnitt 2). Vielmehr hat diese Geschichte durch die Disposition der auf dem Bildträger dargestellten Bildobjekte auf der Diskurs- bzw. Repräsentationsebene (‚discours'; ‚sujet'; ‚recit')[108] auch eine klare Plotstruktur mit einem unterlegten „Komplikation-Lösung"-Schema,[109] mit der der Rezeptionsvorgang der dem monochronen Bild eigenen Temporalität bei der Bildbetrachtung geordnet gesteuert wird.

Demgegenüber wird aus der hier eingenommenen, kognitionsnarratologisch angereicherten Perspektive von der gerade für Alltagserzählungen besonders relevanten

---

Textnarrative „sind" so gesehen für sich genommen nicht mehr „Erzählung" als Bilder, auch sie müssen kompetent als Narrative rezipiert werden. Ich danke Frederik Rogner für eine angeregte Diskussion zu diesem Punkt.

106 Zum auf Lessing (1839 [1766]: 21) zurückgehenden Begriff des ‚fruchtbaren Augenblicks' vgl. z.B. Wolf 2011: 148 m. Anm. 8 u. 153–154 m. Anm. 17; zur ägyptologischen Rezeption vgl. Braun 2020: 50–51.

107 Im grundsätzlich rezeptionsorientierten Ansatz von Frederik Rogner 2022: 33–37 ist das monochrone Einzelbild insofern kein eigenständiger Problemfall, als hier von der generellen Narrativierbarkeit von Bildern durch Bildbetrachtende ausgegangen wird. Bilder haben über ihre „Bestimmtheit, […] Dynamik und […] Detailliertheit" eine „Referenz auf die Realität" von Betrachtenden, wobei der jeweilige „Grad" dieser Faktoren die Stärke des jeweiligen „narrativen Eindrucks" bestimmt, welches ein Bild bei Betrachtenden erweckt (Zitate: 35, 36, 33). Über die Frage, ob und wann ein Bild eine Erzählung *ist* oder nicht, will die Studie keine Auskunft geben, vgl. Rogner 2022: 33 u. 34.

108 Zur Forderung einer verstärkten kunstgeschichtlichen Konzentration auf eben diese Diskursebene vgl. zuletzt Kemp 2018: 482 mit weiterer Literatur.

109 Zum Plot als „cornerstone of virtually all conceptions of narrativity" vgl. Wolf 2003: 182; s.a. Speidel 2018b: 57–59.

„Wahrnehmungsnähe“[110] von Bildern ausgegangen: einfache gegenständliche Bildmedien machen häufig Kommunikationsangebote von hoher relativer Salienz bzw. gesteigerter intersubjektiver Belastbarkeit.[111] Zum einen lassen sich auf der Bildfläche dargestellte Konturen und Formen über ihren Rekurs auf mental gespeicherte Objektschemata und ihre konventionalisierte Ikonographie als konkrete Bildobjekte identifizieren.[112] Zum anderen lassen sich diese Bildobjekte vor dem Hintergrund alltäglicher Weltwahrnehmung und Welterfahrung[113] und unter Rekurs auf mental gespeicherte narrative Verstehensschemata (‚Frame‘; ‚Skript‘) recht voraussetzungslos zu einem Gesamtbild – dem bereits mehrfach angesprochenen ‚Situationsmodell‘ – z.B. einer typischen menschlichen Aktivität mit klarer Intentionalität und temporalisierter Kausalstruktur zusammenfügen und so im kognitiven Prozess automatisiert narrativ strukturieren.

4.2.2 Kausalitätsgesetze und Geschehenslogiken I: Körperflüssigkeiten und Ausscheidungen

Von besonderer Bedeutung ist dabei die Annahme einer auf ununterbrochener menschlicher Erfahrung basierenden Kontinuität von Kausalitätsgesetzen und diesbezüglicher als Schemata abrufbarer Geschehenslogiken, welche die Repräsentationen von Ereignissen auch über kulturelle und historische Grenzen und mit diesen potentiell verbundene unterschiedliche kognitive Stile hinaus verstehbar hält.[114] Dazu gehören neben Gesetzen der Schwerkraft z.B. das Wissen um die Kausalbedingungen menschlicher und tierischer Absonderung von Körperflüssigkeiten. So etwa ist die Darstellung von Blut z.B. im Bild des *Großen Katers*, der die Apophisschlange unter dem Ischedbaum in Heliopolis mit einem Messer bearbeitet, als ein Temporalität, Ereignishaftigkeit und Kausalität involvierender Verweis auf eine intentional herbeigeführte Verletzung zu verstehen. Das Bild aus dem Neuen Reich dient nicht nur als Vignette zu TB 17, sondern ist auch in Gräbern und auf Ostraka belegt.[115] Auch Nadja Braun analysiert dieses Bild als „narrativ“, da es als „Illustration“ zu einem bekannten mythologischen Text dient und es sich zudem um die Darstellung einer normabweichenden Handlung (=> ‚tellability‘) handelt, wenn eine Katze wie ein Mensch ein Messer führt.[116] Doch selbst ohne eine auf Vorwissen beruhen-

---

110 Speidel 2020: 165; Veits 2020: 132, 134; Wilde 2020: 96.

111 Wilde 2020: 94–96.

112 Veits 2020: 135.

113 Hier ist auch die von Monika Fludernik in ihrer *Natural Narratology* zum Hauptkriterium von Erzählung erhobene „experientiality“ (Erfahrungshaftigkeit) anschlussfähig (Fludernik 1996: 12, 311, passim), welches allerdings in der von Martínez 2017: 5 vorgeschlagenen Definition von Erzählung nur als fakultatives Narratem geführt wird. Zur Diskussion des von Fludernik quasi verabsolutierten Kriteriums vgl. Wolf 2003: 182, 185–186.

114 Speidel 2018b: 39–41 u. Speidel 2020: 168–169, 198; s.a. Wilde 2020: 100 und Veits 2020: 139 speziell zum im hiesigen Kontext besonders relevanten „Wissen über Bewegungseffekte“.

115 pBM EA 9901,8 Hunefer (https://www.britishmuseum.org/collection/object/Y_EA9901-8; Budge 1899: Taf. 11), TT 1 Sennedjem (Shedid 1994: 63) und oBerlin 23675 (Brunner-Traut 1956. 92–93 m. Taf. XXXIV).

116 Braun 2020: 105 u. 114; vgl. die entsprechende Textpassage „I am the Great Cat …“ in TB 17 bei Faulkner 1985 [1972]: 48.

de rezipierendenseitige ‚Narrativierung' des Bildes als „Illustration zu" oder den durch die normabweichende Darstellung der menschlichen Handlung eines Tieres vom Bild bei Betrachtenden induzierten Narrativierungsimpuls wäre das dargestellte Blut nicht anders aufzufassen als die Repräsentation einer temporal und kausal strukturierten Ereignis*folge* aus Schnitt durch Akteur*in A und dadurch hervorgerufener Verletzung bei Akteur*in B. Grundsätzlich handelt es sich bei diesem Bild also auch dann um *eine* (Minimal-)Erzählung nach den oben (s. Abschnitt 2) vorgestellten Kriterien *Konkretheit*, *Temporalität*, *Kontiguität*, wenn man es nicht auf den mythologischen Prätext bezieht, auf den das Bild als Illustration in diesem Fall tatsächlich bezogen werden kann. Die Tatsache, dass Varianten der Szene bekannt sind, in denen kein aus dem Hals der Schlange hervortretendes Blut gezeigt ist,[117] legt zudem nahe, dass die Wiedergabe von Blut in diesem Fall bewusst und zielgerichtet als Mittel zur Steigerung der bildeigenen Narrativität eingesetzt wurde – Frederik Rogner würde wohl vom gesteigerten ‚narrativen Effekt' dieses Bildes sprechen[118] –, insofern es die Kausalität des dargestellten Ereignisses expliziter und deutlicher temporal strukturiert. In ähnlicher Art kann auch die Darstellung sich übergebender Personen in einigen Bankettszenen des Neuen Reiches als deutlich narrativitätssteigernd interpretiert werden.[119] Explizit erzählt wird in diesen Bildern, dass sich die Festteilnehmenden übergeben, *weil* sie *zuvor* exzessiv gefeiert haben. Wer geschnitten wird, blutet *immer*, und wer exzessiv feiert, wird sich *möglicherweise* übergeben. Das ist im Übrigen und in beiden gewählten Beispielen auch dort mitzudenken, wo es in entsprechenden Motivvarianten nicht dargestellt ist. Tatsächlich handelt es sich bei der Darstellung von sich beim Bankett übergebenden Personen in narratologischer Terminologie um ein sogenanntes ‚disnarrated' Element – dem Erzählen von etwas, das passieren *könnte*, ohne dass es zwangsläufig passieren *muss*.[120] Aber wenn es dargestellt ist, wird damit explizit(er) erzählt.

4.2.3 Kausalitätsgesetze und Geschehenslogiken II: Bewegungswissen

Jenseits der Darstellung von Körperflüssigkeiten als bildspezifische Kodierungen von Narrativität ist es aber vor allem das menschliche Bewegungswissen, welches kognitiv in sog. ‚Motorschemata', z.B. den basalen Bewegungsschemata ‚Weg' bzw. ‚Transportaktivitäten', ‚Transferaktivitäten' oder ‚Kraftaktivitäten' gespeichert ist.[121] Diese ‚Motor-

---

117 Vgl. z.B. pLeiden T2 (SR) (Leemans 1882: Taf. XI).

118 Rogner 2021: 574–575 u. Rogner 2022: 33 zum ‚narrativen Effekt'; Rogner (2022: 103) verweist bei der Analyse solcher von ihm als „kontingent" (s.a. Rogner 2019: 77) bezeichneten Eigenschaften von Bildobjekten ebenfalls auf die temporalitäts- und kausalitätssteigernde Funktion der Darstellung von Blut im Kontext von Schlachtungsdarstellungen. Ähnliches ist auch von dreidimensionalen Darstellungen bekannt, so etwas vom Holzmodell des Wirtschaftshofes des Gemniemhat aus der Ny Carlsberg Glyptotek Kopenhagen AE. I.N. 1631, vgl. Jørgensen 2002: 83. Ich danke meiner Wiener Kollegin Elisabeth Kruck für den Hinweis auf dieses Objekt.

119 Vgl. z.B. Schott 1953: Taf. XI; weitere Belege auch bei Rogner 2022: 111, der das Motiv allerdings in anderem Kontext bespricht.

120 Prince 1988.

121 Zur Bewegung als „Vokabular" der Bilderzählung vgl. Kemp 2018: 473: „Basismaterial der Erzählung in Bildern sind soziale Akte (Handlungen), die aus Aktionen (*körperlichen Bewegungen*

schemata‘ werden abgerufen, wenn bei der Bildrezeption in Bildern repräsentierte Bewegungsposen – u.a. auch Gesten[122] – zu intersubjektiv anschlussfähigen narrativen ‚Situationsmodellen‘ (s.o. Abschnitte 2 u. 3) transformiert werden können. Grundsätzlich kann ein solcher zielgerichtet-wissensbasierter (äg. *rḫ*) Einsatz von Bewegungsposen im Rahmen standardisierter Formgebungsprozesse bei der Herstellung ägyptischer Bilder nicht nur ägyptologisch rekonstruiert werden,[123] er ist durch explizite Aussagen aus durchaus narrativen Selbstthematisierungen ägyptischer Handwerker auch ägyptisch gut belegt. Dies zeigt z.B. die Stele des Handwerksmeisters Irtisen aus dem Mittleren Reich.

> „Ich bin ein Handwerker, der fähig ist in seinem Handwerk und sich hervorgetan hat durch das, was er erlernt (*rḫ*) hat. […] Ich kenne das Gehen eines männlichen Bildes und das Kommen eines weiblichen Bildes, den Stand des gefangenen Vogels und die aggressive Haltung dessen, der einen Gefangenen erschlägt, den Blick eines Auges in die andere seiner beiden Pupillen, das in Furcht versetzte Gesicht des Feindes, das Anheben des Armes dessen, der nach einem Nilpferd wirft, und den Schritt des Läufers.“[124]

Die Passage veranschaulicht – mit an Sicherheit grenzender Wahrscheinlichkeit bezogen unter anderem auf das Ikon vom *Erschlagen der Feinde*[125] – zudem eine konkrete Funktion des Einsatzes von Bewegungsposen bei der handwerklichen Produktion von identifizierbaren Bildobjekten: Bewegungsposen wie Gesten sind nicht zuletzt Ikonographien von Basisemotionen, über die die Rezeption von Bildbetrachtenden aktiv gesteuert wird, insofern sie in die Lage versetzt werden, in dargestellten Körpern Gefühle wie Angst und damit verbundene Motivationslagen zu erkennen, die aus vorgängigen Handlungen resultieren.[126]

[Kursive G.M.]) bestehen“; zur umfassenderen kognitionsnarratologischen Perspektive vgl. Wege 2017: 347–349 und insbesondere Veits 2020: bes. 135–141.
In Bildern dargestellte Bewegung wurde auch ägyptologisch immer wieder als Indiz für die meist nicht näher definierte Narrativität vor allem von *polychronen Bildern* und von *Bildreihen* wie Feldzugsdarstellungen interpretiert, vgl. dazu die Diskussion der älteren Wahrnehmungen bei Rogner 2022: 29–30. Bei sog. Alltagsdarstellungen ohne ‚tellability‘ reicht nach (oben kritisierter) ägyptologischer Ansicht die Darstellung von Bewegung allerdings auch in diesen Bildtypen nicht hin, um als Hinweis auf die Narrativität dieser Bilder gewertet werden zu können, vgl. Braun 2020: 27, 51, 84, 144, 153.

122 Zu ägyptischen Gesten vgl. Dominicus 1994, zur zielgerichteten Bild-Kommunikation mit ikonographisch konventionalisierten Gesten vgl. nun Rogner 2023, allerdings ohne spezifisch narratologische Perspektive.

123 Je nach gewählter Perspektive handelt es sich um Phänomene, die ägyptologisch u.a. als die „Kanonizität“ ägyptischer Bilder (z.B. Davis 1989) oder als das in ihnen wirkende Prinzip „Dekorum“ (z.B. Baines 1990) wahrgenommen werden.

124 Stele Louvre C14, 9–11 vgl. (jeweils mit weiterer Literatur) Landgráfová 2011: 80–82 und zuletzt Morenz 2020: 31–78 sowie, mit einigen neuen Interpretationsvorschlägen, Fitzenreiter 2019. Die Interpretationen der Lexik des Textes variieren je nach ägyptologischer Zielvorstellung erheblich; die Auffassung, dass die hier wiedergegebenen Passage konventionalisierte Bewegungsposen bei der Bildherstellung thematisiert, wird demgegenüber in allen Bearbeitungen geteilt.

125 Vgl. nochmals Fitzenreiter 2019: 52–53 u. Morenz 2020: 56–57.

126 So auch Braun 2020: 37–39, 187.

Exkurs: narrative Infinitive und Bilder ritualisierter Alltäglichkeit

In diesem Zusammenhang empfiehlt sich auch ein kurzer Blick auf die wohlbekannte Darstellung auf einem Kairener Ostrakon, die einen hockenden Nubier zeigt, der seine Arme im Abwehrgestus angstvoll erhoben hält, *weil* ihn ein Löwe von hinten am Kopf gepackt hat.[127] Auch hier ist die Darstellung einer Bewegungspose ein Indikator für das Vorliegen einer potentiell autonomen Bildgeschichte, die auch dann über *Konkretheit, Temporalität* und *Kontiguität* verfügt, wenn man sie weder als bildmetaphorische Variante (Löwe = König) des *Erschlagen der Feinde*-Ikons,[128] noch als eine Illustration zu einem entsprechenden Prä-Text wie z.B. den narrativen Infinitiven *dȝ(j) ḫȝsw.t* „Abwehren der Fremdländer" (z.B. König Snofru in einer Felsinschrift im Wadi Maghârah auf dem Sinai)[129] oder *ptpt ḫȝsw.t* „Niedertrampeln der Fremdländer" (z.B. Ramses III auf einem Bildostrakon aus Brüssel, vgl. Abb. 2)[130] ansieht, die dem Ikon regelmäßig beigegeben sind.

Die im Bildobjekt kodierte Bewegungspose der abwehrend erhobenen Arme reichert das Bild mit ebenfalls temporal und kausal strukturierter Emotionalität an: Der Fremde erhebt die Arme vor *Angst*, weil ihn ein Löwe am Kopf gepackt hat, denn man weiß: wessen Kopf von einem Löwen ins Maul genommen wird, hat Angst – selbst bei entsprechenden heutigen Zirkusattraktionen dürfte dies aufgrund des auch bei gezähmten Löwen verbleibenden Restrisikos der Fall sein. Auch bei diesem Beispiel wird allerdings nicht behauptet, dass nur dies die Erzählung *ist*, die mit dem Bild erzählt wird, sondern dass die dargestellten Bildobjekte eine autonome Erzählung konstituieren *könnten*, wenn das Bild nicht in konventionalisierter ägyptologischer und möglicherweise auch ägyptischer Wahrnehmung als Variante des Ikons vom *Erschlagen der Feinde* narrativiert werden würde.

Wie nun andererseits die schon angesprochenen Bild-Text-Kombinationen zum Ikon vom *Erschlagen der Feinde* zeigen, sind die in solchen Darstellungen häufig verwendeten und ägyptologisch sinnfällig als *narrativ* bezeichnete Infinitive[131] wie *dȝ(j) ḫȝsw.t* oder *ptpt ḫȝs.wt* nichts anderes als sprachlich transmedialisierte Analogien der im *monochronen* Ikon vom *Erschlagen der Feinde* durch die Wiedergabe schematisierter Bewegungsposen (s.o. Irtisen) repräsentierten komplexen Temporalität des *fruchtbaren* Augenblicks der Bilderzählung. Tatsächlich sind *dȝ(j) ḫȝsw.t* oder *ptpt-ḫȝs.wt* im Kontext der ägyptischen Kultur *Skript*bezeichnungen und damit Nomen, die, wie Mieke Bal in anderem Zusammenhang ausgeführt hat, „eine Erzählung implizier[en]"[132] – hier das *Narrativ* (die

---

127 oDeM 2226, vgl. Vandier d'Abbadie 1936: Taf. XXVI; s.a. https://www.ifao.egnet.net/bases/archives/ostraca/docs/vues/GS_2013_0073.jpg.

128 So etwa Minault-Gout 2002: 79–80 mit Abb. 54.

129 Gardiner & Peet 1952: Taf. II, Abb. 5.

130 oBrüssel MRAH E.07359 (Minault-Gout 2002: 76–79 m. Abb. 52; Photo zugänglich nach Eingabe der Nummer E.07359 in die Suchmaske „Search the collection" unter https://www.carmentis.be/eMP/eMuseumPlus?service=ExternalInterface&module=collection&moduleFunction=highlight&lang=en.

131 Zur Diskussion der Form vgl. Gardiner 1957: 230 (§ 306.2); zu ihrer Unterscheidbarkeit vom wahrscheinlich fälschlich postulierten sog. narrativen *sḏm.t=f* (Gardiner 1957: 320 [§ 406. B]) vgl. Schenkel 1973. Ich danke Orly Goldwasser für eine längere diesbezügliche Diskussion.

132 Bal 1999: 25. Vgl. ferner den Exkurs zum *narrativen* Infinitiv bei Claus Jurman, *Je ne regrette rien!*, in diesem Band. Weitere ägyptische Beispiele für die narrative Verwendung von Nomen bei Gardiner 1957: 67–68 (§89.2).

Meistererzählung; le grand récit) der *ritualisierten*, von jedem König durch gewalttätige Oppression des Fremden zu jeder Zeit immer wieder hergestellten Suprematie Ägyptens.[133] Mit Klaus Speidel müsste man sich daher grundsätzlich fragen, ob ein solches *Ritualbild* tatsächlich als *monochrones* Einzelbild zu bewerten ist oder nicht vielmehr doch als ein *äonochrones* Einzelbild, welches eine auf Dauer gestellte oder zirkulär wiederkehrende Handlung zeigt.[134] Jedenfalls würde die Ansprache des Ikons vom *Erschlagen der Feinde* als *äonochrone* Bilderzählung die Relevanz der ägyptologischen Frage unterlaufen, ob man es bei entsprechend individualisierten Darstellungen wie im Falle König Snofrus oder König Ramses' III. mit Darstellungen zu tun hat, die auf ein konkretes historisches Ereignis rekurrieren oder nicht.[135]

Abb. 2 | oBrüssel MRAH E.07359

Die an der Bild-Text-Kombination von Darstellungen des Ikons vom *Erschlagen der Feinde* vollzogene Analyse ließe sich weiter generalisieren. Sie kann auch für die in jeglicher Hinsicht konventionalisierten, d.h. in diesem Sinne ‚alltäglichen' und in ägyptologischer Standardwahrnehmung per definitionem *nicht-narrativen* (s.o. Abschnitt 4.1) Darstellungen der *ritualisierten* Interaktion zwischen *König*innen* und *Göttinnen/Göttern* zur Anwendung gebracht werden.[136] Diese zeigen zwar im Bild tatsächlich ebenfalls nur genau einen ‚fruchtbaren' Moment in der Zeit, allerdings ist, sofern man der linguistischen Analyse der den Bildern beigegebenen Textsequenzen vertrauen darf, auch diesen monochronen Einzelbildern ein ganz spezifisches temporales Programm inhärent. *Erzählt* wird das ritualisierte Geschehen als die Bildgeschichte *zweier* zwar reziproker, aber aufeinander folgender Übergabeakte von materiellen oder immateriellen Objekten durch *zwei* Akteur*innen,[137] die im Text beidseitig durch zwei narrative Präteritalformen, das sog. ‚performative Perfekt (*sḏm.n=f*)' (‚Koinzidenzfall' *dj.n(=j) n=ṯ/=k* *"Ich habe dir X gegeben" => „Hiermit gebe ich Dir X"), begleitet werden, welche den Moment des Abschlusses einer Handlungssequenz zum Ausdruck bringen.[138]

Alternativ kann, wie z.B. auf dem Türsturz Louvre E 13983 Sesostris' III. aus dem Month-Tempel von Medamud (Abb. 3),[139] das performative Perfekt (*sḏm.n=f*) auf Seiten

133 Vgl. etwa Moers 2004: 88–127 oder Moers 2011. Nadja Braun (2020: 349) spricht in diesem Zusammenhang von einem „patriotischen Schlüsselbild".

134 Vgl. Speidel 2018b: 27, 30, 32.

135 Zur Diskussion vgl. etwa Braun 2020: 349, 353–355.

136 Vgl. dazu etwa Eaton 2013 zum ägyptischen Tempelritual.

137 Zur Funktion von Ritualen im Rahmen der Performanz kultureller Narrative vgl. die Diskussion bei Di Biase-Dyson 2019: 43–45 mit weiterer Literatur.

138 Vgl. Werning 2015: 69: „Dass im Ägyptischen hier der Anterior benutzt wird, zeigt, dass ein performativer Akt im Ägyptischen so verstanden wird, dass die Schaffung neuer Fakten sich erst (gleichzeitig) mit dem *Abschluss* [Kursive D.W.] des Sprechaktes vollzieht".

139 Photo unter https://collections.louvre.fr/en/ark:/53355/cl010010164.

Abb. 3 | Türsturz Sesostris' III. aus Medamud = Louvre E 13983

von König*in durch einen *narrativen* Infinitiv ersetzt sein, wenn z.B. standardisierte Opferhandlungen wie das „Darreichen von Schat-Kuchen" (*dj.t šˁ.t*) dargestellt sind.

Beide Verbalformen können im Rahmen einer solchen Verwendung daher als linguistische Affordanzen zur Aktivierung mental gespeicherter Skripten verstanden werden, vor deren Hintergrund der jeweilige sprachliche Ausdruck als narrative Struktur aufgefasst wird. Dies gilt insbesondere auch für eine produktive Form des Gebrauchs des *narrativen* Infinitivs, wenn er z.B. in unterschiedlichen Manuskripten der *Erzählung von Sinuhe* im Kontext von Darstellungen von Bewegungsaktivitäten (=> ‚Motorschemata') als allofunktionale Variante der narrativen Präteritalform *sḏm.n=f* eingesetzt wird.[140]

4.3 Das monochrone Einzelbild oDeM 2070 = oLouvre E 14367 (Abb. 4)

Am Beispiel des monochrone Einzelbildes oDeM 2070 = oLouvre E 14367[141] soll nun dargelegt werde, wie dargestellte Bewegungsposen und die konkrete Repräsentation eindeutig identifizierbarer Bildobjekte als narrative Strukturen zu interpretieren sind, die nicht nur situationsspezifische Zusammenhänge und Kausalitätstrukturen einer autonomen Erzählung mit Konkretheit, Temporalität und Kontiguität im Sinne des narratologischen Begriffs der ‚fabula' (‚story', ‚histoire') konstituieren, sondern diese Erzählung auf der Ebene des Bilddiskurses (‚sujet'; ‚discours'; ‚récit') auch mit einer klaren, temporal orga-

140 Vgl. etwa Sinuhe B4–5 und R28 *rd.t=j wj* vs. AOS *rd.n=j wj*, Sinuhe B5–6 und R29 *jr.t=j šm.t* vs. C5 *jr.n=j šm.t* oder Sinuhe B16 *rd.t=j wꜣt* vs. Sinuhe R41–42 *rd.n=j wꜣ.t* (Koch 1990: 12, 17). Die drei Fälle werden von Frank Feder im Rahmen seiner editionsphilologischen Bearbeitung des Textes für den *Thesaurus Linguae Aegyptiae* als Fehler interpretiert: „Der ‚narrative Infinitiv' wird nur als ‚Überschrift zu Abschnitten' verwendet und kann hier in R und B nicht gestanden haben kann" (https://aaew.bbaw.de/tla/servlet/S02?wc=143602&db=0; Fall 1) bzw. „der Anfang sollte nach R […] berichtigt werden, da der ‚narrative' Infinitiv hier fehl am Platze ist" (https://aaew.bbaw.de/tla/servlet/S02?wc=143729&db=0; Fall 3). Diese Einschätzung verdankt sich einer normativen Verabsolutierung *einer* der Leistungen dieser Form und verkennt die offensichtliche Produktivität ihrer Verwendbarkeit, die sich an den genannten Stellen durch sämtliche Sinuhe-Manuskripte zieht.

141 oDeM 2070= oLouvre E 14367 (Vandier d'Abbadie 1936: Taf. XXVI; Minault-Gout 2002: 130 m. Abb. 102; s.a. https://collections.louvre.fr/en/ark:/53355/cl010008504). Zu einer möglicherweise ähnlichen Darstellung auf oMM 14039 (Peterson 1973: 94 u. Taf. 47, Nr. 86) s.u.

nisierten Plotstruktur versehen.

Abb. 4 | oDeM 2070 = oLouvre E 14367

Im initialen Moment der Betrachtung zeigt das Bild zentral und als größtes Bildobjekt einen Stier im Sprung, der sich mit schräg-senkrecht vom Boden abgestoßenen Hinterläufen und gestreckt nach vorn erhobenen Vorderläufen nach rechts auf einen Menschen zubewegt. Dieser ist am rechten Bildrand als zweitgrößtes Bildobjekt mit um ca. 15° nach rechts verschobener vertikaler Körperachse gegen den Stier positioniert dargestellt und wird vom linken Vorderhuf des Stieres auf Höhe seines Bauchnabels und von dessen rechtem Vorderhuf wohl auf Höhe seines Oberschenkels berührt. Bei genauerer Betrachtung kann erkannt werden, dass der Stier mit nach hinten erhobenem Schwanz und erigiertem Phallus gezeigt wird. Als weitere, kleinere Bildobjekte sind hinter dem Stier direkt unterhalb seines Schwanzansatzes zwei Kugeln zu erkennen. Der Mensch ist seinerseits mit vor dem Oberkörper nach vorn erhobenen Unterarmen dargestellt, beide Hände befinden sich auf Höhe seines Gesichts. In seiner rechten Hand hält er vor dem Stierkopf als weiteres Bildobjekt einen an der Spitze nach vorn gebogenen Gegenstand, während seine linke Handfläche vor seinem eigenen Gesicht in Richtung des Stieres gedreht ist. Ein letztes Bildobjekt, ein offensichtlich eingerollter Gegenstand mit bis auf die Höhe der Schultern herunterhängendem Ende, ist über bzw. hinter dem Kopf des Menschen dargestellt.

Die Differenzqualität dieses Bildes als vollwertige und autonome Bilderzählung lässt sich anhand der in ihm über spezifischen Bewegungsposen kodierten Besonderheiten und der spezifischen Verteilung der in der Bildfläche dargestellten Bildobjekte nun recht eindeutig analysieren. Um einen Vergleichskontext herzustellen, müssen andere Bilder, die die Interaktion zwischen Stieren und Menschen zeigen, etwas detaillierter vorgestellt werden. Grundsätzlich sind solche Interaktionen in der ägyptischen Bildwelt aus Grabdarstellungen und vor allem durch die Objektgattung der ramessidischen Bildostraka aus dem thebanischen Bereich ebenso gut belegt wie die alleinigen Darstellungen von Stieren.[142] Die konventionalisierte Ikonographie all dieser Darstellungen macht die auf der Bildflä-

142 Im Rahmen dieser Fallstudie ist ein vollständiger Katalog vorhandener Stierdarstellungen und Stier-Hirten-Szenen irrelevant. Die Stücke finden sich bei Daressy 1901, Schäfer 1916, Vandier d'Abbadie 1936, Keimer 1941, Hayes 1942, Werbrouck 1953, Brunner-Traut 1956, Vandier d'Abbadie 1959, Peterson 1973, Brunner-Traut 1979, Page 1983, Gasse 1986, Leospo 1989 und Dorn 2011. Eine gute zusammenfassende Übersicht gibt Dorn 2011: 106–108. Die entsprechenden Motive sind im in Theben-West zu Tage getretenen ‚archäologischen' Material zu bestimmten

Abb. 5 | oMM 14084. Source: National Museums of World Culture – Mediterranean Museum, Sweden (CC BY)

Abb. 6 | oBrüssel MRAH E.06314

che präsentierten Formen durch den rezipierendenseitigen Rückgriff auf mental gespeicherte Objektschemata zunächst eindeutig identifizierbar. Aus einem Vergleich der Darstellung der auch im obigen Bild (Abb. 4) gezeigten, in anderen Bildern aber nicht oder anders dargestellten oder auch anders positionierten Formen (Stiere – Menschen – weitere Gegenstände) geht für jede ägyptische Kommunikationsteilnehmer*in mit Diskurskompetenz zunächst ganz allgemein hervor, dass es sich bei der dargestellten menschlichen Figur im hier analysierten Stück zweifelsfrei um einen Stierhirten[143] handelt, dem mit Hirtenstab (an der Spitze gebogenen Gegenstand) und Lasso (eingerollter Gegenstand) typische Arbeitsinstrumente beigegeben sind. Wenn hier von Diskurskompetenz die Rede ist, bedeutet das nichts anderes, als dass die Bilder von ihren Hersteller*innen als anschlussfähige, intersubjektiv verstehbare Kommunikationsangebote intendiert waren und als entsprechend lesbar eingestuft werden können.[144]

Der Variantenreichtum von Darstellungen, die Hirten mit oder ohne Einsatz ihrer Arbeitsgeräte in verschiedenen Graden von Interaktion mit Stieren zeigen, ist groß. Bei ramessidischen Bildostraka aus Theben-West, die Hirten mit nur einem Stier zeigen, verläuft die dargestellte Bewegung häufiger von links nach rechts als von rechts nach links und findet in der Mehrzahl der Bilder auf einer Standlinie statt. Die Hirten sind vor, hinter oder im Hintergrund des Stieres neben diesem positioniert und interagieren mit diesem in verschiedener Art und Weise und in verschiedene Stufen von Mittelbarkeit und Kontakt. Die jeweilige Art der Interaktion ist einerseits über die Darstellung spezifischer Bewegungsposen und andererseits über die Darstellung des Einsatzes der als Hirtenstab und Lasso identifizierbaren Bildobjekte kodiert. Die Reihung in der folgenden Vorstellung relevanter Bildmotive orientiert sich grob am Eindruck zunehmender Bewegtheit und/oder

Zeiten offensichtlich so präsent und bei Käufern so nachgefragt gewesen, dass auch sie gefälscht wurden, vgl. Keimer 1941: 23 m. Abb. 13.

143 Zu Hirtenbildern generell siehe jüngst Guth 2018.

144 Dies setzt auch Dorns (2011: 107) Ansprache einiger der Stücke als „Gelegenheitsbilder zur Unterhaltung und Belustigung“ voraus, s.o.

Agitation der beteiligten Akteure und setzt damit selbstverständlich eine Lesbarkeit der Bilder im Sinne der hier vorgelegten Analyse voraus.

Das fragmentarische oMM 14084[145] (Abb. 5) zeigt einen rechts vor einem (unvollständigen) Boviden sitzenden Hirten. Beide sind nach rechts orientiert. Der Hirte sitzt mit nach vorn gebeugtem Oberkörper auf seinem rechten Unterschenkel, während sein linkes Bein im Knie abgewinkelt auf dem Boden steht. Ein Arm des Hirten ist gerade von seiner Schulter nach hinten geführt und am Ellenbogen senkrecht nach oben abgewinkelt. In der Hand dieses Armes, die sich direkt unter dem Maul des Tieres befindet, hält der Hirte einen Strick, der wohl durch die Nase des Tiers geführt ist. Der Strick verläuft über die Schulter und den Oberkörper des Hirten zur Hand seines anderen Armes, der am Ellenbogen auf Höhe des linken Knies nach vorn abgewinkelt ist. In dieser Hand hält der Hirte zusätzlich einen Stab. Offensichtlich verharrt der Hirte mit einem Stier an kurzer Leine (Motorschema „Transferaktivität ruhende Kontrolle") in einer Ruheposition.[146]

Das Basismotiv[147] einer bewegten Interaktion von Hirten und Stieren zeigt im Hintergrund des Stierkörpers neben diesen abgebildete Hirten, die den Stier durch einen Griff an dessen hinteren Oberschenkel sowie einen gleichzeitigen Griff an dessen Gehörn in die von ihnen gewünschte Richtung führen. Die Bewegung verläuft wie z. B. in oBrüssel MRAH E.06314 (Abb. 6)[148] in der Regel auf einer Standlinie von links nach rechts,[149]

145 Peterson 1973: 96 m. Taf. 49, Abb. 93; s.a. https://collections.smvk.se/carlotta-mhm/web/object/3006082.

146 Eine Variante der Szene ist im ebenfalls fragmentarischen oMM 14042 (Peterson 1973: 95 m. Taf. 49, Abb. 92; s.a. https://collections.smvk.se/carlotta-mhm/web/object/3005163) dargestellt. Hier sitzt der Hirte bei identischer Beinhaltung mit aufrechtem Oberkörper. Sein rechter Arm ist vor der Brust abgewinkelt, sein linker Arm vor dem Bauch, sodass die Hände übereinander zu stehen kommen. In der linken Hand hält der Hirte einen Strick, dessen unteres Ende auf den Boden fällt, während er nach über den rechten Ellenbogen wahrscheinlich zum Kopf des Stieres verläuft. Möglicherweise hält die in Griffhaltung dargestellte rechte Hand einen anderen Teil desselben Strickes, einen weiteren Strick oder einen anderen Gegenstand. Auch hier verharrt der Hirte offensichtlich mit einem Stier an kurzer Leine in einer Ruheposition.

147 In Anlehnung an Dorn 2011: 107, der Begriff allerdings für das Motiv „allein schreitender Stier" verwendet.

148 oBrüssel MRAH E.06314 (Werbrouck 1953: 110 m. Abb. 14; Photo zugänglich nach Eingabe der Nummer E.06314 in die Suchmaske „Search the collection" unter https://www.carmentis.be/eMP/eMuseumPlus?service=ExternalInterface&module=collection&moduleFunction=highlight&lang=en).

149 oBerlin 21441 (Schäfer 1916: 27, 44 m. Abb. 24; Brunner-Traut 1956: 105 m. Taf. XXXVII, Abb. 106), oBerlin 21440 (Brunner-Traut 1956: 105 m. Taf. XXXVII, Abb. 107), oMünchen 1656 (Stier mit erhobenem Schwanz; Brunner-Traut 1956: 105 m. Taf. XXXVII, Abb. 108), oMM 14085 (Peterson 1973: 95 m. Taf. 49, Abb. 90; s.a. https://collections.smvk.se/carlotta-mhm/web/object/3005196), oDeM 2067 (Vandier d'Abbadie 1936: Taf. X), oDeM 2069 = oLouvre N 1562 (Vandier d'Abbadie 1936: Taf. XI; s.a. https://collections.louvre.fr/en/ark:/53355/cl010026719), oDeM 2074 (Vandier d'Abbadie 1936: Taf. XIII; s.a. https://www.ifao.egnet.net/bases/archives/ostraca/docs/vues_th/NU_2006_01555.jpg), oDeM 2076 (Vandier d'Abbadie 1936: Taf. X; s.a. https://www.ifao.egnet.net/bases/archives/ostraca/docs/vues_th/NU_2006_01548.jpg), oDeM 2081 (Vandier d'Abbadie 1936: Taf. XIII; s.a. https://www.ifao.egnet.net/bases/archives/ostraca/docs/

Abb. 7 | oKeimer 1 (Privatbesitz)

oder seltener auch von rechts nach links[150]. In Ausnahmefällen kann auch ein Objekt wie der Hirtenstab abgebildet sein.[151]

Das oKeimer 1[152] (Abb. 7) zeigt einen nach rechts orientierten und nach vorn auf die Knie gegangenen Stier, dessen Hinterläufe noch aufrecht stehen. Ihm gegenüber ist ein Hirte dargestellt, der auf seinem linken Bein kniet, während sein rechtes Bein im Knie abgewinkelt auf dem Boden steht. Mit seiner linken Hand hält der Hirte auf Höhe seines rechten Knies den Stier an dessen rechtem Horn. Der rechte Unterarm des Hirten ist vor seiner Brust zum Schlag mit einem in seiner Hand befindlichen Stab erhoben. Offensichtlich zwingt der Hirte den Stier durch einen gekonnten Hebel am Gehörn (Motorschema „Transferaktivität erzwungene Kontrolle") sowie durch Schlageinsatz (Motorschema „Kraftaktivität Schlag") mit dem Stab in die Knie.

In oDeM 2062 = oKairo JE 63759[153] bewegen sich Stier und Hirte sich auf Standlinie nach rechts. Der Stier folgt seinem Hirten schreitend mit auf Höhe der Schultern gesenktem Kopf und einem wohl von der Nase hängenden Strick. In seiner rechten Hand hält der Hirte einen Stab, den er bei angewinkeltem Arm rechts geschultert trägt. In seiner linken Hand trägt er ein Gefäß. In dieser Anordnung der dargestellten Bildobjekte befinden sich Mensch und Stier ganz offensichtlich im Zustand größtmöglicher Entspanntheit und bewegen (Motorschema „Weg") sich ohne direkten Kontakt in die vom Hirten vorgegebene Richtung.

In oMM 14083[154] (Abb. 8) bewegen sich Stier und Hirte auf einer Standlinie nach rechts. Der schreitende Stier folgt seinem Hirten mit auf Höhe der Schultern gesenktem

---

vues_th/NU_2006_01549.jpg), oDeM 2753 (Vandier d'Abbadie 1959: Taf. XCIX; s.a. https://www.ifao.egnet.net/bases/archives/ostraca/docs/vues_th/NU_2006_03000.jpg).

150 oDeM 2068 = oLouvre 14296 (Vandier d'Abbadie 1936: Taf. X; s.a. https://collections.louvre.fr/en/ark:/53355/cl010026236).

151 oDeM 2083 Hirte mit Stab in Hand an Gehörn des Stieres (Vandier d'Abbadie 1936: Taf. XIII: s.a. https://www.ifao.egnet.net/bases/archives/ostraca/docs/vues_th/NU_2006_01556.jpg).

152 Keimer 1941: 1 m. Taf. I, Abb. 1.

153 Vandier d'Abbadie 1936: Taf. IX u. Minault-Gout 2002: Abb. 100. Das Bild wurde von Minault-Gout 2002: 128–129 eher tentativ mit dem Zweibrüdergeschichte des *pD'Orbiney* in Verbindung gebracht, die Idee wurde von Braun 2020: 256–257 dahingehend aufgegriffen, dass sie die Möglichkeit zur rezipient*innenseitigen Narrativierung des Bildes „als Anspielung auf diese Erzählung" bei „entsprechendem Vorwissen" grundsätzlich für möglich hält. Was aber gerade diese Szene als besonders passende ‚Illustration' zur Zweibrüdergeschichte qualifizieren würde, ist auch für Nadja Braun nicht einsichtig. Tatsächlich ist Minault-Gouts Assoziation ein gutes Beispiel dafür, wie übereifrige Rezipierende grundsätzlich jedes Bild narrativieren *können*, selbst wenn das Bild gar nicht als autonome Erzählung oder Illustration zu einem verbalen Prätext konzipiert worden wäre.

154 Peterson 1973: 95 m. Taf. 47, Abb. 88; s.a. https://collections.smvk.se/carlotta-mhm/web/object/3005195.

Kopf. Durch die Nase des Stieres ist ein Strick geführt, an dem der Hirte ihn mit herabhängendem rechtem Arm an seiner rechten Hand, in der der Strick doppelt gelegt ist, vergleichsweise kurz führt. In seiner linken Hand hält der Hirte mit ebenfalls herabhängendem Arm einen Stab. Offensichtlich bewegt der Hirte den Stier vergleichsweise entspannt mit wenig Zug am Strick (Motorschema „Transferaktivität ruhig leitende Kontrolle") in die von ihm gewünscht Richtung.[155]

Abb. 8 | oMM 14083
Source: National Museums of World Culture – Mediterranean Museum, Sweden (CC BY)

In oDeM 2064 = oLouvre 14302[156] (Abb. 9) bewegen sich Stier und Hirte auf einer Standlinie nach links. Der schreitende Stier folgt seinem Hirten mit auf Höhe der Schultern gesenktem Kopf. Der Hirte führt den Stier an einem durch dessen Nase geführten Strick, den er zusammen mit einem Stab in seiner bei angewinkeltem Arm linken erhobenen Hand hält. Auch der rechte Arm ist mit nach vorn geöffneter Handfläche angewinkelt erhoben. Offensichtlich bewegt der Hirte den Stier vergleichsweise entspannt mit mittlerem Zug am Strick (Motorschema „Transferaktivität ruhig leitende Kontrolle") in die von ihm gewünschte Richtung.

Im fragmentarischen oUC 33202[157] bewegen sich Hirte und Stier auf einer Standlinie nach rechts. Der Hirte folgt direkt auf den schreitenden Stier und berührt diesen mit seiner linken Hand möglicherweise an dessen linker Hüfte oder fasst ihn am Schwanz. In seiner linken Armbeuge trägt der Hirte wohl ein aufgerolltes Lasso, in seiner rechten Hand trägt er mit herabhängendem Arm einen Stab. Offensichtlich bewegt der Hirte den Stier durch eine leichte Berührung entspannt (Motorschema „Transferaktivität ruhig antreibende Kontrolle") in die von ihm gewünschte Richtung.

In oEGA 4228-1943[158] bewegen sich Hirte und Stier auf einer Standlinie nach rechts. Der Hirte folgt in direkter Nähe (ein Fuß des Hirten steht

Abb. 9 | oDeM 2064 = oLouvre 14302

155 Eine Variante der Darstellung, allerdings mit einem im Verhältnis zum Hirten überdimensionierten Stier, findet sich in oTurin inv. Suppl. 9549 (Leospo 1989: 236 m. Abb. 356).
156 Vandier d'Abbadie 1936: Taf. IX; s.a. https://collections.louvre.fr/en/ark:/53355/cl010026233.
157 Page 1983: 39 m. Abb. 57.
158 Brunner-Traut 1979: 62 m. Abb. 34 und Verweis auf Parallelstücke; online unter: https://www.nino-leiden.nl/download/3938.

auf Höhe eines der Hinterläufe des Stieres) auf einen schreitenden Stier, der seinen Kopf auf Höhe der Schultern gesenkt hält. Der Hirte ist leicht nach vorn gebeugt und hält in seiner linken Hand über der Mitte des Stierrückens einen Strick, der in leichtem Bogen bis zur Brust des Stieres hinabführt, um von dort wieder zu dessen Nase aufzusteigen, durch die er gezogen ist. In seiner rechten Hand hält der Hirte einen Stab, den er bei angewinkeltem Arm rechts geschultert trägt. In seiner rechten Armbeuge trägt er zusätzlich ein aufgerolltes Lasso. Offensichtlich bewegt der Hirte den Stier vergleichsweise entspannt am mit wenig Zug durchhängenden Strick (Motorschema „Transferaktivität ruhig antreibende Kontrolle") in die von ihm gewünschte Richtung.

Abb. 10 | oKairo CG 25142 (Daressy 1901: Taf. XXVIII)

Im fragmentarischen oKairo CG 25142[159] (Abb. 10) bewegen sich Hirte und Stier auf einer Standlinie nach rechts. Der Hirte folgt auf einen schreitenden Stier und hält in seiner rechten Hand ein Lasso, dass straff über den Rücken des Stieres nach vorn (zum verlorenen Kopf?) geführt ist. Das Ende des Lassos ist zumindest einmal in seiner Hand aufgerollt. Sein rechter Ellenbogen ist dabei hinter die Körperachse nach hinten geführt, sein rechter Unterarm verläuft parallel zur Standlinie. Straffes Lasso und Armhaltung signalisieren damit eine deutliche Zugbewegung. In seiner linken Hand hält der Hirte bei mit zum Schlag erhobenem Arm einen Gegenstand bzw. Gegenstände, bei dem es sich um ein oder zwei Stäbe oder um einen Stab und eine Peitsche handeln könnte. Offensichtlich bewegt der Hirte den Stier durch Einsatz dieses Gegenstandes bei gleichzeitig straffem Zug am Lasso ebenso nachdrücklich wie kontrolliert (Motorschemata „Transferaktivität antreibende Kontrolle") in die von ihm gewünschte Richtung.

In oDeM 2065 = oLouvre 14345[160] (Abb. 11) bewegen sich Hirte und Stier nach rechts. Der Hirte folgt dem Stier, den er mit seiner linken Hand an dessen linker Hüfte berührt oder am herabhängenden Schwanz hält. In seiner rechten Hand hält er einen Stab erhoben. Der Stier hat seinen Kopf deutlich über seine Schultern erhoben, seine beiden Vorderbeine stehen in kurzer Distanz zueinander. Offensichtlich dirigiert der Hirte den möglicherweise verharrenden Stier durch direkte Berührung und Stockeinsatz (Motorschemata „Transferaktivität antreibende Kontrolle" und „Kraftaktivität Schlag") in die von ihm gewünschte Richtung.[161]

159 Daressy 1901: Taf. XXVIII.

160 Vandier d'Abbadie 1936: Taf. XI; s.a. https://collections.louvre.fr/en/ark:/53355/cl010026753.

161 Eine Variante des Motivs findet sich möglicherweise im stark fragmentarischen oMM 14039 (Peterson 1973: 94–95 m. Taf. 49, Abb. 87; s.a. https://collections.smvk.se/carlotta-mhm/web/object/3005156). Hier fasst ein hinter einem nach rechts orientieren Stier stehender Hirte diesen

Abb. 11 | oDeM 2065 = oLouvre 14345

Abb. 12 | oDeM 2066 = oLouvre 14344

In oDeM 2066 = oLouvre 14344[162] (Abb. 12) bewegen sich Hirte und Stier auf einer Standlinie nach rechts. Der Hirte folgt einem schreitenden Stier, der seinen Kopf auf Höhe der Schultern gesenkt hält. Der linke Vorderlauf des Stieres ist leicht über die Standlinie erhoben. Durch die Nase des Stieres ist ein nach unten hängender Strick geführt, der leicht nach vorn baumelt. Der Hirte hält mit leicht nach vorn geführtem Arm einen Stab in seiner linken Hand. Mit seiner rechten Hand wirft er von hinten ein Lasso über Rücken und Gehörn des Stieres, die Schlinge des Lassos befindet sich vor dem Kopf des Stieres, das Ende des Lassos hängt aus der Hand des Hirten bis fast an den Boden.[163] Offensichtlich fängt der Hirte einen sich gerade selbständig machenden Stier (erhobener linker Vorderlauf, baumelnder Nasenstrick) mit dem Lasso ein (Motorschema „Transferaktivität ruhiger Versuch der Wiedergewinnung von Kontrolle“).

Das fragmentarische oMM 14077[164] (Abb. 13) zeigt einen Stier im Sprung, der sich mit gestreckt nach vorn erhobenen Vorderläufen und über die Schultern erhobenem Kopf nach links bewegt. Am Gehörn des Stieres ist ein horizontal über seinen Rücken nach hinten verlaufendes Lasso befestigt. Vom Hals des Stieres baumelt ein weiterer Strick nach vorn.[165] Offensichtlich hat ein (im Stück weggebrochener) rechts hinter dem Stier positionierter Hirte das sich schon selbständig gemacht habende Tier (Sprung, baumelnder Halsstrick) mit dem Lasso eingefangen und versucht ihn nun am straffen Strick zu halten (Motorschema „Transferaktivität versuchte Wiedergewinnung straffer Kontrolle“).[166]

am allerdings nach oben aufgerichteten Schwanz. Möglicherweise ist über dem Kopf des Hirten ein zum Schlag erhobenen Stab gezeigt.

162 Vandier d’Abbadie 1936: Taf. XI; s.a. https://collections.louvre.fr/en/ark:/53355/cl010008503.

163 Eine Variante des Motivs liegt möglicherweise vor im fragmentarischen oDeM 3102 (Gasse 1986: Taf. I; s.a. https://www.ifao.egnet.net/bases/archives/ostraca/docs/vues_th/NU_2006_03363.jpg). Ein Hirte folgt von rechts nach links einem Stier, den er an einem straff über dessen Rückenlinie verlaufenden Lasso führt.

164 Peterson 1973: 96 m. Taf. 50, Abb. 94; s.a. https://collections.smvk.se/carlotta-mhm/web/object/3006080.

165 Von Peterson 1973: 96 nicht beschrieben.

166 Peterson 1973: 96 setzt einen Hirten am anderen Ende des Lassos an. oDeM 2071 (Vandier d'Abbadie 1936: Taf. XII; s.a. https://www.ifao.egnet.net/bases/archives/ostraca/docs/vues/GS_2013_0073.jpg) jedenfalls zeigt eine entsprechende Darstellung, in der ein Hirte einen Stier mit einem um dessen Horn geschlungenen Lasso zurückzuhalten versucht, der im Sprung einen anderen Stier attackiert.

Abb. 13 | oMM 14077. Source: National Museums of World Culture – Mediterranean Museum, Sweden (CC BY)

Im fragmentarischen oKV/3.491[167] bewegt sich der Stier auf einer Standlinie nach rechts auf einen Hirten zu, der ihm zugewandt auf der rechten Seite des Bildes gegenübersteht. Der Stier schreitet mit auf Höhe seiner Schultern gesenktem Kopf. Der Hirte schultert mit angewinkeltem Arm seinen Stab mit der linken Hand. Mit der rechten Hand, die sich unmittelbar vor der Nase des Stieres befindet, hält der Hirte den Stier gleichzeitig an einem sichtbar durch dessen Nase geführten Stick und einem an seinem Gehörn befestigten Lasso, dessen größter Teil sich zusammengerollt in der der Hand des Hirten befindet. Offensichtlich führt der Hirte den erhöhte Aufmerksamkeit verlangenden Stier recht ruhig an einer vergleichsweise kurzen Leine (Motorschema „Transferaktivität ruhige straffe Kontrolle“).

In oBerlin 21439[168] (Abb. 14) bewegt sich ein Stier nach rechts auf einen Hirten zu, der ihm zugewandt auf der rechten Seite des Bildes gegenübersteht. Der Stier schreitet mit auf Höhe seiner Schultern gesenktem Kopf und ist mit heraushängender Zunge und erigiertem Phallus dargestellt. Der Hirte ist mit leicht angewinkelten Knien sowie mit leicht nach hinten versetztem und ebenso leicht nach vorn gebeugtem Oberkörper dargestellt. In seiner rechten Hand hält der Hirte mit zum Schlag erhobenem Arm einen Stab, der zweimal abgebildet ist. Während Emma Brunner-Traut die doppelte Abbildung des Stabes für eine „Verbesserung“ hält,[169] wäre sie auch als die Darstellung der Bewegung des Gegen-

---

167 Dorn 2011: 197, 301–302 m. Taf. 242–243 (Nr. 263). Eine Variante des Motivs mit einem auf einer Standlinie nach links schreitendem Stier vor einem ihm auf der linken Seite des Ostrakons gegenüberstehenden Hirten findet sich im fragmentarischen oDeM 2752 (Vandier d'Abbadie 1959: Taf. XCIX; s.a. https://www.ifao.egnet.net/bases/archives/ostraca/docs/vues_th/NU_2006_03033.jpg). Der Hirte trägt seinen Stab rechts geschultert und hält mit seiner direkt unter dem Stiermaul befindlichen Hand den Stier an einem Strick, der wahrscheinlich durch die Nase des Stieres geführt ist. Der Strick ist zwischen Stier und Hirtenhand deutlich sichtbar gespannt, während das lose Ende des Strickes, das der Schwerkraft geschuldete Verhalten eines ansonsten fest umgriffenen Strickes realistisch darstellend, aus der Hand des Hirten herausbaumelt. Offensichtlich führt der Hirte den erhöhte Aufmerksamkeit verlangenden Stier an einer sehr kurzen Leine. Ähnliche Darstellungen sind auch in Gräbern belegt. In TT 82 (De Garis Davies 1915: Taf. VIb) ist ein Stier dargestellt, der sich mit auf Höhe der Schultern befindlichem Kopf nach links auf einen ihm zugewandten Hirten zubewegt. Der aufrecht stehende Hirte berührt den Stier mit seiner rechten Hand am Kopf, während er ihn mit seiner linken Hand an einem straff gespannt dargestellten kurzen Strick führt, der am Maul des Stieres befestigt ist. Das Ende des Strickes verläuft aus der Hand des Hirten hinaus Richtung Boden. Offensichtlich beruhigt der Hirte den Stier durch seine Berührung am Kopf und führt ihn an einer sehr kurzen straffen Leine.

168 Schäfer 1916: 27, 43 m. Abb. 23; Brunner-Traut 1956: 106 m. Taf. XXV (Nr. 110)

169 Brunner-Traut 1956: 106.

standes zu zwei verschiedenen Zeitpunkten in einem *polychronen* Einzelbild interpretierbar. Mit seiner linken Hand hält der Hirte den Stier möglicherweise[170] gleichzeitig an einem durch dessen Nase geführten Stick und einem an seinem Gehörn befestigten Lasso, dessen größter Teil sich zusammengerollt in der der Hand des Hirten befindet. Offensichtlich dirigiert[171] der Hirte den deutlich aufgebrachten Stier mit erhöhtem Körpereinsatz und unter Stockschlägen an kurzer Leine in die von ihm gewünschte Richtung (Motorschemata „Transferaktivität engagierte straffe Kontrolle" und „Kraftaktivität Schlag").

Abb. 14 | oBerlin 21439 (Schäfer 1916: 43)

oMM 14058[172] (Abb. 15) schließlich zeigt eine Darstellung, die mit der auf oDeM 2070 = oLouvre E 14367 (Abb. 4) gezeigten die größte Ähnlichkeit hat. Auch hier springt ein Stier mit schräg-senkrecht vom Boden abgestoßenen Hinterläufen und gestreckt nach vorn erhobenen Vorderläufen nach rechts auf einen ihm zugewandten auf der rechten Seite des Bildes dargestellten Hirten zu und berührt diesen möglicherweise auf Höhe von dessen Knien. Der Schwanz des Stieres ist allerdings nach vorn um seine linke Hüfte geschwungen[173] und sein Phallus ist nicht erigiert. Der Mensch steht im Gegensatz zu oDeM 2070 = oLouvre E 14367 (Abb. 4) mit leicht angewinkelten Knien aufrecht gegen den Stier gewandt. Möglicherweise hält er mit vor seinem Oberkörper zum Schlag nach vorn abgewinkeltem Arm in seiner rechten Hand einen länglichen Gegenstand (Stab?), der vor dem Hals des Stieres dargestellt ist.[174] In seiner linken, vor seinen Oberschenkel positionierten Hand hält der Hirte wahrscheinlich einen straffen Strick, der vom Kopf des Stieres herabführt und dessen unteres Ende aus seiner Hand heraushängt.[175] Offensichtlich versucht der Hirte einen ihn angehenden Stier durch straffen Zug am Strick und Schläge gegen dessen Kopf unter Kontrolle zu bringen (Motorschemata „Transferaktivität aufgeregte Kontrolle" und „Kraftaktivität Schlag").

So, wie aus dem Vergleich des hier thematischen Bildes mit den soeben vorgestellten Stücken klar hervorgeht, dass es sich bei der in oDeM 2070 = oLouvre E 14367 (Abb. 4) dar-

170 Brunner-Traut 1956: 106 spricht von *einem* Seil, das der Hirte „um den Nacken des Stieres geworfen hat".

171 Schäfer 1916: 27: „Ochse von einem sich zurückwendenden Mann an *Leinen* nach r. *gezogen* [Kursive G.M.]".

172 Peterson 1973: 94 u. Taf. 47, Nr. 86; s.a. https://collections.smvk.se/carlotta-mhm/web/object/3006073.

173 Eine ähnliche – offensichtlich ebenfalls agitierte – Schwanzpose zeigt das fragmentarische oDeM 3109 (Gasse 1986: frontispice rto.; s.a. https://www.ifao.egnet.net/bases/archives/ostraca/docs/vues_th/NU_2006_03372.jpg).

174 Alternativ könnte der Gegenstand auch als ein um den Hals des Tieres gelegter Strick angesprochen werden.

175 Alternativ könnte der Gegenstand auch als ein Stab interpretiert werden.

Abb. 15 | oMM 14058. Source: National Museums of World Culture – Mediterranean Museum, Sweden (CC BY)

gestellten Person um einen Hirten handelt, der sich im Gegensatz zu den variantenreichen Darstellungen von Bewegungsposen von Hirten in unterschiedlichen Stadien von Kontrolle aufgrund seiner besonderen Pose sowie der in seiner direkten Nähe markant positionierten Bildobjekte wie Stab und Lasso in einer sehr spezifischen Situation befindet, ist auch jeder ägyptischen Kommunikationsteilnehmer*in mit Diskurskompetenz klar, dass es sich bei dem in diesem Bild dargestellten Stier um ein Exemplar handelt, dessen Zustand seinerseits als Grund für die spezifische Bewegungspose des Hirten namhaft gemacht werden kann: Es handelt sich um einen Stier im Zustand gesteigerter Aufgeregtheit.

Dies kann aus dem Vergleich zwischen vielfach belegten Darstellungen geschlossen werden, die allein das „Basismotiv *Schreitender Stier*“[176] oder Stiere in Interaktion miteinander zeigen, in die dann auch Hirten involviert sein können. Jenseits von Szenen wie z.B. der des oDeM 2062, in denen Hirten mit ihren Arbeitsgeräten Stab und Lasso beim Hüten von Bovidenherden gezeigt sind,[177] sind hier besonders Darstellungen von kämpfenden Stieren von Relevanz, die zwischen dem Alten Reich und der 18. Dynastie in Grabdarstellungen und später in ramessidischen Bildostraka immer wieder abgebildet sind.[178] Aus den Beischriften solcher Grabdarstellungen geht hervor, dass Stierkämpfe nicht nur als Spektakel „angesehen“ (*m33 k3.w*) wurden,[179] sondern Stierhirten auch aktiv in solche

176 So Dorn 2011: 107 mit einer Liste solcher Darstellungen auf Ostraka des Neuen Reiches ebd.: 107–108.

177 oKairo JE 63794 (Vandier d’Abbadie 1936: Taf. IX; Minault-Gout 2002: Abb. 101). Das Bild zeigt zwei Hirten, die sich vor und hinter einer in zwei Registern dargestellten Herde schreitender Langhornrinder mit dieser in einer Marschlandschaft nach rechts bewegen. Der hintere Hirte, der ein Lasso um den Oberkörper gewickelt hat und in dessen beiden erhobenen Händen sich jeweils ein Stab befindet, treibt die Stiere voran, während sich der vordere Hirte mit Oberkörper und Armen nach hinten zur Herde umgewandt hat. Ein Arm ist erhoben, die zugehörige Hand ist weggebrochen, in der anderen Hand hält der Hirte auf Hüfthöhe ebenfalls einen Stab.

178 Einen guten und aktuellen Einstieg in die Kulturgeschichte ägyptischer Stierdarstellungen mit einem Fokus auf Bilder kämpfender Stiere bietet Mathieu 2019 mit exemplarischem Bildmaterial und relevanter älterer Literatur in Anm. 14. Die ebd.: 85–92 gegebene Interpretation der Bilder als Metaphern im Rahmen mythologischer oder königsideologischer Kontexte (s.o. den Exkurs zum narrativen Infinitiv) muss nicht nachgezeichnet werden, sie ist für die hier verfolgten Darstellungsziele zweitrangig und betrifft nicht die Ebene der hier analysierten ikonographischen Kodierung autonomer Bildnarrativität.

179 So etwa die Beischrift zur Stierkampfszene aus TT 82 (De Garis Davies 1915: Taf. VIb; s.a. http://www.osirisnet.net/popupImage.php?img=/tombes/nobles/amenemhat82/photo/amenemhat82_bs_38023.jpg&lang=en&sw=2560&sh=1440).

Abb. 16 | „Trennen" und „Lösen" der Stiere (Blackman 1915: Taf. XV)

Auseinandersetzungen eingriffen, indem sie die Stiere „trennten" (*wp.t*) oder voneinander „lösten" (*sfḫ*).[180]

Auf Ostraka ist eine solche Szene z.B. in oDeM 2071[181] dargestellt, die zwei kämpfende Stiere zeigt. Der linke Stier steht, der rechte Stier springt den linken mit erhobenen Vorderläufen an. Auf der rechten Seite des Bildes ist ein nach links orientierter Hirte mit einem in der Hand zum Schlag erhobenem Stock gezeigt, der den rechten Stier von hinten mit einem um dessen rechtes Horn geschlungenen Lasso zurückzuhalten versucht, dass über den Rücken des Stieres zur linken Hand des Hirten führt.[182] Die ikonographischen Details solcher Stierkampfszenen zeigen nun im Vergleich zu einfachen schreitenden Stieren und auch zu den oben besprochenen Darstellungen von schreitenden Stieren mit Hirten, wie der Zustand gesteigerter oder extremer Rage der Tiere in konventionalisierter Form kodiert ist.

Die Sprungpose „Stier im Angriff" mit vom Boden abgestoßenen Hinterläufen und gestreckt nach vorn erhobenen Vorderläufen, die in oDeM 2070 = oLouvre E 14367 (Abb. 4) gezeigt ist, ist ganz offensichtlich ikonographisch konventionalisiert. Das zeigen zwei bis ins Detail weitgehend identische Darstellungen, die auf oBrüssel MRAH E.06435[183]

180 Belege vom Alten Reich bis in die 18. Dynastie bei Mathieu 2019: 95–99, 101 mit Abb. 5, 6, 9, 11, 12a/b–14, 16, 20. Tatsächlich handelt es sich auch hier in der Regel um narrative Infinitive, mit deren Hilfe die mental gespeicherten Skripte zur Narrativierung solcher Szenen aktiviert werden, s.o. Exkurs.

181 Vandier d'Abbadie 1936: Taf XII.

182 Eine vergleichbare Szene ist auf oUC 33200 (Page 1983: 40 m. Abb. 58) belegt, das zwei auf einer Standlinie stehende Stiere mit jeweils verschieden hoch angehobenem Schwanz zeigt, die sich mit gesenktem Kopf gegenseitig auf die Hörner nehmen. Über dem rechen Stier ist ein auf einer Standlinie nach links schreitender Mann mit erhoben angewinkeltem Arm in Schlagpose dargestellt. Ob sich in der in Griffpose dargestellten entsprechenden Hand ursprünglich ein Gegenstand (z.B. ein Stab) befunden hat, ist nicht zu sagen.

183 oBrüssel MRAH E.06435 (Minault-Gout 2002: 132 m. Abb. 104); Photo zugänglich nach Eingabe der Nummer E.06435 in die Suchmaske „Search the collection" unter https://www.carmentis.be/eMP/eMuseumPlus?service=ExternalInterface&module=collection&moduleFunction=highlight&lang=en.

Abb. 17 | oBrüssel MRAH E.06435

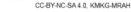

Abb. 18 | oMM 14076. Source: National Museums of World Culture – Mediterranean Museum, Sweden (CC BY)

(Abb. 17) sowie auf oMM 14076[184] (Abb. 18) realisiert sind und beide einen über der Standlinie nach rechts springenden Stier zeigen.

Darüber hinaus lassen sich mit dem nach hinten erhobenen Schwanz, dem erigierten Phallus und dem abgehenden Kot der Tiere (die aufgrund ihrer Größe und Positionierung eindeutig dem Stier zuzuordnenden Kugeln) weitere Details ausmachen, die durch ihre standardisierte ikonographische Kodierung auf das situativ gesteigerten Temperament der betreffenden Stiere verweisen. Exemplarisch macht dies ein Blick auf oMMA 24.2.27 (Abb. 19) deutlich. Das Stück zeigt mit erhobenen Schwänzen, erigierten Phalli und Kotkugeln ebenfalls sämtliche relevanten Details, mit denen ikonographisch standardisiert auf die Rage der Tiere verwiesen wird.[185]

---

184 oMM 14076 (Peterson 1973: 96 u. Taf. 50, Nr. 95; s.a. https://collections.smvk.se/carlotta-mhm/web/object/3005191). Peterson hält das Stück potentiell für das Fragment eines Stierkampfes, Ähnliches vermutet Leospo 1989: 237 m. Abb. 357 für das fragmentarische oTurin inv. Suppl. 6293, das ebenfalls einen nach rechts springenden Stier zeigt. Das Brüsseler Stück kann diese Vermutungen weder verifizieren noch widerlegen. oDeM 2111 (Vandier d'Abbadie 1936: Taf. XVIII) zeigt sehr skizzenhaft einen nach rechts springenden Stier ohne weitere Details.

185 Photo unter https://www.metmuseum.org/art/collection/search/544744. Weitere Darstellungen von Stier(kämpf)en mit entsprechenden Details:
(1a) Komplett nach oben erhobener Schwanz: oSenenmut 15 (Hayes 1942: 12 m. Taf. III, Abb. 15, rechter Stier. Der Schwanz des Tieres ist mehrfach dargestellt, originär wohl hängend wie beim linken Stier, dann aber in verschiedenen Stadien nach oben erhoben. Es wird sich um eine Korrektur handeln, die deutlich zeigt, dass es sich bei der Darstellung des erhobenen Schwanzes um ein konventionelles Mittel zum Ausdruck der gesteigerte Agitiertheit des Tieres handelt, und dass es dafür eine ideale Pose gibt); oSenenmut 16 (Hayes 1962: 12 m. Taf. III Abb. 16; linker Stier); oBrüssel MRAH E.06435 (Minault-Gout 2002: 132 m. Abb 104); oMM 14076 (Peterson 1973: 96 u. Taf.50, Nr. 95); oTurin inv. Suppl. 6293 (Leospo 1989: 237 m. Abb. 357); oDeM 2071 (Vandier d'Abbadie 1936: Taf. XII; linker Stier); oDeM 2122 (Vandier d'Abbadie 1936: Taf. XVI); oMM 14086 (Peterson 1973: 96 m. Taf. 52, Abb. 99, Kälbchen im Sprung); oBrüssel

Abb. 19 | oMMA 24.2.27 (Public Domain)

5 Zusammenfassung: Das monochrone Einzelbild oDeM 2070 = oLouvre E 14367 als autonome Erzählung

Die etwas längere Besprechung der Darstellung des nuancierten Variantenreichtums von Bildobjekten und Bewegungsposen in Bildern, die mit Stieren interagierende Hirten zeigen, war notwendig, um im Vergleich deutlich zu machen, warum die ikonographische Kodierung von Bildobjekten und Bewegungsposen sowie deren kompositorische Verteilung auf der Bildfläche des untersuchten oDeM 2070 = oLouvre E 14367 (Abb. 4) für antike und moderne Betrachter*innen gleichermaßen eindeutig eine Lesbarkeit des Bildes als autonome (Alltags-)Erzählung anbietet.[186] Der Stier ist, erkennbar an seiner

MRAH E.06372 (Kälbchen im Sprung; Photo zugänglich nach Eingabe der Nummer E.06372 in die Suchmaske „Search the collection“ unter https://www.carmentis.be/eMP/eMuseumPlus?service=ExternalInterface&module=collection&moduleFunction=highlight&lang=en.

(1b) leicht erhobene Schwänze: oUC 33200 (Page 1983: 40 m. Abb. 58); oCG 25.062 vso. (Daressy 1901: Taf. XIII).

(1c) Schwanzende um die Hüfte schlagend: oDeM 3109 (Gasse 1986: frontispice rto.); oMM 14039 (Peterson 1973: 94 u. Taf. 47, Nr. 86).

(2) erigierter Phallus: oCG 25.062 vso. (Daressy 1901: Taf. XIII); oBrüssel MRAH E.06435 (Minault-Gout 2002: 132 m. Abb. 104); oMM 14076 (Peterson 1973: 96 u. Taf.50, Nr. 95); oDeM 2071 (Vandier d'Abbadie 1936: Taf. XII, rechter Stier).

(3) abgehender Kot: oBrüssel MRAH E.06435 (Minault-Gout 2002: 132 m. Abb. 104); oMM 14076 (Peterson 1973: 96 u. Taf.50, Nr. 95); oDeM 3109 (Gasse 1986: frontispice rto.); oDeM 2071 (Vandier d'Abbadie 1936: Taf. XII, linker Stier).

186 In einem persönlichen Gespräch äußerte mein Wiener Kollege Manfred Bietak die Ansicht, dass es sich beim hier untersuchten Bild (Abb. 4) um die Darstellung eines „Stierspringers“ handelt, wie sie auch aus Tell el Dab'a bekannt geworden sind, vgl. etwa Marinatos & Bietak 2007. Die ikonographische Differenz der Darstellungen von Stierspielen (s. etwa Decker 2003) zum Kontinuum der in Stier-Hirten-Szenen dargestellten Bewegungsposen und Bildobjekten (Lasso, Stab) sprechen allerdings deutlich gegen eine solche Interpretation.

Sprungpose, seinem nach hinten erhobenen Schwanz, seinem erigierten Phallus und dem abgehenden Kot, im Moment höchster Rage dargestellt (Motorschema „wilder Angriff"). Der Hirte seinerseits ist, erkennbar an seiner spezifischen Bewegungspose mit gegenüber dem Oberschenkel nach hinten versetztem Oberkörper, im Moment des Zurückweichens (Motorschema „Rückzug bei Angriff") dargestellt. Gleichzeitig ist der Hirte, erkennbar an der Bewegungspose der vor das Gesicht erhobenen Hände, bei einer intuitiv ausgeführten Abwehraktion (Motorschema „Selbstschutz") dargestellt. Die spezifische Positionierung des Bildobjekts Stab in der direkt vor dem Kopf des Stieres erhobenen Hand (Motorschema „Kraftaktivität Schlag") verstärkt die Abwehrreaktion zu einem Selbstverteidigungsversuch. Besonders bemerkenswert ist die Positionierung des Lassos über dem Kopf des Hirten und ohne Zugriff durch eine seiner Hände. Während dieses Objekt aufgrund seiner geringen Größe und der Position in direkter Nähe zum Hirten diesem auch ohne den Vergleich mit anderen Bildern zuzuordnen gewesen wäre,[187] sichert ein solcher Vergleich nicht nur die Identifizierbarkeit des Objektes als Lasso. Die Darstellung des Lassos über dem Kopf des Hirten und ohne seinen Zugriff macht im Gegensatz zu den Bildern, in denen der Hirte das Gerät bewusst nicht einsetzt oder gekonnt und kontrolliert verwendet (Motorschema „Transferaktivität Kontrolle"), vor allem klar, dass der Hirte in einem Moment unmittelbaren Kontrollverlustes gezeigt wird. Die besondere Positionierung des Lassos verdichtet damit den Eindruck von Intensität, der bereits durch den direkten Kontakt der Vorderhufe des Stieres mit dem Körper des Hirten hervorgerufen wird.

Die Geschichte, definiert als ein *Geschehen* mit *Konkretheit*, *Temporalität* und *Kontiguität* (s.o. Abschnitt 2) und verstanden zunächst im Sinne des narratologischen Begriffs der ‚fabula'[188] ist damit recht einfach erzählt: Ein wütender Stier greift einen Hirten an. Dieser weicht zurück, verliert dabei sein Lasso und verteidigt sich durch Schläge mit seinem Stab auf den Kopf des Stieres. Dies oder Ähnliches jedenfalls wäre eine rezipientenseitige Narrativierung des Bildinhalts zu einem ‚Situationsmodell' (s.o. Abschnitte 2–3), die das Bild im Rahmen einer kognitionsnarratologisch informierten Interpretation nachgerade zwangsläufig induziert. Die im Bild ikonographisch konventionalisierte Repräsentation von Akteuren, Objekten und Bewegungsposen aktiviert bei Rezipient*innen unter Rückgriff auf ihr Erfahrungswissen Objekt- und Bewegungsschemata sowie situationsspezifische Verhaltensskripte, die als narrative Strukturen mit je eigener Temporalität und Kausalität wirken: Der Stier greift an, *weil* und *nachdem* er in Rage geraten war, und der Hirte verliert sein Lasso und weicht zurück, *weil* und *nachdem* er angegriffen wurde, und er weicht zurück und wehrt sich mit Stockschlägen, *weil* es ihm ein situationsbedingt natürliches *Bedürfnis* ist, seine Gesundheit zu erhalten.[189] Aus einer kognitionsnarratologisch angereicherten und genuin mediensensiblen Perspektive auf die Erzählfähigkeit von Bildern würde dies allein schon ausreichen, um das hier analysierte Bild darüber hinaus auch noch als eine *eigenständige* Erzählung („a narrative proper", s.o. Abschnitt 2) anzusprechen:

187 S. dazu Veits 2020: 141.

188 Vgl. nochmals Wellek & Warren 2019 [1942]: 194: „the temporal-causal sequence which is, however it may be told, the ‚story' or story-stuff […,] an abstraction from the ‚raw materials'", s.o. Abschnitt 1.

189 Zur Relevanz dieser Art von Erfahrungswissen vgl. Veits 2020: 138–141.

Die dem Bild eigene simultane ‚Bildzeit' organisiert die impliziten Temporalitäts- und Kausalitätsstrukturen der über die Bildfläche verteilten und miteinander kontextualisierten Bildobjekte in medienspezifischer Weise zu einer auf Diskurs- bzw. Repräsentationsebene (‚Plot', ‚Text', ‚Sujet')[190] nicht linear, sondern grundsätzlich simultan vermittelten narrativen Sinnstruktur (s.o. Abschnitt 3).

Es kann aber überdies argumentiert werden, dass das Bild wohl ebenfalls aus der Perspektive der klassischen, implizit „medienblind" verbliebenen Bildnarratologie als Erzählung gewertet werden müsste, obwohl diese am Primat des textuellen Erzählens als Prototyp festhält und monochronen Einzelbildern die Fähigkeit zum Erzählung-Sein unter Hinweis auf deren angeblich fehlende ‚doppelte Temporalität' abspricht. Tatsächlich kann im hier analysierten Fall aber sogar auf Ebene des piktorialen Erzähldiskurses eine ebenso klar temporalisierte Plotstruktur und damit auch die strukturierte Steuerung des Rezeptionsvorgangs ausgemacht werden. So wird zunächst über die Größe der Bildobjekte und deren Bewegungsrichtung von links nach vermittelt, dass die erzählte Geschichte mit dem Stier als Subjekt beginnt: *Ein Stier greift einen Hirten an. Dieser weicht daraufhin vor ihm zurück, um sich in Sicherheit zu bringen.* Ein zweiter Blick auf kleiner dargestellte Details (Schwanz, Phallus, Kot) ermöglicht dann eine situationsspezifische Kausalisierung des dargestellten Geschehens. *Der Stier war nämlich in Rage geraten.* Auf der Suche nach weiteren Details finden Betrachtende dann auch zum Hirten gehörende Zusatzinformationen mit situativer Kausalität: *Beim Zurückweichen verliert der Hirte zwar sein Lasso, er verteidigt sich aber durch Stockschläge gegen den Kopf des Stieres.* Die Geschichte bekommt damit nicht nur eine deutliche Plotstruktur mit einem klaren Verlauf von „Komplikation" zu „Lösung", sondern kann bei Rezipierenden zudem auch noch *Spannung*[191] erzeugen, insofern nicht ganz sicher ist, wie der Vorfall für den Hirten am Ende tatsächlich ausgehen wird.

Die vorgelegte Studie bestätigt damit die in jüngster Zeit häufiger vertretene Ansicht, dass auch *monochrone* Einzelbilder autonome Erzählungen sein können. Dass dies auch für Ägypten gilt, ist aus adäquat zugeschnittener narratologischer Perspektive am Ende wohl weniger überraschend als aus einem ägyptologischen Blickwinkel, aus dem schon ägyptische Alltagszenen für nicht-narrativ gehalten wurden und der mit einem klassisch-narratologischen Kriterienkatalog an die Bearbeitung ägyptischer Objekte ging. Das Ergebnis der Studie zeigt zweierlei: Narratologische Kriterien wirken von sich aus weder transmedial noch transhistorisch noch transkulturell. Werden sie aber nicht einfach nur in einem solchen trans-Verständnis angewendet, sondern medien- oder kulturspezifisch zugeschnitten wie z.B. das an ägyptische Erwartbarkeiten angepasste Verständnis von ‚Tellability', dann handelt es sich um eine echte „Konfrontation"[192] von narratologischer

190 Vgl. nochmals Wellek & Warren 2019 [1942]: 194: „the ‚narrative structure' [of] the artistically ordered presentation", s.o. Abschnitt 1.

191 Vgl. dazu Speidel 2018b: 54–56, 60–62, 66–70 vor allem in kritischer Auseinandersetzung mit Werner Wolfs Argument der „deficiency of teleology" in monochronen Einzelbildern, vgl. Wolf 2003: 197–188, 192 (Zitat); s.a. Wolf 2002: 55. Wolfs Position wurde ägyptologisch von Nadja Braun (2020: 37) übernommen.

192 Zum Gegensatz von „application" and „confrontation" vgl. Bal 2002: 24.

Theoriebildung und ägyptischen Gegenständen. Eine solche „Konfrontation“ ermöglicht zweierlei: Erstens wird die Ägyptologie adäquatere und auch interdisziplinär anschlussfähige Wahrnehmungen von ägyptischen Gegenständen „on their *own terms* [Kursive: Mieke Bal]“[193] pflegen können als solche, die bisher gepflegt wurden. Und die Narratologie bekommt im Gegenzug kontextsensiblere Kriterien zurück, ohne dass dadurch ihre Stellung als erzählwissenschaftlicher Leitdiskurs in Frage gestellt wäre. Beide Disziplinen treffen sich damit im Feld der *Historischen Narratologie*.[194] Das kann passieren, wenn *Konzepte reisen*.[195]

Bibliographie

Abbot, H. Porter. 2000. The Evolutionary Origins of the Storied Mind: Modelling the Prehistory of Narrative Consciousness and Its Discontents, in: *Narrative* 8/3, 247–256.

Alber, Jan & Monika Fludernik. 2010. Introduction, in: Jan Alber & Monika Fludernik (Hgg.), *Postclassical Narratology: Approaches and Analyses*, Theory and Interpretation of Narrative, Columbus, 1–31.

Baines, John. 1990. Restricted Knowledge, Hierarchy, and Decorum: Modern Perceptions and Ancient Institutions, in: *Journal of the American Research Center in Egypt* 27, 1–27.

Bal, Mieke. 1999. Close Reading Today: From Narratology to Cultural Analysis, in: Walter Grünzweig & Andreas Solbach (Hgg.), *Grenzüberschreitungen: Narratologie im Kontext – Transcending Boundaries: Narratology in Context*, Tübingen, 19–41.

Bal, Mieke. 2002. *Travelling Concepts in the Humanities: A Rough Guide*, Toronto, Buffalo & London.

Bamberg, Michael. 2013. Identity and Narration, in: Peter Hühn et al. (Hgg.), *The Living Handbook of Narratology*, Hamburg, URL = https://www-archiv.fdm.uni-hamburg.de/lhn/node/29.html [last view date 28 April 2023].

Baroni, Raphaël. 2014. Tellability, in: Peter Hühn et al. (Hgg.), *The Living Handbook of Narratology*, Hamburg, URL = https://www-archiv.fdm.uni-hamburg.de/lhn/node/30.html [last view date 28 April 2023].

Barthes, Roland. 1975 [1966]. An Introduction to the Structural Analysis of Narrative, in: *New Literary History* 6, 237–272.

Blackman, Aylward M. 1915. *The Rock Tombs of Meir II: The Tomb-Chapel of Senebi's Son Ukh-Hotp (B, No. 2) with Two Appendixes on Hieroglyphs and Other Details in B, Nos. 1, 2, 4*, Archaeological Survey of Egypt 23, London.

Blümel, Claudia. 2013. Augenblick und Gleichzeitigkeit – Zur Simultanität im Bild, in: Philipp Hubmann & Till Julian Huss (Hgg.), *Simultanität: Modelle der Gleichzeitigkeit in den Wissenschaften und Künsten*, Kultur und Medientheorie, Bielefeld, 37–55.

Boehm, Gottfried. 1987. Bild und Zeit, in: Hannelore Paflik (Hg.), *Das Phänomen Zeit in Kunst und Wissenschaft*, Acta Humanoria, Weinheim, 1–23.

Boehm, Gottfried. 2018. Die Sichtbarkeit der Zeit und die Logik des Bildes, in: Michael Moxter & Markus Forchow (Hgg.), *Die Zeit der Bilder: Ikonische Repräsentation und Temporalität*, Hermeneutische Untersuchungen zur Theologie 73, Tübingen, 38–60.

Braun, Nadja S. 2020. *Bilder erzählen: Visuelle Narrativität im alten Ägypten*, Ägyptologische Studien Leipzig 2, Heidelberg.

---

193 Bal 2002: 8.

194 Vgl. nochmals Gerald Moers, Egyptological narratology as *historical narratology*, in diesem Band: Abschnitt 4.

195 Zum Konzept der *traveling concepts* vgl. grundsätzlich Bal 2002: bes. 3–55.

Breithaupt, Fritz. 2022. *Das narrative Gehirn: Was unsere Neuronen erzählen*, Berlin.

Brockmeier, Jens. 2012. Narrative Scenarios: Toward a Culturally Thick Notion of Narrative, in: Jaan Valsiner (Hg.), *The Oxford Handbook of Culture and Psychology*, Oxford & New York, 439–467.

Brunner-Traut, Emma. 1956. *Die altägyptischen Scherbenbilder (Bildostraka) der deutschen Museen und Sammlungen*, Wiesbaden.

Brunner-Traut, Emma. 1979. *Egyptian Artists' Sketches: Figured Ostraka from the Gayer-Anderson-Collection in the Fitzwilliam Museum, Cambridge*, Uitgaven von het Nederlands Historisch-Archaeologisch Instituut te Istanbul XLV, Leiden.

Budge, E. Wallis A. 1899. *The Book of the Dead: Facsimiles of the Papyri of Hunefer, Anhai, Kerāsher and Netchemet; with Supplementary Text from the Papyrus of Nu with Transcripts, etc.*, London.

Chatman, Seymour. 1978. *Story and Discourse: Narrative Structure in Discourse and Film*, Ithaca, N.Y. & London.

Chatman, Seymour. 1990. *Coming to Terms: The Rhetoric of Narrative in Fiction and Film*, Ithaca, N.Y. & London.

Daressy, Georges. 1901. *Ostraca*, Catalogue général des antiquités égyptiennes du musée du Caire Nos. 25001–25385, Le Caire.

Davis, Withney. 1989. *The Canonical Tradition in Ancient Egyptian Art*, Cambridge, New York & Melbourne.

Davis, Whitney. 1992. *Masking the Blow: The Scene of Representation in Late Prehistoric Egyptian Art*, Berkeley, Los Angeles & Oxford.

Decker, Wolfgang. 2003. Zum Stand der Erforschung des ‚Stierspiels' in der Alten Welt, in: Reinhard Dittmann, Christian Eder & Bruno Jacobs (Hgg.), *Altertumswissenschaften im Dialog: Festschrift für Wolfram Nagel zur Vollendung seines 80. Lebensjahres*, Alter Orient und Altes Testament: Veröffentlichungen zur Kultur und Geschichte des Alten Orients und des Alten Testaments 306, Münster, 31–79.

De Garis Davies, Nina. 1915. *The Tomb of Amenemhēt (No. 82)*, The Theban Tomb Series 1, London.

Di Biase-Dyson, Camilla. 2019. Narrative by Ancient Egyptians and of Ancient Egypt: A State of the Art, in: Dina Serova & al. (Hgg.), *Narrative: Geschichte – Mythos – Repräsentation. Beiträge des achten Berliner Arbeitskreises Junge Aegyptologie (BAJA 8) 1.12.–3.12.2017*, Göttinger Orientforschungen IV/65, Wiesbaden, 39–63.

Dominicus, Brigitte. 1994. *Gesten und Gebärden in Darstellungen des Alten und Mittleren Reiches*, Studien zu Archäologie und Geschichte Altägyptens 10, Heidelberg.

Dorn, Andreas. 2011. *Arbeiterhütten im Tal der Könige: Ein Beitrag zur altägyptischen Sozialgeschichte aufgrund von neuem Quellenmaterial aus der Mitte der 20. Dynastie (ca. 1150. v. Chr.)*, Aegyptiaca Helvetica 23, Basel.

Eaton, Katherine. 2013. *Ancient Egyptian Temple Ritual: Performance, Pattern, and Practice*, Routledge Studies in Egyptology 1, New York.

Eco, Umberto. 1979. *Lector in fabula: la cooperazione interprtativa nei testi narrative*, Milano.

Fahrenwald, Claudia. 2011. *Erzählen im Kontext neuer Lernkulturen: Eine bildungstheoretische Analyse im Spannungsfeld von Wissen, Lernen und Subjekt*, Wiesbaden 2011.

Faulkner, Raymond O. 1985 [1972]. *The Ancient Egyptian Book of the Dead, Revised Edition*, London.

Fitzenreiter, Martin (Hg.). 2009. *Das Ereignis: Geschichtsschreibung zwischen Vorfall und Befund, Workshop vom 03.10 bis 05.10.08*, IBAES – Internet-Beiträge zur Ägyptologie und Sudanarchäologie / Studies from the Internet on Egyptology and Sudanarchaeology 10, London.

Fitzenreiter, Martin. 2019. Schon wieder Stele Louvre C 14 des Irtisen, in: *Göttinger Miszellen: Beiträge zur ägyptologischen Diskussion* 257, 49–61.

Fludernik, Monika. 1996. *Towards a "Natural" Narratology*, London.

Förster, Frank. 2022. A Pretty Happy Hippo: Pictorial Narrativity in the Early Naqada Period, in: Gunnar Sperveslage (Hg.), *Early Egyptian Miscellanies: Discussions and Essays on Predynastic and Early Dynastic Egypt*, IBAES – Internet-Beiträge zur Ägyptologie und Sudanarchäologie / Studies from the Internet on Egyptology and Sudanarchaeology 26, Berlin & London, 37–50.

Frank, Hilmar & Tanja Frank. 1999. Zur Erzählforschung in der Kunstwissenschaft, in: Eberhard Lämmert (Hg.), *Die erzählerische Dimension: eine Gemeinsamkeit der Künste*, Literaturforschung, Berlin, 35–51.

Gardiner, Alan H. & T. Eric Peet [Second Edition Revised and Augmented by Jaroslav Černý]. 1952. *The Inscriptions of Sinai Part I: Introduction and Plates*, Oxford.

Gardiner, Alam H. 1957 [[1]1927]. *Egyptian Grammar: Being an Introduction to the Study of Hieroglyphs*, Third Edition, revised, Oxford.

Gasse, Anni. 1986. *Catalogue des ostraca figurés de Deir el Médineh n°s 3100–3372 (5e fascicule)*, Documents de fouilles publié par les membres de L'Institut Français d'Archéologie orientale du Caire XXIII, Le Caire.

Gnirs, Andrea. 1996. Die ägyptische Autobiographie, in: Antonio Loprieno (Hg.). *Ancient Egyptian Literature: History and Forms*, Probleme der Ägyptologie 10, Leiden, New York & Köln, 191–241.

Guth, Sonja. 2018. *Hirtenbilder: Untersuchungen zur kulturimmanenten Sicht auf eine altägyptische Personengruppe*, Studien zur altägyptischen Kultur, Beiheft 21, Hamburg.

Hausken, Liv. 2004. Coda: Textual Theory and Blind Spots in Media Studies, in: Marie-Laure Ryan (Hg.), *Narrative across Media: The Language of Storytelling*, Lincoln & London, 391–403.

Hayes, William C. 1942. *Ostraka and Name Stones from the Tomb of Sen-Mūt (No. 71) at Thebes*, Publications of the Metropolitan Museum of Art Egyptian Expedition XV, New York.

Herman, David. 2013. Cognitive Narratology (revised version; uploaded 22 September 2013), in: Peter Hühn et al. (Hgg.), *The Living Handbook of Narratology*, Hamburg, URL = https://www-archiv.fdm.uni-hamburg.de/lhn/node/38.html [last view date Nov. 08 2022].

Honold, Alexander & Ralf Simon. 2010. Vorwort, in: Alexander Honold und Ralf Simon (Hgg.), *Das erzählende und das erzählte Bild*, eikones, München, 9–24.

Huber, Martin & Wolf Schmid (Hgg.). 2018. *Grundthemen der Literaturwissenschaft: Erzählen*, Grundthemen der Literaturwissenschaft, Berlin & Boston.

Huck, Christian. 2009. Coming to Our Senses: Narratology and the Visual, in: Peter Hühn, Wolf Schmid & Jörg Schönert (Hgg.), *Modeling Mediacy: Point of View, Perspective, Focalization*, Narratologia: Contributions to Narrative Theory / Beiträge zur Erzähltheorie 17, Berlin & New York, 201–218.

Hübner, Gert. 2015. Historische Narratologie und mittelalterlich-frühneuzeitliches Erzählen, *Literaturwissenschaftliches Jahrbuch* 56, 11–54.

Hühn, Peter. 2015 Visual Narratives: Narration in Paintings and Photographs, in: *Literaturwissenschaftliches Jahrbuch* 56, 349–365.

Imdahl, Max. 1996 [1980]. *Giotto, Arenafresken: Ikonographie, Ikonologie, Ikonik*, München.

Iser, Wolfgang. 1994 [1976]. *Der Akt des Lesens: Theorie ästhetischer Wirkung*, Uni-Taschenbücher 636, 4. Aufl., München.

Jørgensen, Mogens Schou. 2002. *Gravskatte fra det Gamle Ægypten / Tomb Treasures from Ancient Egypt*, Kopenhagen.

Kafalenos, Emma. 1996. Implications of Narrative in Paintings and Photography, in: *New Novel Review* 3/2, 54–65.

Kafalenos, Emma. 2006. *Narrative Causalities*, Theory and Interpretation of Narrative, Columbus.

Keimer, Ludwig. 1941. *Études d'Égyptologie III*, Le Caire.

Kemp, Wolfgang. 1987. *Sermo Corporius: Die Erzählung der mittelalterlichen Glasfenster*, München.

Kemp, Wolfgang. 1989. Ellipsen, Analepsen, Gleichzeitigkeiten: Schwierige Aufgaben für die Bilderzählung, in: Wolfgang Kemp (Hg.), *Der Text des Bildes: Möglichkeiten und Mittel eigenständiger Bilderzählung*, Literatur und andere Künste 4, München, 62–88.

Kemp, Wolfgang. 1992. Kunstwissenschaft und Rezeptionsästhetik, in: Wolfgang Kemp (Hg.), *Der Betrachter ist im Bild: Kunstwissenschaft und Rezeptionsästhetik*, Neuausgabe, Berlin 7–28.

Kemp, Wolfgang 1996. Narrative, in: Robert S. Nelson (Hg.), *Critical Terms for Art History*, Chicago, 58–69.

Kemp, Wolfgang. 2018. Erzählen in Bildern, in: Martin Huber & Wolf Schmid (Hgg.), *Grundthemen der Literaturwissenschaft: Erzählen*, Grundthemen der Literaturwissenschaft, Berlin & Boston, 472–484.

Kibédi Varga, Aron. 1990. Visuelle Argumentation und visuelle Narrativität, in: Wolfgang Harms (Hg.), *Text und Bild, Bild und Text*, DFG-Symposion 1988, Stuttgart, 356–367.

Klauk, Tobias & Tilman Köppe. 2014. Telling vs. Showing, in: Peter Hühn et al. (Hgg.), *The Living Handbook of Narratology*, Hamburg, URL = https://www-archiv.fdm.uni-hamburg.de/node/84.html [last view date: 21 Feb 2023].

Koch, Roland. 1990. *Die Erzählung des Sinuhe*, Bibliotheca Aegyptiaca XVII, Brüssel.

Kreiswirth, Martin. 1992. Trusting the Tale: The Narrativist Turn in the Human Sciences, in: *New Literary History* 23, 629–657.

Landgráfová, Renata [with contribution by Hana Navrátilova]. 2011. *It is My Good Name that You Should Remember: Egyptian Biographical Texts on Middle Kingdom Stela*, Prag 2011.

Leemans, Conrad. 1882. *Monumens égyptiens du Musée d'antiquités des Pays-Bas à Leide. 3. Partie, Monuments funéraires, Section T, Papyrus égyptien funéraire hiéroglyphique du Musée d'antquités des Pays-Bas à Leide*, 2, Leiden.

Leospo, Enrichetta. 1989. Propitiatory Rites, Aspects of Daily Life, Work and Free Time Activities as Depicted on Painted Linen and Wall Decorations, in: Anna Maria Donadoni Roveri (Hg.), *Egyptian Museum of Turin: Egyptian Civilization, Monumental Art*, Turin, 186–247.

Lessing, Gotthold Ephraim. 1839 [1766]. *Laokoon: oder über die Grenzen der Mahlerey und Poesie*, fünfte, neu durchgesehene Auflage, Berlin.

Marinatos, Nannó & Manfred Bietak. 2007. Taureador Scenes in Tell el-Dab'a (Avaris), in: Manfred Bietak & Nannó Marinatos (Hgg.), *Taureador Scenes in Tell el-Dab'a (Avaris) and Knossos*, Untersuchungen der Zweigstelle Kairo des Österreichischen Archäologischen Instituts 27, Denkschriften der Gesamtakademie 43, Wien, 13–112.

Martínez, Matías. 2017. Was ist Erzählen?, in: Matías Martínez (Hg.), *Erzählen: Ein interdisziplinäres Handbuch*, Stuttgart, 2–6.

Martínez, Matías (Hg.). 2017. *Erzählen: Ein interdisziplinäres Handbuch*, Stuttgart.

Mathieu, Bernard. 2019. Taureau contre taureau. Une motif iconographique de l'Égypte pharaonique et ses implications idéologiques, in: Sidney Aufrère (Hg.), *Les taureaux de l'Égypte ancienne: Publication éditée à l'occasion de la 14e rencontre d'égyptologie de Nîmes*, Nîmes, 75–106.

Meister, Jan Christoph. 2018. Erzählen: Eine anthropologische Universalie, in: Martin Huber & Wolf Schmid (Hgg.), *Grundthemen der Literaturwissenschaft: Erzählen*, Grundthemen der Literaturwissenschaft, Berlin & Boston, 88–112.

Mellmann, Katja. 2017. Anthropologie des Erzählens, in: Matías Martínez (Hg.), *Erzählen: Ein interdisziplinäres Handbuch*, Stuttgart, 208–317.

Meyers, Elizabeth l. 1985. Component Design as a Narrative Device in Amarna Tomb Art, in: Herbert L. Kessler (Hg.) *Pictorial Narrative in Antiquity and the Middle Ages*, Studies in the History of Art 16, Symposium Series / Centre for Advanced Study in the Visual Arts 4, Washington, 35–51.

Minault-Gout, Anne. 2002. *Carnets de pierre: L'art des ostraca dans l'Égypte ancienne*, Paris.

Moers, Gerald. 2004. »Unter den Sohlen Pharaos« – Fremdheit und Alterität im pharaonischen Ägypten, in: Frank Lauterbach, Fritz Paul & Ulrike Christine Sander (Hgg.), *Abgrenzung – Eingrenzung: Komparatistische Studien zur Dialektik kultureller Identitätsbildung*, Abhandlungen der Akademie der Wissenschaften in Göttingen, Philologisch-Historische Klasse 3/264, Göttingen, 81–160.

Moers, Gerald. 2011. Broken Icons: The Emplotting of Master-Narratives in the Ancient Egyptian *Tale of Sinuhe*, in: Fredrik Hagen et al. (Hgg.), *Narratives of Egypt and the Ancient Near East: Literary and Linguistic Approaches*, Orientalia Lovaniensia Analecta 189, Leuven, Paris & Walpole/MA, 165–176.

Moers, Gerald. Im Druck [avisiert für 2025]. Strategic Discourse in the Ancient Near East and Egypt: Egypt, in: Henriette van der Blom & Harvey Yunis (Hgg.), *The Cambridge History of Rhetoric Cambridge, Vol. I: Rhetoric of the Ancient World (to 250 CE)*, Cambridge.

Morenz, Ludwig D. 2020. *Vom Kennen und Können: Zur Mentalitäts- und Mediengeschichte des Mittleren Reiches im Horizont von Abydos*, Thot: Beiträge zur historischen Epistemologie und Medienarchäologie 5, Berlin.

Müller, Günther. 1974 [1946]. Die Bedeutung der Zeit in der Erzählkunst. Bonner Antrittsvorlesung 1946, in: Elena Müller (Hg.), *Günther Müller: Morphologische Poetik – Gesammelte Aufsätze*, 2. unveränderte Aufl., Tübingen 1974, 247–268.

Nünning, Ansgar. 2003. Narratology or Narratologies: Taking Stock of Recent Developments, Critique, and Modest Proposals for Future Usages of the Term, in: Tom Kindt & Hans-Harald Müller (Hgg.), *What is Narratology? Questions and Answers Regarding the Status of a Theory*, Narratologia: Contributions to Narrative Theory / Beiträge zur Erzähltheorie 1, Berlin & New York, 239–275.

Nünning, Vera & Ansgar Nünning (Hgg.). 2002. *Erzähltheorie transgenerisch, intermedial, interdisziplinär*, WVT – Handbücher zum literaturwissenschaftlichen Studium 5, Trier.

Page, Anthea. 1983. *Ancient Egyptian Figured Ostraca in the Petrie Collection*, Warminster.

Peterson, Bengt. E. J. 1973. *Zeichnungen aus einer Totenstadt: Bildostraka aus Theben West, ihre Fundplätze, Themata und Zweckbereiche mitsamt einem Katalog der Gayer-Anderson-Sammlung Stockholm*, Medelhavsmuseet – The Museum of Mediterranean and Near Eastern Antiquities Bulletin 7–8, Stockholm.

Pier, John. 2018. Von der französischen strukturalistischen Erzähltheorie zur nordamerikanischen postklassischen Narratologie, in: Martin Huber & Wolf Schmid (Hgg.), *Grundthemen der Literaturwissenschaft: Erzählen*, Grundthemen der Literaturwissenschaft, Berlin & Boston, 59–87.

Prince, Gerald. 1988. The Disnarrated, in: *Style* 22/1, 1–8.

Prince, Gerald. 1999. Revisiting Narrativity, in: Walter Grünzweig & Andreas Solbach (Hgg.), *Grenzüberschreitungen: Narratologie im Kontext – Transcending Boundaries: Narratology in Context*, Tübingen, 43–51.

Ranta, Michael. 2011. Stories in Pictures (and Non-Pictorial Objects): A Narratological and Cognitive Psychological Approach, in: Contemporary Aesthetics (Journal Archive) 9, article 6, URL = https://digitalcommons.risd.edu/liberalarts_contempaesthetics/vol9/iss1/6/ [last view date: 21 Feb 2023].

Ranta, Michael. 2013. (Re)Creating Order: Narrative and Implied World Views in Pictures, in: *Storyworlds: A Journal of Narrative Studies* 5, 1–30.

Reuter, Guido. 2003. Zeitaspekte der Skulptur, in: Andrea von Hülsen-Esch, Hans Körner & Guido Reuter (Hgg.), *Bilderzählungen – Zeitlichkeit im Bild*, Europäische Geschichtsdarstellungen 4, Köln, Weimar & Wien, 65–84.

Rimmon-Kenan, Shlomith. 2006. Concepts of Narrative, in: Matti Hyvärinen, Anu Korhonen & Juri Mykkänen (Hgg.), *The Traveling Concept of Narrative*, Studies across Disciplines in the Humanities and Social Sciences 1, Helsinki, 10–19.

Römer, Inga. 2017. Narrative Identität, in: Matías Martínez (Hg.), *Erzählen: Ein interdisziplinäres Handbuch*, Stuttgart, 263–269.

Rogner, Frederik. 2019. Zeit und Zeitlichkeit im ägyptischen Flachbild: Wege zur Analyse bildlicher Narrativität im Alten Ägypten, in: Dina Serova & al. (Hgg.), *Narrative: Geschichte – Mythos – Repräsentation. Beiträge des achten Berliner Arbeitskreises Junge Aegyptologie (BAJA 8) 1.12.–3.12.2017*, Göttinger Orientforschungen IV/65, Wiesbaden, 93–116.

Rogner, Frederik. 2021. Narrativity – Storytelling – Reference: On Some Fundamental Distinctions in the Discussion of Images (Review of Nadja S. Braun, *Bilder erzählen: Visuelle Narrativität im alten Ägypten*, Ägyptologische Studien Leipzig 2, Heidelberg, 2020), in: *Bibliotheca Orientalis* 78, 568–596.

Rogner, Frederik. 2022. *Bildliche Narrativität – Erzählen mit Bildern: Rezeption und Verwendung figürlicher Darstellungen im ägyptischen Neuen Reich*, Swiss Egyptological Studies 3, Basel & Frankfurt a.M.

Rogner, Frederik. 2023. Reden – Zeigen – Lesen: Multimodale Formen der Ansprache in altägyptischen Bild-Text-Kompositionen, in: *Lingua Aegyptia: Journal of Egyptian Language Studies* 31, 161–184.

Roussin, Philippe. 2017. What is Your Narrative? Lessons from the Narrative Turn, in: Per Krogh Hansen et al. (Hgg.), *Emerging Vectors of Narratology*, Narratologia: Contributions to Narrative Theory / Beiträge zur Erzähltheorie 57, Berlin & Boston, 383–404.

Ryan, Marie-Laure (Hg.). 2004. *Narrative across Media: The Language of Storytelling*, Lincoln & London.

Ryan, Marie-Laure. 2004a. Introduction, in: Marie-Laure Ryan (Hg.). 2004. *Narrative across Media: The Language of Storytelling*, Lincoln & London, 1–40.

Ryan, Marie-Laure. 2004b. Still Pictures, in: Marie-Laure Ryan (Hg.). 2004. *Narrative across Media: The Language of Storytelling*, Lincoln & London, 139–144.

Ryan, Marie-Laure. 2005. On the Theoretical Foundations of Transmedial Narratology, in: Jan Christoph Meister (Hg. in Collaboration with Tom Kindt & Wilhelm Schernus), *Narratology beyond Literary Criticism: Mediality, Disciplinarity*, Narratologia: Contributions to Narrative Theory / Beiträge zur Erzähltheorie 6, Berlin & New York, 1–23.

Ryan, Marie-Laure. 2014. Narration in Various Media, in: Peter Hühn et al. (Hgg.), *The Living Handbook of Narratology*, Hamburg, URL = https://www-archiv.fdm.uni-hamburg.de/lhn/node/53.html [last view date: 08 Nov 2022].

Schäfer, Heinrich. 1916. Ägyptische Zeichnungen auf Scherben, in: *Jahrbuch der Königlich Preussischen Kunstsammlungen* 37, 23–51.

Schaeffer, Jean-Marie. 2001. Narration visuelle et interprétation, in: Mirielle Ribière & Jan Baetens (Hgg.), *Time, Narrative and the Fixed Image*, Faux Titre: Études de langue et literature françaises 208, Amsterdam & Atlanta, 11–27.

Scheer, Brigitte. 2001/2002. Zur Zeitgestaltung und Zeitwahrnehmung in den bildenden Künsten, in: *Zeitschrift für Ästhetik und allgemeine Kunstwissenschaft* 46/2, 255–269.

Schenkel, Wolfgang. 1973. Das Ende des narrativen *sḏm.t=f*, in: *Göttinger Miszellen: Beiträge zur ägyptologischen Diskussion* 4, 23–28.

Schneider, Ralf. 2018. Kognitivistische Narratologie, in: Martin Huber & Wolf Schmid (Hgg.), *Grundthemen der Literaturwissenschaft: Erzählen*, Grundthemen der Literaturwissenschaft, Berlin & Boston, 380–396.

Schott, Siegfried. 1953. *Das schöne Fest vom Wüstentale: Festbräuche einer Totenstadt*, Abhandlungen der geistes- und sozialwissenschaftlichen Klasse, Akademie der Wissenschaften und der Literatur Mainz, Wiesbaden.

Schöttler, Tobias. 2016. Pictorial Narrativity: Transcending Intrinsically Incomplete Representation, in: Nalia Igl & Sonja Zeman (Hgg.), *Perspectives on Narrativity and Narrative Perspectivation*, Linguistic Approaches to Literature 21, Amsterdam & Philadelphia, 161–182.

Shedid, Abdel Gaffer [unter Mitarbeit von Anneliese Shedid]. 1994. *Das Grab des Sennedjem: Ein Künstlergrab der 19. Dynastie in Deir el Medineh*, Mainz.

Sommer, Roy. 2012. The Merger of Classical and Postclassical Narratologies and the Consolidated Future of Narrative Theory, in: *Diegesis: Interdisziplinäres E-Journal für Erzählforschung* 1, 143–157.

Speidel, Klaus. 2013. Can a Single Still Picture Tell a Story? Definitions of Narrative and the Alleged Problem of Time in Single Still Pictures, in: *Diegesis: Interdisziplinäres E-Journal für Erzählforschung* 2, 173–194.

Speidel, Klaus. 2018a. What Narrative Is: Reconsidering Definitions Based on Experiments with Pictorial Narrative. An Essay in Descriptive Narratology, in: *Frontiers of Narrative Studies* 4, 76–104.

Speidel, Klaus. 2018b. Jak pojedyncze obrazy opowidają historie. Krytyczne wprowadzenie do problematyki narrracji ikonicznej w narratologii, in: Katarzyna Kaczmarczyk (Hg.), *Narratologia transmedialna. Wyzwania, teorie, praktyki*, Krakow, 65–148. (for the uncorrected English original see https://www.academia.edu/35764470/Klaus_Speidel_How_single_pictures_tell_stories_A_critical_introduction_to_narrative_pictures_and_the_problem_of_iconic_narrative_in_narratology_).

Speidel, Klaus. 2020. Empirische Rezeptionsforschung zum Einzelbild: Von der Theorie zum Experiment und zurück, in: Andreas Veits, Lukas R. A. Wilde & Klaus Sachs-Hombach (Hgg.), *Einzelbild und Narrativität: Theorien, Zugänge, offenen Fragen*, Köln, 161–203.

Steiner, Wendy. 1988. *Pictures of Romance: Form against Context in Painting and Literature*, Chicago & London.

Steiner, Wendy. 2004. Pictorial Narrativity, in: Marie-Laure Ryan (Hg.). 2004. *Narrative across Media: The Language of Storytelling*, Lincoln & London, 145–177.

Titzmann, Michael. 1990. Theoretisch-methodologische Probleme einer Semiotik der Text-Bild-Relation, in: Wolfgang Harms (Hg.), *Text und Bild, Bild und Text*, DFG-Symposion 1988, Stuttgart, 368–384.

Vandier d'Abbadie, Jaques. 1936. *Catalogue des ostraca figurés de Deir el Médineh (n°s 2001 à 2255)*, Documents de fouilles publié par les membres de L'Institut Français d'Archéologie orientale du Caire II/1, Le Caire.

Vandier d'Abbadie, Jaques. 1959. *Catalogue des ostraca figurés de Deir el Médineh (n°s 2734 à 3053)*, Documents de fouilles publié par les membres de L'Institut Français d'Archéologie orientale du Caire II/4, Le Caire.

Veits, Andreas. 2020. Narratives (Bild-)Verstehen: Zum narrativen Potential von Einzelbildern, in: in: Andreas Veits, Lukas R. A. Wilde & Klaus Sachs-Hombach (Hgg.), *Einzelbild und Narrativität: Theorien, Zugänge, offenen Fragen*, Köln, 124–160.

Veits, Andres, Lukas R. A. Wilde & Klaus Sachs Hombach. 2020. Einzelbild und Narrativität: Zur Einleitung, in: Andreas Veits, Lukas R. A. Wilde & Klaus Sachs-Hombach (Hgg.), *Einzelbild und Narrativität: Theorien, Zugänge, offenen Fragen*, Köln, 9–20.

Wege, Sophia. 2017, Kognitive Aspekte des Erzählens, in: Matías Martínez (Hg.), *Erzählen: Ein interdisziplinäres Handbuch*, Stuttgart, 346–354.

Weitzmann, Kurt. 1957. Narration in Early Christiandom, in: *American Journal of Archaeology* 61/1, 83–91.

Weixler, Antonius. 2019. Bild – Erzählung – Rezeption: Narrativität in Erzählforschung und Kunstwissenschaft, in: Elisabeth Wagner-Durand, Barbara Fath & Alexander Heinemann (Hgg.), *Image – Narration – Context: Visual Narration in Cultures and Societies of the Old World*, Freiburger Studien zur Archäologie und visuellen Kultur 1, Heidelberg, 83–108.

Weixler, Antonius. 2020. Story at First Sight? Bildliches Erzählen zwischen diachroner Zustandsfolge und synchroner Zustandshaftigkeit, in: Andreas Veits, Lukas R. A. Wilde & Klaus Sachs-Hombach (Hgg.), *Einzelbild und Narrativität: Theorien, Zugänge, offenen Fragen*, Köln, 56–87.

Wellek, Rene & Austin Warren. 2019 [1942]. *Theory of Literature*, New York.

Werbrouck, Marcelle. 1953. Ostraca à figures, in: *Bulletin des musées royauxd'art et d'histoire*, 4/25, 93–111.

Werning, Daniel A. 2015. *Einführung in die hieroglyphisch-ägyptische Schrift und Sprache: Propädeutikum mit Zeichen und Vokabellektionen, Übungen und Übungshinweisen*, Berlin [https://edoc.hu-berlin.de/handle/18452/14302].

Wilde, Lukas R. A. 2020. Vom Bild zur Diegese und zurück: Bildtheoretische Rahmenüberlegungen zum narrativen Verstehen, in: Andreas Veits, Lukas R. A. Wilde & Klaus Sachs-Hombach (Hgg.), *Einzelbild und Narrativität: Theorien, Zugänge, offenen Fragen*, Köln, 88–123.

Wolf, Werner. 2002. Das Problem der Narrativität in Literatur, bildender Kunst und Musik: Ein Beitrag zu einer intermedialen Erzähltheorie, in: Vera Nünning & Ansgar Nünning (Hgg.), *Erzähltheorie transgenerisch, intermedial, interdisziplinär*, WVT – Handbücher zum literaturwissenschaftlichen Studium 5, Trier, 23–104.

Wolf, Werner. 2003. Narrative and Narrativity: A Narratological Reconceptualization and its Applicability to the Visual Arts, in: *Word and Image: A Journal of Verbal/Visual Enquiry*, 180–197.

Wolf, Werner. 2011. Narratology and Media(lity): The Transmedial Expansion of a Literary Discipline and Possible Consequences, in: Greta Olsen (Hg.), *Current Trends in Narratology*, Narratologia: Contributions to Narrative Theory / Beiträge zur Erzähltheorie 27, Berlin, 145–180.

Appendix

„Erzählte Räume“ in nicht-narrativen Texten

Der Schauplatz als Erzählkategorie am Beispiel von PT 412

Kristina Hutter & Dina Serova[1]

Abstract

Der vorliegende Beitrag betrachtet Schnittstellen zwischen narrativen Raumkategorien und „erzählten Räumen“ in altägyptischen Funerärtexten. Unter Rückgriff auf Betrachtungsmethoden aus der Narratologie werden textimmanente Konstruktionen von Raumbezügen in dem *per se* nicht als narrativ zu bezeichnenden Korpus der Pyramidentexte analysiert. Am Einzelbeispiel von Pyramidentextspruch 412 (§§721a–733d) wird die Versprachlichung komplexer räumlicher Strukturen diskutiert sowie mithilfe der Sequenzierung von Handlungssträngen emergente narrative Muster aufgezeigt. Durch den Einsatz narratologischer Instrumentarien bei der Analyse altägyptischer Funerärtexte stellt der Beitrag die narrative Funktionsweise eines nicht-narrativen Textes zur Diskussion.

1 Einleitung

In der Erzählforschung wurde Raum als hintergründige Kulisse zugunsten der temporalen Kategorie, die die sequenziellen Handlungsstränge einer Erzählung ausmacht, lange Zeit vernachlässigt.[2] Spätestens jedoch seit der narratologischen Wende in den Geistes- und Kulturwissenschaften geht es nicht mehr um die bloße narrative Attribution von Texten, sondern um das „Narrative“ selbst: wo es vorkommt und was es ausmacht.[3] Die narrati-

---

1 Dieser Beitrag ist in Kooperation entstanden und ist von Seiten der Humboldt-Universität durch die Deutsche Forschungsgemeinschaft (DFG), SFB 1412, 416591334, finanziert und vom Internationalen Forschungsinstitut Kulturwissenschaften (IFK) der Kunstuniversität Linz in Wien unterstützt worden. Wir möchten uns sehr herzlich für den regen Austausch und Diskussionen mit Frank Kammerzell, Silvia Kutscher und Gerald Moers bedanken. Zudem danken wir Silke Grallert von der Berlin-Brandenburgischen Akademie der Wissenschaften, die uns den Zugang zum Abklatscharchiv des historischen Wörterbuchunternehmens der Berliner Akademie (1897–1963) und somit eine Kollationierung der Hieroglyphen des Textes (A. 1302, 1A–B, 2A–B) ermöglichte (siehe Taf. 1). Ebenso danken wir dem anonymen Gutachter für das konstruktive Feedback. Unser besonderer Dank gilt Gerald Moers für die Aufnahme des Beitrags in den vorliegenden Band.

2 Zur Geschichte der Narratologie siehe etwa die Übersichten bei Herman (2005); Fludernik (2005). Zu aktuellen Strömungen in der Narratologie siehe etwa die Zusammenstellung in Dinnen & Warhol (2018).

3 Für einen Überblick zu Raumdiskurs und Narratologie siehe Ryan, Foote & Azaryahu (2016: 16–43); zur Auseinandersetzung innerhalb der Ägyptologie siehe u. a. Jay (2021: 83–92); Braun (2020: 19–38); Di Biase-Dyson (2019: 39–63); Eyre (2018: 89–102); Suhr (2016); Pehal (2014);

Gerald Moers (ed.), *Narrative and Narrativity in Ancient Egypt*, 263–303
DOI: https://doi.org/10.37011/studmon.29.05

ven Aufgaben einer Raumkategorie umspannen dabei ein weites Einsatzspektrum, in dem Räume als Elemente zur Perspektivierung, als Symbolträger oder strukturelle Organisationsprinzipien verarbeitet und der Verräumlichung diverser Erzählmomente dienen.

Wie die Erzählforschung die Raumkategorie vernachlässigte, so wurde in der ägyptologischen Betrachtung altägyptischer Funerärtexte deren potenzielle Narrativität nur selten thematisiert oder überhaupt anerkannt. Der Grund dafür scheint jedoch weniger in der konkreten Struktur und Beschaffenheit der betreffenden Texte zu liegen, sondern ist vielmehr den Grenzen eines nicht transkulturell anwendbaren klassischen Narrationsbegriffs geschuldet, dessen Anwendung die altägyptischen Texte nach modernen, westlichen Gesichtspunkten als nicht-narrativ ausweist. Der vorliegende Beitrag zielt auf eine Annäherung zwischen dem narratologischen Raumdiskurs und den *per se* nicht-narrativen Pyramidentexten ab. Dabei wird das Konzept der „erzählten Räume" als narrative Raumkategorie herangezogen und als sprachlich generierte Schauplätze verstanden, die Handlungsstränge nicht lediglich akkommodieren, sondern vielmehr zusammenhängend miterzeugen. Die Fallstudie zu PT 412 bringt narrative Funktionsweisen und Modalitäten eines nicht-narrativen Textes zum Vorschein und stellt somit einen Beitrag zur Entwicklung eines ägyptologischen Kohärenzbegriffes dar.

2 „Erzählter Raum" als Bewegung und Interaktion

Der „erzählte Raum" ist der Schauplatz einer Erzählung.[4] Es ist ein sich im Akt des Erzählens konstituierendes Gefüge, ein erdachter, geplanter oder imaginierter Raum, der sich auf der diegetischen Textebene manifestiert und dem Rezipienten[5] (Modell-Leser/Hörer) eröffnet wird. Dieser Raum kann entweder fiktiv sein oder sich nach reellen physischen und sozialen Räumen mimetisch orientieren, verfügt jedoch über eigene Beschaffenheiten, Normzuschreibungen und Gesetzmäßigkeiten. In diesen textimmanenten Räumen (*story world*) leben, interagieren und kommunizieren Figuren. Diese räumlichen Gefüge sind zudem ausgestattet mit Rauminventar, d. h. mit Objekten, mit denen Protagonisten in Berührung kommen und auf die sie deiktisch verweisen können.[6] Oftmals werden solche Requisiten[7] selbst zu aktiven Handlungsträgern, die den Verlauf des Erzähl*plots* mitbestimmen.

Moers (2001); Suhr (1999: 91–129); Quirke (1996: 263–276); Loprieno (1988); sowie ausgewählte Beiträge in den Sammelbänden von Roeder (2009) und (2018).

4 Dennerlein (2014: 1–25), (2011: 158–165) und (2009).

5 Um die spezifische Verwendung bestimmter narratologischer Termini und deren kontextuelles Verständnis zu gewährleisten, wurde im vorliegenden Beitrag zu Gunsten einer lesefreundlichen Vereinheitlichung von einer genderneutralen Sprache abgesehen.

6 Vgl. Lazaridis (2018: 72–73).

7 Es wird hier bewusst der aus dem Theater stammende Begriff „Requisit" verwendet. Hier liegt die Vorstellung zugrunde, dass der Textproduzent/Autor Raum wie eine Bühne mithilfe sprachlicher Mittel erzeugt und im Sinne der Erzählwürdigkeit und Salienz nur diejenigen Gegenstände in das Blickfeld des Modell-Adressaten rückt, die in einem bestimmten Zusammenhang zum Plot bzw. Text stehen oder „notwendig" sind.

Da in altägyptischen Erzähltexten nur allgemeine oder gar keine Angaben zur diegetischen Verortung der Handlung erfolgen, wird das räumliche und zeitliche Setting meist vorausgesetzt und nicht expliziert.[8] Wenn auf das Setting direkt verwiesen wird, dann vor allem durch die Nennung topographischer Schauplätze (z. B. *Jwnw* ‚Heliopolis‘), räumlicher Gegebenheiten (Landschaften, Wege, Grenzen, usw.) sowie ihrer prototypischen Eigenschaften (z. B. architektonische Bestandteile) und Requisiten. Solche raumreferentiellen Ausdrücke, zu denen auch deiktische Adverbialausdrücke (z. B. ‚hier‘, ‚dort‘ oder ‚da‘), bestimmte Konkreta und Abstrakta (z. B. ‚Innen‘, ‚Außen‘) zählen, dienen dazu, Raum und Lokalisation narrativ zu generieren.[9] Die Erzeugung von Raum im Text kann jedoch auch ohne explizite Orts- und Raumangaben, sondern allein durch das Zusammenspiel textlicher Informationen und Kontiguität bewerkstelligt werden.[10]

So wird Raum bevorzugt durch Verweise auf die *Bewegung* und *Interaktion* der Akteure in der Erzählung indiziert.[11] Auf textimmanenter Ebene des Textes passiert Bewegung nicht nur dann, wenn ein Subjekt sich von einem Ort an einen anderen begibt oder ein Objekt an einen anderen Ort versetzt wird (*Ereignisraum*), sondern auch im Rahmen von Kommunikationssituationen, d. h. immer dann, wenn zwei oder mehr Protagonisten der Erzählung aufeinandertreffen (*Kommunikationsraum*). Bewegung im Kontext der Interaktion lässt sich in Bewegungen des Gesichts und des Körpers (Mimik, Gestik, Pantomimik), Taxis (Blick-, Kopf- und Rumpforientierung) und Haptik (Berührungen des eigenen Körpers und/oder des Gegenübers) aufschlüsseln, deren explizite Erwähnung oder Beschreibung in altägyptischen Texten jedoch seltener Artikulation finden. Am häufigsten trägt Proxemik, d. h. die Regulierung von Nähe und Distanz etwa durch Verlagerung des Standorts zwischen zwei oder mehr Akteuren zur Generierung von „erzähltem Raum“ bei.

Basierend auf der Vorstellung, dass sich jegliche zwischenmenschliche Kommunikation durch Multimodalität auszeichnet,[12] lassen sich auch Erzähltexte auf diegetischer Ebene dahingehend analysieren. Mit multimodaler Kommunikation ist hier der Rückgriff auf verschiedene semiotische Ressourcen gemeint, die über auditive, visuelle, taktile, olfaktorische und gustatorische Sinnesmodalitäten verarbeitet werden.[13] Jedoch wird dieser Facettenreichtum als Zusammenspiel von Klang, Intonation, Lautstärke, Mimik, Gestik, Körperhaltung, Berührung, usw. bei der mündlichen Interaktion zunächst im Zuge der Versprachlichung selektiert und dann bei der Fixierung aufs Schriftliche transkribiert:[14] Konzeptionell Gesagtes und Gehörtes[15] wird dabei auf das Graphisch-visuelle, den rein

---

8 Lazaridis (2018: 71).

9 Dennerlein (2009: 75–84 und 209, Tabelle 2) für eine weitestgehend vollständige Auflistung raumreferentieller Ausdrücke.

10 Dennerlein (2009: 83).

11 Lazaridis (2018: 71–72).

12 Siehe u. a. Bateman, Wildfeuer & Hiipala (2017: 7); Kress (2010: 32–37); Norris (2004: 1).

13 Stöckl (2016: 6–9); vgl. Kutscher (2020: 81–82).

14 Vgl. Schmitz (2016: 327–347); bei einer solchen Übertragung in die Diegese und „Planierung“ wird eine multimodale Interaktion demnach vermeintlich monomodal in Form eines rein schriftlichen Textes umgesetzt.

15 Zur Unterscheidung zwischen Medium und Konzeption gesprochener und geschriebener Sprache siehe Koch & Oesterreicher (1986: bes. 17–19).

schriftlichen Text, reduziert und z. B. in Form der direkten Redewiedergabe repräsentiert. Die anderen Sinneseindrücke und Ressourcen der non-verbalen Kommunikation können dabei nur durch (optionale) Kommentare oder „Regieanweisungen" der Erzählerinstanz vermittelt werden. Das bedeutet, dass bestimmte Zeichenmodalitäten in der Erzählung allein durch die Modi Zeigen (*showing*) und Erzählen (*telling*) vermittelt werden können.[16] Dabei gilt, dass, je mehr Angaben gemacht werden, umso lebendiger, authentischer und nahbarer der Erzähltext auf den Modell-Leser/Hörer wirkt. Dies unterliegt jedoch der Entscheidung des Textproduzenten im Rückbezug auf den Modell-Adressaten des Textes. Da Texte nicht nur sprachliche, sondern zugleich materielle Objekte darstellen, sind ferner visuelle Bestandteile wie Schriftart, -größe, -richtung, Layout, Textplatzierung, optische Gliederungsmittel und die Inkorporation von bildlichen Darstellungen (z. B. Vignetten) bedeutungstragend.[17] Diese Mittel können die sprachlichen Elemente nicht nur begleiten, sondern mit diesen interferieren bzw. diese akzentuieren (vgl. „Schriftbildlichkeit"[18]).

Abgesehen von der Verwendung explizit raumreferentieller Ausdrücke, sowie der strukturell-inhaltlichen und visuell-formalen Aspekte[19] eines Erzähltextes kann Bewegung im Raum innersprachlich mithilfe weiterer lexikalischer Mittel ausgedrückt werden. Als implizit raumindizierende Einheiten sind dabei zunächst Verben zu nennen, da durch sie *Dynamik* und *Stillstand* vermittelt werden können. Bei der Selektion durch den Textproduzenten ist dabei relevant, ob sich das ausgesuchte Lexem aus den Verbklassen der Zustands-, Vorgangs- oder Handlungs- bzw. Tätigkeitsverben rekrutiert, da sich diese im Hinblick auf ihre Eigenschaften (±dynamisch; ±agentiv; ±telisch) unterscheiden. Das bedeutet, die Verben vermitteln unterschiedliche Informationen in Bezug auf das Ereignis, die Bewegungsintensität und Bewegungsrichtung, die Dauer und Frequenz, die Zielgerichtetheit und die Beteiligung bzw. das Fehlen eines Akteurs. Besonders Bewegungsverben besitzen ein starkes Potenzial, kognitiv komplexe räumliche Relationen zu beschreiben, da sie Bewegungstypen repräsentieren, die bestimmte semantische Konzepte (z. B. PATH und MANNER) lexikalisieren.[20] Zum anderen sind Präpositionen zu nennen, mit denen vor allem statische Raumrelationen zum Ausdruck kommen.[21] Hier sind vor allem Lokalisationen, d. h. die Angaben zur Position oder Ausrichtung einer Entität, von Interesse. Präpositionalphrasen dienen dabei der textinternen Konfiguration eines topologischen Referenzsystems, das die räumlichen Beziehungen zwischen Akteuren und Dingen im Hinblick auf Inklusion/Inkorporation, Kontakt und Nähe konkretisiert.[22]

---

16 Siehe Lahn & Meister (2016: 127–128).

17 Kutscher (2020, 83–84); vgl. Schmitz (2016: 327–329).

18 Zum Begriff siehe Krämer (2003: 157–176).

19 Vgl. z. B. die Wechsel der Schriftausrichtung von Kolumnen zu Zeilen und *vice versa* im „Schiffbrüchigen" (Z. 123–124; Z. 176–177), die sich mit inhaltlichen Aspekten der Geschichte in Verbindung bringen lassen.

20 Tschander (1999: 25–26).

21 Siehe für das Altägyptische: Werning (2012: 293–346) und (2014: 195–325).

22 Dennerlein (2009: 53, 79–80 mit Anm. 20): topologische Referenzangaben zählen hierbei zu den absoluten und intrinsischen Bezugssystemen.

Eine Untersuchung dieser lexikalischen und grammatischen Einheiten innerhalb des Textes kann somit tiefere Einblicke in die Gestaltung des diegetischen Raumes bieten. Jedoch darf nicht außer Acht gelassen werden, dass alle raumkonstituierenden Angaben innerhalb des Textes stets dem Prinzip der Erzählwürdigkeit (*tellability*) bzw. Salienz unterliegen. Dies gilt zumindest für narrative Text- und Bildkompositionen.[23] Das bedeutet, nur wenn der Autor/Texturheber/Auftraggeber die jeweilige Information als relevant für die Entfaltung des Plots oder Erzählstrangs empfand, schlugen sich diese in der Textstruktur nieder. Dieser Ansatz kann jedoch auch für nicht-narrative Texte fruchtbar gemacht werden.

3 Narrative Texte in der rezenten Erzählforschung

Gemäß der rezenten sprachwissenschaftlich orientierten Erzählforschung zeichnen sich narrative Texte durch eine Mehrzahl spezifischer, teils obligatorischer und teils fakultativer Merkmale aus.[24] Zunächst ist festzuhalten, dass zwischen erzählten Ereignissen (die abstrakte Substanz der Geschichte; Was?) und der Art deren Darstellung (Repräsentation innerhalb des Diskurses; Wie?) unterschieden wird.[25] Im Bereich des Diskurses sind dabei wichtige Beobachtungen gemacht worden:

Als mikrostrukturelles (satzbasiertes) Hauptcharakteristikum von Narration wird meistens als erstes die „ikonische Ereignisabfolge" angeführt (ereignisbezogene Definition).[26] Damit geht die Vorstellung einher, dass im Rahmen der Erzählung mindestens zwei Ereignisse in einen temporalen oder kausalen Zusammenhang gestellt werden. Ihre dargestellte Abfolge entspricht dabei ihrer temporalen Sequenzialität in der erzählten Welt.[27] Als zweites Merkmal wird Erzählungen auf makrostruktureller (textbasierter) Ebene eine Doppelstruktur auf Diskursebene zugesprochen.[28] Das bedeutet zunächst, dass Ereignisse nicht einfach aufeinander folgen, sondern *repräsentiert* bzw. dargestellt werden (Prinzipien der Mittelbarkeit und Perspektivierung).[29] Der Diskursbereich ist dabei doppelschichtig modelliert und verfügt 1) über eine Ebene des präsentierenden Erzählers und 2) die Ebene der dargestellten Ereignisse.[30] Die zweite Ebene ist der ersten untergeordnet (Abb. 1):

---

23 Braun (2020: 12–13) und (2019: 20); Di Biase-Dyson (2019: 40); vgl. hierzu Rogner (2022: 21).

24 Vgl. Zeman (2016a: 3–4).

25 Zeman (2020a: 449–450) und (2018: 179–180); Martínez (2011: 1–2); siehe hierzu die dichotomischen Begriffspaare *fabula* vs. *sjužet* (Tomaševskij 1985 [1931]: 214ff.), *histoire* vs. *discours* (Todorov 1966: 125–151) und *story* vs. *discourse* (Chatman 1978); zur kritischen Diskussion dieser Begrifflichkeiten siehe Pier (2008: 73–98); vgl. hingegen die von Genette (2010: 11–15, 181) vorgeschlagene trichotomische Aufteilung in den Erzählakt (*narration*), den Inhalt der Erzählung (*histoire*) und den narrativen Diskurs (*récit*).

26 Zeman (2020a: 451–452) und (2018: 175–178), vgl. (2016a: 3–4); siehe auch Martínez (2011: 2–5).

27 Zeman (2020a: 451), vgl. (2016a: 3).

28 Zeman (2018: 178–180).

29 Zeman (2018: 179), (2016a: 7–9) und (2016b: 17–42); Martínez (2011: 2); vgl. Genette (2010: 11).

30 Zeman (2018: 179), vgl. (2016b: 28).

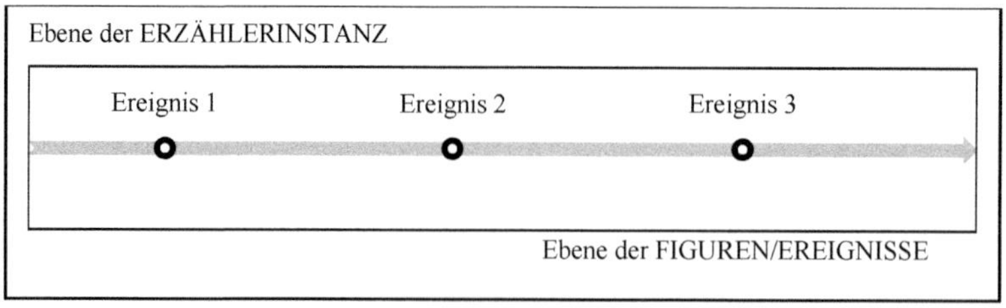

Abb. 1 | Doppelstruktur des narrativen Diskurses: Einbettung der Ebene der Figuren/Ereignisse in die Ebene des Erzählers, nach Zeman (2018: 179, Abb. 3).

Mit dieser Doppelstruktur des Diskursbereiches einhergehend, finden auf verschiedenen Ebenen des Textes kontextuelle Verlagerungen statt, die sich unter anderem durch die Verschiebung des deiktischen Zentrums und folglich mit Wechsel der lokalen und temporalen Deiktika auszeichnen. Damit geht einher, dass sich das Zeitgefüge in drei bis mehr Zeitmomente aufspalten lässt, wobei Sprechzeit (Äußerungssituation), Ereigniszeit (Intervall, in dem das erzählte Ereignis stattfindet) und Referenzzeit differenziert werden.[31] Je nachdem, ob die Ereigniszeit auf der Zeitachse vor, simultan oder hinter dem deiktischen Zentrum, d. h. der Ich-Jetzt-Hier-Origo bzw. dem Sprecherstandpunkt verortet wird, kommen unterschiedliche zeitliche Relationen wie Vor-, Gleich- und Nachzeitigkeit zum Ausdruck (vgl. Bsp. 1 und Abb. 2).[32] Zusammen mit der Doppelstruktur des Textes ergibt sich z. B. die folgende als narrativ zu bezeichnende Informationsstruktur:

(1) Ausschnitt aus P. Berlin ÄMP 3033 (P. Westcar), Z. 5,1–4
ḏd.jn n=f Ḏꜣḏꜣ-m-ꜥnḫ [...] *jb n ḥm=k r qbb n mꜣꜣ ẖnn=sn ẖn.t m-ḫd m-ḫnt*
„Da sagte *Ḏꜣḏꜣ-m-ꜥnḫ* zu ihm: ‚[...] Das Herz deiner Majestät wird sich beim Anblick ihres stromab stromauf Ruderns erquicken.'"

Wie am Beispiel aus dem P. Westcar deutlich wird (Abb. 2), lassen sich hier drei Zeitmomente identifizieren, die jeweils einer anderen Instanz zuzuordnen sind und dabei unterschiedliche Stufen der Einbettung aufweisen. Rechts auf der Zeitachse ist die Position des Erzählers verortet (*tn*), der eine bestimmte Zeit benötigt, um die Erzählung in Gang zu setzen oder zu kodieren. Aus seinem Kontext heraus referiert er auf ein Ereignis in der Vergangenheit (te_1), wobei die Rede des Protagonisten *Ḏꜣḏꜣ-m-ꜥnḫ* eingeleitet und direkt wiedergegeben wird. Diese nimmt eine bestimmte Zeit in Anspruch, nämlich das Zeitintervall *ts* bis *ts'*. *Ḏꜣḏꜣ-m-ꜥnḫ* referiert dabei aus seiner Perspektive heraus auf ein Ereignis in der Zukunft ($te_2 = tr$), das jedoch der Erzählzeit (*tn*) vorgelagert ist.

Solche Wechsel im Zeitmoment bedingen in den meisten Fällen auch Wechsel im Raum („Deixis am Phantasma"[33]). Somit bestehen in einer Erzählung mehrere lokal-

31 Vgl. Zeman (2016b: 23–26); zur Lokal- und Temporaldeixis siehe u. a. Fricke (2007: bes. 13–51) mit einer detaillierten Besprechung wichtiger Ansätze in der Deixisforschung; siehe auch Meibauer (2001: 12–17); Levinson (2000: 59–105).

32 Der Begriff der „Ich-Jetzt-Hier-Origo" geht auf Bühler (1934: 102ff.) zurück; vgl. dazu z. B. Fricke (2007: 18–24).

33 Bühler (1934: 121–140).

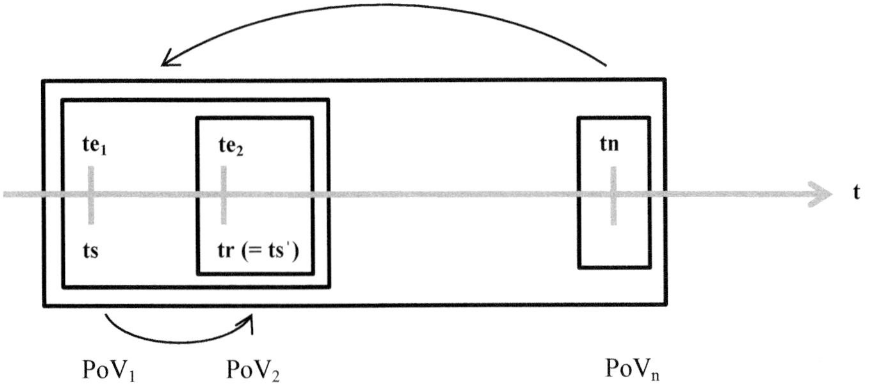

tn: narration time (Erzählzeit); **te**: event time (Ereigniszeit); **ts**: speech time (diegetische Sprechzeit); **tr**: reference time (Bezugs- bzw. Referenzpunkt); **PoV**: point of view

Abb. 2 | Temporales Verhältnis zu Textbeispiel (1) zwischen Erzählzeit (Standpunkt des Erzählers), Ereigniszeit 1 bzw. Sprechzeit (Rede des *Ḏꜣḏꜣ-m-ꜥnḫ*) und Ereigniszeit 2 (Zukunftsreferenz in Bezug auf den König) (Modellierung des Schemas nach Zeman (2018: 187).

temporale Referenzrahmen, die miteinander in eine komplexe Relation treten: der Kontext des Erzählers (die Erzählwelt) und der Kontext der Charaktere (die erzählte Welt).[34] Narration als ein inhärent multiperspektivisches Textgefüge inkorporiert demnach stets unterschiedliche Rede- und Gedankeninhalte der Figuren-Ebene, die durch eine Erzählerinstanz perspektiviert bzw. fokalisiert werden können.[35] Somit unterscheiden sich z. B. Ich-Erzählungen von Berichten in 1. P. Sg. dadurch, dass in Berichten die Sprecher- und Betrachter-Subjekte und somit auch die Erzähler- mit den Figureninstanzen zusammenfallen.[36] In narrativen Texten hingegen sind die einzelnen Instanzen ausdifferenziert und zeichnen sich durch Distanz voneinander aus, wodurch Akzentuierungen und Perspektivenwechsel ermöglicht werden.[37] Auch wenn Erzähler und Protagonist dabei referentiell eine Einheit bilden (z. B. in Ich-Erzählungen),[38] ist von einer Divergenz zwischen dem Wissensstand des Erzählers und dem der Figur auszugehen.[39] Es liegt somit eine „Spaltung des Ich“ bzw. des erzählenden und erlebenden Ich, oder anders gesagt, ein *Doppel-Ich* vor: eines, das die Ereignistrajektorie noch zu durchlaufen hat und eines, das aus der temporalen Distanz heraus auf die Ereignistrajektorie zurückblickt.[40] Darin spiegeln sich

34 Zeman (2020b: 467–470); vgl. das Begriffspaar „Erzählzeit“ und „erzählte Zeit“: für einen Überblick siehe Werner (2011: 150–151).

35 Zeman (2020b: 469); in der altägyptischen Textkultur, die narrative Merkmale aufweist, ist stets eine overte Erzählerinstanz auszumachen; eine Abkehr vom Erzähler und vom „naiven Erzählen“ (siehe Lambrecht (2018: 10–21)) sind als Phänomene der klassischen Moderne zu bezeichnen.

36 Zeman (2020b: 469), (2018: 191) und (2016b: 18–19, 29–30).

37 Zeman (2020b: 469) spricht hier von der „Aktualisierung verschiedener Betrachterstandorte“.

38 Vgl. den „homodiegetischen“ bzw. „autodiegetischen“ Erzähler bei Genette (2010: 158–164, 225–240); siehe auch Lahn & Meister (2016: 78–84).

39 Zeman (2020b: 469).

40 Zeman (2018: 191, 193–194) und (2016b: 23–24); vgl. Lahn & Meister (2016: 82).

zentrale Eigenschaften von Narration wieder, nämlich „Mehrstimmigkeit“ und das inhärente Perspektivenpotenzial.

Als weitere Merkmale von Erzähltexten wurden prototypische Vertextungs- bzw. Themenentfaltungsmuster,[41] Temporalität, Kausalität, Ereignishaftigkeit, Erzählwürdigkeit, Zustandswechsel, Agentivität, Erfahrungshaftigkeit und Mittelbarkeit vorgeschlagen.[42] Dass merkmalsbasierte Definitionen von Narration nicht unproblematisch sind und zudem die mehr als berechtigte Frage nach der Universalität dieser Kriterien aufwerfen, sei dahingestellt. Dennoch bieten sie mögliche Ansätze, um Texte nicht nur besser analysieren, sondern auch klassifizieren zu können.

4 Pyramidentexte als nicht-narrative Texte

Dass Pyramidentexte als nicht-narrative Texte anzusprechen seien, kam im Zuge der Diskussion um die Mythen und Mythenbildung zutage, die bereits 1942 und 1945 von S. Schott aufgeworfen und von J. Assmann 1977 weitergeführt wurde.[43] Dies hängt mit Assmanns vielschichtiger Definition von Mythos zum einen als formale Erzählung über die Götterwelt und zum anderen als gattungs- und medien-transzendenten Geno-Text zusammen.[44] Demnach werden Pyramidentexte in dem Bereich der Rituale, des Verklärens sowie der handlungsbezogenen Textfunktion verortet.[45] Sie stehen somit den Mythen und mythischen Aussagen, dem Akt des Erzählens und Göttergeschichten entgegen.[46]

Pyramidentextsprüche zeichnen sich nach überwiegender Forschungsmeinung dadurch aus, dass sie aus text-narratologischer Sicht weitestgehend weder eine „narrative Kohärenz“ noch eine typische Themenentfaltung (Anfang – Mitte – Ende) aufweisen.[47] Mit „Kohärenz“ sind in der ägyptologischen Sekundärliteratur jedoch nicht pragmatische, diskursive oder inhaltliche Aspekte gemeint,[48] sondern das Fehlen einer kontinuierlichen

41 Labov & Waletzky (1967: 16–44) plädieren für eine Universalstruktur narrativer Texte, die aus den Elementen „Orientierung“, „Komplikation“, „Auflösung“, „Evaluation“ und „Coda“ besteht. Ob dies auch bei altägyptischen Erzähltexten zu beobachten ist, wurde bislang nicht untersucht; vgl. jedoch z. B. Überlegungen zur Themenentfaltung und Handlungsstrukturierung am Beispiel von drei Texten bei Vinson (2004: 33–54); vgl. dazu Simon (2013: 32–34).

42 Zeman (2020a: 452) und (2016a: 3–4) mit weiteren Literaturhinweisen; Martínez (2011: 5–11); Titzmann (2008: 175–204).

43 Assmann (1977: 7–43); Schott (1945: 110ff., 135–136) und (1942: 1–27, bes. 26); siehe dazu Pehal (2014: 28–34); Di Biase-Dyson (2019: 43–45).

44 Assmann (1977: 37–39, 40); vgl. Kommentare und Diskussion bei Pehal (2014: 28–34); Goebs (2002, 28–34, bes. 33): „If narrativity is not one of the features displayed in the early sources, then it was probably not required.“; Broze (1996: 221–223); Zeidler (1993: 86–87); Baines (1991: 83–84, 85–92).

45 Assmann (1977: 15ff., 23).

46 Vgl. hingegen Zeidler (1993: 105–107).

47 Assmann (1977: 20–21); siehe Kommentare von Baines (1991: 85 mit Anm. 29 und 94); vgl. Zeidler (1993: 91–93, 108–109), der Pyramidentexte nach der funktionalen Methode von V. Propp untersucht und somit auf eine „Handlungskohärenz“ schließt; Baines (1996: 361–377); Goebs (2002: 30); Pehal (2014: 28, 33); Hellum (2014: 125); Di Biase-Dyson (2019: 43–45).

48 Zu diesen einzelnen Aspekten siehe Martínez (2011: 2–4).

Ereignistrajektorie ($E_1 \rightarrow E_2 \rightarrow E_3 \rightarrow \ldots E_n$), die sich zu einer Geschichte verbinden/verdichten lässt.[49] Was die aristotelische trichotomische Handlungsstruktur betrifft, so muss auch hier auf die Vielschichtigkeit sowie Heterogenität des Korpus der Pyramidentexte verwiesen werden.[50] Makrostrukturelle Elemente wie Anfang, Mitte, Ende sind als Begrifflichkeiten und Konzeptualisierungen möglicherweise nicht nur zu weit gegriffen, sondern schlichtweg unzureichend, um den Aufbau und die sequentielle Themenentfaltung einzelner Pyramidentextsprüche adäquat zu beschreiben.[51] Vielmehr erscheint es sinnvoll, nach mikrostrukturellen Merkmalen und Kategorisierungen zu suchen.[52]

Ein weiterer Aspekt, der gegen die narrative Qualität von Pyramidentexten angeführt wurde, ist die „raumzeitliche Verankerung“ der Texte, die sie als rituelle und performative Funktionsträger in der „Sphäre der Wiederholung“ verortet.[53] Letztendlich ist damit die funktionale Ausrichtung der Texte als Rezitative im Rahmen von Bestattungs-, Balsamierungs- oder Opferritualen, usw. gemeint.[54] Im Gegenteil dazu werden erzählende Texte als situationsabstrakt verstanden und somit von solchen expliziten Handlungen und Handlungssituationen losgebunden.[55] Nach Assmann vermitteln Pyramidentexte demnach statt Mythen und Göttererzählungen lediglich „Konstellationen“, d. h. (Götter)Rollen und typische Handlungsbezüge.[56] Des Weiteren wurde argumentiert, dass Mythen als Erzählungen über Gottheiten und die göttliche Welt universell stets in der dritten Person erzählt werden und Abweichungen davon nur dann auftreten, wenn z. B. die direkte Rede von Gottheiten wiedergegeben wird.[57] In den Pyramidentexten ist die Personenstruktur und Perspektivierung komplex, da oftmals Wechsel stattfinden.[58] Viele Sprüche richten sich direkt und appellativ an die verstorbene Königsfigur in der zweiten Person und setzen sie in Relation zu anderen Gottheiten, auf die in der dritten Person verwiesen wird.[59] Die Person der sprechenden/erzählenden Instanz muss dabei nicht expliziert werden, aber eine Trennung zwi-

---

49 Assmann (1977: 20–21); ähnlich auch Hellum (2014: 127) zum Fehlen „linearer Narrative“; vgl. Zeidler (1993: 86–89); vgl. Goebs (2002: 33, 37).

50 Dies wird bereits im Hinblick auf die Prozesse der „Verschriftung“ und „Verschriftlichung“ der Pyramidentexte deutlich: Morales (2016: 69–130).

51 Baines (1991: 85 mit Anm. 29 und 94); vgl. Assmann (1982: 30–31, 54, Anm. 85–86); vgl. Hellum (2014: 127, 131), die diese Strukturen in der physischen und metaphysischen Einbettung der Pyramidentexte in der Grabkammer des Königs vermittelt sieht.

52 Siehe z. B. Zeidler (1993: 97, 101, 104); vgl. hingegen Pehal (2014: 34); ähnlich Hellum (2014: 125–126).

53 Assmann (1977: 21); vgl. Baines (1991: 105); vgl. Zeidler (1993: 89–90).

54 Hingegen versteht Zeidler (1993: 89) darunter die „Verankerung einer ‚Geschichte‘ in einer unbestimmten Vergangenheit (in illo tempore)“.

55 Assmann (1977: 33); vgl. Baines (1991: 88).

56 Assmann (1977: 15, 20, 23); vgl. dazu Baines (1991: 86, 92–93); Zeidler (1993: 90–91); Baines (1996: 364) mit dem Begriff „narrative situations“; Goebs (2002: 31–32).

57 Pehal (2014: 33–34); Baines (1991: 87).

58 Entsprechend der Sprecher-Adressaten-Struktur identifiziert Hays (2012: 125–203, 313–314) zwei verschiedene Texttypen („discourse genres“) innerhalb der PT, nämlich „sacerdotal“ und „personal texts“.

59 Hays (2012: 127–131, 181–185).

schen der sprechenden und adressierten Person liegt eindeutig vor („sacerdotal type").[60] Alternativ können diese auch in der ersten Person zusammengeführt werden („personal type"), sodass sich der Text dann an andere Instanzen richtet.[61] Oftmals lassen sich in den Pyramidentextsprüchen auch inkonsequente Schwankungen zwischen der ersten, zweiten und dritten Person ausmachen, die das Leseverständnis hinsichtlich der grammatisch bedingten Textkohärenz erschweren und in vielen Fällen auf redaktionelle Anpassungen und Überarbeitungen dieser Sprüche zurückzuführen sind.[62]

Häufig wirken Pyramidentextsprüche wie direkte Äußerungen bzw. Redewiedergaben, da sie regelmäßig ohne erzählende, einleitende Instanz, d. h. unvermittelt, auftreten (vgl. „autonome direkte Rede"[63]). Eine Einbettung wird durch den Vermerk *ḏd-mdw* ‚Rezitation' bzw. *mḏw* < *mdw* ‚Wort, Rede; Angelegenheit'[64] zu Beginn des Spruches umgesetzt. Dabei handelt es sich faktisch um eine Markierung von direkter Rede im Sinne von Anführungszeichen. Textpassagen, die die einzelnen Redebeiträge einleiten, Sprecherwechsel anzeigen, steuern oder in Bezug setzen (*Inquit*-Formeln), scheinen auf das Verb *j* ‚sagen' beschränkt zu sein, welches, dennoch, wenig weitere kontextuelle Informationen bietet.

Der (nicht-)narrative Charakter eines Textes wird ferner durch dessen Funktion gekennzeichnet. Da das Funktionsspektrum der Pyramidentexte in Zusammenhang mit der Heterogenität des Korpus nach wie vor unzureichend verstanden ist, ist eine allgemeine nicht-narrative Attribuierung kritisch zu hinterfragen. Nach Maßgabe der modernen Narratologie haben die Sprüche grundsätzlich dann als nicht-narrativ zu gelten, wenn sie nicht wie Erzählungen primär zum Zwecke der Unterhaltung, Selbstdarstellung, emotionalen Involvierung, Wissensvermittlung, Veranschaulichung eines Sachverhalts oder Reflexion konzipiert, angedacht oder verfasst wurden.[65] Selbst wenn dies für die Sprüche des vorliegenden Korpus angenommen wird, können diese dennoch zum Teil narrative Elemente auf mikro- und makrostrukturellen Ebenen inkorporieren,[66] die jedoch meist nur auf der Ebene der direkten Äußerung der sprechenden Person bzw. der Protagonisten vermittelt werden. Wie man spätestens seit Bühlers Ausführungen zur „Deixis am Phantasma" weiß, können auch nicht-narrative Texte „erzählten" bzw. imaginierten Raum entstehen lassen

60 Hays (2012: 125–126, 127) mit dem Beispiel PT 425 und 128 mit einer weiterführenden Auflistung.

61 Siehe z. B. Hays (2012: 136–137 mit PT 227, 158–161, 185–187).

62 Zahlreiche Beispiele hierfür finden sich bereits bei Sethe (1922) und vor allem bei Allen (1984); für eine systematische Untersuchung siehe Hays (2012: 136–175). Vgl. auch das Phänomen der „complete role transplantation" bei Hays (2012: 167–175) mit PT 532 als Beispiel.

63 Lahn & Meister (2016: 132–133).

64 Die Lesung *mḏw* geht zurück auf Kammerzell & Peust (2002: 295–296); für einen verbalen Handlungsvorgang durch *mdwi͗* ‚sprechen' spricht jedoch die in den Pyramidentexten gelegentlich vorkommende Agensmarkierung mit *jn* sowie die selten vorkommende Angabe zur Rezitierhäufigkeit durch *zp* + Zahl.

65 Zu den verschiedenen Funktionen von Erzählungen siehe z. B. Kotthoff (2020: 467); vgl. Lahn & Meister (2016: 12–15): hier werden im Bereich des faktualen und fiktionalen Erzählens rhetorische, kognitive, reflexive, soziale und wirkungsästhetische Funktionen unterschieden; vgl. Goebs (2002: 37, 38–42) zu den Funktionen der Mythen.

66 Siehe z. B. die von Zeidler (1993: 95–104, 108–109) detailliert analysierten Sprüche PT 356, PT 359 und PT 477; vgl. Baines (1991: 94–95).

und auf diesen verweisen. Dies ist auch bei den Pyramidentexten der Fall, da sie mehr oder minder festgelegte strukturelle, jedoch gleichzeitig flexible topologische Bezüge zwischen Figuren und Dingen aufweisen.[67] Dieses Phänomen ist bereits unter Berücksichtigung verschiedener methodologischer und theoretischer Ansätze (mit teilweise unterschiedlichen Schlussfolgerungen) als „Konstellation“,[68] „konfigurative Kohärenz“[69], „mythische Schemata bzw. Bilder“[70] oder „Ikonizität“[71] bezeichnet und bei der Sequenzierung[72] der Handlungsstränge methodisch angedacht worden. Auf welche Weise Raum und Raumbezüge in den Pyramidentexten erzeugt werden können, soll in diesem Beitrag am Beispiel von PT 412 (T) veranschaulicht werden.

5 PT 412: Anbringungsorte und funktionale Zuschreibungen

Der Pyramidentextspruch PT 412 §§721a–733d[73] findet sich in den Pyramiden von Teti, Pepi I., Merenre, Pepi II., sowie in zweifacher Ausführung bei Neith (siehe Abb. 3).[74] Der Spruch nimmt bei seinem erstmaligen Vorkommen in der Pyramide Tetis die Nordwand der Durchgangspassage zwischen der Vorkammer und dem Serdab (T/A-S) ein (siehe Tabellen 1 und 2).[75] Danach wandert er von der Serdabpassage an das Westende der Sargkammer in die unmittelbare Nähe zum Sarkophag und wird dort ein fester Bestandteil des Textrepertoires. Bei Pepi I. kommt der Spruch am westlichen Ende der Südwand vor, bei Merenre am westlichen Ende der Nordwand, bei Pepi II. beginnt PT 412 im mittleren Textfeld der Nordwand und setzt sich in der ersten Kolumne des unteren Teils der Westwand fort. In der Pyramide der Neith tritt er auf der Südwand jeweils einmal am westlichen und östlichen Ende auf (Abb.3):[76]

---

67 Goebs (2002: 42–44 und 46–49) mit Beispielen aus den Pyramidentexten in Bezug auf Thot und Horus.

68 Assmann (1977: 15, 20, 23, 41).

69 Pehal (2014: 35–44).

70 Otto (1958: 6–8, 15–16).

71 Assmann (1982: 39–40); vgl. Zeidler (1993: 104–108).

72 Willems (2017: 599–619).

73 Sethe (1908: 395–402) und (1935: 333–359); Mercer (1952: 357–365); Faulkner (1969: 135–136); Allen (2013) und (2015, 90–91); Carrier (2009: 360–365); Tobin (2003: 252–254); Assmann & Kucharek (2008: 54–57, 702); Hays (2012: 104–105 [G. Anointing and wrapping], 109–110 [M. Ascent to the sky], 219–220, 383, 682 [Group G], pl. 13); Shmakov (2014: 194–197) und (2015: 225–228); Mathieu (2018: 296–298); Pierre-Croisiau & Mathieu (2019: 153, 286).

74 Für die Überlieferung von PT 412 siehe die Übersicht bei Allen (1950: 82); Allen (2006: 336–338): Särge B9C und B10C; Morales (2013: bes. 157, 405–406, 419, 422–424, 427).

75 Labrousse (1996: 57–58, 137); Gundacker (2009: II 253); siehe auch Leclant & Berger (1997: 271–277); Bène (2006). Die Nord- und Südwand des Durchgangs folgen dabei einem parallelen Aufbau mit ca. 1,5 m Länge und 1,13 m Höhe sowie einem 0,08 m hohen gemalten Sockel, über dem sich das Textfeld mit jeweils 27 Kolumnen mit komplett erhaltenen Texten erstreckt

76 Die hier zusammengestellten Pläne und schematischen Wandaufteilungen orientieren sich nach den Ausführungen und Plänen bei Hays (2012: 655 [Plan 13: Teti], 658 [Plan 16: Pepi I.], 670 [Plan 28: Pepi II.]); Pierre-Croisiau & Mathieu (2019: 18); Jéquier (1933: 17, Abb. 8 und Tafeln 17–18 [Version a] sowie Tafel 24 [Version b]).

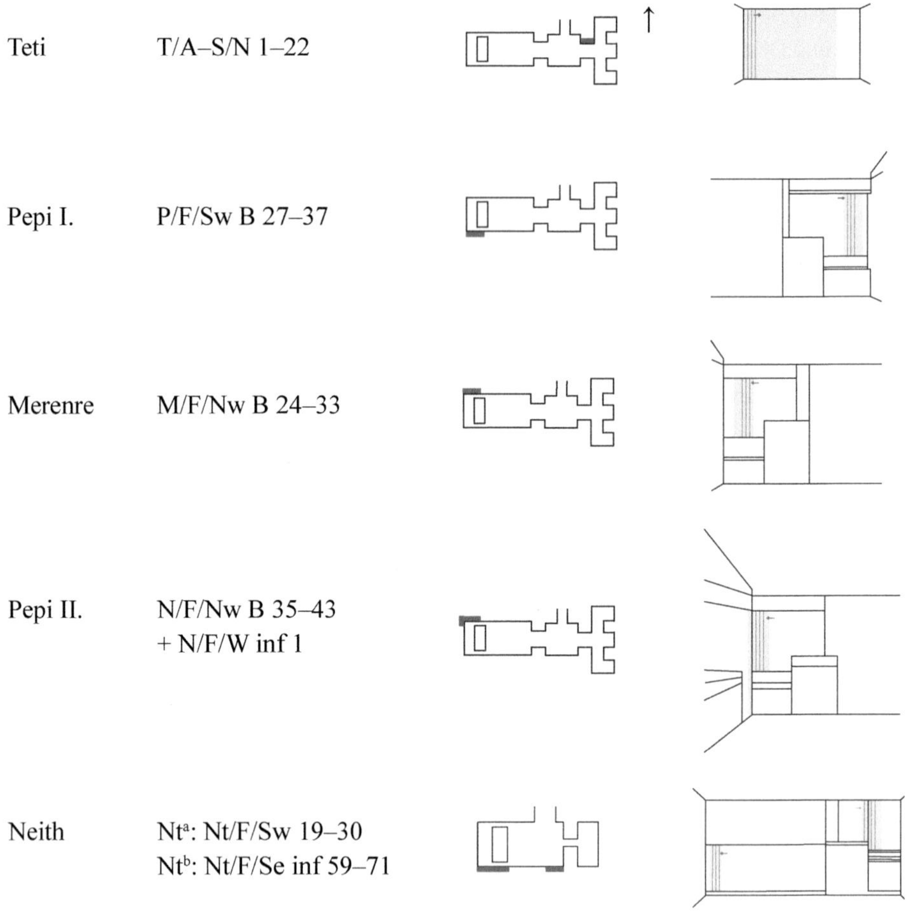
Teti
T/A–S/N 1–22
Pepi I.
P/F/Sw B 27–37
Merenre
M/F/Nw B 24–33
Pepi II.
N/F/Nw B 35–43
+ N/F/W inf 1
Neith
Nt[a]: Nt/F/Sw 19–30
Nt[b]: Nt/F/Se inf 59–71

Abb. 3 | Übersicht der Anbringungsorte von PT 412 in den Pyramiden des Alten Reiches.

H. M. Hays deutet PT 412 aufgrund des Vokativs (Verwendung der 2. P. Sg.) sowie den darin vorkommenden priesterlichen Motiven (*priestly motifs*) als *sacerdotal text* und somit zum Typus der priesterlichen Rezitationen zugehörig. Zudem weist Hays den Spruch der Sequenz 84A, den Untersequenzen 185A und 192,[77] sowie den Gruppen G (*Anointing and Wrapping*)[78] und M (*Ascent to the Sky*)[79] zu. Gruppe G, eine nicht-kanonische und heterogene Zusammenstellung von Sprüchen, umfasst drei Themenkomplexe, nämlich das Ölen und das Darreichen von Stoffen bzw. Bekleiden des Verstorbenen sowie das

77 Hays (2012: 383). Darüber hinaus ist PT 412 teil der Sequenz 126 aus der gemischten Folge (*Mixed series: sacerdotal and personal*).

78 Hays (2012: 104–105). Zur Gruppe G gehören 39 Sprüche in 57 Attestierungen; im Kern handelt es sich um PT 418–421, sowie PT 301, 364, 456, 466 und f723. In Hays (2008–2009: 84) werden die Spruchfolgen in G.1 und G.2 unterteilt, wobei PT 412 zum Letzteren zählt und exklusiv bei Teti vorkommt.

79 Hays (2012: 109–110). Zur Gruppe M gehören 59 Sprüche in 103 Attestierungen.

Besitzen der *wrr.t*-Krone.[80] Während die Gruppe G bei Unas fehlt, wurde sie bei Teti in der Serdabpassage angebracht, wo sie auch bei Pepi I. zu finden ist – allerdings in anderer Zusammenstellung, da hier bereits PT 412 in die Sargkammer wandert und dort in der thematischen Umgebung der Gruppe M platziert ist. Die Gruppe G wurde später bei Merenre und Pepi II. auf der Ostwand der Vorkammer fortlaufend vom Ostgiebel zum unteren Register platziert, wobei die Serdabpassage unbeschriftet blieb.[81]

Tabelle 1 | Spruchumgebung und Leserichtung von PT 412 in Tetis Serdabpassage

Nordwand	T/A–S/N 1–27	PT 412 §§721a–733d – PT 413 §§734a–736c	[→]
Südwand	T/A–S/S 1–27	PT 414 §§737a–f – PT 421 §§751a–b	[←]

Auch die Gruppe M erscheint erstmals bei Teti auf der Westwand der Sargkammer, hier allerdings noch ohne PT 412. Bei Merenre und Pepi II. kommt diese Gruppe in der Sargkammer am westlichen Ende der Nordwand vor, während sie bei Pepi I. am westlichen Ende der Südwand sowie auf der Nordwand in der Vorkammer und dem herabsteigenden Korridor angebracht wurde.[82] Die Verschiebung des Spruches PT 412 in späteren Pyramiden ist besonders unter Berücksichtigung des Spruchkontextes und der Gruppenzuordnung bemerkenswert. So wandert PT 412 von den Sprüchen der Nordwand zur thematischen Gruppe des Himmelsaufstiegs des Verstorbenen (Gruppe M; PT 413 kommt in den anderen Pyramiden nicht vor), während die Sprüche der Südwand (bis auf PT 414) bevorzugt auf der Ostwand der Vorkammer bzw. bei Pepi I. ebenfalls im Durchgang der Serdabpassage anzutreffen sind (vgl. hierzu Tabelle 2).

Die Verteilung dieser Sprüche in den anderen Pyramiden lässt vermuten (Tabelle 2), dass die Nord- und Südwände der Passage thematisch (jedenfalls nach Teti) nicht korrelieren bzw. es möglicherweise zu einer Umdeutung der kontextuell-bedingten themenbezogenen Zugehörigkeit von PT 412 gekommen ist. Nach Untersuchungen zur Korrelation zwischen Spruchinhalt und Anbringungsort konnte B. Mathieu ferner feststellen, dass PT 412 stets eine strategisch wichtige Position in den jeweiligen Pyramiden einnimmt.[83]

Anders als Hays deutet J. P. Allen die Sprüche der Serdabpassage bei Teti als „A Morning Ritual“. Dabei wird PT 414–418 der Südwand mit „Arraying the spirit“ betitelt, während der Rest der Südwand (PT 419–421) gemeinsam mit der Nordwand (PT 412–413) thematisch unter „Sending the spirit to the sky“ zusammengefasst wird. Mit einer solchen Betitelung wird impliziert, dass ein Teil der Texte des Serdabdurchgangs sich mit der allmorgendlichen Ausstattung, Reinigung und Bekleidung des verstorbenen Königs befasst, während der andere Teil den Himmelsaufstieg des Königs thematisiert. Da die Reinigung am Ende von PT 412 als Grundvoraussetzung für das Zusammentreffen zwischen verstorbenem König und Re angesprochen wird,[84] erscheint eine solche inhaltliche Korrelation zum Teil

80 Hays (2012: 104).

81 Hays (2012: 104). Zur späten Überlieferung von PT 412 und der Gruppe G siehe Morales (2017: 487).

82 Hays (2012: 109).

83 Mathieu (2017: 435).

84 Siehe §§733b–c.

Tabelle 2 | Verteilung der Sprüche aus Tetis Serdabpassage in anderen Pyramiden

	Gruppe	T	P	M	N	Nt
PT 412	G, M	A-S/N (G)	F/Sw B (M)	F/Nw B (M)	F/Nw B + F/W inf (M)	Nt^{a}: F/Sw (M?) Nt^{b}: F/Se inf (G?)
PT 413	G	A-S/N (G)	—	—	—	—
PT 414	A, C, D, G	A-S/S (G)	F/Ne II (A)	F/W inf (D)	N^{a}: F/E inf (C) N^{b}: F/Ne IV (A)	
PT 415	G	A-S/S (G)	A-S/S (G)	—	—	—
PT 416	G	A-S/S (G)	A-S/S (G)	—	—	—
PT 417	G	A-S/S (G)	—	—	—	—
PT 418	G	A-S/S (G)	—	A/E sup (G)	N^{a}: F/E inf (G) N^{b}: A/E inf (G)	—
PT 419	G, J	A-S/S (G)	—	A/E sup (G)	A/S (J)	—
PT 420	G	A-S/S (G)		A/E sup (G)	A/E sup (G)	
PT 421	G, J	A-S/S (G)	P/A/S (J)	A/E sup (G)	A/E inf (G)	—

plausibel. Auch J. Spiegel sah in den Sprüchen von Tetis Serdabpassage ein Ritual, wobei die Sprüche PT 412–413 der Nordwand nach Meinung des Autors den Eintritt des Bas in den Serdab begleiten.[85] PT 412 habe ferner mit der Krönung der Statue zu tun.[86]

Dahingegen wurde der Spruch von R. O. Faulkner als „A 'resurrection' text"[87] sowie von V. A. Tobin als „A spell for resurrection"[88] interpretiert. Dies bedeutet, dass die Bearbeiter diesen Spruch in Zusammenhang mit der Wiederauferstehung der verstorbenen Königsperson sehen, die z. B. im Rahmen ritueller Handlungen rezitativ eingeleitet oder unterstützt wurde. Obwohl sich der Spruch in bestimmten Textteilen direkt an das Fleisch des Verstorbenen richtet und somit bestimmte Reaktivierungen wie eine gewisse Mobilisierung des Körpers evoziert werden sollen,[89] lassen sich neben der Wiederauferstehung des Toten weitere zentrale Motive (wie z. B. der Aufstieg in den Nachthimmel) ausmachen. Ähnlich versteht N. Billing den Spruch PT 412 als komplexe Exposition der osirianischen Auferstehung und des Himmelsaufstiegs (*transference to the sky*) und verweist auf die Verschiebung von der osirianischen zur himmlischen Sphäre, die er in der Durchschreitung der Himmelstüren manifestiert sieht.[90] Das Ziel der damit verbundenen Reise ist laut Billing das Hinausgehen zu Re.

Auf Grundlage von Belegen auf Särgen des Mittleren Reiches und Papyri aus der Ptolemäerzeit gruppieren J. Assmann und A. Kucharek PT 412 zusammen mit anderen Pyra-

85 Spiegel (1971: 392, Anm. 16).
86 Spiegel (1971: 454, Anm. 82).
87 Faulkner (1969: 135–136).
88 Tobin (2003: 247–262, bes. 252–254).
89 So sollen z. B. Verwesungs- und Zerfallsprozesse aufgehalten oder gar rückgängig gemacht werden (§§722a–b, §§725a–b). Des Weiteren soll sich der Verstorbene von einer Seite auf die andere Seite begeben (§730a).
90 Billing (2018: 175–177).

midentextsprüchen[91] zu einer Totenliturgie, deren dritte Sequenz als Spruchsammlung zum Opferkult verstanden wird.[92] PT 412 wird dabei in zwei Abschnitte mit jeweils drei Szenen gegliedert, von denen der letztere Teil eine Variante von PT 675 darstellt.[93] Der erste Abschnitt des Spruches umfasst in dieser Einteilung somit die Szenen der 1) Erweckung, der 2) Erscheinung und der 3) Huldigung, während der zweite Abschnitt die Szenen der 4) Himmelsöffnung, des 5) Weckrufs und der 6) Erscheinung beschreibt.[94] Die erste Szenenfolge behandelt laut Assmann und Kucharek den Weg des Toten zum Himmel, wo er als Ba erscheint und als Sohn des Sonnengottes empfangen wird.[95] Die initialen Äußerungen sind somit als „Weckrufe“ und „Vorgangsverkündigungen“ zu verstehen, die den Toten aus dem „Nullzustand des Todesschlafs“ herauslösen sollen.[96] Die zweite Szenenfolge umfasst nochmals den Himmelsaufstieg in Zusammenhang mit der Türöffnung durch die beiden Kronengöttinnen als Mütter der verstorbenen Person. Darauf folgt ein Weckruf, wobei sich der Verstorbene auf seine andere Seite hin zum Opfer umwenden soll. Im Anschluss wird der Verstorbene in seiner himmlischen Erscheinung und Herrschaft über den Himmel gefeiert.[97] Assmann und Kucharek sehen eine enge Verbindung zwischen dem Himmelsaufstieg und der Opferspeisung der verstorbenen Königsperson, da der Themenkreis der Krönung, Herrschaft und Huldigung nicht losgelöst von der Opferpräsentation betrachtet werden kann.[98]

Darüber hinaus wurden aufgrund der vielfältigen Motivassoziationen in PT 412 bereits häufig einzelne Spruchpassagen diskutiert, unter anderem hinsichtlich der astronomischen Motive bei R. Krauss[99], A. Maravelia[100] und ähnlich bei K. Goebs[101], in Zusammenhang mit verschiedenen Aspekten eines jenseitigen Fortlebens der verstorbenen Königsperson bei W. Barta[102] und Allen[103], sowie unter Berücksichtigung schöpfungsrelevanter Passagen bei J. Popielska-Grzybowska.[104]

---

91 Es handelt sich dabei um die Sprüche PT 468, PT 723, PT 690 und PT 674–676.

92 Assmann & Kucharek (2008: 52, 689, 706–707).

93 Assmann & Kucharek (2008: 54–57, 702).

94 Assmann & Kucharek (2008: 54–57).

95 Assmann & Kucharek (2008: 702).

96 Assmann & Kucharek (2008: 706).

97 Assmann & Kucharek (2008: 702).

98 Assmann & Kucharek (2008: 706).

99 Krauss (1997: 133–136, §55).

100 Maravelia (2020: 251–253).

101 Goebs (2008: 76) in Verbindung mit lunaren Aspekten der Mizut/Merezut-Krone, siehe auch 166–168, 170, 182, 188–189, 232, 309.

102 Barta (1981: 81 und 150 [zur Anfangssequenz, §§721a–c], 144 [zum Leichnam, §§722a–b, §§725a–b], 102–103 [zum Ba des Verstorbenen, §723b], 108–109 [zur Macht des Verstorbenen, §723b], 127 [Erscheinen mit dem Sonnengott, §723a], 91 [Zirkumpolarsterne, §724d], 131 [zum Schrecken, §724a], 97 und 123 [Tore des Himmels, §727a], 127 [Menschenmutter, §§728b–c], 139 [als Wildstier soll sich der Verstorbene mit seiner Mutter Nechbet als Wildkuh vereinigen, §729a], 143 [Drehen auf die Seite, §730a], 115 [zu den Insignien, §731b], 119 [zu den Reichsheiligtümern, §731c], 123 [Verstorbener im Sonnenschiff?, §732a], 130 [allmonatliche Wiedergeburt wie der Mond §732b], 113 [zur Reinigung des Verstorbenen, §733c], 115 [der Verstorbene an der Spitze der Jenseitigen, §733a], 141 [§733d]).

103 Allen (1989: 2 [zur Unveränderlichkeit des erworbenen posthumen Status der Königsperson, §§724d–725c], 4 [zum *sḥdw*-Sternenhimmel, §727a], 24 [§732a, §733a]).

104 Popielska-Grzybowska (2020: 36 [Himmelsaufstieg, Re stützt sich auf den Verstorbenen], 37 [Re

6 Konstruktion „Erzählter Räume“ in PT 412: Methodisches Vorgehen

Im Spruch PT 412 werden auf verschiedenen Ebenen raumindizierende Informationen vermittelt. Über die linguistisch-lexikalische und die konzeptuell-semantische Ebene können kognitive Raumschemata greifbar gemacht werden, die zur inhaltlichen Strukturierung und thematischen Entfaltung des Textes beitragen.[105] Der Ausgangspunkt der Analyse liegt daher in raumreferenziellen Ausdrücken auf lexikalischer Ebene, deren raumsemantisches Bedeutungsspektrum extrinsisch-kontextuell greifbar gemacht wird. So wird zunächst das entsprechende Vokabular des Spruches methodisch vorselektiert und auf den raumsemantischen Aussagewert hin analysiert. In einem ersten Schritt (6.1) wird die lexikalisch-semantische Spannbreite der einzelnen Wortarten betrachtet. Besonders berücksichtigt werden dabei Verben, Nomina sowie Präpositionen als topologisch relationierende Ausdrücke. Darauffolgend (6.2) werden satzbasierte und satzübergreifend indizierte Raumsemantiken hinsichtlich der schematischen Bewegungs- und Interaktionsmuster betrachtet und miteinander in Beziehung gesetzt. In einem letzten Schritt sollen im Rahmen der Sequenzierung (6.3) die einzelnen aus der Ereignisebene abgeleiteten und teilweise kausal verbundenen Handlungsstränge hinsichtlich ihrer Verknüpfung mit den Ereignisräumen einander gegenübergestellt werden. Dabei werden besonders die Schauplätze innerhalb der Ereigniskette bei der Entfaltung des Spruches beleuchtet, um einen ganzheitlichen Blick darauf zu ermöglichen, wie diese in PT 412 charakterisiert, inszeniert und strukturiert werden.

Die Grundlage für die folgende Gesamtanalyse bildet die Übersetzungsarbeit an PT 412, die im Anhang (8) präsentiert wird (vgl. dazu den hieroglyphischen Text in Taf. 1). Darüber hinaus werden stellenweise relevante Parallelstellen einzelner Spruchaussagen innerhalb der Pyramidentexte vergleichend herangezogen. Die Präsentation der Ergebnisse beschränkt sich vornehmlich auf exemplarisch aussagekräftige Schlüsselpassagen, während sich der Erkenntnisgewinn auf die oben erwähnten raum-narratologischen Parameter der Bewegung und Interaktion im Rahmen der Beschaffenheit textimmanenter Räume fokussiert.

6.1 Raumreferenzielle Ausdrücke auf lexikalischer Ebene

PT 412 weist unter den Verben eine ausgeprägte lexikalisch-semantische Spannbreite auf. Von insgesamt 307 Worteinheiten (Tokens) des Spruches bilden 18% die Gruppe der Ver-

als Vater des Verstorbenen], 40 [Erscheinen von Re und dem Verstorbenen], 51–52 [Rolle von Re im Übergang des Verstorbenen], 83–84 [über die Dauernden], 141–142 [über die Milchkuh, besonders auch in Verbindung mit der späteren Himmelskuh], 241 [über das Verb *ḫpr* im nichtschöpferischen Kontext]).

105 Die im Weiteren vorgebrachten Überlegungen zur Analyse der Raumkonstruktion in den Pyramidentexten entspringen der laufenden Dissertation von K. Hutter, Wisdom Dwells in Pyramids: The Conceptual Structure of the Rites of Passage in the Ancient Egyptian Pyramid Texts, Universität Wien.

ben. Dies entspricht 56 Tokens und 48 Types.[106] Dies bedeutet, dass die meisten Verben nur einmal im Spruch belegt sind, sodass die im Spruch beschriebenen Ereignisse und Zustände unter Rückgriff auf ein sich variierendes Verbvokabular versprachlicht wurden. Dies mag auf den ersten Blick zwar nicht ungewöhnlich erscheinen, deutet jedoch an, dass der Text in Bezug auf seine Lexik und Wortwahl einen gewissen Grad an kompositorischer Elaboriertheit aufweist. Einige der Verben, die mehrfach innerhalb von PT 412 belegt sind,[107] oszillieren in ihrer kontextuellen Verwendung zwischen den jeweiligen zur Verfügung stehenden Lesarten bzw. Gebrauchsmodalitäten der Verballexeme: so z. B. *ꜥḥꜥ* ‚stehen'[108] (+agentiv, -telisch, -dynamisch) und ‚stellen'[109] (+agentiv, +telisch, +dynamisch) oder *msỉ* ‚gebären'[110] und ‚zeugen'[111] (+agentiv, +telisch, +dynamisch), die zwar raumsemantisch unterschiedliche Richtungen implizieren (OUTSIDE ↔ INSIDE), jedoch beide jeweils aktivisch gebraucht sind, während bei der dritten Verwendung mit ‚geboren werden'[112] (-agentiv, +telisch, +dynamisch) ein passivischer Gebrauch vorliegt.

Bei den meisten in PT 412 vorkommenden Verben (insgesamt 65%) handelt es sich um Handlungs- oder Tätigkeitsverben, d. h. sie bezeichnen Aktionen des Subjekts und implizieren somit stets ein Agens.[113] Die Tätigkeiten sind dabei oftmals zielgerichtet und können dynamisch sein. Zehn dieser Verben in PT 412 sind als Bewegungsverben anzusprechen und gehen mit unterschiedlichen Raumzeitbezügen einher,[114] während zwei weitere Äußerungsverben darstellen.[115] Die zweitgrößte Gruppe unter den Verben bilden die Zustandsverben (insgesamt 25%). Diese erfassen stetiges, undynamisches Geschehen, das keiner Veränderung unterliegt.[116] Dabei handelt es sich größtenteils um Zustände und Erfahrungen, die inhärent oder inkorporiert sind (CONTAINMENT-Prinzip). Fünf dieser Verben sind eindeutig negativ konnotiert[117] und werden zum Teil in ihrer Bezugnahme auf den Verstorbenen verneint.[118] Andere hingegen dienen der positiven, außenwirksamen Charakterisierung des Toten und sind somit erwünschte Qualitäten.[119] Hinzu kommen drei

---

106 Die Berechnungen erfolgten anhand der Glossierung (siehe Anhang) und des Part-of-Speech-Tagging des Textes.

107 Es handelt sich insgesamt um sechs Verben: *ꜥḥꜥ* ‚stehen; stellen' (2 Belege), *jmỉ* ‚nicht sein' (3), *wꜣš* ‚angesehen sein' (2), *bꜣ* ‚ba-mächtig sein' (2), *msỉ* ‚gebären; zeugen' und *twꜣ* ‚stützen' (2).

108 Siehe §723c.

109 Siehe §731c.

110 Siehe §728b.

111 Siehe §728b.

112 Siehe §732b.

113 Siehe z. B. Hentschel & Weydt (2013: 31).

114 Es handelt sich dabei um *nmnm* ‚sich hin und her bewegen', *swꜣ* ‚passieren; vorbeigehen', *šꜣs* ‚niedertrampeln', *ḫnd* ‚treten', *ḫsfi* ‚stromauf fahren', *ḫdỉ* ‚stromab fahren', *hꜣỉ* ‚herabsteigen', *šmsỉ* ‚folgen', *jwỉ* ‚kommen', *prỉ* ‚hinausgehen'.

115 Damit sind die Verben *ḏsw* ‚rufen, rezitieren' und *wḏꜥ-mdw* ‚richten' im semantischen Sinne von ‚Worte zuweisen/trennen' als Univerbierung gemeint.

116 Hentschel & Weydt (2013: 32).

117 Zu den negativ besetzten Verben zählen *ḏwỉ* ‚schlecht sein', *šwỉ* ‚leer sein' sowie die drei Emotionsverben *bwt* ‚verabscheuen', *msḏỉ* ‚hassen' und *zwnḫ* ‚leiden'.

118 Siehe hierzu die Textstellen §722b, §725a, 733d.

119 Diese sind *spd* ‚effektiv sein', *bꜣ* ‚ba-mächtig sein' und *wꜣš* ‚angesehen sein'.

weitere Verben, die eine dauerhafte und raumgreifende Präsenz implizieren, dies jedoch mit abweichenden topologischen Bezügen.[120] Die kleinste Gruppe besteht aus Vorgangsverben, d. h. solchen Verben, die keine eigenständigen Handlungen, sondern Prozesse bezeichnen, die sich an einem Subjekt vollziehen.[121] Es fällt auf, dass bei den insgesamt fünf Lexemen der Aspekt der Transformation, sei es inchoativ, egressiv oder durativ, stark hervorgehoben ist.[122]

Ferner sind auf lexikalischer Ebene besonders auch Nomina als raumreferenzielle Ausdrücke zu betrachten, die in PT 412 mit insgesamt 106 Tokens (35%) und 70 Types (45%) vertreten sind.[123] Davon entfällt ein Teil auf Eigennamen (11 Personennamen[124] und sieben Toponyme[125]), während die anderen Nomina eine kleinere heterogene Gruppe von 12 Abstrakta[126] und eine größere Gruppe von 40 Konkreta bilden. Die raumindizierenden Eigenschaften von Nomina umfassen zunächst die Explizierung konkreter toponymisch-geographischer Lokalisierungen, die einerseits die Schauplätze[127] von PT 412 benennen und andererseits als attributive Hintergrundinformationen zu verstehen sind, da sie der Verortung göttlicher Akteure im Rahmen ihrer Herkunfts- und Kultorte dienen.[128] Die Gruppe der Konkreta beinhaltet unter anderem 14 Gattungsnamen (Appellativa), die auf der Figurenebene als aktive[129] oder passive[130] Akteure auftreten. Eine Sonderrolle kommt dabei räumlich assoziierten Namen zu, die auf eine implizit ausgewiesene Raumsphäre

---

120 Diese sind *ꜥḥꜥ* ‚stehen', *mn* ‚dauern; bleiben' und *pẖr* (/*pšr*) ‚umgeben'.

121 Hentschel & Weydt (2013: 32–33).

122 Es sind die Verben *hwꜣ* ‚faulen', *ḫpr* ‚entstehen', *ḥtm* ‚vergehen' und *jmk* ‚verwesen'. Im Falle von *ḫr* ‚fallen' ist die Transformation auf übertragener Ebene impliziert, da der Ausdruck *ḫr ḥr gs* ‚auf die Seite fallen' (§721a) als Metapher für TOD verstanden werden kann; vgl. zu dieser Textstelle Sethe (1935: 338); Mercer (1952: 357).

123 Von dieser Zählung sind Pronomina (Personal- und Demonstrativpronomen) mit insgesamt 64 Tokens und 7 Types ausgenommen. Demonstrativpronomina und Nominaladverbien sind jeweils nur einfach belegt. Lokaladverbien kommen in PT 412 nicht vor.

124 Götternamen (*Jnpw* ‚Anubis', *Jm(.j)-Ndj.t* ‚Der-in-Nedit', *Wpjw* ‚Wepiu', *Wsrw* ‚Osiris', *Psḏ.tj* ‚die beiden Neunheiten', *Rꜥw* ‚Re', *Ḥrw* ‚Horus'), den Königsnamen (*Ttj* ‚Teti'), Sternenbezeichnungen (*Nṯr-dwꜣ* ‚Morgengott', *Sꜣḥ* ‚Orion', *Spd.t* ‚Sothis'), ein Ethnonym (*Mnṯw* ‚Mentju-Nomaden'). Von diesen kommen als Akteure explizit nur Teti, Re und Horus von Iru vor, sowie ferner auch Osiris (als Großer und als Der-in-Nedit).

125 Diese sieben Toponyme sind *ꜣḫ.t* ‚Achet', *Jwnw* ‚Heliopolis', *Jrw* ‚Iru', *Pi* ‚Buto', *Nḫn* ‚Hierakonpolis', *Ḥb* (/*Nḫb*) ‚Elkab', sowie ferner *Ndj.t* ‚Nedit' im Namen *Jm(.j)-Ndj.t* ‚Der-in-Nedit'.

126 Diese umfasst Vorstellungen (*bꜣ* ‚Ba', *p.t* ‚Himmel', *sḫdw* ‚Firmament'), einen Zeitbegriff (*ꜣbd* ‚Monat'), Zustandsbezeichnungen (*jy-m-ḥtp* ‚Willkommen(sein)', *qdd* ‚Schlaf', *bꜣg* ‚Müdigkeit', *ḥwꜣ.t* ‚Fäulnis'), Vorgangsbezeichnungen (*nmt* ‚Schreiten', *ḏd-mdw* ‚Rezitation') und Eigenschaftsbezeichnungen (*s.t* ‚Stellung', *šꜥ.t* ‚Schrecken').

127 Nur zwei Orte sind als Schauplätze der Handlung(en) in PT 412 expliziert: *ꜣḫ.t* ‚Achet' (§732c) und *p.t* ‚Himmel' (§723a). Alle anderen Ereignisräume müssen kontextuell erschlossen werden.

128 Diese umfassen *Jwnw* ‚Heliopolis' (§§727c, 728a), *Jrw* ‚Iru' (§723c), *Ḥb* (/*Nḫb*) ‚Elkab' (§729a), und ferner *šmꜥw(.j)* als Nisbe zu Oberägypten (§727b).

129 Diese sind *j:ḫm.w-sk* ‚Nicht-Untergehende', *wr* ‚Großer', *ḥwn.t(-wr.t)* ‚(Großes) Mädchen', *smꜣ.t(-wr.t)* ‚(Große) Auerochsenkuh', *smnt.t* ‚Klagefrau', *nḥḥ.w* ‚Dauernde'.

130 Diese sind: *jꜥḥ* ‚Mond', *jtj* ‚Vater', *bjt* ‚König von Unterägypten', *mw.t* ‚Mutter', *nzw* ‚König von Oberägypten', *nṯr.w* ‚Götter', *rmṯ.w* ‚Menschen', *zꜣb(-šmꜥw.j)* ‚(Oberägyptischer) Schakal'.

verweisen.[131] Ferner können personifizierte Figurennamen eine Verkörperung des Ereignisraumes darstellen,[132] während umgekehrt auch Orte selbst metonymisch als Akteure auftreten und eine personifizierte Verräumlichung produzieren können.[133] Zu den Konkreta zählen ferner 17 Bezeichnungen von Körperteilen und körperlichen Eigenschaften,[134] die ebenfalls als aktive Handlungsträger vorkommen können und somit über die Raumrelationen und -beschaffenheiten informieren. Im Falle der Glieder des Teti kann z. B. ihre Separation raumtechnisch durch das Verhältnis von NEAR–FAR modelliert werden und ist somit als metaphorischer Prozess des Kontrollverlustes seitens des Verstorbenen zu verstehen. In diesem Zusammenhang sind auch Gegenstandsbezeichnungen[135] als Rauminventar und somit als Teil des körperlichen Interaktionsraumes zu deuten, die topologische Relationen des Ereignisraumes bezüglich der Bewegungsmuster bedingen und somit den Verlauf des Erzählplots raumsemantisch mitbestimmen. Dies hängt damit zusammen, dass z. B. das Ergreifen, Halten oder Tragen eines Szepters als soziokulturell normierte oder festgeschriebene Körpertechniken zu verstehen sind. Solche Bewegungsmuster sind dem Modell-Rezipienten des Textes bekannt und werden kognitiv aufgerufen. Durch ihre implizite Bewegungsaussage sind ferner raumgenerierende Vorgangsbezeichnungen (z. B. *nmt* ‚Schreiten‘) zu erwähnen, sowie raumimplizierende Zustandsbezeichnungen, die aufgrund der Abwesenheit von Bewegung bzw. der Bewegungslosigkeit entstehen (*qdd* ‚Schlafen‘, *bꜣg* ‚Müdigkeit‘). Unter den Nomen befinden sich ferner durchgehend raumsemantisch geladene Konkreta mit impliziten topologischen Relationen wie INSIDE–OUTSIDE (z. B. *ꜥꜣ* ‚Türflügel‘), oder mit intrinsischen Orientierungsmerkmalen FRONT–BACK (z. B. *jtr.tj* ‚die beiden Schreine‘), LEFT–RIGHT (z. B. *gs* ‚Seite‘) oder UP–DOWN (z. B. *p.t* ‚Himmel‘). Am Rande seien auch Adjektive als raumreferenzielle lexikalische Sprachmittel erwähnt, die in PT 412 besonders als Präpositionalnisben lokal- und direktionaldeiktische Aussagen betreffen, aber auch raumdimensionale Eigenschaften und die Bewegungsfähigkeit von Objekten charakterisieren.[136]

---

131 Dies umfasst allgemein Himmelskörper: *jꜥḥ* ‚Mond‘, *Rꜥw* ‚Re‘ (als Sonne) und Sterne: *Nṯr-dwꜣ* ‚Morgengott‘, *nḥḥ.w* Dauernde, *j:ḫm.w-sk* ‚Nicht-Untergehende‘.

132 Damit ist speziell *Jm(.j)-Ndj.t* ‚Der-in-Nedit‘ (§721b) gemeint, wobei Nedit derjenige Ort ist, an dem Osiris (als der Große) fällt.

133 Dies betrifft *Pi* ‚Buto‘ und *Nḫn* ‚Hierakonpolis‘ (§725d): ‚Buto wird dir zuliebe stromauf fahren, Hierakonpolis wird dir zuliebe stromab fahren.‘ Dabei entfaltet sich auf der diegetischen Textebene kein direkter Interaktionsraum zwischen Buto, Hierakonpolis und Teti, da aber deren Handlungen (stromauf- bzw. stromabfahren) für Teti ausgeführt werden, kann die Verortung eines möglichen Ziels der Fahrt bei Teti als deiktisches Zentrum geographisch als dazwischenliegend impliziert werden.

134 Als körpereigene Eigenschaften sind zu nennen *fd.t* ‚Schweiß‘ und *stj* ‚Geruch‘, ferner *ḥwꜣ.t* ‚Fäulnis‘.

135 Hierzu zählen vor allem *Ḥrw-sj* ‚Horus-Szepter‘, *ḥḏ* ‚Keule‘ und *(j)ḫ.t-ḥꜣ.t* ‚Kopftuch des Königs‘.

136 §729b: *ꜣwi* ‚breit‘, §730a: *jꜣb* ‚links‘ und *jmn* ‚rechts‘, §728a, §729a: *wr* ‚groß‘, §729b: *nḫꜣḫꜣ* ‚baumelnd‘. Adjektive (inkl. Nisbenbildungen) sind in PT 412 mit 13 Types und 19 Tokens vertreten. Präpositionalnisben werden im Folgenden aufgrund ihrer relationierenden Eigenschaften gemeinsam mit den Präpositionen betrachtet.

Die Erzeugung von „erzähltem Raum" und Lokalisation wird in PT 412 nicht zuletzt auch über Präpositionen vermittelt. Mit 8 Types (5%) und 43 Tokens (14%) (zzgl. Präpositionalnisben mit 10 Tokens) strukturieren sie die Verhältnisse zwischen den Verweisobjekten (*trajector*) und den Bezugsobjekten (*landmark*).[137] Präpositionen transportieren dabei zwar intrinsisch-semantische Rauminformationen auf lexikalischer Ebene, sind jedoch aufgrund ihrer hochgradigen Polysemie vor allem kontextabhängig auf der extrinsisch-konzeptuellen Ebene zu deuten. Sie bilden das wichtigste Instrumentarium, um statische Raumverhältnisse zu kodieren und dienen ferner dem Aufzeigen diverser Bewegungsmuster.[138] Der semantische Wert der Präposition ist aber nicht nur vom Verb, sondern auch von zusätzlichen Adverbialien, dem Bezugsobjekt, sowie der kontextuellen Pragmatik abhängig. Räumliche Präpositionen können, beispielsweise, grundsätzlich statisch oder dynamisch (kinetisch) sein, wobei die statische Deutung nicht auf die Beschreibung des Weges abstellt, sondern auch das Ziel bzw. die Konfiguration vor/nach der Bewegung beschreibt.[139] Während es sich bei der Bewertung der Verhältnisse aus topologischer Perspektive stets um konzeptuelle Raumsemantiken handelt, werden mit den produzierten Schemata nicht nur „erzählte Räume" generiert, vielmehr werden hiermit kognitive Versprachlichungsprozesse strukturiert. Die Grundverhältnisse, die in PT 412 mittels Präpositionen hergestellt werden, umfassen die Lokalität, die Temporalität, die Kausalität und die Modalität.[140] Dabei gilt, dass dieselbe Präposition kontextabhängig verschiedene konzeptuelle Felder bedienen kann.[141] Das Grundverhältnis der Lokalität betrifft unter anderem die räumliche Verortung der Handlung,[142] die Verortung von Figuren mittels Herkunftsangabe[143] und von Objekten mittels Adjunktion,[144] sowie orientierungstechnische Positionsangaben[145]. Die lokal-direktionalen Aussagen können als Zielangabe[146] vorkommen oder eine ordnende Struktur mit raumzeitlicher, sozialer, hierarchischer oder funktionaler Semantik erzeugen.[147] Darüber hinaus kann das Direktionale an das Bezugsobjekt verbindend (CONNECTION), distanzierend (NEAR–FAR) oder gegenüberstellend (OPPOSITION)

137 Zum deiktischen, intrinsischen und extrinsischen Gebrauch der Präpositionen siehe die bereits ältere aber übersichtliche Zusammenstellung bei Retz-Schmidt (1988: 95–105). Zur intrinsisch-lexikalischen und extrinsisch-kontextuellen Bedeutung siehe ferner etwa Zelinsky-Wibbelt (1993: 1–24). Zur semantischen Klassifizierung von Präpositionen siehe u. a. Saint-Dizier (2005: 145–157) und (2006: 1–25).

138 Siehe dazu Werning (2014: 197) und (2012: 324ff); Nyord (2010: 27–44).

139 Werning (2014: 199–201).

140 Modale Verhältnisse kommen mit 25 Stellen am häufigsten vor (47%), gefolgt von Lokalverhältnissen (20 Stellen, 38%), Verhältnissen der Kausalität (7 Stellen, 13 %) und schließlich der Temporalität (1 Stelle, 2%).

141 So z. B. die Präposition *m*: *m* ‚in' (CONTAINER), *m* ‚als' (MERGING), *m* ‚(einer) von' (PART–WHOLE).

142 Dies betrifft §732c: *m ꜣḫ.t*, vgl. ferner die Verortung durch Personifikation mittels einer Präpositionalnisbe in §721b: *Jm(.j)-Ndj.t*.

143 §723c: *Ḥrw ḥr(.j)-jb Jrw*, §728a: *ḥwn.t wr.t ḥr.t-jb Jwnw*.

144 Hier mit der Präpositionalnisbe *dp.j*, siehe §§724b–c.

145 Lateral (§§721a, 730a: *ḥr gs*), ventral (§727c: *ḥr ẖ.t=f*).

146 §733c: *pr=k n Rꜥw*.

147 Diese sind z. B. raumzeitlich: §732a: *nḥḥ.w* [...] *dp.w-ꜥ.wj nṯr-dwꜣ*, sozial/funktional: §731c: *Ttj m-ḫnt jtr.tj*, §727c: *Wpjw ḫnt Jwnw*.

gerichtet sein.[148] Die Temporalität, die mittels einer Präpositionalphrase vermittelt wird, ist nur an einer Stelle als Frequenz ausgedrückt,[149] während die Kausalität grundsätzlich dativisch erfasst ist. Demgegenüber stellt die Modalität eine heterogene Gruppe an unterschiedlich strukturierten Grundverhältnissen dar. Interessant ist dabei die Nuancierung bei der Konstruktion und Vermittlung von sozialer Identität und Zugehörigkeit der Hauptfigur, die in PT 412 eine tragende Semantik einnimmt. Diese variiert zwischen dem Vergleichen als MATCHING (mit *mr* ‚wie‘) und dem Gleichsetzen als MERGING (mit *m* ‚als‘) und kann ferner auch mit dem Genitivadjektiv *n(.j)* ‚zugehörig zu‘ gebildet werden. Letzteres kann – abhängig vom Kontext – beide genannte Schemata erzeugen.[150] Darüber hinaus kann die Zugehörigkeit zu einem sozialen Gefüge schließlich auch nach der Metapher CATEGORIES ARE CONTAINERS als CONTAINER oder aber partitiv als PART–WHOLE strukturiert werden.

6.2 Raumerzeugung auf Kontextebene

Im folgenden Abschnitt werden drei ausgewählte Kontexte von PT 412 diskutiert, die mit der Erzeugung solcher Ereignisräume einhergehen, die im Hinblick auf Bewegungs- und Interaktionsmuster der Figuren als zentral zu deuten sind. Diese umfassen (i) die Verkörperung von Ereignisräumen, (ii) die Verräumlichung der prozessualen Todeserfahrung, sowie (iii) Interaktionsräume als Orte der Identitätsstiftung und der sozialen (Re)Integration.

i) Verkörperung des Ereignisraumes (§§721a–721d):
ḏd-mdw j:ḫr wr ḥr gs=f nmnm Jm(.j)-Ndj.t ṯz dp=f jn Rꜥw bwt=f qdd msḏ=f bꜣgj
‚Zu Rezitieren: Der Große fiel auf seine Seite, doch Der-in-Nedit regte sich, nachdem sein Kopf von Re hochgehoben wurde, denn er (Der-in-Nedit) verabscheut den Schlaf, er hasst die Müdigkeit.‘

Die zentralen Handlungen in der einleitenden Passage des Spruches PT 412 (der Fall des Großen und die Wiederauferstehung des ‚Der-in-Nedit‘ mithilfe von Re) enthalten zahlreiche topologische Raumbezüge. Über den Motiv- und Themenkreis zu Nedit in den Parallelstellen aus den Pyramidentexten ist zu erschließen, dass sich der ‚Große‘ und ‚Der-in-Nedit‘ auf den durch Seth gefallen Osiris beziehen, sowie dass beide Ereignisse an demselben Ort stattfinden: in Nedit.[151] Der Handlungsort wird in der vorliegenden Eingangspassage jedoch nicht expliziert, sondern in der Figur ‚Der-in-Nedit‘ verkörpert, die zugleich auch die mit Nedit assoziierten Handlungen konnotiert. Die Todeserfahrung, die dort stattfindet, sowie der Interaktionsraum zwischen Osiris und Re repräsentiert zugleich auch einen Ort der Grenzüberschreitung und Transformation, der über den Körper als zugleich Erfahrungs- und Ereignisraum versprachlicht wird (*Fallen* → Schlaf = Tot

148 Im Sinne von ‚zu‘ (§728a: *rḏ.n* [...] *ꜥ.w=s jr=k*), ‚von‘ (§725b: *ḥr ꜥ.[w]t=k jr=k*) oder ‚gegen‘ (§724a: *ẖpr šꜥ.t=k r jb nṯr.w*).

149 §732b: *ms=k jr ꜣbd.w=k.*

150 Vgl. MERGING als körperliche Zugehörigkeit in §722a. *jf n(.j) Tij* vs. MATCHING als soziale Zugehörigkeit in §732a: *n(.j) ṯw nḫḫ.w.*

151 Siehe v. a. PT 442 §§819a–b, PT 576 §§1500a–b, PT 677 §2018a, PT 701A §2188a. Auch im Falle von *m* ‚als‘ handelt es sich um das CONTAINMENT-Prinzip.

sein / *Kopf heben* → Aufwachen = Leben). Die dabei generierten Bewegungs- und Interaktionsmuster ergeben ein Schema der reziproken Vertikalität als einer Form der Invertierung (↓ *ḫr* ‚fallen' und ↑ *ṯzỉ* ‚hochheben'). Ferner wird durch die Bewegungsfähigkeit der Protagonisten eine Temporalität (= Bewegung im Raum) geschaffen: Re als Prinzip der Bewegungsfähigkeit und -befähigung trifft auf den gefallenen Osiris als Verkörperung der Bewegungslosigkeit, auf die auch multimodal mit der Hieroglyphe des gefallenen und gefesselten Stiers (E174F , §721a) verwiesen wird. In PT 412 erstreckt sich die Metaphorik des Motivs *fallen auf seine Seite* bzw. *auf seiner Seite liegen* als TOD auf den Hauptprotagonisten Teti, der aufgefordert wird, sich von seiner Seite zu erheben (§730a). Bedeutend ist dabei für das Gesamtverständnis des Spruches, dass sich die grammatische Nähe zum Hauptprotagonisten durch den Imperativ bzw. die 2. P. Sg., die PT 412 als rituellen Spruch ausweist, auf der diegetischen Textebene stets an die auf seiner Seite liegende (*tote*) Figur richtet.

ii) Verräumlichung des Todesprozesses (§§722a–723c):
n swꜣꜣ rd=k n šꜣss nmt=k n ḫnd=k ḥr ḥwꜣ.t Wsrw sꜣḫ=k p.t mr Sꜣḥ j:bꜣ=k bꜣ.tj ꜥḥꜥ bꜣ=k m-m nṯr.w m Ḥrw ḥr(.j)-jb Jrw
‚Dein Fuß wird nicht passiert werden, dein Schreiten wird nicht getrampelt werden. Du wirst nicht auf die Fäulnis des Osiris treten. Du wirst den Himmel erreichen wie Orion, dein Ba wird effektiv (/spitz) sein wie Sothis. Du wirst ba-mächtig ba-mächtig sein, du wirst angesehen angesehen sein. Dein Ba wird unter den Göttern stehen als Horus aus Iru.'

Anschließend an die Anfangssequenz wird die oben erwähnte grammatische Nähe zum Hauptprotagonisten aufgebaut, die sich durch den Vokativ und das deiktische Pronomen (§722a: ‚Fleisch dieses Teti') ausdrückt. Dem eingangs erwähnten Tot*sein* als einem kognitiven Schlafzustand wird ein Todes*prozess* als körperliche Verwesung gegenübergestellt. Ferner ergibt sich aus der Semantik der Bewegungsverben (*swꜣ* ‚passieren; vorbeigehen', *šꜣs* ‚niedertrampeln', *ḫnd* ‚treten') und anderer Lexeme (*rd* ‚Fuß' und *nmt* ‚Schreiten'), die metonymisch für das Gehen/den Weg (PATH) des Verstorbenen stehen, die topologische Figur der Prozesshaftigkeit. Das Bild der verräumlichten Todeserfahrung entsteht durch die Kombination dieser raumindizierenden Lexeme im Zusammenspiel mit der Klangfigur der Paronomasie,[152] die auch die lautliche und kontextuell plausible Anspielung von *ḥwꜣ.t* (*Wsrw*) ‚Fäulnis (des Osiris)' (§722d) mit *wꜣ.t* ‚Weg' assoziiert. Ferner suggeriert diese Textstelle die Möglichkeit zweier Todeswege: einen Weg der Verwesung, auf den der Verstorbene nicht treten soll (§722d), und einen Weg in den Himmel, den der Verstorbene erreichen wird (§723a). Das Erreichen des Himmels als Motiv kommt dabei durch die im Spruch immer wiederkehrenden stellaren Bezüge sowie Verweise auf die Sichtbarkeit bestimmter nächtlicher Himmelsphänomene zum Ausdruck.

152 Die Klangfigur beruht auf den Konsonanten *s*, *w*, *ꜣ* und tritt auf in §§722b–723b (vgl. *ḥꜣw*, *swꜣꜣ*, *šꜣss*, *ḥwꜣ.t*, *sꜣḥ*, *Sꜣḥ*, *spd*, *Spd.t*, *wꜣš*, *wꜣš.tj*).

iii) Interaktionsräume als Orte der Identitätsstiftung und der sozialen (Re)Integration (§§730c–732a):
sṯj=k m sṯj=sn fd.t=k m fd.t psḏ.tj j:ḫꜥ=k Ttj m (j)ẖ.t-ḥꜣ.t j:mḥ ḏr.t=k m Ḥrw-sj ẖfꜥ ẖfꜥ=k ḥr ḥḏ ꜥḥꜥ Ttj m-ḫnt jtr.tj wḏꜥ-mdw nṯr.w n(.j) ṯw nḥḥ.w pẖr.w Rꜥw
‚Dein Geruch ist ihr Geruch, dein Schweiß ist der Schweiß der Beiden Neunheiten. Du wirst erscheinen, Teti, mit dem Kopftuch des Königs, deine Hand wird das Horus-Szepter ergreifen, (und) deine Faust die Keule packen. Teti, stell dich vor die beiden Schreine und richte die Götter! Du gehörst zu den Dauernden, die Re umgeben, die vor dem Morgengott sind.‘

Mit dem Erreichen des Himmels geht eine soziale (Re)Integration einher, die dem Verstorbenen seine Identität vermittelt und bestimmte rollenspezifische Funktionen verleiht. In der besprochenen Spruchpassage finden auf vier verschiedenen Ebenen identitätsstiftende Momente statt: zunächst auf der Ebene der Gleichsetzung von Körpereigenschaften des Protagonisten mit den göttlichen (MERGING) (§§730c–d: Geruch, Schweiß), dann auf der Ebene der Attribution (SURFACE) (§§731a–b: Kopftuch, Horus-Szepter, Keule), weiter auf der Ebene der Funktion (FORCE) (§731c: vor den beiden Schreinen stehen und Götter richten), und schließlich auf der Ebene der sozialen Zugehörigkeit (COLLECTION) (§732a: ‚Du gehörst zu den Dauernden‘).

Als Veräußerlichungsformen der Identität kann auf den Ebenen der Gleichsetzung und Attribution teilweise auch von dem konzeptuellen Schema INSIDE–OUTSIDE gesprochen werden, wobei sich durch deren potenziell transformativen Effekt die Frage nach der Wirkweise der Insignien als Machtobjekte stellt, die das Schema umgekehrt als OUTSIDE–INSIDE strukturieren würden: Während z. B. *fd.t* ‚Schweiß‘ im Zuge der Transpiration eine aus dem Körper des Verstorbenen heraustretende Erscheinung darstellt, die ihn inhärent mit der Götterneunheit gleichsetzt, ist die Darreichung von spezifischen Machtinsignien von außen wie z. B. des *Ḥrw-sj* ‚Horus-Szepters‘ zwar gleichermaßen identitätsstiftend, bezieht sich jedoch auf erworbene Statuseigenschaften. Aufgrund ihrer unterschiedlichen Ausrichtungen operieren die Prinzipien der Identitätsstiftung folglich in einem Spannungsverhältnis zwischen Sichtbarkeit und Funktionalität. Die dabei entstandenen Interaktionsräume (Erscheinungs- und Wirkräume), die sich in der Verbalsemantik niederschlagen (*ḫꜥi* ‚erscheinen‘, *wḏꜥ-mdw* ‚richten‘), bedingen ein soziales Gefüge als Gegenüber. Die Sichtbarmachung des Verstobenen am Himmel impliziert ferner eine Phase der Nicht-Sichtbarkeit, wobei aber zu klären wäre, ob es sich dabei konzeptuell um die liminale Phase des Überganges handeln würde oder um eine zyklische Phase, die in den astronomischen Kontexten des Spruches angesprochen wird (vgl. §732b).

6.3 „Erzählte Räume“ in der Sequenzierung der Handlungsstränge

Raumtopologische Verweise in PT 412 können in Anlehnung an das Sequenzierungsverfahren von H. Willems[153] erfasst werden, welches hier adaptiert wurde, um den darunterliegenden Referenzrahmen des Spruches hinsichtlich der Bedeutungsbeziehungen

153 Willems (2017: 599–619).

zwischen Raum, Zeit und den Figuren freizulegen. Räumliche und zeitliche Elemente bilden dabei die kausalen Komponenten zur Kohärenzfeststellung der Handlungszusammenhänge und liefern zugleich die Strukturen für deren Figuration (d. h. Interdependenzgeflecht). Aufgrund der einzelnen Propositionen in PT 412 und unter Berücksichtigung der temporalen und lokalen Textinformationen konnten folgende sechs Sequenzen (a–f) erschlossen werden:

Vergangenheit	*mythologisch:*	a) mythologischer Präzedenzfall
	unmittelbar:	b) Todeserfahrung → Türöffnung
Gegenwart	*zeitlos, dauerhaft:*	c) Identitätsvermittlung
	unmittelbar, ausständig:	d) Aufforderungen zum Handeln
Zukunft	*unmittelbar:*	e) Übergang → Türdurchschreitung
	dauerhaft:	f) soziale (Re)Integration

Abb. 4 | Temporale Sequenzierung von PT 412 mit entsprechenden thematischen Schwerpunkten.

Der Erzählmoment, der den Spruch eröffnet und in einer mythologischen Zeit in Nedit spielt, dient als mythologischer Präzedenzfall und Ausgangspunkt für die Informationsvermittlung und Rahmung der darauffolgenden Ereignisse. Das deiktische Zentrum des Spruches im Hier-und-jetzt zeichnet sich v. a. durch den Zusammenfall der Sprech- und Ereigniszeit aus und ist über die grammatische Nähe zum Hauptprotagonisten mittels direkter Anrede in der Gegenwart auszumachen. Die Räumlichkeiten, in denen sich die Handlungen abspielen,[154] die sich aus der unmittelbaren Vergangenheit über die Gegenwart in die unmittelbare Zukunft erstrecken, werden im Text nicht expliziert, sondern ausschließlich über Verweise auf Interaktionsräume versprachlicht. Eindeutig ist jedenfalls, dass der Verstorbene dabei auf seiner Seite liegt, wodurch eine Angleichung der Verhältnisse zur Eingangssequenz mit Osiris bewirkt wird, der auf seine Seite gefallen ist. In unmittelbarer Vergangenheit wurden infolge von Tetis Todeserfahrung die Himmelstore geöffnet und das ‚Große Mädchen' hat ihm seine Hände gereicht.

Aufgrund der Verbalsemantik und Textentfaltung ist abzuleiten, dass sich der gesamte Spruch in einem Spannungsverhältnis zwischen einem Schlaf/Stillstand als Todeszustand einerseits und der Bewegung/Dynamik als Wachzustand andererseits entfaltet. Diese *lebens*relevante Beziehung wird ferner in der mythologischen Anfangssequenz gemäß der konzeptuellen Metapher ACTIVE IS ALIVE vorweggenommen. Während die diegetische Verortung und Lokalisation der Handlungen in PT 412 zwar nur zweimal expliziert ist (Achet, Himmel), wird darüber hinaus auf das räumliche Setting mittels der beiden Schreine, der beiden Türflügel des Himmels und des Firmaments verwiesen.

Als prototypische Eigenschaft eines Gebäudes ist die Tür ein konzeptueller Bestandteil der Himmelsmetaphorik: Der Himmel/das Firmament ist somit ein Gebäude, in welches der Verstorbene eintreten soll. Satzübergreifende raumsemantische Zusammenhänge

154 Damit ist die Frage gemeint, ob Ritualgeschehen z. B. in der Balsamierungswerkstatt oder in der Grabkammer selbst vollzogen werden.

verdeutlichen in einem Zusammenspiel textlicher Informationen und Kontiguitäten, dass die Öffnung der Himmelstüren, auf die in der Mitte des Spruches verwiesen wird,[155] zeitlich in der Vergangenheit verortet ist (§727a mit Perfekt Passiv: *wn ꜥꜣ.wj* ‚geöffnet wurden die beiden Türflügel‘). Die Himmelstür soll jedoch erst in der Zukunft (implizit und am Spruchende) durchschritten werden (§733c mit Subjunktiv: *pr=k n Rꜥw* ‚mögest du hinausgehen zu Re‘). Somit charakterisiert dieses Türmotiv den gesamten Ereignisraum der Gegenwart und repräsentiert einen liminalen Schwellenbereich, der vom Ort der Todeserfahrung zum dahinter referenzierten Himmelsraum als einem in der Zukunft liegenden Schauplatz führt.

Das Motiv der Türöffnung und -durchschreitung ist somit das pivotale Zentrum des Spruches, das die Handlungsstränge im deiktischen Zentrum zusammenhält (siehe Abb. 5). Dabei ist die Temporalität in der Vermittlung der Türöffnung semantisch gedehnt und erstreckt sich aus der unmittelbaren Vergangenheit bis in die unmittelbare Zukunft:

Türöffnung	→ vor der Durchschreitung	→ bei der Durchschreitung	→ nach der Durchschreitung

Abb. 5 | Die Trajektorie der Durchschreitung der Himmelstüren.

Die Zwischenräume, die eröffnet werden, beziehen sich auf die liminale Phase des Überganges, der vom Tod bis zur (Re)Integration führt. Der Übergang selbst als Durchschreitung assoziiert ferner Bilder zu Bestattungspraktiken im Übergangsritual (§§725d–726b).

Der Wechsel zwischen Stillstand und Dynamik ist ferner an den Handlungen, in die der Hauptprotagonist eingebunden ist, abzulesen und beispielsweise im Motiv des Reichens der Arme zu veranschaulichen, welches zweimal aus unterschiedlicher Perspektive vorkommt. Das erste Mal spielt die Handlung in der Zukunft, in der Teti als aktiver Akteur die Arme der ‚Nicht-Untergehenden‘ ergreifen soll (§724d mit *nḏr*). An zweiter Stelle werden Teti durch das ‚Große Mädchen‘ aus Heliopolis die Arme entgegengereicht (§728a mit *rḏi*), während er noch unbeweglich auf seiner Seite liegt. In der Sequenzierung geht die zweite Handlung der ersten voraus, das schematische Raumgefüge ist aber in beiden Fällen als vertikal aufzufassen: einmal liegt Teti auf seiner Seite (UNTEN), einmal ist das Gegenüber ein Himmelskörper (OBEN). Das Ziel, das mit dem Ergreifen der Hände verfolgt wird, gleicht somit einem Wechsel der Raumbedingungen von einer Ebene auf die andere (UP–DOWN) und setzt einen dazwischenliegenden Weg (PATH) voraus, dessen Überwindung in beiden Stellen einer Höhenüberwindung als Grenzüberschreitung

155 An dieser Stelle ist auf einen Kommentar von Frank Kammerzell zu verweisen, der sich mit der metrischen Struktur und Verseinteilung von PT 412 auseinandergesetzt hat. Für die Zurverfügungstellung seiner Daten möchten wir an dieser Stelle nochmal sehr herzlich danken. Nach Kammerzells Analyse weist PT 412 insgesamt 58 Verse nach dem Muster 8–10–10–2–10–10–8 auf. Seinen Erkenntnissen zufolge lassen sich abgesehen von dieser ausgewogenen Struktur, achsensymmetrische Klangbezüge ausmachen, die darauf hindeuten, dass der Text zentrifugal um die Mittelverse 29–30 herum komponiert wurde. Diese Verse – es handelt sich dabei um §727a: *wn n=k ꜥꜣ.wj p.t jzn n=k ꜥꜣ.wj sḥdw* – bilden somit nicht nur das inhaltliche Zentrum des Spruches, sondern auch den Dreh- und Angelpunkt auf formal-struktureller Ebene.

gleicht. Während die Identitätsstiftung des Verstorbenen in der Gegenwart verankert ist und dessen Bewusstwerdung repräsentiert, liegen diejenigen Interaktionsräume, die vor allem soziale Räume evozieren, vornehmlich in der Zukunft und repräsentieren somit die soziale (Re)Integration, die nach der Türdurchschreitung erfolgt.

Die Sequenzierung von PT 412 verdeutlicht hiermit, dass der strukturelle Aufbau von Raum- und Zeitsequenzen hinsichtlich der Ereigniskette durchdacht, intentional, präzise und teils assoziativ generiert wird. Die thematische Textentfaltung verläuft dabei asymmetrisch mit komplexen emergenten Verweisen innerhalb der Textstruktur.

7 Abschließende Überlegungen

In diesem Beitrag wurden unterschiedliche methodische Herangehensweisen u. a. aus der Erzählforschung, Multimodalität, sowie Textlinguistik miteinander vereint, mit dem Ziel, neue Impulse für die Untersuchung von altägyptischen Konzeptualisierungen von Raum in ihrer Versprachlichung zu bieten. Als Textgrundlage hierzu diente Pyramidentextspruch 412, der erstmals unter Teti belegt ist. Die Auswahl dieses Spruches ermöglichte das Konzept des „erzählten Raumes", d. h. der Konstruktion von Räumen und Raumrelationen auf diegetischer Ebene des Textes, im Detail zu analysieren und die dahinterstehenden sprachlichen Mechanismen in unterschiedlichen Granularitätsstufen (lexikalisch, satzbasiert, satzübergreifend und ganzheitlich) anhand von ausgewählten Beispielen zu beleuchten.

Wie am Beispiel von PT 412 gezeigt wurde, eignen sich Pyramidentexte besonders dafür, inhaltliche, semantische und kontextuelle Raumverweise in den Sprüchen mit ihrer physischen Distribution und Spruchumgebung im Monument des Königsgrabes zu korrelieren. Dies liegt zum einen in ihrer einzigartigen Anbringungssituation in der Substruktur des Königsgrabes begründet. Zum anderen lassen sich viele Pyramidentextsprüche aufgrund ihrer über das Alte Reich hinausgehenden Tradierung gut greifen und nachvollziehen. So können Wechsel in der räumlichen Anbringung, Verteilung und Spruchumgebung der Pyramidentexte dabei aufs engste mit den im Text explizit und implizit genannten raumsemantischen Informationen verknüpft sein.

Darüber hinaus bietet die Untersuchung „erzählter Räume" als mikro-strukturelle Merkmalkategorie neue Perspektiven auf das Verständnis von (nicht-)narrativen Texten aus dem Alten Ägypten fernab der modernen Narratologie, wobei der universale Anspruch rezenter erzähltheoretischer Definitionen am Beispiel der Pyramidentextsprüche kritisch beleuchtet wurde. Ganz im Sinne der „historischen Narratologie" wird in diesem Beitrag dafür plädiert, emische Zugriffe auf Texte zu suchen, um über ihren narrativen oder nichtnarrativen Status Auskunft zu erlangen. Dies wurde durch eine detaillierte Auseinandersetzung mit dem Sprachgut von PT 412 (d. h. die Transkription und Kollation vom Abklatsch, Transliteration, Glossierung, Sequenzierung) bewerkstelligt. Die Auswertung der Morphosyntax und Lexik des Spruches bot hierbei die notwendige Grundlage, um sich mit der innertextuellen kognitiv-semantischen Konstruktion von Raum in diesem Funerärtext zu beschäftigen. Der hier vorgeschlagene methodische Zugriff am Beispiel von PT 412 veranschaulicht, dass die Raumkategorie als (narratologisches) Untersuchungskriterium eigenständiger tiefgreifender Analysen bedarf und der temporalen Kategorie nicht nachgestellt sein sollte, da sie aufs engste miteinander verbunden sind und einander bedingen.

8 Anhang: PT 412 Transkription, Glossierung und Übersetzung

§721a | SP/N1 (346)

| SP/N1 (346) *ḏd-mdw* | *j:ḫr* | *wr* | *ḥr=* | *gs=f*

sprechen:INF=Wort(M.COLL) | fallen:PFV | Großer(M.SG) | auf= | Seite(M.SG)=3SG.M

Zu Rezitieren:[156] Der Große fiel auf seine Seite,

§721b

nmnm | *Jm(-j)=Ndj:t*

sich_bewegen:PFV | in-[ADJZ.M.SG]=Nedit:F

doch Der-in-Nedit regte sich,

§721c

ṯz | *dp=f* | *jn=* | *Rʿw*

heben:PRF.PASS | Kopf(M.SG)=3SG.M | AGT= | Re(M)

nachdem sein Kopf von Re hochgehoben wurde,

§721d

bwt=f | *qdd* | | SP/N2 (347) | *msḏ=f* | *bꜣgj*

verabscheuen:IPFV=3SG.M | Schlaf(M.SG) | hassen:IPFV=3SG.M | Müdigkeit(M.SG)

denn er (Der-in-Nedit) verabscheut den Schlaf, er hasst die Müdigkeit.

§722a

jf | *n(j)=* | *Ttj* | *pn*

Fleisch(M.SG) | von[-M.SG] | Teti(M) | DEM:M.SG

Fleisch dieses Teti,

§722b

m | *ḥwꜣ* | *m* | *jmk*

nicht_sein:IMP | faulen:ADVZ | nicht_sein:IMP | verwesen:ADVZ

faule nicht, verwese nicht!

m | *ḏw* | *stj=k*

nicht_sein:SBJV | schlecht_sein:ADVZ | Geruch(M.COLL)=2SG.M

Dein Geruch sei nicht schlecht!

§722c | SP/N3 (348)

| SP/N3 (348) *n=* | *swꜣ⌜ꜣ* | *rd=k*

NEG= | passieren~PROS.PASS | Fuß(M.SG)=2SG.M

156 Der Rezitationsvermerk steht in der Originalfassung am Beginn einer jeden Kolumne, wird hier jedoch nur einmal am Beginn des Spruches angegeben.

n= *šꜣsꜥ s* *nmt=k*
NEG= trampeln~PROS.PASS Schritt(M.SG)=2SG.M

Dein Fuß wird nicht passiert werden, dein Schreiten wird nicht getrampelt werden.

§722d *n=* *ḫnd=k* (sic) *ḥr=* *ḥwꜣ-t* *Wsrw*
NEG= treten:PROS=2SG.M auf= Fäulnis-F.COLL Osiris(M)

Du wirst nicht auf die Fäulnis des Osiris treten.

§723a | SP/N4 (349) *sꜣḥ=k* *p-t* *mr=* *Sꜣḥ*
erreichen:PROS=2SG.M Himmel-F wie= Orion(M)

Du wirst den Himmel erreichen wie Orion,

spd *bꜣ=k* *mr=* *Spd-t*
spitz_sein:PROS Ba(M.SG)=2SG.M wie= Sothis-F

dein Ba wird effektiv (/spitz) sein wie Sothis.

§723b | SP/N5 (350) *j:bꜣ=k* *bꜣ-tj*
ba-mächtig_sein:PROS=2SG.M ba-mächtig_sein:RES-2SG

Du wirst ba-mächtig ba-mächtig sein,

wꜣš=k *wꜣš-tj*
angesehen_sein:PROS=2SG.M angesehen_sein:RES-2SG

du wirst angesehen angesehen sein.

§723c *ꜥḥꜥ* *bꜣ=k* *m-m=* *nṯr-w* | SP/N6 (351) *m=* *Ḥrw*
stehen:PROS Ba(M.SG)=2SG.M unter= Gott-M.PL als= Horus(M)

ḥr(-j)=jb= *Jrw*
inmitten= Iru

Dein Ba wird unter den Göttern stehen als Horus aus Iru.

§724a *ḫpr* *šꜥ-t=k* *r=* *jb* *nṯr-w*
entstehen:PROS Schrecken-F=2SG.M zu= Herz(M.SG) Gott-M.PL

Der Schrecken vor dir wird gegen den Wunsch[157] der Götter entstehen,

157 Alternativ ist eine Übersetzung als ‚gemäß dem Wunsch' denkbar.

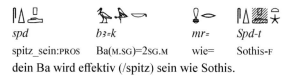

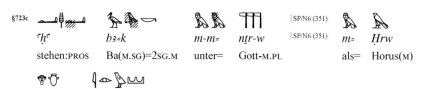

§724b *mr=* *n-t* | SP/N7 (352) *dp-t=* *bjt*
wie= Rote_Krone-F auf-[ADJZ:]F König_von_Unterägypten(M.SG)
wie die Rote Krone auf dem Kopf des Königs von Unterägypten,

mr= *mrzw-t* *dp-t=* *nzw*
wie= Merezut_Krone-F auf-[ADJZ:]F König_von_Oberägypten(M.SG)
wie die Weiße Krone auf dem Kopf des Königs von Oberägypten,

§724c *mr=* sic *ḥnzk-t* | SP/N8 (353) *dp-t=* *mnṯw-w*
wie= Haarflechte-F auf-[ADJZ:]F Mentju_Nomade-M.PL
wie die Haarflechte auf dem Kopf der Mentju-Nomaden.

§724d *nḏr=k* *=jr* *ʿ* *j:ḫm-w=sk*
greifen:PROS=2SG.M =PTCL Arm(M.SG) nicht_kennen:PTCP.IPFV-M.PL=Untergang(M.SG)
Du wirst doch den Arm der Nicht-Untergehenden ergreifen,

§725a *n=* *ḥtm* *qs-w=k*
NEG= vergehen:PROS Knochen-M.PL=2SG.M
deine Knochen werden nicht vergehen,

n= *zwn:w* *jf=k* | SP/N9 (354) *Ttj*
NEG= leiden:PROS Fleisch(M.SG)=2SG.M Teti(M).VOC
dein Fleisch wird nicht leiden, Teti,

§725b *n=* *ḫr* *ʿ-(w)t=k* *jr=k*
NEG= entfernen:PROS Glied-F.PL=2SG.M von=2SG.M
deine Glieder werden sich nicht von dir entfernen,

§725c *n=* *ṯwt* *=js* *wʿ* *m=* *nṯr-w*
weil= 2SG.M =CMPZ einer(M.SG) von= Gott-M.PL
denn du bist einer von den Göttern.

§725d *ḫsf* *n=k* *Pi*
stromauf_fahren:PROS für=2SG.M Pe
Buto wird dir zuliebe stromauf fahren,

§725d *ḫd* *n=k* *Nḫn*
stromab_fahren:PROS für=2SG.M Nechen
Hierakonpolis wird dir zuliebe stromab fahren.

§726a | SP/N10 (355)
| SP/N10 (355) *ḏsw* *n=k* *smnt-t*
rufen:PROS für=2SG.M Klagefrau-F
Die Klagefrau wird dir zuliebe schreien,

swḥ *n=k* *mḫnt-w*[158]
bekleiden:PROS für=2SG.M Antlitz:M.PL
die Antlitze werden sich dir zuliebe verhüllen:

§726b *jy-m=ḥtp* *jr=k* *Ttj* *n=* *jt=k*
Willkommen(M.SG) PTCL=2SG.M Teti(M).VOC von= Vater(M.SG)=2SG.M
„Ein Willkommen an dich, Teti, von deinem Vater,

| SP/N11 (356)
| SP/N11 (356) *jy-m=ḥtp* *jr=k* *n=* *Rʿw*
Willkommen(M.SG) PTCL=2SG.M von= Re(M)
ein Willkommen an dich von Re!“

§727a *wn* *n=k* *ʿ3-wj* *p-t*
öffnen:PRF.PASS für=2SG.M Türflügel-M.DU Himmel-F
Die beiden Türflügel des Himmels wurden dir geöffnet,

jzn *n=k* *ʿ3-wj* *sḥdw*
entriegeln:PRF.PASS für=2SG.M Türflügel-M.DU Firmament(M.SG)
die beiden Türflügel des Firmaments wurden dir entriegelt,

§727b *h3-n* *Ttj* *m=* *z3b* *šmʿw(-j)*
herabsteigen:PRF Teti(M) als= Schakal(M.SG) Oberägypten:[ADJZ.M.SG]
Teti ist als oberägyptischer Schakal herabgestiegen,

§727c | SP/N12 (357)
| SP/N12 (357) *Jnpw* *=js* *ḥr=* *ẖ-t=f*
Anubis(M) =wie auf= Bauch-F=3SG.M

158 Die Übersetzung als „Antlitz“ wird hier alternativ zur Übersetzung mit *(j)m(.j)-ḫnt.w* „Kammerherren“ o. ä. aufgrund metrischer Überlegungen vorgeschlagen. Wir möchten an dieser Stelle Frank Kammerzell für seinen Vorchlag danken. Es sei allerdings darauf hingewiesen, dass die späteren Abschriften von PT 412 bei Pepi II und Neith (Nt[b]) durch die Personenklassifikatoren letzteres näher legen.

wie Anubis auf seinem Bauch,

Wpjw *=js* *ḫnt=* *Jwnw*

Wepiu(M) =wie vor= Heliopolis

wie Wepiu an der Spitze von Heliopolis.

§728a 

rḏ-n *n=k* *ḥwn-t* *wr-t* *ḥr-t=jb=* *Jwnw*

geben-PRF für=2SG.M Mädchen-F groß-F inmitten= Iunu

| SP/N13 (358) 

| SP/N13 (358) *ʿ-wj=s* *jr=k*

Arm-M.DU=3SG.F zu=2SG.M

Das Große Mädchen aus Heliopolis hat dir seine beiden Arme entgegengereicht,

§728b 

n-jwt= *mw-t=k* *m=* *rmṯ-w* *ms:tj* *=ṯw*

für-NEG_SBRD= Mutter-F=2SG.M unter= Mensch-M.PL gebären:PTCP.PRF-F[159] =2SG.M

denn du hast unter den Menschen keine Mutter, die dich geboren hat,

§728c 

n-jwt= *jt=k* *m=* *rmṯ-w*

für-NEG_SBRD= Vater(M.SG)=2SG.M unter= Mensch-M.PL

| SP/N14 (359) 

| SP/N14 (359) *ms:j* *=ṯw*

zeugen:PTCP.PRF-M.SG =2SG.M

denn du hast unter den Menschen keinen Vater, der dich gezeugt hat.

§729a 

mw-t=k *sm3-t* *wr-t* *ḥr-t-jb=* *Ḥb*[160]

Mutter-F=2SG.M Wildkuh-F groß-F inmitten= Necheb

ḥḏ-t *ʿfn-t*

weiß-F Kopftuch-F

Deine Mutter ist die Große Auerochsenkuh aus Elkab, mit weißem Kopftuch,

159 Die feminine Partizipalendung *-tj* mit der im folgenden Satz als *-j* angegebenen maskulinen Entsprechung ist problematisch. Gunn (1924: 35–36) deutet die Endung als eine ursprüngliche prospektive aktive Partizipform, die durch das futurische Partizip *sḏm.tj=fj* verdrängt wurde, aber seinen Ausführungen zufolge immer noch anzutreffen sei. Als Beispiel führt er die zweimal vorkommende Stelle mit *ms.tj ṯw* in den Pyramidentexten an (§§659c–d und §§728b–c), die einmal als Variante zu *ms.tj=s* belegt ist (§728b N) und übersetzt diese als Prospektiv bzw. Subjunktiv ‚die dich gebären könnte‘ (‚who could beget thee‘). Allen (1984: 48–49, §70b) lehnt dies für die betreffende Textstelle ab, wobei er für einen Fall von Metathese oder Fehlschreibung bei *tj* und *s* argumentiert. In der vorliegenden Glossierung wird in §§728b–c mit Allen ein aktives perfektisches Partizip angesetzt.

160 Lesung nach Kammerzell (2021: 27).

§729b

ꜣw-t	*š(w)-tj*	| SP/N15 (360)	*nḥꜣḥꜣ-t*	*mnḏ-wj*
weit-F	Feder-F.DU		baumelnd-F	Brust-M.DU

breiten Flanken und zwei baumelnden Brüsten.

§729c

snq=s	*=ṯw*	*n=*	*wḏḥ=s*	*=ṯw*
säugen:PROS=3SG.F	=2SG.M	NEG=	entwöhnen:PROS=3SG.F	=2SG.M

Sie wird dich säugen, sie wird dich nicht entwöhnen.

§730a

j:dr	*=ṯw*	*ḥr=*	*gs=k*	| SP/N16 (361)	*jꜣb*
entfernen:IMP	=2SG.M	von=	Seite(M.SG)=2SG.M		links(M.SG)

Entferne dich von deiner linken Seite,

ḥms	*ḥr=*	*gs=k*	*jmn*	*Ttj*
sitzen:IMP	auf=	Seite(M.SG)=2SG.M	rechts(M.SG)	Teti(M):VOC

und setze (dich) auf deine rechte Seite, Teti.

§730b

j:mn	*s-(w)t=k*	*jm-t=*	*nṯr-w*
dauern:SBJV	Platz-F.PL=2SG.M	unter-[ADJZ:]F	Gott-M.PL

Deine Stellung unter den Göttern wird beständig sein,

twꜣ	*Rꜥw*	*ḥr=k*	| SP/N17 (362)	*m=*	*rmn=f*
stützen:PROS	Re(M)	auf=2SG.M		mit=	Arm(M.SG)=3SG.M

Re wird sich mit seinem Arm auf dich stützen.

§730c

sṯj=k	*m=*	*sṯj=sn*
Geruch(M.COLL)=2SG.M	als=	Geruch(M.COLL)=3PL

Dein Geruch ist ihr Geruch,

§730d

fd-t=k	*m=*	*fd-t*	*psḏ-tj*
Schweiß-F=2SG.M	als=	Schweiß-F	Neunheit-F.DU

dein Schweiß ist der Schweiß der Beiden Neunheiten.

§731a

| SP/N18 (363)	*j:ḫꜥ=k*	*Ttj*	*m=*	*(j)ḫ-t-ḥꜣ-t*
	erscheinen:SBJV=2SG.M	Teti(M).VOC	mit=	Sache-F=Vorderseite-F

Du wirst erscheinen, Teti, mit dem Kopftuch des Königs,

§731b *j:mḥ* *ḏr-t=k* *m=* *Ḥrw=sj*
fassen:SBJV Hand-F=2SG.M mit= Horus(M)=3SG.F
deine Hand wird das Horus-Szepter ergreifen,

hfꜥ *hfꜥ=k* | SP/N19 (364) *ḥr=* *ḥḏ*
greifen:SBJV Faust(M.SG)=2SG.M nach= Keule(M.SG)
(und) deine Faust die Keule packen.

§731c *ꜥḥꜥ* *Ttj* *m-ḫnt=* *jtr-tj*
stehen:IMP Teti(M).VOC vor= Schrein-F.DU

wḏꜥ=mdw *nṯr-w*
trennen:IMP=Wort(M.COLL) Gott-M.PL
Teti, stell dich vor die beiden Schreine und richte die Götter!

§732a *n(-j)* *=ṯw* *nḥḥ-w* *pḫr-w* *Rꜥw*
von[-M.SG] =2SG.M Dauernder-M.PL umgeben:PTCP.IPFV-M.PL Re(M)

| SP/N20 (365) *dp-w=ꜥ-wj=* *nṯr=dwꜣ*
vor= Gott(M.SG)=Morgen(M.SG)
Du gehörst zu den Dauernden, die Re umgeben, die vor dem Morgengott sind.

§732b *ms=k* *jr=* *ꜣbd-w=k* *mr=* *jꜥḥ*
gebären:PROS.PASS=2SG.M zu= Monat-M.PL=2SG.M wie= Mond(M.SG)
Du wirst gemäß deiner Monate geboren werden wie der Mond.

§732c *twꜣ* *Rꜥw* *ḥr=k* *m=* *ꜣḫ-t* | SP/N21 (366) *Ttj*
stützen:PROS Re(M) auf=2SG.M in= Achet-F Teti(M).VOC
Re wird sich in der Achet auf dich stützen, Teti.

§733a *šms* *=ṯw* *j:ḫm-w=sk*
folgen:PROS =2SG.M nicht_kennen:PTCP.IPFV-M.PL=Untergang(M.SG)
Die Nicht-Untergehenden werden dir folgen.

§733b 

j:ʿbꜣ	*=ṯw*	*jr=*	*jw*	*Rʿw*	| SP/N22 (367)	*Ttj*
ausstatten:IMP	=2SG.M	PTCL=	kommen:SBJV	Re(M)		Teti(m).VOC

Statte dich doch aus, damit Re kommt, Teti![161]

§733c 

wʿb=k	*pr=k*	*n=*	*Rʿw*
reinigen:SBJV=2SG.M	hinausgehen:SBJV=2SG.M	zu=	Re(M)

Du sollst dich reinigen und zu Re hinausgehen!

§733d 

n=	*šw*	*p-t*	*jm=k*	*Ttj*	*ḏ-t*
NEG=	leer_sein:PROS	Himmel-F	von=2SG.M	Teti(M).VOC	ewiglich

Der Himmel wird dich nicht missen, Teti, unendlich.

Glossierungsabkürzungen[162]

-	Segmentierung von Morphemen	IMP	Imperativ
=	Verbindung von sinntragenden Einheiten in Komposita; Markierung klitischer Grenzen	INF	Infinitiv
		IPFV	Imperfektiv
~	Markierung von Redublikationsmorphemen	M	Maskulinum
:	nicht weiter spezifizierte Segmentierung	NEG	Negation
( )	inhärentes bzw. unmarkiertes Merkmal	PASS	Passiv
[ ]	Glossierung enthält ein Element, das im Textbeispiel nicht expliziert wird	PFV	Perfektiv
		PL	Plural
1	1. Person	PRF	Perfekt
2	2. Person	PROS	Prospektiv
3	3. Person	PTCP	Partizip
ADJZ	Adjektivierer, adjektiviert	PTCL	Partikel
ADVZ	Adverbialisierer, adverbialisiert	REL	Relativform, Relativpronomen
AGT	Agens markierende Partikel	RES	Resultativ
COLL	Kollektivum	SBJV	Subjunktiv
DEM	Demonstrativum	SBRD	Subordinierende Partikel
DU	Dual	SG	Singular
F	Femininum	VOC	Vokativ

161 Alternativ kann hier ‚für das Kommen des Re‘ gelesen werden.

162 Di Biase-Dyson, Kammerzell & Werning (2009: 343–366, bes. 350–351, 357–358).

Literatur

Adey, Peter. ²2017. *Mobility*, New York, N.Y.

Allen, James P. 1984. *The Inflection of the Verb in the Pyramid Texts*, BiblAeg 2, Malibu.

Allen, James P. 1989. The Cosmology of the Pyramid Texts, in: William K. Simpson (ed.), *Religion and Philosophy in Ancient Egypt*, YES 3, 1–27.

Allen, James P. 2006. *The Egyptian Coffin Texts, VIII: Middle Kingdom Copies of Pyramid Texts*, OIP 132, Chicago.

Allen, James P. 2013. *A New Concordance of the Pyramid Texts, II: PT 247–421*, Providence.

Allen, James P. ²2015. *The Ancient Egyptian Pyramid Texts*, Writings from the Ancient World 38, Atlanta, GA.

Allen, Thomas G. 1950. *Occurrences of Pyramid Texts with Cross Indexes of These and Other Egyptian Mortuary Texts*, SAOC 27, Chicago.

Assmann, Jan. 1977. Die Verborgenheit des Mythos in Ägypten, in: *GM* 25, 7–43.

Assmann, Jan. 1982. Die Zeugung des Sohnes: Bild, Spiel, Erzählung und das Problem des ägyptischen Mythos, in: Jan Assmann, Walter Burkert & Fritz Stolz (eds.), *Funktionen und Leistungen des Mythos: Drei altorientalische Beispiele*, Freiburg, Schweiz–Göttingen, 13–61.

Assmann, Jan & Andrea Kucharek. 2008. *Ägyptische Religion: Totenliteratur*, Frankfurt am Main–Leipzig.

Baines, John. 1991. Egyptian Myth and Discourse: Myth, Gods, and the Early Written and Iconographic Record, in: *JNES* 50/2, 81–105.

Baines, John. 1996. Myth and Literature, in: Antonio Loprieno (ed.), *Ancient Egyptian Literature: History and Forms*, Leiden–New York, N.Y.–Köln, 361–377.

Barta, Winfried. 1981. *Die Bedeutung der Pyramidentexte für den verstorbenen König*, MÄS 39, München–Berlin.

Bateman, John, Janina Wildfeuer & Tuomo Hiippala. 2017. *Multimodality: Foundations, Research and Analysis*, Berlin.

Bène, Élise. 2006. *Recherches sur les textes de la pyramide du roi Téti. Restitution des parois et étude comparative du programme d'inscription*, unpublizierte Dissertation, Montpellier.

Billing, Nils. 2018. *The Performative Structure. Ritualizing the Pyramid of Pepy I*, HES 4, Leiden.

Braun, Nadja. 2019. Von der Erzählung zum Narrativ, in: Dina Serova, Burkhard Backes, Matthieu Götz & Alexandra Verbovsek (eds.), *Narrative: Geschichte – Mythos – Repräsentation, Beiträge des achten Berliner Arbeitskreises Junge Aegyptologie (BAJA 8), 1.12.–3.12.2017*, GOF IV/65, Wiesbaden, 19–38.

Braun, Nadja. 2020. *Bilder erzählen: Visuelle Narrativität im alten Ägypten*, Ägyptologische Studien Leipzig 2, Heidelberg.

Broze, Michèle. 1996. *Mythe et roman en Égypte ancienne: Les aventures d'Horus et Seth dans le papyrus Chester Beatty I*, OLA 76, Leuven.

Bühler, Karl. 1934. *Sprachtheorie: Die Darstellungsfunktion der Sprache*, Jena.

Canzler, Weert, Vincent Kaufman & Sven Kesselring. 2008. Tracing Mobility: An Introduction, in: Weert Canzler, Vincent Kaufman & Sven Kesselring (eds.), *Tracing Mobilities: Towards a Cosmopolitan Perspective*, Aldershot, 1–12.

Carrier, Claude. 2009. *Textes des Pyramides d'Égypte Ancienne, I: Textes des Pyramides d'Ounas et de Téti*, MELCHAT 12, Paris.

Chatman, Seymour. 1978. *Story and Discourse: Narrative Structure in Fiction and Film*, Ithaca, NY.

Cresswell, Timothy. 2006. *On the Move: Mobility in the Western World*, New York, N.Y.

Dennerlein, Katrin. 2009. *Narratologie des Raumes*, Berlin–Boston, MA.

Dennerlein, Katrin. 2011. B. Grundbegriffe der Erzählanalyse, 5. Raum, in: Matías Martínez (ed.), *Handbuch Erzählliteratur. Theorie, Analyse Geschichte*, Stuttgart–Weimar, 158–165.

Dennerlein, Katrin. 2014. *Theorizing Space in Narrative*, Online Manuskript: https://www.germanistik.uni-wuerzburg.de/fileadmin/05010200/TheorizingSpaceinNarrative.pdf, 25.4.2023.

Di Biase-Dyson, Camilla. 2019. Narratives by Ancient Egyptians and of Ancient Egypt: A State of the Art, in: Dina Serova, Burkhard Backes, Matthieu Götz & Alexandra Verbovsek (eds.), *Narrative: Geschichte – Mythos – Repräsentation, Beiträge des achten Berliner Arbeitskreises Junge Aegyptologie (BAJA 8), 1.12.–3.12.2017*, GOF IV/65, Wiesbaden, 39–63.

Di Biase-Dyson, Camilla, Frank Kammerzell & Daniel Werning. 2009. Glossing Ancient Egyptian. Suggestions for adapting the Leipzig Glossing Rules, in: *LingAeg* 17, 343–366.

Dinnen, Zara & Robyn Warhol (eds.). 2018. *The Edinburgh Companion to Contemporary Narrative Theories*, Edinburgh.

Eyre, Christopher. 2018. The Accessibility of Ramesside Narrative, in: Sabine Kubisch & Ute Rummel (eds.), *The Ramesside Period in Egypt: Studies into Cultural and Historical Processes of the 19th and 20th Dynasties*, Berlin–Boston, 89–102.

Faulkner, Raymond O. 1969. *The Ancient Egyptian Pyramid Texts translated into English*, Oxford.

Fludernik, Monika. 2005. Histories of Narratology (II): From Structuralism to the Present, in: James Phelan & Peter J. Rabinowitz (eds.), *A Companion to Narrative Theory*, Malden, MA.

Fricke, Ellen. 2007. *Origo, Geste und Raum: Lokaldeixis im Deutschen*, Berlin–Boston, MA.

Genette, Gérard. 2010. *Die Erzählung*. UTB 8083: Literatur- und Sprachwissenschaft, Paderborn.

Goebs, Katja. 2002. A Functional Approach to Egyptian Myth and Mythemes, in: *JANER* 2, 27–59.

Goebs, Katja. 2008. *Crowns in Egyptian Funerary Literature. Royalty, Rebirth and Destruction*, Griffith Institute Monographs, Oxford.

Gundacker, Roman. 2009. *Studien zu Genese und innerer chronologischer Schichtung der Pyramidentext, I–II*, unpublizierte Dissertation, Wien.

Gunn, Battiscombe. 1924. *Studies in Egyptian Syntax*, Paris.

Hays, Harold M. 2008–2009. Old Kingdom Sacerdotal Texts, in: *JEOL* 41, 47–94.

Hays, Harold M. 2012. *The Organization of the Pyramid Texts: Typology and Disposition*, PdÄ 31. Leiden–Boston, MA.

Hellum, Jennifer. 2014. Toward an Understanding of the Use of Myth in the Pyramid Texts, in: *SAK* 43, 123–142.

Hentschel, Elke & Harald Weydt. 2013. *Handbuch der deutschen Grammatik*, Berlin–Boston, MA.

Herman, David. 2005. Histories of Narratology (I): A Genealogy of Early Developments, in: James Phelan & Peter J. Rabinowitz (eds.), *A Companion to Narrative Theory*, Malden, MA.

Jay, Jacqueline E. 2021. Who Tells the Story? Objective Narration versus Subjective Discourse in Egyptian Narrative Literature, in: Christina Geisen, Jean Li, Steven Shubert & Kei Yamamoto (eds.), *His Good Name: Essays on Identity and Self-Presentation in Ancient Egypt in Honor of Ronald J. Leprohon*, Atlanta, GA, 83–92.

Jäger, Ludwig. 2010. Intermedialität – Intramedialität – Transkriptivität: Überlegungen zu einigen Prinzipien der kulturellen Semiosis, in: Arnulf Deppermann & Angelika Linke (eds.), *Sprache intermedial: Stimme und Schrift, Bild und Ton*, Berlin–New York, N.Y., 299–324.

Jéquier, Gustave. 1933. *Les Pyramides des Reines Neit et Apouit*, Kairo.

Jéquier, Gustave. 1936–1940. *Le monument funéraire de Pépi II, I–III*, Kairo.

Jin, Shoufu. 2004. Über die direkte Rede im alten Ägypten, in: *DE* 59, 31–46.

Kammerzell, Frank. 2021. Reading Multimodal Compositions from Early Dynastic Egypt, (with an Appendix on Previously Unlisted, Reinterpreted or Otherwise Noteworthy Signs), in: Eva-Maria Engel, Anke I. Blöbaum & Frank Kammerzell (eds.), *Keep out! Early Dynastic and Old Kingdom Cylinder Seals and Sealings in Context*, Menes 7, Wiesbaden, 1–98.

Kammerzell, Frank & Carsten Peust. 2002. Reported Speech in Egyptian: Forms, Types and History, in: Tom Güldemann & Manfred von Roncador (eds.), *Reported Discourse: A Meeting Ground for Different Linguistic Domains*, Amsterdam–Philadelphia, PA, 289–322.

Koch, Peter & Wulf Oesterreicher 1985. Sprache der Nähe – Sprache der Distanz. Mündlichkeit und Schriftlichkeit im Spannungsfeld von Sprachtheorie und Sprachgeschichte, in: *Romanistisches Jahrbuch* 36/1, 15–43.

Kotthoff, Helga. 2020. Erzählen in Gesprächen, in: Karin Birkner, Peter Auer, Angelika Bauer & Helga Kotthoff (eds.), *Einführung in die Konversationsanalyse*, Berlin–Boston, MA, 415–468.

Krauss, Rolf. 1997. *Astronomische Konzepte und Jenseitsvorstellungen in den Pyramidentexten*, Wiesbaden.

Kreiswirth, Martin. 1995. Tell me a Story: The Narrativist Turn in the Human Sciences, in: Martin Kreiswirth & Thomas Carmichael (eds.), *Constuctive Criticism: The Human Sciences in the Age of Theory*, Toronto, 61–87.

Kreiswirth, Martin. 2005. Narrative Turn in the Humanities, in: David Herman, Manfred Jahn & Marie-Laure Ryan (eds.), *Routledge Encyclopedia of Narrative Theory*, London–New York, N.Y., 377–382.

Kutscher, Silvia. 2020. Multimodale graphische Kommunikation im pharaonischen Ägypten: Entwurf einer Analysemethode, in: *LingAeg* 28, 81–116.

Krämer, Sybille. 2003. Schriftbildlichkeit oder: Über eine (fast) vergessene Dimension der Schrift, in: Sybille Krämer & Horst Bredekamp (eds.), *Bild, Schrift, Zahl*, München, 157–176.

Kress, Gunther. 2010. *Multimodality. A social semiotic approach to contemporary communication*, London.

Labov, William & Joshua Waletzky. 1967. Narrative analysis, in: June Helm (ed.), *Essays on the Verbal and Visual Arts*, Seattle, 12–44.

Labrousse, Audran. 1996. *L'architecture des pyramides à textes, Bd. I.1–2: Saqqara Nord*, BdE 114/1–2, Kairo.

Lahn, Silke & Jan C. Meister. 2016. *Einführung in die Erzähltextanalyse*, Stuttgart.

Lambrecht, Tobias. 2018. *Nicht-Naives Erzählen: Folgen der Erzählkrise am Beispiel biografischer Schreibweisen bei Helmut Krausser*, Berlin–Boston, MA.

Lazaridis, Nikolaos. 2018. Action and Private Space in Ancient Egyptian Narrative, in: Gaëlle Chantrain & Jean Winand (eds.), *Time and Space at Issue in Ancient Egypt*, Hamburg, 71–80.

Leclant, Jean & Catherine Berger. 1997. Les textes de la pyramide de Téti. État des travaux, in: Catherine Berger & Bernard Mathieu (eds.*), Études sur l'Ancien Empire et la nécropole de Saqqâra dédiées à Jean-Phillipe Lauer*, II, OrMonsp IX, Montpellier, 271–277.

Leclant, Jean, Catherine Berger-El Naggar, Bernard Mathieu & Isabelle Pierre-Croisiau 2001. *Les Textes de la Pyramide de Pépy Ier I*, MIFAO 118.1–2, Kairo.

Lee, Yoon Sun. 2018. Questions of Scale, in: Matthew Garrett (ed.), *The Cambridge Companion to Narrative Theory*, Cambridge, 29–45.

Levinson, Stephen C. 2000. *Pragmatik*. Tübingen.

Loprieno, Antonio. 1988. *Topos und Mimesis: Zum Ausländer in der ägyptischen Literatur*, ÄA 48, Wiesbaden.

Maravelia, Alicia. 2020. The Function and Importance of Some Special Categories of Stars in the Ancient Egyptian Funerary Texts, 2: The Nature of the *Sbꜣ Wꜥty*, the *Wꜥꜣ*- and the *Nḫḫw*-Star(s), in: Alicia Maravelia & Nadine Guilhou (eds.), *Environment and Religion in Ancient Egypt and Coptic Egypt: Sensing the Cosmos through the Eyes of the Divine. Proceedings of the 1st Egyptological Conference of the Hellenic Institute of Egyptology, 1–3 February 2017*, Archaeopress Egyptology 30, Oxford, 243–256.

Martínez, Matías. 2011. A. Theorie der erzählenden Literatur, I. Grundbestimmungen, 1. Erzählen, in: Matías Martínez (ed.), *Handbuch Erzählliteratur*, Stuttgart, 1–12.

Mathieu, Bernard. 2017. Re-reading the Pyramids. Repères pour une lecture spatialisée, in: Susanne Bickel & Lucía Díaz-Iglesias (eds.), *Studies in Ancient Egyptian Funerary Literature*, OLA 257, Leuven–Paris–Bristol, CT, 375–462.

Mathieu, Bernard. 2018. *Les textes de la pyramide de Pépy Ier: Traduction*, MIFAO 142, Kairo.

Meibauer, Jörg. 2001. *Pragmatik: Eine Einführung*, Tübingen.

Mercer, Samuel A. B. 1952. *The Pyramid Texts in Translation and Commentary, II: Commentary on Utterance 1, Line 1a, to Utterance 486, Line 1045a–c*, New York, N.Y.–London–Toronto.

Moers, Gerald. 2001. *Fingierte Welten in der ägyptischen Literatur des 2. Jahrtausends v. Chr.: Grenzüberschreitung, Reisemotiv und Fiktionalität*, PdÄ 19, Leiden.

Morales, Antonio J. 2013. *The transmission of the Pyramid Texts into the Middle Kingdom. Philological Aspects of a Continuous Tradition in Egyptian Mortuary Literature*, unpublizierte Dissertation, Pennsylvania.

Morales, Antonio J. 2016. From Voice to Papyrus to Wall: Verschriftung and Verschriftlichung in the Old Kingdom Pyramid Texts, in: Markus Hilgert (ed.), *Understanding Material Text Cultures: A Multidisciplinary View*, Berlin–Boston, MA, 69–130.

Morales, Antonio J. 2017. Unraveling the Thread. Transmission and Reception of Pyramid Texts in Late Period Egypt, in: Susanne Bickel & Lucía Díaz-Iglesias Llanos (eds.), *Studies in Ancient Egyptian Funerary Literature*, OLA 257, Leuven–Paris–Bristol, CT, 463–496.

Norris, Sigrid. 2004. *Analyzing Multimodal Interaction: A Methodological Framework*, New York, N.Y.–London.

Pavel, Thomas G. 1986. *Fictional Worlds*, Cambridge, MA.

Pehal, Martin. 2014. *Interpreting Ancient Egyptian Narratives: A Structural Analysis of the Tale of Two Brothers, the Anat Myth, the Osirian Cycle, and the Astarte Papyrus*, Nouvelles Études Orientales, Fernelemont.

Peust, Carsten. 1996. *Indirekte Rede im Neuägyptischen*, GOF IV/33, Wiesbaden.

Pier, John. 2008. On the Semiotic Parameters of Narrative: A Critique of Story and Discourse, in: Tom Kindt & Hans-Harald Müller (eds.), *What Is Narratology? Questions and Answers Regarding the Status of a Theory*, Berlin–New York, N.Y., 73–98.

Pierre-Croisiau, Isabelle & Bernard Mathieu. 2019. *Les textes de la pyramide de Mérenrê: Édition, description et analyse*, MIFAO 140, MAFS 9, Kairo.

Popielska-Grzybowska, Joanna. 2020. *Everything as One: A linguistic view of The Egyptian Creator in the Pyramid Texts*, IKŚiO PAN 5, Warschau–Wiesbaden.

Retz-Schmidt, Gudula. 1988. Various Views on Spatial Prepositions, in: *AI Magazine* 9/2, 95–105.

Richardson, Brian. 2005. Causality, in: David Herman, Manfred Jahn & Marie-Laure Ryan (eds.), *Routledge Encyclopedia of Narrative Theory*, London–New York, N.Y., 48–52.

Roeder, Hubert. 1993. Themen und Motive in den Pyramidentexten, in: *LingAeg 3*, 81–119.

Roeder, Hubert. (ed.) 2009. *Das Erzählen in frühen Hochkulturen I: Der Fall Ägypten*, Ägyptologie und Kulturwissenschaft 1, München.

Roeder, Hubert. (ed.) 2018. *Das Erzählen in frühen Hochkulturen II: Eine Archäologie der narrativen Sinnbildung*, Ägyptologie und Kulturwissenschaft 2, München.

Rogner, Frederik A. 2022. *Bildliche Narrativität – Erzählen mit Bildern. Rezeption und Verwendung figürlicher Darstellungen im ägyptischen Neuen Reich*, SES 3, Basel–Frankfurt am Main.

Ryan, Marie-Laure 1991. *Possible Worlds, Artificial Intelligence, and Narrative Theory*, Bloomington.

Ryan Marie-Laure, Kenneth Foote & Maoz Azaryahu. 2016. *Narrating Space / Spatializing Narrative. Where Narrative Theory and Geography Meet*, Theory and Interpretation of Narrative, Columbus.

Saint-Dizier, Patrick (ed.) 2006. *Syntax and Semantics of Prepositions*, Text, Speech and Language Technology 29, Dordrecht, 1–25.

Saint-Dizier, Patrick. 2005. PrepNet: A Framework for Describing Prepositions. Preliminary Investigation Results, in: *Proceedings of the Sixth International Workshop on Computational Semantics* (IWCS 05), Tilburg, 145–157.

Schmitz, Ulrich. 2016. 14. Multimodale Texttypologie, in: Nina-Maria Klug & Hartmut Stöckl (eds.), *Handbuch Sprache im multimodalen Kontext*, Berlin–Boston, MA, 327–347.

Schott, Siegfried. 1942. Spuren der Mythenbildung, in: *ZÄS* 78, 1–27.

Schott, Siegfried. 1945. *Mythe und Mythenbildung im alten Ägypten*, UGAÄ 15, Leipzig.

Sethe, Kurt. 1908. *Die altaegyptischen Pyramidentexte nach den Papierabdrücken und Photographien der Berliner Museums, I: Text, erste Hälfte, Spruch 1–468 (Pyr. 1–905)*, Leipzig.

Sethe, Kurt. 1922. *Die altägyptischen Pyramidentexte nach den Papierabdrücken und Photographien des Berliner Museums, III: Kritischer Apparat, Beschreibung der Inschriften, Konkordanz der Texte*, Leipzig.

Sethe, Kurt. 1935. *Übersetzung und Kommentar zu den altägyptischen Pyramidentexten, III: Spruch 326–425 (§§ 534–787)*, Glückstadt–Hamburg–New York, N.Y.

Simon, Henrike. 2013. *„Textaufgaben“: Kulturwissenschaftliche Konzepte in Anwendung auf die Literatur der Ramessidenzeit*, SAK Beihefte 14, Hamburg.

Shmakov, Timofey T. 2014. *Древнеегипетские тексты пирамид*, Omsk.

Shmakov, Timofey T. 2015. *New Readings in the Pyramid Texts*, updatable working version, Anapa–Omsk–Moskau.

Spiegel, Joachim. 1971. *Das Auferstehungsritual der Unas-Pyramide: Beschreibung und erläuterte Übersetzung*, ÄA 23, Wiesbaden.

Stöckl, Hartmut. 2016. 1. Multimodalität – Semiotische und textlinguistische Grundlagen, in: Nina-Maria Klug & Hartmut Stöckl (eds.), *Handbuch Sprache im multimodalen Kontext*, Berlin–Boston, MA, 3–35.

Suhr, Claudia. 1999. Zum fiktiven Erzähler in der ägyptischen Literatur, in: Gerald Moers (ed.), *Definitely: Egyptian Literature. Proceedings of the Symposion "Ancient Egyptian Literature: History and Forms", Los Angeles, March 24–26, 1995*, Göttingen, 91–129.

Suhr, Claudia. 2016. *Die ägyptische „Ich-Erzählung“: Eine narratologische Untersuchung*, GOF IV/61, Wiesbaden.

Titzmann, Michael. 2008. The Systematic Place of Narratology in Literary Theory and Textual Theory, in: Tom Kindt & Hans-Harald Müller (eds.), *What is Narratology? Questions and Answers Regarding the Status of a Theory*, Berlin–New York, N.Y, 175–204.

Tobin, Vincent. A. 2003. Selections from the Pyramid Texts, in: William K. Simpson (ed.), *The Literature of Ancient Egypt: An Anthology of Stories, Instructions, Stelae, Autobiographies, and Poetry*, New Haven, CT–London, 247–262.

Todorov, Tzvetan. 1966. Les catégories du récit littéraire, in: *Communications*. Recherches sémiologiques: L'analyse structurale du récit 8, 125–151.

Tomaševskij, Boris V. 1985. Theorie der Literatur, Poetik [1931], in: Klaus-Dieter Seemann (ed.), *Slavistische Studienbücher:* Neue Folge 1, Wiesbaden.

Tschander, Ladina B. 1999. Bewegung und Bewegungsverben, in: Ipke Wachsmuth & Bernhard Jung (eds.), *KogWis99: Proceedings der 4. Fachtagung der Gesellschaft für Kognitionswissenschaft*, Bielefeld, 25–30.

Otto, Eberhard. 1958. *Das Verhältnis von Rite und Mythus im Ägyptischen*, SHAW 1, Heidelberg.

Quirke, Stephen G. 1996. Narrative Literature, in: Antonio Loprieno (ed.), *Ancient Egyptian Literature: History and Forms*, Leiden–New York, N.Y.–Köln, 263–276.

Vinson, Steve. 2004. The Accent's on Evil: Ancient Egyptian „Melodrama“ and the Problem of Genre, in: *JARCE* 41, 33–54.

Werner, Lukas. 2011. B. Grundbegriffe der Erzählanalyse, 4. Zeit, in: Matías Martínez (ed.), *Handbuch Erzählliteratur*, Stuttgart, 150–158.

Werning, Daniel A. 2012. Ancient Egyptian Prepositions for the Expression of Spatial Relations and their Translations: A Typological Approach, in: Eitan Grossman, Stéphane Polis & Jean Winand (eds.), *Lexical Semantics in Ancient Egyptian*, Hamburg, 293–346.

Werning, Daniel A. 2014. The Semantic Space of Static Spatial Prepositions in Hieroglyphic Ancient Egyptian: A Comparison with Nine Indo-European and Afro-Asiatic Languages Based on the Topological Relations Picture Series, in: Silvia Kutscher & Daniel A. Werning (eds.), *On Ancient Grammars of Space: Linguistic Research on the Expression of Spatial Relations and Motion in Ancient Languages*, Berlin, 195–325.

Willems, Harco. 2017. The Method of „Sequencing“ in Analyzing Egyptian Funerary Texts: The Example of Coffin Texts Spell 283 and 296, in: Susanne Bickel & Lucía Díaz-Iglesias Llanos (eds.), *Studies in Ancient Egyptian Funerary Literature*, OLA 257, Leuven–Paris–Bristol, CT, 599–619.

Zeidler, J. 1993. Zur Frage der Spätentstehung des Mythos in Ägypten, in: *GM* 132, 85–109.

Zelinsky-Wibbelt, Cornelia. 1993. Introduction, in: Cornelia Zelinsky-Wibbelt (ed.), *The Semantics of Prepositions: From Mental Processing to Natural Language Processing*, Natural Language Processing 3, Berlin–New York, N.Y., 1–24.

Zeman, Sonja. 2016a. Introduction, in: Natalia Igl & Sonja Zeman (eds.), *Perspectives on Narrativity and Narrative Perspectivization*, Linguistic Approaches to Literature 21, Amsterdam–Philadelphia, Penn., 1–14.

Zeman, Sonja. 2016b. Perspectivization as a Link between Narrative Micro- and Macro-Structure, in: Natalia Igl & Sonja Zeman (eds.), *Perspectives on Narrativity and Narrative Perspectivization*, Linguistic Approaches to Literature 21, Amsterdam–Philadelphia, Penn., 15–42.

Zeman, Sonja. 2018. What is a Narration – and why does it matter?, in: Markus Steinbach & Annika Hübl (eds.), *Linguistic Foundations of Narration in Spoken and Sign Language*, Amsterdam–Philadelphia, Penn., 173–206.

Zeman, Sonja. 2020a. Narrativität als linguistische Kategorie: Schlaglichter auf ein sprachliches Grundkonzept, in: *Zeitschrift für germanistische Linguistik* 48/3, 447–456.

Zeman, Sonja. 2020b. Grammatik der Narration, in: *Zeitschrift für germanistische Linguistik* 48/3, 457–494.

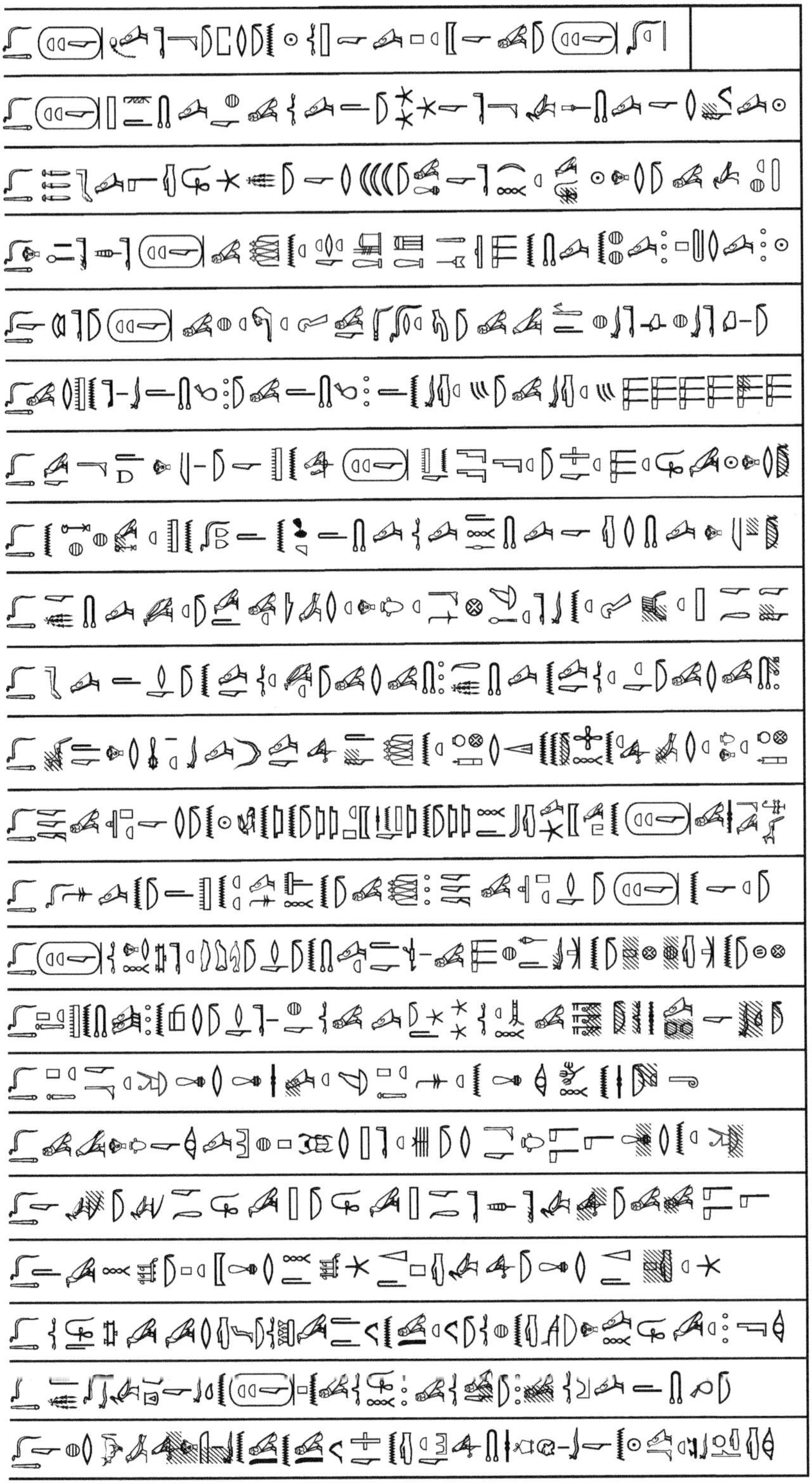

Taf. 1 | Hieroglyphische Inschrift von PT 412 (T) nach der Kollation der Abklatsche BBAW, A. 1302, 1A–B, 2A–B.

9 783943 955293

LINGUA AEGYPTIA
Studia Monographica 26

Transitivity and Aspect in Sahidic Coptic

Nina Speransky

Widmaier Verlag
Hamburg